SOCIETY, ETHICS, AND THE LAW

A Reader

David A. Mackey, PhD
Kathryn M. Elvey, PhD

JONES & BARTLETT
LEARNING

World Headquarters
Jones & Bartlett Learning
5 Wall Street
Burlington, MA 01803
978-443-5000
info@jblearning.com
www.jblearning.com

Jones & Bartlett Learning books and products are available through most bookstores and online booksellers. To contact Jones & Bartlett Learning directly, call 800-832-0034, fax 978-443-8000, or visit our website, www.jblearning.com.

Substantial discounts on bulk quantities of Jones & Bartlett Learning publications are available to corporations, professional associations, and other qualified organizations. For details and specific discount information, contact the special sales department at Jones & Bartlett Learning via the above contact information or send an email to specialsales@jblearning.com.

20024-9

Production Credits

VP, Product Management: Amanda Martin
Director of Product Management: Laura Pagluica
Product Specialist: Audrey Schwinn
Product Coordinator: Paula-Yuan Gregory
Project Specialist: Kathryn Leeber
Digital Project Specialist: Angela Dooley
Marketing Manager: Suzy Balk
Manufacturing and Inventory Control Supervisor: Amy Bacus

Product Fulfillment Manager: Wendy Kilborn
Composition: Exela Technologies
Project Management: Exela Technologies
Cover Design: Michael O'Donnell
Text Design: Kristin E. Parker
Senior Media Development Editor: Troy Liston
Rights Specialist: John Rusk
Cover Image (Title Page, Part Opener, Chapter Opener): © Sergii Gnatiuk/Shutterstock
Printing and Binding: LSC Communications

Library of Congress Cataloging-in-Publication Data

Names: Mackey, David A., author. | Elvey, Kathryn M., author.
Title: Society, ethics, and the law : a reader / David A. Mackey & Kathryn M. Elvey.
Description: Burlington, MA : Jones & Bartlett Learning, [2021] | Includes
    bibliographical references and index.
Identifiers: LCCN 2019039964 | ISBN 9781284199642 (paperback)
Subjects: LCSH: Criminal justice, Administration of--Moral and ethical
    aspects. | Law enforcement--Moral and ethical aspects. | Social ethics.
Classification: LCC HV7419 .M347 2021 | DDC 172/.1--dc23
LC record available at https://lccn.loc.gov/2019039964

6048

Printed in the United States of America
24 23 22 21 20   10 9 8 7 6 5 4 3 2 1

This book is dedicated to my wife, Lisa,
and sons, Ryan and Tyler.
—DM

This book is dedicated to my parents, Will
and Wren.
—KE

Brief Contents

SECTION 9   Ethics and Social Change   336

SECTION 10   Juveniles and Ethics   380

Contents

© Sergii Gnatiuk/Shutterstock

SECTION 5 Ethics and the Judicial System 145

Article 18 Ethics Within the Court System . . . 146

Article 19 Lawyers, Clients, and Ethics in Class Action Cases 156

Article 20 Ethical Responsibilities and Challenges in the Courtroom Work Group. 162

Article 21 Christian Burial Speech. 170

Article 22 The Ethics of Prosecutors 180

Preface

The issues discussed and illustrated in this text not only are timely, significant, and helpful in shaping our society but also are great opportunities to explore and to understand how our society interacts with the law from multiple perspectives and viewpoints. Although the views in this text can range from left to right on the political ideological spectrum, each topic discusses individual rights and responsibilities and notions of what is just and fair. We strive to include topics not traditionally covered in a criminal justice ethics course to make the book appealing to ethics courses offered in philosophy and social science departments while also remaining relevant to criminal justice students. Furthermore, we have included an ethics and popular culture section that includes a variety of topics with a broad appeal.

The coeditors of the book regularly teach the Plymouth State University course titled "Society, Ethics, and the Law," a required course for our criminal justice and criminology degree programs. It is also a course that fulfills two of the seven connection requirements, the Integrative Connection and the Diversity Connection, for the university's general education model. The course is also an elective in four academic disciplines: philosophy, peace and social justice, pre-law, and criminal justice. For this reason, we routinely have students enrolled in the course from a range of academic disciplines, and they have an equally diverse exposure to and understanding of the two disciplines central to the book: criminal justice and philosophy. We often see students who have some background in one academic field but not the other, as well as students who are drawn to the course because of the interesting nature of the course's content and topics.

Society, Ethics, and the Law: A Reader is a book informed by these experiences in the classroom. Among the wide range of topics covered in the book, we draw from a range of contemporary issues where controversies involving ethics and morality intersect with law, notions of justice, and the operations of the criminal justice system. These issues have consequences for society. However, some of the topics may even directly impact the students enrolled in our classes. Some of the issues addressed in the articles will have a central theme of how our legal system treats people in our society; other topics focus on the identification and enjoyment of rights in our society as well as the application of force and deprivation of individual liberties by the criminal justice system. The book contains several articles titled as a Character in Context article. These have been written by a criminal justice practitioner, educator, or individual whose life and work experience are connected to the theme of the section. The Character in Context articles are intended to be written in a more conversational format than the other articles. For example, in Article 39 Jim Obergefell, the plaintiff in the Supreme Court case *Obergefell v. Hodges* (the case that legalized gay marriage), gets to explain, write, and provide his perspective on society, ethics, and the law—something he has yet to do in a text. Another example is Article 42 by LaVerne Bell-Tolliver, who lived through desegregation and gets to discuss the issue of desegregation in Arkansas.

We are fortunate to have a wonderful group of contributors for the book. The authors of individual articles were selected for both their subject matter expertise and their ability to effectively communicate their ideas in relatively short articles. Our goal is to provide readers with a thorough, well-researched, and informative book. Many chapters are designed to provide the reader with a range of viewpoints to inform the reader yet still provide the opportunity to formulate positions on, deliberate, and debate the ethical issues raised. The course explores ethical theories and legal concepts with particular attention to legal issues connected to age, race, class, ideology, and gender. It allows the reader to become aware of and appreciate viewpoints other than those to which they have been acculturated.

▶ Format and Organization

Section 1 begins with a discussion of the foundation for ethical theories. This key section allows students and instructors to apply and contrast theories of ethical and moral development to criminal justice scenarios later in the book. Fundamental views such as utilitarianism, deontology, character, and virtues are presented. The section also explores aspects of cultural relativism and cultural absolutism that are discussed in the context of African culture, practices, and traditions. These foundational ethical concepts are reinforced throughout the text.

The next series of articles in Section 2 delve into the realm of ethics and the lawmaking process. Fundamental issues explored include the constitutional foundation, which provides the framework to protect and enjoy individual rights. For some, the topic may seem distant and abstract, yet the functions of government in the lawmaking area, separation of powers, and the principle of federalism are literally seen every day. The articles explore the myriad of ways laws are created and enforced, reflecting different ideological points of view whether through legislative actions, executive orders, or administrative regulations. These issues include sanctuary cities, decriminalization of marijuana, firearms ownership, needle-exchange programs, same-sex marriage, desegregation, panhandling, and mental health.

Section 3 of the book then explores aspects of ethics and the common good. The issues explored here are far ranging such as eminent domain, gun ownerships and concealed carry laws, and needle exchanges. These articles are aimed at questioning laws (some of them discussed in the previous section) and how those laws may infringe on the rights of the individual. A common theme explored in these articles is, "Who should the law benefit, or whose interests are served?"

Sections 4, 5, and 6 explore the ethics of the three major components of the criminal justice system: police, courts, and corrections. We include articles on topics central to the criminal justice system and its role in regulating society through social control. Contemporary issues such as police use of force, body-worn cameras, prosecutorial ethics, the role of incarceration in jails, community corrections, and aging offenders are discussed. Building from the corrections articles, Section 7 then addresses issues integral to special populations in the criminal justice system. This section not only defines and discusses special populations but also raises questions about how best to deal with special populations in an ethical manner.

Section 8 addresses issues concerning surveillance, security, and crime control. These issues range from ethics of surveillance and privacy to freedom of speech and approaches to catastrophic incidents. These topics and articles appear to raise more questions than they can answer and provide students with some interesting discussion points regarding laws and ethics.

Section 9 explores ethics and social change, bringing up topics that have been debated for decades. Some of these topics involve how courts have changed laws to reflect public opinion on issues in society such as gay marriage, school desegregation, the right of liberty and equality, as well as the right to die. Again, students are pushed to think about issues; however, in this case these are issues they may have some knowledge or personal connection with. These articles offer a new perspective from which to view issues they may have already considered.

Sections 10 and 11 examine the ethics and rights of two particular populations: juveniles and college students. These sections are aimed at addressing issues that our readers in the classroom may be more in tune with. The topics discussed in the articles may have personally affected them or people they know, either recently or during their high school careers. For example, Title IX is an issue that may affect our readers in ways they may not even be aware of. Both sections provide an opportunity for applied discussion and dissection of the course material.

Finally, Section 12 covers ethics and popular culture. Again, this section is something that may be easily consumed and discussed by students. The applications for ethics and discussion of them in our popular culture are vast. Every day we are exposed to news and commentary, social media, imagery, and marketing, all of which provide questions regarding the ethics of these companies and entertainers. It provides an opportunity for students to reflect on their consumption of popular culture and how that popular culture interacts with ethics and society.

▶ Teaching Tools

A range of ancillary materials are available to accompany this text. These resources are meant to aid instructors in planning for their courses and help students gain a deeper understanding of the information at hand.

- Recommended Reading lists provide a starting point for further exploration of selected topics.
- Web Links give instructors and students quick access to internet resources relevant to articles in the text.
- A Sample Syllabus gives instructors an example of how to format their course to fit with the book.
- The Test Bank provides questions for use in assessments and discussions.
- Slides in PowerPoint format give instructors a great starting point for lecture presentations.

For information on how to access these resources, please contact your Jones & Bartlett Learning Account Manager at go.jblearning.com/findmyrep.

Acknowledgments

We would like to thank the contributors to the book. Without their efforts, the book would not be possible. We would also like to thank the team at Jones & Bartlett Learning. In particular, Laura Pagluica, Director of Product Management; Audrey Schwinn, Product Specialist; Suzy Balk, Marketing Manager; and Upendra Kumar Pandey, Vendor Project Manager.

—*David A. Mackey and Kathryn M. Elvey*

I would personally like to thank my co-editor David Mackey for being an excellent colleague, wonderful mentor, and amazing friend. Without his hard work this project would never have become a reality.

—*Kathryn M. Elvey*

The authors and publishers would like to specifically thank the following reviewers for providing valuable feedback during the development of this text:

Diana M. Concannon, PsyD
Associate Provost, Strategic Initiatives
and Partnerships, Dean
California School of Forensic Studies
Alliant International University

Comeka Anderson Díaz
Program Chair—Public Service
Leadership
University of Houston—Clear Lake:
College of Human Sciences and
Humanities

Jennifer C. Gibbs, Ph.D.
Associate Professor
Penn State Harrisburg

Jonathan Gibson
John Jay College of Criminal Justice

Barbara King
Internship Coordinator
Department of Criminal Justice and
Criminology
Georgia Southern University

E. Jay Kolick, M.S., M.B.A., C.C.J.P.
Director, Criminal Justice, Forensic
Psychology, and Homeland Security
Programs
Rosemont College

Richard Powers
Adjunct Professor
University of Houston Downtown

Dr. Joseph L. Richmond, LP.D., MPA
Assistant Professor
Arkansas State University

PJ Verrecchia, Ph.D.
Associate Professor of Criminology
and Criminal Justice
York College of Pennsylvania

Nick Zingo, MPA, TBR-CT
California State University Northridge

About the Authors

David A. Mackey is Professor of Criminal Justice at Plymouth State University in Plymouth, New Hampshire. He earned his BS and MA in Criminal Justice from University of Massachusetts, Lowell and his PhD in Criminology from Indiana University of Pennsylvania. At Plymouth State University, he teaches Technology in Criminal Justice; Society, Ethics, and the Law; and Criminology. Dr. Mackey received the Northeastern Association of Criminal Justice Sciences Regional Fellow Award in 2011 and served as the Association President in 2019–2020. With Kristine Levan (University of Idaho), he coedited *Crime Prevention* published by Jones & Bartlett Learning. Some of his work in the area of criminal justice ethics include "Moral Dilemmas and Worst-Case Scenarios: Using Post-Apocalyptic Fiction to Teach Criminal Justice Ethics," "Employing Surveillance in Situational Crime Prevention," "The 'X-Rated X-Ray': Reconciling Liberty, Privacy, and Community Safety," and "The Ethics of New Surveillance."

Kathryn M. Elvey is an assistant professor of Criminal Justice at Plymouth State University. She earned her BA from University of Mary Washington (Virginia), her MA from Wake Forest University (North Carolina), and her PhD at the University of Cincinnati (Ohio). At Plymouth State University, she teaches Women and Crime; Society, Ethics, and the Law; and Corrections. Dr. Elvey has been appointed by the governor of New Hampshire to serve on the Women's Prison Civilian Advisory Board to help discuss policy and procedure within the prisons as well as best practices. She has published in several peer-reviewed journals but finds her passion is in teaching.

Contributors

Michael E. Antonio, PhD
West Chester University,
West Chester, PA

Shavonne Arthurs, PhD
Seton Hill University, Greensburg, PA

LaVerne Bell-Toliver, PhD, MSW, MABC, LCSW
University of Arkansas at Little Rock,
Little Rock, AR

Christopher M. Bellas, PhD
Youngstown State University,
Youngstown, OH

Christopher Benedetti, PhD
Plymouth State University,
Plymouth, NH

Michele P. Bratina, PhD
West Chester University,
West Chester, PA

Robert Brooks, JD, PhD
Worcester State University,
Worcester, MA

Danielle Marie Carkin, PhD
Stonehill College, Easton, MA

Benecia Carmack, MBA, JD
University of Central Missouri,
Warrensburg, MO

Kelly Carrero, PhD, BCBA
Texas A&M University—Commerce,
Commerce, TX

Adam M. Carrington, PhD
Hillsdale College, Hillsdale, MI

Bryce M. Carter, BS
Appalachian State University,
Boone, NC

David R. Champion, PhD
Slippery Rock University, Slippery
Rock, PA

Kaitlyn Clarke, PhD
Saint Anselm College, Manchester, NH

Jeffery E. Clutter, PhD
Marywood University, Scranton, PA

Derek Cohen, PhD
Texas Public Policy Foundation,
Austin, TX

Gary F. Cornelius, BA
George Mason University, Fairfax,
VA; Fairfax County Office of the
Sherriff, VA (ret)

Kevin E. Courtright, PhD
Edinboro University of Pennsylvania,
Edinboro, PA

Tim Dees, MS
Reno Police Department, Reno,
NV (ret.)

Sherri DioGuardi, PhD
University of Central Missouri,
Warrensburg, MO

Vivian J. Dorsett, PhD
Texas A&M University—Commerce,
Commerce, TX

Adam Dunbar, PhD
University of Florida, Gainesville, FL

Robert E. Fitzpatrick, MA
Plymouth State University,
Plymouth, NH

Tina Fryling, JD, MS,
Mercyhurst University, Erie, PA

Shaun M. Gann, PhD
Boise State University, Boise, ID

Brandon J. Haas, PhD,
Plymouth State University,
  Plymouth, NH

W. Chris Hale, PhD
Louisiana State University Shreveport,
  Shreveport, LA

Stacy H. Haynes, PhD
Mississippi State University,
  Mississippi State, MS

Don Hummer, PhD
Pennsylvania State University
  Harrisburg, Middletown, PA

Veronyka James, PhD
Shenandoah University, Winchester, VA

Richard J. Klonoski, PhD
University of Scranton, Scranton, PA

Sarah Lageson, PhD
Rutgers University-Newark, Newark, NJ

Kristine Levan, PhD
University of Idaho, Moscow, ID

Kweilin T. Lucas, PhD
Mars Hill University, Mars Hill, NC

Paul A. Lucas, PhD
Appalachian State University, Boone, NC

Arelys Madero-Hernandez, PhD
Shippensburg University of
  Pennsylvania, Shippensburg, PA

Rimonda R. Maroun, PhD
Endicott College, Beverly, MA

Philip D. McCormack, PhD
Saint Anselm College, Manchester, NH

Joshua L. Mitchell, PhD
University of Arkansas, Fayetteville, AR

Jim Obergefell, BS
Columbus, OH

Michael Potts, PhD
Methodist University, Fayetteville, NC

Rosemary Ricciardelli, PhD
Memorial University of
  Newfoundland, St. John's, NL

Frank A. Rodriguez, PhD
North Carolina Central University,
  Durham, NC

John J. Rodriguez, PhD
Prairie View A&M University,
  Arlington, TX

Amy J. Samuels, EdD
University of Montevallo,
  Montevallo, AL

Gregory L. Samuels, PhD
University of Montevallo,
  Montevallo, AL

Cadin Sanner
Fort Hays State University, Hays, KS

Yosef S. Schiff, JD
Ohio Legislative Service Commission,
  Columbus, OH

Eric S. See. PhD
Methodist University, Fayetteville, NC

Sarah A. See, MA
Methodist University, Fayetteville, NC

Beau Shine, PhD
Indiana University Kokomo,
  Kokomo, IN

Michael E. Solimine, JD
University of Cincinnati,
  Cincinnati, OH

Dennis J. Stevens, PhD
Justice Writers of America,
  Charlotte, NC

Jason Stevens, PhD
Ashland University, Ashland, OH

Victoria Time, LLB, PhD
Old Dominion University, Norfolk, VA

Brendan Toner, PhD
Arkansas Tech University,
   Russellville, AR

Daniel Trigoboff, JD
North Carolina State University,
   Fayetteville, NC

Arthur Vasquez, MS, MEd, MPA
University of Texas at Arlington,
   Arlington, TX

Wendy C. Vonnegut, JD
Methodist University, Fayetteville, NC

Patricia B. Wagner, JD
Youngstown State University,
   Youngstown, OH

Edward Gregory Weeks III, PhD
Lasell College, Newton, MA

Stephen T. Young, PhD
Marshall University, Huntington, WV

David Zehr, PhD
Plymouth State University,
   Plymouth, NH

SECTION 1

Ethical Theories

ARTICLE 1

Ethical Theories: An Introduction

Kathryn M. Elvey

What makes a person a "good" person? What makes an act a "good" act? What about a "bad" person or a "bad" act? Does one "bad" act by a "good" or moral person make that person a "bad" person; if not, then how many "bad" acts before he or she is considered immoral or bad? To answer many difficult ethical questions, people turn to **normative ethics**. Normative ethics is the study of ethics—more specifically, the study of right and wrong. To answer the questions just asked, ethical theorists and theories try to find underlying principles of what is right and what is wrong. For example, most people agree that lying, cheating, and stealing are wrong, but why? What makes them wrong? Therefore, normative ethics tries to answer these questions as well as the broader question of what is right and what is wrong. Often this can be broken down further into different ethical theories.

This article will examine three classical ethical theories: first, the study of duty, which is known as *deontology*; second, the study of consequences, which is referred to as *utilitarianism*; and third, the study of the character of an individual, which is known as *virtue ethics*. Virtue ethics is different from deontology and utilitarianism because it is concerned with the *character of the individual*, whereas deontology and utilitarianism are more concerned with the *action itself*. This article will next address religious ethics, peacemaking ethics, and ethical absolutism and ethical relativism.

▶ Classical Ethical Theories

The following is a discussion of each classical ethical theory and how it tries to answer the question "What is right and what is wrong?" Before beginning, note that there are tomes written on the following theories, and debates over "right" and "wrong" have taken place for thousands of years. The following is just a *small* sample of some of the most basic concepts and principles that guide these theories—and even then they can be debated endlessly.

Deontology

The word *deontology* literally means the study of (*logos*) duty (*deon*) (Spinello, 2005a). Deontologists argue that humans have certain duties they *must* perform regardless of the consequences of those duties. For example, if you cheat on a test, it is the duty of your professor to turn you in to academic integrity or the administration, even if the professor likes you as a person or knows that you will be kicked out of school; it is the professor's duty. This scenario—despite what some students may think—is not fun or enjoyable for the professor or the student. It may actually pain the professor to turn the student in knowing what it will cost the student, but according to deontology it is his or her duty and so the professor must do it. This is considered the ethical act, the right choice.

Immanuel Kant is considered the most famous deontologist. He is neither always easy to follow or understand nor brief in his explanations of duty (Uleman, 2010). Kant wanted to define duty so that people could fulfill their duty and be ethical. To define duty, he believed that all people are morally obligated to follow the **categorical imperative**. There are many iterations, but we will stick to his first one. The categorical imperative is best defined as something a person *must* or *ought* to do. This imperative then is **universalizable** in nature, which means that you should want everyone to act the same way, even if you yourself would not want to act that way; it is something you would *will* others to do (Kant, 1785/1949). For example, if someone loans you money, you may not want to pay that person back, but you should because if you loaned someone money you would want to be repaid. Some have commented this is similar to the **golden rule**: "Do unto others as you would have them do unto you" (Petrik, 2005). However, there is a notable difference: Some people have different ideas about what they would like someone to do or not do to them. For example, maybe you enjoy being humiliated; therefore, you humiliate others because that is what you want them to do to you. But as a general rule, the majority of people do not enjoy being humiliated; therefore, people should act in a way that you would wish all other *rational* people to follow as if it were universal law (Kant, 1785/1949, p. 38). In other words, if someone was rational, then he or she should be able to understand and follow duty as bound by universal law. One final note on understanding the categorical imperative is that Kant specified that people should never be used as a means to an end. He believed that people have intrinsic value, and they should never be used as a tool (Kant, 1785/1949, p. 45). **FIGURE 1.1** shows the deontological thought process in which a person starts with a duty and ends with an ethical choice.

Some of the issues with this theory involve two competing duties; how do you decide which duty is the right choice? Let's return to the previous example of turning in a student for cheating. As a professor, it is my duty to report the student; on the other hand, it is also my duty as a person and a professor to show compassion, understanding, and possibly even give second chances. So what is the right choice? Furthermore, there is an assumption of rationality on the part of the actors. But how can one assume that everyone is rational and understands what their duty is?

Utilitarianism

A second classical theory is *utilitarianism*. According to utilitarians, an act is good or right if it produces the greatest good for the greatest number. Just as Kant set the tone for deontology, **Jeremy Bentham** (1789/1961) and **John Stuart Mill**

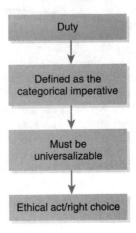

FIGURE 1.1 Thought process of a deontologist.

(1863/1961) were two of the most famous utilitarians and defined many of its founding concepts. The basis of utilitarianism is rooted in **consequentialism** (Habibi, 2005). Consequentialism is, as it is sounds, based on consequences. Mill believed if an act produced good consequences then it was an ethical act. But, as we started this article, the question must be asked: what makes an act a "good" act? Also, how do we know if the consequences are "good" and who are they "good" for?

Bentham and Mill were proponents of **hedonistic utilitarianism** (Habibi, 2005). The "good" that everyone seeks is **happiness**, and happiness according to these men is defined as **pleasure** and the **absence of pain**. What things are pleasurable to you? According to Mill (1863/1961), pleasure, included food, drink, and sex. It might also include intellectual and emotional pleasures. So, according to the utilitarian, a moral or ethical act would produce pleasure and a bad or unethical act would cause pain. So the question becomes, who is receiving the pleasure and who is receiving the pain? As previously stated, the ethical act will produce the greatest amount of pleasure for the greatest number of people while reducing the pain of the greatest number. For example, you murder someone and this brings you pleasure! However, the person who is dead clearly experienced no pleasure, and this person's family is inconsolable. Therefore, Bentham and Mill would tell you to consider all of the affected parties; therefore, your act is unethical. Conversely, you buy everyone at work pizza and everyone is happy. You performed an ethical act. The consequences of your actions and the people affected by them are what is most important in this theory. **FIGURE 1.2** shows the utilitarian thought process by which a person starts with an act, and the decision about whether the act was ethical or not can be determined.

Critics have two major issues with consequentialist ethical theories. First, they do not take into account motivation, or why a person acted the way he or she did. Second, there are some things that produce the greatest good for the greatest number but that use other people as a means to an end—slavery, for example.

▶ Virtue Ethics and Character

Although utilitarianism and deontology are considered two of the most popular forms of normative ethics, virtue ethics stands out as a popular third. Unlike deontology and utilitarianism, which examine the act, virtue ethics examines the actor

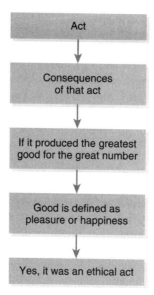

FIGURE 1.2 Thought process of a utilitarian.

and the character of the actor. Contemporary virtue ethics was inspired by Aristotle, though Plato and Socrates also play a role (Aristotle, 1954). Aristotle did not want to answer what one must do or how one must act, but rather what sort of person someone should become in order to live the "good life" (also called an "ethical life") (Barnes, 2004). Aristotle believed that if someone developed their character, then good acts would follow, as well as a good ethical life.

Aristotle focused on virtue and vices in the development of character. He considered virtues to be strength of character, whereas vices were weaknesses. Socrates and Plato had only a short list of virtues: wisdom, courage, temperance, justice, and piety (Rachels, 1999). According to James Rachels (1999), Aristotle's list of virtues included:

- Benevolence
- Civility
- Compassion
- Conscientiousness
- Cooperativeness
- Courage
- Courteousness
- Dependability
- Fairness
- Friendliness
- Generosity
- Honesty
- Industriousness
- Justice
- Loyalty
- Moderation
- Reasonableness
- Self-Confidence
- Self-control
- Self-discipline
- Self-reliance
- Tactfulness
- Thoughtfulness
- Tolerance

According to Aristotle, to reach the "good life" one needed to achieve happiness, and a bad life would be filled with unpleasantness or unhappiness. Aristotle seems to suggest that it is through contemplation and the virtuous life that one can achieve happiness, and that this happiness will lead to fulfillment (Barnes, 2003).

Furthermore, an individual striving for perfect virtue should do so by following the **golden mean**. The golden mean is a way for someone to judge whether his or her virtuous act is appropriate or not. Aristotle argues there are clearly two far ends of the spectrum people can go to when it comes to virtuous traits, and they must choose the most balanced form of the virtuous trait (Slomski, 2005). For example, let's look at self-control. You are on a diet and want to lose 10 pounds; to do this you need self-control. On the one hand, someone without self-control would continue to stuff his face with food, and someone who is overly zealous in pursuit of weight loss decides to eat nothing for a week. Both of these are extreme ends of self-control or lack thereof. The golden mean would have the person use portion control and lose the weight over a period of time and thus exhibit the most thoughtful form of self-control. The idea of the golden mean is to help people balance their virtues in a meaningful way because not everyone has the same abilities. **FIGURE 1.3** shows the process by which one starts with virtue and develops it to obtain the good life.

Much like deontology and utilitarianism, virtue ethics has its own issues. The biggest question is, how do people actually learn virtues? There is an assumption that people are raised in a community or society that supports moral strengths while eschewing moral weaknesses, but is that always the case?

An Applied Example of Classical Ethical Theories

Let's break each theory down into an example:

You see a man drowning in the distance at the beach. You know there is a fairly strong undercurrent, and you also know you are an excellent swimmer and a trained lifeguard. Not only is this man drowning, but also his family is watching on the shore sick with fear.

- A deontologist would have you save the man because it is your duty to do so, you are an excellent swimmer, and you have the capability. You would want someone to save you if you were in distress and the person had the capability

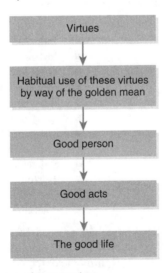

FIGURE 1.3 The thought process of a virtue ethics.

to do so. You want nothing from the man for a rescue because humans have intrinsic value.

- A utilitarian would save the man knowing that the act would produce the greatest good (happiness) for the greatest number—the drowning man and his family. Maybe you were motivated by the thought of receiving honor or a reward for your acts, so you were acting out of your own self-interest. But it does not matter because the consequences unto themselves were the only important thing. The man and his family were happily and safely reunited.
- Finally, as a virtue ethicist you would save the man because you have courage. You understand the risks of saving him, but your character and virtue of courage push you into doing the right thing. You know there is some risk, but by using the golden mean you are able to discern the risk is not too high because you are a trained professional. You are clearly living the good life because you are practicing courage and building character.

▶ Other Ethical Concepts and Theories

Religious Ethics

Religious ethics are based on a particular religion's teachings and moral code. Therefore, it can be somewhat difficult to define religious ethics without discussing the specific religion being examined. These moral codes developed by religions often come from divine revelations and are written in the canonical text of that religion. For example, the Bible (both the Old and New Testament) is often considered *the* moral standard for Christians, with the Ten Commandments being at the center of this moral code. Some believe that to live ethically an individual *must* follow a religious code. Many ethicists note that there appears to be underlying similarities between many religious codes, but that does not mean there is or cannot be a difference between religion and ethics (Jones, 2005).

Peacemaking Ethics and Nonviolence

A more recent ethical perspective that has become popular in the field of criminal justice is **peacemaking ethics**. This is sometimes referred to as **transformative** or **restorative justice**. It comes from the evolution of the humanist perspective combined with a push toward social justice in America. It is influenced by different Eastern and Western religions (Dondson, Bush, & Braswell, 2012). Put simply, peacemaking ethics is meant as a move away from retribution and punitive sanctions toward compassion and restoration for all parties involved in a conflict.

According to Braswell and Gold (1998), peacemaking ethics has three main parts: connectedness, care, and mindfulness. The first concept, **connectedness**, assumes that all people are connected through their environment, whether physically or emotionally. This sense of connectedness means that when something is done to hurt someone, we are all hurt. Next, **care** refers to a need in society to be concerned about and nurturing of other individuals and groups. This can be seen as a way to make sure that discrimination of individuals and groups does not take place. Finally, **mindfulness** is meant to persuade individuals to look beyond themselves and examine the needs of others (Braswell & Gold, 1998; Dondson et al., 2012). Again, the goal of peacemaking ethics is to make sure all parties in a society—if they have been treated unjustly—are brought to a of sense of justice. Overall, peacemaking ethics is considered a process rather than necessarily a theory for how one should live. Because it is a process, it can be carried out in many different ways.

Peacemaking ethics takes many forms and is often practiced in the criminal justice system as a form of **conflict resolution**. Many different types of conflict resolution try to bring about wholeness for all parties involved or affected by an action. A common form of peacemaking for those who are practitioners of peacemaking ethics are **sentencing circles**. The National Institute of Justice (NIJ) (2010) defines a sentencing circle as "a community-directed process, conducted in partnership with the criminal justice system, to develop consensus on an appropriate sentencing plan that addresses the concerns of all interested parties" (p. 1). A sentencing circle is an excellent example of peacemaking ethics for several reasons. First, it includes all affected parties and ensures they are heard throughout the process of trying to achieve justice; this shows care and mindfulness for all affected parties. Second, it focuses on bringing about a solution to a problem or injustice that is respectful and considerate of all affected parties, which takes into account connectedness.

Other forms of conflict resolution that have developed from peacemaking ethics include victim and offender mediation, conferencing, increased emphasis on restitution, community panels or restorative boards, community service, victim-impact panels, and victim-impact classes (NIJ, 2010).

Ethical Absolutism and Ethical Relativism

A final consideration for all of the theories discussed in this chapter is the difference between ethical absolutism and ethical relativism. **Ethical absolutism** assumes that there is a capital "T" truth—a universal moral code that is inherent to all humans. For example, killing is wrong or bad; this might be considered a "truth." This means there is one ethical standard that is indeed applicable to everyone (Serembus, 2005). Conversely, **ethical relativism** assumes there are varying ethical or moral codes that depend on the society or culture one is raised in. It is based on the premise that what is ethical is relative to individuals and groups of people (Spinello, 2005b). An example of ethical relativism might be the practice of animal sacrifice. In some cultures, animal sacrifice is abhorrent and unethical, but in others it is routinely practiced and considered ethical and even necessary. The question that needs to be answered based on these two views is: can there ever really be a universal truth, or is ethics relative based on how you think, feel, and act?

▶ Conclusion

Many different viewpoints and considerations define ethics, what defines an ethical act, and what defines an ethical person. Ethics is in constant flux and requires careful consideration for different viewpoints, theories, and contexts. The application of ethics as it relates to law and society is something that should be considered as society changes and grows and how laws reflect that change.

▶ References

Aristotle (1954). *The Nicomachean ethics*. (J. A. K. Thomson, Trans.). New York, NY: Penguin Classics.

Barnes, J. (2004). Introduction and further reading. In *The Nicomachean ethics*. (J. A. K. Thomson, Trans.). New York, NY: Penguin Classics.

Bentham, J. (1961). Principles of morals and legislation. In *The utilitarians* (7-398). Garden City, NY: Doubleday & Co. (Original work published 1789)

Braswell, M., & Gold, J. (1998). Peacemaking, justice, and ethics. In M. Braswell, B. McCarthy, & B. McCarthy (Eds.), *Justice, crime and ethics* (pp. 25–39). Cincinnati, OH: Anderson.

Dodson, K. D., Bush, M. D., & Braswell, M. (2012). Teaching peacemaking in criminal justice: Experiential applications. *Journal of Criminal Justice Education, 23*(4), 500–516.

Habibi, D. A. (2005). Utilitarianism. In J. K. Roth (Ed.), *Ethics* (Rev. ed., pp. 1531–1533). Pasadena, CA: Salem Press.

Jones, J. F. (2005). Religion. In J. K. Roth (Ed.), *Ethics* (Rev. ed., pp. 1254–1258). Pasadena, CA: Salem Press.

Kant, I. (1949). *Fundamental principles of the metaphysics of morals*. (T. K. Abbott, Trans.). New York, NY: The Bobbs-Merrill Co. (Original work published 1785)

Mill, J. S. (1961). Utilitarianism. In *The utilitarians* (pp. 401–472). Garden City, NY: Doubleday & Co. (Original work published 1863).

National Institute of Justice (NIJ). (2010). Sentencing circles. Retrieved from http://www.courts .ca.gov/documents/SentencingCircles.pdf

Petrik, J. (2005). Golden rule. In J. K. Roth (Ed.), *Ethics* (Rev. ed., pp. 597–598). Pasadena, CA: Salem Press.

Rachels, J. (1999). *The elements of moral philosophy* (3rd ed.) Boston, MA: McGraw-Hill College.

Serembus, J. H. (2005). Absolutism. In J. K. Roth (Ed.), *Ethics* (rev. ed., pp. 10–11). Pasadena, CA: Salem Press.

Slomski, G. (2005). Golden mean. In J. K. Roth (Ed.), *Ethics* (rev. ed., pp. 596–597). Pasadena, CA: Salem Press.

Spinello, R. A. (2005a). Deontological ethics. In J. K. Roth (Ed.), *Ethics* (rev. ed., pp. 367–368). Pasadena, CA: Salem Press.

Spinello, R. A. (2005b). Relativism. In J. K. Roth (Ed.), *Ethics* (rev. ed., pp. 1252–1253). Pasadena, CA: Salem Press.

Uleman, J. K. (2010). *An introduction to Kant's moral philosophy*. New York, NY: Cambridge University Press.

ARTICLE 2

Character in Context: Policing Realities

Tim Dees

The image of police work that most people outside of law enforcement have usually comes from portrayals in entertainment media. Hero cops are often rebels or rogues who seldom follow policy, but they're kept around because they get things done and always bring the bad guy to justice. In reality, *Lethal Weapon*'s Martin Riggs or *Dirty Harry*'s Inspector Callahan would be the focus of multiple expensive lawsuits and—if allowed to keep their jobs at all—they would be relegated to the third sub-basement of an evidence warehouse, filing mug shots until they reached retirement age.

TV and the movies seldom consider the organizational culture of police agencies and the effect of internal politics on the careers and lives of the people who work there. In fact, these two factors have far more influence on law enforcement officers' professional lives than any of the work they do—good, bad, or otherwise.

An exception to the inaccurate emphasis on internal politics was *The Wire*, a cable-network TV series from the early 2000s. *The Wire* examines the street narcotics trade in Baltimore, Maryland from multiple perspectives, including that of cops, dealers, users, schoolteachers, state and local politicians, and the news media. If nothing else, it is some of the best work the television industry has ever done.

Characters in *The Wire* come and go (when they go, they're usually killed) over the five seasons it ran, but the central continuing character is Detective Jimmy McNulty. At the program's outset, McNulty is a homicide detective ("a murder police" in *The Wire*'s vernacular) who is especially good at his job but despised by a high-ranking officer. Despite McNulty nearly always getting his man, he is relegated to uniformed harbor patrol, an assignment he hates. He recovers a body floating in the water, follows up on the case in his own tenacious way, and eventually makes it back to the homicide division. His boss still hates him, and no matter how much good McNulty manages to do, that cloud is always over him.

This dynamic mirrors the way things are in many, if not most, law enforcement organizations. Although police work is widely thought to be a meritocracy in which the best investigators become detectives and the most effective leaders rise to management, this is seldom true. Far more than competency or accomplishment, loyalty and personal alliances are the keys to a successful police career. If you don't have or manage to make friends in high places, you're never going anywhere. Get on the bad side of the wrong people, and you won't even be able to keep your job.

▶ Politics and Loyalty

I experienced this praxis firsthand during my brief tenure as a police sergeant, a first-line supervisor in a medium-sized city police department. I was hired as a rookie police officer after completing my bachelor's degree in biology, a failed medical doctor. New hires with college degrees were the exception at the time, and they were not prized. Most managers and administrators did not have degrees, and they were disdainful of those who did, often characterizing us as "educated idiots." I don't know that the college grads were responsible for any more mistakes than anyone else, but when they happened, everyone was reminded that the college kid was the one who screwed up.

Traditionally, promotional examinations were devised in-house. This allowed management to tailor the exams for the sort of candidate they most desired, but a larger benefit is that the exam could be leaked to candidates who were preordained to be successful. Anyone who kept an eye on the internal machinations of the police department could predict who the top promotional candidates would be.

At the time, the chief of police was relatively new and prone to doing things differently just to put his own mark on the process. In this case, he outsourced the exam to a private testing firm, and thus the process was kept confidential. When the testing was done, I came out number two in a field of some 30 candidates. To give you an idea of the competition, the number three slot went to a woman who eventually retired as the first female assistant director of the FBI. Had the test been done the old way, it's unlikely I would have placed in the top 10.

The day I was promoted, I was told by a lieutenant who was friendly with me that I would not pass my probationary period of one year. The word was out. I was not management material, meaning I was not regarded as sufficiently loyal to my masters.

There was something of an object test. One duty of sergeants is to write performance evaluations on the officers assigned to them. One officer who reported to me was slightly senior to me in tenure and regarded as a loose cannon. He was outspoken on several internal issues, something that was not encouraged. Despite this, he did above-average police work. He followed up cases more and better than most patrol officers. He often took incidents that started as minor crime reports and turned them into solid felony arrests. He was my own Jimmy McNulty.

As it happened, he and I did not get along well. He resented being supervised by someone who had less experience than he did and who frankly didn't have the native police skills he possessed. When his performance review came around, I think he expected me to give him a poor rating. In fact, I rated him as "superior" or "above standard" in nearly every category, adding only that he could try to be a bit easier to work with under "Performance Goals." I didn't believe that my personal feelings about him should have any impact on my professional assessment.

In the assessment process, the supervisor would write the evaluation and give it to his supervisor, a lieutenant. The lieutenant would review it and pass it along to the patrol captain, who would in turn send it to the chief of police. After all these management levels had signed off on the evaluation, only then would it be given to the employee.

My lieutenant—the one who warned me about the doomed fate of my supervisory career—told me that my evaluation would never fly because the captain hated this guy. I needed to rewrite it and not only take down my categorical ratings a bit but also add in negative comments about his performance. My response was that I was the one charged with doing the assessment, and this was my take on it. He could relieve me of this and write his own assessment, but the one I gave him was the one I was willing to put my name to. The lieutenant reluctantly passed the evaluation up the chain, and it was signed off at all levels without comment.

Of course, when I got within a couple of weeks of the end of my probationary year, I was told I wasn't being "confirmed" in the job, and I was demoted. I was told privately that I might have had a chance if I had decided to "play ball" with that performance review.

The method by which one gets internal approval or disapproval varies widely. It might be something more overt—like being asked to void a traffic citation issued to a friend of a supervisor or administrator in the department. When a captain did just that, he thought he would just owe a minor favor to the officer who had written the ticket. A few months later, the same officer was about to be suspended for some minor act of misconduct, and he called in his marker with the captain, asking the captain to intercede on his behalf. The chief of police was not thrilled. The officer avoided his suspension, but the captain got five days off without pay. The officer also spent the rest of his career in uniformed patrol, serving as a warning to others.

▶ Organizational Culture

Organizational culture is also a major determiner in one's career success. If one has a working personality that is already consistent with the organizational culture or can adapt to it, then working life will be a lot easier. Buck the tide of the organizational culture and you'll find yourself at the bottom of the pecking order.

A police agency's organizational culture manifests itself in many ways. One element common to the culture of police agencies in appearance-conscious Southern California is personal appearance and fitness. Although outfits such as the Los Angeles Police Department have their fat cops, you will see far fewer of them there than in agencies that don't strongly emphasize fitness. Law enforcement agencies outwardly encourage their employees to stay in shape for multiple reasons (fewer injuries, less sick time used, better performance, etc.) and often offer incentives for employees who do well on periodic fitness tests. However, there is seldom much of a disincentive because police unions oppose penalizing cops who get out of shape—even if they become morbidly obese.

One cultural element of the police department where I worked was the acceptance of gratuities. I worked in a city with a significant tourist industry, and there were more restaurants than most other cities of similar size. Most of the working-class eateries, coffee shops, and fast-food places provided free food to cops, although some placed conditions on their largesse. One place allowed police to order anything from one side of the menu—sandwiches, salads, and soups—but not from the side with more expensive entrees. Another discouraged cops from coming in between 5 p.m. and 7 p.m., which was the restaurant's peak dinner trade. Still another would provide anything on the menu, but it had to be consumed at a table in the kitchen where employees took their meals. When I was a new rookie, one of my field training officers took it on himself to ensure I thoroughly understood the protocols at the various places on our beat so as not to mess up a good thing with some faux pas.

Some of the faux pas were legendary. One lieutenant, who usually worked Monday to Friday on day shift, would dress up in his uniform on Sunday and take his largish family out to eat at a breakfast restaurant chain, graciously leaving a dollar for the server. Another officer stopped by a Mexican fast-food outlet and ordered enough food for six people, with many requests for special additions such as extra meat, sour cream, guacamole, and so on—and all of it "to go." He would then drive to the station, log off for the night, and take the bag of tacos and such home to his family.

Movie theaters were another opportunity for freebies. Police officers could show their badge at the box office, where they were asked to sign in with their names, badge numbers, and agencies. They could then see any movie they liked for free (they still had to buy any desired snacks). I didn't usually take advantage of this, but one day when I opened my wallet to pay for my ticket the cashier saw the gold star there and told me, "Oh, you can just show your badge and get in for free." Not thinking this through, I did this. While standing in line at the snack bar, I saw that the guy who had been in line behind me was giving me the stink eye. It occurred to me, "I probably make more money than this guy, and he resents having to pay when I didn't."

▶ Going Against the Tide

It was something of an epiphany. For this and other reasons, I started rejecting the offers of free food at the places where I took my meal breaks, and I went back to paying for movies as I had before. This occasionally caused difficulties. Some servers had clear instructions from their managers that cops were not to pay for food and said they would get into trouble if they took my money. I usually resolved this by telling them they could accept the payment as a tip, but even that got difficult if I didn't have anything close to the right change.

When I took meals with one of my fellow officers who wasn't of the same mind (and most of them weren't), they often thought I was trying to make them look bad or force them to follow my lead. There were several high-temperature discussions about this. Some took the attitude that I viewed myself as ethically superior to them, and others were just concerned that I was about to ruin a good thing. Many regarded the gratuities as all but a birthright, and I was screwing up the natural order of the universe.

Over time, the conflicts resolved themselves, in part because fewer establishments were giving away food to the cops. I doubt that I had much to do with this. It was more likely the effect of the rapacious behavior of some of my colleagues, who conducted themselves boorishly when they should have been gracious and appreciative.

There was one long-term effect, one I didn't find out about for several years. My rejection of the free movie tickets caused many officers to impersonate me at theaters, signing my name and badge number when they got their admission. If those sign-in logs still exist anywhere, they will show that I saw most every movie that played in theaters in the 1980s, most of them multiple times, and, in some cases, several at the same time.

▶ Compromise of Moral Authority

The cops who availed themselves of the free goods either didn't appreciate that there could be a transactional consequence to the practice or, just as likely, didn't care. When they took the free food or movie ticket, they didn't ask, "Does this have the potential to compromise my authority?"

In fact, it did. Now and then, a food server or business manager would be on the bad end of an enforcement action when they would bring up that they had been paying their fines on the installment plan for years. Some kept boxes of voided receipts for meals consumed by cops at their establishments, and they brought those boxes into the police station or courtroom when they got a ticket. They may not have had a great legal argument, but they caused enough discomfort for the judge or police administrator that the practice was regarded as a bad one.

The practice of accepting gratuities varies widely and tends to be regional. In the South and Midwest, where cops are often paid low wages, free or discounted meals are frequently commonplace. In the Pacific Northwest, where I live now, an officer who accepts a gratuity will almost certainly be disciplined, if not fired outright.

Police salary compensation has an influence here, but the more critical concern is the effect on the officer's moral authority and social status. The officer who gets his free lunch every day from the man he has stopped for a traffic violation is going to have difficulty making an unbiased discretionary decision on whether to issue a citation or a warning. There are many reasons to do one or the other, but how much food you've taken from the driver's business shouldn't be one of them.

The other concern is the social cubbyhole the officer takes up by accepting gratuities. We routinely offer gratuities or tips to people in certain occupations: food servers, valet parking attendants, bellmen in hotels, taxi drivers, and so on. These are all people who occupy, at least for the moment, the status of servant to our master. They often rely on the tips for a significant fraction of their income, and they are beholden to our generosity. A police officer needs to maintain some semblance of authority, and anything that compromises that authority undermines his effectiveness. The situation is bad enough if the officer is underpaid because we often associate social status with income. If the officer further denigrates himself by ingratiating himself to the violator, he doesn't have a lot to fall back on.

▶ Summary

Politics and organizational culture are underrated influences on professional success and accomplishment in law enforcement. A cop can be great at his job and never be recognized or even used to maximum potential because he isn't well liked or just doesn't fit in. The individual officer may constantly negotiate a compromise between his personal and professional values and the need to go along with the unwritten ethos of his employer.

Classical and Modern Ethical Theory: A Brief Survey

Richard J. Klonoski

Ethics concerns the best life for humans. The notion of the ideal human life has a long rich history, one that pervades the various cultures of the world. Ethical theory in the West has largely developed in response to its ancient origins that go back to pre-Homeric society in the Aegean (MacIntyre, 2007). Although the rumblings of virtue ethics were present in *Iliad* and *Odyssey*, the great heroic epic poems of Homer, virtue ethics *theory*—that is, a philosophical reasoned account of virtue—emerges most clearly and coherently in the dialogues of Plato.[1] In these philosophical dramas of ideas, Plato's teacher, Socrates, is seen conversing with a variety of interlocutors about all manner of things philosophical, including the nature of virtue and the possibility of acquiring it. Classical ethical theory, although developed in Plato's writings, is laid out most systematically in the writings of Plato's student Aristotle. Other Hellenic thinkers such as the hedonistic philosopher Epicurus and several Greco–Roman stoics such as Epictetus, Marcus Aurelius, and Seneca, as well as philosopher and statesman Cicero, made significant contributions to virtue ethics theory.

Foundational principles of classical ethical theory include a robust theory of human nature—specifically, a theory of the human soul—that serves as the basis of ethics and the idea that the goal of ethics or the ethical life is human flourishing, a condition often characterized as the human good or happiness. This condition is achieved by perfecting or making excellent the functions of the various capacities of the soul—that is, by acquiring the virtues. Also characteristic of classical virtue theory is that human excellence or virtue is attained by way of knowledge and a kind of "self-mastery," or by a deliberate rational process of self-development. The result of this cultivation of human moral excellence is virtuous character. Further, the development of virtuous character by and for the individual person is the necessary condition for individual ethical conduct, ethical relationships with other human beings, and with the human community. Finally, for the classical ethical theorists, the good of the society is intrinsically tied to the good of the individual because the society is the necessary context for the development of virtue and because the good of society, or the common good, is the natural end or purpose of the moral development of the members of society.

These fundamental notions are clearly at work in the ethical theories of Plato and Aristotle. In Plato's dialogue *Republic*, he has the main character, Socrates, delineate a tripartite conception of the human soul. For Plato, the soul has the capacities of reason, spiritedness or passion, and desire (Plato, 1991, pp. 118–120, 439a–441a). In his *Nicomachean Ethics*, Aristotle lays out a similar but more detailed conception. For Aristotle, the soul is divided into nonrational and rational elements and each element is further divided, respectively, into the nutritive or vegetative, which is the seat of all biophysiological functions of the body, and the appetitive, the seat of the passions, which are numerous.[2] The rational element has two parts: the calculative or deliberative and the scientific or theoretical.

For both Plato and Aristotle, by using reason the human soul can be developed so as to function with greater and greater excellence or virtue. For Plato, when the soul is rightly ordered—that is, when the various parts function in accord with excellence or such virtues as wisdom, courage, and moderation—the individual becomes "entirely one" and achieves real unity (Plato, 1991, pp. 123, 443e), which he also refers to as *justice* or the *inner harmony* among the parts of the whole soul.[3] Aristotle argues that through early education and prudent deliberation about our passions and actions that are aimed at ethically noble ends, we can acquire a wide range of virtues.[4] For both Plato and Aristotle, the ethical life comes about through a process of self-mastery and the acquisition of the virtues, the goal of which is human flourishing. Of importance here is the centrality of reason governing the passionate and desirous parts of the soul. Both believed that the cultivation of virtue—and, in Aristotle's case, virtuous character—was the basis for ethical action or conduct and ethical relationships, especially the individual's relationship to the human community or the city.[5] Morally good people—that is, those with virtuous character or who are well ordered within—make morally good decisions.

Although Hellenistic philosopher Epicurus argued for a hedonistic life, one in which the pursuit of pleasure and avoidance of pain was the guiding principle (something both Plato and Aristotle argue against), he also saw that the end of ethics was human flourishing, describing the goal of the blessed life as health of the body and freedom from disturbance in the soul (Epicurus, 1994). He famously said that living the pleasant life was inseparable from living the virtuous life, and living virtuously was inseparable from living pleasantly (Epicurus, 1994). The Stoics, Epictetus, and the Roman representatives of Stoicism,[6] Seneca and Marcus Aurelius, all championed tranquility or freedom from disturbance as the ideal condition for a human being. According to these thinkers, a rational self-mastery and acquisition of virtue was the basis for discharging one's moral responsibilities to others and to one's state. Roman philosopher and statesman Cicero argued that virtue was critical to discharging one's duties to the community. In his text, *On Duties*, Cicero outlines the nature of the four cardinal virtues and their relationship to moral duties (Cicero, 2005, p. 17, I. 15–17). These are wisdom, justice, fortitude, and temperance. He argues that by following nature and her laws we will develop in ourselves moral goodness by acquiring these virtues (Cicero, 2005, p. 103, I. 100). We will then not only enlist others in social cooperation but also rightly serve the community of our fellow man. In Cicero we see an early hint of *natural law* ethical theory that would develop more expansively in the Medieval period in the history of philosophy.

Natural law ethics must be considered as part of the traditional of classical ethical theory even though it was developed most substantially during the Medieval period by Catholic theologian and philosopher Saint Thomas Aquinas.[7] One reason for this is that Aquinas' philosophical system is profoundly influenced by Aristotle, whom Aquinas constantly refers to simply as "the philosopher," and because Aquinas' ethical theory is another emendation of virtue ethics.[8]

Key to Aquinas' natural law theory of ethics is the centrality of reason as a capacity given purposively to human beings by God. According to Aquinas, the universe is rationally ordered and governed by God's divine and eternal reason (Aquinas, 1981, Pt I–II, Q, 91, a.1, p. 996). The proper function of human reason, in its "practical employment"—that is, with regard to ethical choices—is to discern the proper end of human action, which is the good. The rational human being "is subject to Divine providence in the most excellent way, in so far as . . . it [the rational human being] has a share of the Enteral Reason [of God]" (Aquinas, 1981; Pt I–II, Q. 91, a2, p. 997). Human beings then have a natural God-given inclination to seek the proper end for human beings: what is good, virtuous, or what contributes to human flourishing. In using practical reason properly, human beings can grasp the first precept of natural law "that good is to be done and pursued, and evil is to be avoided. All other precepts of natural law are based upon this . . ." (Aquinas, 1981, Pt I–II, Q. 94, a.2, p. 1009). This means that by way of natural practical reason we could determine what is morally good and evil for human beings. "The participation of the eternal law in the rational creature is called the natural law" (Aquinas, 1981, pp. 1010–1011). Further, all just or legitimate human or human-made laws are derived from the one natural law (Aquinas, 1981, pp. 1014–1015) as do all ethical responsibilities human beings have to one another and to the human community.[9]

Although natural law ethical theory developed in some good measure in response to Greek and Roman ethics, modern ethical theory developed as a consequence of the birth of modern science, which was a crucial factor in the development of modern philosophy as such. In the 16th and 17th centuries, philosophers Francis Bacon and René Descartes and scientists such as Nicolaus Copernicus, Galileo Galilei, Johannes Kepler, and Tycho Brahe advanced a new scientific method that repudiated and displaced not only medieval scholasticism and Thomistic metaphysics but also so much of Greek philosophy, especially that of Aristotle (Gilson & Langan, 1963, pp. 449ff). Through the lens of this new method, the world was now viewed as composed of a heterogeneous matter in motion that could be studied and explained mathematically. This was contrary to the presumptions of Aristotle's teleological view of nature[10] and Aquinas' notion that the world is governed by God's divine providence. In both cases, the universe is purposely ordered, as are all things in it, including human beings. The best or ethical life would be found in understanding and bringing to full fruition the essential capacities of the human person in accordance with nature's purpose or God's intention or plan in creating these capacities. Once philosophy, now made "scientific," was separated from theology and religion (Gilson & Langan, 1963, p. 3), and once the universe was no longer seen as having an inborn purpose or the beings in it as having a natural telos or end, human beings were thrown back on themselves to determine the nature of ethical good and evil. Man would be the measure of the best life. A variety of ethical theories were born; among the most prominent were ethical egoism, utilitarianism, deontology, and various theories of justice.

In his momentous *Leviathan*, early modern philosopher Thomas Hobbes outlines a presocial, prepolitical condition of humans in a theoretical state of nature. In this circumstance, human beings are isolated, self-interested individuals, according to Hobbes. In this state of nature, human beings fear one another and have both a desire and willingness to hurt or even kill one another to preserve their lives and their interests (Hobbes, 1966, Pt 1.13). For Hobbes, human beings are not social–political creatures by nature as Aristotle and Aquinas would maintain, and society or political association does not develop organically as the natural end and final and most complete association of human beings. Actually, society comes about as a sort of accident and ultimately as a result of a compact or social contract (Hobbes, 1966, Pt 1.14).

The effect of Hobbes' characterization of human nature and human society on his ethical theory is profound. Human beings are driven by their passions and are self-interested in all they do; we are "psychological egoists." Hobbes says that "a general inclination of all mankind [is] a perpetual and restless desire of power after power that ceaseth only in death" (Hobbes, 1966, Pt 1.11, pp. 85–86). This psychological egoism is the basis of Hobbes' "ethical egoism" or the ethical prescription that human beings "ought" to pursue their own interest and satisfy their own desires.[11] Moreover, for Hobbes, society is an artificial construct entered into to avoid existence in a savage state of nature; it is not the human end but merely a means for giving human beings the security to pursue their own interests. Traditional Greco–Roman and Christian virtues such as justice, modesty, mercy, and gratitude are "conventional tools" as opposed to objective human excellences by which we perfect our character in service to human flourishing. Outside the bounds of society the virtues are meaningless as they are "contrary to our natural passions . . ." (Hobbes, 1966, Pt. 1.17, pp. 153–154), which incline us to seek the power necessary to satisfy every desire. This ethical theory is modern by repudiating classical virtue theory and by holding that human beings determine moral good and evil as individuals based on a modern theory of human nature. Neither religion nor the soul—that is, the perfectible hierarchical structure or essence of humankind—is the basis for determining the best or ethical life for human beings and human communities.[12]

Also in the modern period, utilitarian consequentialist ethical theory arose out of the British philosophical tradition of empiricism. Utilitarian ethics is represented most famously by Jeremy Bentham and John Stuart Mill. Bentham argued that "nature has placed man under the governance of two sovereign masters, pain and pleasure . . . the principle of utility recognizes this subjection, and assumes it for the foundation" of the ethical theory utilitarianism (Bentham, 1996, p. 11). Every action of an individual person or any measure of government—that is, law or public policy—should conform to the normative principle of utility. That is to say, actions are judged ethical or not based on the actual or prospective consequences of the action, specifically the tendency that the action or law has to promote the utility or happiness of the party or parties whose interest is in question. To be deemed ethical, actions should guarantee the greatest good for individuals or for the community of individuals insofar as the community is affected by the consequences of the action (Bentham, 1966, pp. 11–12). Bentham developed and employed what can be called a "hedonistic calculus" to measure and quantify the value of pleasures and pains—that is, what has utility and what entails disutility. John Stuart Mill, initially influenced by Bentham, developed his own utilitarian ethical theory, although Mill eventually reacted against Bentham's view that only the quantity of pleasure was relevant to moral decision making. Mill argued that in deciding what was good or evil, what promoted human happiness, utility, benefit, and so on, and what diminished it, the quality of pleasure and pain had to be considered (Scruton, 2002, pp. 237–238). Mill, who prized liberty for human beings and their societies, also believed in the importance of a robust cultivation of the person and in the importance of education through which such development of the self could be furthered as well as the way the individual promotes the greatest good for the greatest number. Nonetheless, Mill advocated for a consequentialist ethical theory (Mill, 1979), divorcing the moral character of the agent from the goodness of the act.

The most profound and most influential reaction against consequentialism come from 18th-century German philosopher Immanuel Kant. In his *Groundwork for the Metaphysics of Morals*, Kant sets out to investigate the "ground" or "foundation" of morality, a paradigmatic modern, quasi-scientific sort of concern. He examines what he calls "ordinary rational knowledge of morality," digs beneath the surface of that ordinary understanding, and uncovers the categorical imperative, the fundamental normative principle of his deontological—that is, duty-based—ethical theory. Kant argues that we ought not to determine the moral goodness or evilness of actions based on the consequences of our action but on the motive of the action. The only moral motive there is for Kant is respect for universal ethical principles— that is, principles that would be valid for and binding on any rational being without exception. Human beings determine whether their action is motivated by or for the sake of duty alone by asking themselves if the motivational principle of the action— the maxim or statement of the rationale for one's action—can become a universal moral law. The categorical imperative is: "I ought never to act except in such a way that I can also will that my maxim should become a universal [moral] law" (Kant, 1981, p. 14). And further, "An action, performed from duty has its moral worth . . . in the maxim according to which the action is determined" (Kant, 1981, p. 13) and is not based in the consequences of the action. The demand for the universality of moral rules indicates that Kant opposes ethical relativism, utilitarian consequentialism, and any ethical theory that derives the ethical legitimacy of actions from pleasure or pain, desire, or passion or emotions. For Kant, reason alone determines what duty is, and that determination occurs when reason commands our will to act from duty alone independently of inclination or desire. Kant argues that human beings have unconditional value or worth, that they are subjects rather than objects, persons rather than things. This is to say that human beings are "autonomous"—that is, literally self-legislating or free. In service to explaining this claim more fully, Kant reformulates the categorical or practical imperative as follows: "Act in such a way that you always treat humanity, whether in your own person or in the person of another, always at the same time as an end and never simply as a means" (Kant, 1981, p. 36). Human beings deserve respect because they are rational, free, and self-governing and may not be used as mere means to anyone else's purposes. Human beings are persons not things, subjects not objects, and ends in themselves not means.

Fueled by a skepticism about classical Greco–Roman philosophy and religion, the birth of modern science was characterized by a search for new foundations not only for metaphysics and epistemology but also for ethics. The modern scientific method—with its focus on rules, principles, and physical laws of nature that govern the movement of matter in space—coupled empirical observation with mathematical analysis and was aimed at uncovering the true nature of reality and the basis or ground of knowledge and truth. Moved by the spirit of modern science, modern philosophers attempted to use scientific methodology applied not only to understanding and solving problems about nature but also to problems in human affairs, including ethics and politics. Ethical theory becomes a kind of problem-solving endeavor using normative principles such as the principle of utility and the categorical imperative as templates or as the basis of ethical decision-making models. Ethical theory became a kind of applied science of good and evil.[13]

With the development of greater and more refined specialization in the sciences (a development that extends Aristotle's original division of the arts and sciences), modern science to this day proceeds as a process of progressive refinement in terms of both scientific disciplines and, most especially, scientific methodology as key to scientific progress. Modern philosophy followed a parallel path of development, and in the academy today we see an increased specialization of ethical theory in the development of applied ethical theory in virtually every area of academic study, including business, communication, biomedical science and research, medicine, environmental studies, engineering, law, politics, and criminal justice, among others. In a word, applied ethics has become a kind of quasi-scientific theoretical attempt at solving ethical problems. The approach to ethics stands opposed to classical ethical theory, which was aimed at the ideal or best life for humans, this is a life rooted in an understanding of what morally improves or debilitates human beings and their communities, what leads to the perfection or corruption of human faculties, and what contributes to or diminishes the possibility of human flourishing. Modern, and much contemporary ethical theory, specifically applied ethics, focuses in a rather technical way on establishing rules for application and addressing ethical issues, problems, dilemmas. The most frequently employed ethical theories in the analysis of ethical problems are consequentialism and deontology, although there have been a variety of texts published on ethical theory that include discussions and applications of virtue ethics, natural law theory, and contemporary theories of justice[14] to contemporary ethical problems.

However, given the predominance of consequentialist and deontological ethical theories, especially in applied ethics, a distinctive ethical theory, the feminist ethics of care is neither utilitarian nor deontological in nature. Although some have argued that care ethics is a kind of virtue ethics, Virginia Held, a proponent of this theory, argues that it is not. The ethics of care is actually a response to and rejection of these aforesaid traditional ethical theories.[15] Held maintains that "the ethics of care focusses on social relations and the social practices and values that sustain them" (Held, 2006, p. 20). This is a feminist ethical theory having roots in the work of psychologist Carol Gilligan. Traditional ethical theories, both classical and modern, emphasize "rational control over the emotions, rather than on cultivating desirable forms of emotion" (Held, 1993, p. 52). According to Held and other proponents of caring and care ethics, "caring, empathy, feeling for others, being sensitive to each other's feelings—all may be better guides to what morality requires in actual contexts than many abstract rules of reason or rational calculation" (Held, 1993, p. 52). The ethics of care aims at cultivating "moral sensibilities," many of which have been manifest in women's practices, work, and experiences (Held, 1993, p. 50; also Noddings, 1984, p. 26ff).

A criticism of feminist care ethics is that it is difficult to apply consistently to the solution of concrete and complex contemporary ethical problems, but this would be the case with any non-normative ethical theory like the classical ethical theories. The development of applied normative ethical theories like modern utilitarian and deontological theories, not to mention some theories of justice, escape this criticism, at least to some extent. That said, it is also true that modern ethical theory has brought to the fore the importance of human rights, liberty, and justice and the importance of having ethics address human problems on a social level. And contemporary applied ethics is a systematic effort to do just that. However, such ethical theories are subject to another criticism—that is, they tend to depend on a narrow and even attenuated conception of human nature. Modern thinkers such as Hobbes and Locke atomize human beings, construing them as isolated individuals largely either subject to desire or pleasure and pain or as simply autonomous and rational. According to classical ethical theories, human beings are a collage of faculties and capacities. In other words, the classical theories recognize the richness of human nature and takes this as the starting point of ethics. The ethics of care, with its focus on the development of moral sensibilities, takes this complexity of human persons into account in a way that modern ethical theories, especially applied ethical theories, do not. And even though it might be argued that the ethics of care smacks of relativism, so does consequentialist applied ethical theory, not to mention the difficulty of predicting the occurrence and adequately determining the relative value of consequences. It is also true that deontological ethical theorists face the challenge of adjudicating between conflicting duties that appear equally, ethically compelling and supporting in all cases the universality of ethical principles. However, applied ethical theory informed by a robust theory of human nature, characteristic of classical ethical theory and also feminist ethics, might be a more effective if not a more thoroughgoingly human way of addressing complex contemporary ethical problems, problems that are a reflection of the complexity of human nature itself. At the risk of being overly simplistic, ethics might best begin with the fundamental principle that virtuous people make morally good decisions, as might human beings with highly developed moral sensibilities. Ethical theory then might begin with a clear conception of what it is to be human, what it means to treat human beings ethically or well, and what is the natural end or telos of human beings—that is, what is human flourishing.

▶ Endnotes

1. In Plato's *Crito*, for example, Socrates is portrayed on death row having been charged, tried, and convicted for having committed crimes against the city of Athens. Presented with a variety of arguments by his friend Crito to escape from prison, Socrates says that in moral matters he "only listens to the argument that seems best" (Plato, 2000, p. 46, 46b) and that he will not violate long-held ethical principles that he has lived his life by (Plato, 2000, 46c) by escaping from prison. Such principles include doing no harm not even in return for a harm done to oneself and keeping just agreements (Plato, 2007, pp. 47–50). Plato develops his ethical theory in several other dialogues including *Republic, Meno, Charmides, Laches,* and others. We should also note that in the *Crito* dialogue there is a three-fold contrast among Socrates, who represents the philosophical view of the importance of virtue and the moral integrity of the soul, his friend Crito, who represents the view of the many and/or the customs or conventions of society, and the laws of Athens personified by Plato, as he has them "speak" to Socrates and Crito about the plan to escape from prison.

2. For Aristotle, the passions or emotions include desire, anger, fear, confidence, envy, joy, friendly affection, hatred, yearning, emulation, and pity (Aristotle, 2011, pp. 32, 1105b).

3. According to Plato, the soul is brought into a harmony because of knowledge about the function of each part of the soul and what makes each part function with excellence or virtue. Thus, Plato's doctrine that "virtue is knowledge." The real unity of the soul or justice is a kind of health of the soul, injustice being a kind of disease or corruption of good order (Plato, 1991, pp. 124, 444a-e).

4. Aristotle argues that there are two kinds of virtue: moral (there are 11 of these) (Aristotle, 2011, pp. 54–114) and intellectual (art, science, prudence, wisdom and intellect) (Aristotle, 2011, pp. 115–134). The former are virtues of character or "intermediate states of character," and the latter virtues of thought or excellent modes of rational activity. The moral virtues are made manifest for Aristotle in morally virtuous actions that precipitate from expressing the right passion in the right way in relation to the right person and rationally by determining the right action as a means to the acquisition of that virtue. These virtues and the passions and actions that undergird them stand "intermediate" between vices of deficiency and excess. For example, generosity is intermediate between stinginess and wastefulness, and courage is intermediate between cowardice and rashness.

5. In the *Republic*, Plato's central analogy is that between the soul and the city. The soul has three parts that are analogous to the three classes of the city: rulers, warriors, and craftsmen. Justice is harmony among the parts of each the soul and the city, the same in each. The individual citizen whose soul has real unity "acts . . . either concerning the acquisition of money, or the care of the body, or something political, or concerning private contracts," justly or ethically (Plato, 1991, pp. 123, 443d-e). The acquisition of virtue by the individual allows them to contribute to the good of the city, or the common good. Note that Aristotle also speaks about human good, happiness or human flourishing, saying that it is "the same thing for one individual or for a city; [and further that] to secure and preserve the good of the city, appears to be something greater and more complete; the good of the individual by himself is certainly desirable enough, but that of a nation and of cities is noble and more divine" (Aristotle, 2011, p. 3, 1094b). The private good of the individual then is put in service to the good of the city or society and which is even its end or purpose. This is a key characteristic of classical ethical theory.

6. The Greek and Roman philosophers acquired the name stoics because they frequented the stoas or porches of the public buildings where they taught philosophy. However, stoicism soon came to refer to the teachings themselves. A stoical person has extraordinary self-control and an undisturbed demeanor, is seemingly emotionless, and is able to endure hardship with equanimity or calmness. The Stoics prized wisdom and courage, moderation and justice, among other virtues, and crafting a tranquility in the soul, the ideal condition of the sage (Aurelius, 1983; Epictetus, 1983).

7. As Howard P. Kainz points out, there were earlier rumblings or intimations of natural law theory in Plato's dialogue *Laws* (890e) and *Republic* (444d) (Kainz, 2004, p. 5).

8. Kainz notes further that, in his *Politics*, Aristotle argues that human beings are "political animals and that the state is a creation of nature itself" (1984, I. 2, 1253a, 1–9), an argument that elicits a natural law that governs the creation of the state, which is the natural end of all human associations. See also Kainz (2004), pp. 10–13, on Stoic and Ciceronian natural law.

9. Fourth-century A.D. philosopher and theologian St. Augustine argued that God's "eternal law has been impressed upon our minds; it is the law by which it is just that everything be ordered in the highest degree" (Augustine, 1983, p. 15). This highest ordering of all things refers to the human person who governs her will by reason, as well as to temporal laws that govern states. Just human-made laws are derived from eternal law.

10. Aristotle believed that nature was "purposeful" or end oriented, meaning that all things have a telos or an end toward which they strive or develop. For humans, this natural end is happiness, the human good, the most excellent expression of our rational nature.

11. Perhaps the most famous if not the most infamous modern or contemporary version of ethical egoism can be found in the writings of philosopher Ayn Rand. She argues for a "rational egoism" in *The Virtue of Selfishness* (Rand, 1964) and depicts this theory in her novels *The Fountainhead* (Rand, 1994), and *Atlas Shrugged* (Rand, 1957).

12. Given the modern notion that society comes about as a result of a social contract and is a conventional or artificial construct, rights of the individual become primary. The common

good of society becomes secondary to the good of the individual, and society is only a means to the good of the individual. This is especially evident in the modern turn of John Locke, as his political philosophy turned away from natural law and toward natural rights (Pakaluk, 2017).

13. At the end of Section I of the *Groundwork* titled "Transition from the Ordinary Rational Knowledge of Morality to the Philosophical," we see Kant ask whether "science or philosophy is needed in order to know what one must do to be honest and good and even wise and virtuous" (Kant, 1981, p. 16). He decides that a systematic analysis of ordinary rational knowledge of morality or a quasi-scientific, philosophical analysis is indeed necessary, the result of which is the uncovering of fundamental principles of morality.

14. In a brief overview of ethical theory such as this, a full discussion of contemporary philosophical or political theories of justice is not in any way possible. Among the most important of these is *A Theory of Justice* (Rawls, 1971). I mention this in particular because of his modern approach to the question of ethical and political justice—Rawls takes an approach that sees ethics as procedural—and because Rawls responds to utilitarian and deontological ethical theorizing.

15. Some care ethics theorists have addressed the issue of justice, often in response to Rawls in particular. For example see Baier (1987), pp. 47–55, and Friedman (1987), pp. 61–77 in Held (1995).

▸ # References

Aquinas, T. (1981). *Summa theologica* (Vol. 2). Westminster, MD: Christian Classics.

Aristotle. (1984). *The politics*. (C. Lord, Trans.) Chicago, IL: University of Chicago Press.

Aristotle. (2011). *Aristotle's Nicomachean ethics*. (R. B. Collins, Trans.) Chicago, IL: The University of Chicago Press.

Augustine. (1983). *On the free choice of the will*. (T. Williams, Trans.). Indianapolis, IN: Hackett Publishing.

Aurelius, M. (1983). *The meditations*. Indianapolis, IN: Hackett Publishing.

Baier, A. (1987). The need for more than justice. In V. Held, *Justice and care: Essential readings in feminist ethics* (pp. 47–58). Boulder, CO: Westview Press.

Bentham, J. (1996). *An introduction to the principles of morals and legislation*. (J. Burns & H. Hart, Eds.) New York, NY: Oxford University Press.

Cicero. (2005). *On duties*. (Miller, Trans.) Cambridge, MA: Harvard University Press.

Epictetus. (1983). *The handbook*. (N. White, Trans.) Indianapolis, IN: Hackett Publishing.

Epicurus. (1994). *The Epicurus reader*. (B. Inwood, & L. Gerson, Trans.) Indianapolis, IN: Hackett Publishing.

Friedman, M. (1987). Beyond caring; The de-moralization of gender. In V. Held, *Justice and care: Essential readings on feminist ethics* (pp. 61–78). Boulder, CO: Westview Press.

Gilson, E., & Langan, T. (1963). *Modern philosophy; Descartes to Kant*. New York, NY: Random House.

Held, V. (1993). *Feminist morality*. Chicago IL: University of Chicago Press.

Held, V. (2006). *The ethics of care; Personal, political, and global*. New York, NY: Oxford University Press.

Hobbes, T. (1966). *The English works of Thomas Hobbes: Leviathan* (Vol. III). Germany: Scientia Verlag Aallen.

Kainz, H. (2004). *Natural law: An introduction and re-examination*. Chicago, IL: Open Court Publishing.

Kant, I. (1981). *Grounding for the metaphysics of morals*. (3rd ed.). (J. Ellington, Trans.) Indianapolis, IN: Hackett Publishing.

MacIntyre, A. (2007). *After virtue*. Notre Dame, IN: University of Notre Dame Press.

Mill, J. (1979). *Utilitarianism*. Indianapolis IN: Hackett Publishing.

Noddings, N. (1984). *Caring: A feminine approach to ethics and moral education*. Berkley, CA: University of California Press.

Pakaluk, M. (2017). From natural law to natural rights in Locke. In M. Rohlf, *The modern turn* (pp. 89–111). Washington, DC: Catholic University of America Press.

Plato. (1991). *The republic of Plato* (2nd ed.). (A. Bloom, Trans.) New York, NY: Basic Books.

Plato. (2000). *The trial and death of Socrates* (3rd ed.). (G. M. Grube, Trans.) Indianapolis, IN: Hackett Publishing.

Rand., A. (1957). *Atlas shrugged.* New York, NY: Random House.

Rand, A. (1964). *The virtue of selfishness.* New York, NY: Penguin.

Rand, A. (1994). *The fountainhead.* New York, NY: Plume.

Rawls, J. (1991). *A theory of justice.* Cambridge, MA: Harvard University Press.

Scruton, R. (2002). *A short history of modern Philosophy* (2nd ed.). New York, NY: Routledge Classics.

Cultural Relativism and Cultural Absolutism: How Does the Discussion Relate to Africa's Affairs?

Victoria Time

▶ Introduction

When we discuss culture, it is about the way of life of a people that identifies them of the same stock while at times distinguishing them from others, even when trait characteristics are similar. Lako (2004) discusses culture in light of the socialization process and furthers her discussion by explaining that culture dominates people's consciousness and experiences. Even though her explanation of culture introduces the concept of female subjugation through a culture of patriarchal domination, her point of what culture entails is eloquently stated.

Any discussion of culture also requires differentiating it from values and norms. This is necessary because certain practices that may simply be values are mistaken for culture. Flynn (2009) explains that values are qualities or beliefs held by a given society, and they delineate certain qualities and characteristics that denote values. They are:

- Values cannot be observed.
- Values are different from other social and psychological states.
- Values vary based on history and culture.

Flynn (2009) also distinguishes values from norms. Norms, Flynn contends, relate to those conditions or ways of behavior that typically are evident in a group or a society that are different from those of other groups or societies. Although a person may hold a particular value as Flynn (2009) elucidates, groups subscribe to norms. Put in context, one may detach oneself from group norms while following values that one deems right. The thrust of this discussion is that, even though one may be depicted as belonging to a particular culture, at any time one may decide to refrain from complying with norms that are destructive or contrary to one's values. One may also engage in a particular norm with the belief that it is the right way of life because it is steeped in culture—and yet others may condemn that way of life. There are diverse cultures in the world, and in Africa—even within a particular country—it is not uncommon to find multiple cultures. What regard do we place on these cultures? Are some cultures antiquated or barbaric? Are some cultures superior to others? What are the bases for any judgments? These are questions that form the basis of this study, and about which cultural relativists and absolutists have incessantly debated.

▶ What Is Cultural Relativism?

In a simplistic sense, cultural relativism means that because there is a vast array of cultures worldwide, it would be unwise to apply an ethnocentric assumption that one culture or way of life is superior to others and must be the standard for all others. As Park (2011) explains, cultural relativism requires that a person's behavior should be evaluated only on the basis of the person's culture. So, if a behavior is culturally accepted, it is not for outsiders to castigate it or call it immoral (see also Rachels & Rachels, 2010; Schick & Vaughn, 2010).

▶ What Is Cultural Absolutism?

Cultural absolutism stands for the premise that, regardless of the existence of diverse societies, we all are of the human species and thus must subscribe to and be judged by the same ethical code. In this regard, absolutists promote the idea that ethically what is deemed wrong or right is universal. In essence, everyone is on the same moral scale and must be judged on that basis. Park (2011) explains that cultural absolutism rests on the premise that a culture may be deemed superior and the "right standard" for other cultures.

Also relevant to the discussion is ethical pluralism. *Ethical pluralism* relates to the premise that there are divergent perspectives on rightness or wrongness that may clash with one's moral compass. Berlin's (1997) explanation of pluralism resides on the point that there are several values, and one may appreciate multiple values even if subsequently one chooses those that are most meaningful to oneself. So, even though a practice is customary and constitutes the norms of one's society, one's values or ethics can be in conflict with the norms of one's society.

In the African context, ethical quagmires exist when culture, norms, and practices cross paths with cultural absolutists' viewpoints. As well understood, culture is practice that can factually be researched and explained, although ethics on the other hand is normative. Practices that may not sit well with many ethicists are at times referred to as "primitive cultures" (Wall, 1967). To the people immersed in the culture, it is a way of life, a continuity of practice that spans decades if not centuries, and to them they find no wrongness in what they do.

In this article, some practices that exist in some African countries will help advance the discussion between cultural relativism and cultural absolutism.

▶ Forced Marriages and Bride Price

Accounts of the practices of forced marriages, bride price, levirate, and clitoridectomy can be found in several articles and books (see Bentheim, 2010; Chigbu et al., 2010; Kiragu, 1996; Lionnet, 2005; Welstead, 2009). Forward UK (n.d.) defines *forced marriage* as a union "conducted without the valid consent of one or both parties and is a marriage in which duress—whether physical or emotional is a factor." Along with forced marriage is bride price. "Bride price is a sum, either in cash or kind, used to purchase a bride for her labour and fertility" (Forward UK, n.d.). In some villages in the eastern part of Burkina Faso, kidnapping a girl for the purpose of marriage is considered an act of bravery.

> Kidnapping a girl is showing to the community that one has become mature. Kidnapping girls helps one earn social status of an accomplished adult. Very often, after kidnapping a girl, a man will raise a flag in his compound to serve as a testimony to the community that he is now to be considered among the strongest and most respectable men in the village. (Kabore, Yaro, & Dan-Koma, 2008, p. 24)

Martin Mogwanja, who in 2014 was deputy executive director of UNICEF, revealed that women between the ages of 20 and 24—that is, four of every 10 of them—married before adulthood (SBS News, 2014). Projections by the regional director of the U.N. Population Fund are that there will be at least 16 million child brides in Africa every year (SBS News, 2014). In response to such findings, 50 African heads of states and representatives from the United Nations met at a summit in Addis Ababa, Ethiopia, in 2014. The basis of this meeting was to launch a campaign to ban marriages contracted with girls younger than 18 years of age. Refworld (2006) states that in countries like Mali, girls as young as 12 are forced to marry. This is not unique to Mali; reports of 12-year-old girls being forced to marry have come out of Niger (see Smith, 2016) and Burkina Faso (Kabore et al., 2008). In South Africa and other African countries, it is not uncommon to find 14-year-old brides (see Mchunu et al., 2012). Birech (2013), explains that South African law respects traditional marriages even when the girl is as young as 12 and the boy 14.

The predicament suffered by girls does not end with being forced to marry at tender ages. Health issues following infectious diseases add to the suffering of the young bride (see Nawal, 2006). Following surveys among parents in several African countries, it is clear that there is still a preference that boys, not girls, receive an education (Plan International, 2012). The preference rests on the mistaken belief that boys are smarter, would eventually be breadwinners, and remain custodians of the family lineage, whereas girls would marry and then leave the home (Plan International, 2012). Take the example of Mali, where 48% of parents favor sending sons but not daughters to school; if forced to send their daughters to school, only 28% indicate that they would have their daughters stay on in school. In the Ashanti region of Ghana, 50% of parents indicate a preference for sons to go to school, and just 10% favor their daughters (Plan International, 2012).

▶ Levirate

Kiragu (1996) explains *levirate* as a practice whereby surviving brothers of deceased men inherit their widows. This practice is still prevalent in some parts of some African states such as Senegal, Burkina Faso, and Nigeria, among others (Alewo & Olong, 2012; Plateau et al., 2000).

▶ Female Circumcision or Clitoridectomy

Althaus (1997) explains clitoridectomy as the cutting of the outward genitalia. This practice is intended to mark a girl's transition to womanhood by increasing fertility and reducing a woman's interest in being promiscuous (see Maluleke, 2012). The practice occurs in at least 28 African countries, particularly those in the northern part of the continent (Althaus, 1997; Toubia, 1995).

Clearly, girls are disproportionately affected by these practices. Plan International (2012, p. 25) puts things in perspective:

> Constraints of poverty, location, gender stereotypes, social norms, customs and harmful practices all form a shifting and interconnected web through which girls, their families and their communities have to navigate on a daily basis. In particular, students, teachers and parents highlighted the way in which poverty lies at the heart of many of the challenges that hinder girls' access to, and experience of, education. The pressures of poverty mean that parents must constantly make decisions about how to utilize extremely limited resources and how best to provide a secure future for their family. In the context of the range of factors explored below, the choices made often mean that girls' opportunities and life chances are severely constrained.

▶ The Debate

Locke (1989, p. 67) advances three ideas as necessary ingredients for a "peaceful culturally plural world" that include (1) cultural equivalence, (2) cultural reciprocity, and (3) limited cultural convertibility.

With regard to a "cultural plural world," Locke advocates a world in which cultures are complementary, or connected; with cultural reciprocity, he projects a state of affairs where no one culture is superior to the other. Cultural reciprocity, as Locke explains, relates to some sort of parity among cultures.

Locke's viewpoints are evocative of the cultural pluralist viewpoints that William James (1842–1910), Max Weber (1864–1920), Isaiah Berlin (1909–1997), and others espoused. To further understand the vitality of diverse cultural acceptance, Menand (2001) advocates accepting cultural diversity by primarily absorbing those aspects of each culture that contribute to enrich society. This, as Menand (2001) discusses, is a premise accepted by John Dewey, a cultural pluralist in his time. Berstein (2015) contributes to the dialogue by concluding that discussions that incorporate cultural pluralistic views are necessary in democratic societies.

The debate about cultural pluralism versus absolutism cannot make sense in this study without hearing from Africans themselves. Pluralists see culture as a way of inherited life; they do not endorse barbarism but give deference to the way of life of a people. Althaus (1997), for example, explains how Sudanese men favor the ritual of female circumcision because to them it is a way to promote culture, and many women who have gone through the practice are slow to condemn it because it is a cultural heritage. With regard to forced marriages and bride price, it is not uncommon to hear parents approve of such unions as a way of not only promoting culture but also as a way of cementing family friendships, providing financial security, and lifting the burden of taking care of the daughter and shifting it to her husband (ghanabusinessnews.com, 2013). Birech (2013) explains that the practice of forcing little girls to marry in South Africa is defended by village elders. The custom is seen as a tribal tradition—notwithstanding the fact that the country ratified the Convention on the Rights of the Child in 1995, which imposes 18 years as minimum age for marriage. African women who accept levirate obligation base their support on the psychological balance and financial stability that the widow and her children get from the marriage (see Plateau et al., 2000). One can deduce a connection of the viewpoints of the Africans already noted to Locke's cultural equivalence. The conclusion is that they do not think their culture is less valuable; if anything, they think it is desirable.

Certainly, there are detractors to such perspectives even within the regions where those practices occur. Take the practice of levirate, for example. African women who are opposed to it contend that it is not a relation based on love or physical attraction, and such a state of affairs generates cruelty and violence (Plateau et al., 2000). With regard to female circumcision, objections are centered on the physical, psychological, and health issues that at times ensue in the process (see Obiora, 2005). Girls forced into early marriages have raised objections through legal action—for instance, the lawsuit filed by Hadijatou Koraou (forced at 12 years old to marry a 46-year-old man) against the Republic of Niger (see *Hadijatou Mani Koraou v. The Republic of Niger*, 2008). See also the case of 11-year-old Mwaka of Malawi who fled from her 63-year-old husband back to her parents, who gladly received her back (LaFraniere, 2005; Time, 2017). Her father gave her away to settle a loan of 2,000 Malawian kwacha, around $16. In a study among women in the Wakiso district of Uganda, Kaye et al. (2005) found out through 14 in-depth interviews and 10 focus group discussions that the women saw the practice as a way to subjugate women by limiting their ability to make decisions that directly affect them. In a one-on-one interview with a woman in her 70s in Cameroon in 2014, the woman expressed grave disgust and condemnation of the persistence of child marriages. Although she acknowledged the practice persists because of poverty, she was nonetheless emphatic on her conviction that "under no circumstance should a parent sacrifice a child for their needs" (Time, 2017, p. 21).

Opinions of Western observers have been critical, and for the most part objections hinge on human rights violations. Lionnet (2005, p. 99), for example, views the debate as "two apparently conflicting versions of human rights, one based on the Enlightenment notion of the sovereign individual subject, and the other on a notion of collective identity grounded in cultural solidarity."

In making the point that no culture is better than another and that there is relativity in morality, Park (2011, p. 161) puts forth the following analogy:

A beef-eating culture, for example, is no better than a beef-abstaining culture, and vice versa, so the latter should not accuse the former of eating beef, and the former should not denigrate the latter for refraining from eating beef. Consequently, they ought to tolerate each others' practices, and they are justified in keeping their different customs without interfering with one another.

Setting the stage for the arguments raised by cultural absolutists are some of the assumptions made by researchers regarding these cultural practices in Africa. With regard to female circumcision, they state that it is:

1. a sinister vestige of barbarism that violates universal standards of modern civilization,
2. an oppressive system of patriarchy that attempts to control female sexuality through physical violence,
3. a culturally sanctioned form of torture that violates every human's right to bodily integrity and individual autonomy,
4. a despotic assertion of parental power that places the emotional and physical well-being of children at grave risk, and
5. an alien practice of Islamic affiliation that African Muslims are transplanting to the West. (Steffen, 2011)

As universal moralists conclude, "Equals should be treated equally is not the only self-evident moral truth. Another is: Unnecessary suffering is wrong" (Schick & Vaughn, 2010, p. 365). In essence, values of rightness cannot be compromised regardless of cultural setting, cultural beliefs, or cultural practices. In dismissing that viewpoint, Park (2011) explains that cultural relativists only examine rightness or wrongness of an act with respect to a particular culture and that no culture is superior to another. Furthermore, it is not that cultural relativists dismiss the idea of rightness or wrongness in toto but that they accept the fact that there may be convergence among various cultures. In this regard, if Africans state that female circumcision and child marriages are wrong, then it is not because universal moralists state the practices are wrong but because Africans themselves decry the practices as immoral.

Using the example of slavery, Park (2011) explains that social reformers were wrong to have denounced it, and the wrongness was only because they were condemning a past culture, but they are right to condemn it as a current culture. This argument would make sense in the African context if the cultural practices in question were vestiges of the past. But that is not the case with the cultural practices in Africa discussed here. These practices are ongoing in societies in Africa where they are reported to take place. What is more meaningful in this discussion following Park's (2011) trend of thought is that if those who perpetuate these cultures in Africa were cultural relativists, then they would understand that their practice or culture is in no way better than the culture of those who oppose and abhor the practice or culture. In essence, selling children into marriages, depriving girls of education, and submitting them to genital mutilation is more reflective of an absolutist viewpoint of wrongness than that of a relativist. At the same time, following Park's (2011) argument, even if these abhorrent practices were abandoned, the cultural relativist would see this only as stepping toward equality, but not as stepping toward absolutism.

In raising objections to the perspectives of cultural relativists, Pojman (2008) asserts that cultural relativism is a flawed concept because it affords no clarity with regard to what constitutes a society or how many persons are required to form a culture. Park's (2011) response is that the number of persons who constitute a society or culture is irrelevant both to relativists and absolutists. If numbers were the issue, then some of the practices that have come under criticism in Africa would not be talked about because even within a country with dozens and dozens of tribes, only one or just a few tribes engage in the practice. Take Ghana, for instance. Child marriage is more common in just some parts of the country such as Volta, parts of the Ashanti, and the Brong Ahafo communities (Cooper, 2019). In the Imo State in Nigeria, the practice of forced marriages still goes on (Alewo and Olong, 2012). In Mali, levirate is practiced just among the Supyire tribe (Jemphrey, 2011). And in some parts of South Africa, the supposed "virgin cure" exists, a mythical belief that having sex with extremely young girls cures HIV or AIDS (Lutya, 2012).

▶ Conclusion

As Time (2017, p. 182) states, "[C]ulture identifies a people and some aspects of it distinguish a set of people from another. To the extent that the culture of the people promote healthy values, it is endearing." However, when cultural practices produce negative consequences—as, for instance, denying girls the benefit of an education or childhood experiences by forcing them to marry men the age of their grandparents—such a culture is antiquated. Souryal (1992) explains that Greek philosophers considered the promotion of a "good life" as exemplifying the best of the moral character of a person or persons and further explains how Plato described human goodness as the "achievement of an intelligent and a rational order of thinking" (Souryal, 1992, p. 19). It should not take a debate of cultural relativists and absolutists to decide the rightness or wrongness of a practice. Common sense suffices. Forcing a child to marry for pecuniary benefit, depriving a child of formal education, having a widow marry her late husband's brother, and subjecting girls to clitoridectomy may be practices acceptable to a culture, but they violate human goodness. Each person should be left to live her or his life happily and be free to choose a lifestyle carved out for her- or himself.

▶ References

Alewo, A., & Olong, M. (2012). Cultural practices and traditional beliefs as impediments to the enjoyment of women's rights in Nigeria. *International Law Research, 1*(1), pp. 134–143.

Althaus, F. (1997). Female circumcision: Rite of passage or violation of rights? *International Family Planning Perspectives, 23*(3), 130–133.

Bentheim, C. (2010). Forced marriage in Africa: Examining the disturbing reality. Consultancy Africa Intelligence. Retrieved October 7, 2010 from http://www.consultancyafrica.com/index .php?opinion=com_content&view=article&id290

Berlin, I. (1997). *The proper study of mankind: An anthology of essays.* H. Hardy & R. Hausheer (Eds). London, UK: Chatto & Windus.

Berstein, R. (2015). Cultural pluralism. In A. Ferrara, K. Volker, & R. David (Eds.), *Philosophy and Social Criticism, 41*(4–5), 347–356.

Birech, J. (2013). Child marriage: A cultural health phenomenon. *International Journal of Humanities and Social Sciences, 3*(17), 97–103.

Chigbu, C., Ekeazi, K., Chigbu, C., & Iwuji, S. (2010). Sexual violation among married women in south eastern Nigeria. *International Journal of Gynecology and Obstetrics, 110*(2), 141–144.

Cooper, N. (2019). Ghana: Ending child marriage: The time is now. allAfrica. Retrieved from https://allafrica.com/stories/201905130564.html

Flynn, S. (2009). Culture and conformity. Research Starters Sociology [online]. Retrieved from http://www.academicpub.com/map/authors/Fylnn%2C+Simone+l.html

Forward UK. (n.d.). Eradicating child marriage in Africa. Retrieved October 4, 2014 from http://www.forwarduk.org.uk/key-issues/child-marriage

Ghanabusinessnews.com. (2013). Forced marriages impede education in Karaga—ISODEC. Retrieved December 30, 2013, from http://www.ghanabusinessnews.com/2013/09/05/forced-marriages-impede-education-in-karaga-isodec/#respond

Hadijatou Mani Koraou v. The Republic of Niger (ECW/CCJ/JUD/06/08 of 27 October 2008).

Jemphrey, M. (2011). The levirate custom of inheriting widows among the Supyire people of Mali: Theological pointers for Christian marriage. Retrieved January 1, 2014, from Http://scholar.google.co.uk/citations?user=s7BmsVQAAAAJ&hl=en

Kabore, W., Yaro, Y., & Dan-Koma, I. (2008). Background study of the inter-agency joint programme on violence against women. Burkina Faso. The Inter-Agency Network on Women and Gender Equality Task Force on Violence Against Women. Retrieved August 5, 2012, from www.un.org/women-watch/ianwge/taskforces/vaw/version_anglaise_l_etude_de_baseVEF_2009-ud.docx

Kaye, D., Mirembe, A., Ekstrom, A., Kyouhendo, G., & Johansson, A. (2005). Implications of bride price on domestic violence and reproductive health in Wakiso District of Uganda. *African Health Sciences, 5*(4), 300–303.

Kiragu, J. (1996). Policy overview: HIV prevention and women's rights—Their promotion goes hand in hand. *AIDS Captions,* 8–14. Secondary Source ID: PIP/118343.

LaFraniere, S. (2005). Forced to marry before puberty, African girls pay lasting price. *The New York Times.* Retrieved December 26, 2013, from www.nytimes.com.

Lako, W. (2004). Gender difference masquerading as a tool for women oppression in cultural discourse. *The Ahfad Journal, 21*(1), 4–17.

Lionnet, F. (2005). Women's rights, voices, and identities: The limits of universalism and the legal debate around excision in France. In O. Nnaemeka (Ed.), *Female Circumcision and the Politics of Knowledge.* Westport, CT: Praeger.

Locke, A. (1989). *The philosophy of Alain Locke: Harlem Renaissance and beyond.* L. Harris (Ed.). Philadelphia, PA: Temple University Press.

Luyta, T. (2012). Human trafficking of young women and girls for sexual exploitation in South Africa. Retrieved from https://repository.up.ac.za/bitstream/handle/2263/20132/Lutya%20_Human%282012%29.PDF?sequence=1

Maluleke, M. (2012). Culture, tradition, custom, law and gender equality. South African Legal Information Institute (SAFLII). Retrieved January 4, 2014, from http://www.saflii.org/za/journals/PER/2012/1.html

Mchunu, G., Peltzer, K., Tutshana, T., & Seutlwadi, L. (2012). Adolescent pregnancy and associated factors in South African youth. *African Health Science, 12*(4), 426–434.

Menand, L. (2001). *The metaphysical Club: A story of ideas in America.* New York, NY: Farrar, Straus, & Giroux.

Nawal, N. (2006). Health consequences of child marriage in Africa. *Emerging Infectious Diseases, 12*(11), 1644–1649.

Obiora, L. (2005). The anti-female circumcision campaign deficit. In O. Nnaemeka (Ed.), *Female Circumcision and the Politics of Knowledge.* Westport, CT: Praeger.

Park, S. (2011). Defence of cultural relativism. *Cultura. International Journal of Philosophy of Culture and Axiology, 8*(1), 159–170.

Plan International. (2012). Because I am a girl. Retrieved August 2, 2014, from https://plan-international.org/because-i-am-a-girl

Plateau, J., Abraham, A., Gaspart, F., & Stevens, L. (2000). Traditional marriage practices as determinants of women's land rights: A review of research-articles prepared based on research by Jean-Philippe Plateau, Anita Abraham, Frederic Gaspart, and Luc Stevens. CRED Centre de Recherche en Economie du Développment. University of Namur, Belgium. Retrieved January 2, 2014, from http://www.fao.org/docrep/008/a0297e/a0297e05.htm

Pojman, L. (2008). "Who's to judge what's right or wrong?" In S. Satris (Ed.), *Taking sides: Clashing views on moral issues* (11th ed., pp. 13–21). Dubuque, IA: McGraw-Hill Companies.

Rachels, J., & Rachels, S. (2010). *The elements of moral philosophy* (6th ed.). New York, NY: McGraw-Hill Companies.

Refworld. (2006). Ghana: Forced marriages; prevalence of such marriages; whether a woman can refuse such a marriage, and the consequences of the refusal; available state protection and redress (2004–2006). Retrieved December 29, 2013, from http://www.refworld.org/docid/45f1473720.html

SBS News. (2014). Child brides' big issue in Africa. Retrieved July 4, 2014, from http://www.sbs .com.au/news/article/2014/05/30/child-brides-big-issue-africa

Schick, T., Jr., & Vaughn, L. (1990). *Doing philosophy: An introduction through thought experiments* (4th ed.). New York, NY: McGraw-Hill.

Souryal, S. (1992). *Ethics in criminal justice: In search of the truth*. Cincinnati, OH: Anderson.

Steffen, C. (2011). *Mutilating Khalid: The symbolic politics of female genital cutting*. Trenton, NJ: Red Sea Press.

Smith, A. D. (2016, August 10). Threat of marriage hangs over young Malian refugee girls in Mauritania/Global/Development. *The Guardian* (UK). Retrieved July 12, 2017, from https:// www.theguardian.com/global-development/2016/aug/10/threat-of-marriage-young-malian -refugee-girls-mauritania-mbera-camp

Time, V. (2017). *Women's social and legal issues in African current affairs: Lifting the barriers*. Lanham, MD: Rowman & Littlefield.

Toubia, N. (1995). *Female genital mutilation: A call for global action*. New York, NY: RAINBO.

Wall, G. (1967). Primitive cultures and ethical universals. *International Philosophical Quarterly, 1*, 471–482.

Welstead, M. (2009). Forced marriage: Bifurcated values in the U.K. *Denning Law Journal, 21*, 49–65.

SECTION 2

Ethics and the Lawmaking Process

ARTICLE 5

Introduction to Ethics and the Lawmaking Process

Paul A. Lucas

▶ Lawmaking Process

A legislature is defined as "a group of individuals elected or selected as members of a government assembly of individuals established by a state or national constitution" (Lippman, 2018, p. 102). Legislators are sometimes referred to as *lawmakers* because they are responsible for proposing statutes that, if voted on and passed, will become part of state or federal law. In the United States, lawmaking responsibility is shared by both federal and state legislators. Although there are differences between state and federal legislatures, the lawmaking process is quite similar between the two.

At the federal level, the first step in the lawmaking process is introduction of a bill into either the House of Representatives or the Senate. Once a committee with specific knowledge regarding the proposed bill reviews and discusses its suitability, it returns to the floor for a vote. If the bill passes, it moves directly to the other chamber for a committee review and discussion of its appropriateness before a vote is held. If there are recommended revisions to the bill, it will return to the appropriate committee for any necessary changes before another vote is held, which begins the review process once more. If there are no changes or the recommended changes are sufficiently made and the vote passes, the bill then goes to the president (or governor at the state level) for final approval. At this point, the president has two options: (1) sign the bill to have it become law or (2) veto the bill, which prevents it from becoming law. However, even if vetoed, the bill can still become law if two-thirds of the both House and Senate vote to override the veto. The same process is followed at the state level, with the exception of Nebraska, which has a unicameral (single chamber) rather than bicameral (dual chamber) legislature that is responsible for both approval and rejection of proposed legislation. There exists yet another option for the creation of federal law, which occurs through an executive order issued by the president, which is discussed specifically in the following paragraphs. It is important to note that although the legislature at the state and federal levels is responsible for creating law, this does not necessarily mean that the laws they enact are lawful in and of themselves.

Laws created by federal or state legislatures cannot infringe on the rights granted by the United States Constitution or individual state constitutions. So, what happens when a law violates one of our individual rights? The answer to that question lies within the process of *judicial review* when courts exert their power to examine the law and decide whether it is constitutional or unconstitutional. This power was granted to the U.S. Supreme Court after the landmark case of *Marbury v. Madison* (1803). In *Marbury*, the Court ruled that it was the Court's own job to review the laws passed by other branches of the government to ensure that they align with our constitution. This landmark case gave the Court the right to judicial review. This right was extended to the review of decisions made by the state courts in the case of *Martin v. Hunter Lessee* (1816) 13 years later. The *Marbury* and *Martin* decisions ensure that even though federal and state legislators have the ability to create laws, they must do so while not infringing on individual liberties. Our court system, through the use of judicial review, ensures that this occurs.

▶ State and Federal Law

The United States uses a dual-court system that operates simultaneously under the federal court system and the court systems operating within each state. Each system is similar in that it includes trial courts, intermediate appellate courts, and a supreme court (with the U.S. Supreme Court being the highest court in our nation and thus the court of last resort) (Hemmens, Brody, & Spohn, 2017). The United States is governed based on federalism. Under federalism, states grant the federal government certain powers that are set forth within the Constitution. States maintain power within their jurisdictions on any matter not granted to the federal government. Powers granted to the federal government include the regulation of interstate commerce, declaring war, providing for national defense, coining money, collecting taxes, operating post offices, and the regulation of immigration.

But what happens when state and federal law comes into conflict? The simple answer is the Supremacy Clause, which is found within the U.S. Constitution (where it is termed the *preemption doctrine*) and states that federal law is superior to state law if a conflict arises (Lippman, 2019). However, there is a constitutional counter to the Supremacy Clause found in the 10th Amendment's anticommandeering doctrine, which states that the federal government cannot commandeer states by requiring them to enact laws or have state officers assist the federal government in enforcing federal laws within their states. This does not stop the federal government from enforcing federal law within the states, but it cannot force states to abide by federal law or their state and local authorities to enforce it (Chemerinksy, Forman, Hopper, & Kamin, 2015). The interaction between state and federal law is discussed in more detail, including recent examples, in the following articles.

▶ Executive Orders and States' Rights

As previously noted, a president who wishes to advance a policy agenda has two options: (1) recommend legislation to Congress for consideration, discussion, review, and possible passage; or (2) exercise unilateral presidential powers in the form of executive orders, agreements, directives aimed at national security, or memoranda. This form of policy creation circumvents formal endorsement and passage of law by the House of Representatives and the Senate. This is not without limitation because the sitting president must justify his or her actions through statutory, treaty, or constitutional power. If not, the proposed legislation must be approved by Congress before its adoption and enforcement (Howell, 2005). This provides enormous power to the sitting president. As Paul Begala, an adviser to former President Bill Clinton, once stated, " 'Stroke of the pen . . . Law of the Land. Kind of cool' " (Kennedy, 2015, p. 60). Although the debate surrounding whether granting such power to one individual is not new (see Cooper, 2002, 2005; Mayer, 2001), there exists one large obstacle once an executive order is signed: Do the bureaucrats in charge of instituting the orders actually follow the directive or attempt to circumnavigate it?

When an executive order is issued, this does not necessarily mean the order will be implemented by all agents who are responsible for doing so. This may be the result of the monetary cost of implementation, unclear orders on who should take action and how, or political disagreement surrounding the nature of the order. This bureaucratic unresponsiveness has been explained using principle-agent theory (PAT) (Spence & Zeckhauser, 1971). PAT states that there is difficulty in overseeing an agent's actions when implementing an order. This may be confounded by incentives for not following the orders by the agent (the president in the case of executive orders), with such incentives coming from Congress, which is responsible for allocating resources to different agencies within the executive branch (Kennedy, 2015; Weingast, 2005; Weingast & Morgan, 1982). This partially explains why, on gaining the presidency, there is directed change within departments overseen by the president in an attempt to place loyal departmental heads in charge and thus reduce the chances of noncompliance. This is especially true when directives are received from multiple principles, who may have differing goals and objectives for the agents to oversee. Research does indicate that noncompliance can be reduced by directly naming the agency responsible for instituting the executive order through promulgation (Kennedy, 2015), but this does not ensure that the executive order itself will not be contested.

There has been a recent shift toward states combating executive orders through the use of local governmental orders (Ross & Goelzhauser, 2018). Conversely, through the use of preemption, state governments have been passing legislation preventing certain localities from enacting statutes contrary to federal law and executive orders. As previously stated, the United States uses a federalist system, which divides power between the federal and state governments. Although Republicans controlled both houses of Congress for two years, unilateral executive orders were increasingly used by President Donald Trump to roll back Obama-era policies and circumnavigate divisions within the Republican Party, which stymied the passage of legislation focused on improving health care, addressing immigration, and managing environmental issues. The orders were met and continue to be met with both support and resistance in the form of preemptive legislation and lawsuits filed on behalf of individual states.

Democratic and Republican states alike have taken a variety of actions against administrative policies and executive orders. States have resisted many executive orders by lawsuits directly filed by state attorneys general. Lawsuits have been filed to undermine key provisions of the Affordable Care Act (ACA) by Republican-run states during the Obama administration, immigration policies such as the Deferred Action for Childhood Arrivals policy, marijuana legalization at the state level and enforcement of the Controlled Substances Act at the federal level, the role of the federal government on educational policies, and the limiting of environmental protections (Ross & Goelzhauser, 2018). The judicial battles also extend to local governments. For example, in an issue discussed in an article following this section's introduction, local governments have passed so-called sanctuary legislation limiting local law enforcement cooperation with federal immigration officials in an attempt to protect undocumented immigrants living within their communities. These statutes directly oppose federal directives, and they are a strong assertion of state's rights and their ability to govern in a way that they believe to be in their best interests. However, local governments are often seen as a product of state governments, and legislation is often produced at the state level to limit what smaller localities and jurisdictions are able to enact. These preemptive policies are enacted to control what some jurisdictions *may* do in the future. Certain states, in response to cities within California which have made themselves sanctuary cities for undocumented immigrants, have passed preemptive policies that state a local police force's cooperation with federal law enforcement cannot be limited. This preempted future local ordinances from being created because the state legislature had already decided against such action. Regardless of whether opposition or support comes in the form of lawsuits or preemptive legislation, our nation looks to the judiciary to settle disagreements over state's rights and federal oversight.

▶ Judicial Review

In 1803, *Marbury v. Madison*—arguably the most famous and important court case decided by the Supreme Court—effectively established the concept of judicial review at the federal level. Essentially, *Marbury* granted the Court the right to review whether acts of Congress or the president are aligned with the rights stated within the U.S. Constitution. Thirteen years later, *Martin v. Hunter Lessee* (1816) granted the Court the right to exercise judicial review in matters concerning the states. However, although these cases established the right to judicial review, there has been much controversy concerning judicial activism and restraint.

Judicial activism and restraint are at two opposite ends of the judicial review spectrum. When demonstrating judicial activism, judges disregard *stare decisis* (meaning "let the decision stand") and overturn state and federal law when *interpreting* the Constitution. On the other hand, when exhibiting judicial restraint, judges defer to precedent and, as implied in the name, "restrain" from overturning previous rulings or laws enacted by the legislature by adhering to originalism (faithfulness to the original meaning of the Constitution). Although so-called activist judges are typically framed as being liberal Democrats and judges favoring judicial restraint are seen as conservative Republicans, there are instances of each political side exhibiting activism and restraint, usually to the chagrin of opposing political parties (Lippman, 2018). However, there have been judges and scholars who have argued that the terms *activism* and *restraint* are overused and used out of context.

A court decision that an individual disagrees with for any reason can be lauded as activism, whereas a decision that is more favorable (to that individual or group) is seen as an appropriate ruling, regardless of how it was reached. Justice Thomas R. Lee of the Utah Supreme Court (2013) argues that the term *activism*, or as he calls it, the "A word," is used in three distinct ways within public and political discourse. First, a judge may be considered activist when he or she hands down a decision that overturns the passage of legislation at the legislative or executive levels. This is sometimes seen as a show of power, which can be met by those in disagreement with calls of activism and questions about whether a group of unelected judges should hold power over the passage of legislation by democratically elected branches of government. President Barack Obama, in a preemptive call to disarm the possibility of the Supreme Court ruling against the health insurance mandate of the ACA, stated that judicial activism had no place concerning a duly constituted and passed law. Conversely, on the Republican side of the aisle, there were cries of activism when the Supreme Court ruled in favor of same-sex marriage. Senator Ted Cruz (R–TX) decried judicial activism in this case because it negated the will of the people in California, who had voted against same-sex marriage. In both of these instances, the "A word" was used to decry the judicial branch overruling the will of the people either directly (in the case of same-sex marriage) or through striking down legislature arrived at by elected officials in office.

The second concept of activism, according to Justice Lee (2013), is overruling previous court decisions. Striking down the precedent of past rulings is met with charges of activism, depending on whether the decision is agreed on or not. Although the "A word" is seldom used in judicial opinions, it is used by, in the words of Justice Lee (2013), "the politicians and the pundits . . . to up the ante in criticizing judicial decisions" (p. 14). As in the *Roper v. Simmons* (2005) decision striking down the use of capital punishment for juveniles, then–presidential candidate John McCain called the ruling one of activism, disregarding the principles and facts used to review and decide that particular case, simply because it overruled past precedent that he and many in his party saw as correct. This leads us into the third use of the term *activism*: when a decision is labeled activist if it is assumed to have been wrongly decided based on legal facts. In these instances, court decisions are seen to be incorrect on their legal merits, such as judges being out of touch with the realities of certain issues within American society.

In each of these three instances, and conversely within the use of judicial restraint, the term *activism* is used to frame judicial disagreements with individual political ideology or crafted legislation by elected officials. However, these claims do not hold up when reviewing what activism and restraint accurately entail: the use of judicial review to ensure justice through the rights that our Constitution grants each individual in our society. Given that the ruling in *Marbury v. Madison* grants the judicial branch the power to curtail the actions of the executive and legislative branches, the negative use of the term *activism* does not apply here; it is the purpose of the courts to check the constitutional powers of the other branches to uphold our individual rights. Similarly, when a court disregards precedent in favor of a new ruling, those in disagreement will call it *activism*, as if to slight or diminish the ruling. However, some of the Supreme Court's most influential rulings would not be decried as activism in this manner. Take the decision of *Brown v. Board of Education* (1954), which ignored both precedent (overturning the decision in *Plessy v. Ferguson*, 1896) and duly constituted legislation passed by states within the South claiming segregation under the separate-but-equal premise. No one would state that this ruling was one of activism solely because it went against precedent and the decisions of the elected officials within the Southern states. This is because legal scholars would agree that this was an appropriate use of judicial power, which is how the terms *activism* and *restraint* should be critiqued.

If we begin to view judicial activism and restraint as each term pertains to judicial power, we can be much more effective in using these terms accurately and not based on personal opinion. As Justice Lee (2013) states,

> our use of these terms ought to be informed by a careful delineation of the meaning of the nature of judicial powers. And we ought to chide a judge's activism only where it exceeds that definition of judicial powers, just as we ought to applaud a judge's restraint only where it respects that definition. (p. 18)

Essentially, judicial activism should pertain only when a judge uses a personal opinion to change and shape the law, and judicial restraint should pertain only to when judges *do not* allow their personal opinions to influence their judicial powers. In this sense, we can take the often-used and loaded terms of *activism* and *restraint* to consider purely the interpretation of the law outside of what a judge may feel should happen, which is the truest form of interpretation of our Constitution.

The following articles will take a more in-depth look into the broad discussion of the lawmaking process, state and federal law, executive orders and states' rights, and judicial review. Although these topics were simplified within this article, when they are applied at the federal and state levels, both within and outside of legislative laws and executive orders, they become more complex. The remaining articles of this section will present and discuss these complex issues and more to enable you to better understand how each pertains to our daily lives.

▶ References

Brown v. Board of Education, 347 U.S. 483 (1954).

Chemerinksy, E., Forman, J., Hopper, A., & Kamin, S. (2015). Cooperative federalism and marijuana regulation. *UCLA Law Review, 62*, 74–122.

Cooper, P. J. (2002). *By order of the president: The use and abuse of executive direct action*. Lawrence, KS: University Press of Kansas

Cooper, P. J. (2005). George W. Bush, Edgar Allan Poe, and the use and abuse of presidential signing statements. *Presidential Studies Quarterly, 35*, 515–532.

Hemmens, C., Brody, D. C., & Spohn, C. (2017). *Criminal courts: A contemporary perspective* (3rd ed.). Thousand Oaks, CA: Sage.

Howell, W. G. (2005). Unilateral powers: A brief overview. *Presidential Studies Quarterly, 35*(3), 417–439.

Kennedy, J. B. (2015). Do this! Do that! and nothing will happen: Executive orders and bureaucratic responsiveness. *American Politics Research, 43*(1), 59–82.

Lee, T. R. (2013). Judicial activism, restraint, & the rule of law. *Utah Bar Journal, 26*(6), 12–20.

Lippman, M. (2018). *Law and society* (2nd ed.). Thousand Oaks, CA: Sage

Lippman, M. (2019). *Contemporary criminal law: Concepts, cases, and controversies* (5th ed.). Thousand Oaks, CA: Sage.

Marbury v. Madison, 5 U.S. 137 (1803).

Martin v. Hunter Lessee, 14 U.S. 1 (1816).

Mayer, K. R. (2001). *With the stroke of a pen: Executive orders and presidential power*. Princeton, NJ: Princeton University Press.

Plessy v. Ferguson, 163 U.S. 537 (1896).

Roper v. Simmons, 543 U.S. 551 (2005).

Ross, S., & Goelzhauser, G. (2018). The state of American federalism 2017–2018: Unilateral executive action, regulatory rollback, and state resistance. *Journal of Federalism, 48*(3), 319–344.

Spence, M., & Zeckhauser, R. (1971). Insurance, information, and individual action. *American Economic Review, 61*, 380–387.

Weingast, B. R. (2005). Caught in the middle: The president, congress, and the political-bureaucratic system. In J. D. Aberbach & M. A. Peterson (Eds.), *The executive branch* (pp. 312–343). New York, NY: Oxford University Press.

Weingast, B. R., & Morgan, M. J. (1982).The myth of runaway bureaucracy: The case of the FTC. *Regulation, 6*, 33–38

The Conservative Rationale for Criminal Justice Reform

Derek M. Cohen

Conservative criminal justice reform's rapid ascendancy in spite of decades' worth of entrenched "tough-on-crime" policy and rhetoric has surprised many observers (Khimm, 2012). The campaign has been mystifying to some because it takes a seemingly opposite philosophical position from accepted conservative orthodoxy and argues antithetical ideas on conservatism's own terms. This incomplete analysis can be simply summarized as "prisons are expensive, therefore society should rely upon them less" (see, e.g., Gottschalk, 2016). It is correct insofar as conservative lawmakers are willing to reevaluate existing positions on a policy issue when that position directly conflicts with their beliefs and they have an identifiable peer group doing the same (see, e.g., Cohen, 2003). However, the lone fiscal argument is not enough to substantiate why a group so ideologically multifaceted as conservatives were the first to adhere to tough-on-crime rhetoric and why a growing chorus of them have begun advocating for alternatives.

▶ What Conservatives Believe

Conservatism is not monolithic. There is no revered central tome of conservative doctrine; "no Holy Writ and no *Das Kapital* to provide dogmata" (Kirk, 1993, p. 15). Rather, conservative belief is an aggregation of what conservative intellectuals put forth, a body of work that on the margins can be in self-conflict. As a result, conservatives frequently find themselves involved in minor schisms and internal disagreements on matters seemingly of fundamental importance (Kirk, 1953).

It is equally important to note that conservatism is not rote resistance to change. To the contrary, conservative philosophers throughout history have recognized that a maturing and evolving civil society must have appropriate mechanisms for altering or eliminating key institutions. Irish statesman and early conservative scholar Edmund Burke recognized this need, stating that a nation "without the means of some change is without the means of its conservation" (1790, p. 19). However, it is in the measured degree and deliberate process afforded to societal changes that marks philosophy as "conservative."

In the most thorough compilation on contemporary conservative thought, political theorist Russell Kirk (1993) articulated the most common elements of conservative philosophy from Burke to the modern age. Along this timeline, Kirk identifies 10 key principles that all facets of conservative thought include, even if under different interpretations. It is in the interpretation of these principles that the conservative philosophy of conservative criminal justice reform diverges from tough-on-crime rhetoric.

The first tenet of conservative thought is the belief in an enduring moral order, meaning that for society to persist and function there must be harmony from the chaotic Hobbesian state of nature. Conservatives believe that when a society has common values and a shared sense of morality and subscribes to a ubiquitous understanding of justice, then that society "will be a good society—whatever political machinery it may utilize" (p. 18). Commonly, the "order" contained in "law and order" refers explicitly to this idea—that is, that through rule of law, which was previously interpreted as strictly punitive sentencing policy, society will be able to flourish.

Second and perhaps most emblematically, conservatives ascribe to "custom, convention, and continuity" (p. 18). This principle holds that contemporary society and subsidiary institutions have achieved their present form through generations of trial and error. To quickly depart from the established orthodoxy is seen not only as rejecting this deliberate process but also as gambling with the continuance of society's order. This belief represented the fundamental schism in conservative thought surrounding the American revolution between traditionalist conservatives such as Burke and more classically liberal conservatives such as Thomas Paine. Burke recognized the grievances aired by the colonists and advocated for peaceful and political redress. Conversely, Paine was one of the ideological architects of the revolution seeking to martially cast off the tyrannical, oppressive rule of King George III. Both interpretations were in favor of achieving a state of tranquility, whether that was under continued social order or in the return to previously granted liberties.

In fact, it is the effort to reinvigorate previously granted liberties that typify conservatives' belief in prescription—the third principle. On their founding, the English colonies were given great latitude for autonomy and self-rule. Having migrated to the colonies before the Revolutionary War, Paine witnessed firsthand the gradual restrictions of colonial freedoms by English administrators. The conservative belief in prescription holds that those in the present are unlikely to make new discoveries in morality or behavior and should err to reinforcing the past. This applies both to positive and negative change; just as conservatives believe that no institution should be created that mimics the role of another, no right identified or liberty once conferred can be stripped from an individual without satisfying extremely high standards. For example, a prosecutor must prove the case against an accused criminal "beyond a reasonable doubt" before the state is permitted to take property, freedom, or even life. The tenet of prescription partially explains conservatives' collective belief in the rule of law and procedural sanctity.

Fourth, conservatives believe in prudence when changing institutions. Kirk (1993, p. 20) suggests that individuals rushing into action in the name of reform run "the risk of new abuses worse than the evils they hope to sweep away." Therefore, conservatives must consciously deliberate on change, and any change must be adequately complex to effectuate the desired outcome. In the present context, prudence is why conservatives broadly bristle at ambitious criminal justice reform campaigns such as Cut50, an effort to reduce the nation's incarcerated population by 50% over a decade. It is not that conservatives are opposed to reducing the prison population or even doing so by such a substantial margin, but that such a goal is an abstract and arbitrary reduction that takes no consideration of justice or public safety.

The fifth principle conservatives ascribe to is that of variety. Variety dictates that society must not only be diverse in both individual thought and behavior but also will experience some degree of inequality. Conservatives believe that equality of outcome can only be achieved through damaging other tenets of conservative thought such as property rights. In an applied context, this tenet represents Justice Louis Brandeis's "laboratories of democracy," allowing similar governments to experiment with novel solutions to their problems for successful solutions to be emulated by others. Most notably, it is the want for variety that reinforces the importance of equality guaranteed before a court of law lest the court become a tyrannical mechanism in itself (Kirk, 1953).

Sixth, conservatives believe in humanity's imperfectability. In the religious context, conservatives feel that mankind is unsalvageable outside of the divine providence of Jesus Christ, Mahdi, or another relevant redeemer. In a secular context, imperfectability refers to the error in striving for a utopian society in the face of society's fickle passions—a view contrary to progressive ideology. Imperfectability also mandates both prudence and prescription because imperfect humans seeking sweeping reforms will be unlikely to succeed in accounting for all contingencies.

The seventh pillar of conservative thought is the inextricability of freedom and property rights. Deeply entrenched in the writings of John Locke and the founding documents of the United States, conservatives consider personal property rights as tantamount to liberty. The sanctity of property rights is why conservatives fervently resist the forced redistribution of resources such as in progressive tax policies. If citizens cannot choose how their property is used and how (or on whom) their money is spent free of government interference, then the property belongs to the collective. "Separate property from private possession," Kirk (1993, p.21) writes, "and Leviathan becomes the master of all."

This concept of the collective is nuanced in conservative thought. Conservatives do not categorically reject collectivism; however, they do reject *involuntary* collectivism. Institutional mainstays in conservative life, such as the church or the neighborhood, are seen as ideal because individuals can freely associate and disassociate should the institution no longer reflect their values. The eighth belief—voluntary community—is also why conservatives are proponents of states' rights over centralized federal authority: An individual is free to choose the relationships that best facilitate his or her desired ends.

The ninth tenet of conservative philosophy is the belief in prudent restraints on power. With humanity seen as ultimately fallible, arbitrary, and capricious, conservatives naturally believe that those who rise to leadership are equally faulty. When vested with both authority and power, conservatives are fearful of the harm these individuals could bring. Therefore, as a matter of course conservatives seek to bind those in power, requiring increasing levels of collective support for change, depending on its permanence.

Finally, conservatives believe that society must adapt—that it must reconcile both change and permanence in order to preserve the elements of society that they value. Cultural stagnation is likely to damage all institutions, including those most closely held by conservatives. Conservatives also believe that, more often than not, when one institution is ascending, another is declining. It is the prudent balance of which change is most preferable to societal functioning over the long term.

Even with these common threads running through the whole of conservative thought, it is impossible to state with certainty that "the conservative position on X is Y." By conservatism's own internal beliefs, two diametrically opposed philosophical beliefs might be equally valid under common conservative doctrine. Still, there have been countless attempts to establish a "conservative purity test," a method for separating the true conservative firebrands from weak-willed apostates, with modern iterations so doctrinally rigid that President Ronald Reagan would be expected to be found wanting if he were alive and espousing similar beliefs today (Cunningham, 2014). This aspiration of reaching their interpretation of unflinching doctrinal conservativism is what motivates many of today's remaining tough-on-crime champions and poses a threat to Right on Crime activities in the future.

▶ Understanding Tough-on-Crime Philosophy Through the Conservative Lens

Outside of rational political gamesmanship, little analysis was given to conservatives' internal thought process that had led—and in some cases, continues to lead—well-meaning, right-leaning people to adhere to tough-on-crime beliefs. In fact, conservative reform efforts such as Right on Crime wholly recognize the founding rationale of the tough-on-crime thought and, in fact, agree with it nearly uniformly. However, it is in the reanalysis of these beliefs where reform-minded conservatives part company with the once-prevailing orthodoxy.

Although tough-on-crime rhetoric and policy have been present in American politics since the mid-1960s, not until the mid-1970s did the idea find purchase among criminological scholars. For two-thirds of the century, liberals and progressives held near-hegemonic control of the academic discourse surrounding crime and punishment. Predictably, this uniform pattern of thought shaped the prevailing concepts accordingly. Nearly all theories of crime posited some external loci of control and decision making from the "social disorganization theory" of the Chicago School of Criminology to criminal-creating "labeling theory" to societal valuation of success under "anomie theory," prevailing criminological theory divested the criminal of some, if not all, of the agency of their actions. Each successive theory seemed to further minimize individuals' personal responsibility for their behavior.

With the scholastic body of criminology straying further afield of conservative principles and advancing theories incongruous with conservative philosophy, right-leaning scholars pioneered a heterodox theory of criminal behavior. Although "conservative criminology" as it came to be known was seen as a "fringe" or reactionary theory, it is quite similar to the tenets of classical criminology, such as those outlined by Cesare Beccaria (1775). As a criminal-centric theory of crime, conservative criminology rejects what left-leaning scholars consider the "root causes" of criminal behavior such as social inequality and racially biased institutions. In these causes' stead, conservative criminologists reinvigorated the economic decision-making process at the center of classical criminology and the more-recent rational choice theory (Wilson, 1975).

Under this theory of crime, a to-be criminal performs a rational economic calculus of the potential positives and negative outcomes of criminal behavior. If the likely positives outweigh the negatives consequences, then the individual will commit the crime (Becker, 1968). The central components of the calculus are largely constant across individuals, although the moral and virtuous individuals in society are further encumbered by the harm their behavior would visit on others. Therefore, it is the role of policy makers to alter this calculus as much as possible, creating an insurmountable disincentive to criminal behavior. Because the "moral poverty" highlighted by Bennett, DiIulio, and Walters (1996) is largely beyond the ambit of common public policy, the only recourse to alter this balance lies in deterrence (Wilson, 1975).

The adoption of deterrence and rational choice theories both in criminology and public policy was the most predictable outcome in retrospect. The United States was facing steadily increasing crime rates throughout the majority of the tough-on-crime era. This increase in crime occurred in tandem with what many saw as the destruction of social institutions. Because morality cannot be easily legislated into being, lawmakers were left with increasing the "pain"—the punitive harm delivered in the name of justice—that offenders are to endure upon being found guilty of or pleading guilty to an offense. This toughening has been nearly uniformly expressed in the lengthening of sanctions, prohibiting punishments seen as lenient such as probation or parole, or by suspending certain procedural protections in pursuit of law and order. To deliver these punitive sanctions more effectively, lawmakers have enacted policies that rely heavily on prosecutorial discretion.

Currently, tough-on-crime rhetoric and policy proposals are seen in the federal and most state legislatures, albeit less frequently than in years past. This often entails specific enhancements on certain offenses or for habitual offenders. However, no longer is there collective support for the broad toughening of criminal sanctions. The already burdensome prison system coupled with fiscal realities makes overreliance on simple incarceration an unpopular goal for both policy makers and the voting public (see, e.g., Thielo, et al., 2016).

▶ Understanding Right on Crime Through the Conservative Lens

Starting in Texas in 2005 and engaging nationally in 2010, Right on Crime is a relative newcomer to the criminal justice policy discussion. This affords campaign personnel and signatories the advantage of hindsight. When a particular policy question arises, Right on Crime is able to draw on a half-century of criminal justice policy to consider in tandem with its conservative beliefs. Early policy scholars had no such advantage and were constrained to the information at hand, rationally leading them to the quintessential tough-on-crime stance on public policy. Once these policies began leading to political advantages, they were adopted wholesale in public policy discussions.

This position flourished for decades. As crime increased, so did penalties. Among the proximate outcomes of this policy, the criminal justice system was now better equipped to intercede in habitual criminal offending, even if through no other mechanism than incarceration. There is a modicum of support to this claim, with studies identifying as much as one-third of the observed crime decline in the 1990s as being attributable to the rote increase in incarceration (Levitt, 2004). However, reliance on incarceration eventually reached a point of diminishing returns. One dollar spent on incarceration or one person incarcerated in 1980 lost a great deal of its ability to translate into a reduction in crime in 2000. Further, a growing body of research illustrated that one public dollar would be more effective in crime reduction when spent on other criminal justice endeavors such as policing (p. 189). Although tough-on-crime proponents are not antipolice in any respect, the philosophy's overreliance on incarceration expresses a preference for a costlier intervention, even in the face of weakening empirical support. With governments at all levels hesitant to raise spending on criminal justice in the face of collective falling crime rates, this creates a natural tension between the desire to fund incarceration versus the use of less expensive forms of criminal justice sanctions. In light of this tension, the tough-on-crime philosophy can exist only if criminal justice—as a core government function—is not held to the same standards of efficiency to which conservatives hold other institutions.

As illustrated in the first declaration of the Statement of Principles, Right on Crime explicitly rejects granting this pass. "As with any government program, the criminal justice system must be transparent and include performance measures," it states, "that hold it accountable for its results in protecting the public, lowering crime rates, reducing re-offending, collecting victim restitution and conserving taxpayers' money" (Right on Crime, 2010). With scarce resources available for the protection of public safety from both first-time and repeat offenders, it is critical that each dollar spent in the pursuit of public safety has both a quantifiable and proximate benefit rather than if it were spent in another manner toward the same pursuit. Reckless public spending with no eye to effectiveness can exist only under confiscatory tax policy coupled with burdensome spending, both antithetical to the beliefs of conservatives.

It is important here to distinguish Right on Crime's nuanced belief on criminal justice spending from a common false dichotomy frequently used by liberal and progressive policy advocates: that states spend more incarcerating prisoners than on the education of law-abiding students (see, e.g., Ingraham, 2016). Implicit in this observation is that crime can be reduced by redirecting public funding from criminal justice and law enforcement to education. This claim was explicitly advanced in a U.S. Department of Education (2016) policy brief that called for policy makers "to make investments in education that we know work . . . including significantly increasing teacher salaries" to reduce crime (p. 13). However, omitted from the brief is any citation that demonstrates that fungible public money spent on education versus incarceration produces any collective or individual effect.

Second, the growth of the criminal justice system has also led to a marginalization of crime victims and their role within the criminal justice process. Just as the Texas Public Policy Foundation's Center for Effective Justice was originally established to research policy advancements that would prioritize the victim in the criminal process, Right on Crime advocates for victim-centric policies that prioritize restitution above and concurrent with punishment. This includes policies that, as monetary punishment is assessed and collected, the victim is made whole before the state (Cohen, 2013). Further, Right on Crime calls for elevating the preference of the victim, even if the desired outcome is not punitive enough in the eyes of the state.

To that end, Right on Crime rejects undue deference afforded to prosecutors in pursuit of punitive judgments. Right on Crime strongly believes in the role of prosecutors in delivering justice to a community, and that they should have all available tools in pursuit of justice. However, Right on Crime concurrently believes in a balanced, adversarial system that holds the natural rights to liberty and property inviolate, only depriving offenders of such rights only after criminal conduct has been proven. Further, as with all agents of the state, the conservatives of Right on Crime believe that prosecutors must work with reasonable safeguards placed on their activity because they are not immune from individual caprice or malice. Prosecutorial discretion is a necessary tool that must be preserved to maintain a functioning justice system, and so too are the safeguards and limitations that preserve the justice system's legitimacy.

Finally, Right on Crime points out the departure from doctrinal conservatism necessary to facilitate tough-on-crime ideology for the entirety of its existence. It is objectively clear that in the 1960s, crime was on the rise and there was a collective public will to address the problem as illustrated by Barry Goldwater and later Richard Nixon. Taken in tandem with what was perceived as institutions growing more liberal—for example, the due process revolution in the U.S. Supreme Court— few policy options remained that were able to deter would-be criminals save for toughening sanctions.

However, as the decades wore on, sentences kept getting stricter as both crime and incarceration continued to rise. Not once did prominent voices in the tough-on-crime movement call for the reanalysis or reconsideration of the central tenets of their chosen policy. Instead, the choice was to stay the course and continue increasing the length of sanctions for nearly all offenses without any proof that these increases had public safety benefits. This continuance also required deliberate blindness to the human costs of incarceration, making it difficult for even low-level offenders to reenter society after their sentence. Right on Crime believes that criminals should be firmly punished, but also that every avenue should be made available to them to achieve their own redemption.

Although Right on Crime parts company from tough-on-crime proponents on several key issues, the two groups overlap far more often. Many well-known progenitors of conservative criminology—William Bennett, John DiIulio, and George Kelling, for example, all being initial early advocates for tough-on-crime policies—have since signed on to the Right on Crime Statement of Principles without having to retract or be dismissive of their earlier works. Both groups of conservatives recognize the high cost that crime imposes on society, and that crime must be prevented to the extent that public policy can do so. Both groups also realize that the government is both uniquely positioned and justified in being the arbiter of justice. However, the key difference is in the policy prescriptions advocated to achieve that goal.

▶ References

Beccaria, C. (1775). *An essay on crimes and punishment.* Brookline Village, MA: Branden Press.

Becker, G. (1968). Crime and punishment: An economic perspective. *Journal of Political Economy, 76,* 169–217.

Bennett, W., DiIlulio, J., & Walters, J. (1996). *Body count: Moral poverty . . . and how to win America's war against drugs and crime.* New York, NY: Simon and Schuster.

Burke, E. (1790). *Reflections on the revolution in France.* Oxford, UK: Oxford University Press.

Cohen, D. (2013). *Reviving restorative justice: A blueprint for Texas.* Austin, TX: Texas Public Policy Foundation.

Cohen, G. (2003). Party over policy: The dominating impact of group influence on political beliefs. *Journal of Personality and Social Psychology,* 808–822.

Cunningham, J. (2014, February 27). The conservative litmus test, Charles Cooke, and purity. *Redstate.* Retrieved from https://www.redstate.com/diary/joesquire/2014/02/27/conservative-litmus-test-charles-cooke-purity/

Gottschalk, M. (2016, December 1). Wrong on crime. *Cato Unbound.* Retrieved from https://www.cato-unbound.org/2016/12/01/marie-gottschalk/wrong-crime

Ingraham, C. (2016, July 7). The states that spend more money on prisoners than college students. *Washington Post.* Retrieved from https://www.washingtonpost.com/news/wonk/wp/2016/07/07/the-states-that-spend-more-money-on-prisoners-than-college-students/

Khimm, S. (2012, August 31). The GOP platform's surprisingly progressive stance on crime. *Washington Post.* Retrieved from https://www.washingtonpost.com/news/wonk/wp/2012/08/31/the-gop-platforms-surprisingly-progressive-stance-on-crime/

Kirk, R. (1953). *The conservative mind, from Burke to Satayana.* Washington, DC: Regnery.

Kirk, R. (1993). *The politics of prudence.* Bryn Mawr, PA: Intercollegiate Studies Institute.

Levitt, S. (2004). Understanding why crime fell in the 1990s: Four factors that explain the decline and six that do not. *Journal of Economic Perspectives,* 163–190.

Right on Crime. (2010). *Statement of Principles.* Retrieved from Right on Crime at http://rightoncrime.com/statement-of-principles/

Thielo, A., Cullen, F., Cohen, D., & Chouhy, C. (2016). Rehabilitation in a red state: Public support for correctional reform in Texas. *Criminology and Public Policy,* 137–170.

U.S. Department of Education. (2016). State and local expenditures on corrections and education. Washington, DC: Author.

Wilson, J. (1975). *Thinking about crime.* New York, NY: Vintage Books.

ARTICLE 7

From Watergate to Pancakes: Ethics in the Ohio General Assembly

Yosef S. Schiff

▶ Introduction

In the mid-1970s, as America reeled in the wake of the Watergate scandal, a widespread effort to reform the nation's ethics laws was underway. Governments everywhere began enacting new codes of conduct to regulate the behavior of public officials and employees.[1] These codes addressed everything from conflicts of interest and commingling of funds to improper influence and the use of state resources for private gain. Ohio was a pioneer in this initial effort, but the pancaking scandal of the early 1990s led to that state reforming its laws yet again. This article explores the history of the Ohio legislature's attempts to police itself. It begins with an overview of Watergate and initial reforms of the 1970s, followed by the pancaking scandal and subsequent reforms of the 1990s, and ends with a closer look at the current ethics requirements governing Ohio lawmakers and their staff.

▶ History

Watergate

On August 9, 1974, Gerald Ford was sworn in as the 38th president of the United States in the midst of perhaps the most infamous political scandal in modern American history: Watergate. In less than one year, Ford had risen from a mere member of the House of Representatives to the position of vice president and finally president through a series of unlikely, earth-shattering events involving crime and corruption at the highest levels of the United States government. The first of these was the resignation of Vice President Spiro Agnew, who left office on

October 10, 1973, after pleading no contest to charges of tax evasion. The Constitution states, "Whenever there is a vacancy in the office of the Vice President, the President shall nominate a Vice President who shall take office upon confirmation by a majority vote of both Houses of Congress."[2] President Richard Nixon nominated Ford, who was confirmed by Congress and sworn in on December 6, 1973.

At this point in time, media coverage of the Watergate scandal had reached a fever pitch. On June 17, 1972, five burglars were arrested while breaking into Democratic National Committee headquarters in the Washington, D.C., Watergate office complex. The burglars were caught attempting to bug the office, having been unsuccessful in several previous attempts. Over the course of the next two years, as the investigation unfolded, it became clear that the break-in was orchestrated at the highest levels of the Nixon administration. Perhaps Nixon's biggest blunder was recording many of his conversations relating to the break-in on tape. In one of these conversations, the so-called smoking gun, he ordered White House staffers to instruct the CIA to tell the FBI to shut down its investigation. Congress subpoenaed the tapes, and the Supreme Court ordered the administration to comply. On release of the tapes, public support for Nixon plummeted. Facing impeachment on charges of obstruction of justice, abuse of power, and defying subpoenas, Nixon resigned on August 9, 1974, clearing the way for Ford's ascension.

The impact of Watergate on American politics and culture cannot be overstated. It led to reforms at every level of American government. To this day, the suffix *-gate* is often used in connection with scandals of all types; recent examples include Bridgegate, Celebgate, FIFA-gate, and Pizzagate. One positive outcome was an increased focus on the importance of ethics in governing. Governments everywhere began passing new codes of conduct for public officials and employees. Ohio was an early pioneer in these efforts, passing House Bill (HB) 55 in 1973.[3] HB 55 created a new ethics law that would apply to all three branches of government: legislative, executive, and judicial. The remainder of this section will focus on HB 55's application to the legislature and its shortcomings.

House Bill 55

House Bill 55 created ethics committees in both chambers of the Ohio General Assembly. Each committee was composed of six members, three from each political party. Members were appointed by the leaders of the House and Senate and were tasked with recommending new codes of ethics for their respective chambers no later than one month following the first day of each session.[4] The codes adopted by these committees served as internal rulebooks, supplementing the ethics laws codified—and still in force today—in Chapter 102 of the Ohio Revised Code. Among other things, these laws require candidates for office and certain public officials to file annual financial disclosure statements, and they prohibit a public official or state employee from doing any of the following subject to criminal penalties:

- representing clients before the agency he or she served;
- using confidential information he or she obtained while in office; or
- using his or her position to obtain outside compensation or anything of value "that would not ordinarily accrue . . . in the performance of his [or her] official duties."[5]

The reforms of HB 55 were praised as a leap forward in raising the ethical standards of public officials. But the law had its shortcomings, mostly regarding its application to executive branch officials and employees. These shortcomings led to the introduction of HB 285 in 1993. One notable provision in HB 285 directs the Ohio Ethics Commission[6] to "study the need for implementing a program of continuing ethics education for public officials."[7] Such a program was never adopted, and continuing ethics education remains optional. However, initial ethics training is often required as a condition of employment.

The Pancaking Scandal

As HB 285 worked its way through the legislative process, the so-called pancaking scandal—also known as the honoraria scandal—captured the public's attention and led to the introduction of yet another ethics bill, HB 492. The old ethics law (HB 55) required public officials to identify "every source of income over five hundred dollars" on their annual financial disclosure forms.[8] Beyond this disclosure requirement and traditional graft laws, there were no restrictions on the services for which a lawmaker could be paid. One common way lawmakers supplemented their income was through honoraria. An honorarium is "a payment for a service (such as making a speech) on which custom or propriety forbids a price to be set."[9] Lawmakers were often invited to give speeches at receptions hosted by lobbyists. Following these speeches, lawmakers received checks—honoraria—often in the exact amount of $500. Because by law they were required to report any source of income *more than* $500, these speaking fees flew under the radar for years. Although not illegal and not against any ethics rules, when the practice came to light it was viewed by the public as improper pay-to-play.

The practice of receiving honoraria became a full-blown political scandal when two Ohio lawmakers, Senate President Stanley J. Aronoff and legendary House Speaker Vernal G. Riffe, were indicted on charges of failing to report $9,000 in speaking fees they received from The Limited, a Columbus-based clothing company, for attending two company breakfasts (hence the term *pancaking scandal*) in the early 1990s.[10] These fees were well in excess of the $500 reporting threshold. The indictments brought the entire practice of receiving honoraria under fire and led to the introduction of HB 492, which among other things, prohibited the receipt of honoraria altogether, significantly increased financial disclosure requirements, and restructured the way in which the legislature enforced the ethics rules against lawmakers and employees.[11]

▶ The Current Ethics Landscape

The changes effected by HB 285 and 492, subject to occasional tweaks, remain in place today, a quarter-century following their enactment. The remainder of this article explores the current state of legislative ethics in Ohio.

The Joint Legislative Ethics Committee

House Bill 492 significantly changed the legislative ethics rules that had been in place since the passage of HB 55 two decades earlier. First, it combined the previously separate House and Senate ethics committees into one Joint Legislative

Ethics Committee (JLEC) comprised of 12 members, six from each chamber and each political party. The JLEC retained the same duties as the original two committees:

- The JLEC *shall* recommend a code of ethics for the General Assembly;
- It *may* hear and investigate any ethics complaints and recommend sanctions;
- It *may* recommend new ethics legislation; and
- It *shall* act as an advisory body to the General Assembly on questions relating to possible conflicts of interest.[12]

However, several new duties and provisions were added. HB 492 created the Office of Legislative Inspector General (OLIG), required the JLEC to employ an executive director and staff for the OLIG, and created a funding mechanism for the JLEC and OLIG. The bill also provided for the appointment of special counsel as needed and identified certain investigative and disciplinary reports as public records.[13]

As a function of its advisory role, members of the General Assembly can publicly or privately seek advisory opinions on ethics matters from the JLEC. If an opinion is publicly sought, the opinion is published and the member may reasonably rely on the JLEC's conclusions and will be immune from any punishment arising from the set of circumstances described in the opinion.[14] For example, in 2015, a member requested an advisory opinion to determine whether he may continue to provide certain medical services on behalf of the Ohio Bureau of Workers' Compensation (BWC) while serving in the General Assembly. The question was whether continuing to provide these services under his contract with a government agency—the BWC—while serving in the legislature would result in an unlawful interest in a public contract. The JLEC concluded that the services were lawful and that he could continue providing them. The JLEC's opinion has the force of law, and the member may not be prosecuted or otherwise penalized for providing the services described in the opinion.[15]

Specific Laws and Rules

Perhaps as its most important duty, the JLEC must recommend a code of ethics for each General Assembly.[16] The code of ethics in place as of the writing of this article is the Legislative Code of Ethics for Members and Employees of the 132nd Ohio General Assembly, Employees of Any Legislative Agency, and Candidates for the 133rd General Assembly (henceforth, Code of Ethics). The rules for each General Assembly remain largely the same. The following are some of the more noteworthy ethics rules in the current Code of Ethics and the Ohio Revised Code.[17]

Financial Disclosure

Section 102.02 of the Ohio Revised Code and Section 2 of the Code of Ethics require members of the General Assembly and legislative employees to file financial disclosure statements. As previously mentioned, HB 492 significantly strengthened disclosure requirements. The following information is required on all financial disclosure statements:

- The person's name and the names of the person's immediate family members and all names under which the person and his or her immediate family do business.

- All sources of income and a description of any services rendered in exchange for that income.
- If the person is a member of the General Assembly, every source of income received from a lobbyist in the preceding calendar year along with a brief description of the nature of the services rendered. This requirement applies to attorneys, physicians, and other professionals who may be subject to their own codes of ethics. In such cases, the person may withhold certain information such as a client's name or certain details regarding any services rendered that are necessary to comply with confidentiality requirements.
- Any business in which the person holds an investment of more than $1,000 or in which he or she holds office or has a fiduciary relationship, along with details regarding the official duties or relationship.
- Any property owned by the person in Ohio.
- Details regarding certain debts.
- The source of certain gifts received from any lobbyist during the preceding calendar year, except from a lobbyist who is a member of the person's immediate family or gifts received via a deceased lobbyist's will.
- The source of certain expenses such as food and beverages received from any lobbyist during the preceding calendar year.[18]

As you can see, the financial disclosure requirements are extensive. These requirements also apply to public officials in the other two branches of government, not just the legislature. You can read more about gift and meal restrictions below under Compensation and Gifts.

Voting Abstention

The Code of Ethics allows a member of the General Assembly who has a substantial personal interest in a piece of legislation to request permission from the chair of the JLEC to abstain from voting on the legislation. If so requested, the chair must grant the request. Note that the initial request is voluntary under the rules. However, the rules go on to prohibit outright a member from voting on a piece of legislation if that member is an employee, business associate, or contractor of the person advocating for the legislation. The JLEC may fine an offending member not more than $1,000.[19]

Compensation and Gifts

The Code of Ethics prohibits any person under the JLEC's jurisdiction from directly or indirectly receiving compensation in connection with a matter before the General Assembly.[20] Also, as previously discussed, receipt of honoraria is prohibited, although lawmakers and staffers may receive reimbursements for certain expenses such as travel and lodging.[21] The Code of Ethics also prohibits such persons from receiving more than $75 per calendar year from a lobbyist as payment for food or beverages, except as part of certain events such as seminars, conventions, or functions to which all members of the General Assembly or either chamber of the General Assembly are invited. Lastly, there is a separate $75 limit on gifts from lobbyists, although the term *gift* does not include campaign contributions.[22]

The limitation on gifts raises an interesting question: What if a lawmaker or staffer is married to a lobbyist? Are gifts beyond $75 permitted in that case? In 1995, the JLEC issued an advisory opinion on the matter, concluding that spouses are not subject to the limitation on gifts if those gifts are unrelated to the performance of their official duties.[23] The same rule applies to other immediate family members.[24]

An even more interesting question: If unlimited gifts between spouses are permitted, what about unlimited gifts given *before* marriage? What about an engagement ring? Although the rules allow unlimited gifts from a lobbyist spouse to a lawmaker or staffer spouse, they do not allow unlimited gifts between nonmarried romantic partners, meaning the lawmaker or staffer would need to refund the cost of anything resulting in more than $75 from the lobbyist for that calendar year.[25] However, the receipt of an engagement ring does not violate the ethics rules because an engagement ring is considered a conditional gift given in contemplation of marriage; it does not become a true gift until the condition—marriage—is met.[26] At that point, the gift limitation no longer applies.

Revolving Door

Section 102.03 of the Ohio Revised Code (RC) contains several "revolving door" provisions, so described because they attempt to prevent individuals from leaving office and coming right back in as lobbyists. For example, RC 102.03(A)(4) prohibits a member or employee of the General Assembly from representing any person or matter before the General Assembly—lobbying—for a period of one year following the conclusion of that member's or employee's service. Even if it is well-intentioned, however, a revolving door law that limits an individual's ability to lobby can raise First Amendment questions if it constitutes a prior restraint on political speech. Indeed, this specific provision was the subject of a federal case.

In May 2009, Thomas E. Brinkman, Jr., of the Coalition Opposed to Additional Spending and Taxes (COAST), and COAST treasurer Mark Miller sued the JLEC and several officials to prevent enforcement of RC 102.03(A)(4) against Brinkman, who had left his position as state representative a few months before in December 2008 and immediately joined COAST as an uncompensated lobbyist. The court ruled in the plaintiffs' favor, permanently enjoining the law as an unconstitutional infringement on both Brinkman's and COAST's First Amendment rights. In a First Amendment case like this, a court will analyze the facts using a *strict scrutiny* standard under which a law will be upheld only if it is *narrowly tailored* to achieve a *compelling governmental interest.* The court held that, as applied to Brinkman, the defendants failed to establish a compelling governmental interest justifying the law as applied to *uncompensated* lobbying. As applied to COAST, the court held that the law severely burdened COAST's rights to lobby by prohibiting it from using its choice of lobbyist. The court further held that the law was not narrowly tailored to achieve the objectives of avoiding corruption or the appearance of corruption.[27] The lesson here is that sometimes our efforts to reign in unethical behavior go too far.

Use of Official Resources for Personal Gain

Members and employees of the General Assembly are prohibited from using their position to secure anything of value.[28] For example, a member of the House of Representatives may not use his or her title to get a reservation at an exclusive restaurant that he or she would otherwise have difficulty getting. Sometimes, however, the issue is more subtle. In 2007, the JLEC issued an advisory opinion sought by a college professor who was also serving as a state representative. The professor wished to use statehouse hearing rooms and equipment for a class he taught and planned to ask other elected officials to speak to his students. He was concerned that using the rooms and equipment for nonstatehouse purposes and convincing his elected colleagues to speak to his students might constitute an improper use of his position. The JLEC concluded that as long as the resources and speakers were also available to the general public and the professor did not use his position as a representative to obtain them on more favorable terms than he otherwise would have gotten, he was free to hold his classes in the statehouse, although the JLEC suggested that he have a student request the rooms and resources to assuage any doubts.[29]

▶ Conclusion

The ethics landscape now is significantly different than it was in the mid-20th century. Major shocks such as the Watergate and pancaking scandals tend to serve as catalysts for change. We saw this with the significant increase in financial disclosure requirements. But as we've seen with revolving door laws, sometimes well-intentioned changes can go too far and infringe on the rights of those subject to the rules. Ultimately, although many in the general public cast a wary eye on government officials, the reality is that most elected officials and state employees want to do the right thing. Rare is the feature story about an ethical politician; corruption and scandal make better headlines.

▶ Endnotes

1. DeSario, J. P., & Freel, D. E. (1997). Ohio ethics law reforms: Tracing the political and legal implications. *Akron Law Review, 30*(1), Article 5, 1. Retrieved from http://ideaexchange.uakron .edu/akronlawreview/vol30/iss1/5
2. U.S. Const. amend. XXV, § 2.
3. DeSario & Freel (1997), 1.
4. RC 101.34(A) of Amended Substitute House Bill 55 of the 110th Ohio General Assembly.
5. RC 101.34(A) at 102.02, 102.03, 102.04, 102.07, and 102.99.
6. The Ohio Ethics Commission was created by H.B. 55. It was and remains the executive branch's ethics authority.
7. Section 4 of Amended Substitute House Bill 285 of the 120th Ohio General Assembly.
8. RC 102.02(A)(2) of Amended Substitute House Bill 55 of the 110th Ohio General Assembly.
9. Honorarium. (n.d.). Merriam-Webster Online. In Merriam-Webster. Retrieved July 6, 2018, from https://www.merriam-webster.com/dictionary/honorarium
10. Candisky, C. (1996, February 2). Several named in honorarium indictments. *The Columbus Dispatch*, p. 1A.
11. DeSario & Freel (1997), 11.
12. RC 101.34 of Amended Substitute House Bill 492 of the 120th Ohio General Assembly.
13. RC 101.34 of Amended Substitute House Bill 492 of the 120th Ohio General Assembly.
14. RC 102.08(C).
15. Legislative Code of Ethics for Members and Employees of the 132nd Ohio General Assembly, Employees of any Legislative Agency, and Candidates for the 133rd General Assembly, Section 12. Retrieved August 13, 2018 from https://www.legislature.ohio.gov/publications

/legislative-code-of-ethics; JLEC Advisory Opinion 2015-001, issued October 6, 2015. Retrieved August 13, 2018 from http://www.jlec-olig.state.oh.us/PDFs/AdvisoryOpinions/15-001.pdf

16. RC 101.34(B)(1).
17. Note that aside from the rules established by the Code of Ethics, which are only enforceable by the General Assembly, Ohio law contains other provisions governing the conduct of public officials, including members of the General Assembly, that are ultimately enforceable by the courts. The remainder of this article focuses only on the Code of Ethics.
18. RC 102.02(A); Code of Ethics, Section 2.
19. Code of Ethics, Section 4.
20. Code of Ethics, Section 5.
21. Code of Ethics, Section 10.
22. Code of Ethics, Section 5. The exclusion of campaign contributions from the definition of "gift" makes sense because otherwise *any* campaign contribution would be considered a gift, effectively meaning that no one could donate more than $75 to a political campaign. Campaign contribution limits and related requirements are governed by other law.
23. JLEC Advisory Opinion 95-003, issued March 14, 1995.
24. JLEC, Expenditures made for the benefit of spouses or other immediate family members. Retrieved August 13, 2018 from http://www.jlec-olig.state.oh.us/?p=681
25. More accurately, the recipient would need to refund the excess amount to the donor.
26. See, e.g., *Cooper v. Smith*, 155 Ohio App. 3d 218.
27. *Brinkman v. Budish*, 692 F. Supp. 2d 855.
28. RC 102.03(D).
29. JLEC Advisory Opinion 07-001, issued September 12, 2007.

▶ References

Brinkman v. Budish, 692 F. Supp. 2d 855.

Candisky, C. (1996, February 2). Several named in honorarium indictments. *The Columbus Dispatch*, p. 1A.

Cooper v. Smith, 155 Ohio App. 3d 218.

DeSario, J. P., & Freel, D. E. (1997). Ohio ethics law reforms: Tracing the political and legal implications. *Akron Law Review, 30*(1), Article 5, 1. Retrieved from http://ideaexchange.uakron.edu/akronlawreview/vol30/iss1/5

Joint Legislative Ethics Committee (JLEC). (1995, March 14). JLEC Advisory Opinion 95-003. Ohio General Assembly.

Joint Legislative Ethics Committee (JLEC). (2018, August 13). Expenditures made for the benefit of spouses or other immediate family members. Ohio General Assembly.

Merriam-Webster Online Dictionary. (n.d.). Honorarium. Retrieved July 6, 2018, from https://www.merriam-webster.com/dictionary/honorarium

Ohio General Assembly. (n.d.). RC 101.34(A) of Amended Substitute House Bill 55 of 110th Assembly.

Ohio General Assembly. (n.d.). RC 101.34(A) of Amended Substitute House Bill 128 of 120th Assembly.

Ohio General Assembly. (n.d.). RC 101.34 of Amended Substitute House Bill 492 of 120th Assembly.

Ohio General Assembly. (2015). Legislative Code of Ethics for Members and Employees of the 132nd Ohio General Assembly, Employees of any Legislative Agency, and Candidates for the 133rd General Assembly, Section 12.

U.S. Constitution, Amendment XXV, § 2.

ARTICLE 8

Proper Role of Government

Jason W. Stevens

▶ Introduction

The Declaration of Independence asserts that the purpose of government is to secure the equal natural rights of the people on the basis of consent.

This idea was shared by the leading American Founders, as expressed not only in Thomas Jefferson's Declaration but also in many of the other official Founding-era documents of the time. In the Massachusetts Constitution of 1780, for example, John Adams wrote that the end, or purpose, of government "is to secure the existence of the body-politic; to protect it; and to furnish the individuals who compose it, with the power of enjoying, in safety and tranquility, their natural rights, and the blessings of life" (Kurland & Lerner, 1987, p. 11). Likewise, Virginia's 1776 Declaration of Rights, whose principal author was George Mason, argued that government "is, or ought to be, instituted for the common benefit, protection, and security of the people, nation, or community—of all the various modes and forms of Government that is best which is capable of producing the greatest degree of happiness and safety, and is most effectually secured against the danger of mal-administration" (Kurland & Lerner, 1987, p. 6). The American Founders, who may have been bitterly divided over some important questions of administration and policy, stood united in mutual agreement regarding the fundamental principle of the purpose of government.

Although the Declaration of Independence tells us that governments derive their just powers from the consent of the governed to secure rights, it has little if anything to say about the constitutional framework or specific institutional arrangements that would work best to achieve that goal. The Declaration might have provided the initial vision or ends for good and just government, but it was left up to the prudence of statesmen to determine the appropriate means for carrying that vision into effect. For that, we must look to the Constitution and, in particular, its focus on the doctrine of the separation of powers (or the division of governmental power along tripartite lines—legislative, executive, and judicial) as well as the principle of federalism (or the relationship among the different kinds of government—national, state, and local) to determine the proper role of government in guaranteeing the inalienable rights of individuals on the basis of consent.

Therefore, the purpose of this article is to discover how the Declaration and Constitution work together to produce justice in the government by securing the rights of life, liberty, and the pursuit of happiness.

▶ The Declaration of Independence

"Justice," James Madison said in *Federalist* No. 51, "is the end of government. It is the end of civil society. It ever has been and ever will be pursued until it be obtained, or until liberty be lost in the pursuit" (Hamilton, Madison, & Jay, 2003, p. 321). The Declaration of Independence contains the clearest and best expression of the American conception of justice as the end of government. Although no discussion of justice is ever easy or complete, and whereas the words of the Declaration may strike some people as hollow and many others as so familiar and famous as to detract somewhat from their meaning, it still must be admitted that here we find what Jefferson called "an expression of the American mind" (Burkett, 2013, p. 135)—fairly precise principles with definite conclusions about the proper role of government.

At the heart of the Declaration's theory of government is the principle of equality, which states that all men are created equal in terms of their natural rights to life, liberty, and the pursuit of happiness. To say that all men are naturally created equal in terms of their rights is to say that such rights exist independently of civil society and positive law and that no one should rule another without that latter's consent. There are no natural masters and no natural slaves among us, in other words. As Thomas Jefferson put it near the end of his life in 1826, "the mass of mankind has not been born, with saddles on their backs, nor a favored few booted and spurred, ready to ride them legitimately, by the grace of God" (Burkett, 2013, p. 137). Even though there may exist a vast inequality among mankind—for example, in terms of individual attributes, abilities, and talents—no difference is so great and so powerful as to overcome mankind's essential equality of rights, shared alike among all humanity. "Because Sir Isaac Newton was superior to others in understanding," Jefferson also wrote, "he was not therefore lord of the person or property of others" (Whitman, 1960, p. 252). In 1776, for the first time in human history, the self-evident truth of universal human equality provided the fundamental basis for the political experiment in popular self-government.

"That to secure these rights," the Declaration continues, "governments are instituted among men, deriving their just powers from the consent of the governed" (Burkett, 2013, p. 2). The purpose of human beings coming together to establish government is to better secure their individual rights, which, without government, are left unsafe and unprotected, and their enjoyment extremely uncertain (for instance, in what the Founders often called a "state of nature"). Government's first job, therefore, is to protect the equal natural rights of all its members. And because all human beings are equal, no one having a natural or permanent right to rule over another, the powers of government are not "just" unless the people who are subject to that government also consent to its rule. A government may protect the people's rights and liberties, but unless it is a government based on the consent of the governed, it cannot be a just one.

The Declaration's understanding of justice, therefore, is based on two key elements: first, government must protect the equal natural rights of all; and, second, it must be done with the consent of the governed. Any government that fails to observe these ends for which it was established cannot be a just one and cannot long retain the esteem and confidence of the people.

Finally, in light of these observations, the Declaration concludes, "that whenever any form of government becomes destructive of these ends [i.e., securing natural rights on the basis of consent], it is the right of the people to alter or to abolish it, and to institute new government, laying its foundation on such principles and organizing its powers in such form, as to them shall seem most likely to effect their safety and happiness" (Burkett, 2013, p. 2). This is what is commonly called the *right of revolution*, and it provides the final check, or limitation, on the unjust exercise of governmental power. Because the main purpose of human beings entering into civil society in the first place, as has been said, is to better protect and enjoy their natural rights, no government that seeks contrary ends and transgresses this fundamental rule of society can, with justice, long endure. Whenever government violates the end for which it was instituted, endeavoring to destroy that which it was created to secure, it thereupon forfeits any power that it might possess back to the original and supreme fountain of all legitimate authority, the people themselves.

And from there, it is left up to the people, as Madison said in *The Federalist*, to pursue justice "until it be obtained, or until liberty be lost in the pursuit." The American people, after their own bloody revolution, looked for and finally found such a solution in the U.S. Constitution.

▶ The Constitution

In conformity with the principles of the Declaration of Independence, the Preamble of the Constitution declares, on the authority of "We the People," that among the purposes of the new government are to "establish Justice" and to "secure the Blessings of Liberty" (Burkett, 2013, p. 24). To do this, the Framers at the Philadelphia convention of 1787 proposed a strong national government of enumerated (or expressed) powers based in the republican form, meaning "a government which derives all its powers directly or indirectly from the great body of the people, and is administered by persons holding their offices . . . for a limited period, or during good behavior" (Hamilton et al., 2003, p. 237).

Although the Federalists, who favored the new Constitution, and the Anti-Federalists, who opposed its ratification, differed on a great variety of topics related to the maintenance of republican government, the two sides agreed completely on at least one area: the momentous importance of the question now at hand, whether to vote the Constitution up or down. Brutus, one of the most prominent Anti-Federalists, put it this way: "The most important question that was ever proposed to your decision, or to the decision of any people under heaven, is before you, and you are to decide upon it by men of your own election, chosen specifically for this purpose" (Burkett, 2013, p. 38). Alexander Hamilton, writing in the opening salvo of *Federalist* No. 1, repeated Brutus's sentiment with slightly more gusto when he said, "It has been frequently remarked that it seems to have been reserved to the people of this country, by their conduct and example, to decide the important question, whether societies of men are really capable or not of establishing good government from reflection and choice, or whether they are forever destined to depend for their political constitutions on accident and force" (Hamilton et al., 2003, p. 27). Both men argued that the ratification question ought not to be taken lightly by the American people because, for the first time in human history, they were given the unheard of opportunity to choose a form of government for themselves and their posterity, instead of being forced to rely on conditions outside of their control, as had always been the case in the past. The stakes could not have been higher as the future of self-government, or the capacity of mankind to govern itself, hung in the balance. America was now in the unique position to prove to the world that human beings not only should in theory but also actually could in practice rule themselves.

Success in this endeavor would require what James Madison called, in *Federalist* No. 51, certain "auxiliary precautions" or "inventions of prudence" (Hamilton et al., 2003, p. 319) in the constitutional framework of government, chief among which was the doctrine of the separation of powers along tripartite lines—legislative, executive, and judicial.

Separation of Powers

Like the principles of the Declaration of Independence, students of American politics and government sometimes have a difficult time thinking clearly about the separation of powers as a whole. The various intricacies of the system can, with not a little bit of effort, be committed to memory to be recalled at will at some later time and place. But this is not why the separation of powers is worth studying and taking seriously. It is a relatively easy task to memorize the different parts of the system; for example, how the president's veto power works, that all revenue measures must originate in the House of Representatives, that the minimum age requirement for a member of the Senate is 30 years, that justices in the federal judiciary serve for good behavior, and so on. It is much more difficult, however, to begin to comprehend and appreciate the whole, and to not mistake the trees for the forest. When it comes to the separation of powers, if we may borrow Aristotle's famous maxim, the whole really is greater than the sum of its parts. The reason for this is explained by *The Federalist*.

James Madison, writing as Publius in *Federalist* No. 47, did something rare, at least in the pages of *The Federalist*: he heaped lavish praise on the Anti-Federalists who were opposed to the ratification of the new Constitution. In particular, he praised them for their respectable concern over the tripartite division of power in the Constitution. "No political truth is certainly of greater intrinsic value, or is stamped with the authority of more enlightened patrons of liberty than that on which the objection is founded," Madison said. "The accumulation of all powers, legislative, executive, and judiciary, in the same hands, whether of one, a few, or many, and whether hereditary, self-appointed, or elective, may justly be pronounced the very definition of tyranny" (Hamilton et al., 2003, p. 298). In other words, the Anti-Federalists were absolutely right, according to Madison, to be so concerned about the separation of powers. Because without the separation of powers, the result will always be tyranny; or, to put it another way, the definition of tyranny is the absence of the separation of powers.

Many of the Anti-Federalists questioned the idea of the separation of powers proposed by the Constitution. The author Centinel, for example, provided perhaps the most scathing indictment when he said that he could trace "the constitution of every form of government that ever existed, as far as history affords materials, [without finding] a single instance of such a government [in practice]" (Kurland & Lerner, 1987, p. 349). Nothing even close to the kind of institutional arrangements proposed by the Framers had existed at any time throughout history, not even among the ancient Greek and Roman states. And even though Hamilton, writing as Publius in *The Federalist*, admitted that "experience" remains the "best oracle of wisdom" (Hamilton et al., 2003, p. 105), he also claimed that "the science of politics" has undergone many great and recent improvements, "which were either not known at all, or imperfectly known to the ancients," including "the regular distribution of power into distinct departments" (Hamilton et al., 2003, p. 67). Hamilton meant that although Centinel was correct about the broad history of politics lacking any example of a constitutional system similar to that of the United States, the innovations incorporated into the new Constitution (e.g., the separation of powers) would allow the American system to succeed and prosper where all others had previously failed.

Far from being a weakness, therefore, the separation of powers was actually the Constitution's greatest strength. The reason for this was to prevent the abuse of governmental power by requiring each branch to control itself, while at the same time encouraging it to resist encroachments by the others in order to secure the people's rights and liberties with their consent. As Madison put it in *Federalist* No. 51, "In framing a government which is to be administered by men over men, the great difficulty lies in this: you must first enable the government to control the governed; and in the next place oblige it to control itself" (Hamilton et al., 2003, p. 319).

The main purpose of the doctrine of the separation of powers, according to the Framers of the Constitution, was to prevent tyranny, the concentration of all powers—legislative, executive, and judicial—in one set of hands to the destruction of the rights of the people. The proper role of governmental power might be to protect the people's natural rights, but because "power is of an encroaching nature" (Hamilton et al., 2003, p. 305), it is absolutely necessary to provide a check on government itself to prevent it from destroying that which it was instituted to protect and descending into chaos, possibly requiring another revolution to correct.

Although the separation of powers remains the primary means to controlling the government, a secondary precaution exists in the principle of federalism, or the relationship among the different kinds of government—national, state, and local. Thus, the constitutional framework of the United States provides a double security to the rights of the people.

Federalism

In addition to the separation of powers, the other fundamental part of the constitutional framework that protects the people's natural rights and prevents governmental tyranny by dividing power is the principle of federalism. *Federalism* refers to the division of power between the different kinds of government existing in the compound republic of the United States. James Madison explained in *The Federalist* why the separation of powers and federalism were both absolutely necessary to the maintenance of good and just government:

"In the compound republic of America," Madison said in *Federalist* 51,

the power surrendered by the people is first divided between two distinct governments [i.e., the national government and the state governments], and then the portion allotted to each subdivided among distinct and separate departments [i.e., legislative, executive, and judicial]. Hence a double security arises to the rights of the people. The different governments will control each other, at the same time that each will be controlled by itself (Hamilton et al., 2003, p. 320).

In other words, state and local governments are not just an afterthought when it comes to the proper role of government in America's constitutional framework; they are an indispensable element of the entire system and, in many ways, the power that is most immediately felt and more intimately familiar in the daily lives of citizens than that of the national authority.

The national government, on the one hand, has authority only over matters of a truly general concern to the entire nation, such as national security, foreign policy, maintaining a national currency, and the regulation of commerce among the states and with foreign nations. Its business is national in scope and remains constant and uniform throughout the entire country.

The state and local governments, on the other hand, have authority over matters of a more particular and pressing concern, such as education, police and fire departments, internal improvements (e.g., building roads and bridges), and the regulation of commerce within the states. Their business is much more localized and varies widely from place to place.

Taken together, they are an expression of self-government by the people for identical ends—namely, to prevent government oppression by dividing government power and to secure equal natural rights on the basis of consent.

▶ Conclusion

The purpose of government, according to the American Founders, is to protect the people's natural rights on the basis of the consent of the governed. This is the main lesson of the Declaration of Independence as well as the U.S. Constitution.

At some point after his election as the 16th president of the United States, but before the scheduled inauguration in March 1861, Abraham Lincoln reflected on the proper relationship between the Declaration of Independence and the Constitution. Lincoln wrote that the principle of "Liberty to all" from the Declaration was an "apple of gold," while the Constitution and the Union were a "picture of silver" subsequently framed around it. "The picture was made," Lincoln explained, "not to conceal, or destroy the apple; but to adorn and preserve it. The picture was made for the apple—not the apple for the picture" (Burkett, 2013, pp. 275–276).

The Constitution of the United States is grounded in the principles of the Declaration of Independence. This means that the Constitution was necessary to bring to life the unfulfilled promises of the American Revolution and, in some measure, complete the revolutionary vision of a government of, by, and for the people. The Declaration contemplated certain ends for just government, whereas the Constitution embodied the institutional means essential for its support. The result was an inseparable bond between the Declaration's "golden apple" and the Constitution's "silver frame."

The intricate constitutional framework was designed to secure the people's natural rights. The separation of powers guaranteed that political power was not concentrated in one set of hands, thus avoiding tyranny and promoting individual liberty. Federalism again sought to divide power, but this time between national and state authorities for the benefit of the public welfare and the safety and happiness of all.

The result may not have been perfect, and none of the Founders claimed it was. "A faultless plan," James Madison warned, "was not to be expected" (Hamilton et al., 2003, p. 222). And in many ways the nation is still struggling to live up to its original creed as expressed by the Founders in the Declaration of Independence.

The American experiment in self-government remains a work in progress. But without the American Founders, there is a good chance that the apple of gold ensconced in a frame of silver would have been lost to the world forever.

▶ References

Burkett, C. (Ed.). (2013). *50 core American documents: Required reading for students, teachers, and citizens*. Ashland, OH: Ashbrook Press.

Hamilton, A., Madison, J., & Jay, J. (2003). *The Federalist papers*. Clinton Rossiter (Ed.). New York, NY: New American Library.

Kurland, P. B., & Lerner, R. (Eds.). (1987). *The Founders' constitution* (Vol. 1). Chicago, IL: University of Chicago Press.

Whitman, W. (Ed.). (1960). *Jefferson's letters*. Eau Claire, WI: E. M. Hale and Co.

Federal Law, State Law, and City Enforcement Issues

Paul A. Lucas
Bryce M. Carter
Cadin D. Sanner

▶ Immigration Law Enforcement

Immigration is a topic that has divided the United States for decades. This was a topic of high interest during the 2016 presidential campaign. Immigration law is complex and involves every level of government. Laws surrounding immigration within the United States will be reviewed at the local, state and federal levels.

▶ Federal Law

Under the administration of President Donald Trump, the importance of strong borders has been emphasized through the proposed building of a border wall and increased detainment of illegal immigrants. As a result, Immigration and Customs Enforcement (ICE) raids have been increasingly focused in Latino communities, and are not as politically silent, as in the Obama administration (Hing, 2015). Increased enforcement and the perception of "anti-immigration" policy are having adverse effects on marginalized groups in the United States. An increase in enforcement and an increased "anti-immigrant" attitude and law in the United States is leading to a decrease in the physical and mental health in Latino communities (Vargas, Sanchez & Juárez, 2017). Though the focus of enforcement has fallen mainly on immigrants of Hispanic origin, there are other marginalized groups that have been impacted by the immigration policies of recent administrations.

During Trump's campaign, he called for increased vetting of immigrants entering the United States. An early executive order from his administration temporarily banned travel from six different countries that were pulled from a list of countries that pose a threat to the United States; the list had been created by the Obama administration. Trump used the provision in the Immigration and Nationality Act that allows for halting a person's travel if his or her country of origin poses a threat to the United States (Starr, 2017). There was conflict between executive and state legislatures in this regard. The travel ban was deemed unconstitutional because it focused on Muslim-majority nations. Media coverage of topics such as this have highlighted the harsh nature of current immigration-enforcement methods. Historically, immigration enforcement has used two approaches: deporting unauthorized immigrants and using prosecutorial discretion. The detainment of potential illegal persons and their deportation can often involve questionable methods such as profiling based on race (Vargas et al., 2017). An example of prosecutorial discretion in the Obama administration was the protection of certain groups from the detainment and deportation method. The Deferred Action for Childhood Arrivals Act was created as an act of discretion to prevent children who had arrived in the United States illegally from being deported (Starr, 2017). These two methods gained support from opposite ends of the political spectrum. Another potential option would be to employ a cooperative enforcement model.

The cooperative model has been used effectively by other government organizations. The Environmental Protection Agency and the Food and Drug Administration have embraced the idea of working together to ensure those under regulation can come into compliance. These goals can be achieved through educational programs and consultations. There are examples of this in immigration enforcement (such as waivers for family members of U.S. citizens), but those they apply to may have difficulty navigating the naturalization process. Immigration enforcement could be simplified with a streamlined process and assistance to those who may struggle with the naturalization process (Frost, 2017). Changing these processes may be complicated by state-level immigration policy.

▶ State Law

Although immigration enforcement typically falls under the jurisdiction of the federal government, local and state governments still have the ability to decide how they approach undocumented immigrants. The stalemate of immigration reform during the Obama administration led to an increase in states' creation of immigration law. Many of these laws came from officials who pushed racial issues within their campaigns (Johnson, 2016). Two examples of these state laws are Arizona's Senate Bill 1070 and Alabama's House Bill 56.

Arizona's SB 1070, or the Support Our Law Enforcement and Safe Neighborhoods Act, was signed into law by Arizona Governor Janice K. Brewer in 2010. This law gave state and local law enforcement the authority to detain those they believed to be unlawfully present. Arizona has a long history of anti-immigrant policies— from laws requiring schools to report the immigration status of students to laws prohibiting undocumented persons from receiving any damages in an Arizona court (Campbell, 2011). Alabama also has a history of creating anti-immigrant policies that some may view as extreme.

During the 2008 and 2010 elections, organizations such as the Federation for American Immigration Reform were supporting conservative politicians in Alabama who would be tough on immigration issues. In 2011, the multifaceted HB 56 was signed into law. It allowed law enforcement to detain anyone whom officers believed may be undocumented, and it prohibited undocumented peoples from receiving government services and attending schools (Johnson, 2016). As we see with both Alabama's HB 56 and Arizona's SB 1070, immigration enforcement trickles down to the local level of government.

▶ Local Level

The Alabama and Arizona legislatures gave local law enforcement the ability to detain people under reasonable suspicion, which has led to racial profiling. In other communities, the response to increased immigration enforcement has been to aid those targeted. So-called sanctuary cities such as Santa Ana, California, have achieved their status through a combination of methods. These cities limit their cooperation with immigration enforcement by methods such as restricting communication with federal authorities and preventing officers from making arrests based on immigration law (Rice, 2017). Efforts such as this are under increasing scrutiny by President Trump and his administration for "noncooperation" with immigration policy.

Immigration law and enforcement constitutes a complex relationship between various levels of government. Regulation instated at the federal level inherently impacts other levels of government, including how law enforcement enforces such laws. This impacts experiences by the individuals living in certain areas. The inclusion of state-level enforcement has created a clear division in the United States. The dichotomy of opinions on the two methods of immigration enforcement is crystal clear in American politics. Cooperative enforcement via assistance with the naturalization process offers an interesting alternative to deportation without simply excluding groups from deportation.

Sanctuary Cities

Although there is no federal designation for what a sanctuary city is, sanctuary jurisdictions have been defined as any "city, town, and state governments that have passed provisions to limit their enforcement of federal immigration laws" (Bhatt, 2016, p. 139). According to the Immigrant Legal Resource Center (n.d.), four states, 364 counties, and 39 cities currently have limited cooperation with ICE and do not detain noncitizens on their illegal status alone (Martinez, Martinez-Schuldt, & Cantor, 2017). Within these locations, sanctuary ordinances are passed that offer private or public sanctuary. Private sanctuary involves religious and nongovernmental organizations providing food, shelter, and other forms of assistance to undocumented immigrants. Private sanctuary began during the 1980s when many individuals were fleeing Central America to escape war, violence, and political persecution. The United States turned many of these individuals away, but U.S. religious organizations began offering sanctuary to provide assistance to the undocumented immigrants and protect them from deportation, with many claiming that this was the beginning of the current day public practices used by sanctuary cities (Bau, 1994; Ridgely, 2008; Villazor, 2008). Public sanctuary ordinances limit local law enforcement cooperation with federal agencies and increase undocumented immigrant inclusion at the local level (Graauw, 2014; Martinez et al., 2017).

Following the practices used by private sanctuary organizations for reasons that include increasing community cohesion, preventing racial discrimination, and having local law enforcement emphasize other local enforcement issues, public sanctuary cities began to emerge. The emergence of sanctuary cities is claimed to be a response to the 1986 Immigration and Control Act that, while regularizing the immigration status of approximately 3 million immigrants by 1992, also expanded illegal immigration enforcement's reach further into the United States (Massey, Dorand, & Malone, 2003). However, the increased enforcement has not thwarted the number of illegal immigrants within the United States, and the unauthorized immigrant population stands at approximately 11.1 million individuals, with 52% consisting of migrants from Mexico (Passel & Cohn, 2016). Given this inland shift toward enforcement, ICE and the U.S. Customs and Border Protection, who have traditionally been responsible for enforcing immigration laws, have been requesting that state and local officials and law enforcement share some of their responsibility (Martinez et al., 2017). This is highlighted by the Secure Communities, Criminal Alien, and 287(g) programs that allow ICE to enter into agreements with state and local officials to assist with immigration-enforcement duties (Meissner, Kerwin, Chrishti, & Bergeron, 2013).[1] Programs aimed at increasing federal and local partnerships in enforcing immigration laws have been criticized for their overall legality, humanitarian considerations, use of racial profiling, and fiscal constraints (Dreby, 2012; Gardner & Kohli, 2004; Lasch, 2013; Wells, 2004). This has led to a fight between the federal government, which favors enforcement of the law regarding undocumented immigrants, and state and local officials who favor protecting residents within their jurisdictions, whether undocumented or documented (Wells, 2004).

Opponents of sanctuary cities claim they promote unregulated crime because of their lack of law and order and are founded upon and perpetuated by the immigrant-as-threat narratives. These narratives include threats to national security (terrorism), economic security (taking jobs from resident Americans), and cultural security (different languages, customs, and religions) (Ibrahim, 2005). These narratives are echoed by Blalock's (1967) minority threat perspective in which minority groups, including legal and undocumented immigrants, are seen as a threat to the majority. This threat is enhanced during times when resources, such as employment and political capital, are scarce (Stacey, Carbone-Lopez, & Rosenfeld, 2011). The main argument in the opposition to sanctuary cities is that they cause harm to the public's safety through an increase in crime in the localities in which these ordinances have passed. Opponents claim that undocumented immigrants know they will not be deported and intentionally seek these areas out to live and commit crimes, causing social disorganization, a known catalyst for crime. Although violent offenses within sanctuary jurisdictions are prosecuted and not treated differently, opponents still claim that those who are undocumented move to these areas for impunity toward their crimes. This sentiment has recently been promoted politically with emphasis on one case in particular.

The 2015 death of Kathryn Steinle has been repeatedly used by President Trump and other politicians to promote antisanctuary policies. Steinle, 32, was shot and killed by Juan Francisco Lopez-Sanchez, who was living in San Francisco unlawfully. Lopez-Sanchez had been deported from the United States five times prior to Steinle's death. However, San Francisco, a well-known sanctuary city, does not allow local law enforcement to contact federal immigration officials, a policy which has been blamed for allowing Steinle's death to occur. As a result, several federal proposals have been introduced that call for increased penalties for unauthorized reentry and limits on federal grants to sanctuary cities (Marcos, 2017). Although the immigrants-as-threats narrative is currently a politically charged topic highlighted by cases such as Steinle's, research does not support the notion that sanctuary cities, or other cities with large immigrant populations, experience an increase in crime as a result.

Supporters of sanctuary cities contend that social disorganization does not occur and that sanctuary cities actually experience an increase in organization through the promotion of robust networks and enhanced cooperation. These claims are supported by research that has shown that increasing minority populations are positively related to informal and formal social controls, including criminal justice responses (Eitle, D'Alessio, & Stolzenberg, 2002). Research has also indicated that immigrants tend to commit less crime than native-born citizens (Gonzalez, Collingwood, & El Khatib, 2017; Lee, Martinez, & Rosenfeld, 2001; Morenoff, Sampson, & Raudenbush, 2001). When compared to similar cities without such policies, sanctuary cities had lower rates of robbery and homicide (Lyons, Vélez, & Santoro, 2013) and lower overall crime rates (Stowell, Messner, McGeever, & Raffolovich, 2009).[2] In fact, the absence of sanctuary policies may actually promote social disorganization because undocumented immigrants without certain support networks within their communities are less likely to report victimization (e.g., domestic violence) and are more likely to be victims of crimes perpetrated against them (Crenshaw, 1995; Kittrie, 2006; Menjivar & Bejarano, 2004). Clearly, research conducted on sanctuary cities does not support opponents' claims against them and offers support for their creation and incorporation. However, this evidence does not signal an end to the debate over their right to exist anytime soon.

The debate surrounding the use of sanctuary cities will continue, but research shows that many of the threats used to support the opposition against them are unsupported and misplaced.

▶ Drug Legalization

As a country, the United States has a long history of drug consumption and, consequently, an equally long history of punishing drug offenders. North Americans consume more drugs annually than any other region in the world (United Nations Office on Drugs and Crime [UNODC], 2018). The start of the so-called War on Drugs led to an increase in the numbers of arrests of these drug users. As of 2016, 197,200 individuals were serving time in state prisons, 81,900 were incarcerated in federal prisons, and 171,245 were in local jails serving sentences or awaiting sentencing for drug-related crimes (Sentencing Project, 2017). These statistics also include a troubling number of youth drug users. According to the National Institute on Drug Abuse (NIDA) (2015), "In 2013, an estimated 24.6 million Americans aged 12 or older—9.4% of the population—had used an illicit drug in the past month." A combination of treatment services and proper legislation is necessary to correct domestic drug problems.

A look at consumption of illicit substances within the United States shows that marijuana is consumed more than any other substance (Center for Behavioral Health Statistics and Quality, 2016). In 2013, 19.8% of the total U.S. population were actively consuming marijuana (NIDA, 2015). In addition, 70.3% of all drug users consumed marijuana as their first illegal substance (NIDA, 2015). However, when misused or abused, legal drugs such as prescription pain killers, particularly opioids, can become addictive and potentially lead to harder drug use. In North America, 14.2 million people abuse prescription pain killers, making them the second most abused drug in the continent (UNODC, 2018). The biggest difference between opioids and marijuana is the risk of overdose from consumption; the first presents a substantial threat to life, the second does not. According to NIDA (2015), between 2013 and 2016 fatal overdoses directly related to opioids increased from 25,050 to 42,068. This increase has led the U.S. Department of Health and Human Services to recognize such addiction and overdosing as a public health crisis. Legalization and decriminalization of drugs such as marijuana could potentially allow government entities to focus more on the opioid crisis and find better solutions.

Marijuana, the most widely consumed drug in North America (NIDA, 2015), has had a long and complicated history. In recent years, many states passed laws that directly contradict federal laws by legalizing marijuana in some form. In 1937, the Marijuana Tax Act was enacted and allowed the federal government to regulate marijuana for the first time. The tax act authorized the government to heavily tax those involved with marijuana, from growing to distribution and consumption. The tax act was a turning point for marijuana prohibition and set a precedent for the policies that are still in effect today. In 2012, Colorado became the first state to legalize marijuana with Amendment 64, also known as the Colorado Marijuana Legalization Amendment. This amendment legalized consumption of marijuana for citizens 21 and over within the state. In January 2014, it became legal to sell marijuana to individuals 21 or older at licensed facilities. Since then, more states have "followed the example" set by Colorado. According to the National Conference of State Legislatures (2018), "31 states, the District of Columbia, Guam, and Puerto Rico now allow for comprehensive public medical marijuana and cannabis programs." Despite this, there is still pushback from legislatures to maintain the status quo ante on drug enforcement.

Marijuana legislation has been of two main types: medical and recreational. States that have legislation allowing medical marijuana "allow the legal use of botanical cannabis for medicinal purposes" (Michalec, Rapp, & Whittle, 2015). Only patients with a prescription are legally allowed to possess any amount. States that have legalized recreational marijuana allow for anyone to consume given that the individual is old enough and doesn't have more than the maximum amount defined in that state's law. More states have legalized medical marijuana than recreational marijuana because of shifting public opinions. Research conducted by Gaede and Vaske (2017) found that college students who regularly consumed marijuana consistently held more positive views on legalization compared to students who were not regular consumers. A 2017 poll revealed that 64% of Americans believe marijuana should be legal (Rose & Goelzhauser, 2018). Despite this, marijuana remains illegal under federal law.

Examining federal laws, marijuana remains a Schedule I drug. Looking at the scheduling guidelines used by the U.S. Drug Enforcement Agency (DEA), Schedule I controlled substances are "drugs with no currently accepted medical use and a high potential for abuse" (United States Drug Enforcement Agency, 2018). Other Schedule I drugs include LSD, ecstasy, methaqualone, and peyote. Because marijuana is a Schedule I drug, the government currently does not recognize any medicinal benefits resulting from its consumption. However, marijuana and related compounds seem to have therapeutic promise when it comes to movement disorders and neurodegenerative diseases such as Parkinson disease (Babayeva, Assefa, Basu, Chumki, & Loewy, 2016). Despite still being illegal at the federal level, the government has not tried to impede states' policies legalizing marijuana. According to Bushan (2015), "The Department of Justice has left the legalization of marijuana in Colorado and Washington unchallenged" since its passing in 2012. Despite marijuana being deemed a Schedule I drug at the national level, the expansion of the marijuana industry has not stopped and will eventually require a federal decision on its legality. Carefully considered legislation on marijuana and other drugs is the key to correcting and preventing further drug crises.

▶ Endnotes

1. Pressure to enhance local and state law enforcement partnerships increased sharply after the September 11, 2001, terrorist attacks.
2. Localities that begin sanctuary policies may see an increase in *reported* crimes given that the undocumented population is more likely to report victimization absent the fear of being deported for doing so. This is not to be confused with *increasing* crime rates because of lawlessness, but rather previously unreported crimes are now being brought to the attention of local law enforcement, leading to their inclusion in office reports of crimes known to the police (Gonzalez et al., 2017).

▶ References

Babayeva, M., Assefa, H., Basu, P., Chumki, S., & Loewy, Z. (2016). Marijuana compounds: A nonconventional approach to Parkinson's disease therapy. *Parkinson's Disease, 2016*, 1–19. Article ID 1279042. Retrieved from http://dx.doi.org/10.1155/2016/1279042

Bau, I. (1994). Cities of refuge: No federal preemption of ordinances restricting local government cooperation with the INS. *Berkley Law Raza Law Journal, 7*(1), 50–71.

Bhatt, R. (2016). Pushing an end to sanctuary cities: Will it happen? *Michigan Journal of Race and Law, 22*, 140–162.

Blalock, H. M. (1967). *Toward a theory of minority-group relations.* New York, NY: John Wiley.

Bushan, A. (2015). An evaluation of the effects of the legalization of marijuana in Colorado and Washington from an international law perspective. *Canada-United States Law Journal, 39*, 187–201.

Campbell, K. M. (2011). The road to S.B. 1070: How Arizona became ground zero for the Immigrants' Rights Movement and the continuing struggle for Latino civil rights in America. *Harvard Latino Law Review, 14*, 1–21.

Center for Behavioral Health Statistics and Quality. (2016) *National survey on drug use and health: Detailed tables,* Retrieved from https://www.samhsa.gov/data/sites/default/files/NSDUH-DetTabs-2015/NSDUH-DetTabs-2015/NSDUH-DetTabs-2015.pdf

Crenshaw, K. (1995). Mapping the margins: Intersectionality, identity politics, and violence against women of color. *Stanford Law Review, 43*(6), 1241–1299.

Dreby, J. (2012). *Enforcement policies impact children, families, and communities: A view from the ground.* Washington, DC: Center for American Progress.

Eitle, D., D'Alessio, S. J., & Stolzenberg, L. (2002). Racial threat and social control: A test of the political, economic, and threat of black crime hypotheses. *Social Forces, 81*, 557–576.

Frost, A. (2017). Cooperative enforcement in immigration law. *Iowa Law Review, 103*, 1–51.

Gaede, D. B., & Vaske, J. J. (2017). Attitudes toward the legalization of marijuana on Colorado tourism. *Tourism Analysis, 22*(2), 267–272.

Gardner, T. II, & Kohli, A. (2009, September). The CAP effect: Racial profiling in the ICE Criminal Alien Program. Policy Brief, 9–10. The Chief Justice Earl Warren Institute on Race, Ethnicity, & Diversity, Berkeley Law Center for Research and Administration.

Gonzalez, B., Collingwood, L., & El-Khatib, S. O. (2017). The politics of refuge: Sanctuary cities, crime, and undocumented immigration. *Urban Affairs Review*, 1–38.

Graauw, E. D. (2014). Municipal ID cards for undocumented immigrants: Local bureaucratic membership in a federal system. *Politics and Society, 42*(3), 309–330.

Hing, B. O. (2015). Ethics, morality, and disruption of U.S. immigration laws. *Kansas Law Review, 63*, 981–1044.

Ibrahim, M. (2005). The securitization of migration: A racial discourse. *International Migration, 43*, 163–187.

Immigrant Legal Resource Center. (n.d.). Retrieved from https://www.ilrc.org/

Johnson, K. R. (2016). A political explanation of the popularity of unconstitutional state immigration enforcement law. *Journal of American Ethnic History, 35*(3), 68–75.

Kittrie, O. F. (2006). Federalism, deportation and crime victims afraid to call the police. *Iowa Law Review, 91*, 1449–1508.

Lasch, C. (2013). *The faulty legal arguments behind immigration detainers: American immigration special report*. Washington, DC: American Immigration Council.

Lee, M., Martinez, R., & Rosenfeld, R. (2001). Does immigration increase homicide? Negative evidence from three border cities. *Sociological Quarterly, 42*(4), 559–580.

Lyons, C. J., Vélez, M. B., & Santoro, W. A. (2013). Neighborhood immigration, violence, and city level immigrant political opportunities. *American Sociological Review, 78*(4), 604–632.

Marcos, C. (2017, June 29). House passes "Kate's Law" and bill targeting sanctuary cities. The Hill. Retrieved from: http://thehill.com/blogs/floor-action/house/340137-house-passes-kates-law-and-crackdown-on-sacntuary-cities

Martinez, D. E., Martinez-Schuldt, R. D., & Cantor, G. (2017). Providing sanctuary or fostering crime? A review of the research on "sanctuary cities" and crime. *Sociology Compass, 12*, 1–13.

Massey, D., Durand, J., & Malone, N. (2003). *Beyond smoke and mirrors: Mexican immigration in an era of economic integration*. New York, NY: Russel Sage Foundation Publications.

Meissner, D., Kerwin, D. M., Christi, M., & Bergeron, C. (2013). *Immigration enforcement in the United States: The rise of a formidable machinery*. Washington, DC: Migration Policy Institute.

Menjivar, C., & Bejarano, C. L. (2004). Latino immigrants' perceptions of crime and police authorities in the United States: A case study from the Phoenix metropolitan area. *Ethnic and Racial Studies, 27*(1), 120–148.

Michalec, B., Rapp, L., & Whittle, T. (2015) Assessing physicians' perspectives and knowledge of medical marijuana and the Delaware Medical Marijuana Act. *Journal of Global Drug Policy and Practice, 9*, 1–24.

Morenoff, J. D., Sampson, R. J., & Raudenbush, S. W. (2001). Neighborhood inequality, collective efficacy, and the spatial dynamics of urban violence. *Criminology, 39*, 517–559.

National Conference of State Legislatures. (2018). State medical marijuana laws. Retrieved from http://www.ncsl.org/research/health/state-medical-marijuana-laws.aspx

National Institute on Drug Abuse (NIDA). (2015, June). Nationwide trends. Retrieved from https://www.drugabuse.gov/publications/drugfacts/nationwide-trends

Passel, J. S., & Cohn, D. (2016). *Overall number of U.S. unauthorized immigrants holds steady since 2009*. Washington, DC: Pew Research Center.

Rice, J. M. (2017). Looking past the label: An analysis of the measures underlying "sanctuary cities." *University of Memphis Law Review, 48*, 83–143.

Ridgely, J. (2008). Cities of refuge: Immigration enforcement, police, and the insurgent genealogies of citizenship in U.S. sanctuary cities. *Urban Geography, 29*(1), 53–77.

Rose, S., & Goelzhauser, G. (2018). The state of American federalism 2017–2018: Unilateral executive action, regulatory rollback, and state resistance. *Publius: The Journal of Federalism, 48*(3), 327–330.

Sentencing Project. (2017). Criminal justice facts. The Sentencing Project. Retrieved from https://www.sentencingproject.org/criminal-justice-facts/

Stacey, M., Carbone-Lopez, K., & Rosenfeld, R. (2011). Demographic change and ethnically motivated crime: The impact of immigration on anti-Hispanic hate crime in the United States. *Journal of Contemporary Criminal Justice, 27*(3), 278–298.

Starr, B. (2017). Executive power over immigration. *Texas Review of Law and Politics, 22*, 283–296.

Stowell, J. I., Messner, S. F., McGeever, K. F., & Raffalovich, L. E. (2009). Immigration and the recent violent crime drop in the United States: A pooled, cross-sectional time-series analysis of metropolitan areas. *Criminology, 47*, 889–928.

United Nations Office on Drugs and Crime. (2018). Annual prevalence of drug use, by region and globally, 2015. [Data file]. Retrieved from https://data.unodc.org/#state:3

United States Drug Enforcement Administration. (2018). Drug scheduling. Retrieved from https://www.dea.gov/drug-scheduling

Vargas, E. D., Sanchez, G. R. & Juárez, M. (2017). Fear by association: Perceptions of anti-immigrant policy and health outcomes. *Journal of Health, Politics, Policy and Law, 42*(3), 459–483.

Villazor, R. C. (2008). What is a sanctuary? *Southern Methodist University Law Review, 61*(133), 1–20.

Wells, M. J. (2004). The grassroots reconfiguration of U.S. immigration policy. *International Migration Review, 38*(4), 1308–1347.

SECTION 3

Ethics and the Common Good

© Sergii Gnatiuk/Shutterstock

Introduction to Ethics and the Common Good

Sherri DioGuardi

▶ Introduction

This section of the text deals with ethics and the common good. To grasp this inter-secting concept, we must place it within the context of the social contract, and both terms—*ethics* and *the common good*—must be defined. First, looking at the common good, Strang (2005) describes it as an organizing construct that enables individuals to pursue happiness. This correlates closely with the social contract (Hobbes, 1651/1909; Locke, 1689; Rousseau, 1762/2017) which is an implied contract between the government and its citizenry in which individuals willingly (albeit reluctantly) give up some of their natural rights in order to provide the government with the necessary authority to keep them and their property safe. Although the pursuit of happiness is recognized as a natural right, it was realized that such pursuit could be unfairly blocked by other people—that is, one's property could be stolen, one's home invaded, and one's life threatened—thereby making governmental regulation acceptable. There is always, however, an ongoing tension between the role of government to intervene on behalf of the common good and the rights of individuals to be free from government intervention.

▶ The Common Good

The common good is a utilitarian concept because it is concerned with aggregate happiness and refers to interests shared by all people, such as the need for everyone to access high levels of quality for natural resources that belong to all equally—for example, air, water, and public lands (Hussain, 2018). The common good encom-passes many facets of daily life, and to uphold it is a major responsibility and moral obligation that is reciprocally shared by government and the people being gov-erned. It is through the social contract that the common good is pursued because the government is obligated to implement and enforce laws that promote the common good, and the people are obligated to cooperate and assist in that promotion. Ethics become the recognition and the acceptance of this moral obligation. Albanese (2012) states, "Ethics provides the way to see that there is a greater purpose to life than self-interest" (p. 5). Sometimes in the pursuit of the common good, the rights of individuals are sacrificed to benefit the community. Balancing the welfare of society with the rights of individuals is not always a simple or straightforward proposition and will sometimes cause ethical dilemmas to arise, lawsuits to be filed, and trust in government or its agents to be lost.

▶ Ethics, Morality, and the Law

What is *ethics*, and how is it distinguished from morality? Historically, ethicists such as Aristotle, Immanuel Kant, and John Stuart Mill equated an ethical life with a happy one, even though their ethical pathways for pursuing happiness differed. Today, the tendency is for the general public to use the terms *ethics* and *morals* interchangeably (Barry & Ohland, 2009). *Ethics* is often the term used when applying moral obligations to professionals, and many organizations have established codes of ethics as standards for members' conduct—for example, the American Bar Association (2016), the American Correctional Association (1994), the American Medical Association (2018), the International Association of Chiefs of Police (IACP, 1957), and one association of U.S. judges (Administrative Office of the U.S. Courts, 2014).

Black's Law Dictionary defines *ethics* as follows:

> Directives based on one's . . . morality. How one lives with others. The foremost concepts and principles of proper human conduct. Socially, it is the collective of universal values, treating each human equally, acknowledging human and natural rights, obeying the law of land, showing health and safety concerns, caring for natural environment. (Law Dictionary, n.d.a)

In contrast, *morals* are defined as the "general principles of right conduct" (Law Dictionary, n.d.b, para. 1). A broader definition would be that ethics are the guidelines for *being* moral. The term *moral* tends to be used to describe an individual's character, such as "She is a moral person." Morals can, therefore, be defined more generally as the characteristics possessed by individuals (or entities) that enable them to know the difference between right and wrong, presuming these characteristics will also enable them to choose *right* (or ethical) action under any given set of circumstances.

What is the relationship between morality (or ethics) and the law? A common adage is "You can't legislate morality." In response, Dr. Martin Luther King, Jr., stated, "Morality cannot be legislated, but behavior can be regulated. Judicial decrees may not change the heart, but they can restrain the heartless" (King, 1962–1963, p. 484). Despite these declarations, morality is—and has always been—legally regulated because many, if not most, laws have a moral basis, and "[t]he origins of legal ethics are explicitly moral" (Barton, 2005, p. 426). Laws are implemented to serve society by upholding the common good, which maximizes overall happiness. Sometimes, however, the common good conflicts with individual rights.

▶ Conflicts with Individual Rights

The United States is a constitutional democracy because the will of the people cannot supersede the rule of law (Samaha, 2014). Our forefathers wrote the U.S. Constitution to preserve foundational principles of liberty and justice for all. Therefore, the majority was meant to be legally constrained from oppressing the minority, which is why freedom of speech and religion as well as the other amendments within the Bill of Rights were established. Justice Clarence Thomas addressed this in his concurring opinion in *Evenwel v. Abbott* (2016): "The Framers also understood that unchecked majorities could lead to tyranny of the majority. As a result, many viewed antidemocratic checks as indispensable to republican government" (p. 1138). When it comes to a legal contest between the common good and individual rights, however, the common good will usually prevail despite the ruling in *Griswold v. Connecticut* (1965), in which the U.S. Supreme Court declared that the Constitution guarantees a fundamental right of privacy that bars "all governmental invasions of the sanctity of a man's home and the privacies of life" (p. 484).

Although the right to be left alone from governmental interference is not explicitly spelled out within the U.S. Constitution, the Court ruled it is implied by the First, Third, Fourth, Fifth, Ninth, and 14th Amendments (Samaha, 2014). Yet, despite this recognized constitutional right to be left alone, there have been laws implemented for the common good that do affect or infringe on individual freedom. Many of these infringements are as a result of strict liability offenses in which proof of criminal intent is unnecessary because criminalizing these offenses is deemed necessary for public health or welfare reasons—that is, for the *common good*. For example, the Harrison Narcotics Act of 1914 was challenged on *scienter* because the defendant–appellant claimed no knowledge of wrongdoing or no intent to commit a crime. Chief Justice William Howard Taft ruled that "the emphasis of the statute is evidently upon achievement of some social betterment rather than the punishment of the crimes" (*United States v. Balint*, 1922, p. 252).

Adult Pornography and Prostitution

Although most states have decriminalized mere possession of adult pornography as a result of the landmark case of *Stanley v. Georgia* (1969), which established a constitutional *right of privacy*, a few statutes explicitly state that possession of three or more similar images establishes a presumption of distribution, which *is* criminalized across states (see Florida §847.011(b)(b) and Oklahoma §21.1040.24). In effect, this makes mere adult possession of "pornographic images" illegal, which arguably violates the *Stanley* ruling. There is also the oft-claimed defense that computer owners were unaware of illicit images residing within their hard drives (Magid, 2009), which makes the element of mens rea questionable, but intent is also presumptive when sufficient quantities of obscene matter are found.

Adult pornography in recent years has been grouped in with child pornography and declared by numerous state legislators as a public health crisis (Howard, 2016), and momentum may be building to reclassify this offense as a strict liability crime. Also, sex-trafficking research has revealed that, for some of the photographed persons, involvement was involuntary or coerced (Luzwick, 2017), which shatters the previously held belief that there was free-willed consent for all participants over the age of majority. Similar research revelations have been made regarding adult prostitutes.

Although distinctions have been made between sex workers, the term for free-willed persons who voluntarily offer sex for money, and "prostituted persons" (connoting those who are sexually exploited because of some preexisting vulnerability such as addiction, poverty, and having been involuntarily trafficked), the once-clear demarcation line between these two categorizations is now blurred (Luzwick, 2017).

For much of American history, adultery, nonmarital sex, and sodomy have been illegal, and these crimes are still on the statutes in some states (Sweeny, 2014). For the most part, however, they are considered *blue laws* (Finer, 2004) or statutes that are outdated and no longer prosecuted. Not until the 21st century did the U.S. Supreme Court rule a Texas statute making homosexual sodomy a crime unconstitutional (*Lawrence v. Texas*, 2003). The following is an excerpt from Justice Anthony Kennedy's majority opinion:

> This case does not involve minors. . . . It does involve two adults who, with full and mutual consent, engaged in sexual practices common to a homosexual lifestyle. Petitioners' right to liberty under the Due Process Clause gives them the full right to engage in private conduct without government intervention. The Texas statute furthers no legitimate state interest which can justify its intrusion into the individual's personal and private life. (p. 526)

Gambling

Today, gambling in some form or another is statutorily legal in every state except for Hawaii and Utah (Romboy, 2018). When America was first founded, gambling was permitted; however, laborers were often discouraged from participating because gambling was perceived as a sport best reserved for "gentlemen" because they alone were thought to possess requisite means and morality (Chapetz, 1960; Whitebread, 2000). It was around the mid-1700s that gambling began to be formally outlawed, and a Tennessee Supreme Court judge conveyed the general antigambling sentiment that swept the country in the early 19th century:

> Gaming, as a general evil, leads to vicious inclinations, destruction of morals, abandonment of industry and honest employment, a loss of self-control and respect. Frauds, forgeries, thefts, make up the black catalogue of crime, the closing scene of which generally ends in highway robbery and murder. (*State v. Smith*, 1829, p. 278)

Despite a surfeit of recent research that identifies the addictive nature of gaming and the identification of the "pathological gambler" (Dowling et al., 2017), gambling activities are increasingly being permitted across the country (e.g., state-sponsored lotteries, riverboat casinos, electronic gambling devices), in large part because of the enormous revenues they generate for government (National Gambling Impact Study Commission, 1999).

Substance Use

According to the National Highway Traffic Safety Administration (NHTSA), more than 10,000 people die each year from alcohol-involved vehicle accidents (NHTSA, 2017). The majority of states make it illegal to have open containers of any type of alcoholic beverage in a motor vehicle while it is being operated (Fink, 2017), and most state laws have a presumption of driving impairment when blood-alcohol concentration (BAC) levels exceed 0.08%. NHTSA (2017) reports that more than 2,000 people were killed in 2016 when drivers' alcohol levels were lower than that established illegal limit. Further confusing the issue, research has also found that functional impairment varies across individuals; for instance, chronic heavy drinkers may develop a functional tolerance for ingesting alcohol in amounts that would prove "incapacitating or even fatal" for recreational drinkers (National Institute on Alcohol Abuse and Alcoholism, 1995, para. 3). And, for chronic heavy drinkers and alcoholics, functional impairment may actually only occur when BAC levels drop or when symptoms of alcohol withdrawal begin (Becker, 2008). Two studies found that driving when hungover may impact functioning as much as when drivers operate a motor vehicle under the influence of alcohol (McKinney, Coyle, & Verster, 2012; Verster et al., 2014). The Centers for Disease Control and Prevention (2017) estimates that drowsy drivers may be responsible for 6,000 fatal accidents annually. The time may come when measurements exist so that drivers will be randomly stopped and tested to ensure a predetermined, acceptable alertness level, and the legal presumption will be that everyone's driving ability is similarly diminished if the preestablished fatigue threshold is reached.

Prohibition, the so-called Noble Experiment, was legislation enacted for the common good because alcohol use was condemned as criminogenic, poverty-producing, unhealthy, and harmful for society (Thornton, 1991). The 18th Amendment, along with the Volstead Act of 1920, outlawed the manufacture, transportation, and sale of intoxicating liquors and is commonly believed to have caused more harm than good (Lerner, n.d.) by creating a larger market niche for recreational marijuana (Siegel, 1989), allowing organized crime to flourish, and increasing violent crime (Okrent, 2010). However, there are also counterclaims that organized crime had already been fully established in the United States well before Prohibition began, that the violent crime rate was stable during the Prohibition era, and that overall alcohol consumption decreased as a result of the Noble Experiment, as did the incidents of death from cirrhosis of the liver (Moore, 1989). Although imbibing alcohol has a differential effect, Prohibition applied to everyone equally.

Many of the illegal or federally regulated drugs of today such as cannabis (Martin, 2016), cocaine, and opiates (Green, 2015) were legal and available over the counter in the latter part of the 1800s and into the early 1900s. After criminalizing these drugs, enforcement efforts ramped up over time with former President Richard Nixon identifying drugs as "public enemy number one" in 1971 and President Ronald Reagan informally declaring a "War on Drugs" once he took office in 1981 (Encyclopaedia Britannica, 2018). Taxpayers have spent more than $2.5 trillion dollars in almost 50 years regulating illicit drugs (Blackwell, 2014). The vast majority of the arrests, however, were for simple possession charges.

Even though cigarettes are currently legal for adults, smoking is now prohibited in most public areas. Cigarette advertising was banned from broadcast media in 1971 (Madden & Grube, 1994), and smoking has been increasingly stigmatized. This is quite a societal shift because, in the not-so-distant past, not only was smoking allowed everywhere (e.g., on domestic air flights and in grocery stores and movie theaters), but also some medical doctors actually endorsed cigarette smoking as a weight-loss strategy and recommended certain brands of cigarettes to ease sore throat symptoms (Gardner & Brandt, 2006). Everything changed once incontrovertible evidence was produced in the mid-1960s to show that smoking significantly increased the risk of lung cancer and a host of other life-threatening diseases, and there were indicators that merely breathing in secondhand smoke placed people at greater health risk (U.S. Department of Health and Human Services, 2006). States and municipalities continually raise considerable amounts of money by imposing "sin taxes" on cigarettes and other vice-related products, which may create an ethical conflict because, besides profiting, states are increasingly becoming dependent on revenue produced from sin taxes (Saul, 2008). A similar conundrum exists with the more than $100 billion dollars already paid out to state governments from the 25-year, $246 billion settlement reached with the tobacco industry (NPR Staff, 2013). That money was earmarked to offset the high health-care costs being borne by states in treating smoking-related diseases and was expected to help subsidize smoking-cessation programs, but some states may not be using those funds as originally intended (Sloan, Allsbrook, Madre, Masselink, & Matthews, 2005).

▶ Five Ethical Principles

Thiroux (1977) identified five principles that form the basis for every ethical system:

1. concern for the protection and preservation of human life;
2. a tripart rightness principle requiring that (a) goodness be promoted over badness, (b) no harm be caused, and that (c) any potential harm be prevented;
3. fairness;
4. the principle of truth telling or honesty; and
5. respect for individual rights.

Principles 1 and 2(a) reinforce the utilitarian idea that societal benefits outweigh individual right concerns (the last principle listed). However, the prioritizing principles of overall health and welfare must also honor the principles of fairness, honesty, and respect for individual rights. Government policy makers, as well as federal and state lawmakers, have an ethical obligation to promote the common good, to be transparent, to be accountable for any regulations implemented for the common good, and to do everything in their power to limit restrictions that such regulations would place on personal freedom.

▶ Conclusion

The U.S. Supreme Court has made it clear that a compelling state interest is necessary to override the right of persons to be left alone from governmental intrusion. However, a legitimate common good reason provides legal justification for right-of-privacy violations. This introduction identified instances in which conflicts have developed and has touched on areas where government might be confusing revenue generation with the common good. Further articles within this section will explore issues with school safety, eminent domain, and gun control, and one article will delve deeper into the drug dilemma.

Ethics comes into play with the balancing act between the common good and individual liberty. Justice Thomas wrote in *Evenwel v. Abbott* (2016), "As the Framers understood, designing a government to fulfill the conflicting tasks of respecting the fundamental equality of persons while promoting the common good requires making incommensurable tradeoffs" (p. 1139). With population increases as well as technological advances and political upheavals, societal risks multiply, and additional harm reduction policies are implemented. Much of these policies involve citizens being required to forfeit more of their natural rights than initially anticipated in the social contract—including those who never contribute to harmful conditions. The crucial question then becomes, When, if ever, will further forfeitures become unacceptable trade-offs for the American people?

▶ References

Administrative Office of the U.S. Courts. (2014). Code of conduct for United States judges. Retrieved from www.uscourts.gov/judges-judgeships/code-conduct-united-states-judges

Albanese, J. S. (2012). *Professional ethics in criminal justice: Being ethical when no one is looking* (3rd ed.). Upper Saddle River, NJ: Pearson Education.

American Bar Association. (2016). Model rules of professional conduct. Retrieved from www .americanbar.org/groups/professional_responsibility/publications/model_rules_of _professional_conduct/model_rules_of_professional_conduct_table_of_contents.html

American Correctional Association. (1994.) ACA code of ethics. Retrieved from www.aca.org /ACA_Prod_IMIS/ACA_Member/About_Us/Code_of_Ethics/ACA_Member/AboutUs /Code_of_Ethics.aspx?hkey=61577ed2-c0c3-4529-bc01-36a248f79eba

American Medical Association. (2018). Ethics. Retrieved from www.ama-assn.org/delivering-care /ama-code-medical-ethics

Barry, B. E., & Ohland, M. W. (2009). Applied ethics in the engineering, health, business, and law professions: A comparison. *Journal of Engineering Education, 98*(4), 377–388. Retrieved from https://onlinelibrary.wiley.com/doi/abs/10.1002/j.2168-9830.2009.tb01034.x

Barton, B. H. (2005). The ABA, the rules, and professionalism: The mechanics of self-defeat and a call for a return to the ethical, moral, and practical approach of the canons. *North Carolina Law Review, 83*, 411–480.

Becker, H. C. (2008). Alcohol dependence, withdrawal, and relapse. *Alcohol Research Health, 3*(4), 348–361.

Blackwell, J. M. (2014). The costs and consequences of U.S. drug prohibition for the peoples of developing nations. *European Journal of Law Reform, 16*, 665–692.

Centers for Disease Control and Prevention. (2017). Drowsy driving: Asleep at the wheel. Retrieved from https://www.cdc.gov/features/dsdrowsydriving/index.html

Chapetz, H. (1960). *Play the devil: A history of gambling in the United States from 1492 to 1955.* New York, NY: Clarkson N. Potter.

Dowling, N. A. Merkouris, S. S., Greenwood, C. J., Oldenhol, E., Toumbourou, J. W., & Youssef, G. J. (2017). Early risk and protective factors for problem gambling: A systematic review and met-analysis of longitudinal studies. *Clinical Psychology Review, 51*, 109–124.

Encyclopaedia Britannica. (2018). War on drugs: United States history. Retrieved from www .britannica.com/topic/war-on-drugs

Evenwel v. Abbott, 136 S. Ct. 1120 (2016).

Finer, J. (2004). Old blue laws are hitting red lights: Statutes rolled back as anachronisms. *Washington Post.* Retrieved from http://www.washingtonpost.com/wp-dyn/articles/A33552-2004Dec3.html ?noredirect=on

Fink, G. (2017). 11 states that don't have typical "open container" laws for vehicles. HuffPost News. Retrieved from www.huffingtonpost.com/2014/01/24/open-containerlaw_n_4653013.html

Gardner, M. N., & Brandt, A. M. (2006). "The doctors' choice is America's choice": The physician in US cigarette advertisements: 1930–1953. *American Journal of Public Health, 96*(2), 222–232.

Green, S. P. (2015). Vice crimes and preventive justice. *Criminal Law and Philosophy, 9*(3), 561–576. Retrieved from https://law.rutgers.edu/sites/law/files/Vice%20Crimes%20and%20Preventive%20 Justice.pdf

Griswold v. Connecticut, 381 U.S. 479 (1965).

Hobbes, T. (1909). *Leviathan*. London, UK: Menston, Scolar P. Originally published 1651. Retrieved from https://archive.org/details/hobbessleviathan00hobbuoft

Howard, J. (2016). Republicans are calling porn a "public health crisis," but is it really? CNN. Retrieved from www.cnn.com/2016/07/15/health/porn-public-health-crisis/index.html

Hussain, W, (2018). The common good. In E. N. Zalta (Ed.) *The Stanford encyclopedia of philosophy*. Retrieved from https://plato.stanford.edu/entries/common-good/

International Association of Chiefs of Police. (1957). Code of ethics: Law enforcement code of ethics. Retrieved from www.theiacp.org/resources/law-enforcement-code-of-ethics

King, M. L., Jr. (1962–1963). Draft of Chapter II, "On Being a Good Neighbor." Stanford University. Retrieved from https://stanford.app.box.com/s/975wxpb75wqec6hzel5miofz3mommg29

Law Dictionary. (n.d.a). *What is ethics?* Retrieved from https://thelawdictionary.org/ethics/

Law Dictionary. (n.d.b). *What is moral?* Retrieved from https://thelawdictionary.org/moral/

Lawrence v. Texas, 539 U.S. 558 (2003).

Lerner, M. (n.d.) Prohibition: Unintended consequences. A film by Ken Burns and Lynn Novick. Public Broadcasting Service. Retrieved from www.pbs.org/kenburns/prohibition/unintended -consequences/

Locke, J. (1689). *Second treatise of government*. Retrieved from www.gutenberg.org/files/7370/7370 -h/7370-h.htm

Luzwick, A. J. (2017). Human trafficking and pornography: Using the Trafficking Victims Protection Act to prosecute trafficking for the production of internet pornography. *Northwestern University Law Review, 3*, 137–153.

Madden, P. A., & Grube, J. W. (1994). The frequency and nature of alcohol and tobacco advertising in televised sports, 1990 through 1992. *American Journal of Public Health, 84*, 297–299.

Magid, L. (2009). A child porn-planting virus: Threat or bad defense? C|NET. Retrieved from www .cnet.com/news/a-child-porn-planting-virus-threat-or-bad-defense/

Martin, S. C. (2016). A brief history of marijuana law in America. Time. Retrieved from http://time .com/4298038/marijuana-history-in-america/

McKinney, A., Coyle, K., & Verster, J. (2012). Direct comparison of the cognitive effects of acute alcohol with the morning after a normal night's drinking. *Human Psychopharmacology: Clinical and Experimental, 27*(3), 295–304. https://onlinelibrary.wiley.com/doi/abs/10.1002 /hup.2225

Moore, M. H. (1989, October 16). Actually, prohibition was a success. *The New York Times*, A.21.

National Gambling Impact Study Commission. (1999). *Final report*. Washington, DC: Author. Retrieved from https://govinfo.library.unt.edu/ngisc/reports/fullrpt.html

National Highway Traffic Safety Administration (NHTSA). (2017). Drunk driving. Washington, DC: U.S. Department of Transportation. Retrieved from www.nhtsa.gov/risky-driving/drunk -driving

National Institute on Alcohol Abuse and Alcoholism. (1995.) No. 28 PH 356. Alcohol alert. Washington, DC: U.S. Department of Health and Human Services. Retrieved from https://pubs .niaaa.nih.gov/publications/aa28.htm

NPR Staff. (2013). 15 years later, where did all the cigarette money go? NPR. Retrieved from www .npr.org/2013/10/13/233449505/15-years-later-where-did-all-the-cigarette-money-go

Okrent, D. (2010). *Last call: The rise and fall of Prohibition*. New York, NY: Scribner.

Romboy, D. (2018, May 14). Utah GOP lawmakers hail decision on sports betting as win for states' rights. *Deseret News*. Retrieved from www.deseretnews.com/article/900018566/utah-gop-lawmakers -hail-decision-on-sports-betting-as-win-for-states-rights.html

Rousseau, J.-J. (2017). *The social contract*. Originally published 1762. Retrieved from https://www .earlymoderntexts.com/assets/pdfs/rousseau1762.pdf

Samaha, J. (2014). *Criminal law and procedure* (9th ed.) Boston, MA: Cengage Learning.

Saul, S. (2008, August 30). Government gets hooked on tobacco tax billions. *The New York Times*. Retrieved from www.nytimes.com/2008/08/31/weekinreview/31saul.html

Siegel, R. K. (1989). *Intoxication: Life in pursuit of artificial paradise*. New York, NY: Dutton.

Sloan, F. A., Allsbrook, J. S., Madre, L. K. Masselink, L. E., & Mathews, C. A. (2005). States' allocations of funds from the tobacco master settlement agreement. *Heath Affairs, 24*(1), 220–227.

Stanley v. Georgia, 394 U.S. 557 (1969).

State v. Smith, 10 Tenn. 272 (1829).

Strang, Lee J. (2005.) The role of the common good in legal and constitutional interpretation. *University of St. Thomas Law Journal, 3,* 48–74.

Sweeny, J. (2014). Undead statutes: The rise, fall, and continuing uses of adultery and fornication criminal laws. *Loyola University Chicago Law Journal, 46,* 127–173.

Thiroux, J. P. (1977). *Ethics: Theory and practice.* Encino, CA: Glencoe Press.

Thornton, M. (1991). Alcohol Prohibition was a failure. Policy Analysis No. 157. Cato Institute. Retrieved from www.cato.org/publications/policy-analysis/alcohol-prohibition-was-failure

United States v. Balint, 258 U.S. 259 (1922).

U.S. Department of Health and Human Services. (2006). *The health consequences of involuntary exposure to tobacco smoke: A report of the Surgeon General.* Washington, DC: U.S. Department of Health and Human Services, Centers for Disease Control and Prevention, National Center for Chronic Disease Prevention and Health Promotion, Office on Smoking and Health.

Verster, J. C., Bervoets, A. C., de Klerk S., Vreman, R. A., Olivier, B., Roth, T., & Brookhuis, K.A. (2014). Effects of alcohol hangover on simulated highway driving performance. *Psychopharmacology, 239*(150), 2999–3008.

Whitebread, C. H. (2000). "Us" and "them" and the nature of moral regulation. *Southern California Law Review, 74,* 361–370.

ARTICLE 11

The Ethics of Eminent Domain

Kathryn M. Elvey

D oing the greatest good for the greatest number sounds great in theory, but in practice it may not be so wonderful, particularly when you are not part of the greatest number.

▶ Introduction

Imagine you have inherited your childhood home. This beautiful old farmhouse has been in your family for generations and has many new updates your parents added right before they signed it over to you. It sits in the middle of a picturesque valley overlooking mountains with beautiful sunrises and a lake below; all of this is your property. You plan on living in this home for the rest of your life, sharing it with your spouse, raising your children there, and retiring there. Hopefully one day you can give it to your own child. You love this house and so do your parents who moved to a smaller home just down the street. Five years after settling in the home with your spouse and raising your first child, a government worker comes to your door and tells you that you will be selling your home to the state government because they are putting in a new highway. Furthermore, you will be paid a "fair" market value price for the home, which will be dictated to you. You have a reasonable time to vacate. Best of luck.

The preceding scenario is not that far-fetched and is completely legal. According to *eminent domain*, the government has the right and power to take private property and use it for public interest. This is normally done to create roads, railways, municipal and government buildings, and public utilities (Somin, 2016). However, more recently it has been used for private economic development (*Kelo v. City of New London*, 2005). The right of the government to do this comes from the Fifth Amendment to the U.S. Constitution, which reads:

> No person shall be held to answer for a capital, or otherwise infamous crime, unless on a presentment or indictment of a Grand Jury, except in

cases arising in the land or naval forces, or in the Militia, when in actual service in time of War or public danger; nor shall any person be subject for the same offence to be twice put in jeopardy of life or limb; nor shall be compelled in any criminal case to be a witness against himself, nor be deprived of life, liberty, or property, without due process of law; *nor shall private property be taken for public use, without just compensation.* (U.S. Constitution, Fifth Amendment)

The important part concerning eminent domain has been highlighted. The highlighted section is referred to as the *takings clause.* This clause denotes that as long as a state justly compensates the owner of the private property, the government may take it for *public* use. This has raised many questions such as what is "just compensation" and how much should the public benefit from its use?

Going back to the example of your childhood home in the picturesque valley, how much would you think the government would need to give you to justify turning it into a highway? All of your memories—including your childhood ones and now your memories with your own child—are in that home! So now what? Should the government be required to compensate you for your memories as well as the cost of the home?

▶ Important Legal Cases

The following is a discussion of the important legal cases concerning eminent domain. These legal cases have answered many of the questions surrounding eminent domain, but occasionally they raise more questions than they answer.

First, the Bill of Rights acknowledged the right of the federal government to take land with the Fifth Amendment—but not states. The recognition of states' rights of eminent domain did not come until the ratification of the 14th Amendment in 1868 and was tested later with the case of *Chicago, Burlington & Quincy Railroad Co. v. City of Chicago* (1897). In this case, the city of Chicago wanted to widen a street, which would involve going through private land owned by Chicago, Burlington & Quincy Railroad company. This was clearly a case in which the public would benefit from the widening of the road, but the railway company would lose its land. Illinois state law at the time stipulated that if the government wanted to take private property for public use, a jury had to be brought in to determine what the government would have to pay the private landowner for compensation—this ensured due process was met. The jury ruled that "just compensation" in this case would be $1. The jury's justification for such a low value was because the city of Chicago would not be taking over the land, but would only be interfering with the railroad's use of said land, so there was no reason to pay a full value for the property. Clearly, the railroad company was displeased with such an amount and appealed the case to the Supreme Court of Illinois—which upheld the original decision—and then appealed again to the U.S. Supreme Court, which also upheld the decision.

The Supreme Court has consistently sided with states in determining what is considered "public use" in that state or area of the country. The Court has held that because there are such unique circumstances across the nation, the definition of public use will change, depending on the scenario. For example, in *Clark v. Nash* (1905), the Court ruled that a farmer could expand his irrigation ditch across the land of another farmer to reach a local waterway—in this case, the water was considered for public use—and the Court ruled that both farmers had a right to it. The irrigation expansion was okay as long as the farmer whose land was being cut across was fairly compensated.

Cases of eminent domain often involve *blighted properties*. In legal terms, *blighted* means that the land is unsafe, unsightly, and dilapidated; typically, these properties are abandoned or unoccupied. These blighted properties are easy for the state or local government to take over because they do not require much compensation—and can easily be turned into something more useful for the public.

However, in *Berman v. Parker* (1954) the District of Columbia wanted to tear down a large parcel of blighted properties in southwest Washington, D.C. and transfer the land to redevelopers. This was part of the District of Columbia Redevelopment Act of 1945, which was aimed at modernizing the nation's capital while eliminating the slums and keeping them from returning (*Berman v. Parker*, 1954). The large section of the city that was going to be razed for redevelopment did contain some unblighted properties, including a department store that was still in use, mixed in with blighted properties. Berman—the plaintiff and owner of the department store—argued that taking his property and selling it to redevelopers was like stealing from one landowner or business owner to give to another, and this did not serve the public or public use. However, the courts disagreed and found that the overall effect of eliminating the blighted properties and even those unblighted properties mixed in with the blighted for the purpose of redevelopment and modernization would be an overall benefit to the community as a whole and voted in favor of redevelopment (*Berman v. Parker*, 1954). This case set the precedent for the *Kelo v. City of New London* (2005).

In 2000, the city of New London, Connecticut, wanted to increase jobs and revitalize its waterfront. The city wanted to transform about 90 acres of property from private residences into a river walk, hotels, and restaurants. Much of the property was blighted, but not all. This property was meant to complement the Pfizer research facility, worth $350 million, that had been built near the area (Somin, 2016). This plan boasted of creating 3,169 new jobs and bringing $1.2 million per year to local tax revenues (Cohen, 2006).

Instead of the city carrying out the redevelopment, the New London Development Corporation (NLDC), a private nonprofit, was established (Cohen, 2006; Ryskamp, 2007). The city granted the NDLC the right to seize the 90 acres. Susan Kelo, who had lived in the area and whose property was being seized, sued the city and lost in a 5–4 ruling in the Supreme Court of Connecticut (Cohen, 2006).

The case then moved on to the U.S. Supreme Court with this question in mind: Would a total public good be created? Kelo argued it would not, considering some of the property would not be for the general public and would be going to private businesses. Furthermore, could the predicted benefit—increased tax base—really be considered a total public good (Scott, 2009)? The Court's argument and support of eminent domain relied on the *Berman* case to make its ruling.

Given the comprehensive character of the plan, the thorough deliberation that preceded its adoption, and the limited scope of our review, it is appropriate for us, as it was in Berman, to resolve the challenges of the individual owners, not on a piecemeal basis, but rather in light of the entire plan. Because that plan unquestionably severs a public purpose, the taking challenged here satisfy the public use requirement of the Fifth Amendment. (*Kelo v. City of New London*, 2005, 125 S. Ct. at 2655)

However, this case was not just a replay of Berman, but an extension of the Berman ruling. As Kyle Scott (2009) eloquently states regarding the ramifications of *Kelo*:

> There was no evidence offered by the respondent that the areas were blighted or in need of renovation, only that there was a plan proposed that would be more economically beneficial to the area, without first proving that the area was economically unstable. Therefore, for eminent domain to apply in matter of urban rejuvenation, the area under consideration may be in good condition, but the state—or a private agent of the state—may determine that is not good enough. There is no evidence offered by the respondent or required by the court, to prove that the area was blighted of that the economic plan would be effective. (p. 96)

In other words, the plan did not really show an economic benefit, and the Court did not appear to need a solid plan to be shown for the property to be taken. Many have argued that this set a dangerous precedent by allowing private companies to come to cities and argue that their business would create tax revenue, business, and thus a public good—and property would be more valuable than whatever was currently there, including private residences. The Supreme Court ruled in favor of New London 5–4.

Since the case, Pfizer has closed its research facility—which the whole plan had been anchored around—and took 1,500 jobs out of the area (McGeehan, 2009). The redeveloper was never able to receive financing for its redevelopment project and eventually abandoned the project; therefore, it was not generating any tax revenue for the city (Allen, 2014). In 2011, Hurricane Irene swept through Connecticut, and the property was used as an area to store and transfer debris (Nunes, 2011). The land, which cost the city and state $78 million to purchase from landowners and bulldoze, has never been developed and is still sitting vacant as of 2018 (Collins, 2018).

Putting the Kelo case in context, let's return to the example of your childhood home. Imagine that the government comes to you and says that your property is going to be turned into an IKEA and you need to be out within six months and it will pay you "just compensation." What it offers in no way reflects how you feel about the house, but you have no choice. The government states the IKEA will generate millions of dollars in tax revenue and provide several hundred jobs to the local area. The local government is also convinced that the IKEA will encourage more businesses to build on the land and therefore generate more revenue. The government does not have to prove this will be case but simply needs to make the argument. You move out and a decade later the IKEA still has not been built and you see no public good. How does this make you feel? Do you think the public has really been served? Did this do the greatest good for the greatest number? Keep in mind, the government used money to buy your property as well as the surrounding properties.

▶ Recent Issues in Eminent Domain

Taking private property for necessary public use such as roads and municipal buildings does not seem especially controversial, but taking property that is then turned into commercial use has been widely condemned. In aftermath of *Kelo*, state and nationwide polls showed public opposition to the ruling that cut across gender, racial, ethnic, and political lines (Somin, 2016, p. 137). For example, a 2005 poll by Saint Index found that 81% of the total population disagreed with the *Kelo* decision (Somin, 2016, p. 138). Furthermore, the U.S. House of Representatives denounced *Kelo* in a 365–33 vote (Somin, 2016, p. 137), again crossing partisan lines. But this does not mean that the ruling does not stand. In fact, the issues in eminent domain continue today.

The election of Donald Trump in 2016 has brought several interesting issues in eminent domain to the forefront of American dialog. During Trump's campaign, he continually promised to build a border wall between the United States and Mexico to stop illegal immigration crossings. Trump believes that this would and will help stop violence, keep drugs from entering the United States, and reduce gang crime.

He states on twitter:

> We need the Wall for the safety and security of our country. We need the Wall to help stop the massive inflow of drugs from Mexico, now rated the number one most dangerous country in the world. (@realdonaldtrump, January 18, 2018)

In another tweet he wrote:

> MS-13 gang members are being removed by our Great ICE and Border Patrol Agents by the thousands, but these killers come back in from El Salvador, and through Mexico, like water. El Salvador just takes our money, and Mexico must help MORE with this problem. We need The Wall! (@realdonaldtrump, February 23, 2018)

However, the issue with such a wall is not just the amount of money it would take to build it but also the acquisition of the land that wall would be built upon. The federal government does not own all of the land along the border, and the government will need to buy private properties along the Rio Grande crossing several states to complete this wall (Miller, Collier, & Aguilar, 2017).

This is not the first time Texans and other Southern landowners have dealt with border protection and eminent domain issues. George W. Bush sought to create a border fence during his presidency. During the Secure Fence Act of 2006, the U.S. Department of Homeland Security filed more than 360 eminent domain lawsuits across the states of Texas, New Mexico, Arizona, and California to obtain land for the border fence. The agency paid $18.2 million for the land (Miller et al., 2017).

Proponents of the fence and the wall argue that the United States would be safer and more secure if there was a wall. Clearly, the argument is that eminent domain has been and will be used to make the entire American population safe, even though there will be a heavy burden on taxpayers to buy the property from landowners. It should be noted that many have argued that building a wall will not make America safer and is a waste of taxpayer dollars (Bier, 2017). However, the point of this article is not to debate the issue of illegal immigration but to examine the use of eminent domain (see Article 35 for more on issues in immigration).

▶ Ethical Issues

Cost versus Benefit

Ilya Somin, a scholar of eminent domain, explains that a plethora of issues surrounds eminent domain and the idea of just compensation. Somin (2016) explains that landowners who are poorer and cannot afford lawyers are often shortchanged and do not receive fair compensation, whereas those who are wealthier and can afford to fight the government are able to—and sometimes triple the original offer. To illustrate this point, a joint investigation by ProPublica and the *Texas Tribune* (Miller et al., 2017) found that during the eminent domain cases brought forth during the Secure Fence Act of 2006, Homeland Security "bungled" many cases. This report noted several things. First, the poorer landowners were shortchanged because Homeland Security "circumvented laws" and never did proper appraisals. As a result of improper or no appraisals, lands were undervalued and thus undercompensated. Second, wealthier individuals who could afford lawyers argued to increase the price of their land. To highlight these differences, the report uses two different cases:

Retired teacher Juan Cavazos was offered $21,500 for a two-acre slice of his land. He settled for that, assuming he couldn't afford to hire a lawyer.

> Rollins M. Koppel, a local attorney and banker, did not make the same mistake. A high-priced Texas law firm negotiated his offer from $233,000 to almost $5 million—the highest settlement in the Rio Grande Valley. (p.1)

Third, the report states that Homeland Security mistakenly paid individuals for land they did not even own. The report says, "The agency did not attempt to recover the misdirected taxpayer funds, instead paying for land a second time once it determined the correct owners" (p. 1).

The preceding findings suggest there were a lot of misdirected taxpayer funds. So even though the argument can be made that the federal government was using eminent domain for the protection and security of *all* Americans with a fence, the issue arises that all taxpayers are the ones who are suffering. Somin (2016, pp. 204–208) points out that this leads to competing forces for all cases of eminent domain, whereas people want just compensation for those whose land is being taken. If the price goes up, then taxpayers are the ones to suffer, so is the greatest good really being accomplished? This argument does not include how "just compensation" can be decided when there is often an emotional component to these purchases. These competing interests can be applied to almost all cases of eminent domain and do not resolve the issue of how much is just compensation and if taxpayers really benefit from these purchases (see *Kelo*)?

Who Owns the Land Anyway?

Although public goods, economic benefits, and emotional attachments are all easy arguments to find with eminent domain, there is also the question of who really owns the land. Jeremy Bentham, one of the foremost utilitarians (see introductory article on ethics), stated the following: "Property and law are born together, and die together. Before laws were made there was no property; take away laws, and property ceases" (Bentham, 1802/1882, p. 113). In other words, laws create property. When your parents gave you the house in our opening example, they gave it to you using a legal process, drawing up a deed, having a lawyer examine it, and so forth. Because the law and property are born together, the law is the decider of what can or cannot be done with the property. In other words, property is a "pure creature of law" (Merrill & Smith, 2007), and as such, distributive justice—in this case, eminent domain—is fine, according Bentham.

However, many have questioned this ethical and moral argument. Is property really a creature of law and should the government be able to stake claim to your property when it feels a benefit may be served to others? Merrill and Smith (2007) argue this is not the case and that there must instead be some type of inherent value in property, some type of human right to it. They state:

> Likewise, if the core of property law must rest on a simple foundation of everyday morality, property is unlikely to be wholly the creature of law. If we are right about the necessary connection between property and morality, then Bentham is almost certainly wrong that property arises wholly from law. (p. 1851)

The authors go on to argue that there is a connection between bodily security and integrity and that this is a human right that should be enjoyed by all. They further state that eminent domain is a type of coercion by the government. They argue, "The basic immorality of coercing the innocent to give up their property also helps explain why the payment of compensation to the owner does not validate the taking in the eyes of the public" (p. 1883). Even still, when eminent domain is used to transfer private property not just for the public good but also to private developers, then it becomes even more morally reprehensible because favoritism is being shown to a select few and contradicts the utilitarian argument further.

Thus, the question becomes, do people really have a right to the land they own or is it purely a societal construct? Does the government have the right to take your land as long as what it does with the land has some benefit? Does the benefit have to be for the public or can it be for business and the government itself? Do you have a right to your land intrinsically based on human rights?

What If You Disagree?

Finally, there are questions about whether you are morally opposed to what is being done with your land. What if you are morally opposed to eminent domain in general? The Trump border wall is just one example of moral opposition to eminent domain and what it is used for. A Pew Research poll (Suls, 2017) shows that 62% of Americans oppose the building of a border wall, and just 35% favor it. Many people are arguing that it would not serve its purpose of protecting the United States and that currently the borders are safer than they have ever been (Bier, 2017). Furthermore, there is the moral and legal question of helping those who are trying to migrate to the United States for a better life.

Research shows (UN News, 2018) stricter border laws led to an increase in deaths at border crossings, possibly because individuals trying to flee gang violence and seek economic opportunity are more likely to enter the United States using more dangerous and desperate means (Carrillo, Aja, & Hernandez, 2017). This leads to more questions concerning the border wall beyond economic considerations, such as what is the cost and value of human life as well as the ethical obligation of the United States to these migrants? Although there may be no answer to what individuals or society can do if they object to eminent domain or its uses, some try to stop it at all costs (see Cards Against Humanity Saves America, 2017).

▶ Conclusion

Cases in eminent domain will never go away and will continually be used to help the public, whether it is through building roads or municipal buildings or possibly revitalizing blighted areas of cities. However, there are many moral and ethical questions that surround eminent domain such as: who really owns the land? Is land a right? What is the public good? Who should benefit from the use of eminent domain? All of these questions will need to be answered by the courts as cases in eminent domain continually come forward.

▶ References

Allen, C. (2014, February 10). "Kelo" revisited. *The Weekly Standard*. Retrieved from https://www.weeklystandard.com/charlotte-allen/kelo-revisited

Bentham, J. (1882) *Theory of legislation*. (R. Hilderth, Trans.). London, UK: Trubner & Co., Ludgate Hill. (Original work 1802)

Berman v. Parker 348 U.S. 26 (1954).

Bier, D. (2017). Why the wall won't work. Cato Institute. Retrieved from https://www.cato.org/publications/commentary/why-wall-wont-work

Cards Against Humanity Saves America. (2017). Retrieved from https://www.cardsagainsthumanitysavesamerica.com/

Carrillo, R., Aja, A., & Hernandez, J. (2017). The immorality of Trump's border wall, explained. *Teen Vogue*. Retrieved from https://www.teenvogue.com/story/the-immorality-of-trumps-border-wall-explained

Chicago, Burlington & Quincy Railroad Co. v. City of Chicago, 166 U.S. 266 (1897).

Clark v. Nash. 198 U.S. 361 (1905).

Cohen, C. E. (2006). Eminent domain after Kelo v. City of New London: An argument for banning economic development takings. *Harvard Journal of Law and Public Policy, 29*(2), 491–568.

Collins, D. (2018, May 17). Whoa! Nothing has been built at Fort Trumbull because of DEEP? *The Day*. Retrieved from https://www.theday.com/article/20180517/NWS05/180519401

Kelo v. City of New London, 545 U.S. 469 (2005).

McGeehan, P. (2009, November 12). Pfizer to leave city that won land-use case. *The New York Times*. Retrieved from https://www.nytimes.com/2009/11/13/nyregion/13pfizer.html

Merrill, T. W., & Smith, H. E. (2007). The morality of property. *William and Mary Law Review, 48*, 1849–1895.

Miller, C., Collier, K., & Aguilar, J. (2017, December 14). The taking. ProPublica. Retrieved from https://features.propublica.org/eminent-domain-and-the-wall/the-taking-texas-government-property-seizure/

Nunes, A. (2011, August 30). Residents haul debris to Fort Trumbull. *The Day*. Retrieved from https://web.archive.org/web/20120326171220/http://theday.com/article/20110830/MEDIA0101/110829587

Ryskamp, J. (2007). *The eminent domain revolt: Changing perception in a new constitutional epoch* [e-book]. New York, NY: Algora.

Scott, K. (2009). *The price of politics: Lessons from Kelo v. City of New London* [e-book]. Lanham, MD: Lexington Books.

Somin, Ilya (2016). *The grasping hand: Kelo v. City of New London and the limits of eminent domain* [e-book]. Chicago, IL: The University of Chicago Press.

Suls, R. (2017) Most Americans continue to oppose U.S. border wall, doubt Mexico would pay for it. Pew Research Center. Retrieved from http://www.pewresearch.org/fact-tank/2017/02/24/most-americans-continue-to-oppose-u-s-border-wall-doubt-mexico-would-pay-for-it/

UN News. (2018, February 6). Migrant deaths along U.S.-Mexico border remain high despite drop in crossings. United Nations. Retrieved from https://news.un.org/en/story/2018/02/1002101

The Firearm Debate: The Legality, Morality, and Ethics of Ownership

Eric S. See

Christopher M. Bellas

Sarah A. See

Just hearing the word *gun* can cause a reaction in people, no doubt based on events seared into the national conscience. School shootings such as those that took place at Sandy Hook and Parkland and mass shootings such as the events in Las Vegas and at the Pulse nightclub have become part of our fabric. Police shootings of armed and unarmed suspects have divided the country and forced a critical examination of police tactics and made the use of body cameras popular and, in some locales, mandatory across the country. An armed citizen with an AR-15 confronted and fired at the gunman in a Texas church shooting. The shooting resulted in 26 deaths, but many more could have died had the citizen not intervened with his own weapon and confronted the gunman. Clearly, guns can both take and defend lives.

Regardless of any individual's reaction to guns, the number of firearms in this country is considerable. Figures from 2017 place the population of the United States at approximately 325 million—and the number of firearms owned by U.S. residents at an estimated 393 million. This represents nearly 40% of the estimated 1 billion firearms in the world (Karp, 2018). Estimates of the percentage of households with a firearm range from roughly 30% to 44%. This figure also varies substantially when looking at those living in rural versus urban environments, when comparing men versus women, or when looking at Republicans versus Democrats (Parker, Horowitz, Igielnik, Oliphant, & Brown, 2017).

Few issues in the field of criminal justice are as controversial as the issue of guns. In addition, few issues involve so many separate and distinct controversies. Common gun issues currently being debated include open carry of handguns, concealed carry of handguns, ownership of bump stocks, background checks, 3D printing, semiautomatic guns, assault weapons, large capacity clips, stand-your-ground laws, gun shows, and gun-free zones. We're sure readers can think of many additional issues. The only relatively new issue on this list of controversies is 3D printed guns. They have been in development over the last 6 years, and the plans have been widely available to download online for the last several years. Once downloaded, an individual could 3D print an untraceable firearm made almost entirely of plastic (Koslow, 2018).

Any of the previously stated issues are worthy of extended debate and research. Exploring all of them is outside the scope of this article, but a few of these issues will be touched on as part of our central focus. Although acknowledging the important questions raised by the issues already presented, the focus of this article is much more basic and to the point. Before it can be determined if an individual should be allowed to carry a gun, what places he or she can carry the weapon, what kind of weapon they can carry, and of what materials a gun should be made, far more basic questions must be addressed. Simply put, do private individuals have a right to own a firearm? If so, is it an ethical decision to own one?

How can these questions be addressed? Are they legal questions? Perhaps they are moral questions. Are they best addressed in a political environment? Perhaps the courts are the best place to address them. Should we seek these answers from a criminologist, a philosopher, a politician, a lawyer, or a judge? There are pros and cons to all of these approaches. If a private individual has a right to own a firearm, however, then that right has to come from some place. It must have a source. Perhaps there is a moral or legal right to own a firearm.

This article examines private firearm ownership from a moral, ethical, and legal perspective. Its objective is to provoke thought, discussion, and debate in the minds of the reader and serve as a starting point for further investigation. As a part of the review of the issues involved, basic propositions will be offered for consideration. After this review, the concepts of private firearm ownership and ethical constraints will be answered, and policy recommendations will be offered and addressed.

▶ Moral Ethical Perspective

Is there a moral or natural right to own a firearm? Natural rights are those rights that do not depend on a particular law or government. In fact, they are rights that are so basic and fundamental and agreed to as that they are necessary for human existence. These natural rights are inalienable and universal. They are beyond the reach of any governmental or political entity, and they cannot be stripped away or denied. The rights to self-preservation and self-defense are such rights.

Although it can be a straightforward theoretical exercise to discuss fundamental rights and the origins of such rights, for practical purposes, it is often difficult to separate and distinguish the moral, ethical, and legal rights of self-preservation from the right to own a gun. In discussing fundamental rights, Martin, Lavan, Lopez, Naquin, and Kats (2014) demonstrate how the concepts of essential, fundamental rights become intertwined with the concept of natural law.

At the time the Constitution was being drafted, the right to own firearms already existed. The framers were aware of this as well as the arguments of natural law and the work of John Locke. These factual and philosophical elements played a part in crafting the Second Amendment. The result was a fusion of rights and law. It took more than 200 years for the U.S. Supreme Court to rule directly on the precise meaning of the Second Amendment. That ruling (which will be addressed in the legal section) has done little to satisfy those on either side of the gun issue.

Those on both sides of the debate cite a combination of moral and ethical rights and often seek to establish their case in absolute terms. When this occurs, the debate is framed as either "Repeal the Second Amendment," as argued by the late Supreme Court Associate Justice John Paul Stevens (2018) or "from my cold dead hands" as popularized by the late Charlton Heston of the National Rifle Association. This rhetoric is often based on purely emotional grounds and strays from a discussion of moral and ethical reasoning. Both sides present strong, unified arguments and believe they are on the side of right (Kocsis, 2015).

▶ Proposition One: The Right to Own a Firearm Is a Fundamental Right

Under this perspective, the right to own a firearm is, in fact, a fundamental or basic right. This means that the right stems from a source higher than the law. Attempts to regulate, control, or limit access to firearms must be viewed with suspicion. Attempts to limit any fundamental right must be viewed with suspicion, and this right is no different.

The right to own a firearm gains strength not only from appeals to natural law and the fundamental rights of self-preservation and self-defense but also from the cultural fabric and symbolism that make up the history of the country. Since the founding of this country, firearms have been present and an integral part of the American story. From the establishment of the first colony to the fight for independence, the fulfilment of manifest destiny, and the taming of the West, the firearm has served as both villain and champion. Fact and fantasy have combined to form a mythical aura around the idea of firearms and the ownership of firearms. Regardless of the final consensus of philosophers, the debate in this country has historically focused on the extent of gun control that is desirable, permissible, or legal and not on the fundamental issue of ownership itself. For the most part, the issue of private ownership has been conceded, and the general right of firearm ownership (with certain exclusions) has been accepted.

Not everyone agrees with this perspective. Justice Stevens, with his call to repeal the Second Amendment, clearly did not. He was not alone in believing that there is no fundamental right to own a firearm. Other voices are also not so willing to concede that the right to own a firearm is fundamental or given, even if society acts as though it were. DeGrazia (2014) concedes the moral and legal right to gun ownership for the purposes of proposing what he labels "moderate gun control measures" is assumed, yet he declares that the existence of an actual moral right to bear arms is in fact debatable. The argument is often made that the right to own a firearm is simply not a basic or fundamental right. For those like Stevens and DeGrazia who argue this perspective, the right to self-preservation or self-defense is the fundamental right involved, not the right to own a firearm.

There are, of course, many ways in which an individual could defend him- or herself in response to a violent attack. These responses include everything from cooperation, fleeing the scene, fighting back with fists, or fighting back with a non-lethal or lethal weapon other than a firearm. Even nonlethal weapons such as stun guns and pepper spray are not without controversy. These and similar nonlethal devices are subject to varying regulations, requirements, and are often illegal to own and carry (Volokh, 2009).

If, in fact, the right of self-defense is the fundamental right in question, then the right to own a firearm is merely an extension of that right or one possible way to achieve the fundamental right of self-defense. If this is the case, then the right for a private individual to own a firearm would not be viewed as basic or fundamental, and it would not be essential or inalienable. Federal, state, and local governments would have far more power and authority to regulate, restrict, or simply ban firearms in this scenario.

Self-preservation and self-defense are well-established and basic fundamental rights. The ability to achieve self-preservation is impossible without the right of self-defense. The right of self-defense is often impossible without the aid of a firearm. It is simply not realistic to expect that a citizen under fire can adequately achieve self-preservation and self-defense using fists or evasion. In many cases, the difference between life and death is the ownership and use of a firearm. This makes the ability to own a firearm fundamental and on par with the right to self-preservation and self-defense. Because the right to own a firearm is impossible to separate from the fundamental rights of self-preservation and self-defense, the right to own a firearm is basic and fundamental as well.

Legal

When examining gun issues from a legal perspective, the focus changes from a moral argument to one based on laws and legal documents. As previously noted, basic and fundamental rights are inalienable and do not derive from human-made or governmental sources. Legal rights do, however. An examination of the U.S. Constitution is the logical starting point to determine if a private individual has the right to own a firearm.

The Second Amendment to the United States Constitution is as follows:

> A well regulated Militia, being necessary to the security of a free State, the right of the people to keep and bear Arms, shall not be infringed.

Those 27 words, ratified in 1791, have proven to be complex, controversial, and open to multiple interpretations. What exactly does the amendment mean? Was it written to guarantee the right of a private individual to own a firearm? Was it written to guarantee that those in the "militia" had a right to arm themselves in times of national crisis? What precisely was meant by the term *militia* or the term *arms*? The true intentions of the amendment may be impossible to determine.

Interpreting the Constitution is the job of the courts, and the final authority in the court system is the United States Supreme Court. The primary case of interest here is *District of Columbia v. Heller* 554 U.S. 570 (2008). Although not the first or last case to examine the Second Amendment, it is the most relevant in helping to understand and address the propositions. An extensive examination of *Heller* is beyond our scope here, but a brief analysis is helpful. As a part of this examination, the focus will shift from an examination of basic and fundamental rights to one of individual or collective rights. Individual rights are those that would apply to each and every person, whereas collective rights would require some sort of group affiliation or membership.

▶ Proposition Two: The Right to Own a Firearm Is an Individual Legal Right

In the *Heller* case, the Supreme Court had to determine if private individuals had a constitutional right to own a firearm. In doing so, the court addressed the issue of the proper meaning of the Second Amendment. As a part of the decision, the Court also addressed the language used in the Constitution and how to understand the various terminology found within.

> In interpreting this text, we are guided by the principle that "[t]he Constitution was written to be understood by the voters; its words and phrases were used in their normal and ordinary as distinguished from technical meaning" *United States v. Sprague*, 282 U.S. 716, 731, 51 S.Ct. 220, 75 L.Ed. 640 (1931); see also *Gibbons v. Ogden*, 9 Wheat. 1, 188, 6 L.Ed. 23 (1824). Normal meaning may of course include an idiomatic meaning, but it excludes secret or technical meanings that would not have been known to ordinary citizens in the founding generation. (*District of Columbia v. Heller*, 2008, p. 577)

In essence, the Court is saying that the Constitution should be interpreted as written and is advising the reader not to look for secret meanings or hypertechnical definitions. In the *Heller* decision, the majority of the Court held that there is a right to bear arms. The right belongs to individual citizens, and that right is not connected to service in the militia. This is an individual right as opposed to a collective right (meaning it is not granted only to those individuals who are part of a larger organization such as a militia). The right exists for purposes such as self-defense in the home as well as for hunting.

Assuming that the right to bear arms exists, and assuming that the right is an individual right, what exactly does it allow someone to own? What is meant by the term *arms*? As noted by the late Associate Justice Antonin Scalia, those familiar with gun rights debates have often heard the argument that if a right to bear arms exists, it is limited to arms that existed at the time the Second Amendment was written. The implication is that the right would be largely limited to weapons of the late 18th century and apply mostly to muskets. After all, the framers of the Constitution could have never foreseen the development of semiautomatic weapons, large capacity clips, or high-powered hunting rifles.

Addressing this argument, Scalia writes:

> Some have made the argument, bordering on the frivolous, that only those arms in existence in the 18th century are protected by the Second

Amendment. We do not interpret constitutional rights that way. Just as the First Amendment protects modern forms of communications, e.g., *Reno v. American Civil Liberties Union*, 521 U.S. 844, 849, 117 S.Ct. 2329, 138 L.Ed.2d 874 (1997), and the Fourth Amendment applies to modern forms of search, e.g., *Kyllo v. United States*, 533 U.S. 27, 35–36, 121 S.Ct. 2038, 150 L.Ed.2d 94 (2001), the Second Amendment extends, prima facie, to all instruments that constitute bearable arms, even those that were not in existence at the time of the founding. (*District of Columbia v. Heller*, 2008, p. 582)

The *Heller* decision affirms that private citizens have a right to bear arms and the right to carry those arms in the home for self-defense. It affirms that this right is not limited to muskets but includes modern firearms. Just as First and Fourth Amendment rights have evolved, Second Amendment rights have as well.

Heller is clear. The right to own a firearm is a Constitutional right and it is not connected to military service. The right however, is not unlimited. Having established the right to own firearms and the right to carry those weapons in the home, the court goes on to clarify some of the limits of the Second Amendment.

The Court found as follows:

Although we do not undertake an exhaustive historical analysis today of the full scope of the Second Amendment, nothing in our opinion should be taken to cast doubt on longstanding prohibitions on the possession of firearms by felons and the mentally ill, or laws forbidding the carrying of firearms in sensitive places such as schools and government buildings, or laws imposing conditions and qualifications on the commercial sale of arms. (*District of Columbia v. Heller*, 2008, p. 627)

This supports the foundation and rationale of many of the country's current gun laws. Private individuals may own, purchase, and possess firearms as guaranteed by the Second Amendment. To exercise those rights, individuals must demonstrate that they are not felons or mentally ill. Furthermore, a state may place reasonable restrictions on where individuals may carry firearms outside of their homes.

An examination of the dissent in the *Heller* decision is necessary to fully grasp the difficulty in accurately interpreting the Second Amendment. Again, a full examination of the dissenting opinions is beyond the scope of this article. An examination of two issues, however, is relevant to the discussion here: individual versus collective rights and the role of the militia. The first issue focuses on the right in question as an individual or collective right. Writing in dissent, Justice Stevens says:

The centerpiece of the Court's textual argument is its insistence that the words "the people" as used in the Second Amendment must have the same meaning, and protect the same class of individuals, as when they are used in the First and Fourth Amendments. According to the Court, in all three provisions—as well as the Constitution's preamble, §2 of Article I, and the Tenth Amendment—"the term unambiguously refers to all members of the political community, not an unspecified subset." *Ante,* at 2790–2791. But the Court *itself* reads the Second Amendment to protect a "subset" significantly narrower than the class of persons protected by the First and Fourth Amendments; when it finally drills down on the substantive meaning of the Second Amendment, the Court limits the protected class to "law-abiding, responsible citizens," *ante,* at 2821. But the class of persons protected by the First and Fourth Amendments is *not* so limited; for even felons (and presumably irresponsible citizens as well) may invoke the protections of those constitutional provisions. The Court offers no way to harmonize its conflicting pronouncements. (*District of Columbia v. Heller,* 2008, p. 644)

The exclusions here are key. Justice Scalia is claiming that the Second Amendment applies to everyone. After claiming it applies to everyone, he then excludes certain individuals such as those with felony records or mental illness. The argument is often made that felons and the mentally ill should not have access to firearms. As noted, this is a key part of our gun control laws today and a view endorsed by Justice Scalia and the court majority in *Heller.* The Second Amendment, however, makes no such distinction. This is problematic if the Second Amendment is to be viewed as an individual right. This fits with Justice Stevens's view regarding collective rights and the belief that the right protects only those involved in service to the militia. Felons and the mentally ill still enjoy the right of free speech found in the First Amendment. The fact that the right to bear arms can be denied to some citizens weakens the case for the individual rights perspective.

The second key issue raised by the dissent concerns the role of the militia. The Court majority in the *Heller* decision finds a right to keep and bear arms that exists independent of militia service. The dissenters counter:

This reading is confirmed by the fact that the clause protects only one right, rather than two. It does not describe a right "to keep . . . Arms" and a separate right "to bear . . . Arms." Rather, the single right that it does describe is both a duty and a right to have arms available and ready for military service, and to use them for military purposes when necessary.[13] Different language surely would have been used to protect nonmilitary use and possession of weapons from regulation if such an intent had played any role in the drafting of the Amendment. (*District of Columbia v. Heller,* 2008, p. 651)

This interpretation by Justice Stevens is a clear rejection of the argument by Justice Scalia that the use of firearms is protected for such activities as hunting and protection in the home. In the view of the dissenters, these additional rights could have been easily added to the Constitution had that been the desire of the framers. Justice Scalia and the majority simply have no ability to add them in now.

Although there is dissent and argument among the justices of the Supreme Court, proposition two—that the right to own a firearm is an individual legal right—is clearly supported in the *Heller* decision, the controlling case on this issue. This decision states that private individuals have a right to own and carry a weapon in their home for self-defense unrelated to military service. This right is not without limits, however. Felons and the mentally ill can be excluded, and certain unusual and dangerous weapons can be excluded. However, this does not end the legal or moral discussion. This perspective is not limited to the mere ownership of firearms. It is often extended as follows.

▶ Proposition Three: The Right to Carry a Firearm Outside the Home is a Fundamental Right

The right to own a firearm is fundamental and legal, but what about the right to own *and* carry a firearm outside of the home? Is that a fundamental and legal right as well? The rights to self-preservation and self-defense are not limited exclusively to the home environment. Although their laws are constantly changing, currently, all 50 states and the District of Columbia allow some type of firearm carry outside the home (Hsiao & Bernstein, 2016). Once an individual chooses to carry a firearm outside the home, additional issues come into play. Where can the weapon be carried? Where might it be excluded? The open and concealed carry of firearms often faces limitations by the declaration of gun-free zones and various workplace restrictions.

Anyplace where guns are prohibited by statute or where a sign is posted prohibiting guns is a gun-free zone. This might include such places as schools, churches, and government buildings. Employers might also limit or restrict firearm rights in the workplace. There is little consistency between these various state laws. Different states impose varying requirements and regulations on the ability to carry a firearm in a concealed fashion or in an open and visible fashion and define those acts differently.

Hsiao (2017) examined gun-free zones and concluded that individuals who have a right to own a firearm have a moral right to be allowed to carry it. The right to self-preservation and self-defense do not end once one enters a public space. He states "there exists a moral right to carry a gun, an issue distinct from whether there exists a political or constitutional right to carry guns" (p. 660). This right stems from the right to self-defense. As a basic right, the state cannot deny people the right to carry a gun at will. If the state were to deny citizens the right to carry outside of the home, then the state would then have a special obligation to defend the disarmed citizens. In many parts of the country, the state has, in fact, denied this right while simultaneously failing to protect disarmed citizens. The state is unable to meet the obligation generated by prohibiting the carrying of firearms in public (Hsiao, 2017). Therefore, a ban on carrying guns outside of the home is unjust and immoral. People have a right to protect themselves at home, in public, and at the workplace.

Martin et al. (2014) examined taking guns into the workplace. They acknowledged that the right to bear arms was "fundamentally defined by the Second Amendment" (p. 5). They then examined the right to take a weapon to work from both a legal perspective and from six different ethical perspectives. Concluding that the legal perspective found in the Second Amendment was at best unclear, they then focused solely on the ethical perspectives involved. It is clear from this approach that they were not challenging the proposition of owning a firearm but the further proposition of taking that firearm outside of the home to the work environment. After examining the issues from the ethical perspectives provided by libertarian, fundamental rights, consequentialism, stakeholder, peace, and public health views, they determined that firearms should not be permitted in the workplace. They recommend several policies and procedures, including increasing guards and electronic surveillance, as well as limiting access to company premises (Martin et al., 2014).

Still, these recommendations cannot guarantee the safety of those who have been disarmed. Employers who ban firearms at work are not violating a constitutional right, but are they perhaps violating an ethical right? Gun-free zones and guns in the workplace pose difficult moral and legal questions. Although the rights to self-preservation and self-defense remain, the establishment of a moral right to carry a firearm outside of the home does not make the right a constitutional one.

As clear as we wish the Second Amendment to be, and regardless of how often the Court reminds us that the Constitution was written with common usage in mind, there are many unanswered questions. As long as there are unanswered questions and various interpretations among the public, scholars, and current and former Supreme Court justices themselves, this debate will never be fully settled. The discussion here barely scratches the surface of the Second Amendment debate and touches on only a fraction of the arguments both pro and con in the *Heller* decision.

The evidence supports proposition number three from both a moral and legal perspective. The right to carry a firearm can refer to carry within the home and carry outside of the home. Currently, the Supreme Court has found a right to carry within the home, but it has also recognized limits on the right to carry outside of the home. As of yet, the Court has not fully recognized the right to carry firearms outside of the home. Note, however, that *Heller* explicitly states that the full range and depth of the Second Amendment has not yet been clarified. Even though it acknowledges that others will not share this expanded view, the weight of the evidence supports the basic and fundamental right to self-preservation and self-defense. The legal right to bear arms has been established. There is simply no compelling moral, ethical, or legal rationale to provide that right and protection in the home but to limit it outside of the home.

Private firearm ownership has been established as a fundamental and legal right. That said, is it an ethical decision to own a firearm? How can one best define ethics? In looking at ethics, Pojman (2006) states:

> I use ethics to refer to the whole domain of morality and moral philosophy, since these two areas have many features in common. For example, both areas concern values, virtues, and principles and practices, although in different ways. (p. 2)

In more simple terms, ethics can be understood as the study of "right and wrong, good and evil" (Braswell, McCarthy, & McCarthy, 2015, p.3). Is it right to own a firearm? Does it promote good or evil?

The search for understanding is common to all definitions. Values, virtues, principles, and practices are relatively easy to understand in the general sense but become a bit more difficult when a specific question is asked.

Looking at an individual question such as firearm ownership shifts the focus from theoretical to applied ethics. This is, of course, tricky and must be considered in light of concepts such as right and wrong. To understand firearm ownership from an ethical perspective, the moral intentions of the individual must be examined. Just because a particular action is legal does not necessarily make it right or moral. As noted by Pojman, "ethics may judge that some laws are immoral without denying that they are valid laws" (2006, p. 3). Viewed through this lens, owning a firearm to do harm may be a legal act but not an ethical act.

This brings us back to the fundamental rights of self-preservation and self-defense. Self-preservation and self-defense are fundamental rights, as is the right to own a firearm. As noted by Pojman (2006), ethical systems accept the concept of motive as an important and relevant factor. Taking motive into account is necessary to judge the actions of an individual. Owning a firearm to further the rights of self-preservation and self-defense satisfies an inquiry on ethical grounds. The decision to own a firearm for the purposes of self-preservation and self-defense is therefore an ethical decision.

It has been established that private citizens have an individual right to own a firearm and that it is an ethical decision to own one. Gun ownership represents the merging of a natural and fundamental right with a constitutional and legal one. The right to self-preservation is natural and fundamental. It predates the Constitution. Firearm ownership predates the Constitution as well. The Second Amendment merely reinforced an inalienable right already in existence and provided a constitutional framework.

Exercising this right comes with an ethical responsibility. It is the responsibility of the gun owner to ensure that his or her firearm is used in a moral manner. This is tied in with ethical ownership and a necessary condition and requirement when exercising even a fundamental right.

▶ Policy Recommendations

Academics, law enforcement agencies, and politicians must prioritize the myriad of gun issues facing the country today. Although the issue of 3D-printed guns is indeed important, cost and practicality are still massive hurdles. There are simply few criminals interested in the expense needed to produce an unreliable, often single-use, plastic firearm. The technology will improve, of course, and the price will drop. At that time, policy and law will need to adapt and change. The plans to make 3D guns have already been released on the Internet. They will never not be available, and they will continue to improve in quality and function. We have, however, not yet reached that crossroad.

More important today are the issues of open and concealed carry and the related issue of gun-free zones. Currently, state laws on these topics are contradictory, ever-changing, and ineffective. The training required to obtain a carry–conceal license ranges from moderate to nonexistent. Bordering states have such different laws that a law-abiding citizen can turn into a felon simply by crossing state lines with a firearm. The authors recommend a commonsense approach to concealed and open carry. We recommend one standard for obtaining a license agreeable to all of the states. This will be difficult, but not impossible. If the states cannot find a way to achieve this, then Congress may enact a standard in their absence.

In a similar manner, gun-free zones are often a target for criminal activity. It can no longer be assumed that simply posting a sign banning guns will have any impact or serve any function in reducing crime. A special duty exists to protect citizens when they are forbidden by law to bring a firearm to a given location. Clearly, private organizations as well as the state are unable to meet that burden.

Research on firearms must be expanded on all levels and across all gun-related issues. A fear of the research process and the resulting data stands only to benefit the uninformed and raises additional moral, legal, and ethical questions. Empirical evidence should be used to guide future legislative issues and approaches.

Firearms have always been a part of our society. Viewed as part of a fundamental right to self-preservation or as a constitutionally protected right enshrined in the Second Amendment, the right to own a firearm has been established and preserved. The right is, in fact, an ethical choice to make and comes with corresponding responsibilities. One must always act to ensure that the exercising of his or her fundamental and constitutional rights does not infringe on the fundamental and constitutional rights of another.

▶ References

Braswell, M. C., McCarthy, B. R., & McCarthy, B. J. 2015. Justice, crime, and ethics. Fifth Edition. New York, NY: Routledge.

DeGrazia, D. (2014). The case for moderate gun control. *Kennedy Institute of Ethics Journal, 24*(1), 1–25.

District of Columbia v. Heller, 554 U.S. 570 (2008)

Hsiao, T. (2017). The ethics of gun-free zones. *Philosophia, 45,* 659–676.

Hsiao, T., & Bernstein, C. (2016). Against moderate gun control. *Libertarian Papers, 8*(2).

Karp, A. (2018). Estimating global civilian held firearm numbers. Small Arms Survey. Canberra, Australia: Department of Foreign Affairs and Trade. Retrieved from http://www.smallarmssurvey .org/fileadmin/docs/T-Briefing-Papers/SAS-BP-Civilian-Firearms-Numbers.pdf

Kocsis, M. (2015). Gun ownership and gun control in the United States of America: Philosophy and gun control. *Essays in Philosophy, 16*(2).

Koslow, T. (2018). 2019 3D printed gun report—all you need to know. ALL3DP. Retrieved from https://all3dp.com/3d-printed-gun-firearm-weapon-parts/

Martin, W., Lavan, H., Lopez, Y., Naquin, C., & Kats, M. (2014). An ethical analysis of the Second Amendment: The right to pack heat at work. *Business and Society Review, 119*(1), 1–36.

Parker, K., Horowitz, J., Igielnik, R., Oliphant, B., and Brown, A. (2017). America's complex relationship with guns. Pew Research Center. Retrieved from http://www.pewsocialtrends .org/2017/06/22/the-demographics-of-gun-Ownership/

Pojman, L. (2006). *Ethics: Discovering right and wrong* (5th ed.). Belmont, CA: Thomson Wadsworth.

Stevens, J. P. (2018, March 18). Repeal the Second Amendment. *The New York Times,* p. A23.

Volokh, E. (2009). Nonlethal self-defense (almost entirely) nonlethal weapons and the right to keep and bear arms and defend life. *Stanford Law Review, 62*(1). Retrieved from http://www2.law .ucla.edu/volokh/nonlethal.pdf

Right to Health: The History of Needle-Exchange Programs and State Control

Stephen T. Young

▶ Introduction

The debate surrounding the most appropriate means of combating drug abuse within the United States continues to be contentious. The War on Drugs, while still strongly debated for its disastrous consequences, appears to be relatively ineffective under the current Department of Justice (Lopez, 2018). However, decades of research demonstrate the deleterious effects this so-called war continues to cause for lower-economic disadvantaged groups and communities of color across the country (Alexander, 2012). This multidecade-long implementation of punitive policies led many communities to stand and fight for alternative harm reduction–based programming. Arguably, needle-exchange programs represent the largest of these alternative programs. However, the history and status of these programs face vehement repression from the State as they mirror other social welfare-based programs traditionally geared toward helping exploited populations (see Massey, 2007).

The conversation of needle-exchange programs and state controls of citizens for the purpose of zero-tolerance punitive policies is complex. A single chapter in a text will not address the depth of state reliance on punitive measures and repressive behaviors toward harm-reduction programs. However, the opportunity exists to answer many questions to provide a foundation for future conversations. Specifically, what services or needs do needle-exchange programs attempt to fulfill? What is the history of the development of these programs in the United States? Finally, why have these programs faced continuous contention from the state as a part of a broader control of the bodies of underprivileged and often exploited populations?

▶ Needle-Exchange Programs

To begin, it is important to understand fundamental services provided by needle-exchange programs. Many intravenous drug users face high levels of risk concerning contracting specific blood-borne illnesses (Centers for Disease Control and Prevention [CDC], 2016). *Needle exchanges* will be used to describe these programs throughout; they provide sterile and disposable needles without cost or in some cases without the need for prescriptions. Providing easy access to these clean syringes is meant to promote the use of clean needles over the sharing of "dirty" or previously used needles in the hope of limiting the number of individuals contracting infections (CDC, 2016). These programs use policies created as a part of the harm-reduction prospective to support this population through many interventions (Des Jarlais, McKnight, Goldblatt, & Purchase, 2009). The majority of programs provide access to other important materials such as alcohol swabs, vials of sterile water, and even condoms. In addition, many of these programs provide services such as education on how to inject syringes and care for wounds, referral to treatment programs, overdose prevention, counseling services, and testing for those concerned about HIV and viral hepatitis. The CDC also states that many programs "provide linkage to critical services and programs, such as HIV care, treatment, pre-exposure prophylaxis, and post-exposure prophylaxis (2018, para. 2)." Though extremely contentious, as will be demonstrated, many of these programs receive some level of federal funding through the Consolidated Appropriations Act of 2016. This act provides to states and local communities the opportunity to garner funds to support components of these programs under specific and limited circumstances. This funding is arguably the most vehemently assailed aspect of these programs through state rhetoric and policies because it represents the integral piece in either the success or failure of many programs.

▶ History of Programs and the Control of the State

The services provided help us understand and contextualize the history behind state scrutinization of these programs. However, to truly understand the development of U.S. programs, we must first turn our attention to the development of programs in other countries. The initial purpose of these needle-exchange programs dealt with reducing the spread of hepatitis B (Des Jarlais, 2006). However, shortly after efforts began, the concern for the spread of HIV in the 1980s became an additional imperative. Before the 1970s, many injection-based drug users were limited to areas primarily located in North America and Europe (Cook & Kanaef, 2008). By the early 1990s, injection drug use had spread to 80 countries and territories. By 2008, researchers demonstrated that 158 countries displayed data consistant with injection drug use (Mathers et al., 2008). This led many countries to begin evaluating the usefulness of needle-exchange programs as a measure of battling rising costs of injection-drug use-related illnesses.

In 1984, the Netherlands established the first needle-exchange program and officially established the first national program by 1987. Following a one-year evaluation in 1986, the United Kingdom followed suit by determining that needle-exchange programs demonstrated a significant effectiveness in combating the spread of communicable diseases, a conclusion that warranted the creation of a national U.K. program (Des Jarlais et al., 2006). By the mid- to late 1990s, the majority of industrialized nations apart from the United States and Sweden created some version of universally adopted needle-exchange programs. The United Nations Office on Drugs and Crime and the Joint United Nations Programme on HIV/AIDS developed during this time because of significant governmental and community-based nongovernmental organizations and the World Health Organization support (Cook & Kanaef, 2008).

Today, at least 77 countries provide some form of needle-exchange programs. The level of sophistication and programs offered varies. Countries such as New Zealand provide some of the most comprehensive services globally (Hay, Henderson, Maltby, & Canales, 2007). These more comprehensively oriented countries go as far to provide vending machines that allow users to obtain clean needles. Funding and oversight for these programs also vary widely. However, some degree of oversight by the government is involved and is usually complemented by the support of community-implemented programs (Cook & Kanaef, 2008). Such oversight usually determines whether these programs are provided at cost or are provided through the state. In addition, many individual countries allow legal purchases of sterile injecting equipment through pharmacies (Cook & Kanaef, 2008). Like all other programs, these vary widely with regard to providing disposal services for used needles and support materials to help users contact services.

This brings up a critical question. If these program are so widely accepted globally, why does the United States continue to fight their implementation and argue their effectiveness? U.S. needle-exchange programs faced a significant level of resistance from the beginning. This history of resistance, both governmental and social, is a large factor in why programs continue to grow at a much slower rate than in other countries (Des Jarlais et al., 2006). The majority of this combativeness stems from the timing of the push for such programs and the government's move toward the early stages of the War on Drugs. This fact is especially clear when discussing the creation and later failure of a pilot program by the New York City Department of Health in the early days of 1984 (see Des Jarlais et al., 2006). The majority of this early state resistance stemmed from rhetoric surrounding both drug use as well as strong stigmas related to HIV-infected individuals (Klein, Karchner, & O'Connell, 2002). Many—both socially and governmentally—believed that such programs worked to encourage drug use instead of the tough approach of condemnation then being discussed. Simply, needle-exchange programs at this time did not line up with the sentiment of "Just Say No" being brandished on billboards and commercials of the time (Shoemaker, 2012). This rhetoric, situated firmly in the controls of the state, provided a forum for various groups to oppose the implementation of these programs, including high-ranking government officials and law enforcement personnel (see Des Jarlais, 2006). The state pushed to admonish the creation of needle-exchange programs under the guise of normative state protections (see Lynch, 2002), which were strongly built through the previous "War on Drugs" style rhetoric. Similar to other social progressive programs highly disdained by the state, the powers to control the funding became a central point in the means to appeal implementation.

The nature of drug use faced such demonization during this time that it would be political suicide as a part of the "tough on crime" rhetoric to support such progressive measures as needle policies. The beginnings of the governing through crime policies of the time could not allow such policies to exist (see Simon, 2007). To ensure this, Congress attached an amendment to the U.S. Department of Health and Human Services' budget in 1998 (see Des Jarlais, 2006). The amendment directly supported the claim that the government would not "support" needle-exchange programs through the provision of federal funds. However, the amendment did not come without a caveat. Federal funding could exist following a formal evaluation of U.S.-based programs determining that exchange programs reduced HIV transmission while also proving programs did not increase drug use (Des Jarlais, 2006). This type of proof arguably would be impossible to show with the resources provided at the time and subsequently began a chilling effect of the development of needle-exchange programs nationally.

The resistance to the development of these programs did more than stunt the implementation of needed policies. As known throughout state power literature, many classes of individuals disproportionately felt the brunt of more conservative power-oriented policies (Alexander, 2012; Massey, 2007; Rothe & Friedrichs, 2014; Soss, Fording, Schram, & Schram, 2011). The decision to slow the growth of these programs provided similar results to those directly affected by not having provided services. Estimates demonstrate that between 4,400 and 9,700 avoidable HIV infections occurred because of a lack of programming during the first few decades of debate. These numbers, although staggering, also do not demonstrate the overall number of realistic infections and fall short of explaining the overall cost, both economically and socially, of these infections on the intravenous drug–using population during this time (Heimer, 1998).

As with many other community-oriented programs fighting for relevance under the power of state policies, needle-exchange programs began functioning outside of traditional sanctioned channels. Following the 1998 amendment, needle-exchange programs divided into three major categories: legal, illegal but tolerated, and illegal underground (Sherman & Purchase, 2001). Legal programs operated in states where no law existed to ban the purchase of hypodermic syringes without a prescription. These programs were able to skirt particularly punitive regulations against those who used needles but struggled as little large-scale funding existed for the programs. The fact that many of these programs also needed to charge for their syringes exacerbated the issue of poverty already seen within the drug-usage community (Sherman & Purchase, 2001). Illegal but tolerated programs began appearing in states with laws demanding prescriptions to purchase syringes. However, because of differing political leanings and accounts of how to deal with the issue at hand, many of these states provided formal votes of support or some form of approval from elected officials to provide policies that allowed these programs to operate. Many of these programs were struggling and continue to struggle because of opposition by conservative voices within the federal government (Davidson, Lopez, & Kral, 2017; Sherman & Purchase, 2001).

The final category of needle-exchange programs were known as *illegal* or *underground*. These programs existed in states in which a prescription is mandated and little or no support comes from the elected officials. Because of the lack of support, these programs began to develop "underground" and provided supports for the community in areas where such programming faced vilification and became the brunt of the rhetoric claiming they were responsible for addiction (Sherman & Purchase, 2001). These underground programs began in the United States around 1986 as a way to undermine strict conservative ideologies of the state infiltrating much of society with regard to the control of a citizen's body. Like much of the early history of the creation of state control (Foucault, 2012), this new form of making citizen rights to ensure their own health illegal became an emerging means of widening the net (see Garland, 2001) on what constituted criminality. At this point, a shift began to target not only those who would use the syringes but also those would act in a capacity to provide them "paraphernalia." Despite this, legal exchanges began appearing across the country. Washington state opened the first exchange program in early 1988 (Des Jarlais 2006; Des Jarlais et al., 2006). The research following its creation set forth a final push leading to the endorsement of the U.S. National Commission on AIDS in 1991 (Des Jarlais, 2006). However, such endorsements did little to help the advancement of similar programs.

As discussed, as a part of state control and the complete admonishment of rhetoric beyond the War on Drugs, the government sought a means to limit access to these programs. This led to the creation of some very restrictive laws. Many of the earliest programs struggled to fully operate under the weight of these laws and subsequently provided little impact on the overall prevalence of HIV in their respective areas (Des Jarlais, 2006). The state found legal loopholes to restrict the location of these programs, the number of needles provided, and the number of needles a participant could exchange, and it forced programs toward extensive and costly entrance examinations requiring significant amounts of personal history and even physical examination (Des Jarlais, McKnight, & Milliken, 2004). These requirements became hardships for patients looking for support. The combination of the level of information collected and the close proximity of police stations to many of the programs led many of those seeking help to fear entering these facilities. Many individuals feared surveillance and subsequent harassment by the police. Despite the creation of some "safe zone" understandings between many facilities and law enforcement, many patients refused to take part (Cooper, Moore, & Gruskin, & Krieger, 2005). This, in turn, fueled the state rhetoric behind the usefulness of programs. By legally cutting funding and restricting these programs to the furthest extent it could, the state created a space in which it would be impossible for programs to succeed (Weinmeyer, 2016). This also supported the rhetoric still used today as a means of discrediting the use of such facilities nationally.

The mid- to late 1990s saw a pushback against such restrictive policies from both community and local governments. Many cities used the idea of "public health emergencies" as a means to override legislation targeting the support for the programs (Bluthenthal, 1998; Burris et al., 1996; Stoller, 1998). Resistance to oppressive policies created space for independently funded studies to combat the restrictive controls placed by the state on both funding and placement. A landmark study published in the *Journal of the American Medical Association* in 1994 by Watters et al., began a series of important research projects that would become the voice to combat the stereotypes, rhetoric, and misinformation used to starve specific programs (see Watters, Estilo, Clark, & Lorvick, 1994). This led to an academic back-and-forth between supporters and opponents on the merit of needle-exchange programs (see Alexander, 2012; Bruneau et al., 1997; National Institutes of Health, 1997; Normand, Vlahov, & Moses, 1995; Strathdee et al., 1997). Proponents used positive findings supported through government data, whereas those opposing the programs turned to mixed or ambiguous findings to argue their points. This, however, mostly fell on deaf ears because many state officials, including then-President Bill Clinton, refused to fully address these reports and refused to support programs through lifting of the ban previously discussed (Showalter, 2018). This led to continued service gaps through the early and mid-2000s, creating a large disparity in what independent regions could provide (Bluthenthal, et al., 2008; Guardino et al., 2010). Not until President

Barack Obama signed a compromise bill in 2009 would the ban be temporarily lifted (Showalter, 2018). However, this would be reversed again in a display of state power over the body and lives of civilians with regards to a new emerging surge for the War on Drugs by conservative politicians in 2011 (Showalter, 2018). This reinstatement as a part of a much larger conservative battle against the control of citizens' rights to health care (such as the attacks and subsequent defunding of the Affordable Care Act) falls directly in line with decades' worth of missing programming and support for the poor and communities of color to continually subvert their political power (see Garland, 2001; Karon, Fleming, Steketee, & De Cock, 2001; Massey, 2007).

▶ Needle-Exchange Programs Today

The history behind the tumultuous conflicts for the development of needle-exchange programs under state power did not end in the mid-2000s. Today, with rising abuse of opioids and heroin, the divisive rhetoric for the need of exchange programs is forcing forward. The country again is seeing large numbers of both HIV and hepatitis infections as well as an alarming number of overdoses as opioid addiction ravages large swaths of the country (Dart et al., 2015). Many of those suffering from addiction are making the transition from overprescribed opioids to illicit opioids. Despite being a complex issue, this is partly the result of continued efforts to restrict prescription opioids, structural changes in the heroin market, and the overall drop in street costs for heroin (Alpert, Powell, & Liccardo Pacula, 2017; Ciccarone, 2017; Compton, Jones, & Baldwin, 2016). In fact, drug overdoses involving opioid use took over as the leading cause of injury-related deaths in 2009 (Showalter, 2018). Scholars argue that this uptick in use, infection, and death is the result of continued state efforts to ban funding and to control particular populations nationally (Showalter, 2018; Young, 2017). Such control techniques fall in line with the pervading push to control the most vulnerable. This is demonstrated in the number of cases embedded in poverty-stricken rural areas (Cicero, Ellis, Surratt, & Kurtz, 2014; Quinones, 2015; Young, 2017). However, note the obvious difference in the state's response to this new call for needle-exchange programs. This, some argue, is the direct correlation in how the state determines the worthiness of those seeking help based on race, political worth, and other inequality-based ideals (see Young, 2017).

Particular state biases are clear when looking at the rhetoric and actual decisions made to support programs in particular demographic areas. One example would be the drastic shift that now Vice President Mike Pence made as governor of Indiana in 2015 to support particular exchange programs through the declaration of a "public health emergency" (Showalter, 2018). For decades, Pence vehemently attacked needle-exchange programs and voted on multiple occasions to support the funding ban before he became governor. This trend of conservative state officials supporting programs continued as the discussion focused more on the issue seen in predominantly white areas. CDC data showed that many of the vulnerable areas are located in Appalachia and the so-called Rust Belt (Van Handel et al., 2016) and provided cover for the state to shift political support toward partial programs (Showalter, 2018). As a result, many conservative-led states such as West Virginia, Kentucky, and Florida now allow needle-exchange programs (Auslen, 2016: Vincent, 2016; Watkins, 2017). Moreover, newly found support from conservative state legislators led to the final lifting of the federal ban as increasing numbers of constituents faced issues of overdose deaths and infection outbreaks (Castillo, 2016). Of important note, however, is that state control could not be fully relinquished. The lifting of the ban came with particular caveats allowing the state to determine how much funding would be provided, for what services, and in what areas (Weinmyer, 2016).

▶ Discussion

The preceding discussion of the development of needle-exchange programs demonstrates the struggle many programs face as a part of the states' search for further control of citizens. The process of legislative controls over the past few decades demonstrates the presence of the states' consistent pursuit of widening the net (see Garland, 2001) under the cover of zero-tolerance policies to ensure control over citizens' space and bodies (Foucault, 2012). It also demonstrates a long-established form of control that targets benefits and harm reduction–based programs that support vulnerable populations (Alexander, 2012; Massey, 2007; Young, 2017). In particular, the historical debate and current status of state support for needle-exchange programs demonstrates an obvious bias against particular communities of color, impoverished citizens, and members of other vulnerable communities who deal more with the issues surrounding the lack of support (see Beckett, Nyrop, & Pfingst, 2006; Davidson, Lopez, & Kral, 2017). Specifically, the historical spread of the AIDS epidemic and the resurgence of addiction and disease in predominantly white populations demonstrates the adjustment of policies seemingly because of of the political worth of particular populations. These particular biases of the state toward the implementation of particular programs help identify the overall uneven provision of programs nationally (see Showalter, 2018). Altogether, scholars continue to argue that the lack of support by both the federal and many state governments demonstrates an additional shackle in the chain of state control over vulnerable populations for the purpose of punishment and cultural distancing (Young, 2007). However, this back and forth of support is not over. With more punitive controls once again seen as favorable, many of the needle-exchange programs supported in rural areas are beginning to close (Katz, 2018). This removal marks an emerging or possibly reemerging designation of political usefulness for particular populations and further unwillingness to support harm-reduction programming. Altogether, the debate over the usefulness of needle-exchange programs will continue as opponents of the state push for better treatment, provision of valuable resources, and the overall demonstration of weakening of deeply rooted state controls in historically vulnerable populations.

▶ References

Alexander, M. (2012). *The new Jim Crow: Mass incarceration in the age of colorblindness.* New York, NY: The New Press.

Alpert, A., Powell, D., & Liccardo Pacula, R. (2017). *Supply-side drug policy in the presence of substitutes: Evidence from the introduction of abuse-deterrent opioids.* Cambridge, MA: National Bureau of Economic Research.

Auslen, M. (2016, March 23). Gov. Rick Scott signs needle exchange, rape kit bills into law. *Miami Herald.* Retrieved from https://www.miamiherald.com/news/local/community/miami-dade /article67779477.html

Beckett, K., Nyrop, K., & Pfingst, L. (2006). Race, drugs, and policing: Understanding disparities in drug delivery arrests. *Criminology, 44*(1), 105–137.

Bluthenthal, R.N. (1998). Syringe exchange as a social movement: A case study of harm reduction in Oakland, California. *Substance Use & Misuse, 33*(5), 1147–1171.

Bluthenthal, R. N., Heinzerling, K. G., Anderson, R., Flynn, N. M., & Kral, A. H. (2008). Approval of syringe exchange programs in California: Results from local approach to HIV prevention. *American Journal of Public Health, 98*(2), 278–283.

Bruneau, J., Lamothe, F., Franco, E., Lachance, N., Desy, M., Soto, J., & Vincelette, J. (1997). High rates of HIV infection among injection drug users participating in needle exchanges programs in Montreal: Results of a cohort study. *American Journal of Epidemiology, 146*(12), 994–1002.

Burris, S., Finucane, D., Gallagher, H., & Grace, J. (1996). The legal strategies used in operating syringe exchange programs in the United States. *American Journal of Public Health, 86*(8), 1161–1166.

Castillo, T. (2016, January 20). Congress lifts the ban on federal funding for syringe exchanges. *Huffington Post.* Retrieved from https://www.huffpost.com/entry/congress-lifts-the-ban-on_b_9032362

Centers for Disease Control and Prevention. (2016). Syringes services programs. Retrieved from https://www.cdc.gov/hiv/risk/ssps.html

Ciccarone, D. (2017). Fentanyl in the US heroin supply: A rapidly changing risk environment. *International Journal of Drug Policy, 46,* 107–111.

Cicero, T., Ellis, M., Surratt, H., & Kurtz, S. (2014). The changing face of heroin use in the United States: A retrospective analysis of the past 50 years. *JAMA Psychiatry, 71*(7), 821–826.

Compton, W. M., Jones, C. M., & Baldwin, G. T. (2016). Relationship between nonmedical prescription-opioid use and heroin use. *New England Journal of Medicine, 374*(2), 154–163.

Cook, C., & Kanaef, N. (2008). *The global state of harm reduction 2008: Mapping the response to drug-related HIV and Hepatitis C epidemics.* London, UK: International Harm Reduction Association.

Cooper, H., Moore, L., Gruskin, S., & Krieger, N. (2005). The impact of a police drug crackdown on drug injectors' ability to practice harm reduction: A qualitative study. *Social Science & Medicine, 61*(3), 673–684.

Dart, R., Surratt, H., Cicero, T., Parrino, M., Severtson, G. Bucher-Bartelson, B., & Green, L. (2015). Trends in opioid analgesic abuse and mortality in the United States. *New England Journal of Medicine, 372*(3), 241–248.

Davidson, P., Lopez, A., & Kral, A. (2017). Using drugs in un/safe spaces: Impact of perceived illegality on an underground supervised injecting facility in the United States. *International Journal of Drug Policy, 53,* 37–44.

Des Jarlais, D., (2006). Mathilde Krim, amfAR, and the prevention of HIV infection among injecting drug users: A brief history. *AIDS Patient Care and STDS, 20*(7), 467–471.

Des Jarlais, D., McKnight, C., Goldblatt, C., & Purchase, D. (2009). Doing harm reduction better: Syringe exchange in the United States. *Addiction, 104*(9), 1441–1446.

Des Jarlais, D., McKnight, C., & Milliken, J. (2004). Public funding of US syringe exchange programs. *Journal of Urban Health, 81*(1), 118–121.

Des Jarlais, D., Sloboda, Z., Friedman, S., Tempalski, B., McKnight, C., & Braine, N. (2006). Diffusion of D.A.R.E. and syringe exchange programs. *American Journal of Public Health, 96*(8), 1354–1358.

Foucault, M. (2012). *Discipline and punish: The birth of the prison.* New York, NY: Vintage Press.

Garland, D. (2001). *The culture of control.* Oxford, UK: Oxford University Press.

Guardino, V., Jarlais, D., Arasteh, K., Rothschild, B. E. de, Johnston, R., Purchase, D., Solberg, A., Lansky, A., & Lentine, D. (2010). Syringe exchange programs: United States, 2008. *Morbidity and Mortality Weekly Report, 59*(45), 1488–1491.

Hay, B., Henderson, C., Maltby, J., & Canales, J. (2017). Influence of peer-based needle exchange programs on mental health status in people who inject drugs: A nationwide New Zealand study. *Frontiers in Psychiatry, 7,* 211.

Karon, J. M., Fleming, P. L., Steketee, R. W., & De Cock, K. M. (2001). HIV in the United States at the turn of the century: An epidemic in transition. *American Journal of Public Health, 91*(7), 1060–1068.

Katz, J. (2018, April 27). Why a city at the center of the opioid crisis gave up a tool to fight it. *The New York Times.*

Klein, S., Karchner, W., & O'Connell, D. (2002). Interventions to prevent HIV-related stigma and discrimination: Findings and recommendations for public health practice. *Journal of Public Health Management and Practice, 8*(6), 44–53.

Lopez, G. (2018, January 5). Trump and Session's quiet success: Reinvigorating the federal war on drugs. *Vox.* Retrieved from https://www.vox.com/policy-and-politics/2018/1/5/16851120 /trump-sessions-war-on-drugs

Lynch, M. (2002). The culture of control: Crime and social order in contemporary society. *PoLAR: Political and Legal Anthropology Review, 25*(2), 109–112.

Massey, D. S. (2007). *Categorically unequal: The American stratification system.* New York, NY: Russell Sage Foundation.

Mathers, B., Degenhardt, L., Phillips, B., Wiessing, L., Hickman, M., Strathdee, S., Wodak, A., Panda, S., Tyndall, M., Toufik, A., & Mattick, R. (2008). Global epidemiology of injecting drug use and HIV among people who inject drugs: A systematic review. *The Lancet, 372*(9651), 1733–1745.

National Institutes of Health (1997). Interventions to prevent HIV risk behaviors. *NIH Consensus Statement, 15*(2), 1–41.

Normand, J., Vlahov, D., & Moses, L. (Eds.). (1995). *Preventing HIV transmission: The role of sterile needles and bleach.* Washington, DC: National Academy Press.

Quinones, S. (2015). *Dreamland: The true tale of America's opiate epidemic.* New York, NY: Bloomsbury Press.

Rothe, D., & Friedrichs, D. O. (2014). *Crimes of globalization.* New York, NY: Routledge Press.

Sherman, S. & Purchase, D. (2001). Point defiance: A case study of the United States' first public needle exchange in Tacoma, Washington. *International Journal of Drug Policy, 12*(1), 45–57.

Shoemaker, P. J. (2012). *Communication campaigns about drugs: Government, media, and the public.* New York, NY: Routledge Press.

Showalter, D. (2018). Federal funding for syringe exchange in the US: Explaining a long-term policy failure. *International Journal of Drug Policy, 55,* 95–104.

Simon, J. (2007). *Governing through crime: How the war on crime transformed American democracy and created a culture of fear.* Oxford, UK: Oxford University Press.

Soss, J., Fording, R. C., Schram, S. F., & Schram, S. (2011). *Disciplining the poor: Neoliberal paternalism and the persistent power of race.* Chicago, IL: University of Chicago Press.

Stoller, N. (1998). *Lessons from the damned: Queers, whores, and junkies respond to aids.* New York, NY: Routledge.

Strathdee, S. A., Patrick, D. M., Currie, S. L., Cornelisse, P. G. A., Rekart, M. L., Montaner, J. S. G., Schechter, M., & O'Shaughnessy, M. (1997). Needle exchange is not enough: Lessons from the Vancouver injecting drug use study. *AIDS,* F59–F65.

Van Handel, M., Rose, M., Hallisey, E., Kolling, J., Zibbell, J., Lewis, B., Bohm, M., Jones, C., Flanagan, B., Siddiqi, A., Iqbal, K., Dent, A., Mermin, J., McCray, E., Ward, J., & Brooks, J. (2016). County-level vulnerability assessment for rapid dissemination of HIV or HCV infections among persons who inject drugs, United States. *Journal of Acquired Immune Deficiency Syndromes, 73*(3), 323–331.

Vincent, J. (2016, July 8). West Virginia has four needle exchanges: Are they working? *We Heart WV.* Retrieved from http://weheartwv.com/2016/07/08/west-virginia-needle-exchanges-are -they-working/

Watkins, M. (2017, January 24). Needle exchanges spread in heroin-riddled KY. Courier Journal [KY]. Retrieved from https://www.courier-journal.com/story/news/politics/2017/01/24/needle -exchanges-start-spread-ky/90485098/

Watters, J. K., Estilo, M. J., Clark, G. L., & Lorvick, J. (1994). Syringe and needle exchange as HIV/ AIDS prevention for injection drug users. *Journal of the American Medical Association, 271*(2), 115–120.

Weinmyer, R. (2016). Needle exchange programs' status in US politics. *American Medical Association Journal of Ethics, 18*(30), 252–257.

Young, J. (2007). *The vertigo of late modernity.* Thousand Oaks, CA: Sage Publications.

Young, S. T. (2017). Wild, wonderful, white criminality: Images of "white trash" Appalachia. *Critical Criminology, 25*(1), 103–117.

SECTION 4

Ethics and Law Enforcement

ARTICLE 14

Policing and Ethics: Controversies of Force, Culture, and Society

David R. Champion

▶ Policing and Ethics: A Brief Discussion of Hot Points

Police in the United States currently face an onslaught of scrutiny. Although the Internet and social media have certainly contributed to this through near-instantaneous transmission of videos depicting on-duty law enforcement activities, contemporary cultural factors have also sharpened the focus on police behavior. One of the most contentious issues in contemporary U.S. culture is the use of police force, despite findings that police use of force is relatively rare and its applications usually minimal (National Institute of Justice, 2016). Goldstein's (1977) description of the central conflict that faces police officers in their role as line-level agents of social control in a free society continues to resonate today. Police are armed literally and figuratively with the powers to exert coercive authority on all citizens, who are provisioned with constitutional protections and an assumption of liberty of action (Bittner, 1970; Sherman, 1980). As Sherman (1981) notes, criminal justice professionals hold an unusual role in society in that a fundamental aspect of their function is to force people to do things they do not want to do (as cited in Braswell, McCarthy, & McCarthy, 2015). As Crank (2004) asserts, police identity draws heavily from the use of force and violence of action. Officer force, as a polarizing and conflicting dynamic, clearly demonstrates the dilemma imposed on officers by a mercurial and divided public: Society often demands a police force to quell violence and disorder in the name of the overall protection of the community. At the same time, actual demonstrations of raw force disseminated in the public sphere often invoke revulsion or outrage, regardless of whether the display is legally justified or not. The coercive powers of police, ultimately founded on the potential of physical force, clearly distinguish police from other social control agents (Bittner 1970; Sherman 1980).

Patrol officers are the most visible symbol of this coercive authority. They are highly visible in the community, making regular contact with citizens, and are equipped with firearms, handcuffs, and other gear that provides a constant visual reminder of their role. The coercive function is usually beneath the surface of an encounter, but it is an undercurrent in any police–citizen contact ranging from pleasant consensual (even conversational) encounters to arrest or use-of-force situations. It may well be the mere *potential* of coercive force that divides the citizens from the officer and fuels alienation between the two. At the same time, this authority is necessary for police to effectively investigate and apprehend offenders and accomplish their mission of maintaining collective safety. As Braswell, McCarthy and McCarthy (2015) suggest, this inherently coercive function constitutes a major goal of ethical instruction for law enforcement officers. Further, recognition of this tension is a fundamental aspect of ethical inquiry for criminal justice students and scholars.

▶ Force, Coercion, and Power: Just and Unjust

Numerous scholars have focused on this basic police power of employing state-sanctioned force (Bittner, 1970; Crank, 2004; Goldstein, 1977; and Sherman, 1980, 1981, among many others). As Sherman (1980) asserts, it is this capability to wield physical coercion coupled with the wide range of latitude afforded to police as discretionary powers that may foster officer misconduct.

Current policing controversies often center on racial disparities in the use of police force—particularly lethal force—on suspects. As is often the case, the cultural narrative tends to oversimplify and obfuscate the complexity of the issue. Fryer (2016) reports that even though police use of force on minorities tends to be higher at less-than-lethal levels of force regardless of situational variables, he found little racial difference in the use of deadly force. Others have suggested that police may tend to operate from an implicit rather than an explicit bias in use of force decision making, where the racial disparity in force tends to disappear in high crime neighborhoods (Fridell & Lim, 2016). As scholars continue to examine the issue, it has become apparent that the simplistic narrative of the overtly racist police officer has been become a part of the cultural lore and has emerged as a powerful theme in popular culture. Such cultural distortion fuels the distrust between police and the citizenry.

Although the issue of racially biased law enforcement rightfully demands public and scholarly attention, it should not override other legitimate concerns that have arisen in regard to police conduct. Several studies (Johnson, 1991; Johnson, Todd, & Subramanian, 2005; Neidig, Seng, & Russell, 1992; Zavala, 2013) report disturbingly high prevalence of intimate partner and family violence (including both physical and verbal abuse) perpetrated by police officers, with one author reporting as high as 40% prevalence among officers as offenders (Johnson et al., 2005). Although such off-duty criminal violence against innocent victims would seem to be at least as disturbing as on-duty excessive use of force against suspects, this issue does not receive near the social attention as the latter perhaps because of the private (as opposed to public) nature of the acts. It may also be speculated that, unlike on-duty force (righteously employed or not), videos of private police family violence are not widely disseminated in the media or Internet. In much the same way that the 2014 incident involving then-NFL player Ray Rice assaulting his fiancée did not gain social traction until a video of the event was publicly posted on an entertainment news website, perhaps the current popular culture does not ascribe truth or meaning to an event short of prominent video evidence (TMZ Sports, 2014).

The role of social media and widespread dissemination of videos depicting various police–citizen interactions provide a steady supply of fodder for both pro- and antipolice ideologues, or the so-called YouTube effect (Singh, 2017). These videos are often shared without context or edited to conform to some bias of the channel or website owner. Viewers and commentators to these videos are often ignorant of the use of force continuum and police training protocols in the face of violent resistance, and misguided outrage often ensues. In such an open forum for videos that often appear to be inflammatory, it is predictable that the public frequently gets it wrong when condemning police use of force. Police use of force against violent suspects often looks bad even if it is legitimate, especially to those with little knowledge of law enforcement training or legal deployment of police force.

However, to lament that YouTube and other public forms of recorded police actions serves only to unfairly undermine good-faith police actions would also be wrong. Public recording of police actions—or, as Singh puts it, "anticipatory citizen surveillance of police" (2017, p. 676)—has also shed light on police brutality or criminality that might otherwise have gone undetected. These examples include the 2015 murder of North Carolina citizen Walter Scott by Officer Michael Slager (Trendy Galaxy, 2015), the brutal 2007 assault of a barmaid by off-duty Chicago police officer Anthony Abbate (BadCase, 2007), and the disturbing incident involving Los Angeles Police Department (LAPD) officers David Shin and Jinseok Oh that left Kim Nguyen with a shattered jaw and missing teeth after "falling" from a speeding patrol vehicle ("Kim Nguyen latest victim," 2014). Agency responses to these incidents varied. Slager was arrested and convicted of murder and sentenced to 20 years (Vann & Ortiz, 2017). Abbate was eventually fired and subsequently charged with and convicted of felony battery. A jury also found the Chicago Police Department of attempting to cover up the incident and awarded the victim $850,000 (Sweeney & Meisner, 2012). The LAPD reportedly delayed an internal investigation until Nguyen filed a civil lawsuit, for which she was eventually awarded $3.5 million, although the details of the incident remain unclear ("Kim Nguyen," 2014; Rocha, 2017). In the latter two cases, the institutional reluctance to address allegations of serious criminal actions on the part of the officers may be of even greater concern than the actions of the individual officers. The latter may be rationalized as the occasional rotten apple, but the former depicts a darker scenario of organized suppression of wrongdoing by police leadership.

Of course, the study of policing and ethics extends beyond the issue of force or violence among police (whether these are on- or off-duty, legitimate or criminal). Colorfully termed concepts such as the *Dirty Harry syndrome* (Klockars, 1980) and *noble cause corruption* (Delattre, 2011), the *Blue Wall*, the *Blue Flu*, and *testilying* all relate (in one way or another) to a less than ideal picture of police conduct. The 1970 Kefauver Commission coined the terms *meat eaters* and *grass eaters* to describe organized rather than freelance corruption among New York City Police Department (NYPD) officers (Armstrong, 2012). Among the meat eaters, officers were acting in a manner similar to organized crime operations. Systemized extortion of drug dealers, theft rings, bribery, and other crimes became full-time occupations of on-duty officers. Among the grass eaters, situational graft was described as the "swamp of low-level corruption" that bred more serious police crimes (Armstrong, 2012, Preface, para. 4).

▶ Ethical Theory and Practice

Officers often tend to approach challenges from a utilitarian perspective. This utilitarian approach may operate from both a general societal level (as Klockars describes) or in specific situations such as use-of-force decisions (Fryer, 2016). In an empirical analysis of racial disparities in officer use of force, Fryer posits a model in which police tend to act as "utility maximizers," (abstract, para. 1)—that is, both biased and unbiased officers may use force on suspects depending on the "payoff" (p. 27) they get (e.g., compliance). However, racially biased officers gain emotional reinforcement in inflicting less-than-lethal force on Black suspects, irrespective of the suspects' compliance. Fryer noted that this racial disparity was found to disappear at the lethal force level, however, indicating that the gravity of the consequences for using deadly force on a citizen offset whatever benefit racially biased officers gained.

Klockars's (1980) analyzes a dilemma faced by the 1971 movie character *Dirty Harry*, who uses illicit means, including grinding his heel into the killer's wounded leg, to attempt to save a kidnapped girl. Klockars thus frames a compelling and persistent dilemma for law enforcers: how to deal with a problem in which one is pursuing an end that is undeniably good, but only an illegal ("dirty") method will work to achieve that end. Delattre (1989, and as cited in van Halderen and Koltoff, 2016) later introduced the term *noble cause corruption* to present the question of police breaking minor basic laws to benefit the security of the community.

Both of these represent an essentially utilitarian posture, although the former example includes an illicit (racist) self-serving gain, whereas the Dirty Harry and noble cause corruption dilemmas deal with the question of using illicit means for the greater good without personal benefit.

Police utilitarianism emerges as a central theme in criminal justice ethics discussion, in part because certain aspects of the job could not be accomplished through strict adherence to deontology, duty, or virtue-based ethical systems. Undercover work, interrogation, and the use of confidential informants are only three examples in which police deception is routine and lawful, but they are permitted only when the greater good is the ultimate deciding factor as to an action's moral worth.

However, not all controversies associated with policing are a struggle between questionable means and consequences. To begin with, not all "good" outcomes are "unquestionable and compelling" (Klockars, 1980, p. 43) once all ramifications play out. For example, consider the police practice of *testilying*. This term originated with NYPD officers and refers to police officer perjury and other forms of in-court deception (Cunningham, 1999). In my ethics capstone course, I generally start the first day of class with a hypothetical scenario. I set up the scene with each student in the role of a detective who arrested some heinous criminal (usually some kind of serial killer, sex offender, or child molester). However, through some kind of unspecified glitch (not the detective's fault), key evidence against the suspect has been excluded and will not make it to trial. The student detective is morally certain of the suspect's guilt. The prosecutor does not believe that she can make the case without the excluded evidence. But if the detective were to testify that the suspect made a spontaneous statement confessing to his crimes on arrest, she can surely convict him. However, the suspect never made any such statement, spontaneous or otherwise.

I then put it to the students: Would they testilie to convict a vicious criminal who will no doubt go out and harm more people if he were to be released? Or would they adhere to their sworn duty to testify truthfully?

Although class responses tend to vary, we generally end up in a discussion about how the "good" outcome of a perjury-based conviction may ultimately turn out to be even more socially harmful than an acquittal. If caught, the disgraced detective not only faces job loss and criminal prosecution but also all of his or her testimony in prior cases will be questioned and could lead to new trials and possible release of multiple (righteously) convicted criminals. More broadly, the publicity surrounding such an event would serve to undercut any trust between the police and the public, thereby making future law enforcement efforts even more difficult. It is interesting to note that several students often change their votes from truthful testimony to testilying if I add the qualifier that their perjury would never be discovered in this scenario. Thus, they begin to see that the problem with consequentialist ethical systems is that one cannot always determine which outcome is unquestionably good.

▶ Police Militarization

Another issue of controversy is the "militarization" of police (Doherty, 2016; Lawson, 2018) and the development of a warrior mentality among officers (Kraska, 2007). Later versions of the 1990 National Defense Authorization Act (specifically, the 1033 program) provided for the transfer of military equipment and weapons to federal, state, and later local law enforcement agencies (Fox, Moule & Parry, 2018). However, as Kraska (2007) points out, the militarization model not only refers to gear and weaponry but also to organizational, operational, and cultural dimensions. Although some supporters assert that the militarized model may provide societal benefits in terms of deterrence and reduction of street crime (Bove & Gavrilova, 2017), there is some evidence to indicate that the majority of the public tends to distrust this trend (Mummolo, 2018; Fox, Moule & Parry, 2018). In a national study, Lawson (2018) reports evidence of a positive correlation between militarized police departments and lethal shootings of suspects, not necessarily as a result of the acquisition of military equipment but more as the development of a warlike culture in the departments. This phenomenon is reflected in the "thin blue line" perception of police officers as frontline troops defending law-abiding society from the vicious criminals who would otherwise impose destruction and chaos. Sparked by high profile instances of quasi-military force applied by law enforcement agencies, including the 1993 Waco siege incident, the warrior model has earned bipartisan political condemnation in U.S. society (Ristroph, 2018). Here again, Goldstein's (1977) description of the fundamental problem with on-duty officers resonates—that is, the powerfully authorized agent of state control tasked with the powers to detain, investigate, and use force on its citizens to provide collective safety. And now, as previously discussed, their actions are often recorded for later dissection and analysis, not only by supervisors and lawyers but also often by the public at large through widespread social media dissemination.

▶ Discussion

Police officers are, of course, individuals with their own specific backgrounds, experiences, and moral postures. Any discussion of general tendencies of a collective is intellectually risky, and to draw sweeping conclusions about how individual police officers will make ethical decisions is specious. Still, it is instructive to examine contemporary issues through the lenses of classical ethical theories and to commit to increased ethical training for law enforcement officers at the local, state, and federal level.

This work discussed only a few contemporary issues from an ethical perspective, and, of course, volumes may be written (and have been written) on the intersection of ethical systems, law, morality, justice, and enforcement. At some point, however, the discussion ultimately centers on police powers of coercion and authority and all that may spin off to, including entitlement-driven grass eaters, organized systemic meat eaters, testilying, illegal use of lethal force, racially biased policing, off-duty domestic violence, and other criminal assaults. The essential utilitarian dilemma posed by Klockars (1980) is, in a sense, the same problem posed by Goldstein (1977): At what point does the execution of police power convert from righteous to malevolent? Does the law determine such a bright line indicator, or are there more universal moral principles that should determine it? Some elements, such as a warrior mentality and the use of force, have legitimate applications in the appropriate situations. Others such as assault of defenseless and compliant citizens, sexual assault of suspects, and organized corruption are purely criminal activities with no connection to their duties.

Practicing ethical dilemmas in the classroom (in the academy and the university) may serve to familiarize potential law enforcement officers with the types of challenges they may face in the field. This extends to the temptation to generalize their on-duty authority to off-duty conduct, the source of police criminality in the form of domestic violence and other assaults. There is a mantra in the U.S. Army espousing the principle of "tough, realistic training" based on U.S. Army Field Manual 25-100, *Training the Force* (U.S. Army, 1988). The idea is to challenge troops with as realistic and stressful training scenarios as may be reasonably offered in a training environment. Of course, this principle applied to combat arms training for soldiers. Perhaps the classrooms of both police academies and university criminal justice courses may be the environment for such exercises, offering role play scenarios with realistic ethical stressors. Role-playing through true ethical dilemmas (situations with no good solution, as Klockars, 1980, notes) could provide a wrench or two for the ethical toolbox that all officers should carry.

Contemporary law enforcement faces numerous challenges, including a citizenry that is running a type of countersurveillance on police public actions

(Singh, 2017). Although this new transparency can spotlight true police abuses and crimes, it may also present proper actions out of context at the cost of careers and public funds when paid out in lawsuits. Like police discretion itself, this recent development is a double-edged sword that can cut either for or against the interests of justice. Officers who flout conventional morality and law (and the leadership that backs them through deception and cover-up) serve only to put all police at risk.

▶ References

Armstrong, M. F. (2012). *They wished they were honest: The Knapp Commission and New York City police corruption*. New York, NY: Columbia University Press.

BadCase (2007, September 26). *Chicago police officer Anthony Abbate attacks bartender Karolina Obrycka* [Video file]. Retrieved from https://youtu.be/49kgGOs7lvk

Bittner, E. (1970). *The functions of police in modern society*. Chevy Chase, MD: National Institute of Mental Health, Center for Studies of Crime and Delinquency. Retrieved from https://www.ncjrs.gov/pdffiles1/Digitization/147822NCJRS.pdf

Bove, V., Gavrilova, E. (2017). Police officer on the front line or soldier? The effect of police militarization on crime. *American Economic Journal: Economic Policy, 9* (3), 1–18. Retrieved from https://doi.org/10.1257/pol.20150478

Braswell, M. C., McCarthy, B. R. & McCarthy, B. J. (2015). *Justice, crime and ethics* (8th ed.). Cincinnati, OH: Anderson-Lexis Nexis.

Crank, J. P. (2004). *Understanding police culture*. Cincinnati, OH: Anderson Publishing.

Cunningham, L. (1999). Taking on testifying: The prosecutor's response to in-court police deception. *Criminal Justice Ethics, 18*(1), 26–40.

Delattre, E. J. (1989). *Character and cops: Ethics in policing*. Washington, DC: AEI Press.

Delattre, E. J. (2011). *Character and cops: Ethics in policing* (6th ed.). Washington, DC: AEI Press.

Doherty, J. B. (2016). Us vs. them: The militarization of American law enforcement and the psychological effect on police officers and civilians. *Southern California Interdisciplinary Law Journal, 25*, 1–51. Retrieved from http://gould.usc.edu/students/journals/ilj/

Fox, B., Moule, R. & Parry, M. (2018). Categorically complex: A latent class analysis of public perceptions of police militarization. *Journal of Criminal Justice, 58*(3), 33–46. Retrieved from https://doi.org/10.1016/j.crimjus.2018.07.002

Fridell, L., & Lim, H. (2016). Assessing the racial aspects of police force using the implicit- and counter-bias perspectives. *Journal of Criminal Justice, 44*, 36–48. doi: http://dx.doi.org/10.1016/j.jcrimjus.2015.12.001

Fryer, R. G., Jr. (2016). An empirical analysis of racial differences ins police use of force. Working paper 22399. *National Bureau of Economic Research*. Retrieved from http://www.nber.org/papers/w22399

Goldstein, H. (1977). *Policing a free society*. Cambridge, MA: Ballinger Publishing.

Johnson, L. B. (1991, May 20). On the front lines: Police stress and family wellbeing. Hearing Before the Select Committee on Children, Youth, and Families House of Representatives, 102nd Congress, pp. 32–48. Washington, DC: U.S. Government Printing Office.

Johnson, L.B., Todd, M. & Subramanian, G. (2005). Violence in police families: Work-family spillover. *Journal of Family Violence, 20*, 3–12. doi: 10.1007/s10896-005-1504-4

Kim Nguyen latest victim of LAPD's Olympic division (2014, March 1). Korean Town LA News. Retrieved from https://koreatownlanews.com/kim-nguyen-latest-victim-of-lapd-olympic-division/

Klockars, C. B. (1980, November). The Dirty Harry problem. *Annals of the American Academy of Political and Social Science, 452*, 33–47.

Kraska, P. B. (2007). Militarization and policing—Its relevance to 21st century police. *Policing*, 501–513. Retrieved from https://cjmasters.eku.edu/sites/cjmasters.eku.edu/files/21stmilitarization.pdf

Lawson, E., Jr. (2018). Police militarization and the use of lethal force. *Political Research Quarterly, 52*(1), 1–13. doi: 10.1177/1065912918784209

Mummolo, J. (2018). Militarization fails to enhance police safety or reduce crime but may harm police reputation. *Proceedings of the National Academy of Sciences of the United States of America, 115*(37), 9181–9186. doi: 10.1073/pnas.1805161115

National Institute of Justice. (2016). Police use of force. Washington, DC: U.S. Department of Justice. Retrieved from https://www.nij.gov/topics/law-enforcement/officer-safety/use-of-force/Pages/welcome.aspx

Neidig, P. H, Seng, A. F., & Russell, H. E. (1992). Interspousal aggression in law enforcement personnel attending the FOP biennial conference. *National FOP Journal*, 25–28.

Ristroph, A. (2018). The Thin Blue Line from crime to punishment. *Journal of Criminal Law and Criminology, 108*, 305–334. Retrieved from: https://scholarlycommons.law.northwestern.edu/jclc/vol108/iss2/

Rocha, V. (2017, February 9). Los Angeles to pay $3.5 million to settle lawsuit filed by woman who fell from LAPD cruiser. *Los Angeles Times*. Retrieved from http://www.latimes.com/local/lanow/la-me-ln-35-million-settlement-lapd-20170209-story.html

Sherman, L. W. (1980). Perspectives on police and violence. *Annals of the American Academy of Political and Social Science, 452*, 1–12. Retrieved from https://journals.sagepub.com/doi/abs/10.1177/000271628045200101

Sherman, L. W. (1981). *The study of ethics in criminology and criminal justice*. Chicago, IL: Joint Commission on Criminology and Criminal Justice Education and Standards.

Singh, A. (2017). Prolepticon: Anticipatory citizen surveillance and police. *Surveillance & Society, 15*, 676–688. Retrieved from https://ojs.library.queensu.ca/index.php/surveillance-and-society/issue/view/Open

Sweeney, A. & Meisner, J. (2012, November 12). Jury finds in favor of bartender in cop bar beating case, "Justice was served." *Chicago Tribune*. Retrieved from http://www.chicagotribune.com/news/ct-xpm-2012-11-14-chi-verdict-reached-in-cop-bar-beating-case-20121113-story.html

TMZ Sports (Producer). (2014, September 8). Ray Rice elevator knockout [Video file]. Retrieved from https://www.tmz.com/2014/09/08/ray-rice-elevator-knockout-fiancee-takes-crushing-punch-video/

Trendy Galaxy. (2015, April 8). Dash cam shows moments before shooting of Walter Scott [Video file]. Retrieved from https://youtu.be/MYaYdaFFLoQ

U.S. Army. (1988). *FM 25–100: Training the force*. Retrieved from https://www.globalsecurity.org/military/library/policy/army/fm/25-100/index.html

van Halderen, R. C., & Kolthoff, E. (2016). Noble cause corruption revisited: Toward a structured research approach. *Public Integrity, 19*, 274–293. doi: 10.1080/10999922.2016.1230689

Vann, M., & Ortiz, E. (2017, December 7). Walter Scott shooting: Michael Slager, ex-officer, sentenced to 20 years in prison. NBC News. Retrieved from shooting/walter-scott-shooting-michael-slager-ex-officer-sentenced-20-years-n825006

Zavala, E. (2013). Testing the link between child maltreatment and family violence among police officers. *Crime and Delinquency, 59*, 468–483. Retrieved from https://journals.sagepub.com/doi/abs/10.1177/0011128710389584

Should Big Brother Be Watching? Ethical Concerns of Police Body Cams

Veronyka James

▶ Introduction

As result of many high-profile police-involved shootings occurring across the country, there has been a call for increased police accountability and transparency. After the events in Ferguson, Missouri, where White officer Darren Wilson shot and killed Michael Brown, an unarmed 18-year-old Black male, many called for further accountability for police officers and their use of force, particularly deadly force. Even though many police departments are equipped with dashboard cameras (dash cams), there was a call to have increased accountability and transparency through the use of body-worn cameras (BWCs) (Adams & Mastracci, 2017; Freund, 2016; Novak, Cordner, Smith, & Roberg. 2017). Many promote the use of BWCs as a way to increase the accountability and transparency of police departments and their officers' actions, as well as a way to increase the public's satisfaction with police–citizen interactions and build the legitimacy of police departments (Adams & Mastracci, 2017). "Body-worn cameras have received positive appraisal from the NAACP Legal Defense & Education Fund and the American Civil Liberties Union (ACLU)" (Mateescu, Rosenblat, & Boyd, 2015, p. 1). In addition, BWCs are thought not only to work in the favor of citizens (e.g., capturing misuse of police authority and holding police accountable for their actions) but also to work in favor of police officers (e.g., shielding them from false claims of abuse of power) (Freund, 2016; Mateescu et al., 2015).

Body-worn cameras are a new technological advancement whereby police officers wear a small camera somewhere on their person (e.g., head, shoulder, glasses, chest) to record their interactions with citizens during the course of their duties (Adams & Mastracci, 2017; Mateescu et al., 2015). These recordings are "stored for varying amounts of time, generally dictated by a mixture of law, policy, and subjective sense of the importance of the video" (Adams & Mastracci, 2017, p. 313). These are often not stored by police departments themselves but rather in "the cloud," an Internet-based "facility" offered by manufacturers of specific BWCs or other third-party services. Because of the recent high-profile cases (e.g., Ferguson), these have are being adopted rapidly and hastily by departments without fully investigating the ethical implications of this new technology and with research often occurring in a post hoc manner (Adams & Mastracci, 2017).

Unanswered questions remain regarding the implementation of BWCs and their implications even though these have the ability to enhance interactions between the police and the public (Adams & Mastracci, 2017; Freund, 2016; Novak et al., 2017). BWCs are a relatively new technology within departments, and there has been a slow rate of evaluation by researchers, which allows questions to remain unanswered about how best to use and not abuse this technology. In addition, because BWCs are a new technology, the long-term impact of their use is not fully known (Adams & Mastracci, 2017; Mateescu et al., 2015). Although more than one-third of police departments in the United States have implemented the use of BWCs, "evidence of BWC effectiveness is mixed" (Adams & Mastracci, 2017, p. 315). Although early reports suggest that BWCs do decrease use-of-force incidents and decrease citizen complaints, these claims are "still largely untested from a rigorous scientific standpoint" (Novak et al., 2017, p. 352). Other studies suggest there is either no effect on police use of force or that these actually increase police use of force (Adams & Mastracci, 2017). In addition to mixed results on whether BWCs accomplish what they are meant to (i.e., decreased use of force and increased citizen satisfaction with the police), there still remain questions regarding privacy rights of citizens and police officers and policy and implementation issues. These ethical considerations of using BWCs remain to be addressed. The following will examine some of the ethical considerations of the implementation of BWCs with police departments.

▶ Privacy of Citizens

One issue of concern with the implementation of BWCs is privacy, particularly privacy rights of citizens when they are captured on video during interactions with police. With many departments, because BWCs are new, there are ambiguities with best practices for their use as well as minimal policies regarding their use (Mateescu et al., 2015). Although many departments do have formal policies on certain usage issues (e.g., how long to retain footage), many departments have no clear policies for when the cameras need to be shut off, how best to disseminate footage, or how to address privacy concerns (Butt, 2018; Freund, 2016; Mateescu et al., 2015). Generally, when people interact with police, they are doing so when it is not their best day (e.g., they have been victimized, they are being arrested). As a result, they will be captured on camera at these times, particularly because body-worn cameras are harder for the public to avoid and are more easily able to access private spaces

(Freund, 2016). There are issues with who has access to this footage and how, when, or if this footage should be widely disseminated. What happens if someone who is a victim of domestic violence is captured by a BWC through his or her contact with police and that footage is then posted on social media? What if the victim never disclosed his or her victimization to others? Should this footage be released at all? What about footage of an offender that is released? What happens if the footage of his or her arrest is released on social media and results in the loss of job? What happens if the release of this footage embarrasses or otherwise harms participants captured on camera (Freund, 2016)?

What about police informants or witnesses captured on camera cooperating with police? If this footage is released to the public, this could place these individuals in danger (Freund, 2016). It is not outside the realm of possibility that body-camera footage could be released to the public even if there is no content of public importance (e.g., police misconduct) because "footage from dash cameras has been inadvertently released to the public and spread on the Internet" (Freund, 2016, p. 100). This footage could damage individuals' reputations or place them in danger by its release (Freund, 2016). Policies implemented by departments need to effectively address these issues as well as address who has access to the footage obtained and how this footage will be disseminated to others (both within and without the criminal justice system) (Mateescu et al., 2015).

In addition to the release of BWC footage and the privacy concerns that accompany this, there are other ethical considerations for those within criminal justice and their use of footage obtained from BWCs. Should defense attorneys or prosecutors negotiate pretrial settlements by using this footage? Should it be used as a basis to offer plea bargains or influence the type of pleas offered (Mateescu et al., 2015)? In addition to policies implemented by police departments regarding privacy concerns associated with BWC footage, there need to be policies set forth by court officials on how to use footage obtained by BWCs to make sure citizens' rights and privacy are retained.

Privacy concerns are not limited to victims and offenders, however. If officers respond to a call for service with BWCs recording footage, then innocent bystanders might also be part of the footage. They might not have any indication of being a part of the incident and were not involved with the police-involved incident but were captured on video. These individuals may not want the footage released for a variety of reasons, and their privacy should be protected as well, particularly because they were not participants in the incident. Policies should take into consideration the fact that these individuals also have privacy rights that need protection.

Victim Issues

Complicating the issue of privacy rights in general is the concern about the impact BWCs might have on victims, both directly and with their right to privacy. This is of particular concern for certain victims (e.g., sexual assault victims, children, undocumented victims), and it "is currently undertheorized and entirely unexamined" (Adams & Mastracci, 2017, p. 316). Victims who are already distressed, traumatized, and feeling vulnerable might find this exacerbated by the presence of BWCs recording them in this state (Adams & Mastracci, 2017).

Research has already shown that there is consistently low reporting to law enforcement and other official agencies by victims of sexual assault (Menard, 2005; Planty, Langton, Krebs, Berzofsky, & Smiley-McDonald, 2013). If officers are wearing BWCs, this may exacerbate this lack of reporting. Victims may fear they will experience secondary victimization as a result of this recording if it is shared with employers or probation or parole officers. The embarrassing nature of the victimization and intimate details recounted to officers may raise fears that these would be shared via social media and that it could be used to discredit their account of events (Adams & Mastracci, 2017). If victims are already concerned about reporting and the possibility of not being believed by the criminal justice system, they may fear the footage will be available through social media to friends, family, coworkers, and strangers and thus avoid reporting an assault at all.

Another concern for victims of sexual assault is the legal issue of the BWC recording. There is now a video record of the report by the victim, which could be used within a court of law if the case proceeds that far. The suspect who assaulted the victim could view this video during legal proceedings. In addition, "BWCs record victims in the exact circumstances that are most likely to produce evidence that could harm the victim's interests, especially in court" (Adams & Mastracci, 2017, p. 318). These initial interviews captured by BWCs are under less-than-ideal circumstances that could dissuade a jury (i.e., victim has a difficult personality) (Adams & Mastracci, 2017). During the initial report, a traumatized victim could display memory inconsistencies and perceptual distortion, which could make her or him appear less than reliable in a court of law. "When a defense attorney plays that video and highlights any inconsistency between her initial report and [a later interview], the victim will look like she's lying" (Adams & Mastracci, 2017, p. 319).

The use of BWCs also may breach victims' rights to confidentiality. BWCs can record and then expose the conversations victims have with victim advocates and medical staff to the perpetrator and others (if viewed as part of the legal process or disseminated inappropriately—that is, leaked). "BWC footage, distributed through the legal discovery process, exposes the victim to a higher risk of retaliation" (Adams & Mastracci, 2017, p. 323) and also increases the victim's risk of coercion and intimidation.

▶ Privacy of Police

In addition to the privacy concerns of citizens being captured on film when interacting with the police, there are additional concerns for the privacy of police officers. There is a limited expectation of privacy when interacting with the public, particularly in the current age when many people have cameras on them at all times in the form of cell phones. However, there is an increased expectation of privacy when police retire to the station (either during the course of their shift or at the end of their shift) and when police go home. Yet, depending on the type of camera and the policy of the particular department, officers might now have no privacy during the course of their shift because every moment could (and may) be recorded. Some have argued that the distinction of when an officer should be recorded should depend on where the officer is (e.g., in the public they should be recorded) (Freund, 2016). However, there are certain times, even "on the clock," when it might be more prudent to not record interactions (e.g., communicating with informants) to protect both the safety of officers and those being recorded.

Not only is there the issue of privacy, but these recordings could also be used by supervisors to monitor police officers (Freund, 2016). Supervisors could monitor recordings to see if officers are engaging in any "unwanted" behaviors, whether misconduct or not (e.g., engaging in union activities) (Freund, 2016; Mateescu et al., 2015). "An officer who had displeased his superiors for other reasons [besides misconduct] might be subjected to a thorough review of his footage in retaliation" (Freund, 2016, p. 107). Even if policy does not lead recordings to be examined without a specific reason (e.g., a use-of-force incident during a shift), "simply being recorded at all times . . . might create an oppressive working environment" (Freund, 2016, p. 106)

▶ Data Retention and Future Suspects

Another concern of BWCs is the issue of retaining the recordings and their use. These recordings could potentially be used by departments to identify suspects of future crimes, which leads to a net widening and a virtual surveillance state. Opponents argue that these recording can be combined with facial-recognition technologies (FRTs) and used to identify suspects and discover new suspects from previous recordings (Adams & Mastracci, 2017; Freund, 2016). These videos coupled with the use of FRT software could be used to pressure individuals into complying with investigations, particularly if combining these technologies leads to someone who is on probation or parole or has outstanding warrants. This information could be used to coerce individuals to comply (e.g., testify) in exchange for future charges being dropped. Because "Taser is already developing a body-worn camera with FRT" (Freund, 2016, p. 103), and "departments in Seattle, Chicago, and . . . [the UK] are reportedly already experimenting with combining BWCs . . . and automatic facial recognition software" (Adams & Matracci, 2017, p. 321), it is a distinct possibility that police departments will be using these technologies in the future and will be using these to identify individuals captured on video.

This has implications not only to those captured on video but also for future reporting of crimes to the police. "Individuals might worry that if their face is captured by the camera, it will be compared to a database using [FRT] for outstanding warrants and matches to unsolved cases" (Freund, 2016, p. 104). This may cause people to be even more wary of reporting crimes to the police or even interacting with police officers for fear of being "captured on camera." Although being implemented and used as a tool to watch the police, these could become another surveillance tool to watch citizens, "[reminding] others that their actions are recorded by the state" (Adams & Mastracci, 2017, p. 320). By realizing they can and will be captured on tape, individuals may choose not to interact with law enforcement even when they have a compelling reason to do so (e.g., are victims of crime).

▶ Conclusion

Although BWCs offer the ability to increase police transparency and legitimacy and increase citizen satisfaction with the police, these technologies are not without their potential dangers. These are being rapidly adopted by departments because of these potential benefits, but often this adoption is coming without fully considering their drawbacks as well. Despite the rapid implementation by police departments, there is still little known about the long-term effects of BWCs or their efficiency in increasing transparency and legitimacy of police (Adams & Mastracci, 2017; Novak et al., 2017).

Police departments need to implement policies to make sure the ethical risks of BWCs do not outweigh their potential benefits for departments and officers. These would include making sure no one infringes on the privacy rights of both citizens and officers. In addition, policies need to take into consideration the potential impacts BWCs could have on victims of crime, particularly sexual assault and domestic violence (Adams & Mastracci, 2017). "Policy should demand both considerable officer discretion and the ability to hold officers accountable for misuse of discretion as counterbalance" (Adams & Mastracci, 2017, p. 325). There also should be policies that limit dissemination of BWC footage to protect victims and others "caught on camera" who could potentially be impacted by the release of this footage. Departments also need to be cognizant of how merely using BWCs could impact their interactions with the public, particularly if these technologies start to be used to surveil the public rather than merely keep police accountable.

As with many new technologies, their promise is often more ideal than their practice. With BWCs, departments and the public need to be vigilant to make sure the practice matches their promise (i.e., holding police accountable but not infringing on rights of citizens, victims, or officers) with implementing sound policies and continuing the conduct research into their efficacy.

▶ References

Adams, I., & Mastracci, S. (2017). Visibility is a trap: The ethics of police body-worn cameras and control. *Administrative Theory & Praxis, 39*, 313–328.

Butt, N. (2018). Body worn cameras in law enforcement (unpublished paper). West Chester, PA: West Chester University.

Freund, K. (2016). When cameras are rolling: Privacy implications of body-mounted cameras on police. *Columbia Journal of Law and Social Problems, 49*(1), 91–133.

Mateescu, A., Rosenblat, A., & Boyd, D. (2015, February). Police body-worn cameras. *Data & Society*. Retrieved from https://www.bja.gov/bwc/pdfs/PoliceBodyWornCameras.pdf

Menard, K. (2005). *Reporting sexual assault: A social ecology perspective*. New York, NY: LFB Scholarly.

Novak, K., Cordner, G., Smith, B., & Roberg, R. (2017). *Police and society* (7th ed.). New York, NY: Oxford University Press.

Planty, M., Langton, L., Krebs, C., Berzofsky, M. & Smiley-McDonald, H. (2013). *Female victims of sexual violence, 1994–2010*. Washington, DC: U.S. Department of Justice, Bureau of Justice Statistics.

The Ethics of Police Use of Force

Christopher M. Bellas
Sarah A. See
Eric S. See
Wendy C. Vonnegut

▶ Introduction

Police–citizen encounters rarely involve the use of force, especially the use of excessive force. From the years 2002 to 2011, nearly 44 million U.S. citizens (ages 16 and older) had at least one face-to-face encounter with a police officer; throughout all of those interactions, only 1.6% claimed a threat or had experienced the use of nonfatal police force, with 1.2% cases involving excessive force (Hyland, Langton, & Davis, 2015, p. 1). Although the percentage of use of force cases is small when compared to overall police encounters, the topic of excessive force being used by police has raised ethical concerns about police behavior. The purpose of this article is to discuss whether or not the use of force by police is ethical and by what standard we should draw any conclusions. To come to a consensus, one must first look at all police use of force, both reasonable and excessive. We make the distinction between the two by first discussing reasonable use of police force on citizens and then moving on to excessive force. Whether the use of force by police is ethical is critiqued based on two guiding principles: *moral* (respect for human life, acting in a fair and just manner) and *institutional* (legal doctrine).

▶ Reasonable Uses of Police Force

From the routine traffic stop to the more violent interactions police encounter such as domestic violence, law enforcement is required to have a range of possible responses to public contact so police can maintain public safety. This at times can result in an officer needing to assess a threatening situation and with permission to use the *amount of force necessary* to control the circumstances. The question often becomes, what level of control is necessary for police to apply to get the best result with the least amount of harm? Whatever level is deemed proportional would be seen as a reasonable use of police force—not excessive. Although every situation is different, most police departments have developed a use-of-force continuum often taught in police academies around the country that ranges from the mere presence of law enforcement to verbalization and then physical contact. The continuum generally includes:

1. *Mere presence*—the police are visible to the public by the uniforms and marked cars they patrol in giving the public notice of their presence.
2. *Command*—the verbal level of command to achieve a desired result.
3. *Firm grip*—restraining a suspect in order to control a situation without pain.
4. *Pain compliance*—the infliction of pain without lasting harm (wristlock).
5. *Impact technique*—used to overcome resistance and may involve nonlife-threatening objects or chemicals (e.g., tasers, chemical sprays, batons).
6. *Lethal force*—force capable of killing or likely to kill. (National Institute of Justice, 2015)

Although most police departments include this range of responses for police behavior, the Albuquerque, New Mexico, Police Department spells out a continuum of behavior not only for police but also for citizens. The citizen continuum looks at a citizen's behavior (cooperative, noncooperative, unarmed assailant, armed assailant) along with the policing continuum regarding officer behavior (alert, control, active, and survival); both sets of factors provide a greater depth for understanding a police–citizen situation (Terrill & Paoline, 2016, p. 9).

▶ Excessive Use of Police Force

According to the Bureau of Justice Statistics (2016), police use of excessive force is defined as the application of force greater than that which a "reasonable" and "prudent" law enforcement officer would use under the current circumstances. Police use of excessive force is a highly controversial topic in the field of criminal justice. Both the popular press and social media have underscored many cases of officers' use of excessive force, especially those cases involving the most extreme level of force—that which is lethal. Not since the 1992 police brutality case of Rodney King—when Los Angeles Police Department officers were caught on videotape beating King—had there been such a high-profile case of excessive force until the Michael Brown case in Ferguson, Missouri, in 2014. On August 9, 2014, Police Officer Darren Wilson shot and killed Michael Brown, an African American teenager in Ferguson, Missouri. Although there is much dispute over the events leading up to the fatal shooting, city prosecutors eventually decided not to indict Officer Wilson. This generated massive protests both in Ferguson and around the country, prompting the U.S. Department of Justice (DOJ) to investigate the practices of the Ferguson Police Department. The DOJ ultimately released recommendations on how to improve police–community relations (U.S. Department of Justice Civil Rights Division, 2015). After the Ferguson case, police departments around the country were heavily scrutinized for their use of force. In addition, many cases of lethal force used by police have been captured on video, prompting more public outrage. The so-called Ferguson effect was a term used for the possible impact the Michael Brown case may have had on both citizens and the police departments entrusted to protect them. There is one notion that citizens would be more inclined to report police misconduct by videotaping police encounters. Another perspective is the belief that police would "back off" their proactive duties out of fear of media backlash. For all the media attention since the Michael Brown case, there is research showing that the high-profile case did little to change either citizen or police behavior (Campbell, Nix, & Maguire, 2017, p. 404). Another case sparked massive protests across the country when Eric Garner died in Staten Island, New York, after New York Police Department (NYPD) officers used a chokehold to take Garner down. While lying on the ground, Garner repeatedly stated, "I can't breathe," and police were regarded as causing his death for something that was no more than a petty offense and presented no immediate threat to the officers (Smith, 2016, pp. 315, 331). The fact that the entire incident was caught on video also focused public attention as to whether police behavior, given the situation at the time, was in fact ethical. There are contradictory opinions about the Garner and Brown cases, and what transpired out of the intense media coverage has prompted competing societal ideas about ethics and police use of force.

▶ Is the Use of Force by Police Ethical?

Defining ethics can be a daunting task, especially for those in the field of criminal justice. Agents of the government are entrusted to protect society and its members while also respecting the liberty and freedom afforded to all citizens. One way of deciding which behavior is or is not ethical has to do with the basic respect one has for another's life. Police officer conduct having the most respect for the value of human life not only would be considered moral but also would lend itself to taking the *right* or *just* action in a professional role. According to Apressyan (2009, p. 95), one could claim that a resistance to violence is a moral obligation of each person and inherent in the concept of justice. More specifically, the principle of doing what is just is based on doing no harm to others and respecting individual rights.

Police officers are representatives of the state and are therefore morally obligated to perform their duties in a fair and just manner. With power comes the responsibility to not abuse such power nor use it in an arbitrary way. Police do have an obligation to protect society, but the amount of force they *should use* to carry out this protection should be proportional to the actions of the transgressor (Kleinig, 2014, p. 86). This is where many officers get into trouble. The question is often not whether the officer had a right to use force, but whether the force applied was excessive in relation to the suspect's behavior. Furthermore, there is the question as to whether the police, moral agents of the state, are respecting the very institution they are obligated to protect—the criminal justice system. In criminal justice there is a procedural process, as well as a substantive process, of which officers are aware in their police training. Part of being ethical is abiding by the procedural rules, whether the officers personally agree with them or not. Violating these rules by using excessive force disturbs the norms and standards called for in the criminal justice system.

Police officers who use excessive force may have no intention to act in an unethical way. Yet the actions of police officers, at least as viewed by the public, often do not take into consideration the motivations of the officers at the time excessive force was used. The public does not see the events from the officers' point of view. If the officer does believe he or she is doing what is right, what the law requires him or her to do, is this being unethical? Therefore, when looking at the actions of police and whether they are behaving ethically, we often get into one highly complicated area of criminal law—intent. Does the police officer's intent matter when he or she acts by using excessive force? Of course it does, but proving intent in court is another matter. In litigation where police departments have been sued for using excessive force, many juries have not found criminal guilt or civil liability because the officers believed in that moment that their lives were in danger. Thus, if their motivation for using such force was reasonable, how could this be unethical?

One way we can examine the ethical quandary regarding police use of force is to study two high-profile symbolic counterparts to the debate over the value of human life, an ethical principle explored throughout this article. Passionate in their convictions, the ethical issue for strong opposition to law enforcement's use of force are advocacy groups such as Black Lives Matter, a relatively new organization spurred by recent media cases of unarmed Black men fatally shot by police. The ethical position they subscribe to is that just because police force may be legal does not always make it ethical. The group focuses on high-profile cases, indeed many caught on video, demonstrating racist overtones to police use of force and that some lives (indeed Black lives) are devalued. The counterpart to the Black Lives Matter movement is a pro-law enforcement grassroots organization referred to as *Blue Lives Matter*, which underscores the sacrifice and risk police officers face daily to protect their communities. From a law enforcement perspective, just because force can at times be unavoidably violent (resulting in possible injury or death) does not make its use necessarily unethical. The use of force from their position is an obligation they have to protect and serve the people. We now explore the launch of those two rival social movements and examine their impact on the ethical debate regarding use of force.

The Black Lives Matter movement ignited in 2013 when Alicia Garza, Patrisse Cullors, and Opal Tometi responded via social media to the recent acquittal of George Zimmerman, a man who was charged with killing an unarmed Black teen named Trayvon Martin. The social movement seemed to grow as more media attention focused on the deaths of other unarmed Black men; before long, multistate protests took over the streets, especially after the Ferguson incident. Although the organization has received a lot of media attention, both good and bad, one criticism has been that the group lacks any clear purpose and is doing nothing more than inciting harmful actions against the police (Clayton, 2018, pp. 453–455). Despite detractors, the effort has grown. The Black Lives Matter movement now has roughly 30 chapters and is poised with the mission to expose violence inflicted on the Black community by agents of the state. The guiding principles of the organization specifically include diversity, globalism, restorative justice, a world free of anti-Blackness, and support for other diverse targeted populations (Black Lives Matter, 2018).

In direct response to the Black Lives Matter movement, a rising antithesis crusade was cleverly named *Blue Lives Matter*. Blue Lives Matter was formed after the December 2014 killings of NYPD Officers Rafael Ramos and Wenjian Liu. The mission of Blue Lives Matter is to promote the education and training of police officers as well as counter what is believed by the organization to be a public relations attack on the police. The purpose of Blue Lives Matter supporters is to promote community safety, provide transparency to the public, and deliver comfort and aid to law enforcement and their family members in times of crisis (Blue Lives Matter, 2018). Blue Lives Matter offers a counternarrative against the alleged demonization the Black Lives Matter movement has cast on the law enforcement community. The official websites of both organizations are passionate in their beliefs about what is ethical. Take the Ferguson case as an example. Black Lives Matter views the killing of Michael Brown by Officer Wilson as an abuse of police power—the unlawful killing of a minority member that would likely have never occurred if Brown had not been Black. Brown represented an entire criminal justice system that behaved unethically in how it treated minorities across the country. Contrarily, the position of the Blue Lives Matter movement focuses on Officer Wilson as the victim and how he was demonized in the press after responding to the actions of Brown, a known criminal. Both sides have carefully chosen to emphasize one life over the other, and what they share is a passion for believing their position represents the ethical one. When citizens such as those who form a united cause like Black Lives Matter feel protests are not the only recourse for justice, an individual harmed or the family members of one killed may use the civil court system. One such remedy is a civil lawsuit against the government. Even then, however, police may be protected or immunized from civil litigation by way of qualified immunity.

▶ Qualified Immunity

Qualified immunity is a legal doctrine that is intended to balance "the need to hold government officials accountable when they exercise power irresponsibly as well as the need to shield law enforcement officials from harassment, distraction, and liability when they perform their duties responsibly" (*Pearson v. Callahan*, 2009). The protection it affords police is analogous to the frontline bulletproof vest that protects officers from having their lives "pierced" by a civil lawsuit while performing their professional duties as an officer. Qualified immunity does not apply to criminal proceedings, however, but it does protect officers from being sued for most civil actions.

To fully understand qualified immunity, you must first understand its history. Title 42 § 1983 of the United States Code provides:

> Every person who, under the color of any statute, ordinance, regulation, custom, or usage, of State or Territory or the District of Columbia, subjects or cause to be subjected, any citizen of the United States or other person within the jurisdiction thereof to the deprivation of any rights, privileges, or immunities secured by the Constitution and laws, shall be liable to the party injured in an action at law, suit in equity or other proper proceeding for redress, except that in any action brought against a judicial officer for an act or omission taken in such officers judicial capacity, injunctive relief shall not be granted unless a declaratory was violated or declaratory relief was unavailable.

Nowhere in the statutory language will you find specific reference to the term *qualified immunity*. However, the doctrine has been fashioned by the courts. In *Monroe v. Pape* (1961), the U.S. Supreme Court held that a plaintiff whose constitutional rights have been infringed upon by one acting under "color of state law" can bring a federal cause of action under § 1983 even when the state provides an adequate remedy through its common law of tort. In the case of *Monroe*, the Supreme Court stated that § 1983 provided a remedy to individuals "deprived of constitutional rights, privileges and immunities" as a result of a government official's abuse of his or her position (p. 172). The significance of the *Monroe* decision was that plaintiffs could now seek relief in both state and federal court against individual police officers for violating their constitutional rights, but not municipalities. Since then, §1983 has become the vehicle for considerable litigation. The statute has expanded, challenging state practices that range from police brutality to maternity leave policies. These proceedings, along with other statutory civil rights actions, have occupied a lot of space on the federal court docket. For example, between 1961 and 1979, the number of federal filings under § 1983 (excluding suits by prisoners) increased from 296 to 13,168 (Annual Report of the Director, 1979). In 1976, almost one out of every three nonprisoner suits filed in federal court was a civil rights claim against a state or local official (Whitman, 1980, p. 6).

In law we often turn to a standard or test on which to analyze the facts of a case. In *Scheuer v. Rhodes* (1974), the Supreme Court provided the standard to use for the application of qualified immunity. The Court explained that two criteria must be met for qualified immunity to apply:

1.　An officer must have a *reasonable* basis for the belief that, considering all circumstances existing at the time, the amount of force used was reasonable.
2.　An officer must have believed in *good faith* that the action was lawful.

Qualified immunity thus avoids placing police officers between the proverbial rock and a hard place when tension rises between the officer's law enforcement responsibilities and his or her constitutional obligations (Chen, 1997, p. 16). The standard outlined in *Scheuer*, however, made it more difficult for plaintiffs to bring action in federal court because, just as in criminal law, one must show that the police acted in bad faith, an extremely difficult burden to meet.

Nearly 10 years after the *Scheuer* decision, the standard for qualified immunity was modified. The Court in the case of *Harlow v. Fitzgerald* (1982) provided a more simplistic standard for what is needed for qualified immunity to apply:

1.　Did the defendant violate the plaintiff's constitutional right?
2.　Was a constitutional right clearly established at the time of the violation?

With respect to the second prong of the test, "clearly established" can be interpreted to mean "a right must be sufficiently clear that every reasonable official would have understood that what [the officer] is doing violates that right" (*Taylor v. Barkes*, 2015). Therefore, the constitutional rights violation must be obvious. Although the courts have carved out a legal remedy for citizens to exercise their legal right to be protected from excessive force, being able to bring a case forward is much different than succeeding on the merits. Outside of the legal system, policy changes are needed to deal with police use of force.

▶ Law and Policy Recommendations on Police Use of Force

One obvious recommendation for decreasing police use of force is better community relationships between police and citizens. One cannot overlook racial tensions over the past several years between police officers and the citizens they are obliged to *serve* and *protect*. One of the most significant statements regarding racial tension between police and citizens was the President's Commission on Law Enforcement and Administration of Justice (1967), which showed African Americans were remarkably unsatisfied with police conduct and that the attitude toward police was mirrored by the actions of the officers. As recent as July 2016, there has been no defined standard for a national database on police use of excessive force despite a recommendation by the President's Task Force on 21st Century Policing (2015), which stated that "policies on use of force should require government agencies to collect, maintain, and report data to the Federal Government on *all* officer shootings (lethal or not) as well as any in custody death" (p. 21). One problem with collecting such data, just like the Uniform Crime Report, is that reporting law enforcement statistics is voluntary, not mandatory. Shane (2016) recommends something along the lines of the National Incident Based Reporting System; more complete information regarding officers' actions, the behavior of the offenders, and the environmental conditions of the situation at hand could provide for a more qualitative assessment of what transpired (Shane, 2016, pp. 6–7). More specifically, according to Stum (2016), policy reform efforts can be obtained in several ways: increasing the diversity of police departments, introducing community-based policing, increasing cultural competency training and developing police department policies that take into consideration special needs offenders and victims based on mental health, physical, and psychological impairments, race, religion, sexual orientation, and so on (pp. 14–15). This is important because it tends to show that the policy changes that need to take place can come only from the departments themselves. This may mean that law enforcement training needs to include more skills-based training on culture norms regarding the communities they protect. This will help break ethical misbehavior by many police organizations and allow officers in the future to develop a cognitive ability to adapt to a diverse population (Rivera & Ward, 2017, p. 244). In a sense, this is the "ethics reform" needed to restore faith and political legitimacy to the criminal justice system.

Another policy recommendation is changing the guidelines for police departments. Officers should consider three factors when engaging in use of force. First, there are environmental factors such as the location of where crime normally happens in any given area. Second, there are the individual factors of the suspect the officer is dealing with, which is the focus of most police officer scrutiny. Third, there is the organizational culture of the police department where officers are employed (Fyfe, 1987, p. 79–94). With respect to ethical behavior, the last is important to consider. Specifically, when looking at whether police use of force is, in fact, ethical, we need to examine particular police department protocols in addition to the individual attitude of any one officer (Rivera & Ward, 2017, p. 242). If changes are to be made regarding when police use force, changing the guidelines employed by police departments needs to be examined (White, 2001, p. 131).

Other practical policy considerations have been proposed such as police body cameras and a call for a national database of officer involved shootings (Alpert, 2016). After Michael Brown's death, the DOJ called for major changes in how the Ferguson Police Department was to carry out its duties with a major focus on de-escalation tactics and using the least amount of force necessary when confronting suspects, as well as increased training for police (U.S. Department of Justice Civil Rights Division, 2015). In a study by Obasogie and Newman (2017), the majority of police departments failed to include discussions on a use-of-force continuum (only 45% of the time), de-escalation (just 50% of the time), and proportionality (30% of the time) (p. 287). Within police policies on use of force, one should also be able to identify the moral principles previously discussed. Yet many use-of-force policies across 20 of the largest U.S. cities demonstrate that departmental guidelines are limited to the bare minimum constitutional requirements outlined by the U.S. Supreme Court in *Graham v. Connor* (1989). That case stated that police force must only meet the legal standard of what is objectively reasonable. Precisely, what came out of the *Graham* decision were two important legal standards. First, all constitutional claims involving excessive force by law enforcement against suspects fall under the Fourth Amendment to the U.S. Constitution and cannot be argued under a general claim, again a violation of the due process clause. Second, the legal standard (one can argue whether this should be the ethical standard), regarding the use of force is "objective reasonableness" from the point of view of what a similarly situated officer on the scene would have done at that time. Hence, the Court argued one should not rely on a hindsight analysis in discussing reasonableness. If he or she wants to use a precise definition of whether a police officer's use of force was ethical, then he or she is stuck with the vague legal standard of "it depends."

▶ Conclusion

In conclusion, ethics play a role in the use of force by law enforcement. Ethics are based on the principles of moral rights and the duty to respect human life balanced against the moral rights and the duty to protect society from harm. Although the basic moral values are the same, both the Black Lives Matter and the Blue Lives Matter movements paint two decidedly different portraits of where we as a society stand on police–citizen relations today. The former believes law enforcement engages in immoral action by treating Black lives differently from others, and the latter believes police officers have been treated unfairly by the press and hindered from carrying out their obligation to protect society. Both points of view are to some extent correct and therefore are not mutually exclusive. Police do need to reassess their departmental policies and police training to better understand appropriate police responses to dangerous situations. At the same time, those who are distrustful of the police can better appreciate that the profession calls for maintaining the peace—and understand the police are placed in dangerous situations where force at times is absolutely necessary. Finally, we studied ethics and use of force through legal dogma. Surely the law, in order to be just and fair, is an appropriate standard to measure police behavior as ethical or unethical. The problem is that the law, whether a state or federal statute or case law is routinely vague and gives deference in nearly all cases to police conduct, such as the case with qualified immunity. It is our conclusion that there will never be consensus on whether use of force by police is or is not ethical as long as perceived injustice is felt on both sides. We can only hope that both perspectives are respected enough to open a dialogue, for only then can Americans begin to heal the bitter divide that has caused such tension throughout the country.

▶ References

Annual Report of the Director. (1979). *Annual report of the director for the twelve month period ending June 30, 1979.* Washington, DC: Administrative Office of the United States Courts.

Alpert, G. P. (2016). Toward a national database of officer-involved shootings. *Criminology & Public Policy, 15*(1), 237–242. doi: 10.1111/1745-9133.12178

Apressyan, R. G. (2009). The ethics of force: Against aggression and violence. *Diogenes, 56*(2–3), 95–109. doi: 10.1177/0392192109339679

Black Lives Matter. (2018). What we believe. Retrieved from https://blacklivesmatter.com/about/what-we-believe/

Blue Lives Matter. (2018). Mission Statement. Retrieved from http://archive.bluelivesmatter.blue/organization/#mission-statement

Bureau of Justice Statistics. (2016). *Use of force.* Retrieved from http://www.bjs.gov/index.cfm?ty=tp&tid=84

Campbell, B. A., Nix, J., & Maguire, E. R. (2017). Is the number of citizens fatally shot by police increasing in the post-Ferguson era? *Crime & Delinquency, 64*(3), 398–420.

Chen, A. K. (1997). The burdens of qualified immunity: Summary judgment and the role of facts in constitutional tort law. *American University Law Review, 47*(1–2), 1–104.

Clayton, D. M. (2018). Black Lives Matter and the Civil Rights Movement: A comparative analysis of two social movements in the United States. *Journal of Black Studies, 49*(5), 448–480. https://journals.sagepub.com/doi/abs/10.1177/0021934718764099

Fyfe, J. J. (1987). Police shooting: Environment and license. In J. E. Scott & T. Hirschi (Eds.), *Controversial Issues in Crime and Justice* (pp. 79–94). Newbury Park, CA: Sage.

Graham v. Connor, 490 U.S. 386 (1989).

Harlow v. Fitzgerald, 475 U.S. 800 (1982).

Hyland, S., Langton, L., & Davis, E. (2015). *Police use of nonfatal force, 2002–11.* Special Report NCJ 249216. Washington, DC: U.S. Department of Justice. Retrieved from http://www.bjs.gov/content/pub/pdf/punf0211.pdf

Kleinig, J. (2014). Legitimate and illegitimate uses of police force. *Criminal Justice Ethics, 33*(2), 83–103. https://www.tandfonline.com/doi/abs/10.1080/0731129X.2014.941539

Monroe v. Pape, 365 U.S. 167 (1961).

National Institute of Justice. (2015). The use-of-force continuum. Retrieved from http://www.nij.gov/topics/law-enforcement/officer-safety/use-of-force/Pages/continuum.aspx

Obasogie, O. K., & Newman, Z. (2017). Police violence, use of force policies, and public health. *American Journal of Law & Medicine, 43,* 279–295. doi: 10.1177/0098858817723665

Pearson v. Callahan, 555 U.S. 221 (2009).

President's Commission on Law Enforcement and Administration of Justice. (1967). *Task force report: The police.* Washington, DC: U.S. Government Printing Office.

President's Task Force on 21st Century Policing. (2015). *Final report of the president's task force on 21st century policing.* Washington, DC: Office of Community Oriented Policing Services.

Rivera, M. A., & Ward, J. D. (2017). Toward an analytical framework for the study of race and police violence. *Public Administrative Review, 77*(2), 242–250. doi: 10.1111/puar.12748

Scheuer v. Rhodes, 416 U.S. 232 (1974).

Shane, J. M. (2016). Improving police use of force: A policy essay on national data collection. *Criminal Justice Policy Review, 29*(2), 1–21. doi: 10.1177/0887403416662504

Smith, J. M. (2016). Closing the gap between what is lawful and what is right in police use of force jurisprudence by making police departments more democratic institutions. *Michigan Journal of Race and Law 21*(2), 315–347.

Stum, B. (2016). Recommendations, part 1 of 2, to Spokane mayor David Condon from the police leadership advisory committee. Retrieved from http://media.spokesman.com/documents/2016/01/PLAC_Recommendations_Part_1_1_26_2016_2.pdf

Taylor v. Barkes, 135 S. Ct. 2042 (2015).

Terrill, W., & Paoline, E. A. (2016). Police use of less lethal force: Does administrative policy matter? *Justice Quarterly, 34*(2), 193–216. doi: 10.1080/07418825.2016.1147593

U.S. Department of Justice Civil Rights Division. (2015). Investigation of the Ferguson police department. Retrieved from http://www.justice.gov/sites/default/files/opa/press-releases/attachments/2015/03/04/ferguson_police_department_report.pdf

White, M. D. (2001). Controlling police decisions to use deadly force: Reexamining the importance of administrative policy. *Crime & Delinquency, 47*(1), 131–151. https://journals.sagepub.com/doi/10.1177/0011128701047001006

Whitman, C. B. (1980). Constitutional torts. *University of Michigan Law School, 79*(5), 5–71.42 U.S.C. §1983 (1994).

Ethics and Law Enforcement: Examining the Ethical Considerations of Focused Deterrence Strategies

Jeffrey E. Clutter

▶ Introduction

Ethical considerations play a major role in how law enforcement happens and, perhaps more important, how the actions of the police are perceived by the public. Perceptions of legitimacy, defined as fairness in treatment, have long plagued law enforcement in the United States (Tyler, 2004). Recent pushes towards improvements in police legitimacy, including the emphasis on procedural justice (Tyler, 2006), can be seen in the rise of community-oriented policing (Eck & Rosenbaum, 1994) as well as the results of President Barack Obama's Task Force on 21st Century Policing (President's Task Force on 21st Century Policing, 2015).

General reviews on police ethics, including what ethical policing is and why it is important, have been written on extensively elsewhere (e.g. Barker, 2011). This chapter views ethical considerations of policing by focusing on what citizens expect from their police. While the list of expectations may differ considerably depending in the context, Eck and Rosenbaum (1994) suggest that citizens generally want their police to be effective, efficient and equitable. Viewing ethics in terms of expectations allows for a more nuanced discussion on the police role in the United States and elsewhere. That is, we can adjudge police actions to be ethical if they successfully meet the expectations of the people.

Again, general considerations of how police live up to expectations have been discussed elsewhere. It may be time to begin examining the ethical considerations of specific law enforcement practices, policies, and approaches. This chapter is an attempt to take a specific law enforcement approach—focused deterrence (Kennedy, Piehl, & Braga, 1996)—and examine it from an ethical standpoint. Namely, this chapter argues that focused deterrence approaches satisfy the three expectations Eck and Rosenbaum (1994) suggest that citizens expect from their police.

▶ Ethics and Expectations of Law Enforcement

Generally speaking, ethics is the moral behavior of people or groups of people. Police ethics, then, have to do with the moral actions taken by police generally as well as by individual police officers. Policing itself is an enormously complex task, thus requiring an equally intricate discussion of what is meant by ethical and moral policing. In addition, many situations in which police find themselves are morally ambiguous, thus adding to the complication and complexity of police ethics. General discussions of the complexity of police ethics can be found elsewhere (e.g., Barker, 2011). Suffice to say, most discussion surrounding the role of morality and ethics in policing centers on issues of legitimacy, fairness, and procedural justice.

Even though this tends to be the case, however, other elements of the police role merit discussion as they pertain to police ethics—that is, we expect more from law enforcement than simply fair treatment. Eck and Rosenbaum (1994) summarize our expectations of police into the three E's: effectiveness, efficiency, and equity. Effectiveness is essentially how well police are performing a given function. Police serve many functions, including law enforcement, order maintenance, and service delivery, but the ability to control crime is most often cited as the measure of effectiveness or what is known as "evidence-based policing" (Sherman, 2013).

Related to effectiveness, citizens expect the police to operate in an efficient manner. Because of financial constraints, many police departments have had to refocus their efforts in ways that emphasize cost-effective practices. However, the requirement of being asked to do more with less has not come with a reduced expectation of effectiveness. Despite being asked to maintain or enhance crime reductions with fewer resources, law enforcement has generally risen to the challenge (Bayley & Nixon, 2010). One reason for this stems from improvements in evidence-based policing strategies such as problem-oriented policing (Eck & Spelman, 1987; Goldstein, 1979). By increasing the focus on specific crime problems, police have been able to better allocate resources to address high crime places, repeat offenders, and repeat victims.

The final expectation discussed by Eck and Rosenbaum (1994) is that of equity, or fairness in how police treat those they serve. Issues of equity in law enforcement are often subsumed under the name "police legitimacy." Generally speaking, *legitimacy* refers to impartial treatment of citizens both in terms of police actions and outcomes. Citizens not only want to ensure that police are abiding by the law and ensuring their due process rights, but also want to feel as if the outcomes of police actions are not the result of inequality in treatment. Tyler (2003, 2006) and others define this using the term *procedural justice* and have found that people who feel they have been treated fairly are more likely to obey the law and regard the police as legitimate (Tyler & Fagan, 2008).

Thus, one can assumedly judge the ethics of the police or a specific policing approach based on whether they, or the approach, are effective, efficient, and equitable. However, as Engel and Eck (2015) discuss, many police and criminal justice scholars have assumed that there is an inherent trade-off among the three E's. That is, in order for police to be more effective, they must sacrifice some amount of equity. This perceived trade-off, it is argued, stems from Packer's (1968) influential work on the two competing models of criminal justice processing: the due process model and the crime control model. While the due process model prizes individual rights and fairness, the crime control model values efficiency and crime reductions. Thus, it is said that any particular act, sanction, or aspect of criminal justice processing must give up some level of efficiency for due process and vice versa.

Engel and Eck (2015) argue against this natural trade-off between effectiveness or efficiency and equity. Rather, they maintain that properly crafted police strategies, specifically those that use a problem-oriented or focused approach, can be effective, efficient, and equitable at the same time. In this light, it is important to identify popular police strategies and assess whether they are or can be viewed as ethical. One such popular approach, focused deterrence, is discussed next.

▶ Focused Deterrence

The focused deterrence policing strategy, also known as *pulling levers* or *group violence intervention*, is a problem-oriented policing approach with origins dating to Boston in the early to mid-1990s (Kennedy et al., 1996). The first iteration of focused deterrence was an attempt to combat the increasing problem of youth gun violence. In crafting a response to the problem, four themes emerged. First, the youths involved in gun violence, either as perpetrators or victims (and sometimes both), made up a tiny percentage of the Boston population yet caused a much larger percentage of the violence in city. Second, it became apparent that these youths were arranged in informal, neighborhood-based groups and gangs. Third, the violence perpetrated by youth group and gang members was propelled by issues of respect and driven by the code of the street (Anderson, 1999) as well as by group dynamics. Finally, because of the importance of group dynamics, it was possible to influence behavior (via change in perceptions of deterrence) through group pressure (Kennedy, 2008, 2011).

Because of the convergence of these factors, researchers in Boston created the focused deterrence model, whereby the message promising swift, severe, and certain punishment for future behavior was communicated directly with group members. To deliver this message, offenders were either invited or forced (via conditions of probation or parole) to attend "call-in" sessions. At these call-in sessions, law enforcement informed offenders (and by proxy their friends and fellow group or gang members) that they were under heightened scrutiny and that future incidents that were the focus of the initiative (e.g., gun violence) would invite increased criminal sanctions for all group or gang members.

What makes focused deterrence a problem-oriented policing approach is the use of entities beyond the criminal justice system, including local community leaders, religious leaders, social service providers, and street outreach workers

(National Network for Safe Communities, 2016), who relayed to offenders at these call-in sessions messages of support and invitations to help. However, if a group or gang was found to be involved in an incident after the call-in, law enforcement would deliver on its promise by "pulling every lever," or using every legal tool, in its arsenal. In other words, police would focus on all criminal behavior, not just the types of offenses that triggered their initial involvement (Braga, Kennedy, Waring, & Piehl, 2001).

Eventual evolutions of focused deterrence involved two other types of offenses and offenders. First, police began using this approach to combat street-level drug markets and drug dealers. Drug-based focused deterrence approaches are commonly referred to as *drug market intervention* (DMI) strategies (Kennedy & Wong, 2009). Second, the focused deterrence approach has been used on high-risk individuals who are not necessarily part of a group or gang (e.g. Papachristos, Meares, & Fagan, 2007). Although the targets of these two approaches differ, the strategy overall remains the same.

▶ The Ethics of Focused Deterrence

To recap, it is possible to view the ethics of the police and specific law enforcement approaches as they pertain to whether or not law enforcement delivers on the expectations of citizens. Moreover, although some argue that police cannot be simultaneously effective, efficient and equitable, others suggest otherwise (e.g., Engel & Eck, 2015). Taken together, if a police action or approach is perceived to be effective, efficient and equitable, it could be said to be ethically and morally just. Therefore, when examining the ethics of focused deterrence, one must ask, does this particular strategy meet the three E's of citizen expectations as put forth by Eck and Rosenbaum (1994)?

Effectiveness

As previously discussed, focused deterrence began in the mid-1990s in Boston as a response to the growing problems of youth gun violence and homicide. This initial project, then known as Operation Ceasefire, was evaluated by Braga et al. (2001). Examining seven years of monthly counts of youth homicides, gun assaults, and shots-fired calls for service, their results suggested that Operation Ceasefire had a significant effect on all dependent variables. These results held after introducing relevant control variables, and similar reductions were not seen in other cities throughout the country.

Because of the success of Boston's focused deterrence initiative, an ever-increasing number of police departments around the country and internationally have opted to apply the problem-solving approach to their crime problems. To synthesize what is known about the effectiveness of focused deterrence, Braga, Weisburd, and Turchan (2018) conducted a systematic review and meta-analysis of program evaluations. Their systematic review identified 24 quasi-experimental evaluations, which included strategies centered on groups and gangs, drug markets, and high-risk individuals. In 19 of the 24 studies, researchers reported significant crime reductions. The results of their meta-analysis mirrored this finding, suggesting focused deterrence programs lead to statistically significant yet moderate crime reductions.

Thus, the evidence suggests that focused deterrence programs are likely to be effective, satisfying the first criteria in the current discussion on ethical policing. That said, like most criminal justice approaches, the use of focused deterrence does not guarantee crime reductions, and there are certainly issues that still need sorting out (see, for example, the discussion section of Braga et al., 2018; Corsaro, 2018; and Tillyer, Engel, & Lovins, 2012). However, as with other problem-oriented approaches, proper tailoring of focused deterrence to specific crime problems has been shown to be an empirically effective police strategy.

Efficiency

Despite the wealth of evidence examining the crime-reduction effectiveness of focused deterrence, less is known about its efficiency in terms of cost-effectiveness. In her introduction and discussion of the Braga et al. (2018) systematic review and meta-analysis, Engel (2018) suggests an examination of the cost effectiveness of focused deterrence is critical to its future implementation and success. Despite the lack of direct knowledge of its efficiency, viewing focused deterrence as a problem-oriented approach may aid in this discussion.

In their extensive work on policing in the United States, the National Research Council (2004) identified four general models of policing based on the level of focus and range of interventions: the standard model, the community policing model, the focused-policing model, and the problem-oriented policing model. The standard model of policing involves a low diversity of approaches and low level of focus, often relying only on law enforcement tactics to combat crime across an entire jurisdiction. The community policing model increases the diversity of approaches by including other entities besides law enforcement, yet does so in a less focused way. Focused policing amps up the level of focus by concentrating on high crime places, times, and offenders, yet does so only using law enforcement approaches. Problem-oriented policing maintains this high degree of focus while also allowing for the wide array of approaches offered by community policing strategies.

Taken together and examined through the lens of efficiency, it becomes apparent that problem-oriented approaches offer the best chance at cost-effective police practices. Increasing the focus to concentrate on known offenders, known high-crime places, and known high-crime times while using resources beyond law enforcement allows for the best use of limited police resources. In other words, it allows police to do more with less when compared to policing approaches that fall in the other models described by the National Research Council (2004). In addition, the focused deterrence approach does not ask law enforcement to go beyond their police role—that is, their role in focused deterrence is "business as usual," albeit more concentrated on a certain group of offenders or offenses. Other entities, such as community members, local religious and business leaders, social service providers, and street outreach workers, may incur more costs, but that burden does not fall on the police. That said, those costs may be offset by the reductions in violence, which itself is quite costly (Cook & Ludwig, 2000).

Thus, even though evidence on the cost-effective nature of focused deterrence and its many components is lacking, it is not hard to imagine that it would be at least as efficient as other potential solutions to similar crime issues. And, even though the exact level of efficiency may differ from department to department (like the level of effectiveness and equity would), one benefit of the problem-oriented approach is the ability to update and mold strategies as conditions (be they budgetary or shifts in crime problems) change. That said, future research should heed Engel's (2018) suggestion that future evaluations of focused deterrence should consider issues of efficiency.

Equity

Finally, as with any discussion of ethical policing, it is important to examine issues of equity and fairness as they pertain to focused deterrence. Although the strategy has been shown to be effective and is likely a more efficient use of police resources than other potential strategies aiming at the same crime problems, it must also be perceived as legitimate and procedurally just to be considered an ethical and moral police strategy.

There are numerous ways to examine the equity of a specific police initiative such as focused deterrence. As Eck and Rosenbaum (1994) suggest, two common methods include judging based on legal principles of due process and the distribution of resources or outcomes. As focused deterrence relates to both, one could argue that it is among the most equitable police strategies despite the promise of increased criminal sanctions. In other words, this increased sanction is promised only to those who commit or are involved with those who commit future crimes. These individuals tend to be responsible for a large percentage of crime with a given jurisdiction (Corsaro, 2018; Kennedy et al., 1996), so they are usually not controversial targets of police resources (unlike other community-wide zero-tolerance strategies that have been accused of net widening—e.g., stop–question–frisk). More important, offenders are essentially *warned* about the increased likelihood of future sanctions at call-in meetings. Although these warnings typically come from law enforcement personnel, they are usually done in a respectable manner and accompanied by messages of support and outreach from others. Taken together, focused deterrence concentrates on a small, violent subset of offenders who are then directly warned about the consequences of future violent behavior. Although perceptions of legitimacy are subjective, it is not likely that many would find this process unfair.

A recent chapter by Kennedy, Kleiman, and Braga (2017) examines equity in focused deterrence from the viewpoint of offenders and the communities in which they live. This is important, because their ability to view criminal justice sanctions as fair and just influences the deterrent capability of those sanctions. In addition, focused deterrence initiatives facilitate the community's "moral voice" that allows for informal social control, outreach, and support for those caught up in the life of crime (Kennedy et al., 2017). They even go so far as to say that the term *focused deterrence* is a partial misnomer because the strategy's inclusion of community members, and their importance, have little to do with traditional, sanction-based deterrence.

Additional support for focused deterrence as an equitable solution to violence stems from recent research suggesting that high-rate violent offenders are also at higher risk for victimization. Papachristos, Braga, & Hureau's (2012) examination of a social network of high-risk individuals in Boston found that one's risk of a gunshot injury is directly influenced by others in their social network. Thus, as Kennedy (2019) states, the individuals at risk for increased attention in focused deterrence initiatives are also at risk for victimization themselves and have been exposed to high levels of violence as well as procedurally unjust criminal justice practices.

Recent reviews of focused deterrence (e.g., Kennedy et al., 2017) have begun to incorporate discussions of legitimacy and procedural justice in their examinations of the strategy. This is not because researchers are trying to "sell" focused deterrence to communities and then failing to follow up on the promises of legitimacy. Rather, it is because the strategy offers a unique blend of focusing on the most high-risk individuals in a community who are responsible for the preponderance of violence while also offering them a way out by using key stakeholders in the community. Taken together, this suggests focused deterrence is quite capable of being considered an equitable police practice to serious crime problems.

▶ Conclusion

Police ethics is not a new concept, but recent controversies in American policing have reinforced the need to focus on what it means for law enforcement to be fair, legitimate, and just. This has led to many innovations and advancements in law enforcement training, technology, approaches, and studies into police accountability. Although just policing is vitally important procedurally, it needs to be incorporated into police practices that are efficient and effective. Some might suggest that the police or their policies cannot be effective, efficient and equitable at the same time, but others vehemently argue against this false trade-off (Engel & Eck, 2015).

Focused deterrence strategies are an increasingly popular program used by police to combat several chronic crime problems such as group and gang violence, gun violence, drug markets, and chronic offending. After reviewing Eck and Rosenbaum's (1994) three E's of citizen expectations for police, it appears that focused deterrence checks all the boxes. More work is needed to disentangle certain aspects of focused deterrence, such as which elements are most effective, how cost-effective it is in terms of limited police budgets, and how to best ensure that it fits within the framework of procedural justice, but it seems to be one of the more promising policing strategies that balances the need for effective crime control and ethical standards of American policing.

▶ References

Anderson, E. (1999). *The code of the street: Decency, violence, and the moral life of the inner city.* New York, NY: W.W. Norton & Co.

Barker, T. (2011). *Police ethics: Crisis in law enforcement* (3rd ed.). Springfield, IL: Chares C. Thomas.

Bayley, D.H. & Nixon, C. (2010). The changing environment for policing, 1985–2008. In *New Perspective in Policing*. Washington, DC: Harvard Kennedy School and the National Institute for Justice Executive Session on Policing.

Braga, A.A., Kennedy, D.M., Waring, E.J., & Piehl, A.M. (2001). Problem-oriented policing, deterrence, and youth violence: An evaluation of Boston's Operation Ceasefire. *Journal of Research in Crime & Delinquency, 38*: 195–226.

Braga, A.A., Weisburd, D., & Turchan, B. (2018). Focused deterrence strategies and crime control. *Criminology & Public Policy, 17*, 205–250.

Cook, P. J., & Ludwig, J. (2000). *Gun violence: The real costs.* Oxford: Oxford University Press.

Corsaro, N. (2018). More than lightning in a bottle and far from ready-made: Focused deterrence strategies and crime control. *Criminology & Public Policy, 17*(1), 251–259.

Eck, J. E., & Rosenbaum, D. (1994). The new police order: Effectiveness, equity, and efficiency in community policing. In D. Rosenbaum (Ed.) *Community policing: Testing the promises* (pp. 3–26). Newbury Park, CA: Sage.

Eck, J. E., & Spelman, W. (1987). *Problem solving: Problem-oriented policing in Newport News.* Washington, DC: Police Executive Research Forum.

Engel, R. S. (2018). Focused deterrence strategies save lives: Introduction and discussion of an updated systematic review and meta-analysis. *Criminology & Public Policy, 17*(1), 199–203.

Engel, R.S., & Eck, J.E. (2015). Effectiveness vs. equity in policing: Is a tradeoff inevitable? *Ideas in American Policing, 18,* 1–12.

Goldstein, H. (1979). *Problem-oriented policing.* New York, NY: McGraw-Hill.

Kennedy, D. M. (2008). *Deterrence and crime prevention: Reconsidering the prospect of sanction.* London, UK: Routledge.

Kennedy, D. M. (2011). *Don't shoot: One man, a street fellowship, and the end of violence in inner-city America.* New York. NY: Bloomsbury.

Kennedy, D. M. (2019). Response to "What works with gangs: A breakthrough." *Criminology & Public Policy, 18*(1), E1–E4.

Kennedy, D. M., Kleiman, M. A. R., & Braga, A. A. (2017). Beyond deterrence: Strategies of focus and fairness. In N. Tilley & A. Sidebottom (Eds.) *Handbook of crime prevention and community safety* (2nd ed., pp. 157–182). New York, NY: Routledge.

Kennedy, D. M., Piehl, A. M., & Braga, A. A. (1996). Youth violence in Boston: Gun markets, serious youth offenders, and a use-reduction strategy. *Law and Contemporary Problems, 59,* 147–196.

Kennedy, D. M., & Wong, S-L. (2009). *The high point drug intervention strategy.* Washington, DC: U.S. Department of Justice, Office of Community Oriented Policing Services.

National Network for Safe Communities. (2016). *Group violence intervention: An implementation guide.* Washington, DC: Office of Community Oriented Policing Services.

National Research Council. (2004). *Fairness and effectiveness in policing: The evidence.* Washington, DC: National Academies Press.

Packer, H. L. (1968). *The limits of the criminal sanction.* Stanford, CA: Stanford University Press.

Papachristos, A. V., Braga, A. A., & Hureau, D. M. (2012). Social networks and the risk of gunshot injury. *Journal of Urban Health, 89*(6), 992–1003.

Papachristos, A. V., Meares, T. L., & Fagan, J. (2007). Attention felons: Evaluating Project Safe Neighborhoods in Chicago. *Journal of Empirical Legal Studies, 4,* 223–272.

President's Task Force on 21st Century Policing. (2015). *Final report of the president's task force on 21st century policing.* Washington, DC: Office of Community Oriented Policing Services.

Sherman, L. W. (2013). The rise of evidence-based policing: Targeting, testing and tracking. In M. Tonry (Ed.) *Crime and justice in America 1975–2025. Crime and Justice: A Review of Research, 42,* 377–451. Chicago, IL: University of Chicago Press.

Tillyer, M. S., Engel, R. S., & Lovins, B. (2012). Beyond Boston: Applying theory to understand and address sustainability issues in focused deterrence initiatives for violence reduction. *Crime & Delinquency, 58*(6), 973–997.

Tyler, T. R. (2003). Procedural justice, legitimacy, and the effective rule of law. *Crime and Justice, 30,* 283–357.

Tyler, T. R. (2004). Enhancing police legitimacy. *Annals of the American Academy of Political and Social Science, 593*(1), 84–99.

Tyler, T. R. (2006). *Why people obey the law.* Princeton, NJ: Princeton University Press.

Tyler, T. R., & Fagan, J. (2008). Why do people help the police fight crime in their communities? *Ohio State Journal of Criminal Law, 6,* 231–275.

SECTION 5

Ethics and the Judicial System

ARTICLE 18

Ethics Within the Court System

Benecia Carmack

▶ Introduction

In law school, the phrase "term of art" is often used. This informs the students that the word or phrase means something specific to the profession of law. In this article, the term of art explored is "officer of the court," which means someone who is working within the court system and has a specific duty to uphold the system of justice and codes of conduct required of those individuals, whether they be judges or attorneys.

The judges' administration of court should occur in an orderly and respectful manner; they guard rights of the defendant guaranteed by our Constitution. They ensure no conflicts of interest affect the outcome of the case, that all parties advocate for their side while still conducting themselves with civility, and, most important, that justice results. The prosecutor presents the case of the people in a way that ensures justice for the victim, includes the introduction of legally obtained evidence, but could also include turning over evidence to the defense that may exonerate the defendant. The defense attorney, as an advocate for the defendant, ensures the investigation followed the rules of criminal procedure, advises the defendant through each step of the prosecution, and makes the best decisions for the strategy and theory of their case. All other employees of the court also are required to perform the functions of their positions with competence and respect for all parties and in a manner that keeps court functioning as efficiently and safely as possible without showing favoritism for either side.

▶ Model Rules of Professional Conduct

The Model Rules of Professional Conduct help courts and officers of the court accomplish all of the preceding responsibilities. The American Bar Association (ABA) created the Model Rules, "to serve as a national framework for implementation of standards of professional conduct" (ABA,1983, n.p.). Initially established in 1908 as the Canons of Professional Ethics, the ABA through committees have revised, rewritten, amended, and added as changes within the legal field created new issues for lawyers, such as multijurisdictional practices, globalization, and technology. All states, the federal courts, and the District of Columbia have adopted the Model Rules, some with their variations or amendments, except for California which has continued to use its own rules (ABA & Bloomberg BNA, 2018). These rules apply to all attorneys practicing in all areas of the law. However, this particular article addresses the criminal court system.

As stated in the Model Rule's preamble and scope (ABA, 2018), the rules address the various lawyer roles—as a representative of a client; as adviser, advocate, negotiator, evaluator, and neutral third party; and as a public citizen. The scope preceding the rules also states that these are voluntary, but compliance is necessary with the laws in an open society, and violation of these rules is enforced with disciplinary actions. Lawyers and judges are all members of their state or multiple states' bar associations, which administer disciplinary actions ranging from letters of reprimands to suspensions and, ultimately, disbarment.

The separate ABA Model Code of Judicial Conduct (2011, n.p.) states in its preamble the values we require in our courts: "An independent, fair and impartial judiciary is indispensable to our system of justice. The United States legal system is based upon the principle that an independent, impartial, and competent judiciary, composed of men and women of integrity, will interpret and apply the law that governs our society." When all officers of the court act with independence, fairness, and impartiality, they uphold the defendant's constitutional rights, maintain the rule of law, and serve justice.

▶ Judges

Judges supervise and administer the courts. Our American criminal justice systems require an independent judiciary to apply the facts of the current case to the laws of their current jurisdiction, whether that be state, federal, or administrative agency. If violations of the Model Code occur, disciplinary action can be initiated against the judge from the appropriate authority.

Scope

The word *judge* brings an image of a full-time judge presiding over a civil or criminal trial. There are, however, many forms of judges, and the Model Code applies to all of them with some variations. In the application section of the ABA Model Code of Judicial Conduct (2011, n.p.), *judge* is defined as, "anyone who is authorized to perform judicial functions, including an officer such as a justice of the peace, magistrate, court commissioner, special master, referee, or member of the administrative law judiciary." Administrative law judges work for particular federal or state agencies, or departments therein, such as the Departments of Revenue, Social Security, Workman's Compensation, and Homeland Security, among others. Although there are separate model codes for state and federal administrative law judges, they are beyond the scope of this article. The term *judges* may also include retired judges who are subject to recall. It is not uncommon to appoint retired judges to cases where the presiding judge has to recuse or remove him- or her-self because of a conflict of interest. The Model Code applies to them as well. The Model Code consists of four canons, with rules under each canon providing more guidance and interpretation.

Independence

Arguably, the essential characteristic of a judge is independence. Of the four canons of the Model Code of Judicial Conduct, the first one outlines independence. Canon 1 states, "A judge shall uphold and promote the independence, integrity, and impar-tiality of the judiciary, and shall avoid impropriety and the appearance of impro-priety" (ABA, 2011, n.p.). Within this canon is the caution of not only the actual impropriety but also the mere appearance of impropriety. If a judge is considering removing him- or herself from a case, than it is probably a good indication that he or she should. Canon 1 also cautions judges not to abuse the prestige of their office to advance their own interests or others' interests.

Canon 2 again mentions impartiality and directs judges to perform their duties with competence and diligence. The rules underneath canon 2 instruct judges to give precedence to their duties, apply laws in a fair and impartial manner, and elim-inate the use of bias, prejudice, and harassment. The canon requires that no external pressure influences a judge's conduct, ensures the right to be heard, requires order and decorum within the court, and requires patience, dignity, and courteousness to all parties. Judges are not allowed to participate in ex parte communications—that is, communication with only one side of the dispute. They must also refrain from making public statements on pending cases, disqualify themselves when impartial-ity is questioned, and perform supervisory duties and administrative appointments with competence. Rule 2.15 of the ABA Model Code of Judicial Conduct (2011) illustrates self-governance of the rules by requiring judges to report other judges or attorneys who they know have committed violations of the rules to the appropriate authority, usually the state bar association disciplinary committee. The judges are also required to cooperate with the disciplinary authorities and avoid any retaliation against a person suspected to have cooperated in an investigation of the judge.

Extrajudicial Activities

Canon 3 of the ABA Model Code of Judicial Conduct (2011) cautions judges against extrajudicial activities that interfere with the performance of their duties, activities that would allow for disqualification, undermine their independence, appear to be coercive, or use court assets for tasks other than court activities. Again, the rule addresses issues that would undermine the independence and integrity of the judge or their office. The rules caution against or forbid activities such as testifying as a character witness, using nonpublic information, being appointed to other govern-mental positions, belonging to a discriminatory organization, being appointed to fiduciary positions, practicing law, being involved in other business activities, or accepting gifts or other things of value.

Judges sometimes acquire their positions by appointment. Other judges find their way to the bench through elections. This code not only applies to judges but also to candidates for judicial offices. According to the ABA Model Code of Judicial Conduct, Canon 4 (2011, n.p.), "A judge or candidate for judicial office shall not engage in political or campaign activity that is inconsistent with the independence, integrity, or impartiality of the judiciary."

Pretrial Publicity

The basis of our criminal court system is the fair trial. A fair trial is less likely with celebrated cases, constant media attention, and participants' access to social media. Often in cases of national recognition or even local recognition with well-known defendants, the defense attorney will file a motion for a change of venue; this allows the trial to commence in another county. The judge decides to grant or deny the motion for a change of venue.

The concern here is the potential jury pool and citizens' access to pretrial publicity. What the judge wants within the trial is for jury members to use only the admissible evidence presented at trial to decide the fate of the accused, not outside information. As stated in McEwen and Eldridge (2016), "the conscientiousness and diligence of a decision maker will not necessarily allow them to disregard information they have become aware of as a consequence of prejudicial publicity. Once known, information cannot be unknown" (p. 112). In a bench trial, the judge is the trier of facts; there is no jury. There is also a concern of judges' knowledge of pretrial publicity, even though we assume judges will be able to disregard it. McEwen and Eldridge (2016) note that some studies suggest "that judges may be just as vulnerable to the impact of inadmissible evidence and prejudicial publicity as jurors" (p. 112).

▶ Attorneys

All attorneys are *officers of the court*, a term that conveys specific responsibilities to uphold justice and promote efficient operation of the court. This section generally addresses those responsibilities of all attorneys, and they apply equally to prosecutors and defense attorneys as discussed in the following separate sections.

Confidentiality

Once an attorney and client relationship is formed, and sometimes when information is gained from a prospective client, the duty of confidentiality or the attorney–client privilege attaches. This privilege is one of the oldest from common law and belongs to the client; the information may not be revealed without the client's consent (ABA, 2018). The consent comes in the form of a waiver.

> The privilege applies only if (1) the asserted holder of the privilege is or sought to become a client; (2) the person to whom the communication was made (a) is a member of the bar of a court, or his subordinate and (b) in connection with this communication is acting as a lawyer; (3) the communication relates to a fact of which the attorney was informed (a) by his client (b) without the presence of strangers (c) for the purpose of securing primarily either (i) an opinion on law or (ii) legal services or (iii) assistance in some legal proceeding, and not (d) for the purpose of committing a crime or tort; and (4) the privilege has been (a) claimed and (b) not waived by the client. (*United States v. United Shoe Machinery Corporation*, 1950, pp. 358–359)

Rule 1.6, Confidentiality of Information, of the Model Rules (ABA, 2018, n.p.) states, "A lawyer shall not reveal information relating to the representation of a client unless the client gives informed consent, the disclosure is impliedly authorized in order to carry out the representation or the disclosure is permitted by paragraph (b)." Subsection (b) lists the occasions when the lawyer may disclose privileged information for the furtherance of justice or to prevent harm, injury, or crime from occurring. Marcum and Campbell (2015) state that the boundaries of confidential information is not always clear and that getting a waiver from the client is the best course of action. If that is not possible, however, the attorney should consult others such as judges, courts, or bar associations before releasing the information.

Competence

To offer knowledgeable advice to clients, attorneys are required to provide competent representation that includes keeping current on local court rules, statutes, rules of procedure, evidence, regulations, and skills as stipulated by the ABA Model Rule of Professional Conduct 1.1: Competence (ABA, 2018). Rule 2.1 directs the attorney as an adviser to the client to render advice with consideration to not only the law but also to "moral, economic, social and political factors that may be relevant to the client's situation" (ABA, 2018, n.p.). This is also the reason state bar associations require a certain amount of continuing legal education each year to maintain the attorney's bar license.

Pro Bono Service

Another duty of attorneys essential to the administration of justice is the responsibility to provide legal service to those who cannot afford it. Langton and Farole (2010) note that 49 states and the District of Columbia provide some organized criminal defense representation to indigent defendants, most of these in the form of public defenders. Of these, 22 states fund state public defender offices; the others provide this service locally through counties (Langton & Farole, 2010). However, these organizations are historically and currently underfunded by the states, and public defenders are overwhelmed in the number of cases they assume. Law school teaches students about giving back to the profession in the form of pro bono work or providing legal expertise without cost to the client. Rule 6.1 of the ABA Model Code of Professional Conduct speaks to this issue: "Every lawyer has a professional responsibility to provide legal services to those unable to pay. A lawyer should aspire to render at least (50) hours of pro bono publico legal services per year" (2018, n.p.). Within the rule is a list of possible ways to provide this type of service. Often judges find it necessary to appoint private attorneys to represent defendants unable to afford an attorney, and Rule 6.2 states, "A lawyer shall not seek to avoid appointment by a tribunal to represent a person except for good cause" (2018, n.p.).

> A lawyer should be mindful of deficiencies in the administration of justice and of the fact that the poor, and sometimes persons who are not poor, cannot afford adequate legal assistance. Therefore, all lawyers should devote professional time and resources and use civic influence to ensure

equal access to our system of justice for all those who because of economic or social barriers cannot afford or secure adequate legal counsel (ABA, 2018, Preamble and Scope item 6).

Self-Governance

As previously mentioned, judges are required to report and cooperate with disciplinary authorities when they know of rules violations; so, too, are attorneys assigned with this same obligation with regard to other attorneys and judges. This is part of the self-governance of the profession. Rule 8.3 of the ABA Model Rules of Professional Conduct (2018, n.p.) states,

> (a) A lawyer who knows that another lawyer has committed a violation of the Rules of Professional Conduct that raises a substantial question as to that lawyer's honesty, trustworthiness or fitness as a lawyer in other respects, shall inform the appropriate professional authority.

> (b) A lawyer who knows that a judge has committed a violation of applicable rules of judicial conduct that raises a substantial question as to the judge's fitness for office shall inform the appropriate authority.

It is noteworthy that the same conduct triggering disciplinary action in federal court can initiate action in state courts (Lucio, 2017). When a state bar association finds an attorney or judge in violation of the Model Rules, it can impose sanctions. The Model Rules do not provide for sanctions, although each state bar Association outlines a disciplinary mechanism with sanctions that can include fee forfeiture, monetary sanctions, disbarment, suspension, and prohibition from future representation in particular types of cases (Lucio, 2017).

Conflicts of Interest

Avoiding conflicts of interest is necessary not only for attorneys but also for judges. As stated in the Comments for the ABA Model Rules of Professional Conduct (2018, n.p.), Rule 1.7, "Loyalty and independent judgment are essential elements in the lawyer's relationship to a client." Concurrent conflicts of interest occur when the attorney's representation or potential representation of a client may have a negative consequence for another client. Conflicts can also occur when an attorney has a financial or personal stake in the outcome of a case. Rule 1.7 of the ABA Model Rules of Professional Conduct (2018, n.p.) states,

> (a) Except as provided in paragraph (b), a lawyer shall not represent a client if the representation involves a concurrent conflict of interest. A concurrent conflict of interest exists if:
> > (1) the representation of one client will be directly adverse to another client; or
> > (2) there is a significant risk that the representation of one or more clients will be materially limited by the lawyer's responsibilities to another client, a former client or a third person or by a personal interest of the lawyer.

▶ Prosecutors

In criminal prosecutions, prosecutors represent the victim and the state or the federal government—in essence, us. Prosecutors establish the truth through the presentation of witnesses and challenging defense witnesses. They represent the administration of justice for the victim by charging the accused and convicting the guilty. They also, after investigation, do not pursue charges when the evidence does not support prosecution. Often law enforcement officers complain when prosecutors fail to file charges on those arrested for crimes. This is within their discretion because probable cause to arrest does not always equate to proof beyond a reasonable doubt to prosecute and convict.

Rule 3.8, Special Responsibilities of a Prosecutor, of the ABA Model Rules of Professional Conduct (2018) provide for prosecutors. The rule includes filing charges on those with enough evidence to convict, not filing charges when evidence is slight, ensuring defendants know their rights, not taking advantage of unrepresented defendants, turning over exculpatory evidence to the defense, and maintaining privileged communications between lawyers and clients.

The National District Attorneys Association also has a *National Prosecution Standards*, third edition (n.d.). This organization was formed to support prosecutors in their duties as public servants and to inform Congress and the U.S. Department of Justice about views and policies affecting their own and law enforcement's jobs (https://ndaa.org/about/aboutndaa/). The first standard—1-1.1 Primary Responsibility—states the role of a prosecutor:

> The prosecutor is an independent administrator of justice. The primary responsibility of a prosecutor is to seek justice, which can only be achieved by the representation and presentation of the truth. This responsibility includes, but is not limited to, ensuring that the guilty are held accountable, that the innocent are protected from unwarranted harm, and that the rights of all participants, particularly victims of crime, are respected. (National District Attorneys Association, n.d.).

The prosecutor must prove each element of the alleged offense beyond a reasonable doubt. Proving this starts with the opening statement in which the prosecution must outline the evidence that will show each element of the offense. If the prosecutor fails in this effort, the defense attorney will stand and immediately ask the judge for a directed verdict.

▶ Defense Attorneys

As just stated, good defense attorneys ensure prosecutors do their jobs by requiring each element of the offense or offenses is proven beyond a reasonable doubt. That is why so many closing arguments emphasize the point of reasonable doubt. This is not merely good lawyering—it is also a portion of Rule 3.1: "A lawyer for the defendant in a criminal proceeding, or the respondent in a proceeding that could result in incarceration, may nevertheless so defend the proceeding as to require that every element of the case be established" (ABA, 2018, n.p.).

The defense attorney is an advocate for the defendant charged with a crime and provides a zealous representation within the boundaries of criminal substantive and procedural law. Providing advice is one of the main reasons for hiring an attorney, even though sometimes the client refuses to accept that advice. Laying out possible results for different courses of action can allow clients to make informed decisions on their representation. The Model Rules of Professional Conduct cited can apply to many attorney situations, civil and criminal, but they are used here to address defense attorney obstacles.

The pretrial process and litigation sometimes seem sluggish. However Rule 1.3 provides diligence and promptness in client representation, and ABA Model Rules of Professional Conduct, Rule 3.2 directs the attorney to "make reasonable efforts to expedite litigation consistent with the interests of the client" (2018, n.p.). Judges can be influential here by not allowing every motion for continuance requested. A continuance is a request of the court to delay the hearing or proceeding. The judge's decision to grant or deny a motion for continuance can depend on factors such as the number of other cases pending on the docket, the length of time the case has already consumed, the availability of witnesses, whether the defendant is in pretrial detention, and the availability of the judge him- or herself.

There are many strategic decisions the defense attorney, sometimes in deliberation with the defendant, must make in regard to the defense portion of the case. These can include whether to submit any evidence on behalf of the defense at all, whether the client will testify, and allowing ensuring the testimony is truthful if the defendant testifies. A complicated issue with criminal defense attorneys occurs when clients want to testify. Rule 3.3, Candor Toward the Tribunal, first addresses the truthfulness of the lawyer's statements to the court involving all matters of law and fact and the duty to correct any false statements. Included in this rule is the duty of the lawyer to ensure the defendant, or defense witnesses, offers no material fact that is known by the attorney to be false. If this does occur, it is the attorney's responsibility to inform the court through "reasonable remedial measure, including, if necessary, disclosure to the tribunal" (ABA, 2018, n.p.). A later subsection of the same rule expresses that this duty continues even if the information is protected by the confidentiality of the attorney–client privilege.

▶ Social Media

The previous sections outlined issues that officers of the court must face every day within the court system. As technology and our methods of communication change, the lawyer must continue to make ethical decisions while representing clients and communicating with them. Social media has presented new challenges for lawyers, judges, and the rules of ethics. Although there are no new rules of ethics for this challenging media, a reevaluation of current rules and comments apply to this environment.

The ABA released Formal Opinion 480 in March 2018 titled "Confidentiality Obligations for Lawyer Blogging and Other Public Commentary." Social media can include "blogs, list serves, online articles, website postings, and brief online statement or microblogs" (ABA, 2018, n.p.). Social media also include "LinkedIn testimonials and Facebook postings by satisfied clients" (Dixon, 2018, n.p.).

Dixon (2018) specifies 10 commandments to follow when using social media to avoid violation of the Model Rules. They involve attorney educating themselves on the benefits and risks of social media use, carefully posting comments to ensure no confidential information is revealed, obtaining clients' consent when posting information about them, warning clients of their postings, and using discovery to uncover information helpful to the attorney's case (Dixon, 2018). Also, recognizing the person the attorney is communicating with on social media could be a "witness, represented person, unrepresented adverse party, potential client, etc." (Dixon, 2018, n.p.). Honest representation is also a requirement for the types of services offered on sites that promote the attorney's practice, especially when client testimonials are used (Dixon, 2018).

Judges are not expected to withdraw from all social media. However, the Model Code still applies to the actions of judges in person or in the cyberspace known as the *cloud*. Some of the virtual landmines for judges include befriending lawyers who appear in front of them or connecting with them on LinkedIn, allowing statements of bias or prejudice on their webpages, and "likes," postings, and photos (Gray, 2017a). Judges are warned against friending not only lawyers but also "any persons who regularly appear before the judge in an adversarial role, such as law enforcement personnel, social workers, expert witness or parties" (Gray, 2017a, p. 17; State of Connecticut, 2013). Ex parte communications are not allowed by the Model Code, and this is true on social media. Judges are also prohibited from independently investigating facts of a case (Gray, 2017a). Judges are never allowed to make public comments that could affect the outcome of a case, and this is true online as well (Gray, 2017a). Full-time judges are not allowed to practice law, so they must make sure that their comments are not considered legal advice and that they are not releasing nonpublic information (Gray, 2017b).

▶ Conclusion

This article provides a brief overview of the ethical challenges facing officers of the court within the criminal court system. The Model Rules of Professional Conduct and Model Code of Judicial Conduct cover more issues than are presented here, and the comments under each rule define the rules clearly and with more detail. A safe course of action for judges and attorneys, if confused whether a particular course of action will violate the rules, is to ask the state bar association's ethics advisory committees for opinions before acting. Despite the jokes about lawyers and judges, it is a profession of respect; in times of distress and uncertainty, attorneys can provide guidance and knowledge to help clients make informed decisions. They do this while keeping current on the law, keeping the confidences of their clients, avoiding ex parte communications, reporting violations of rules, cooperating with tribunals investigating violations, and carefully using social media.

Judges and attorneys want to provide their clients with representation that is ethical, intelligent, and in their client's best interest. As stated in the prayer to Oxford-educated and lawyer St. Thomas More, the patron saint of lawyers,

> [T]hat . . . I may be trustworthy with confidences, keen in study, accurate in analysis, correct in conclusion, able in argument, loyal to clients, honest

with all, courteous to adversaries, ever attentive to conscience . . . so that today I shall not to win a point, lose my soul. (Center for Thomas More Studies, 2003)

▶ References

American Bar Association (ABA). (2018). Model Rules of Professional Responsibility. Chicago, IL: ABA. Retrieved from https://www.americanbar.org/groups/professional_responsibility /publications/model_rules_of_professional_conduct/model_rules_of_professional_conduct _preamble_scope/

American Bar Association (ABA). (2011). Model Code of Judicial Conduct. Chicago, IL: ABA. Retrieved from https://www.americanbar.org/groups/professional_responsibility/publications /model_code_of_judicial_conduct.html

American Bar Association (ABA). (1983). *Model Rules of Professional Conduct, chair's introduction.* Chicago, IL: ABA. Retrieved from https://www.americanbar.org/groups/professional _responsibility/publications/model_rules_of_professional_conduct/model_rules_of _professional_conduct_preface/chair_introduction/

American Bar Association (ABA) & Bloomberg BNA. (2018). Lawyer's manual on professional conduct. Retrieved from https://www.americanbar.org/groups/professional_responsibility/publications/aba _bna_lawyers_manual_on_professional_conduct/ababnalawyersmanualorderingandpricing/

Center for Thomas More Studies. (2003). A prayer to St. Thomas More. Retrieved from https:// www.thomasmorestudies.org/docs/Prayer_to_TM.pdf

Dixon, H. B., Jr. (2018). Yes, judges should know about recurring ethical issues involving the use of social media by lawyers. *The Judges' Journal, 57*(2), 37–39. Retrieved from https://www .americanbar.org/content/dam/aba/publications/judges_journal/vol57no2-jj2018-tech.pdf

Gray, C. (2017a). Social media and judicial ethics: Part 1. *Judicial Conduct Reporter, 39*(1), 1–24. Retrieved from https://www.ncsc.org/~/media/Files/PDF/Topics/Center%20for%20 Judicial%20Ethics/JCR/JCR_Spring_2017.ashx

Gray, C. (2107a). Social media and judicial ethics: Part 1. *Judicial Conduct Reporter, 39*(1) 1–24. Retrieved from https://www.ncsc.org/~/media/Files/PDF/Topics/Center%20for%20 Judicial%20Ethics/JCR/JCR_Spring_2017.ashx

Gray, C. (2017b). Social media and judicial ethics: Part 2. *Judicial Conduct Reporter, 39*(2) 1–20. Retrieved from https://www.ncsc.org/~/media/Files/PDF/Topics/Center%20for%20 Judicial%20Ethics/JCR/JCR_Summer_2017.ashx

Langton, L., & Farole, D., Jr. (2010). State public defender programs, 2007. (NCJ 228229). Washington, DC: U.S. Department of Justice, Office of Justice Programs, Bureau of Justice Statistics. Retrieved from https://www.bjs.gov/content/pub/pdf/spdp07.pdf

Lucio, T. (2017). Standards and regulation of professional conduct in federal practice. *The Federal Lawyer,* 50–53. Retrieved from http://www.fedbar.org/Resources_1/Federal-Lawyer -Magazine/2017/July/Features/Standards-and-Regulation-of-Professional-Conduct-in -Federal-Practice.aspx?FT=.pdf

Marcum, T. M., & Campbell, E. A. (2015). The ethical boundaries of the attorney-client privilege. *Journal of Legal Profession, 39*(2), 199–229.

McEwen, R., & Eldridge, J. (2016). Judges, juries and prejudicial publicity: Lessons from empirical legal scholarship. *Alternative Law Journal,* 110–114.

National District Attorneys Association. (n.d.). *National prosecution standards* (3rd ed.). Retrieved from https://ndaa.org/wp-content/uploads/NDAA-NPS-3rd-Ed.-w-Revised-Commentary.pdf

State of Connecticut. (2013, March 22). Informal opinion 2013-06. Connecticut Committee on Judicial Ethics. Hartford, CT: Connecticut Committee on Judicial Ethics. Retrieved from https://www.jud.ct.gov/Committees/ethics/sum/2013-06.htm

United States v. United Shoe Machinery Corporation, 89 F. Supp. 357, (1950).

ARTICLE 19

Lawyers, Clients, and Ethics in Class Action Cases

Michael E. Solimine

Legal ethics is the body of law that governs the relationships of lawyers to their clients, to each other, and to and between other actors in the legal system such as judges. It might seem to be of technical concern only to the legal community, but it addresses issues that are familiar to the general public from watching *Law and Order* and many other legal shows and movies. So, for example, many people likely have at least a passing familiarity with topics such as the attorney–client privilege or conflicts of interests an attorney might have when representing multiple clients.

Legal ethics can and should be of interest to the general public in another way. Many people likely have heard of or even been involved in (whether they realize it or not), a certain type of civil case: the class action. In this type of suit, one party—almost always the party bringing the suit (the plaintiff)—requests the court to permit an attorney to represent a large number or class of people who have the same or a similar legal dispute with the defendant. The members of the class, if one is certified by the court, are not strictly speaking parties to the lawsuit, however; only the plaintiff is. But the class members are *represented* by the plaintiff, and they are usually bound by the result of the case, whichever side wins, or when the case settles out of court. Many people have likely seen references to class actions being filed—to give only one example, in the many electronic data breaches in recent years. That usually means the plaintiff's attorney has filed a suit for one plaintiff and further requested that a class of similarly harmed individuals be certified. (Needless to say, not all such requests are granted. Many are denied or a case is dismissed, settled without a class being certified, or resolved on other grounds.) If a class action settles, as most do, then notifications of a proposed settlement are sent to class members (sometimes informing them for the first time that they are in a class) and frequently posted in the news media. Members of the class can support or object to the settlement, but it needs to be approved by the court.

▶ Class Actions and Legal Ethics

The class action device has been around for hundreds of years. It was first developed in the equity courts in England as a matter of fairness and efficiency to resolve a legal dispute that involved large numbers of individuals who were affected in similar ways. Rather than each plaintiff filing his own suit, which would be a burden to the defendant and the court, they were consolidated in the class action and resolved all at once. In its early stages, class actions were usually limited to cases in which the factual and legal issues for all of the class members were virtually identical. More recently, class actions were used in these types of situations (think of a plane crash) but also began to be certified in broader types of cases in which the alleged harm caused by a defendant was spread out geographically and in time (think of a product sold to many people throughout the country at different times). The broader use of class actions was particularly driven by amendments in 1966 to Federal Rule of Civil Procedure 23, which governs cases in federal courts, and to similar rules that govern litigation in most state courts. Today, it is not unusual for class certification to be sought in such instances as mass accidents, products affecting many people (the Dalkon Shield, asbestos, and many other examples), products that are improperly designed or manufactured (washing machines), or employment disputes involving many workers at one employer to name a handful of examples (Marcus, 2018; Miller, 2018).

So what do class actions have to do with legal ethics? Lots, it turns out. A typical civil case begins with a potential plaintiff reaching out to a lawyer; after consulting with the client, the lawyer may then file suit against a defendant. Consultations continue as the lawsuit proceeds, and the client must be aware of and approve all major decisions made by the lawyer, whether the case is resolved by the court or settles out of court (though, in many instances, especially with unsophisticated clients, the lawyer will run the show). The defendant similarly has a lawyer. A relatively passive judge presides over the suit; the judge takes action only when requested by the lawyers by motions or when, if at all, the case is resolved at a trial. Many of these straightforward relationships may be turned upside down in class action cases. Lawyers may reach out to clients, lawyers make all important decisions, and frequently the lawyers for *both* sides cooperate, especially if they agree to settle. The judge may be actively involved in the case, including in the negotiation and approval of a settlement. As well-known federal judge Jack Weinstein, who has presided over many class action cases, says, our "current general code of ethics assumes a Lincolnesque lawyer strongly bonded to an individual client. In mass torts the facts do not fit this picture" (Weinstein, 1994, p. 481).

▶ Negative Value Suits and Entrepreneurial Litigation

Not every class action case is marked by these unusual ethical problems—or any ethical issue at all. Consider, say, the class actions of African Americans in the 1950s and 1960s seeking injunctive (nondamages) relief to desegregate public schools and other facilities. But the potentially odd nature of ethical issues in class actions is accentuated in those cases marked by both negative value suits and entrepreneurial litigation. John Coffee of Columbia Law School defines such litigation as that "in which the attorney acts as a risk-taking entrepreneur, both financing and managing the litigation for numerous clients, who necessarily have smaller stakes in the litigation than the attorney" (Coffee, 2017, p. 1897).

Negative value suits are those in which the amount of monetary damage to any given person is so small that it is simply not worth the effort for any one person to bring a suit. In fact, the person may not even know he or she has been harmed; think of a breach of electronic data for millions of people kept by a credit agency or Facebook. Nor would it make much economic sense for an attorney to bring suit on behalf of one person. In these cases, an attorney is usually paid on a contingent fee basis, meaning the attorney gets approximately one-third or more of a court award, or a settlement, from the case. (If neither award nor settlement happens, the attorney gets nothing.) One-third of a small amount is even smaller.

Similarly, attorneys in these situations may reach out to potential clients, rather than the other way around. Everyone has seen the ads on TV where attorneys tout their services. (Such ads were prohibited by long-standing ethical rules enforced by states, until they were declared unlawful by the U.S. Supreme Court in the 1970s as violations of free speech guaranteed by the First Amendment.) Typically, these attorneys would contact one or a small number of potential class representatives. And typically, the nature of the suit leads to the lawyer taking the lead role in controlling all of the steps in the litigation—that is, only the class representatives need be consulted; the members of the class, if one is certified, usually are not contacted in any formal way. Thus, the attorneys for the class have little incentive to appreciate variances that may exist among class members.

Richard Posner, another federal judge with extensive experience with class actions, has said that the

> class action is a worthwhile supplement to conventional litigation procedure. . . . [But] control of the class over its lawyers usually is attenuated, often to the point of nonexistence. Except for the named plaintiffs, the members of the class are more like beneficiaries than like parties . . . [and] they have no control over class counsel. In principle the named plaintiffs do have that control, but . . . this is rarely true in practice. Class actions are the brainchildren of lawyers who specialize in prosecuting such actions, and in picking class representatives they have no incentive to select persons capable or desirous of monitoring the lawyers' conduct of the litigation. (*Eubank v. Pella Corp.*, 2014, pp. 719–720)

There's more. Another unusual aspect of ethics in the class action setting is the often counterintuitive degree of cooperation between lawyers for the class and those for the defendant. For different reasons, both sides may find it advantageous to settle the case on terms that may not be particularly helpful for most of the class. We'll consider the settlement of class actions in further detail in the following sections. For the moment, we can say that a plaintiff may seek class certification even if the claim is relatively weak on the merits because a certified class places pressure on any defendant to settle given the potentially large liabilities associated with many class actions (a defendant cannot be certain that an objectively weak case will, in fact, lose). Similarly, rather than fighting tooth and nail, a defendant may not oppose certification and usually follow up by agreeing to some kind of settlement because it resolves legal exposure all at once. Such settlements, as we will see, may pose the danger of giving something modest to the class representatives and little or virtually nothing to the members of the class while providing a generous award of attorneys' fees to class counsel. As Posner has observed, the "defendant cares only about the size of the settlement, not how it is divided between attorneys' fees and compensation for the class. From the selfish standpoint of class counsel and the defendant, therefore, the optimal settlement is one modest in overall amount but heavily tilted toward attorneys' fees" (*Eubank v. Pella Corp.*, 2014, p. 720).

Under Rule 23, there's a right of class members in most suits for damages to opt out of the class and a proposed settlement, but experience has shown that opt-out rates are almost always tiny. Thus, as Robert Gordon of Yale Law School has observed, the "plaintiff and defendant class action lawyers sometimes colluded against the interests of the injured to settle cases early and cheaply, assisted by trial judges trying to clear their dockets" (Gordon, 2019, p. 182).

Despite these numerous ethical problems, is the class action device still worth the trouble? Many people would answer yes, especially when it comes to negative value suits. Generally speaking, civil suits serve the broad purposes of compensating plaintiffs who have been harmed in some way and deterring illegal conduct by defendants. Neither purpose is served if a lawsuit is unlikely to be brought at all except by way of a group of injured individuals in a class action. But class actions come with costs. Yes, they can be efficient for the legal system and society as a whole by resolving large numbers of legal disputes in one courtroom, but there can be significant fairness issues: Class members (and their attorneys) might get more compensation by filing individual actions, especially in non-negative value suits, if they weren't part of the class (Coffee, 1987, pp. 880–881).

▶ Judicial Approval of Class Action Settlements and the Subway Footlong Case

Various proposals have been advanced to ameliorate these ethical problems. Some would more closely regulate or limit the attorneys' fees received by class counsel or directly make it more difficult to certify class actions in the first instance (Marcus, 2018). Others would make it easier for class members to opt out (or even require them to *opt in*), require more individual hearings to take into account the possibly disparate interests of large classes, or provide for greater use of subclasses within one large adjudication (Coffee, 1987, pp. 918–930). Still others might revisit the ethical rules themselves and alternatively enforce them more vigorously in class actions or overtly generate new rules to deal with class actions (Menkel-Meadow, 1995; Weinstein, 1994). The focus here is on one existing mechanism: Rule 23(e). The rule (and its state court counterparts) provides that any settlement of a class action must be approved by the court, and the settlement must be "fair, reasonable, and adequate."

This requirement is unusual in American civil litigation. Many civil cases settle out of court, but the vast majority are not subject to court approval. Rather, the parties agree to settle their differences, the settlement is memorialized in a contract, and the plaintiff then dismisses the case. With rare exceptions, no court intervention or approval is needed. Class actions are different because the class representatives and their attorneys stand in a fiduciary relationship to the members of the class.

Rule 23 generally takes a hands-off stance to that relationship, but it intervenes at the settlement stage to try to ensure that the class representatives and their counsel have acted—as best as the court can tell—consistently with their obligation as fiduciaries to the class.

In theory, the requirement of court approval of settlements has the potential to ameliorate some of the ethical issues previously outlined. But court approval itself has problems. As Posner observes:

> American judges are accustomed to presiding over adversary proceedings. They expect the clash of the adversaries to generate the information that the judge needs to decide the case. And so when a judge is being urged by both adversaries to approve the class-action settlement that they've negotiated, he's at a disadvantage in evaluating the fairness of the settlement to the class.

As Posner further points out, the problem is partially solved by the ability of class members to object to the proposed settlement (that's why they receive notice) (*Eubank v. Pella Corp.*, 2014, p. 720). Indeed, a cadre of professional objectors to class action settlements has arisen (they nominally represent objecting members of the class), and courts have permitted and even welcomed their involvement. True, this newer "hard-look review" (Elia, 2018) is not perfect. Taken to extremes, it may discourage too many settlements, and professional objectors may be said to engage in their own opportunistic behavior (Lopatka & Smith, 2012).

Consider one well-known example of a court considering a class action settlement: *In re Subway Footlong Sandwich Marketing and Sales Practices Litigation* (2017). In 2013, a teenager bought and measured his Subway Footlong sandwich and discovered that it was only 11 inches long. A class action was soon brought in federal district court in Wisconsin on the basis that the failure to sell a foot-long sandwich was unlawful fraud under state consumer protection statutes. The facts soon revealed that, as the appellate court put it, the claims lacked merit. Subway's unbaked bread sticks are uniform and rarely fall short of 12 inches. According to the court, the "minor variations that do occur are wholly attributable to the natural variability in the baking process and cannot be prevented." Plaintiffs proved unable to show any kind of damages, so they requested certification of a class for injunctive relief. Negotiations with Subway took place, and ultimately a settlement was reached, whereby Subway agreed to take some minor steps to ensure that its sandwich rolls measure at least 12 inches long and to pay $520,000 in attorneys' fees for class counsel and $500 for each named plaintiff. The federal trial court approved the settlement.

Ted Frank, a well-known professional class action objector with the Competitive Enterprise Institute, had earlier challenged the proposed settlement on the grounds that it was worthless to the class and then appealed its approval. The U.S. Court of Appeals for the Seventh Circuit in Chicago agreed with Frank and reversed the district judge. After first echoing the concerns of Richard Posner and others and then calling for close scrutiny of class action settlements, the court argued that the status quo for the class was virtually the same before and after the settlement: "[T]here's *still* the same small chance that Subway will sell a class member a sandwich that is slightly shorter than advertised." The court concluded that because the "settlement yields fees for class counsel and 'zero benefits for the class,'" the settlement should not have been approved. Shortly afterward, the plaintiffs reportedly dismissed the entire case (Competitive Enterprise Institute, 2017).

Cognizant of the harder-look review federal courts have recently taken of class action settlements, of which the *Subway* decision is only one example, the federal rule makers amended Rule 23(e) as of December 1, 2018, to codify those cases. It still has the "fair, reasonable, and adequate" language but adds that a proposed settlement must have been negotiated at arm's length, class members must be treated equitably, and that the relief provided for the class is adequate, taking into account the costs, risks, and delay of a trial and appeal, absent a settlement, as well the terms of any attorneys' fees awarded.

The *Subway* settlement seems a textbook example of the ethical problems that can be associated with the pursuit of class action litigation. Its ultimate resolution also seems an example of the legal profession admirably confronting the possible ethical dilemmas faced by lawyers for both sides and indeed the judges in those cases. It shows that class actions, or the current ethical rules, need not be abolished or sharply curtailed. The social utility of class actions can remain while ethical problems can be policed by less drastic means such as more closely examining the settlements of these cases.

▶ References

Coffee, J. C., Jr. (1987). The regulation of entrepreneurial litigation: Balancing fairness and efficiency in the large class action. *University of Chicago Law Review, 54*, 877–937.

Coffee, J. C., Jr. (2017). The globalization of entrepreneurial litigation: Law, culture, and incentives. *University of Pennsylvania Law Review, 165*, 1895–1925.

Competitive Enterprise Institute. (2017, October 26). Consumers win in Subway Footlong settlement as plaintiffs walk away. Retrieved from https://cei.org/content/consumers-win-subway-footlong-settlement-plaintiffs-walk-away

Elia, K. (2018). Hard-look judicial review of class action settlements. *University of Cincinnati Law Review, 85*, 1135–1163.

Eubank v. Pella Corp., 753 F.3d 718 (7th Cir. 2014).

Gordon, R. W. (2019, Winter). Lawyers, the legal profession and access to justice in the United States: A brief history. *Daedalus, 148*(1), 177–189.

In re Subway Footlong Sandwich Marketing and Sales Practices Litigation, 869 F.3d 551 (7th Cir. 2017).

Lopatka, J. E., & Smith, D. B. (2012). Class action professional objectors: What to do about them? *Florida State University Law Review, 39*, 865–929.

Marcus, R. (2018). Revolution v. evolution in class action reform. *North Carolina Law Review, 96*, 903–943.

Menkel-Meadow, C. (1995). Ethics and the settlements of mass torts: When the rules meet the road. *Cornell Law Review, 80*, 1159–1221.

Miller, A. R. (2018). The American class action: From birth to maturity. *Theoretical Inquiries in Law, 19*, 1–45.

Weinstein, J. B. (1994). Ethical dilemmas in mass tort litigation. *Northwestern University Law Review, 88*, 469–568.

Ethical Responsibilities and Challenges in the Courtroom Work Group

Patricia B. Wagner

▶ The Courtroom Work Group

The actors who work closely and consistently together in the criminal trial courts are often referred to as the *courtroom work group*. The core of this group consists of prosecuting attorneys, defense attorneys, and judges. As with any work group, there is a socialization process that occurs. Because prosecutors and defense attorneys are frequent adversaries of each other and because they, in turn, appear repeatedly in front of the same judges, these actors get to know one another and develop working relationships over time.

Members of the courtroom work group labor in the context of the customs and expectations of other members of the group. Consider, for example, that most criminal cases are resolved with plea bargains. To successfully negotiate a plea bargain, the prosecutor and the defense attorney must work together to reach an agreement on what they believe is the best deal for their sides. The defense attorney depends on the prosecutor to be open and forthcoming about the evidence that will be used against the defendant. The prosecutor depends on the defense attorney to represent his or her clients zealously without being dishonest or putting the public in danger. The judge trusts that the prosecutor and the defense attorney are working in the interests of justice and must ultimately approve the plea bargain for it to take effect. In learning to navigate these situations, members of the work group develop norms and practices that influence their behavior. The members of the courtroom work group are interdependent with one another in processing cases despite their differing interests. Their professional success depends not only on developing positive working relationships with other members in the courtroom work group but also working well with other actors in the legal system such as court staff, corrections officials and police. The need for healthy working relationships within the work group motivates courtroom actors to adhere to minimum standards of professional behavior.

The behavior of the members of the courtroom work group is also guided by formal rules that govern attorney and judicial conduct. Attorneys and judges are considered officers of the court. As such they are sworn to uphold the Constitution of the United States and the constitutions of the respective states in which they practice, and they must conduct themselves in a manner that reflects well on the court. All members of the bar have a duty of honesty to the court. Making false statements to the court (perjury) or knowingly enabling false witness testimony (subornation of perjury) are criminal offenses. Beyond these general obligations for officers of the court, there are also highly specific rules that govern each role in the court process.

▶ Codes of Professional Responsibility

All attorneys and judges are required to follow detailed ethical principles and guidelines. Every state has adopted its own code of professional conduct for attorneys licensed to practice in that state. Typically, there is a separate code of judicial conduct, given the special role judges play among members of the bar. The rules set out in these codes, often referred to as *codes of professional responsibility*, impose ethical obligations on the courtroom work group that are enforced by state commissions. In addition, professional associations such as the American Bar Association (ABA) publish standards of conduct of their own. The ABA is the predominant national professional organization for the legal field, and the standards it publishes set expectations for members of the bar throughout the United States. All 50 state codes of conduct, although showing variation from jurisdiction to jurisdiction, are largely modeled after the ABA's Model Rules of Professional Conduct and Model Code of Judicial Conduct. Attorneys and judges are bound by the codes adopted in their jurisdiction. If they violate a provision, they may be subjected to disciplinary proceedings.

Each state maintains its own disciplinary commission that enforce codes of attorney and judicial conduct. The commissions are usually supervised by a branch of the state's supreme court. The state's disciplinary commission may initiate proceedings based on a complaint that a judge or attorney has engaged in some misconduct that violated a rule of professional conduct. The disciplinary commission may take a variety of different actions, depending on the severity of the violation. For minor infractions, they may censure the attorney or judge, which consists of publishing information about the violation in legal publications and including information about the violation in the individual's permanent records. For example, judges or attorneys who fail to complete their continuing legal education requirements in a timely manner may be censured. For more severe violations, the attorney or judge may be suspended from practice for a given term. Assume, for example, that an attorney has been grappling with substance abuse issues that led him to miss an important filing deadline on a case and has been charged with neglect of a legal matter. The commission may sentence the attorney to a one-year suspension and order him to get medical or psychiatric treatment. During the suspension, the attorney cannot practice law. In the most extreme cases, an attorney or judge may be disbarred, meaning the individual is no longer able to practice law and his or her license must be permanently surrendered. Disbarment is mandatory if the attorney or judge is convicted of certain serious crimes. For instance, California attorney Kevin Lee was summarily disbarred in 2019 after he was convicted of arson, criminal threatening, and firearms violations (Kidd, 2019).

If the alleged ethical violation involves a federal judge, the Judicial Conduct and Disability Act of 1980 provides for a process in which a special committee investigates the judge in question. Whether it is a federal investigatory committee or a state commission involved, attorneys and judges all may be disciplined for a wide variety of ethical violations. These include making false statements to a court, conflicts of interest, and failure to report unlawful activity of another member of the bar. There are, however, ethical challenges that are unique to each of the roles of prosecutor, defense attorney, and judge.

▶ Ethical Responsibilities and Challenges of the Prosecutor

Prosecutors are often viewed as the most powerful actors in the criminal justice system because they have the power to decide whom to charge with a crime, what level of crime to charge someone with, and whether to agree to a plea bargain. Prosecutors are protected from retaliation for these decisions by legal immunity. Legal *immunity* means that prosecutors cannot be sued for their charging decisions, even if they engage in misconduct such as making false statements, breaking plea agreements, or failing to disclose important evidence. Although they can still be subject to the attorney discipline processes previously described, including disbarment, they do not have to worry about personally being sued. The enormous discretion wielded by prosecutors in making charging decisions comes with great responsibility. They are public servants who are expected to treat people fairly and not to indiscriminately, selectively, or maliciously pursue charges. The ABA Model Rules of Professional Conduct 3.8(a) (2018b) aim to prevent malicious prosecution by requiring that any prosecutor in a criminal case "shall refrain from prosecuting a charge that the prosecutor knows is not supported by probable cause."

The prosecutor represents all the people in his or her jurisdiction, not just individual victims. One of the most important ethical obligations of the prosecutor was articulated in 1963 by the U.S. Supreme Court in the case of *Brady v. Maryland*. The so-called Brady Rule requires that a prosecutor must disclose any exculpatory evidence to the defense if it is material to the case. Exculpatory evidence is defined as any evidence that may be favorable to the defendant. Exculpatory evidence is considered material to the case if there is a reasonable chance that the case would have a different outcome if the evidence were disclosed. In the landmark *Brady* case, the defendant's death sentence was overturned because the prosecution failed to disclose that another man confessed to killing the victim by himself. The obligation to disclose exculpatory evidence extends to impeachment evidence as well. *Impeachment evidence* is evidence that undermines the credibility of a witness. For example, there may be evidence that a witness committed perjury in a previous proceeding or has a conflict of interest in the current case that gives him or her a motive to lie. The Brady Rule stems from the basic concept that the prosecutor's ethical duty is to pursue justice rather than just to win cases. Clearly, there is no justice in knowingly trying to convict an innocent person, so covering up or ignoring evidence of innocence is inconsistent with a prosecutor's duty to society.

The Brady Rule has subsequently been folded into the ABA's Model Rules of Professional Conduct (2018b). Rule of Professional Conduct 3.8(d) states in pertinent part that prosecutors shall "make timely disclosure to the defense of all evidence or information known to the prosecutor that tends to negate the guilt of the accused or mitigates the offense, and, in connection with the sentencing, disclose to the defense and to the tribunal all unprivileged mitigating information known to the prosecutor." The ABA rules further require that if prosecutors later discover evidence that creates a reasonable likelihood that someone was wrongfully convicted, then they must contact the proper court and attempt to remedy the situation.

The ABA's Model Rules also try to prevent prosecutors from taking advantage of accused individuals who have not had the benefit of legal advice. Rule of Professional Conduct 3.8(b) states that the prosecutor shall "make reasonable efforts to assure that the accused has been advised of the right to, and procedure for obtaining, counsel and has been given reasonable opportunity to obtain counsel."

Another area addressed by the ABA Rules of Professional Conduct has to do with making inappropriate out-of-court statements. Rule 3.8(f) (2018b) admonishes prosecutors not to unfairly prejudice a case in the eyes of the public by requiring that prosecutors, "except for statements that are necessary to inform the public of the nature and extent of the prosecutor's action and that serve a legitimate law enforcement purpose, refrain from making extrajudicial comments that have a substantial likelihood of heightening public condemnation of the accused." Furthermore, the rule provides that prosecutors must also use care to prevent investigators, law enforcement personnel, employees, or others assisting them from making prejudicial out-of-court statements.

Ethical lapses on the part of prosecutors no doubt occur for many reasons— from purely personal failings to the incentives of the adversarial system. In the adversarial system, attorneys are trained to focus on winning, and it is easy to lose sight of other more nebulous goals such as serving justice for all. Prosecutors may be tempted to engage in any number of forbidden activities—from having contact with the judge or defendant without notifying the defense attorney, to intentionally referring to inadmissible evidence during trial in order to prejudice a jury. The pressure to bend the rules in order to succeed is shared by prosecutors and defense attorneys alike.

▶ Ethical Responsibilities and Challenges of the Defense Attorney

Above all, the defense attorney is ethically bound to be a zealous advocate for his or her client. This is true regardless of whether the attorney believes the client to be guilty or innocent. The official comment to ABA Rule of Professional Conduct 1.3 (2018a) states that "[a] lawyer should pursue a matter on behalf of a client despite opposition, obstruction, or personal inconvenience to the lawyer, and take whatever lawful and ethical measures are required to vindicate a client's cause or endeavor. A lawyer must also act with commitment and dedication to the interests of the client and with zeal and advocacy on the client's behalf." Zealous representation requires that the attorney take all reasonable actions to present a viable defense, regardless of his or her own personal feelings. Unlike the prosecutor, whose duty is to society, the defense attorney's duty is to only to the client. Members of the public who do not understand the adversarial system may see defense attorneys as inherently unethical because they are trying to help criminals escape justice. This unfair but common perception does not take into account that our system presumes that everyone is innocent and is entitled to due process.

One of the most important responsibilities of the defense attorney is to keep attorney–client communications confidential. These communications are protected by the attorney–client privilege, which can only be waived by the client. It is unethical for the attorney to disclose privileged communications. This privilege allows defendants to speak candidly to their attorneys without fear of reprisals. ABA Rule of Professional Conduct Rule 1.6(a) explicitly requires that "a lawyer shall not reveal information relating to the representation of a client unless the client gives informed consent." There are some narrow exceptions, such as when the client is threatening specific physical harm to someone or planning a future crime, but these are few. The rationale behind the attorney–client privilege is that the client must be able to trust his or her lawyer for the attorney to be able to defend the client properly.

At times the confidentiality requirement may present ethical challenges for the defense attorney. The defendant may make a full confession to a horrific crime—and the attorney is nonetheless honor bound to fight for an acquittal. The attorney must then set aside any personal repugnance related to the crime and not let it diminish the quality of the representation he or she provides. Also, the attorney–client privilege applies to communications but not to physical evidence. The prosecution can subpoena physical evidence, but there is a dilemma when a client turns over a piece of physical evidence to his or her defense attorney that is unknown to the prosecution. There is no clear guidance under the ABA Model Rules of Professional Conduct, or under current case law, to guide a defense attorney who acquires such incriminating physical evidence. What should an attorney do if a client gives the attorney a knife and says he used it to stab someone? The attorney might inform the prosecution, return it to the defendant, send it to the prosecution anonymously, or just keep quiet, depending on the balance between duty to client and duty to conscience.

Like all attorneys, defense attorneys must avoid conflicts of interest. They cannot, for example, implicate one client in a crime in order to exonerate another. They cannot knowingly allow a client to commit perjury, and this is commonly avoided simply by refusing to allow the client to testify. Often shortcomings in defense attorneys' performance have less to do with intentional misbehavior than with incompetence. Public defenders are notoriously overworked and underpaid, and they may simply not have the time and resources necessary to attain the goal of truly zealous representation. Perennial problems such as missing deadlines, failing to raise viable arguments, poor communication with clients about their options, and even falling asleep in court are subject to claims of ineffective assistance of counsel. Such behavior may result in a case being overturned and the attorney being disciplined by a state commission, despite the lack of any moral turpitude.

Poor performance by defense attorneys is also managed to a certain extent by the threat of malpractice suits. A malpractice suit is a civil lawsuit in which a client sues his or her attorney for failure to represent the client at the minimum standards expected for the legal profession. A defendant might sue an attorney for malpractice if he or she believes the attorney was negligent in handling the case. They must also show that, but for the attorney's negligence, the client would not have been convicted. These suits are relatively rare, but they can be expensive. In a malpractice suit in 2015, Jason Mashaney, a convicted child molester, demanded

$1.6 million from his public defenders, claiming he was innocent and not properly advised of his options before he pled guilty. The suit was eventually settled for an unspecified amount.

▶ Ethical Responsibilities and Challenges of the Judge

The ethical obligations of the judiciary are succinctly summarized by the ABA's Model Code of Judicial Conduct (2010) in four canons:

Canon 1: A judge shall uphold and promote the independence, integrity, and impartiality of the judiciary, and shall avoid impropriety and the appearance of impropriety.

Canon 2: A judge shall perform the duties of judicial office impartially, competently, and diligently.

Canon 3: A judge shall conduct the judge's personal and extrajudicial activities to minimize the risk of conflict with the obligations of judicial office.

Canon 4: A judge or candidate for judicial office shall not engage in political or campaign activity that is inconsistent with the independence, integrity, or impartiality of the judiciary

Pursuant to canon 1, note that even the *appearance* of impropriety raises ethical dilemmas for judges. This often becomes an issue with part-time judges who practice law on the side. If they have cases as attorneys in the same courts where they sit as judges, it gives the appearance of unfair advantage. Unfair advantage may also appear to be an issue, depending on the judge's prior legal experience. If the judge was a career prosecutor before joining the bench, there may be questions about his or her objectivity toward the defense. Especially in smaller communities, judges may be related to or be friends with many of the attorneys or witnesses in their courts. This appears to create a conflict of interest, yet judges are not uniformly prevented from hearing cases in these situations. In addition, most state judges are elected officials and must therefore run for office, raising questions about the judges' political activities and objectivity toward opponents. Avoiding the appearance of impropriety is a lofty goal but difficult for the judiciary to maintain.

Judges are ethically bound to remain neutral and detached. Canon 2 specifically requires that judges be impartial. When they cannot be, they are expected to recuse themselves, meaning that they step down from a case so it can be heard by a different judge. Recusal would be expected, for instance, if the victim in a case was the judge's mother. A judge is expected to act without bias, not only regarding the race, gender, sexual orientation, or religion of those that come before them but also regarding social class. In a recent case, a juvenile court judge offered unusually lenient treatment to a 16-year-old rape suspect, denying the prosecution's motion to try the teenager as an adult. The judge justified his decision because the defendant came from a good family, attended an excellent school, and had good test scores. His decision to keep the case in juvenile court was appealed, and the appellate court sharply rebuked the judge for showing bias toward privileged teenagers (Ferre-Sadurni, 2019).

Canon 3 demands that judges avoid activities that would create conflicts with their work. For this reason, many judges avoid joining civic groups of various kinds, even if they strongly support their goals. Whether it is the National Rifle Organization, Mothers Against Drunk Driving, the American Civil Liberties Union, the Federalist Society, or some other well-known group, membership therein casts doubt on the judge's objectivity. New judges may feel obligated to distance themselves from former legal colleagues and discontinue service on community boards to insulate themselves from claims of bias. Add to this the fact that judges are prohibited from commenting on pending cases, even to their own families, and the experience of a judge can be rather isolating. Ironically, judges are prohibited by Canon 4 from engaging in political activity inconsistent with their impartiality, yet those who are in elected positions must be overtly political animals to obtain their offices.

Judicial misbehavior typically culminates in punishment more serious than a reprimand only when it is blatant and involves willful or repeated misconduct in office, habitual failure to perform duties, substance abuse, or conviction of a crime. For example, Dianne Vettori-Caraballo, a part-time judge in Ohio, was recently sentenced to more than two years in prison after pleading guilty to stealing money from the estate of a client that she represented as a probate lawyer (U.S. Attorney's Office, 2019). She confessed to taking more than $100,000 in cash from the home of her deceased client, money that was intended to go to animal charities. Incompetent or unethical judges can be removed from office in various ways, depending on the jurisdiction. Federal judges can be impeached, as can judges in some states. State disciplinary commissions may order a judge's removal from the bench, and some states allow for recall elections. Because most judges are elected officials, the most common way to unseat bad judges is simply not to reelect them.

In summary, whether it is politics, the pressure to win that is inherent in the adversarial system, or pure human imperfection, numerous factors challenge the ethics of the courtroom work group. There are many laws and regulations that guide the ethics of the work group, but they do not cover every situation. Fortunately, the need for prosecutors, defense attorneys, and judges to work together as a cohesive team to process cases, coupled with a common desire to do the right thing, drives the work group to overcome most ethical challenges.

▶ References

American Bar Association (ABA). (2010). Model Code of Judicial Conduct. Chicago, IL: ABA. Retrieved from https://www.americanbar.org/groups/professional_responsibility/publications/model_code_of_judicial_conduct/

American Bar Association (ABA). (2018a). Model Rules of Professional Conduct 1.3: Diligence Comment. Chicago, IL: ABA. Retrieved from https://www.americanbar.org/groups/professional_responsibility/publications/model_rules_of_professional_conduct/rule_1_3_diligence/comment_on_rule_1_3/

American Bar Association (ABA). (2018b). Model Rules of Professional Conduct 3.8: Special Responsibilities of a Prosecutor. Chicago, IL: ABA. Retrieved from https://www.americanbar.org/groups/professional_responsibility/publications/model_rules_of_professional_conduct/rule_3_8_special_responsibilities_of_a_prosecutor/

Brady v. Maryland, 373 U.S. 83 (1963)

Ferre-Sadurni, L. (2019, July 2). Teenager accused of rape deserves leniency because he's from a "good family," judge says. *The New York Times*. Retrieved from https://www.nytimes.com/2019/07/02/nyregion/judge-james-troiano-rape.html

Judicial Conduct and Disability Act of 1980, 28 U.S.C. Chapter 16 (1980) Kidd, K. (2019, July 11). San Francisco attorney summarily disbarred following 2015 felony arson conviction. Northern California Record. Retrieved from https://norcalrecord.com/stories/512746339-san-francisco-attorney-summarily-disbarred-following-2015-felony-arson-conviction

Mashaney v. Board of Indigents Defense Services, 355 P.3d 667. (2015).

U.S. Attorney's Office. (2019, June 13). Former Mahoning County judge sentenced to more than two years in prison for stealing $1000,000 from deceased client's estate. The United States Attorney's Office, Northern District of Ohio. Retrieved from https://www.justice.gov/usao-ndoh/pr/former-mahoning-county-judge-sentenced-more-two-years-prison-stealing-100000-deceased

ARTICLE 21

Christian Burial Speech

Robert A. Brooks

© Sergii Gnatiuk/Shutterstock

Brewer v. Williams is a complex and fascinating case because of the brutality of the crime, the lengthy appellate record, and the courts' consideration of a rather novel legal question. In addition, the case could not have been more closely decided in the three appellate courts that considered it, with justices vehemently arguing for opposite outcomes based on identical facts. The article begins with a summary of the facts of the case and the appellate court decisions and then raises questions about both police ethics and judicial ethics.

▶ Summary of the Case[1]

On Christmas Eve 1968, the Powers family was at a YMCA in Des Moines, Iowa, when 10-year-old Pamela Powers went to the bathroom and did not return. Robert Williams, then a resident of the YMCA, carried a "bundle" wrapped in a blanket through the YMCA lobby. A boy reported to YMCA staff that he saw legs sticking out of the bundle, but Williams sped away in his car. The vehicle was found Christmas day in Davenport, Iowa, some 160 miles east of Des Moines.

The following day, Williams telephoned his Des Moines attorney, Henry McKnight, who advised Williams to turn himself in. McKnight then went to the Des Moines Police Department to discuss arrangements for his client's transport. In the meantime, Williams turned himself in to Davenport police. Later, he spoke on the telephone with McKnight while Des Moines Chief of Police Wendell Nichols and Detective Cleatus Leaming listened in. McKnight informed the officers that Williams would talk to police when he got back to Des Moines, and the officers agreed not to question Williams during the return trip.

Once the officers were in Davenport, another of Williams' attorneys, Mr. Kelly, asked that Leaming not question Williams and also asked to accompany Williams in the police car; this request was denied. Leaming gave Williams his Miranda warning, and told Williams that the two would be "visiting" on the ride. They then set off on the trip to Des Moines, with Nelson driving and Leaming and Williams sitting in the back seat. Another squad car followed. Leaming and Williams began speaking soon after they got in the car and spoke at length on a variety of topics during the trip. At several points during the trip, Williams told Leaming that he would tell police "the whole story" when they got to Des Moines.

At some point, Leaming gave what has come to be known as the "Christian burial speech." Knowing that Williams considered himself to be deeply religious, Leaming said to Williams:

> I want to give you something to think about while we're traveling down the road. . . . Number one, I want you to observe the weather conditions, it's raining, it's sleeting, it's freezing, driving is very treacherous, visibility is poor, it's going to be dark early this evening. They are predicting several inches of snow for tonight, and I feel that you yourself are the only person that knows where this little girl's body is, that you yourself have only been there once, and if you get a snow on top of it you yourself may be unable to find it. And, since we will be going right past the area on the way into Des Moines, I feel that we could stop and locate the body, that the parents of this little girl should be entitled to a Christian burial for the little girl who was snatched away from them on Christmas [E]ve and murdered. And I feel we should stop and locate it on the way in rather than waiting until morning and trying to come back out after a snow storm and possibly not being able to find it at all. (*Brewer v. Williams*, 430 U.S. 387, 392–393, 1977)

Later, Leaming also told Williams that he "knew" that the girl's body was near Mitchellville, Iowa, a town close to Des Moines. Williams asked how he knew, and Leaming said, "I do not want you to answer me. I don't want to discuss it further. Just think about it as we're riding down the road" (*Brewer v. Williams*, p. 393). Sometime later, Williams led the officers to places where he said he had hidden Pamela Powers' boots and a blanket, and when they got close to the Mitchellville exit, Williams told the officers that he would show them where the body was. He took them to a culvert in Polk County from which Pamela Powers' body was retrieved.

Before trial, McKnight moved to suppress Williams' incriminating statements, alleging a violation of his client's Fifth Amendment right to remain silent and his Sixth Amendment right to counsel. He also asked that Pamela Powers' body be excluded from evidence as "fruit of the poisonous tree" (that is, evidence flowing directly from the initial violation). The trial court denied the motion, and Williams was later convicted and sentenced to life in prison. The Supreme Court of Iowa affirmed his conviction by a vote of 4–3, finding that Williams had voluntarily waived his right to counsel and that his incriminating statements about the clothing were made "suddenly, spontaneously, voluntarily, and with no prompting" (*State v. Williams*, 182 N.W.2d 396, 402, Iowa 1970).

Subsequently, a federal district court granted Williams' habeas corpus petition and overturned his conviction, finding that Leaming had designed his statements to elicit incriminating information (see *Williams v. Brewer*, 375 F.Supp. 170, S.D. Iowa 1974). An Eighth Circuit Court panel upheld this decision by a vote of 2–1 (see *Williams v. Brewer*, 509 F.2d 227, 8th Cir. 1974). The U.S. Supreme Court affirmed the circuit court decision 5–4 (see *Brewer v. Williams*, 430 U.S. 387, 1977). The case resulted in seven opinions among the nine justices. The majority opinion, written by Associate Justice Potter Stewart, held that Leaming had violated Williams' Sixth Amendment right to have an attorney present during questioning, finding that (1) the police had agreed not to interrogate Williams; (2) the police sought to isolate

Williams from his lawyer; (3) the statements made by Leaming, including the Christian burial speech, were "tantamount to interrogation"; and (4) the state did not present "any evidence" that Williams had waived his right to have an attorney present during questioning. Associate Justices Thurgood Marshall, Lewis Powell, and Stewart each wrote a concurring opinion.

There were three strongly worded dissents. Chief Justice Warren Burger wrote that Williams had waived his right to have an attorney present when he voluntarily made the incriminating statements; even if Leaming had wrongfully interrogated Williams, such was merely a "technical violation," and thus the Court made a mistake "in mechanically applying the exclusionary rule without considering" its costs or its goals (p. 420). Associate Justice Byron White believed Williams had waived his Sixth Amendment right to counsel and added, "[t]he police did nothing 'wrong,' let alone anything 'unconstitutional'" (p. 437). Both Justices White and Harry Blackmun both predicted that the state would not be able to retry Williams eight years after his conviction and thus he would go free. This prediction is particularly interesting for two reasons. First, it wasn't accurate, as further discussion will show. Second, it seems to have provoked the majority to write the following in a footnote,

> While neither Williams' incriminating statements themselves nor any testimony describing his having led the police to the victim's body can constitutionally be admitted into evidence, evidence of where the body was found and of its condition might well be admissible on the theory that the body would have been discovered in any event, even had incriminating statements not been elicited from Williams. (p. 406, n. 12)[2]

Although Justice Burger found this to be an "unlikely theory" (p. 416, n. 1), Iowa prosecutors clearly took the hint. In Williams' retrial, they argued for the admission of Pamela Powers' body under the "inevitable discovery" doctrine. The trial court agreed, and a jury found Williams guilty. And again, the Iowa Supreme Court upheld his conviction (*State v. Williams*, 285 N.W.2d 248, Iowa 1979). Williams then filed his second habeas corpus petition in federal court, citing several errors. The district court denied the writ (see *Williams v. Nix*, 528 F.Supp. 664, S.D. Iowa 1981), but the circuit court reversed, finding that the inevitable discovery doctrine does not apply in cases like this one in which police have acted in bad faith (see *Williams v. Nix*, 700 F.2d. 1164, 8th Cir. 1983). The U.S. Supreme Court reversed, finding that bad faith is not an element of the inevitable discovery doctrine and remanded the case to the circuit court for consideration of Williams' other claimed errors (see *Nix v. Williams*, 467 U.S. 431, 1984). On remand, the circuit court found no errors and reinstated Williams' conviction 17 years after the crime occurred (see *Williams v. Nix*, 751 F.2d 956, 8th Cir. 1985). Williams later mounted a third habeas corpus challenge that was denied by the district court. That decision was affirmed (see *Williams v. Thalacker*, 103 F.3d 405, 8th Cir. 1997).

▶ The Ethics of Interrogation

Even though *Brewer v. Williams* was decided under the Sixth Amendment and not the Fifth, it was important to consider whether Leaming had "interrogated" Williams. This is because a suspect who invokes his or her Sixth Amendment right to counsel has a right to have a lawyer present during questioning, and interrogation must cease.[3] Thus, it matters whether Leaming was trying to encourage Williams to make incriminating statements or whether he was merely engaging him in conversation. The Iowa Supreme Court did not clearly rule on the issue, but the federal district court and each federal appellate court majority held that psychological pressure or persuasion, without questions, is the functional equivalent of interrogation and is sometimes even more effective.[4] Counsel for the state of Iowa acknowledged at oral arguments that at least the Christian burial speech was "tantamount to interrogation" (see *Brewer v. Williams*, 430 U.S. 387, 399 n. 6, 1977). The federal court dissenters argued variously that Leaming had not interrogated Williams, that Williams made the incriminating statements spontaneously and not in direct response to Leaming's statements, or that Leaming's statements did not coerce Williams.[5]

The conclusion that Leaming *intended* to obtain incriminating information from Williams is well supported by both the evidence and an understanding of police interrogation methods. As to the evidence, Leaming himself testified at trial that he was "hoping to get all the information [he] could before Williams got back to McKnight" (*Brewer v. Williams*, 430 U.S. 387, 399, 1977). If Leaming's own testimony were not enough, other circumstances indicate the officers intended to seek incriminating information from Williams.[6]

In addition, Leaming appears to have employed many "classic" interrogation tactics found in manuals. Kamisar (1978–1979) summarized Leaming's technique:

> He invoked the trickery, deception, and "psychology" recommended in the "how-to-do-it interrogation manuals" that so aroused the ire of the *Miranda* majority. He appealed in the name of religion to someone he knew to be deeply religious.[7] In effect, he challenged Williams to display some evidence of honor and decency. He addressed Williams as "Reverend,"[8] admittedly to win his friendship and confidence and also probably because someone like Williams would be more vulnerable to such flattery than persons of high social or professional status. In his "speech," Leaming assumed that the girl was dead and that Williams knew where the body was. And he falsely told Williams that he "knew" the girl's body was in the Mitchellville area (p. 7, original footnotes omitted).*

That an officer's statements alone can amount to "interrogation" is clearly correct, objections of the dissenters aside. The U.S. Supreme Court has long made clear that its constitutional concern regards various police *tactics* or *methods* to overcome suspects' defenses rather than strict use of interrogation *questions* only (see, e.g., *Bram v. United States*, 168 U.S. 532, 1897) (after the defendant had invoked his privilege against self-incrimination, a police *statement* to him that a co-suspect had confessed violated the privilege). Shortly after *Brewer v. Williams*, the Supreme Court decided *Rhode Island v. Innis*, 446 U.S. 219 (1980), which made clear that "interrogation" for purposes of the Fifth Amendment "refers not only to express questioning, but also to any words or actions on the part of the police (other than those normally attendant to arrest and custody) that the police should know are reasonably likely to elicit an incriminating response from the suspect" (p. 301).[9]

The legal question as to whether Leaming's statements constituted interrogation in this case is perhaps closer; the answer seems to depend in large part on one's ideological stance, something that is discussed further in the following sections.

---

*Kamisar, Yale. "*Brewer v. Williams, Massiah and Miranda*: What Is 'Interrogation'? When Does It Matter?" Geo. L. J. 67 (1978): 1–101. Reprinted with permission of the publisher, *Georgetown Law Journal* © 1978.

The *Brewer v. Williams* and *Rhode Island v. Innis* decisions, because they are so fact specific, give little guidance to police as to what they can and cannot say to a suspect.

Of interest is the likelihood that *had* the Court found Williams had waived his Sixth Amendment right to counsel, then Leaming's false statement that he "knew" where the body was would not have been found legally problematic. The Supreme Court long ago struck down "first-degree" practices such as physical abuse (e.g., *Brown v. Mississippi*, 297 U.S. 278, 1936), but the decline in coercion has resulted in an increase in deception (Leo, 1992), and the Supreme Court has put few limits on deceptive practices. This is likely because nearly all interrogation involves some deception, ranging from false sympathizing with the suspect to outright fabrication (about, say, positive lab results) (see Magid, 2001). The Reid method (see Inbau, Reid, Buckley, and Jayne, 2013), in popular use today, is based in large part on deception. The way the Supreme Court has sought to protect defendants is mostly by requiring that they be informed of their right not to answer questions (see *Miranda v. Arizona*, 384 U.S. 436, 1966). However, the Court has held that deception that arises to coercion (e.g., the use of a threat or a false promise) may be unconstitutional. The line between "mere deception" and coercion is fuzzy. In *Frazier v. Cupp*, 394 U.S. 731 (1969), the Supreme Court held that police use of the "prisoner's dilemma" technique (separating co-suspects and falsely telling each that the other confessed) was not coercive where "[t]he questioning was of short duration, and petitioner was a mature individual of normal intelligence" (p. 739). Heyl (2013) points out that this "dodges the question" and asks rhetorically, "What if the questioning had gone on for hours? What if the petitioner was not mature, or of below average intelligence?" (p. 942). These and other cases raise the question of when deception goes too far.

▶ The Ethics of the Exclusionary Rule

One of the sharpest points of disagreement in the appellate courts was the application of the exclusionary rule. The Supreme Court created the rule in the case *Weeks v. United States*, 232 U.S. 383 (1914); more than five decades later, it applied the rule to state prosecutions in *Mapp v. Ohio*, 367 U.S. 643 (1961). Under the rule, courts can exclude evidence from trial that law enforcement unconstitutionally seizes. Also barred is further evidence that was found as a direct result of the violation ("fruit of the poisonous tree"). However, in recent years the Court has severely curtailed its applicability by carving out many exceptions, including those based on "good faith" (see *United States v. Leon*, 468 U.S. 897, 1984), and of course, the inevitable discovery doctrine previously discussed. A majority of the Court believes that exclusion should be "our last resort, not our first impulse" (*Herring v. United States*, 555 U.S. 135, 141, 2009, citing *Hudson v. Michigan*, 547 U. S. 586, 591, 2006).

When the Court first fashioned the exclusionary rule, it stated two purposes for it: (1) to deter constitutional violations by law enforcement and (2) to protect the integrity of the courts by disallowing illegally seized evidence. (In more recent years, the justices have limited the doctrinal basis to deterrence only.) Critics have attacked the exclusionary rule since its creation, claiming that it is: (1) immoral because of "the enormous social costs it imposes on society" (*Brewer v. Williams*, 430 U.S. 387, 422, 1977, J. Burger dissenting), and (2) ineffective in actually deterring police misconduct. As to the first point, an early critic, Associate Justice Benjamin Cardozo, famously complained, "the criminal should go free because the constable has blundered" (*People v. Defore*, 242 N.Y. 13, 21, 1926). As to the latter, some commentators have claimed that it is an ineffective deterrent because, among other things, officers are motivated more by arrests than by convictions (e.g., Cicchini, 2010).[10] Proponents claim that the exclusionary rule is the only practical deterrent available; civil lawsuits against police are impractical for many reasons, and criminal prosecutions and internal discipline against police officers for constitutional violations are rare. Proponents also point to empirical research that indicates social costs have been exaggerated. For example, Nardulli (1983) studied the outcomes of 7,500 cases and found that successful motions to suppress were filed in only 46 cases—just 0.6%—and that most of those cases involved potential maximum punishments of six months or less. Nardelli also found that, contrary to Justice Cardozo's concern, evidence suppression did not necessarily mean cases were dismissed.

This article cannot delve into all of these complexities but focuses on the suggestion offered by Justice Burger in his dissent in *Brewer v. Williams* that the Court should conduct a "balancing test" because of the competing interests involved (a practice Court majorities in later cases have instituted). Justice Burger stated that on one side of the scale the Court should place the seriousness of the police conduct; on the other side should be placed the "enormous" social cost represented by hindrance of the "crucial truth-seeking function of a criminal prosecution" (p. 422). Burger concluded that only police conduct that is "outrageous or egregious" (p. 427) should be considered sufficient to override the social costs. Thus, Burger appears to suggest that the social costs are fixed but the level of malfeasance is variable. In other words, the Court should judge how "bad" the police conduct was (and put it on one side of a hypothetical scale) and then put the social costs on the other side (which he seems to say are the same in every case—i.e., the "enormous" social costs of depriving the jury of evidence). However, his later discussion implies that he would place additional considerations on the "social cost" side. First, he claimed that it does not make sense to apply the exclusionary rule to evidence that is highly reliable and probative of the defendant's guilt or innocence. Second, he seemed to suggest that a court should not suppress evidence in cases where the defendant was clearly guilty of the crime. Last, one could infer that Justice Burger believed that the type of crime or its seriousness should also be factors. For example, he wrote, "I find it most remarkable that a *murder* case should turn on judicial interpretation" (p. 419, emphasis supplied), and he later wrote, "a *murder* case ought not turn on such tenuous strands" (p. 420, emphasis supplied). In the context of his statement toward the beginning of his dissenting opinion that "Williams is guilty of the savage murder of a small child" (p. 416), Justice Burger seems to suggest that the application of constitutional remedies, or even a determination of whether a defendant's constitutional rights have been violated, should turn at least in part on the type of crime committed or its seriousness. This brings to mind the old adage, "Hard facts make bad law," which means that cases that are emotionally powerful can interfere with legal judgment.[11] In fact, the dissenting justices in the state case made this clear when they wrote, "I doubt if the majority would have reached this result if defendant's crime had been less reprehensible" (*State v. Williams*, 182 N.W.2d 396, 406, Iowa 1970, J. Stewart dissenting).

This discussion raises many questions. First, putting aside the issue of whether Williams' guilt was undisputed in this case,[12] should the Court consider "how guilty" a defendant is? (In addition, as a practical matter, what would that determination entail? Note that the Court nearly always considers constitutional claims from defendants who have been found guilty because prosecutors cannot appeal "not guilty" verdicts). Second, assuming courts could overcome practical limitations, should the type of crime or its seriousness determine application of the exclusionary rule? (In other words, should constitutional protections be different for different crimes or for varying seriousness of the same crime?). More generally, is the exclusionary rule likely to deter police misconduct, both at the level of the individual officer and the police force? Assuming that it does, is the exclusionary rule the best method for doing so?

▶ Closing Thoughts

Williams was convicted in 1969. His last appeal was settled in 1997, 28 years later. His case resulted in 10 published appellate court opinions, and it consumed all the time and expense that those opinions represent. Whose fault was this? One could argue that it was the result of a justice system that was too permissive and accommodating to defendants.[13] One could also place the fault with Captain Leaming. As Justice Burger noted, not questioning Williams would have been the wiser course. Had Leaming not made the Christian burial speech, there almost certainly would not have been a successful appeal to the U.S. Supreme Court. One could also blame the lack of a recording of their conversation. "In all likelihood the use of a recording device, a tiny administrative and financial burden, would have spared the state the need to contest the admissibility of Williams' disclosures in five courts for eight years" (Kamisar, 1977–1978, p. 238). Kamisar also pointed out that the existence of the speech came out "more or less accidentally" during Leaming's cross-examination. If it hadn't popped out, there never would have been a Christian burial speech case (p. 235).

This lack of an objective record made it necessary to determine the truth through the process of examination and cross-examination, a rather crude method (Kamisar, 1977–1978). Although many commentators have called for universal recording of interrogations (e.g. Leo & Richman, 2007), it is still not a common practice.[14]

▶ Endnotes

1. The factual summary cannot capture the complexity of all the facts and legal arguments. The reader is directed to the cases for more detail. The summary also does not delve into the various inconstancies and ambiguities in the testimony, which Kamisar (1977–1978) has expertly documented.
2. Appellate courts are typically quite careful to consider only the facts before them when ruling. Indirect comments such as Justice Marshall's are called *dicta* and have no force of law. It is even rarer for an appellate court to suggest to one party a strategy for retrial; doing so in this case seems to undercut the decision to overturn the conviction.
3. The legal issues are somewhat complex because the Supreme Court majority opted to decide the case under the Sixth Amendment and *Massiah v. United States*, 377 U.S. 201 (1964) rather than the Fifth Amendment and *Miranda v. Arizona*, 384 U.S. 436 (1966). However, it would appear that resolving the question of whether "interrogation" had occurred would be similar under either amendment.
4. See *Williams v. Brewer*, 375 F.Supp. 170 (S.D. Iowa 1974) (statements "clearly amounted to interrogation . . . [because they] explicitly encouraged incriminating responses");

Williams v. Brewer, 509 F.2d 227, 234 (8th Cir. 1974) ("subtle form of interrogation"); *Brewer v. Williams*, 430 U.S. 387, 399 (1977) ("There can be no serious doubt . . . that Detective Leaming deliberately and designedly set out to elicit information from Williams just as surely as—and perhaps more effectively than—if he had formally interrogated him"). The two dissents in the Iowa Supreme Court agreed. *See State v. Williams*, 182 N.W.2d 396, 408 (Iowa 1970) (Stuart, J., dissenting) ("the fact that [Leaming] was able to get the information by implanting ideas in defendant's mind without direct questioning is unimportant"); *State v. Williams*, 182 N.W.2d 396, 408 (Iowa 1970) (Rawlings, J., dissenting) ("Whether these statements by Officer Leaming be classified as declaratory or interrogatory in form, they were designed to elicit a statement or confession by defendant").

5. See *Williams v. Brewer*, 509 F.2d 227, 237 (8th Cir. 1974) (Webster, J., dissenting) ("A fair reading of the record is that each statement was not in response to a specific inquiry but was spontaneous"); *Brewer v. Williams*, 430 U.S. 387, 416 (1977) (Burger, J., dissenting) ("the Court now holds that because Williams was prompted by the detective's statement—not interrogation but a statement—the jury must not be told how the police found the body"); *Brewer v. Williams*, 430 U.S. 387, 434 (1977) (White, J., dissenting) ("even if [Williams'] statements were influenced by Detective Leaming's above-quoted statement, respondent's decision to talk in the absence of counsel can hardly be viewed as the product of an overborne will"); *Brewer v. Williams*, 430 U.S. 387, 438 (1977) (Blackmun, J., dissenting) ("I am not persuaded that Leaming's observations and comments . . . were an interrogation, direct or subtle, of Williams"). This is not to say that the Iowa Supreme Court or the federal court dissenters approved of Leaming's tactics. See, for example, *State v. Williams*, 182 N.W.2d 396, 405 (Iowa 1970) ("Books may be written on what is or is not proper police procedure in this regard, but we hold here it was not cause to reject the evidence adduced on this trip"); *Williams v. Brewer*, 509 F.2d 227, 236 (8th Cir. 1974) (Webster, J., dissenting) ("To say [that William was not coerced] is not to approve of any techniques which involve misrepresentations to counsel, if in fact Leaming was guilty of such acts"); *Brewer v. Williams*, 430 U.S. 387, 439 (1977) (Burger, J., dissenting) (in hindsight, it would have been "the wiser course" for Leaming to wait until they got to Des Moines to seek information from Williams).

6. The Supreme Court found the following: (1) The police chief sent Captain Leaming, chief of detectives and a 19-year veteran of the force, and homicide detective Nelson, a 15-year veteran; (2) the officers did not allow attorney Kelly to ride with them; (3) Leaming told Williams they would be "visiting" while driving; and (4) Leaming sat in the back seat with Williams. This closeness increased the psychological pressure on Williams (Kamisar, 1977–1978, p. 220, citing Driver [1968], pp. 44–46).

7. Although it is not reported in the Supreme Court opinion, Leaming testified that Williams told him in the car that he thought Leaming hated him and wanted to kill him. Leaming said that he responded by telling Williams, "I myself had had religious training and background as a child, and that I would probably come more near praying for him than I would to abuse him or strike him, and added that he was a good police officer and would protect Petitioner and not allow anyone to molest or abuse him." *Williams v. Brewer*, 375 F.Supp. 170, 174 (S.D. Iowa 1974). This type of statement is a common technique used to create a sense of trust and engender a desire to reciprocate.

8. There are two different versions of the "Christian burial speech." Leaming gave the first version at a pretrial suppression motion. There he testified that he prefaced the speech by referring to Williams as "Reverend." However, when Leaming testified at trial, he gave a different version of the speech in which he did not use the word "Reverend." Kamisar (1977–1978, pp. 217–218) reproduced and compared the two versions. Justice Stewart begins the speech with the word *Reverend* but then quotes the trial version. See *Brewer v. Williams*, 430 U.S. 387, 392 (1977). Kamisar (1977–1978) asked, "*Why* did Leaming call Williams that? *How many times* did he do so on the drive back to Des Moines? These questions were never asked. *No* questions about Williams being addressed as Reverend were ever asked" (p. 221, emphases in original).

9. In *Innis*, police arrested a suspect they believed had robbed a taxi driver at gunpoint. At that time, he was unarmed. While transporting him to be booked, one of the officers mentioned to the other that there was a school for handicapped children in the area and added, "God forbid one of them might find a weapon with shells and they might hurt themselves" (pp. 294–295).

Shortly after, Innis led the officers to the weapon. The Court found that this statement, although "subtle compulsion" (p. 503), did not amount to interrogation because, unlike in *Brewer v. Williams*, there was no evidence that Innis was particularly susceptible to such a ploy.

10. Although Cicchini (2010) presents an economics-based model that he claims demonstrates that the exclusionary rule will not deter officer misconduct, he nevertheless argues for its retention for other reasons, chiefly the protection of the integrity of the judiciary and providing a remedy to the individual whose rights have been violated.

11. The expression dates back at least to the early 19th century. Justice Oliver Wendell Holmes once stated a variant: "Great cases like hard cases make bad law. For great cases are called great, not by reason of their importance . . . but because of some accident of immediate overwhelming interest which appeals to the feelings and distorts the judgment" (*Northern Securities Co. v. United States*, 193 U.S. 197, 400–401, 1904). There is a corollary as to legislation that responds to particularly emotional and sensational crimes or wrongs. Such legislation has been termed "crime control theater" because it often offers an ineffective solution that is based on a distorted conception of the problem (see Griffin & Miller, 2008).

12. At Williams' retrial, the defense claimed that another boarder at the YMCA, who had a history of sexual assault, had murdered Pamela Powers and put her body in Williams' room to throw suspicion onto Williams. Williams claimed that he panicked and fled with the body to dispose of it. In reviewing the evidence in support of that claim, the Eight Circuit posited, "The theory is not so far-fetched as it sounds," and found Williams' "guilt is not undisputed" (*Williams v. Nix*, 700 F.2d. 1164, 168, 1169, 8th Cir. 1983). See also the discussion in Kamisar (1977–1978).

13. The Antiterrorism and Effective Death Penalty Act of 1996 substantially curtailed federal courts' review of habeas corpus petitions. This provision was upheld by the Supreme Court in *Felker v. Turpin*, 518 U.S. 651 (1977). This may not have prevented Williams' first petition, but it most assuredly would have prevented his third.

14. Referring to a different case, Kamisar (1977–1978) noted, "It seems almost incredible that in the 1970's a *murder* suspect such as Mosley could twice be questioned . . . in the *departmental headquarters building* (not in a car or on the street) without any police effort to make an objective record of either interrogation session" (p. 234, n. 102). Forty years later, commentators are wondering still.

▶ References

Bram v. United States, 168 U.S. 532 (1897)

Brewer v. Williams, 430 U.S. 387, 392–393 (1977)

Brown v. Mississippi, 297 U.S. 278 (1936)

Cicchini, M. D. (2010). An economics perspective on the exclusionary rule and deterrence. *Missouri Law Review, 75*, 459–491.

Driver, E. D. (1968). Confessions and the social psychology of coercion. *Harvard Law Review, 82*(1), 42–61.

Felker v. Turpin, 518 U.S. 651 (1977)

Frazier v. Cupp, 394 U.S. 731 (1969)

Griffin, T., & Miller, M. K. (2008). Child abduction, AMBER alert, and crime control theater. *Criminal Justice Review, 33*(2), 159–176.

Herring v. United States, 555 U.S. 135, 141 (2009)

Heyl, D. (2013). The limits of deception: An end to the use of lies and trickery in custodial interrogations to elicit the truth. *Albany Law Review, 77*, 931–953.

Hudson v. Michigan, 547 U. S. 586, 591 (2006)

Inbau, F. E., Reid, J. E., Buckley, J. P., & Jayne, B. C. (2013). *Criminal interrogation and confession*. Burlington, MA: Jones and Bartlett.

Kamisar, Y. (1977–1978). Foreword: *Brewer v. Williams*—A hard look at a discomfiting record. *Georgetown Law Journal, 66*, 209–248.

Kamisar, Y. (1978–1979). *Brewer v. Williams, Massiah* and *Miranda*: What is "interrogation"? When does it matter? *Georgetown Law Journal, 67*, 1–101.

Leo, R. A. (1992). From coercion to deception: The changing nature of police interrogation in America. *Crime, Law and Social Change, 18*(1–2), 35–59.

Leo, R. A., & Richman, K. D. (2007). Mandate the electronic recording of police interrogations. *Criminology & Public Policy, 6*(4), 791–798.

Magid, L. (2001). Deceptive police interrogation practices: How far is too far? *Michigan Law Review, 99*(5), 1168–1210.

Mapp v. Ohio, 367 U.S. 643 (1961)

Massiah v. United States, 377 U.S. 201 (1964)

Miranda v. Arizona, 384 U.S. 436 (1966)

Nardulli, P. F. (1983). The societal cost of the exclusionary rule: An empirical assessment. *Law & Social Inquiry, 8*(3), 585–609.

Northern Securities Co. v. United States, 193 U.S. 197, 400–401 (1904)

People v. Defore, 242 N.Y. 13, 21 (1926)

Rhode Island v. Innis, 446 U.S. 219 (1980)

State v. Williams, 182 N.W.2d 396, 402 (Iowa 1970)

State v. Williams, 285 N.W.2d 248 (Iowa 1979)

United States v. Leon, 468 U.S. 897 (1984)

Weeks v. United States, 232 U.S. 383 (1914)

Williams v. Brewer, 375 F.Supp. 170 (S.D. Iowa 1974)

Williams v. Brewer, 509 F.2d 227 (8th Cir. 1974)

Williams v. Nix, 700 F.2d. 1164, 168, 1169, 8th Cir. (1983)

ARTICLE 22

The Ethics of Prosecutors

Tina Fryling

Attorneys are often given a "bad rap" when it comes to the issue of ethics, especially in the area of criminal law. Defense attorneys are often asked how they can represent people they know are guilty. Their response is that everyone has the right to a fair trial. However, prosecutors are extremely powerful in the criminal justice system. They have the ability to decide what charges to bring against a person and whether to drop any of those charges or negotiate a plea deal, and they have some power in recommending a sentence to the judge when that time arises. This article will discuss some of these powers and analyze how prosecutors abuse their power and what can be done to make sure their decision-making process is as ethical as possible. The decision to charge someone with a crime can affect that individual's life forever, especially if someone ends up being charged with or entering a guilty plea to a crime that he or she did not actually commit. This article will discuss how the ethical codes that prosecutors must follow relate to these issues.

▶ Ethical Codes for Attorneys

Attorneys are bound by ethical rules called the "Rules of Professional Conduct" that are enacted by each state, and most states' rules are fairly similar. In addition to state rules, the American Bar Association has developed its "Model Rules of Professional Conduct," which are nonbinding "recommended" guidelines for attorneys. The Federal Code, in 28 U.S.C. S 530B, makes federal government attorneys subject to the state ethics laws in the state in which they practice. Thus, federal and state prosecutors are bound by the same ethical rules.

When an allegation of ethical misconduct is made against an attorney, the state bar association will serve as the initial fact-finding body, with the highest court in a state (often the state supreme court) having the final say on whether an attorney is disciplined. Possible disciplinary actions can range from something as little as a reprimand all the way up to disbarment, depending on the conduct. Every situation is different, and it can be extremely difficult to determine exactly how an ethical rule will apply to various situations.

▶ Ethical Codes For Prosecutors

The Model Rules created by the American Bar Association are often adopted in whole or in part by states. The rules as they specifically relate to prosecutors follow.

Rule 3.8: Special Responsibilities of a Prosecutor

The prosecutor in a criminal case shall:

(a) refrain from prosecuting a charge that the prosecutor knows is not supported by probable cause;

(b) make reasonable efforts to assure that the accused has been advised of the right to, and the procedure for obtaining, counsel and has been given reasonable opportunity to obtain counsel;

(c) not seek to obtain from an unrepresented accused a waiver of important pretrial rights, such as the right to a preliminary hearing;

(d) make timely disclosure to the defense of all evidence or information known to the prosecutor that tends to negate the guilt of the accused or mitigates the offense, and, in connection with sentencing, disclose to the defense and to the tribunal all unprivileged mitigating information known to the prosecutor, except when the prosecutor is relieved of this responsibility by a protective order of the tribunal;

(e) not subpoena a lawyer in a grand jury or other criminal proceeding to present evidence about a past or present client unless the prosecutor reasonably believes:

> (1) the information sought is not protected from disclosure by any applicable privilege;

> (2) the evidence sought is essential to the successful completion of an ongoing investigation or prosecution; and

> (3) there is no other feasible alternative to obtain the information;

(f) except for statements that are necessary to inform the public of the nature and extent of the prosecutor's action and that serve a legitimate law enforcement purpose, refrain from making extrajudicial comments that have a substantial likelihood of heightening public condemnation of the accused and exercise reasonable care to prevent investigators, law enforcement personnel, employees or other persons assisting or associated with the prosecutor in a criminal case from making an extrajudicial statement that the prosecutor would be prohibited from making under Rule 3.6 or this Rule.

(g) When a prosecutor knows of new, credible and material evidence creating a reasonable likelihood that a convicted defendant did not commit an offense of which the defendant was convicted, the prosecutor shall:

> (1) promptly disclose that evidence to an appropriate court or authority, and

> (2) if the conviction was obtained in the prosecutor's jurisdiction,

>> (i) promptly disclose that evidence to the defendant unless a court authorizes delay, and

>> (ii) undertake further investigation, or make reasonable efforts to cause an investigation, to determine whether the defendant was convicted of an offense that the defendant did not commit.

(h) When a prosecutor knows of clear and convincing evidence establishing that a defendant in the prosecutor's jurisdiction was convicted of an offense that the defendant did not commit, the prosecutor shall seek to remedy the conviction.

Some of these guidelines are highly specific, whereas others are more open to interpretation. They all, however, require prosecutors to be careful when charging and prosecuting a case so that they are not trying merely to prosecute "someone" for a crime but are trying to prosecute the "right person"—that is, the person who actually committed the crime.

▶ The Supreme Court Case of *Bordenkircher v. Hayes*

In 1978, the Supreme Court of the United States considered the actions of a prosecutor as they related specifically to the issue of plea bargaining in the landmark case of *Bordenkircher v. Hayes*.[1] The use of plea bargains is common in the United States criminal legal system, with claims by various studies that up to 95% of cases are disposed of through plea bargains. To understand the Supreme Court's opinion, it is important to first understand what a plea bargain is and why plea bargains are used so often in criminal cases.

A plea bargain is an agreement between a prosecutor and a defendant that permits the defendant to plead guilty to a lesser charge or to plead guilty to one of two or more charges in order to avoid the time, expense, and uncertainty of a jury trial. This type of agreement benefits the prosecutor in that not every case will end up going to trial. It benefits witnesses in that they do not have to take the time to testify at a trial. It benefits victims in that they know that the defendant will be admitting guilt at least to one or some charges, and they also know that they will not have to testify at a trial, which is often stressful, time consuming, and can involve difficult and potentially accusatory cross-examination. Finally, it helps the defendant who may be entering a plea to a lesser crime (such as a misdemeanor rather than a felony) or pleading to fewer crimes overall so that when sentencing takes place, any potential jail time, fines, or time on supervision is lessened overall. Judges can also consider a plea made by a criminal defendant as acceptance of wrongdoing, which can result in the judge handing down a less harsh sentence than she or he might give if the defendant did not admit guilt. As you can see, plea bargains have a lot of benefits to both the government and defendants. A criminal defendant sometimes even enters a "straight plea," which means the defendant would plea to each charge that was filed against him. This type of plea also has some of the benefits just listed, including a judge taking into consideration during sentencing that the defendant accepted responsibility for her actions.

In the *Bordenkircher* case, the defendant, Paul Lewis Hayes, was indicted by a Fayette County, Kentucky, grand jury on a charge of "uttering a forged instrument" for forging a document for a total of $88.30. The offense was punishable by a term of two to 10 years in prison. Mr. Hayes' attorney met with the prosecutor to discuss a plea bargain. The prosecutor stated that he would recommend a sentence of only five years in prison if Hayes would plead guilty to the charge for which he was indicted. Although a judge is not bound by this sort of sentencing recommendation by a prosecutor, it can be highly persuasive to a judge's final sentencing decision.

However, the prosecutor further stated that if Hayes refused to enter the plea and thus "save the court the inconvenience and necessity of a trial," the prosecutor would seek indictment for another charge, adding it on to the current charge. Worse, adding that charge would result in Hayes being subjected to a mandatory sentence of life imprisonment because he had two prior felony convictions.

Hayes chose not to enter the plea, and the prosecutor did exactly what he said he would do, seeking indictment for another charge. The prosecutor had the evidence to support the new charge at the time he requested the indictment for the first charge but had chosen not to move forward with the indictment when he initially charged Hayes. The prosecutor admitted that Hayes' refusal to plead guilty to the original charge was what led him to request that the grand jury indict Hayes for the additional charge.

A jury found Hayes guilty of all of the crimes for which he had been charged, including the new one, and also determined that he had previously been convicted of two felonies, so he was sentenced to a life term in the penitentiary. Mr. Hayes appealed his case to the Kentucky Court of Appeals, which rejected his appeal, and Hayes later filed a petition for a federal writ of habeas corpus, which was also denied. Mr. Hayes ultimately appealed his case to the U.S. Supreme Court, which agreed to hear his case.

Mr. Hayes argued that the prosecutor's actions had violated his right to due process. The Supreme Court had previously ruled that defendants are protected from the "vindictive exercise of a prosecutor's discretion."[2] Was the prosecutor's decision to add a charge as a result of Mr. Hayes refusing to enter a voluntary plea in his case a sort of punishment to Mr. Hayes for exercising his right to have his culpability for his crime decided in a trial? Can a prosecutor's decision to treat a defendant more harshly based on that defendant's failure to enter a plea be considered unethical? Or was it a potential gift to the defendant that entering a plea would save him from being charged with a crime when enough evidence existed for that charge?

The Supreme Court stated that it had agreed to hear Mr. Hayes' case because it involved an important constitutional question relating to our system of justice. However, the Court decided that the prosecutor's actions were proper. The Court relied heavily on the fact that Mr. Hayes knew at the time that he decided not to enter a plea that the new charge would be lodged against him as a result of his choice.

The Court did cite other cases in which it had found prosecutorial misconduct where vindictiveness on the part of the prosecutor was present. One such case involved a prosecutor who reindicted a convicted misdemeanor on a felony charge after the defendant had appealed his conviction for the misdemeanor.[3] Another involved a defendant who was resentenced harshly after appealing his case—the Court decided that a prosecutor could not act vindictively against that defendant in recommending a sentence to a judge.[4] The Court stated that those cases involved obvious retaliation by the state when an accused lawfully attacked his conviction through the appellate process. However, the Court differentiated Hayes' case because he was told what the result would be if he decided not to enter a plea in his case.

Do you think the Supreme Court would have determined that the prosecutor's "vindictiveness" was acceptable in the other two cases if those prosecutors had told the defendants that exercising their appellate rights would result in vindictiveness?

The Court has time and time again determined that the appellate process is a right that cannot be taken away from defendants and that, in fact, defendants even have a right to an attorney at the appellate stage. What makes appealing a case different from turning down a plea? Do the Supreme Court's decisions in these cases seem consistent?

▶ Overcharging by the Prosecutor

Had the prosecutor in the *Bordenkircher* case brought both of the charges against Hayes in the beginning stages of his case, there could have been a different discussion regarding the ability of a prosecutor to overcharge a defendant. Overcharging can encourage the entry of a plea bargain because plea bargaining involves charges being dropped. Consider the following example:

A man is driving downtown in a metropolitan city with an expired license plate. A police officer driving behind the man runs a license plate check and determines that the license is expired. On determining this, the officer turns on his flashing lights, attempting to pull over the vehicle. The vehicle continues through an intersection, moving through a yellow light, and then turns onto a side street without a turning signal. The driver did not notice the police officer's flashing lights until he had traveled for about two blocks after the original violation, but he immediately pulls over once he sees the flashing lights. The officer charges the individual with (1) driving with expired plates, (2) fleeing and eluding a police officer, (3) failure to use a turn signal, (4) driving too fast for conditions, and (5) failing to yield at a yellow light.

The intention of the officer is generally that not all of these charges will remain. The defendant would have a difficult time arguing that his plates were not expired. The failure to use a turn signal is fairly basic, and the defendant did fail to use his signal (although many of us probably also fail to use our turn signals in similar situations). The defendant probably did not intend to flee from the police officer; it just took him some time to notice the lights in his rearview mirror, and there is no proof either way as to whether the defendant was going too fast because no radar or other speed-timing device was used. Most likely this case will result in the defendant entering a plea to driving with expired plates and perhaps one other charge, and the other charges will be dropped.

So what is the point of overcharging? In a case in which the defendant does have some arguments as to whether or not she actually committed the crime or whether the proper police work took place, charging the defendant with so many crimes might encourage her to enter a plea. A defense attorney will warn the defendant that if she fails to enter a negotiated plea and proceeds to trial on all of the charges, she could be found guilty of *all* of the charges, and then the fines and potential other punishments will be much larger. Overcharging can also include using charges that are at a higher level than the charge that could actually be easily proven, such as charging an individual with aggravated assault instead of simple assault. The prosecutor might drop the charge to simple assault if the defendant enters a plea, thereby making the defendant believe that he is being rewarded for entering a plea when there might not have been enough evidence to convict the defendant of the higher charge to begin with.

Is the use of overcharging an ethical issue? The problem, of course, is that it might be inducing defendants to enter a plea even when he is not guilty of a crime because he is afraid of the sheer number of charges or the severity of the highest charge he could be convicted of. Do we want defendants to enter a plea because they are afraid of what might happen if they do not, or do we want defendants to enter a plea because they are guilty? Remember, the Model Rules set forth by the American Bar Association require that a prosecutor refrain from prosecuting a charge that she knows is not supported by probable cause. Arguments can be made in the driving example that this is the case.

▶ Wrongful Convictions

Many wrongful convictions have been overturned in recent years, with more being discovered every day. The most concerning of these include defendants who have spent years on death row only to eventually be exonerated of any guilt. In addition to the death row cases, there are many other cases where people have been exonerated by DNA evidence, new evidence obtained in a case after conviction, a confession by another person after conviction, or a witness or victim admitting he lied to police or at trial. Wrongful convictions are also caused by defense attorneys who do not do their job properly. Finally, some wrongful convictions result from prosecutorial misconduct. Examples of this misconduct include failing to turn over exculpatory evidence to the defense, failing to consider conflicting evidence that is received in a case, failing to examine new leads that suggest someone else might be guilty, or, as previously discussed, overcharging to convince a defendant to plea. If our justice system puts even one innocent person to death or forces a criminal record on someone for something he did not do, can we argue that our system of justice is fair? If the wrong person is in jail, then the person who really committed the crime is not being punished for his actions. Is it ethical for a prosecutor to move forward with a plea bargain knowing that he does not have enough evidence to prove that the defendant is guilty beyond a reasonable doubt? Many exoneration cases involve guilty pleas made by defendants who felt they did not have any other choice. If the purpose of our system of justice is to find the truth rather than to convict someone, then the use of plea bargaining can result in an unfair result.

The American Bar Association Standards for Criminal Justice Prosecution Function and Defense Function 3-3.11(a) provide: "A prosecutor shall not intentionally fail to make timely disclosure to the defense, at the earliest feasible opportunity, of the existence of all evidence which tends to negate the guilt of the accused or mitigate the offense charged or which would tend to reduce the punishment of the accused." The rule does not say what the "earliest feasible opportunity" is. How is a defendant to know when the prosecution has completed its investigation and has all of the information it will obtain? If the rule specifically stated that the evidence should be exchanged before the plea bargain stage, then the defendant would be able to enter a plea while being aware of all of the evidence the prosecution has. In the case of *Brady v. Maryland*,[5] the Supreme Court ruled that a prosecutor must turn over to the defense all "exculpatory evidence" that is "material." "Exculpatory evidence" is basically anything that could help to exonerate a defendant. The Court stated that evidence is "material" if "there is a reasonable probability that his conviction or sentence would have been different had these materials been disclosed." In other words, if the prosecution had evidence that showed that the DNA left at a rape scene did not belong to the defendant, or that a bullet that killed a person did not come from the gun fired by the defendant, then those items must be turned over to the defense. The doctrine has been interpreted to also mean that any evidence that could assist the defense in finding witnesses who would testify in opposition to that evidence must also be turned over. The *Brady* case also does not specifically mandate the time period for when this evidence must be turned over; it states only that it should be before trial. Thus, once again, it is difficult to argue that the evidence in the prosecutor's possession must be given to the defense before discussion and negotiation of a plea bargain. Although many prosecutors will turn over all of the evidence they have in their files to the defense, there are still times when evidence will be held back or is arguably not "exculpatory" or "material." If the defense does not know that this evidence exists, there will never be a method for the defense to request to the court that the evidence be turned over.

Often, a plea bargain is offered to a defendant early in a criminal case and before discovery would even be turned over by the prosecution. Thus, a defendant might be entering a plea without even knowing for sure what documents and other evidence the prosecutor has that could result in a conviction. The chances, then, are high that a defendant will enter a plea to a crime he did not commit based on fear that evidence will be fabricated or a witness will lie. In fact, the National Association of Criminal Defense Lawyers recently concluded that evidence exists that federal criminal defendants often plead guilty because the penalty for exercising their constitutional rights is too high to risk. The report theorized that defendants who choose to exercise their constitutional rights and have a trial rather than enter a plea receive higher sentences than those who choose to plea.[6] The federal sentencing guidelines provide extremely severe penalties—up to life sentences—for certain types of crimes. To plead guilty to a lesser crime and receive the guarantee a lesser sentence is tempting to defendants. Basically, defense attorneys often spend their time trying to negotiate pleas rather than focusing on whether or not police and the government respect the boundaries of the law.

▶ How Can Prosecutors Be Held Accountable for These Ethical Violations?

Given that courts are overloaded with cases, how can the process be regulated so that overcharging and overzealously using plea bargains are less of an issue? Plea bargains help resolve cases early in the process. Obviously, one of the most effective ways to solve this problem is to require a prosecutor to turn over her entire case file to the defense as soon as possible and before any plea bargain is entered. This way, the prosecutor does not have to decide what evidence is exculpatory or material; rather, the defense can evaluate the material. Another remedy would involve requiring prosecutors to provide data regarding the charges, convictions, and ethics violations that took place in the prosecutor's office each year. Finally, it can help to pass laws that limit prosecutorial immunity so that if a prosecutor violates a person's due process rights via overcharging or failing to provide the defense with all information relevant to the defense of the case, then the prosecutor will be held liable. Currently, laws provide that prosecutors generally have immunity from suit for all decisions that are made in the course of their duties.

Of course, defense attorneys must also be cognizant of these issues. A good defense attorney will look at all of the discovery provided by the prosecutor and demand that all relevant documents be turned over. A good defense attorney will also pursue any possible defenses, including search-and-seizure issues and other constitutional issues that might result in evidence being suppressed (excluded from trial). Although certainly some cases should be concluded with a plea, every defendant should receive clear information about her options to go to trial and the fact that it is her constitutional right to do so. Further, it has been suggested that possible remedies include limiting plea bargains to certain lower-level crimes and involving judges in the process. Plea bargains are certainly never going to be eliminated from the criminal justice system, but policies should be put in place to regulate how they are being used.

▶ Conclusion

The issue of plea bargaining as a prosecutorial tool is a difficult ethical topic to dissect. Eliminating plea bargains entirely would prejudice defendants and overwhelm the court system, as well as tax already burdened prosecutorial and public defense offices. However, the current method of plea bargaining sometimes leads people who are not guilty to enter guilty pleas. The use of plea bargains involves many ethical issues and should be overseen by the courts, with defense attorneys demanding to obtain all evidence available before any plea is entered, and with prosecutors charging defendants only with crimes that are truly appropriate based on the actual actions of the offender.

▶ References

1. *Bordenkircher v. Hayes*, 434 U.S. 357 (1978).
2. *Blackledge v. Perry*, 417 U.S. 21 (1974).
3. *Blackledge v. Perry*, 417 U.S. 21 (1974).
4. *North Carolina v. Pearce*, 395 U.S. 711 (1969).
5. *Brady v. Maryland*, 373 U.S. 83 (1963).
6. Palvo, W. (2018, July 31). Are innocent people pleading guilty? A new report says yes. Forbes.com. Retrieved from https://www.forbes.com/sites/walterpavlo/2018/07/31/are-innocent-people-pleading-guilty-a-new-report-says-yes/#423881eb5193

SECTION 6

Ethics and the Correctional System

ARTICLE 23

Introduction to Correctional Ethics

Kweilin T. Lucas

▶ Introduction

There has never been a more pressing time to demand the ethical treatment of correctional populations than now. As it stands, correctional facilities in the United States house 2.2 million individuals in jails and prisons across the country—the highest incarceration rate in the world (Bureau of Justice Statistics, 2016a; World Prison Brief, 2016). Moreover, more than 7 million individuals are supervised in the community on probation or parole (Bureau of Justice Statistics, 2016c). As these numbers demonstrate, the lives of literally millions of people are impacted by the criminal justice system. Maintaining the system is also incredibly costly. The United States spends an estimated $81 billion each year to operate prisons, jails, parole, and probations (Bureau of Justice Statistics, 2017b). Alarmingly, however, annual spending costs are likely significantly higher when considering policing and court costs, as well as costs paid by families to support incarcerated individuals. Recently, the Prison Policy Initiative (2017) released an investigative report that found that mass incarceration costs state and federal governments and American families around $182 billion a year, $100 billion more than was previously thought (Equal Justice Initiative, 2017). Although lawmakers across the country have enacted new policies to reduce incarceration and spending on prisons and jails, the report indicates that not much progress has been in made in terms of reducing crime. Rather, our current criminal justice system has not done much to enhance public safety or reduce crime (Equal Justice Initiative, 2017). With so many lives hanging in the balance and the massive amount of correctional spending taking place in the United States, reflecting on how deep mass incarceration and over-criminalization have affected our communities must be examined.

▶ Correctional Ethics

The criminal justice system is an important public service system that has the challenge of protecting and defending the public from crime. As such, the criminal justice system is obligated to maintain the highest ethical standards possible, even if those standards and subcultures are uniquely distinct from other fields and occupations (Belshaw & Johnstone, 2015). It is important that institutions establish guidelines that are specific to each criminal justice agency. In addition, criminal justice agencies must reinforce rules, regulations, and sanctions to maintain structure and order between individuals and those responsible for governing them. Above all, however, criminal justice agencies must consider ethicality and moral reasoning in the decisions they make (Belshaw & Johnstone, 2015).

Ethics generally refers to the study of right and wrong (Braswell, McCarthy, & McCarthy, 2017). Being ethical thus pertains to how an individual makes conclusions about what is right and wrong behavior (Belshaw & Johnstone, 2015). To better understand the relationship between justice, crime, and ethics, researchers point to the process that human beings go through when analyzing the context of situations. For example, from a personal point of view, individuals first determine if a behavior represents their individual sense of justice. Next, people process the behavior from a social justice perspective and determine how the community is affected in a broader sense—that is, we seek to understand how conditions and environments contribute to someone's criminality. Finally, individuals should consider the complex interrelationships between personal beliefs, social factors, and the criminal justice system, as well as their consequences (Braswell et al., 2017). Our beliefs and values, which are shaped by family and friends, guide us in determining the difference between what is right and what is wrong. The media also heavily influences individual perceptions of the criminal justice system, particularly correctional agencies (Banks, 2017). Indeed, examination of the correctional system presents a plethora of ethical dilemmas and questions concerning the nature and goals of punishment (Braswell et al., 2017).

▶ Ethics of Punishment

In the United States, each state is responsible for inflicting punishment on individuals who violate important social norms that are intended to protect the common interests of members of a political community (Bennett, 2008; Beyleveld & Brownsword, 2008; Duff, 2001; Kleinig, 2008). Researchers indicate that several elements of punishment are necessary components in the criminal justice system. For example, the actions that constitute punishment must be officially authorized by the state, and they must be intentionally directed at an outcome that benefits the larger society. In addition, punishments should be reprobative, meaning that they reflect disapproval of a behavior. Finally, the punishments must also follow a wrongful act and should be viewed by the offender as being harmful (Boonin, 2008). Deliberately inflicting harm on another is generally considered morally wrong and requires ethical justification (Ward & Salmon, 2009). Therefore, there are ethical issues in justifying punishment because offenders can experience harm or suffering and because it can lead to additional hardships for others who are involved, such as family, friends, and the broader community (Ward & Salmon, 2009).

Utilitarianism and deontology serve as foundations for specific philosophies of punishment (Braswell et al., 2017). From these perspectives, several classical justifications to warrant punishment include retribution, deterrence, rehabilitation, and incapacitation (Kleinig, 2016). Retribution, or *lex talionis*, is an ancient principle that outlines punishment as an appropriate response to a wrongdoing if it is like the offense originally committed (Shichor, 2006; Waldron, 1992). Ultimately, retribution is based on the idea that if a person commits an offense and breaks the law, he or she deserves to be punished (Braswell et al., 2017). Often, this philosophy is expressed in the phrase "An eye for an eye, a tooth for a tooth" (Waldron, 1992). Deterrence is a punishment philosophy that attempts to discourage offenders from breaking the law by ensuring that punishment outweighs the benefits of a crime (Braga, Hureau, & Papachristos, 2014). This penal strategy considers the calculation of costs that people make before engaging in crime and can be categorized as either general—which relies on fear of punishment to deter crime—or specific, which prevents individuals from reoffending again in the future (Braswell et al., 2017).

Modern eras of punishment emphasize rehabilitation, or individualized treatment that aims to address the root causes of crime (Cullen & Gilbert, 2013; MacKenzie, 2001). Ultimately, this strategy emphasizes that individuals who commit crime are in need some of intervention once criminogenic risk factors are identified (Braswell et al., 2017). Such risk factors for criminality include antisocial behavior, associations with criminal peers, lack of parental support, poor school performance, and substance abuse (Andrews & Dowden, 2007). Finally, incapacitation, a punishment philosophy that promotes removing offenders from society, is justified by maintaining physical control over those who break the law (Braswell et al., 2017). Although these efforts purport to address mainly chronic offenders, the scope of these strategies is broad and often targets larger groups of offenders in the form of punitive sanctions, such as three-strike laws and mandatory minimum sentences (Braswell et al., 2017; Harris, 1995; Welch, 2005). In addition, punitive strategies such as incarceration are often criticized because they do not appear to contribute much to public safety (Andrews & Dowden, 2007). The types of punishment generated from the philosophies that are often justified in the criminal justice system include intermediate sanctions and imprisonment, as well as capital punishment, which is reserved for the most serious offenses (Kleinig, 2016). Each punishment type presents its own unique challenges in relation to correctional ethics.

Intermediate Sanctions

Intermediate sanctions are often implemented for offenders who pose little to no risk to society but require punishment that is harsher than ordinary probation (Byrne, Lurigio, & Petersilia, 1992). Although intermediate sanctions are not as severe in nature as imprisonment or capital punishment, they still raise questions in terms of ethical implementation. Although intermediate sanctions aim to provide cost-effective alternatives to incarceration, deter offenders, protect the community, and rehabilitate offenders, there are still areas in need of reform to ensure that measures effectively meet the stated objectives. For example, fines and forfeitures have been at the forefront of the discussion as researchers voice skepticism about their usefulness and application given the fact that not all offenders can afford to pay and because these sanctions are often implemented alongside other forms of punishment (Hillsman & Greene, 1992). Community corrections have also been criticized, especially those issues that relate to probation (Morris & Tonry, 1990; Muraskin, 2001b; Petersilia, 1998; von Hirsch, 1990; Whitehead, 1996). Scholars point to various ethical issues, including the appropriate conditions for probationers (Kleinig, 2016), as well as the role probation officials play, especially regarding training, caseloads, supervisory issues, conditions of probation, curfews, and drug testing (Kleinig, 2016; Mills, 1980; Turner, Petersilia, & Deschenes, 1994). Alternatives to incarceration such as drug courts (Harrison & Scarpitti, 2002; Nolan, 2002), community service (McDonald, 1992), boot camps (MacKenzie & Armstrong, 2004), and electronic monitoring (Mainprize, 1992; Prison Reform Trust, 1999) have also been examined to include ethical implications.

Imprisonment

One of the many ethical issues that arise in the criminal justice system is that relating to imprisonment. Specifically, issues often relate to which offenders should be imprisoned for their crimes. Researchers have taken notice of the disproportionate rates of incarceration among offender groups (Petersilia, 1983; Prison Reform Trust, 1999; Tonry, 1994; Visher, 1983), as well as judicial discretion, sentencing guidelines, and assistance departures for those who are returning to their communities following incarceration (Kleinig, 2016; Schwartz, 2004: von Hirsch & Greene, 1993). One of the most controversial aspects to sentencing is plea bargaining (Alschuler, 1979, 1981). In the criminal justice system, plea bargaining is used by prosecutors as a tool for negotiating guilty pleas in return for reduced charges or penalties (Braswell et al., 2017). Although plea bargains help to speed up prosecution, ethical issues arise when defendants must weigh a guilty plea with a wrongful conviction. Indeed, this strategy allows prosecutors a great amount of discretion since they can determine the charges for defendants. Relatedly, critics of plea bargaining have also pointed to the fact that plea bargains can affect decisions made by individuals who are held in pretrial detention for lengthy periods of time (Braswell et al., 2017). Therefore, prosecutors must exercise caution in how their decisions will impact individuals accused of a crime if they are to perform their job duties in a responsible, ethical manner.

The sentencing of juveniles is also littered with ethical implications. Although the juvenile justice system is geared more toward rehabilitation than the adult criminal justice system, some aspects of juvenile corrections take a more punitive approach to punishment yet do nothing to prevent recidivism (Braswell et al., 2017). For example, evidence suggests that boot camps, shock incarceration, and counseling programs that do not address individual risk factors are not effective (Sherman, Farrington, Welsch, & MacKenzie, 2002). Moreover, research on "Scared Straight" programs indicate that they can have countereffects on juveniles and contribute to delinquency rates (Klenowski, Bell, & Dodson, 2010). Fortunately, the public supports alternatives to incarceration, particularly for juveniles (Braswell et al., 2017). A recent survey conducted by the National Council on Crime and Delinquency found that respondents did not support jail or prison time for all offenses, which can be encouraging for juvenile corrections (Hartney & Marchionna, 2009). Regardless of these findings, however, certain issues need to be addressed such as overcrowding (Braswell et al., 2017), housing juveniles in adult institutions (Centers for Disease Control and Prevention, 2007; Redding, 2010), sexual victimization (Beck, Cantor, Hartge, & Smith, 2013; Beck, Harrison, & Adams, 2007; Snyder & Sickmund, 2006), and high suicide rates among incarcerated juveniles (Bureau of Justice Statistics, 2016d; Turner, Finkelhor, Shattuck, & Hamby, 2012).

More recently, privatization in the criminal justice system has been met with criticism, having been applied to various agents of corrections, including those that take place in the community and in institutional settings (Braswell et al., 2017). Opponents of privatization argue that it is unethical for the government to allow private businesses to supervise offenders because they will ultimately profit from their punishment (Shichor, 1995). Some researchers also point out that conditions of confinement suffer because of privatization, and corrections professionals lack substantial support from the agencies in which they are employed, which can create dangerous environments for both inmates and officers (Blackely, 2005; Braswell et al., 2017).

Indeed, the conditions of confinement present challenges for correctional institutions. For example, certain ethical issues relate to basic conditions of confinement, including cell size, double celling, overcrowding, smoking policies, noise, temperature control, and food (Gaes, 1985, 1994; Levenson, 1999). In addition, corrections agents are met with requirements to provide basic rights to incarcerated individuals, and they must abide by policies to uphold provisions for religious observance, free speech, privacy, safety, and physical and mental health care (Kleinig, 2016). Often, correctional institutions are also met with challenges that relate to recreational activities, educational and vocational programming, and labor (Chang & Thompkins, 2002; Duwe & Clark, 2014; Gendreau & Goggin, 1996). Imprisonment also presents barriers for family members of incarcerated individuals in the form of visitation, phone policies, and conjugal visits (Carlson & Cervera, 1991; Christian, 2005; Jackson, 2002). In institutional settings, there are ethical implications for security issues as well, including strip searches (MacGregor, 2003), surveillance of illicit drug use (Brewer, Banta-Green, Ort, Robel, & Field, 2016), lockdowns (Correctional Association, 2003), and the use of solitary confinement (Shalev, 2011). In addition, studies indicate that children of incarcerated individuals experience negative consequences, including risk of future offending and poor development (Nesmith & Ruhland, 2008). Certainly, much work needs to be done to address these ethical issues in institutional settings.

Capital Punishment

Perhaps one of the most controversial issues related corrections is the use of capital punishment (Mandery, 2005; Pojman & Reiman, 1998). Also known as the *death penalty*, capital punishment is applied to the most egregious offenses, including murder, treason, espionage, war crimes, crimes against humanity, and genocide (Kronenwetter, 2001). According to Amnesty International (2018), by the end of 2017, 106 countries (most of the world's states) had abolished the death penalty in law for all crimes, and 142 countries (more than two-thirds) had abolished the death penalty in law or practice. Figures indicate that 56 countries use capital punishment (Amnesty International, 2018). Currently, the United States is the only Western country to use the death penalty, although not every state actively pursues it in practice (Bienen, 2010). According to the Death Penalty Information Center (2018b), 31 states currently use capital punishment, but only a handful have initiated executions since 1976. In 2017, most executions in the United States took place in Texas (7), Arkansas (4), Florida (3), Alabama (3), Ohio (2), Oklahoma (2), Missouri (1), and Georgia (1) (Death Penalty Information Center, 2018b).

Researchers point to several ethical issues in relation to capital punishment. First and foremost is the controversy and debate surrounding the death penalty as a form of punishment. Proponents of this practice emphasize that it is a just penalty that deters crime, is useful in plea bargaining, and prevents criminals from offending in the future (Blecker, 2013, 2014). Opponents, however, argue that capital punishment is expensive (American Civil Liberties Union of Northern California, 2009), inhumane, irreversible, and not an effective deterrent to crime (National

Research Council, 2012). Further, capital punishment is criticized for discriminatory treatment toward minorities and the poor and for encouraging a culture of violence (American Civil Liberties Union, 2012).

One of the most discussed elements concerning capital punishment's application is the controversy behind the methods used on inmates. American states that use the death penalty have the option of using several methods of execution, including electrocution, gas chambers, hanging, and firing squads, but lethal injection is the most commonly used (Death Penalty Information Center, 2018d). States that rely on lethal injections have been met with the challenge of accessing the drugs needed to execute individuals because pharmaceutical companies are becoming increasingly reluctant to provide correctional facilities with the chemicals needed to initiate death (Vivian, 2013). In addition, there is evidence of botched executions, especially among those involving lethal injection (Death Penalty Information Center, 2018d; Sarat, 2014). As a result, corrections officials have resorted to exploring nontraditional means. For example, Oklahoma, Alabama, and Mississippi have authorized nitrogen for executions despite no scientific data to support executing people in this manner (Grady & Hoffman, 2018). In addition, Nevada recently proposed the use of fentanyl, the first state to do so. The move is certainly controversial, given the opioid epidemic that is occurring in the United States (McGreal, 2018). Alcoven, the pharmaceutical company that produces the drug, filed a lawsuit against the Nevada Department of Corrections after stating that it does not condone the use of its products in state-sponsored executions (Kennedy, 2018). Recently, the state reported that they will utilize pentobarbital rather than fentanyl when they resume federal executions at the end of 2019 (Allen, 2019).

▶ Role of Corrections Officials and Administrators

Correctional officials and administrators are in a unique position because they hold authority over those whose liberties have been compromised by criminal conviction. Individual beliefs vary and are shaped by a multitude of effects, but criminal justice professionals should achieve positions that are fair, equal, and respectful of others' individual beliefs (Belshaw & Johnstone, 2015). Correctional professionals are mandated to maintain high standards of ethical behavior and must perform their duties within the constraints of correctional policies and practices (Bush, Connell, & Denny, 2006; Haag, 2006; Levenson & D'Amora, 2005). The American Correctional Association (ACA) clearly outlines expectations of correctional staff in its Code of Ethics. To summarize, members are expected to respect and protect civil and legal rights, and each professional situation must be met with concern for the welfare of those involved, with no intention of personal gain. In addition, members should criticize colleagues and agencies only in situations where it is warranted. Members also must refrain from using their positions to secure privileges and cannot allow any formal or informal activity that presents a conflict of interest or hinders their work performance. Ultimately, ACA standards require that members respect, promote, and contribute to a safe and healthy working environment (American Correctional Association, 1994).

There are various issues related to the ethics of correctional personnel. For example, researchers point to prison administrators' responsibilities and responsiveness to wider community and political overseers, as well as the supervision of officers and the development of correctional policies that consider changing demographics (DiIulio, 1987; Wright & Goodstein, 1989). Prison officers, on the other hand, are exposed to a wide variety of ethical issues (Johnson & Price, 1981; Lombardo, 2001; Muraskin, 2001a). For example, men and women in positions of authority must deal with issues related to defensible training policies (Conover, 2001), relationships with colleagues and inmates (Griffin, 2006; Schaufeli & Peeters, 2000; Vartia & Hyyti, 2002; Walters, 1992), the use of force (Griffin, 2002; Henry, Senese, & Ingley, 1994), and deception and corruption (McCarthy, 1991). For executioners, those who implement state or legal sanctioned capital punishment, there is evidence to suggest that the role can be traumatizing for those involved, which brings one's own morality into question (Bandes, 2016; Connelly, 1997). Researchers, in fact, question the role of medical personnel in performing capital punishment because this practice goes against standards outlined by the American Medical Association and the American Board of Anesthesiology, as well as the Hippocratic oath that ensures physicians do no harm to their patients (Diep, 2015). Indeed, as this summary suggests, it is vital that correctional professionals should be competent and properly trained so that they are better prepared for whatever role they play in the correctional system (Kleinig, 2008).

▶ References

Allen, J. (2019, September 13, 2019). Exclusive: While battling opioid crisis, U.S. government weighed using fentanyl for executions. *Reuters*. Retrieved from https://www.reuters.com /article/us-usa-executions-exclusive/exclusive-while-battling-opioid-crisis-u-s-government -weighed-using-fentanyl-for-executions-idUSKCN1VY0YS.

Alschuler, A. (1979). Plea bargaining and its history. *Columbia Law Review, 79*, 1–43.

Alschuler, A. (1981). The changing plea-bargaining debate. *California Law Review, 69*, 652–730.

American Civil Liberties Union (2012). *The case against the death penalty*. New York, NY: Author. Retrieved from https://www.aclu.org/other/case-against-death-penalty

American Civil Liberties Union of Northern California (2009). *The hidden death tax: The secret cost of seeking execution in California*. San Francisco, CA: Author. Retrieved from https://www .aclunc.org/sites/default/files/asset_upload_file358_8069.pdf

American Correctional Association. (1994, August). *ACA Code of Ethics*. Alexandria, VA: Author. Retrieved from http://www.aca.org/ACA_Prod_IMIS/ACA_Member/About_Us/Code_of _Ethics/ACA_Member/AboutUs/Code_of_Ethics.aspx?hkey=61577ed2-c0c3-4529 -bc01-36a248f79eba

Amnesty International. (2018). *Death sentences and executions 2017*. London, UK: Author. Retrieved from https://www.amnesty.org/download/Documents/ACT5079552018ENGLISH.PDF

Andrews, D., & Dowden, C, (2007). The risk-need-responsivity model of assessment and human service in prevention and corrections: Crime-prevention jurisprudence. *Canadian Journal of Criminology and Criminal Justice, 49*(4), 439–464.

Bandes, S. A. (2016). What executioners can—and cannot—teach us about the death penalty. *Criminal Justice Ethics, 35*(3), 183–200.

Banks, C. (2017). *Criminal justice ethics: Theory and practice* (4th ed.). Thousand Oaks, CA: Sage.

Beck, A. J., Cantor, D., Hartge, J., & Smith, T. (2013). *Sexual victimization in juvenile facilities reported by youth, 2012*. Washington, DC: U.S. Department of Justice, Bureau of Justice Statistics.

Beck, A. J., Harrison, P. M., & Adams, D. B. (2007). *Sexual violence reported by correctional authorities, 2006*. Washington, DC: U.S. Department of Justice Statistics.

Belshaw, S. H., & Johnstone, P. (2015). *Ethics in the criminal justice system*. Dubuque, IA: Kendall Hunt.

Bennett, C. (2008). *The apology ritual: A philosophical theory of punishment*. Cambridge, UK: Cambridge University Press.

Beyleveld, D., & Brownsword, R. (2008). *Human dignity in bioethics and law*. New York, NY: Oxford University Press.

Bienen, L. B. (2010). *Murder and its consequences: Essays on capital punishment*. Evanston, IL: Northwestern University Press.

Blackely, C. (2005). *America's prisons: The movement toward profit and privatization*. Boca Raton, FL: Brown Walker Press.

Blecker, R. (2013). *The death of punishment: Searching for justice among the worst of the worst*. New York, NY: Palgrave Macmillian.

Blecker, R. (2014, April 6). The death penalty needs to be an option for punishment. *The New York Times*. Retrieved from https://www.nytimes.com/roomfordebate/2014/04/06/what-it-means -if-the-death-penalty-is-dying/the-death-penalty-needs-to-be-an-option-for-punishment

Boonin, D. (2008). *The problem of punishment*. New York, NY: Cambridge University.

Braga, A., Hureau, D., & Papachristos, A. (2014). Deterring gang-involved gun violence: Measuring the impact of Boston's Operation Ceasefire on street gang behavior. *Journal of Quantitative Criminology, 30*(1), 113–139.

Braswell, M. C., McCarthy, B. R., & McCarthy, B. J. (2017). *Justice, crime, and ethics* (9th ed.). New York, NY: Routledge.

Brewer, A. J., Banta-Green, C. J., Ort, C., Robel, A. E., & Field, J. (2016). Wastewater testing compared with random urinalyses for the surveillance of illicit drug use in prisons. *Drug & Alcohol Review, 35*(2), 133–137.

Bureau of Justice Statistics. (2016a). *Annual probation survey and annual parole survey*. Washington, DC: Department of Justice. Retrieved from https://www.bjs.gov/index.cfm?ty=dcdetail&iid=271

Bureau of Justice Statistics. (2017b). *Justice expenditure and employment*. Washington, DC: Department of Justice. Retrieved from http://www.bjs.gov/index.cfm?ty=pbdetail&iid=6310

Bureau of Justice Statistics. (2016c). *National prisoner statistics program*. Washington, DC: Department of Justice. Retrieved from https://www.bjs.gov/index.cfm?ty=dcdetail&iid=269

Bureau of Justice Statistics. (2016d). *Mortality in local jails, 2000-2014 – Statistical tables*. Washington, DC: Department of Justice. Retrieved from https://www.bjs.gov/content/pub/pdf /mlj0014st.pdf)

Bush, S. S., Connell, M. A., & Denny, R. L. (2006). *Ethical practice in forensic psychology: A systematic model for decision making*. Washington, DC: American Psychological Association.

Byrne, J. M., Lurigio, A. J., & Petersilia, J. (1992). *Smart sentencing: The emergency of intermediate sanctions*. Thousand Oaks, CA: Sage.

Carlson, B. E., & Cervera, N. (1991). Inmates and their families: Conjugal visits, family contact, and family functioning. *Criminal Justice and Behavior, 18*(3), 318–331.

Centers for Disease Control and Prevention (CDC). (2007). *Prosecuting youths as adults creates younger repeat offenders: Separate justice system is essential to reduce recidivism*. Retrieved from http://www.campaignforyouthjustice.org/Downloads/PressReleases/CJYJ_CDC_Report _11-29-07.pdf

Chang, T. F. H., & Thompkins, D. E. (2002). Corporations go to prisons: The expansion of corporate power in the correctional industry. *Labor Studies Journal, 27*(1), 45–69.

Christian, J. (2005). Riding the bus: Barriers to prison visitation and family management strategies. *Journal of Contemporary Criminal Justice, 21*(1), 31–48.

Connelly, R. J. (1997). Role morality and the executioner's intention. *Professional Ethics, 6*(1–2), 77–102.

Conover, T. (2001). *Newjack: Guarding Sing Sing*. New York, NY: Vintage Books.

Correctional Association. (2003). Lockdown New York: Disciplinary confinement in New York state prisons. Retrieved from https://www.prisonpolicy.org/scans/lockdown-new-york-1.pdf

Cullen, F., & Gilbert, K. (2013). *Reaffirming rehabilitation* (2nd ed.). New York, NY: Routledge.

Death Penalty Information Center. (2018a). Botched executions. Retrieved from https:// deathpenaltyinfo.org/some-examples-post-furman-botched-executions

Death Penalty Information Center. (2018b). Facts about the death penalty. Retrieved from https:// deathpenaltyinfo.org/documents/FactSheet.pdf

Death Penalty Information Center. (2018c). Lethal injection. Retrieved from https://deathpenaltyinfo .org/lethal-injection

Death Penalty Information Center. (2018d). Methods of execution. Retrieved from https:// deathpenaltyinfo.org/methods-execution

Diep, F. (2015, March 12). The psychology of the executioner. *Pacific Standard*. Retrieved from https://psmag.com/social-justice/ready-aim-fire

DiIulio, J. (1987). *Governing prisons: A comparative study of correctional management*. New York, NY: Free Press.

Duff, R. A. (2001). *Punishment, communication, and community*. New York, NY: Oxford University Press.

Duwe, G., & Clark, V. (2014). The effects of prison-based educational programming on recidivism and employment. *The Prison Journal, 94*(4), 454–478.

Equal Justice Initiative. (2017, February 6). Mass incarceration costs $182 billion every year, without adding much to public safety. Retrieved from https://eji.org/news/mass-incarceration-costs -182-billion-annually

Gaes, G. G. (1985). The effects of overcrowding in prisons. In M. Tony and N. Morris (Eds.). *Crime and Justice*, Vol. 6 (pp. 265–346). Chicago, IL: University of Chicago Press.

Gaes, G. G. (1994). Prison crowding research re-examined. *Prison Journal, 73*(3), 329–364.

Gendreau, P., & Goggin, C. (1996). Principles of effective correctional programming. *Forum on Correctional Research, 8*(3), 38–41.

Grady, D., & Hoffman, J. (2018, May 7). States turn to an unproven method of execution: Nitrogen gas. *New York Times*. Retrieved from https://www.nytimes.com/2018/05/07/health/death -penalty-nitrogen-executions.html

Griffin, M. L. (2002). The influence of professional orientation on detention officers' attitudes toward the use of force. *Criminal Justice and Behavior, 29*(3), 250–277.

Griffin, M. L. (2006). Gender and stress: A comparative assessment of sources of stress among correctional officers. *Journal of Contemporary Criminal Justice, 22*(1), 5–25.

Haag, A. D. (2006). Ethical dilemmas faced by correctional psychologists in Canada. *Criminal Justice and Behavior, 33*, 93–109.

Harris, J. (1995). Sentencing enhancement—"Three Strikes" law: Memorandum for all United States attorneys. Retrieved from https://www.justice.gov/jm/criminal-resource-manual-1032 -sentencing-enhancement-three-strikes-law

Harrison, L. D., & Scarpitti, F. R. (2002). Special issue: Drug treatment courts. *Substance Use & Misuse, 37*(12–13), 1441–1832.

Hartney, C., & Marchionna, S. (2009). *Attitudes of US voters toward nonserious offenders and alternatives to incarceration*. Oakland, CA: National Council on Crime and Delinquency.

Henry, P., Senese, J. D., & Ingley, G. S. (1994). Use of force in America's prisons: An overview of current research. *Corrections Today, 56*(4), 108–112.

Hillsman, S., & Greene, J. (1992). The use of fines as an intermediate sanction. In J. Byrne, A. Lurigio, & J. Petersilia (Eds.). *Smart sentencing: The emergence of intermediate sanctions* (pp. 123–141). Newbury Park, CA: Sage.

Jackson, S. J. (2005). Ex-communication: Competition and collusion in the U.S. prison telephone industry. *Critical Studies in Media Communication, 22*(4), 263–280.

Johnson, R., & Price, S. (1981). The complete correctional officer: Human service and the human environment of prison. *Criminal Justice and Behavior, 8*(3), 343–373.

Kennedy, M. (2018, July 11). Nevada postpones planned execution using fentanyl. National Public Radio. Retrieved from https://www.npr.org/2018/07/11/628050984/nevada-postpones -planned-execution-using-fentanyl

Kleinig, J. (2016). Correctional ethics. In J. Kleinig (Ed.). *Correctional Ethics*. New York, NY: Routledge.

Kleinig, J. (2008). *Ethics and criminal justice: An introduction*. Cambridge, UK: Cambridge University Press.

Klenowski, P. M., Bell, K. J., & Dodson, K. D. (2010). Evidence-based assessment of faith-based programs: Do faith-based programs "work" to reduce recidivism? *Journal of Offender Rehabilitation, 50*(6), 367–383.

Kronenwetter, M. (2001). *Capital punishment: A reference handbook* (2nd ed.). Santa Barbara, CA: ABC-CLIO.

Levenson, J. (1999). *A system under pressure: The effects of prison overcrowding.* London, UK: Prison Reform Trust.

Levenson, J., & D'Amora, D. (2005). An ethical paradigm for sex offender treatment: Response to Glaser. *Western Criminology Review, 6*, 145–153.

Lombardo, L. X. (1981). *Guards imprisoned: Correctional officers at work.* New York, NY: Elsevier.

MacGregor, D. L. (2003). Stripped of all reason? The appropriate standard for evaluating strip searches of arrestees and pretrial detainees in correctional facilities. *Columbia Journal of Law and Social Problems, 36*(2), 163–207.

MacKenzie, D. (2001). Corrections and sentencing in the 21st century: Evidence-based corrections and sentencing. *Prison Journal, 81*(3), 29–312.

MacKenzie, D. L., & Armstrong, G. S. (2004). *Boot camps: Studies examining military basic training as a model for corrections.* Thousand Oaks, CA: Sage.

Mainprize, S. (1992). Electronic monitoring in corrections: Assessing cost effectiveness and the potential for widening the net of social control. *Canadian Journal of Criminology, 34*(2), 161–180.

Mandery, E. J. (2005). *Capital punishment: A balanced examination.* Sudbury, MA: Jones & Bartlett.

McCarthy, B. J. (1991). Keeping an eye on the keeper: Prison corruption and its control. In M. Braswell, B. McCarthy, & B. McCarthy (Eds.). *Justice, crime, and ethics* (pp. 239–253). Belmont, CA: Wadsworth.

McDonald, D. (1992). Punishing labor: Unpaid community service as a criminal sentence. In J. Byrne, A. Lurigio, & J. Petersilia (Eds.). *Smart sentencing: The emergence of intermediate sanctions* (pp. 182–193). Newbury Park: CA: Safe.

McGreal, C. (2018, July 10). Nevada to become first state to execute inmate with fentanyl. *The Guardian* [UK]. Retrieved from https://www.theguardian.com/us-news/2018/jul/10/nevada -fentanyl-execution-opioid-crisis-drug-death-row

Mills, R. B. (1980). Ethical guidelines in corrections. In R. B. Mills (Ed.). *Offender assessment: A casebook in corrections* (pp. 51–55). Cincinnati, OH: Anderson.

Morris, N., & Tonry, M. (1990). *Between prison and probation: Intermediate punishments in a rational sentencing system.* New York. NY: Oxford University Press.

Muraskin, R. (2001a). Corrections/punishment: Ethical behavior of correctional officers. In R. Muraskin & M. Muraskin (Eds.), *Morality and the law* (pp. 119–129). Upper Saddle River, NJ: Prentice Hall.

Muraskin, R. (2001b). Probation and parole officers: Ethical behaviors. In R. Muraskin, & M. Muraskin (Eds.). *Morality and the Law* (pp. 119–129). Upper Saddle River, NJ: Prentice Hall.

National Research Council. (2012). *Deterrence and the death penalty.* Washington, DC: National Academies Press.

Nesmith, A., & Ruhland, E. (2008). Children of incarcerated parents: Challenges and resiliency, in their own words. *Children and Youth Services Review, 30*(10), 1119–1130.

Nolan, J. L. (2002). *Drug courts in theory and practice.* New York, NY: Aldine de Gruyter.

Petersilia, J. (1983). *Racial disparities in the criminal justice system.* Santa Monica, CA: RAND Corporation.

Petersilia, J. (1998). *Community corrections.* New York, NY: Oxford University Press.

Pojman, L., & Reiman, J. (1998). *The death penalty: For and against.* Lanham, MD: Rowman & Littlefield.

Prison Policy Initiative. (2017, January 25). Following the money of mass incarceration. Retrieved from https://www.prisonpolicy.org/reports/money.html

Prison Reform Trust. (1999). *Electronic tagging: Viable options of expensive diversion.* London, UK: Prison Reform Trust.

Redding, R. E. (2010). Juvenile transfer: An effective deterrent to delinquency? Washington, DC: U.S. Department of Justice, NCJ 220595. Retrieved from www.ncjrs.gov/pdffiles /ojjdp/220595.pdf

Sarat, A. (2014). *Gruesome spectacles: Botched executions and America's death penalty.* Stanford, CA: Stanford University Press.

Schaufeli, W. B., & Peeters, M. C. (2000). Job stress and burnout among correctional officers: A literature review. *International Journal of Stress Management, 7*(1), 19–48.

Schwartz, A. (2004). A market in liberty: Corruption, cooperation, and the federal criminal justice system. In W. C. Hefferman and J. Kleinig (Eds.). *Private and public corruption* (pp. 173–222). Lanham, MD: Rowman & Littlefield.

Shalev, S. (2011). Solitary confinement and supermax prisons: Human rights and ethical analysis. *Journal of Forensic Psychology Practice, 11*(2), 151–183.

Sherman, L. W., Farrington, D. P., Welsh, B. C., & MacKenzie, D. L. (2002). *Evidence-based crime prevention.* New York, NY: Routledge.

Shichor, D. (1995). *Punishment for profit: Private prisons/public concerns.* Thousand Oaks, CA: Sage.

Shichor, D. (2006). *The meaning and nature of punishment.* Long Grove, IL: Waveland.

Snyder, H. N., & Sickmund, M. (2006). *Juvenile offenders and victims: 2006 national report.* Washington, DC: U.S. Department of Justice, Office of Justice Programs.

Tonry, M. (1994). Racial disproportion in U.S. prisons. *British Journal of Criminology, 34,* 97–115.

Turner, H.A., Finkelhor, D., Shattuck, A., & Hamby, S. (2012). Recent victimization exposure and suicidal ideation in adolescents. *Archives of Pediatrics and Adolescent Medicine, 166*(12), 1149–1154.

Turner, S., Petersilia, J., & Deschenes, E. P. (1994). The implementation and effectiveness of drug testing in community supervision: Results of an experimental evaluation. In D. MacKenzie & C. Uchida (Eds.). *Drugs and crime: Evaluating public policy initiatives* (pp. 231–251). Thousand Oaks, CA: Sage.

Vartia, M., & Hyyti, J. (2002). Gender differences in workplace bullying among prison officers. *European Journal of Work and Organizational Psychology, 11*(1), 113–126.

Visher, C. (1983). Gender, police arrest decisions and notions of chivalry. *Criminology, 21*(1), 5–28.

Vivian, J. C. (2013, October 18). Lethal injections, drug shortages, and pharmacy ethics. *U.S. Pharmacist.* Retrieved from https://www.uspharmacist.com/article/lethal-injections-drug-shortages-and-pharmacy-ethics-44470

von Hirsch, A. (1990). The ethics of community-based sanctions. *Crime and Delinquency, 36*(1), 162–173.

von Hirsch, A., & Greene, J. (1993). When should reformers support creation of sentencing guidelines? *Wake Forest Law Review, 28,* 329–343.

Waldron, J. (1992). Lex talionis. *Arizona Law Review, 34,* 25–51.

Walters, S. (1992). Attitudinal and demographic differences between male and female corrections officers: A study in three midwestern prisons. *Journal of Offender Rehabilitation, 18*(1–2), 173–190.

Ward, T., & Salmon, K. (2009). The ethics of punishment: Correctional practice implications. *Aggression and Violent Behavior, 14*(4), 239–247.

Welch, M. (2005). *Ironies of imprisonment.* Thousand Oaks, CA: Sage.

Whitehead, J. T. (1996). Ethical issues in probation and parole. In M. Braswell, B. McCarthy, & B. McCarthy (Eds.). *Justice, crime and ethics* (pp. 243–259). Cincinnati, OH: Anderson.

World Prison Brief. (2016). World prison brief data. Retrieved from http://prisonstudies.org/highest-to-lowest/prison-population-total?field_region_taxonomy_tid=All

Wright, K. N., & Goodstein, L. (1989). Correctional environments. In L. Goodstein & D. L. MacKenzie (Eds.). *The American prison: Issues in research and policy* (pp. 253–270). New York, NY: Plenum Press.

ARTICLE 24

Ethics and Manipulation in Corrections: Having One Combats the Other

Gary F. Cornelius

▶ Introduction

In any discussion of ethics, the problem of inmate manipulation must be a critical part. In the last several years, ethical breaches by correctional staff, both sworn and civilian, have been seen in several facilities across the country. In 2015, two convicted murderers serving life sentences without parole escaped from the Clinton Correctional Facility in upstate New York, after manipulating two employees into helping them. In 2013, at the Baltimore City Detention Center in Maryland, a scandal revealed a lack of ethics with some employees, sex with inmates, contraband smuggling, and inmates fathering children. There are other incidents, but the common thread running through these and similar others is the lack of professional ethics among staff members, allowing themselves to be targeted and manipulated by inmates. Inmates will look for and seek out staff—sworn and non-sworn—who appear to have weak ethical foundations. This opens a door through which the inmate schemer—and there are some brilliant ones—can move right on in. In a related note, the public should realize that correctional officers (COs), guards, deputies, and so on are *law enforcement officers* and a vital part of the criminal justice system. They deserve the public's gratitude, respect, and thanks. However, popular culture at times portrays police officers as brutal and corrupt and correctional officers as "people not being smart enough to be cops." These characterizations are unfair and biased. Police officers arrest the criminal offenders; correctional officers keep them locked up. Both groups serve the public and both serve the public trust. But it is embarrassing to a criminal justice agency when some of its members put aside their ethics, fall victim to manipulation, and violate that public trust. This article will discuss ethics and manipulation and training in both areas.

▶ Ethics in Corrections

Corrections staff—both sworn (officers) and nonsworn (civilians)—are an important part of the criminal justice system. Police officers arrest criminal offenders, and correctional officers maintain their incarceration. However, in some movies and television shows corrections staffers are portrayed as using excessive force, being corrupt, or being easily duped by inmates who are depicted as much more intelligent. COs are portrayed as rejects from the police academy who just sit around, except for taking head counts, feeding inmates, or breaking up the occasional fight. As a corrections professional for more than 30 years, I am always amazed at the ignorance and misinformation that citizens have about the local jail in the community and the types of inmates—often dangerous or mentally ill—confined there. Statistics paint a portrait of jail and prison COs dealing with inmates who are mentally ill, substance abusers, functionally illiterate, violent, lacking in social skills, and aligning themselves with or becoming members of security threat groups (gangs, racists, etc.). It takes a special type of professional to deal with inmates, maintain composure, and not fall under the spell of manipulation by inmates.

Ethics: The Definition

Culturally, we see and are amused by the characterizations of unethical lawyers, politicians, and used car salesmen. The term *ethics* has a simple definition. Goodman (2008, p. 6) defined it as the study of morals. This includes questions of what is right, what is wrong, what is good, and what is bad. She also defines ethics as a choice—a conscious decision to act correctly or wrongly. Because of the aspect of rational choice, it is not surprising that the public—the taxpayer—has little or no sympathy for correctional officers who engage in sex with inmates, bring in contraband for them, or help them escape custody. Ethical violations incur the wrath of the taxpayer and are clear violations of the public trust. Law enforcement officers wearing guns, uniforms, and badges are supposed to keep us safe. Ethical violations taint the entire profession. A CO who works at a state prison that has been spotlighted in the media because of reported widespread sexual misconduct with inmates may feel violated—even though he or she is innocent. When telling citizens where they work, they may experience responses such as, "Oh yeah! Everybody knows what goes on inside *that* place."

The Public Trust

There is little debate as to what is meant by *public trust*. Simply, holding any public office is the public trust. A police officer, correctional officer, probation officer, elected official, and so on are all part of the public trust. It is supported by the axiom that in a participatory democracy, confidence is required in the integrity of the government. This is the "heart" of the public trust—ethical demands on these public servants and establishing baseline guidelines for behavior. These guidelines, laws, and standards establish the minimum standards of conduct (Whisenand, 2007, p. 55). As a result, when the public sees correctional personnel engaging in sexual misconduct, smuggling contraband, being lax in facility security, or helping inmates escape, they feel that their trust in our criminal justice system has been violated.

A clear example is the so-called Animal House jail scandal in Montague County, Texas, in 2008–2009. Investigations by law enforcement authorities revealed that inmates—not the deputies—ran the jail as far back as 2006. Inmates had sex with female deputies, took drugs, conversed on cell phones brought in by deputies or friends, and relaxed in recliners. Security was lax in the 100-bed jail; several security surveillance cameras were disabled, two cellblock doors did not lock, and inmates made weapons out of nails. Inmates also used extension cords to keep deputies out of certain areas. People in the community had heard rumors about inmate–deputy sex, but had dismissed them as gossip. An official received a handwritten letter from a jail inmate describing his sexual relationship with a female deputy. A Texas grand jury returned a 106-count indictment against the 62-year-old sheriff, 16 of his deputies, and four jail inmates. The sheriff pleaded guilty to an unrelated federal civil rights charge involving sexual assault. He told a woman that unless she had sex with him, she would be sent to jail on drug charges (Associated Press, 2009a, 2009b, 2009c). The taxpaying moral citizen wants to feel safe; in this case, it would have been difficult to feel safe.

▶ Acts of Co-Deviance

Acts of deviance and violation of ethics by correctional personnel do not have to be headline-grabbing incidents. *Deviance* is related to ethics and is defined as an "action or behavior that violates generally accepted norms." From society's norms, laws and policies are developed. Also, agencies will codify these unacceptable behaviors into general orders (Ross, 2008, pp. 190–192). Every CO is or should be familiar with his or her agency's code of conduct and the consequences for violating them, including criminal prosecution and being subject to civil lawsuits. There is a range from minor to major acts of deviance, but line staff and supervisors adhering to policy and not committing them is critical to a professionally run and staffed correctional facility. Inmates will tempt staff to not follow policies, trying to discover a weak moral compass within an officer or civilian.

Ross (2008, pp. 192–196) describes 12 primary types of deviance committed by correctional officers and staff:

1. *Improper use or misuse of agency equipment and property.* Examples include running a private business using agency office supplies or looking at pornography on agency computers, among other violations.
2. *Mishandling or theft of inmate property.* Stealing money, personal items, or jewelry from inmates as they are processed in or "losing" or misplacing property.
3. *Drinking on the job.* This can be expanded to include usage of illegal drugs or abusing alcohol. The effects of such substance abuse can impair a CO from being alert and safe while carrying out his or her duties.
4. *Accepting gifts from inmates and contractors.* The door to manipulation opens when a staff member accepts a gift from an inmate—most often a letter, note, or so on. Also, if an inmate worker (a trustee) observes a staff member accepting a gift from a contractor or vendor, this shows that the staff member can be "bought"—and word will get around.

5. *Discrimination.* COs must be impartial and fair. They must treat inmates with basic human respect and dignity and not discriminate on the basis of race, gender, sexual orientation, sexual preference, ethnicity, or national origin.

6. *Abuse of authority.* Like police officers, COs have a lot of power. Abuse of this power in the form of harassment, humiliation, or preferential treatment is unprofessional and will result in anger and resentment in the inmate population.

7. *General border violations.* More simply, crossing the line with inmates will blur the line and minimize the professional distance that COs and staff must maintain. Doing favors for inmates, granting favors, and overlooking rule violations allow inmates to have power over the staff and circumvent security.

8. *Sexual harassment of colleagues.* This creates a hostile, tense work environment. Staff inappropriately touching staff, asking for and pressuring for dates, telling off-color jokes, and so on constitute sexual harassment. Also included are the display of pornographic material and making comments about body parts of physiques.

9. *Sexual relations with inmates.* This is the "dark cloud" that hovers over corrections. Most if not all states have statutes that make carnal knowledge with a person in custody a crime. Many scandals involving correctional staff and inappropriate behavior with inmates include sexual acts with inmates.

10. *Smuggling contraband.* Although the informal CO code stresses safety and watching out for each other, smuggling contraband, including weapons, into a facility shows flagrant disregard for the safety of others. Smuggled drugs and alcohol alter inmates' behavior and can result in injury or death to staff and other inmates.

11. *Theft of correctional facility property.* Illegally taking property can range from institutional food to office supplies.

12. *Violence against inmates.* The United States has a humane correctional system, but force has to be used for self-protection, to protect staff and other inmates, and to prevent destruction of property and escape. Unfortunately, some COs have used excessive force on inmates, resulting in serious injury or death. Some "rogue officers" have committed psychological violence against inmates, such as performing humiliating strip searches, harassing inmates, tearing up mail, ignoring legitimate requests, and so on. Punishment for these crimes can be severe. For example, a 30-year prison sentence was handed down to an Alabama shift lieutenant who assaulted an inmate, including "stomping" on his head to "send a message" to other inmates. The lieutenant was angry that the inmate had assaulted a subordinate CO. (Cornelius, 2017, p. 359)

An effective training program for corrections staff, both sworn and civilian, must include a training policy that emphasizes the type of manipulative inmate population that COs and staff deal with rather than a cursory glossing over of the topic. It must emphasize that lapses in ethical behavior will be dealt with firmly, including all the way up to termination or criminal prosecution. This training must be presented in a frank and relevant manner using actual examples from reputable corrections sources. The goal is not to unnecessarily scare staff but to *inform* them.

▶ The Mechanics of Ethical Behavior in Corrections

There are guidelines to correctional staff making ethical decisions: common sense, adhering to staff and institutional policies, remembering training, and being aware of the public trust. It is the A-B-C-D formula (Goodman, 2008, p. 7):

Actions: How COs or nonsworn staff members conduct themselves in front of the inmate population will show how ethical they are. Following policy, not engaging in deviance, and keeping security at the front of all duties being carried out shows the inmate that this staff person is no "pushover." Ethical actions call for awareness and conscientious decision making: "Doing the right, proper thing."

Beliefs: Staff members should believe in the profession of corrections, their peers, their families, and so on. Staff can have *empathy* toward inmates because some want to change and stay out once released. A CO's belief should be in the job and the mission of the agency, not in always believing what manipulative inmates tell him. Discretion and verification are key.

Conduct: Self-examination is necessary before a staff member decides to bend the rules, do a favor for an inmate that may circumvent policy, or engage in romantic conduct with a prisoner. In particular, when contemplating a sexual act with an inmate, staff members should ask themselves. "Would I want my family, friends, colleagues, the public, or the media to see this?"

Discipline: Staff must have the self-discipline to resist doing the *wrong* things—and the strength to do the *right* things. Doing the right things and adhering to good ethics requires energy. If a CO is lazy, takes shortcuts, and treats inmates like friends, he or she should find another profession.

▶ Ethical Failures in Correctional Institutions

The past several years have seen several well-publicized incidents in which the manipulation of correctional staff members caused COs and civilians to consciously abandon positive ethical values and effectively compromise security, embarrassing the field of corrections and ending their careers. For example, in the 2015 Clinton Correctional Facility escape of inmates Richard Matt and David Sweat (two so-called lifers), their goal was to successfully breach the prison's perimeter and escape. In the 2013 Baltimore City Detention Center scandal, escape was not a priority of the inmates—having sex with female COs and running a criminal enterprise were. In both cases, inmates manipulated staff into doing their bidding, from smuggling in tools to help them tunnel out to smuggling in drugs. Both events are textbook cases of manipulation defeating ethics—and staff members allowing it.

Baltimore City Detention Center

In spring 2013, authorities began to investigate widespread misconduct by correctional officers at the Baltimore City Detention Center. A high-ranking member of the Black Guerilla Family (BGF) reportedly "ran" the jail, fathering four children with female COs, and boasting of making nearly $16,000 in drug sales in one month. Percocet pills were valued at $30 each, and one-ounce bags of marijuana went for $50. Besides drugs, cell phones were brought in by COs who hid the phones in their hair, shoes, and underwear. One media report stated that the names of 14 female COs who would engage in sex with inmates were scrawled on one wall along with their fee ($150). One CO was allowed to drive a car, one of two purchased by an inmate; two had the gang leader's name tattooed on them and talked about having his children. Informal arrangements were devised in which the BGF inmates would keep the jail calm if COs would ignore smuggling and other illicit activities. Some COs participated in the smuggling solely for the money (Marimow & Wagner, 2013; Vargas, Marimow, & Shin, 2013).

The manipulation of the correctional officers was a critical factor. The BGF leader instructed inmates to target female COs with "low self-esteem, insecurities, and certain physical attributes." One CO witnessed a brutal attack on an inmate. Apparently shaken, she needed advice—but she went to the BGF leader to get solace, not to staff or supervisors. In Baltimore, paying COs to bring in cigarettes and writing love letters to them began the "game" and persuaded the COs to act unethically. Worse yet, they believed that the inmates really cared for them (Vargas et al., 2013). The manipulation schemes target the actions and beliefs of the ethics A-B-C-D paradigm. The consequences are ignored because of an irrational decision, and the discipline can be severe, including criminal prosecution and termination. Any professional COs who want to keep their jobs should take their duties and training seriously and avoid engaging in these types of acts.

Clinton Correctional Facility

In June 2015, Richard Matt and David Sweat, two inmates serving life without parole, escaped from the Clinton Correctional Facility in Dannemora, New York, through the underground infrastructure of the prison. By manipulating civilian worker Joyce Mitchell, the two inmates developed a friendly and romantic relationship with her and convinced her to bring in tools and other items to facilitate their digging out of the facility through its underground network of steam heating pipes. Mitchell engaged in sexual activity with Matt, brought in contraband for the escapees, and agreed to be the getaway driver once the escape occurred. The staff "middleman" was CO Gene Palmer, who brought food to the inmates, reportedly unaware that escape tools were being hidden in packages of frozen meat. Matt bribed Mitchell with sex, and Palmer was bribed with paintings and drawings given to him by Matt (Eastman, 2016).

Time is a factor. Inmates who are out to manipulate look for lapses in ethics and then target those staff members who show those lapses. According to the report of the New York Inspector General (2016), Sweat and Matt planned the escape for six months, starting in January 2015. They used the time to manipulate Mitchell and used the good intentions of Palmer, who wanted to be the inmates' friend. Sweat did the digging, and sloppy staff security procedures allowed for both his absences from his cell and hiding of contraband to go undiscovered. Mitchell was performing improper favors for the inmates, including smuggling in personal items, making phone calls to Matt's daughter on his behalf, and sharing food in the tailor shop where she supervised the inmates. She agreed to obtain cash, guns, camping gear, a compass, and clothing for Sweat and Matt (New York Office of the Inspector General, 2016, pp. 2–5).

However, this escape cannot be solely blamed on just Mitchell and Palmer. As in many breaches of institutional security, the failings resulted from several factors. At the Clinton facility, Mitchell and the inmates took advantage of breakdowns in security, ranging from failures to search her bag at the front gate to CO Palmer failing to search inmates when they returned from the tailor shop. He also did not require the inmates to pass through a metal detector; if they had, the contraband from Mitchell would have been discovered. Discarded scrap metal lying around the underground digging site and unsecured tools were used by Sweat to fashion tools for digging. Night counts by COs were sloppy or negligent, Sweat's cell was not searched, and security and supervision of civilians and inmates were complacent. Combine the lack of ethics and CO reports that security and compliance standards were being met became a textbook example of manipulation, complacency, and lack of ethics (New York Office of the Inspector General, 2016, pp. 2–8). Less than three weeks after their escape, Matt was killed by law enforcement officers, Sweat was recaptured, and Palmer and Mitchell were arrested and later prosecuted.

▶ Maintaining Ethics and Combatting Manipulation

Correctional supervisors and trainers frequently ask, "Can proper ethics be taught?" There is no easy answer. Corrections staffs comprise individuals; when they are hired, it is hoped the facility will receive good and moral people to work inside. Because ethics and manipulation are interrelated, there must be clear, plain-speaking approaches to both.

Ethics Training

Any approach to training correctional staff in the importance of and adherence to ethics should work to build a sense of self-worth and confidence. Pride in the profession and keeping a good positive sense of morale are two good tools in maintaining ethics. This training cannot be a soft approach: CO veterans will say that the job of working with and among criminal offenders must be described early on in both positive and negative terms, a version of "warts and all" or the good, the bad, and the ugly. Supervisors and trainers must make it clear to subordinates that the benefits of a professional career outweigh the risks and consequences of inappropriate behavior. They must also avoid letting personal bias or negative views of the field dominate any discussions of the correctional field because it will tear down the positive morale they are working to build (Jones & Carlson, 2004, p. 43). Also, informing staff members that they are not on the lower level of the criminal justice system must also be clear. Some police officers who have retired and become COs in a second career have said that they had no idea that correctional officers have a tough job. The training for COs has continued to improve, and in many jurisdictions the pay scale and benefits have reached parity with those of police departments.

In addition, every agency must have a clear but flexible code of conduct that is clearly discussed and periodically reviewed for ongoing training. Such a review must use clear examples such as the New York state and Baltimore cases. COs and staff must be made aware of the personal and professional costs of ethical lapses: divorce, humiliation, suspension, demotion, criminal prosecution, and termination. Flexibility must address new developments in society such as the use of social media; in fact, an effective code of conduct will state clearly the parameters of proper social media use.

Inmate Manipulation Training

A primary rule for corrections staff is that if inmates see unethical behavior, they will be your new best friends. And that "friendship" will exact a price. Inmate manipulators will hand staff members a bill sooner or later. All corrections staff can defend themselves against manipulation by adhering to good ethics and understanding manipulation—how it is defined and how to resist it. The decision to abandon ethics and be manipulated is a conscious one; manipulated COs have no one to blame but themselves.

Manipulation: Definition

Not all inmates manipulate staff, but staff members must use universal precautions with a dose of healthy skepticism. As their careers progress, COs and civilian staff will learn through actions and behavior which inmates want to change, get out, and stay out and which ones want to use people for their own ends. The definition of manipulation has the following three components, and each must be placed in a correctional context (Cornelius, 2009, pp. 69–97).

1. *To control or play upon.* Inmates want to control contraband trafficking, where they are housed, their communications with fellow inmates, and so on. They also want to make incarceration as comfortable as possible. Inmates know that staff has access to the outside world—and want to control that access and make it work for them. They also will target and work on staff who display poor ethics, complacency, and inattentiveness to the job. In New York state, the inmates wanted escape. In Baltimore, they wanted sex with staff and contraband.

2. *By artful and unfair means.* This is the most dangerous aspect of manipulation by inmates. These means include lying, exaggerating, professing love and affection, "buttering up," looking tearful, acting depressed, and so on. The manipulative inmate's acting ability and imagination have few limits.

3. *To achieve a desired end.* Some inmates want to escape, and others use ploys to get transported to a hospital to escape or to see scenery outside the facility. An inmate may cry and say he or she needs to get into a drug program—not to get clean and sober but to get some sympathy from a jury or judge. Another desire is to see the staff "dance" to the inmates' tune by having sex, doing errands, getting an inmate a desirable worker position, and so on. A staff member does not know what is in the mind of an institutionalized, hard-core inmate.

▶ The CHUMPS Approach

The CHUMPS approach for correctional staff is a device that reminds staff members about ethics and resisting manipulation. It can be easily incorporated into any training or discussion about ethics and manipulation (Cornelius, 2009, pp. 200–206).

Control, not complacency. Correctional institutions must control all inmate movements, living areas, and allowed items. Control also means having the ability to say no to inmate requests to bend the rules.

Helping the inmates help themselves. Correctional institutions have programs and counselors that can help inmates regain their lives and overcome their problems. Like everything in life, it requires effort and work. Instead of inmates using people to solve their problems, they should be steered to programs and staff members that can help them—and take it from there.

Understanding the offender subculture and understanding yourself. Corrections staff strive to be ethical; this is the opposite of inmates who have not lived their lives by a moral code. Also, self-awareness is important—and difficult. A CO should ask him- or herself, "Am I too friendly with inmates?" "Am I easily distracted"?

Maintaining a professional distance. Ethics means maintaining boundaries by not telling inmates anything personal about themselves, especially their relationships and any financial problems they might have. Inmates will use personal information to cloud the objectivity of staff members.

Professionalism in adhering to policies and procedures. Commitment to following all rules provides a foundation for the ethical CO. Inmates target staff members who do not perform their duties in accordance with regulations.

Stressed out staff are vulnerable. Because correctional staff members can be highly talkative, inmates will work to find out who is "stressed out." Any staff member experiencing burnout or having trouble dealing with the stress of the job should seek help from supervisors, families, friends, and employee-assistance programs—not inmates.

▶ Summary

Maintaining ethics in correctional facilities and resisting inmate manipulation are interrelated objectives. Ethics means more than doing the right thing. To be ethical, one must act appropriately, believe in the profession and its moral makeup and expectations, conduct oneself appropriately, and have self-discipline. Deviant acts by correctional staff vary from minor to major. Two well-known recent examples are the Baltimore City Detention Center in 2013 and the Clinton Correctional Facility in upstate New York in 2015. In these cases, inmates had sex with staff, and corrupted staff smuggled in contraband. Training in ethics must be blunt and ongoing. Training in inmate manipulation must illustrate both the definition and the CHUMPS approach as tools to combat it.

▶ **References**

Associated Press. (2009a, January 3). Jail shut after cops discover recliners in cells. NBCNews.com. Retrieved from: http://www.nbcnews.com/id/28475274/ns/us_news-crime_and_courts/t/jail-shut-after-cops-discover-recliners-cells/#.W2SWLHkm4Sk

Associated Press. (2009b, February 28). 17 charged in drug, sex probe at Texas jail. NBCNews.com. Retrieved from http://www.nbcnews.com/id/29439918/ns/us_news-crime_and_courts/t/charged-drug-sex-probe-texas-jail/#.W2SVRHkm4Sk

Associated Press. (2009c, March 16). Texas jail was an Animal House, authorities say. *Mercury News.* Retrieved from https://www.nbcdfw.com/news/local/Texas-Jail-Was-An-Animal-House-Authorities-Say--.html

Cornelius, G. F. (2009). *The art of the con: Avoiding offender manipulation* (2nd ed.). Alexandria, VA: American Correctional Association.

Cornelius, G. F. (2017). *The correctional officer: A practical guide* (3rd ed.). Durham, NC: Carolina Academic Press.

Eastman, K. (2016, June 7). Inspector general's report on Dannemora prison break: Lack of searches pervasive at Clinton jail. Time Warner Cable News. Retrieved from http://spectrumlocalnews.com/nys/new-york-state/clinton-prison-break/2016/06/6/inspector-general-s-report-on-dannemora-prison-break-released

Goodman, D. J. (2008). *Enforcing ethics: A scenario-based workbook for police and corrections recruits and officers* (3rd ed.). Upper Saddle River. NJ: Pearson Prentice Hall.

Jones, J. R., & Carlson, D. R. (2004). *Reputable conduct* (2nd ed.). Upper Saddle River, NJ: Pearson Prentice Hall.

Marimow, A. E., & Wagner, J. (2013, April 23). 13 corrections officers indicted in Md., accused of aiding gang's drug scheme. *Washington Post.* Retrieved from https://www.washingtonpost.com/local/thirteen-correctional-officers-indicted-in-maryland/2013/04/23/6d2cbc14-ac23-11e2-a8b9-2a63d75b5459_story.html?noredirect=on&utm_term=.9db4c5b1f98d

New York Office of the Inspector General. (2016, June). Investigation into the June 5, 2015, escape of inmates David Sweat and Richard Matt from Clinton Correctional Facility. Retrieved from https://ig.ny.gov/sites/g/files/oee571/files/2016-11/DOCCS%20Clinton%20Report%20FINAL_1.pdf

Ross, J. I. (2008). *Special problems in corrections.* Upper Saddle River, NJ: Pearson Prentice Hall.

Vargas, T., Marimow, A. E., & Shin, A. (2013, May 6). Baltimore case depicts jail culture ruled by drugs, money, sex. *Saratogian News.* Retrieved from http://www.saratogian.com/general-news/20130506/baltimore-case-depicts-corrupt-jail-culture-ruled-by-drugs-money-sex

Whisenand, P. M. (2007). *Supervising police personnel: The fifteen responsibilities* (6th ed.). Upper Saddle River, NJ: Pearson Prentice Hall.

The Increase of Aging and Elderly Inmates in Local Jails, State Prisons, and Federal Correctional Facilities: Likely Causes, Current Problems, and Possible Solutions

Michael E. Antonio

A ging in jails or prisons is a contemporary issue and one of great importance to consider for penal systems and correctional populations throughout the world. In the United States, the study of aging and elderly inmates is complicated because any examination must consider the total number of inmates involved, the causes of incarceration, the physical and mental health needs of this group, and the viable options available to address these concerns. This chapter will address these issues by reviewing available research findings on the topic, and it will consider specific findings about trends among elderly inmates incarcerated in Pennsylvania's Department of Corrections (PADOC) from 2007 through 2016.

▶ Extent of the Problem

Recent years have brought a surge in literature about the "graying" of U.S. jail and prison populations. What specific age denotes an aging or elderly inmate from a younger one is still up to debate, but some research has categorized this population as those 50 years of age and older (Maschi, Morrisey, & Leigey, 2013), whereas other studies use age 55 as the threshold (Ahalt, Trestman, Rich, Greifinger, & Williams, 2013; Anno, 2004; Greene, Ahalt, Stijacic-Cenzer, Metzger, & Williams, 2018; Parks, 2018). An inmate can be sentenced to a jail or prison at a young age, then grow old over the years from extensive incarceration, or the individual may be committed at a later stage in life and live out his or her final years behind bars. Regardless, the circumstances of when an inmate was incarcerated, the dilemmas of aging, and elderly inmates equally affects all jails and prisons at the local, state, and federal levels.

Aging and elderly inmates represent a growing segment of the population in U.S. jails and prisons. The increase in this population has been documented by multiple sources. For example, the Office of the Inspector General (OIG) (2015) showed that inmates in federal correctional facilities who were 50 or older were the fastest-growing group in prison, increasing by 25% from 2009 to 2013. Bureau of Justice Statistics (BJS) compared changes in the number of older inmates in prisons from 1993 to 2013 and found that the number of inmates in state correctional facilities who were 50 or older was 131,500 in 2013, which represented an increase of more than 400% from the 26,300 older inmates incarcerated in 1993 (Carson & Sabol, 2016). The BJS findings also showed that in 2013 most elderly inmates were male (96.6%), White (60.7% White males and 73.4% White females), and serving time for violent offenses (65%). Many spent at least 10 years in prison (40%) or were admitted to prison at age 55 or older (40%).

Pennsylvania's Department of Corrections

PADOC examined trends among the number and percentage of aging and elderly inmates. **TABLE 25.1** shows data about annual inmate population totals from 2007 through 2016 (Pennsylvania's Department of Corrections, 2018). As the table shows, the annual inmate population peaked in 2011 (51,638) and fluctuated but steadily declined until 2016 (49,301). The number of inmates committed to Pennsylvania prisons was, on average, approximately 10,000 individuals annually during this time frame. The number of new inmate commitments reached its highest in 2013 (11,520) and was lowest in 2016 (9,183). Finally, the table shows that the number of new inmate commitments age 55 and older fluctuated but increased steadily and peaked in 2013 (703) and remained consistently high from 2014 through 2016.

FIGURE 25.1 shows trends among elderly inmates committed to PADOC. The figure shows the percentage of elderly inmates in Pennsylvania prisons increased slightly but remained steady from 2007 (.70%) through 2016 (1.19%). Moreover, the percentage of new inmate commitments age 55 or older was lowest in 2007 (3.16%) but more than doubled by 2016 (6.41%). Overall, these findings show the general prison population and new commitments have been decreasing in recent years even though the percentage of new commitments age 55 and older has been increasing. The findings from Pennsylvania are consistent with trends for aging and elderly inmates in jails and prisons at the local, state, and federal levels.

TABLE 25.1 PA DOC Annual Population Figures from 2007 through 2016 by General Population, New Commitments, and Age

	2007	2008	2009	2010	2011	2012	2013	2014	2015	2016
PA DOC inmate population	46,028	49,307	51,487	51,321	51,638	51,184	51,512	50,756	49,914	49,301
New inmate commitments	10,222	10,783	10,798	10,781	10,969	10,810	11,520	10,321	9,798	9,183
Commitments age 55 or older	323	348	391	460	451	524	703	545	581	589

Data from Pennsylvania's Department of Corrections. (2019). Monthly Population Reports.

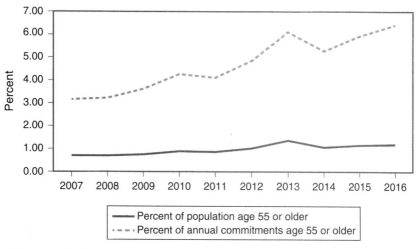

FIGURE 25.1 Elderly inmates in PA DOC.

Data from Pennsylvania's Department of Corrections. (2019). Monthly Population Reports. Office of Planning, Research & Statistics.

▶ Causes for Population Increase

As the previous description of available data shows, the U.S. penal system is facing a true crisis related to an ever-increasing population of elderly inmates. How did this come to be? The general population in the United States is gradually getting older. According to the U.S. Census Bureau, it was predicted that by 2050 the percentage of the general population aged 65 and older will be 88.5 million, which is more than double the estimated population of 40.2 million in 2010 (Vincent & Velkoff, 2010). With this information about population statistics, one may reasonably expect the number of elderly prisoners to rise as well. However, is this enough of an explanation to account for the robust trends in our prisons or is there more to the story? One issue that should be considered, according to research about correctional populations, is how federal and state governments responded to rises in crime rates in the 1970s and 1980s.

Sentencing Reform

Historically, the period between 1960 and 1980 was a restless time in the United States. The baby boomers, those born in the 20 years following World War II, were entering an age of more delinquent and criminal behavior. The War on Drugs had begun, and acts of egregious violence, including murders and rapes, increased dramatically (Peak, 2015; Schmalleger, 2018; Stohr & Walsh, 2016). Americans expressed outrage and concern about being victimized in their own communities, and politicians and the news media seized on an opportunity to exploit this level of fear (Dilulio, 1995; Lane & Meeker, 2000). In response to growing crime rates, policy makers set out to create strict sanctions and extended prison sentences to control incidents of crime in society.

The 1980s and 1990s marked a time of great change for the U.S. criminal justice system. Both federal and state governments enacted numerous laws that would ensure harsh punishments and guaranteed incarceration time for convicted criminals. One example from the federal government was passage of the Sentencing

Reform Act of 1984, which eliminated parole opportunities for federal inmates convicted of crimes (Tonry, 2015). During the same time, numerous states enacted policies and initiatives aimed at decreasing and deterring delinquent and criminal behaviors. Although many changes occurred in sentencing policy, some popular initiatives were adopted by various jurisdictions throughout the country (Peak, 2015; Stohr & Walsh, 2016). For example, so-called three-strikes legislation was passed that required all persons to serve a minimum of 25 years in prison if convicted of a third felony offense. Also, mandatory sentencing was imposed, with persons convicted of certain crimes required to serve a minimum number of months or years in prison. Some jurisdictions passed truth-in-sentencing laws that mandated persons convicted of certain crimes serve at least 85% of their sentence before being considered for release from prison. Finally, sentences of life without the possibility of parole meant persons convicted of certain crimes would spend the rest of their lives behind bars.

Crime rates started showing a marked decline in the early to mid-1990s. It is debated whether this drop in crime was the result of sentencing reforms in the previous decade, changes in demographic characteristics, or an upswing in economic development reflecting American society at the time (Peak, 2015; Stohr & Walsh, 2016). Regardless of the reason for decreases in crime, the result it had on prison populations was clear: The numbers of incarcerated persons at the state and federal levels soared. Current problems associated with the increased number of aging and elderly prisoners in the penal system today may have resulted in large part because of strict and lengthy sentences imposed on criminals convicted during the period of change decades ago.

▶ Problems and Concerns

The increased number of aging and elderly inmates in America's jails and prisons poses significant problems for the modern correctional system. Like the general population, the need for specialized care related to physical, mental, and emotional health increases as individuals age. Some research suggests the nature of correctional environments may accelerate the aging process, with inmates displaying symptoms of failing health earlier than nonincarcerated populations (Anno, 2004; Maschi, Kwak, Ko, & Morrissey, 2012).

Physical Health

Research findings about inmates' physical health needs revealed numerous problems and concerns. At a minimum, elderly inmates may experience poor or failing vision and have difficulties with movement or mobility issues, which puts them at greater risk for injury from loss of balance and falls. This is especially true for inmates who are required to climb stairs in a correctional facility or cell block, those who use canes or walkers, and those who must access top bunks to sleep (Gross, 2007; Maruschak, 2006; Ollove, 2016). Correctional populations in general also may put elderly inmates at higher risk for injury. For example, younger and more agile inmates may pose a threat to the physical health of elderly inmates by victimization through attacks or assaults (Baidawi, Trotter, & Flynn, 2016).

Elderly inmates face other serious physical health concerns in prison. Research findings show that elderly inmates suffer from hypertension, cardiovascular disease, ulcer disease, respiratory disorders, diabetes, hepatitis C, severe lung disease, and unstable seizure disorder, and some need dialysis (Brown, 2012; Hayes, Burns, Turnbull, and Shaw, 2012; Maruschak, Berzofsky, & Unangst, 2016; U.S. Department of Justice, 2004). Diagnoses of cancer were found among both male and female inmates, but cancers are more prevalent among female prisoners (Maruschak, 2006). Bratina (2018) showed that a sample of elderly PADOC inmates self-reported experiencing one or more serious medical problems, including arthritis, breathing problems, dizziness, diabetes, glaucoma, macular degeneration, heart disease, high blood pressure, stroke, and cancer. These physical health problems are typical among any aging population, but some research suggests these problems are more severe among inmates.

The rate of physical diseases and ailments among elderly inmates exceeds that of the nonincarcerated elderly population. Research revealed that elderly inmates in jails and prisons displayed symptoms of poor health at younger ages and more acutely or with more severe forms of disease and disorders than did the nonincarcerated elderly (Greene et al., 2018; Maruschak et al., 2016). Some research suggested that elderly inmates' physical health problems could be heightened by their living environments, which are marked by stress, overcrowding, poor diet, temperature fluctuations, limited exercise, reduced interactions with family members and friends, threat of victimization, poor monitoring and detection of health problems, and lack of access to proper medical care (Brown, 2012; Burnett, 2016; Williams, 2006). Moreover, the decision-making and lifestyle choices these individuals made before being incarcerated might have included excessive and chronic alcohol consumption or illicit substance abuse, which facilitated their poor health and more acute problems as elderly inmates (Bratina, 2018).

Mental and Neurological Health

In addition to physical health problems, aging and elderly inmates have other ailments and require specialized treatment for mental health issues and neurological disease. Research findings gathered from inmates housed in jails, state prisons, and federal correctional institutions suggest "the rates of mental illness among inmates are thought to be higher than among the U.S. population as a whole" (Wilper et al., 2009, p. 670). Moreover, elderly inmates are more likely to suffer from mental health disorders, including anxiety, depression, schizophrenia, mood disorders, and co-occurring disorders, than the general population (Ollove, 2016; Williams, Goodwin, Baillargeon, Ahalt, & Walter, 2012).

Other findings about mental illness among elderly inmates were gathered from various state departments of corrections. For example, findings among inmates from Utah's Department of Corrections showed inmates 50 years and older were frequently diagnosed with depression, bipolar disorder, and schizophrenia spectrum disorders at rates that exceeded the nonincarcerated elderly population (Caverley, 2006). Also, findings from a sample of elderly PADOC inmates showed that approximately half self-reported being previously diagnosed with emotional or mental health problems, and three-quarters reported actively taking medication for current mental health-related issues (Bratina, 2018).

Some of these mental health problems were reported more frequently among elderly women than men. For example, some research suggested elderly incarcerated women may be more afflicted with severe anxiety and depression

(Covington, 2001) and suffer from posttraumatic stress disorder more than men (Wolff, Huening, Shi, & Frueh, 2014).

Along with mental illness, elderly inmates also suffer from neurological diseases. Research findings indicated elderly inmates developed dementia and Alzheimer's disease more rapidly than the elderly residing in the community (Maschi et al., 2012; Nelson, 2017). Overall, more specific information needs to be gathered about the prevalence of the neurological and mental health needs of aging and elderly inmates for treatment inside the correctional facility or for referral to competent specialists in the community.

Financial Costs

As the cost of medical care for the nonincarcerated aging and elderly population in the United States is increasing, so too are the medical expenses for elderly inmates. Correctional systems at all levels must allocate increasingly larger portions of their annual budgets to defray costs for the physical, mental, and emotional health-care needs of aging inmates (Ollove, 2016).

The financial costs associated with caring for elderly inmates comes from multiple sources. Each is necessary for the proper care and treatment of this aging population. Obviously, prescription drugs and other medications are expensive, as are the actual medical procedures performed on individual inmates to treat specific diseases, disorders, and general health problems. Correctional facilities may not be equipped to perform complex medical procedures on site and therefore will assume the expense for transporting inmates to hospitals and medical clinics where individual procedures can be performed (Ahalt et al., 2013; Williams et al., 2012). Personnel costs are also associated with hiring quality and knowledgeable physicians who are trained to assess, diagnose, and treat specific diseases, as well as skilled staff who are responsible for the daily care—including bathing, dressing and feeding—of elderly inmates who cannot look after themselves (Ahalt et al., 2013). Finally, correctional facilities may require remodeling or new construction to provide special accommodations for physically disabled inmates, including ramps, elevators, and grab bars in cells, showers, and toilets (U.S. Department of Justice, 2004).

Information about an exact dollar amount required to care for elderly inmates varies, but most sources agree that medical care for older inmates far exceeds the costs incurred from younger ones. For example, Nelson (2017) reported that U.S. correctional systems spent an average of $60,000 to $70,000 per elderly inmate, which is two to three times larger than the cost for younger ones, whereas other research estimated correctional systems spent between four and eight times more for medical care of elderly inmates than for younger prisoners (Ollove, 2016). Research findings specific to federal correctional institutions reported 19% of budgetary expenses in 2013—approximately $881 million—were allocated to defray costs associated with incarcerating elderly inmates (OIG, 2015).

▶ Possible Solutions

As the research findings shown here illustrate, there are multiple problems and concerns related to the aging and elderly inmate population that involve physical health, mental health, and financial burdens. The problems are plentiful, but the viable solutions are scarce. One reaction from correctional administrators, politicians, or the public may simply be to do nothing. For many jurisdictions, the costs associated with caring for an elderly inmate population further drains an already overextended fiscal budget. Inmates in these jails and prisons will continue to suffer without getting the necessary treatment and care that meets their unique needs. This option is worrisome to those who advocate more humane and rehabilitative approaches to criminal sanctioning.

Changes to Infrastructure

Other possibilities to consider about the growing elderly inmate population include changes to the infrastructure such as the physical design of the correctional facility and training opportunities available for correctional staff. First, as previously mentioned, some prisons are now being designed or retrofitted to accommodate older inmates' needs by installing ramps instead of stairs, affixing grab bars in bathrooms around toilets and showers, creating in-house assisted-living centers, or equipping prison infirmaries with hospice-level care alternatives (McKillop & Boucher, 2018; Ollove, 2016). Other practical changes include housing elderly inmates on the first floor of a cell block, allowing them the bottom bunks, and replacing weight rooms and basketball courts with walking trails, bingo, board games, or shuffleboard courts (Ollove, 2016; U.S. Department of Justice, 2004). Finally, as increasing numbers of elderly inmates are being admitted into prisons, correctional systems may consider constructing residential care facilities for placement of these older individuals (Barton, 2018; OIG, 2015). These facilities should be designed to include the necessary medical equipment and space to perform procedures and surgeries required for elderly inmates.

Second, in addition to making physical and practical changes to the infrastructure of a jail or prison setting, some jurisdictions are focused on staff training to address the major concerns identified with elderly inmates. For example, correctional staff will be called on to address and deescalate episodes of anxiety, depression, schizophrenia, and mood disorders among elderly inmates. Research indicates that few staff members—who will be the first to respond to these incidents—possess the necessary skills, knowledge, and confidence to address issues related to mental health (Bratina, 2017). In recent years, two programs, Crisis Intervention Team and Mental Health First Aid, have been used in the United States to provide information and training about signs and symptoms of mental illness and general techniques to effectively respond to individuals with mental health problems (Bratina, 2018). Additional training that targets the physical needs of elderly inmates could address mobility issues and first aid, as well as the need for overseeing their physical safety and harm from victimization, including sexual assault (Baidawi et al., 2016; Maruschak et al., 2016; OIG, 2015; Wilper et al., 2009).

Early Release

Another consideration for the increased number of elderly inmates in prison is the terms and conditions of their release. Some states are releasing nonviolent, elderly inmates back into their communities because research indicates this population is the least likely to commit offenses compared to younger offenders (Barton, 2018; OIG, 2015) and because incarceration for the chronically or terminally ill may no longer be a deterrent for future crime (Jefferson-Bullock, 2015). The idea behind such policy initiatives, referred to as *compassionate release*, was first introduced in the Sentencing Reform Act of 1984, with federal courts allowed to reduce a prison sentence under extraordinary circumstances (Wylie, Knutson, Greene, & Lamb, 2018). Often inmates are released specifically for reasons of poor health and chronic illness (Barton, 2018).

Specific outcomes for these programs to reduce the elderly inmate population have been overwhelmingly unsuccessful in large part because of restrictions regulating release. For example, jurisdictions that have this type of release may require the inmate be a certain age, be a nonviolent offender, and have served a minimum or maximum amount of time on his or her sentence to be eligible for release (Barton, 2018; Parks, 2018). With these restrictions, only a small percentage of elderly inmates are eligible for early release (OIG, 2015).

▶ Conclusion

The previous review of available data about elderly inmates in U.S. jails and prisons showed clear evidence of a contemporary problem facing the correctional system. Even though the initial causes of this problem may have started decades ago with harsh criminal sanctions for delinquent and criminal behaviors, current sentencing standards contribute to the growing number of aging and elderly inmates behind bars today. This population, in comparison to younger inmates, has unique physical and mental health needs that few correctional facilities and staff are equipped to address. Further discussion is needed on making the infrastructure of jails and prisons more accessible for elderly inmates and on expanding efforts to release elderly inmates who served many years behind bars and who no longer pose a threat of danger to society.

▶ References

Ahalt, C., Trestman, R., Rich, J., Greifinger, R., & Williams, B. (2013). Paying the price: The pressing need for quality, cost, and outcomes data to improve correctional health care for older prisoners. *Journal of the American Geriatrics Society, 61*(11), 2013–2019.

Anno, B. (2004). *Correctional health care addressing the needs of elderly, chronically ill, and terminally ill inmates.* Washington, DC: U.S. Department of Justice, National Institute of Corrections.

Baidawi, S., Trotter, C., & Flynn, C. (2016). Prison experiences and psychological distress among older inmates. *Journal of Gerontological Social Work, 59*(3), 252–270.

Barton, G. (2018, April 18). Release programs for sick and elderly prisoners could save millions. But states rarely use them. *Milwaukee Journal Sentinel.* Retrieved from https://projects.jsonline.com /news/2018/4/18/release-programs-for-sick-elderly-prisoners-could-save-millions.html

Bratina, M. P. (2017). *Forensic mental health: Framing integrated solutions.* New York, NY: Routledge-Taylor & Francis.

Bratina, M. P. (2018). Management and care of older offenders with mental illness (OOMI) in the criminal justice system. In P. C. Kratcoski & M. Edelbacher (Eds.), *Perspectives on elderly crime and victimization* (pp. 225–244). New York, NY: Springer.

Brown, M. (2012). Empathy and punishment. *Punishment & Society, 14*(4), 383–401.

Burnett, J. (2016, September 12). Texas prisoners sue over "cruel" conditions, citing extreme heat. National Public Radio. Retrieved from http://www.npr.org/2016/09/12/493608371/with-no -air-conditioning-texas-prisoners-live-in-cruel-conditions-suit-alleges

Carson, E., & Sabol, W. (2016). *Aging of the state prison population, 1993–2013* [Special report]. Washington, DC: U.S. Department of Justice, Office of Justice Programs, Bureau of Justice Statistics.

Caverley, S. (2006). Older mentally ill inmates: A descriptive study. *Journal of Correctional Health Care, 12*(4), 262–268.

Covington, S. (2001). Creating gender-responsive programs: The next step for women's services. *Corrections Today, 63*(1), 85–87.

Dilulio, J. (1995, November 27). The coming of the superpredator. *Weekly Standard.* Retrieved from https://www.weeklystandard.com/john-j-dilulio-jr/the-coming-of-the-super-predators

Greene, M., Ahalt, C., Stijacic-Cenzer, I., Metzger, L., & Williams, B. (2018). Older adults in jail: High rates and early onset of geriatric conditions. *Health & Justice, 6*(1), 1–9.

Gross, B. (2007). Elderly offenders: Implications for correctional personnel. *The Forensic Examiner, 16*(1), 56–61.

Hayes, A. J., Burns, A., Turnbull, P., & Shaw, J. J. (2012). The health and social needs of older male prisoners. *International Journal of Geriatric Psychiatry, 27*(11), 1155–1162.

Jefferson-Bullock, J. (2015). Are you (still) my great and worthy opponent? Compassionate release of terminally ill offenders. *UMKC Law Review, 83*(3), 521–564.

Lane. J., & Meeker, J. W. (2000). Subcultural diversity and the fear of crime and gangs. *Crime Delinquency, 46*(4), 497–521.

Maruschak, L. (2006). *Medical problems of jail inmates* [Special report]. Washington, DC: U.S. Department of Justice, Office of Justice Programs, Bureau of Justice Statistics.

Maruschak, L. M., Berzofsky, M., & Unangst, J. (2016). *Medical problems of state and federal prisoners and jail inmates, 2011–12* [Special report]. Washington, DC: U.S. Department of Justice, Office of Justice Programs, Bureau of Justice Statistics.

Maschi, T., Kwak, J., Ko, E., & Morrissey, M. (2012). Forget me not: Dementia in prison. *The Gerontologist, 52*(4), 441–451.

Maschi, T., Morrisey, M., & Leigey, M. (2013). The case for human agency, well-being, and community reintegration for people aging in prison. *Journal of Correctional Health Care, 19*(3), 194–210.

McKillop, M. & Boucher. A (2018, February 20). Aging prison populations drive up costs. Pew Charitable Trusts. Retrieved from http://www.pewtrusts.org/en/research-and-analysis/articles/2018/02/20/aging-prison-populations-drive-up-costs

Nelson, F. (2017). The graying and incarcerated: Shawshank Redemption was right on target. *Corrections Today, 79*(4), 54.

Office of the Inspector General (OIG). (2015). *The impact of an aging inmate population on the Federal Bureau of Prisons.* Washington, DC: U.S. Department of Justice.

Ollove, M. (2016). Elderly inmates burden state prisons. Pew Charitable Trusts. Retrieved from http://www.pewtrusts.org/en/research-and-analysis/blogs/stateline/2016/03/17/elderly-inmates-burden-state-prisons

Parks, E. (2018). Elderly and incarcerated: Preventing the medical deaths of older people in Texas prisons. *Texas Journal on Civil Liberties & Civil Rights, 23*(2), 145–164.

Peak, K. J. (2015). *Introduction to criminal justice: Practice and process.* Los Angeles, CA: Sage Publications.

Pennsylvania's Department of Corrections. (2018). *Annual statistical report.* Harrisburg, PA: Office of Planning, Research, and Statistics. Retrieved from https://www.cor.pa.gov/About%20Us/Statistics/Pages/Reports.aspx

Schmalleger, F. (2018). *Criminal justice: A brief introduction* (12th ed.). Boston. MA: Pearson.

Stohr, M. K., & Walsh, A. (2016). *Corrections: The essentials.* Los Angeles, CA: Sage Publications.

Tonry, M. (2015). Federal sentencing "reform" since 1984: The awful as enemy of the good. *Crime & Justice, 44*(1), 99–164.

U.S. Department of Justice. (2004). *Correctional health care: Addressing the needs of elderly, chronically ill, and terminally ill inmates.* Washington, DC: National Institute of Corrections.

Vincent, G., & Velkoff, V. (2010). *The next four decades: The older population in the United States: 2010 to 2050* (Current population reports. Series P-25, Population estimates and projections no. 1138). Washington, DC: U.S. Department of Commerce, Economics and Statistics Administration, U.S. Census Bureau.

Williams, B. A., Goodwin, J. S., Baillargeon, J., Ahalt, C., & Walter, L. C. (2012). Addressing the aging crisis in U.S. criminal justice healthcare. *Journal of the American Geriatrics Society, 60*(6), 1150–1156.

Williams, J. L. (2006). *The aging inmate population: Southern states outlook.* Proceedings from the Southern Legislative Conference, Atlanta, GA.

Wilper, A. P., Woolhandler, S., Boyd, J. W., Lasser, K. E., McCormick, D., Bor, D. H., & Himmelstein, D. U. (2009). The health and health care of U.S. prisoners: Results of a nationwide survey. *American Journal of Public Health, 99*(4), 666–672.

Wolff, N., Huening, J., Shi, J., & Frueh, B. C. (2014). Trauma exposure and posttraumatic stress disorder among incarcerated men. *Journal of Urban Health, 91*(4), 707–719.

Wylie, L., Knutson, A., Greene, E., & Lamb, M. E. (2018). Extraordinary and compelling: The use of compassionate release laws in the United States. *Psychology, Public Policy, and Law, 24*(2), 216–234.

ARTICLE 26

Jail and Social Class

Kaitlyn Clarke and Philip D. McCormack

▶ Introduction

Jails have been used for custodial supervision of suspected and convicted criminal offenders for nearly 1,000 years. In this time, their purpose and function have remained largely unchanged. In 1166, through the Assize of Clarendon, King Henry II mandated each county sheriff in England to establish a jail—originally referred to as *gaols* (Siegel, 2018). Ever since, across the globe, jails have served as institutions of confinement for those suspected of criminal behavior and awaiting trial. Over time, the function of jails has expanded to hold individuals who are awaiting trial or sentencing, are being transferred to another jurisdiction, have been denied bail (e.g., were deemed flight risks or dangers to society) or cannot afford bail, have been sentenced to terms of incarceration of one year or less (or longer than one year in some states), are being held for another jurisdiction, are being held for a federal agency such as the U.S. Immigration and Customs Enforcement or U.S. Marshals Service, or, more recently, have been transferred from a state or federal prison as a result of overcrowding.

Despite the ubiquitous and long-standing use of jails, this area of the criminal justice system has received less attention with respect to research than areas such as law enforcement, courts, and probation. Reiter (2014) argues that carceral research has become a "social black site . . . physically located outside our communities, invisible to the public and researcher alike" (p. 417). More recently, scholars have begun to explore how social control and punishment play out in the carceral facilities (Cochran, Toman, Mears, & Bales, 2017; McKendy, 2018; Phelps, 2011). However, there remains a dearth of literature that focuses on the experience and social world of jails. As an institution, jails remain theoretically and empirically improvised and neglected within the penal scholarship (Irwin, 1985; McKendy, 2018; Riley et al., 2018). Klofas (1990), now three decades ago, suggested this neglect might be attributed to the assumptions that researchers have regarding how inmates in jails and prisons experience incarceration similarly or, as a result of the brief stay, how many of the issues encountered by the jail population are not as serious or consequential compared to those of the prison population. Yet it is clear jails are different from prisons in their purpose, conditions of the carceral stay, and inmate demographics (Greenberg & Rosenheck, 2008; Irwin, 1985; McKendy, 2018; Walker, 2014).

The purpose and use of jail facilities differ from those of a prison, but legislation and administrative policy affect them similarly. This can be seen in the punitive nature of the jail facility—diverged from previous rehabilitative efforts observed before the 1970s. During this time, the consensus that "nothing works" fueled a shift toward more punitive policies. This shift in penal philosophy was supported by a so-called tough-on-crime approach embraced by high-ranking and influential politicians of the last few decades. Many of the policies that were supported involved tougher penalties for those convicted of quality-of-life and drug-related charges—crimes that are more likely to be committed by those who are young, of color, and of low social class (Irwin, 1985; Phelps, 2011; Tonry, 1996). The disproportionate effect of the tough-on-crime policies has by no means gone unnoticed. McKendy (2018) notes that jails operate to manage society's underclass, and Irwin (1985), states, "instead of 'criminals,' the jail receives and confines mostly detached and disreputable persons who are arrested more because they are offensive than because they have committed crimes" (p. xxv). Relatedly, Welch (1999) discusses how jails function as a "warehouse reserved mostly for the urban underclass" (p. 89). Thus, carceral facilities, and particularly jails, are not reserved necessarily for dangerous offenders but for those viewed as society's undesirables—the disempowered and marginalized low social class. Though the definition and measurement of class have long been in dispute and lack consensus and consistency (see early discussions by Cattell, 1942; Cox, 1945; Goldschmidt 1950; Gordon, 1949), this chapter defines *class* as groups of individuals who occupy similar positions in labor markets and political systems—typically measured by individual factors such as education level, employment status, and wealth and discussed as a hierarchy of "low" or "under," "middle," and "upper."

▶ The Jail Population

Most recent data show the size of the U.S. jail population has remained relatively stable since its peak in 2008. In 2016, approximately 740,000 persons were supervised by local jails, down from 780,000 persons in 2007 and representing a 0.7% decrease over that time period (Kaeble & Cowhig, 2018; Zeng, 2018). Of these, 31% were held in a facility outside the jurisdiction in which the apprehension or conviction occurred or in which the custodial agency has jurisdiction. Approximately 42% of jail inmates were White, 37% Black, and 16% Hispanic or Latino, with the remaining 5% of inmates identifying as another race or multiracial. The majority of inmates were adult males (86%). Adults females represented 13% of the jail population, and the remaining 1% consisted of juveniles. The criminal status of inmates varied greatly. Nearly 63% of inmates were not convicted at the time of detention, and 71% were charged with or convicted of a felony, 24% a misdemeanor, and 5% another offense type (U.S. Department of Justice, 2017.

The significant number of unconvicted inmates warrants particular attention. This is known as *pretrial detention*, which is the holding of a person before his or her criminal trial. This can be a result of a pretrial detention statute, denial of bail (based on a judge's discretion), or failure to secure release because of the inability to afford the bail amount set forth by the court. The effects of these conditions on lower-class suspects are staggering. For 15 years beginning in 1992, the average bail amount set by a court more than doubled (Neal, 2012). In a study examining urban counties, nine out of 10 individuals charged with a felony for which bail was availed could not afford it (Reaves, 2013).

It has been argued that pretrial detention presents several ethical concerns. First, individuals of low social class are disproportionately represented in jails. It has long been documented that carceral facilities are filled with the destitute (Wheelock & Uggen, 2008) and increasing numbers of low-level offenders (Raphael & Stoll, 2013). As McKendy (2018) notes, "most of the individuals confined in jails do not conform to stereotypical images of the 'dangerous criminal'" (p. 4). Instead, their stay reflects how jails are used to deal with social problems (Irwin, 1985; McKendy, 2018; Wacquant, 2000, 2001), and such discrimination on the basis of social class—particularly economic status—has long been officially admonished (see U.S. President's Commission on Law Enforcement and Administration of Justice, 1967). Second, and related, it is common for the large unconvicted population—many of whom are of low social class—to be detained, in addition to the inability to afford the amount set forth by the court, because of the nature of the alleged offense, by the evidence against the accused, or by being deemed high risk by the absence of a permanent residence, or by being perceived as a threat to public safety—among other factors (Arnold, Dobbie, & Yang, 2018; Emmelman, 2003).

The overrepresentation of individuals of low social class in jails is not only a function of being detained on the basis of the inability to afford bail, being denied bail on the basis of a condition related to one's social class position, or on the basis of perceived dangerousness, but also by the inability to navigate the criminal justice system (Cantrell, 2002). Further, the strategies employed by law enforcement to initially apprehend those detained have long been cited as disproportionate in their application. Disenfranchised groups are significantly more likely to experience the law's power and mechanisms of social control (Black, 1976, 1980; Wilson, 1968), as evidenced by findings that suggest neighborhood characteristics influence police strategies (Klinger, 1997; Sampson, 1986). Poor areas have seen policies such as order maintenance and zero tolerance (Wilson & Kelling, 1982), hot spot policing (Weisburd, Mastrofski, McNally, Greenspan, & Willis, 2003), and the expanded use of police stops (Spitzer, 1999). These areas, which already have high crime rates, experience increased police presence and law enforcement. These aggressive targeted strategies have helped fill local jails—particularly those in urban areas—with the American "underclass" (Meeks, 2006).

▶ Effects of Jailing

Health

The health effects of a jail stay on those detained can be profound. Although jails are generally physically smaller, detain fewer individuals, and detain those individuals for a significantly shorter time than prisons, jails nonetheless have the same adverse conditions—and some of those are considered worse than their state-run counterparts. According to Walker (2014), "jails are significantly more punitive than prisons" (p. 16). An inmate must learn to process such environmental challenges as inadequate bedding, clothing, nutrition, overcrowding, and structural conditions involving facility plumbing, lack of natural light, and extreme temperatures. Welch (1999) further explains how "like the persons detained there, jails are the most neglected institution within the criminal justice system" (p. 92). Physical deterioration of jails poses its own risks to the health and safety of those detained. They are also a reflection of other conditions that are often seen in these facilities.

Inadequate institutional living conditions associated with overcrowding, unsanitary conditions, and a poor diet have all been factors that have increased the likelihood of contracting a disease. It is not uncommon for inmates to contract hepatitis C, AIDS or HIV infection, tuberculosis, methicillin-resistant *Staphylococcus aureus*, or other infectious and deadly diseases (Dannenberg, 2007). These diseases pose a threat to all inmates, including the innocent or those who, even if found guilty, would not be given an "in-house sentence." Other common ailments of inmates are skin rashes, asthma, premature aging, malnutrition, muscular atrophy, heart-related problems, and high blood pressure (Norris, 2012), which are particularly unjust to those who are innocent of their suspected crimes (Humphrey & Clarke, 2018). These conditions and more have a significantly higher prevalence among jail inmates than the general population. Furthermore, jail inmates have higher rates of these ailments, including chronic conditions, than state and federal prison inmates. This is observed across nearly all monitored conditions, including hypertension, stroke-related problems, diabetes, heart-related problems, asthma, and cirrhosis. The prevalence of infectious disease is no different. Jail inmates have higher rates of tuberculosis, hepatitis, sexually transmitted diseases, and HIV and AIDS. The difference is observed across all age groups, with the greatest found among young adults (Maruschak, Berzofsky, & Unangst, 2015).

Safety and Treatment

Further contributing to the prevalence of these health risks is the inability of institutions to prevent and address these conditions when they arise or when an inmate has a preexisting condition. Mirroring the differences observed between inmates and the general population and inmates in jail and state and federal prison, inmates who have been sentenced to jail have higher rates of drug dependence and current or previous regular use of drugs. The difference is pervasive across drug types. For example, the Bureau of Justice Statistics (BJS) found jail inmates have significantly higher rates for past use across nine drug types, and across eight of nine drug types for regular use (Bronson, Stroop, Zimmer, & Berzofsky, 2017). Jails and the agencies that operate them are ill equipped to deal with these issues. They are often understaffed and underfunded. Jails are plagued with high rates of correctional officer turnover and have to overcome limited resources, making treatment and services difficult to obtain. Even when available, they are limited. Not all inmates receive them, and those who are lucky enough to receive them do not receive individualized care. Even with a relatively short time in custody, treatment and services can be essential for a jail inmate because this has been deemed the most difficult part of the carceral stay (Toman, Cochran, & Cochran, 2018).

Because of the conditions endured when jailed, data also suggest mental health problems are more prevalent in jail than in prison—and certainly more than in the general population. Jail inmates are more likely to have expressed major depressive or mania symptoms. The BJS found this to be evident in eight of 10 categories examined. Jail inmates are also more likely to exhibit psychotic symptoms, including delusions and hallucinations (James & Glaze, 2006). When untreated—and even when treated—these conditions can have dire consequences. According to the BJS, 2014 saw the most suicides by jail inmates in a study spanning the years 2000–2014. Suicide was the leading cause of death, and more than a third of the deaths occurred within the first seven days of detention (Mumola, 2005; Noonan, 2016). For those who have been denied or cannot afford bail, the stress of not being in control and the uncertainty of their future may contribute to the high rate of suicide. This may also be exacerbated when an individual is jailed in a jurisdiction away from friends and family.

Social

Social isolation can substantially and negatively impact the jail population. This isolation can be a function of communication restraints or restrictions governing visits that have been put in place by the facility or by restrictions imposed by a judge or magistrate. Isolation can also be a function of the inmate's inability to afford social contact—particularly for those being detained in a facility far away from their support systems. For example, some inmates must use a collect call system, a mode of communication that depends on the recipient of the call. These calls may also be limited to family or legal consultants such as lawyers (McKendy, 2018). More troublesome is the fact that it has become increasingly unlikely for households to have a landline, especially for those of lower class (Blumber & Luke, 2014), reducing the opportunity to even use the collect call system.

Isolation may be a by-product of alienation, with the inmate outcast because of his or her detention. Alienation may occur even with those who would otherwise be the basis of the inmate's support system, whether it be coworkers and employers, friends, or family. Alienation may also be the result of stigmatizing attitudes or dramatic change in the inmate's environment, whether or not he or she is convicted or pleads guilty. Alienation from coworkers and employers may limit the job prospects available when an inmate is released. Not only can stigma contribute to these reduced opportunities, but so can the gap in employment and peripheral effects of untreated or insufficiently treated health conditions. Alienation from friends and family may result in long-term or even permanent changes in interpersonal relationships, whether or not he or she is convicted or pleads guilty. The effects of alienation on the mental health of those jailed can be profound. Most notably, morale may deteriorate to the extent that the inmate experiences conditions associated with mental health problems and with similar dire consequences such as suicide (Durkheim, 1897/1965).

Criminal Status

Being of low social class can also have several consequences related to the outcome of a pending criminal case and the inmate's resultant criminal status. Those who are detained pretrial, such as the disproportionate number of individuals who cannot afford or were not afforded bail, are more likely to plead guilty. This is often the result of requiring the use of a designated public defender. This is shown to be associated with harsher outcomes than the use of privately hired attorneys. Furthermore, those who are detained pretrial and then found guilty are more likely to be given longer prison sentences (Williams, 2003). According to Stevenson (2016), pretrial detention increases guilty pleas by 13%, and the length of the stay increases by 42%. This can be partly attributed to being unable to bargain with the prosecutor when detained. Consideration of plea offers is of great importance because any amount of jail time can disrupt an inmate's life. Employment status can be affected, as can parental rights and housing (Riley et al., 2018). These considerations may be of greater concern for those in the lower social class, which can increase their odds of accepting unfavorable plea bargains (Dobbie, Goldin, & Yang, 2018). Perhaps more determinantal is the fact that current laws restrict this population by impeding their "access to welfare, public housing, Pell Grants, and student loans" (Rabuy & Kopf, 2015).

Plea bargains are also more likely to be seen in jurisdictions without specialized courts such as veterans' courts, mental health courts, and drug courts. Jurisdictions with these courts allow for and encourage an offender to remain in the community, employed, and in contact with friends and family—all of which maintain the social ties that detention may sever. These specialized courts also provide treatment services and resources than jails cannot—treating conditions that are more likely to be seen in jail and in the lower class and be associated with recidivism. These courts have been shown to affect future criminality, because those who participate have lower rates of recidivism and remain in the community for longer periods of time (Finigan, Carey, & Cox, 2007). When detained in jail, similar resources are not provided. Rarely do jails offer treatment and educational classes or employment training to assist with successful reentry and to reduce the likelihood of recidivism. When programs do exist, they are extremely limited (Soloman, Osborne, LoBuglio, Mellow, & Mukamal, 2008). In addition, the areas in which the jail is located—and in which the individual is released—can greatly affect the likelihood of recidivism. The risk of recidivism increases for many individuals of low social class who are released in or returned to disadvantaged areas (which may or may not be the jurisdiction in which they reside and where support and resources are located) (Kubrin & Stewart, 2006; Mears, Wang, Hay, & Bales, 2008).

▶ Summary

Serving time in jail is not only associated with adverse physical and mental health conditions but also with diminished economic and social opportunities among those who are already the most socioeconomically disadvantaged (Western & Pettit, 2010). The highest incarceration rate for this group is seen in young adults. This is problematic because these are typically the years in which they begin their life journey, finding themselves on pathways that shape their professional and personal developments (Western & Pettit, 2010). This includes reaching such milestones as finding employment, securing housing, and starting a family. These are important for establishing oneself while entering adulthood. Time spent in jail, by taking time away from participation in the labor force, reduces earning potential and social mobility. In addition, any stigma produced by this detention may affect chances of being hired on release and affect the maintenance of social ties. As a result, there are fewer economic opportunities available to those released, which continues to further divide the social classes. When educational attainment is considered with social class and age, social class inequalities are further made apparent. According to Harlow (2003), "47% of inmates in local jails . . . had not completed high school or its equivalent while about 18% of the general population failed to attain high school graduation" (p. 2). Low educational attainment by those incarcerated and subsequently released from jails also contributes to the pervasive and long-standing inequalities observed across the social classes.

Some of the poorest people are being sent to jail as a result of the tough-on-crime policies enacted in the last few decades. It is important to remember that indigents sent to jail leave just as penniless—or even further in debt—than before their carceral stay. Those who are serving time in jail are returning home less employable and more detached from their families, especially when they are being housed in different jurisdictions. To break the cycle of poverty and incarceration, policies need to be revised that eliminate the disproportionality observed in law enforcement, pretrial detention, and sentencing and make it less difficult for inmates to succeed on reentry into their communities. If not, penal confinement will continue to perpetuate social and economic disadvantage, transferring their effects to the next generation.

▶ References

Arnold, D., Dobbie, W., & Yang, C. S. (2018). Racial bias in bail decisions. Technical report, National Bureau of Economic Research [unpublished working paper]. Retrieved from https://www.princeton.edu/~wdobbie/files/racialbias.pdf

Black, D. (1976). *The behavior of law.* New York, NY: Academic Press.

Black, D. (1980). *The manners and customs of the police.* New York, NY: Academic Press.

Blumber, S. J., & Luke, J.V. (2014). Wireless substitution: Early release of estimates from the National Health Interview Survey, January–June 2014. Hyattsville, MD: National Center for Health Statistics. Retrieved from https://www.cdc.gov/nchs/data/nhis/earlyrelease/wireless201412.pdf

Bronson, J., Stroop, J., Zimmer, S., & Berzofsky, M. (2017). *Drug use, dependence, and abuse among state prisoners and jail inmates, 2007–2009.* Washington, DC: U.S. Department of Justice, Bureau of Statistics. NCJ 250546.

Cantrell, D. J. (2002). Justice for interests of the poor: The problem of navigating the system without counsel. *Fordham Law Review, 70,* 1573–1590.

Cattell, R. B. (1942). The concept of social status. *Journal of Social Psychology, 15,* 293–308.

Cochran, J. C., Toman, E. L., Mears, D. P., & Bales, W. D. (2017). Solitary confinement as punishment: Examining in-prison sanctioning disparities. *Justice Quarterly, 35*(3), 381–411.

Cox, O. C. (1945). Estates, social classes, and political classes. *American Sociological Review, 10*(4), 464–469.

Dannenberg, J. (2007, August 15). Prisons as incubators and spreaders of disease and illness. *Prison Legal News.* Retrieved from https://www.prisonlegalnews.org/news/2007/aug/15/prisons-as-incubators-and-spreaders-of-disease-and-illness/

Dobbie, W., Goldin, J., & Yang, C. S. (2018). The effects of pre-trial detention on conviction, future crimes, and employment: Evidence from randomly assigned judges. *American Economic Review, 108,* 201–240.

Durkheim, E. (1965). *Suicide: A study in sociology* (Originally published 1897). Glencoe, IL: Free Press.

Emmelman, D. (2003). Social class effects on criminal client. In M. R. Pogrebin (Ed.), *Qualitative approaches to criminal justice: Perspectives from the field.* Thousand Oaks, CA: Sage Publications.

Finigan, M.W., Carey, S. M., & Cox, A. (2007). *The impact of a mature drug court over 10 years of operation: Recidivism and costs.* Portland, OR: NPC Research.

Goldschmidt, W. (1950). Social class in America: A critical review. *American Anthropologist, 52*(4), 483–498.

Gordon, M. M. (1949). Social class in American sociology. *American Journal of Sociology, 55*(3), 262–268.

Greenberg, G. A., & Rosenheck, R. A. (2008). Jail incarceration, homelessness, and mental health: A national study. *Psychiatric Services, 59*(2), 170–177.

Harlow, C. W. (2003). *Bureau of Justice Statistics special report: Education and correctional populations.* Washington, DC: U.S. Department of Justice, Office of Justice Programs. NCJ 195670.

Humphrey, J. A., & Clarke, K. (2018). *Wrongful conviction: From prevention to the reversal of injustice.* Springfield, IL: Charles C. Thomas.

Irwin, J. (1985). *The jail: Managing the underclass in American society.* Berkeley, CA: University of California Press.

James, D. J., & Glaze, L. E. (2006). *Mental health problems of prison and jail inmates.* Washington, DC: Bureau of Justice Statistics. NCJ 213600.

Kaeble, D., & Cowhig, M. (2018). *Correctional populations in the United States, 2016.* Washington, DC: U.S. Department of Justice, Bureau of Justice Statistics. NCJ 251211.

Klinger, D. A. (1997). Negotiating order in patrol work: An ecological theory of police response to deviance. *Criminology, 35,* 277–306.

Klofas, J. M. (1990). The jail and the community. *Justice Quarterly, 7*(1), 69–102.

Kubrin, C. E., & Stewart, E. A. (2006). Predicting who reoffends: The neglected role of neighborhood context in recidivism studies. *Criminology, 44*(1), 165–197.

Maruschak, L. M., Berzofsky M., & Unangst, J. (2015). *Medical problems of state and federal prisoners and jail inmates, 2011–12.* Washington, DC: U.S. Department of Justice, Bureau of Justice Statistics. NCJ 248491.

McKendy, L. (2018). The pains of jail imprisonment: Experiences at The Ottawa-Carleton Detention Centre. PhD thesis, Carleton University, Ottawa, Ontario, Canada.

Mears, D. P., Wang, X., Hay, C., & Bales, W. D. (2008). Social ecology and recidivism: Implications for prisoner reentry. *Criminology, 46,* 301–340.

Meeks, D. (2006). Police militarization in urban areas: The obscure war against the underclass. *Journal of Black Studies and Research, 35*(4), 33–41.

Mumola, C. (2005). *Suicide and homicide in state prisons and local jails.* Washington, DC: Bureau of Justice Statistics. NCJ 210036.

Neal, M. (2012). *Bail fail: Why the U.S. should end the practice of using money for bail.* Washington, D.C.: Justice Policy Institute.

Noonan, M. E. (2016). *Mortality in local jails, 2000–2014. Statistical tables.* Washington, DC: Bureau of Justice Statistics. NCJ 250169.

Norris, R. J. (2012). Assessing compensation statues for the wrongly convicted. *Criminal Justice Policy Review, 23*(3), 352–374.

Phelps, M. S. (2011). Rehabilitation in the punitive era: The gap between rhetoric and reality in U.S. prison programs. *Law and Society Review, 45*(1), 33–68.

Rabuy, B. & Kopf, D. (2015, July 9). Prison of poverty: Uncovering the pre-incarceration incomes of the imprisoned. Prison Policy Initiative. Retrieved from https://www.prisonpolicy.org/reports/income.html

Raphael, S., & Stoll, M. A. (2013). *Why are so many Americans in prison?* New York, NY: Russell Sage Foundation.

Reaves, B. A. (2013). *Felony defendants in large urban counties, 2009-statistical tables.* Washington, DC: U.S Department of Justice, Bureau of Justice Statistics. NCJ 243777.

Reiter, K. (2014). Making windows in walls: Strategies for prison research. *Qualitative Inquiry, 20*(4), 417–428.

Riley, R. W., Kang-Brown, J., Mulligan, C., Valsalam, V., Chakraborty, S., & Henrichson, C. (2018). Exploring the urban-rural incarceration divide: drivers of local jail incarceration rates in the United States. *Journal of Technology in Human Services, 36*(1), 76–88.

Sampson, R. J. (1986). Effects of socioeconomic context on official reaction to juvenile delinquency. *American Sociological Review, 51,* 876–885.

Siegel, L. (2018). *Corrections Today* (4th ed.). Boston, MA: Cengage Learning.

Stevenson, M. T. (2016). Distortion of justice: How the inability to pay bail affects case outcomes [Unpublished working paper]. Retrieved from https://www.econ.pitt.edu/sites/default/files/Stevenson.jmp2016.pdf

Soloman, A. L., Osborne, J, W. L., LoBuglio, S. F., Mellow, J., & Mukamal, D. A. (2008). *Life after lockup: Improving reentry from jail to the community.* Washington, DC: The Urban Institute.

Spitzer, E. (1999). *The New York City Police Department's "stop & frisk" practices: A report to the people of the State of New York from the Office of the Attorney General.* New York, NY: Office of the Attorney General of the State of New York.

Toman, E., Cochran, J. C., & Cochran, J. (2018). Jailhouse blues? The adverse effects of pretrial detention for prison social order. *Criminal Justice and Behavior, 45*(3), 316–339.

Tonry, M. (1996). *Malign neglect: Race, crime, and punishment in America.* New York, NY: Oxford University Press.

U.S. Department of Justice. (2017). *Annual survey of jails, 2017.* Ann Arbor, MI: Inter-University Consortium of Political and Social Research.

U.S. President's Commission on Law Enforcement and Administration of Justice. (1967). *The challenge of crime in a free society.* Washington, DC: U.S. Government Printing Office.

Wacquant, L. (2000). The new "peculiar institution": On the prison as surrogate ghetto. *Theoretical Criminology, 4*(3), 377–389.

Wacquant, L. (2001). Deadly symbiosis: When ghetto and prison meet and mesh. *Punishment & Society, 3*(1), 95–133.

Walker, M. L. (2014). Punishment and coping in "Golden County:" An ethnography of jail living. PhD thesis, University of California, Riverside.

Weisburd, D., Mastrofski, S., McNally, A. M., Greenspan, R., & Willis, J. (2003). Reforming to preserve: Compstat and strategic problem solving in American policing. *Criminology and Public Policy, 2,* 421–456.

Welch, M. (1999). *Punishment in America: Social control and the ironies of imprisonment.* Thousand Oaks, CA: Sage.

Western, B., & Pettit B. (2010). Incarceration & social inequality. *Daedalus: Journal of the American Academy of Arts & Sciences* (pp. 8–19). Retrieved from https://www.amacad.org/content/publications/pubcontent.aspx?d=808

Wheelock, D., & Uggen, C. (2008). Race, poverty, and Punishment: The impact of criminal sanctions on racial, ethnic, and socioeconomic inequality. In D. Harris & A. C. Lin (Eds.), *The colors of poverty: Why racial and ethnic disparities persist* (pp. 261–292). New York, NY: Russell Sage.

Williams, M. R. (2003). The effect of pretrial detention on imprisonment decisions. *Criminal Justice Review, 28,* 299–317.

Wilson, J. Q. (1968). *Varieties of police behavior: The management of law and order in eight communities.* Cambridge, MA: Harvard University Press.

Wilson, J. Q., & Kelling, G. L. (1982, March). Broken windows: Police and neighborhood safety. *Atlantic Monthly, 249,* 29–38.

Zeng, Z. (2018). *Jail inmates in 2016.* Washington, DC: U.S. Department of Justice, Bureau of Statistics. NCJ 251210.

ARTICLE 27

Ethics and Community Corrections[1]

Kevin E. Courtright

▶ Introduction

In the United States, nearly 4.5 million offenders are serving probation or parole in their communities (Kaeble & Cowhig, 2018). Those who teach or work in corrections are well aware that the vast majority (roughly 60%) of the correctional population resides in the community. It is also clear to professionals, however, that other components of the criminal justice system (particularly prisons and policing) absorb much of the public's attention, as well as a large share of the corrections budgets of the federal, state, and local governments. Petersilia (2011) notes that nine out of 10 correctional dollars go to prisons. Although the corrections population is large and growing, that growth has not translated into commensurate resources to adequately manage the largest segment of the correctional population—those on probation and parole. As caseloads increase and staffing levels decrease, probation and parole (p/p) officers are often asked to do more with less (Ross, 2016). When compared to prison systems, community supervision of offenders has typically been cost-efficient (see, e.g., Courtright, Berg, & Mutchnick, 1997). Nevertheless, community corrections, perhaps the most professionalized sector of corrections (more on this later), has long suffered a resource and credibility problem, and mass media rarely if ever depict this part of the corrections system positively (Lutz, 2014).

Community corrections—also known as *community-based corrections* (CBCs)—are sanctions or programs that offenders serve or participate in while in the community instead of being incarcerated. In addition to cost efficiency, there are several reasons why the number of offenders serving terms of correctional supervision in their communities is so high. In addition to having the largest player on the "team" (probation), community corrections encompasses a myriad array of other (also community-based) sanctions such as parole, community corrections centers (formerly known as halfway houses), and intermediate sanctions or punishments (IPs). IPs are sanctions that fall somewhere between probation on the left and incarceration on the right of the supervision-and-control continuum. As versatile sanctions, some CBCs such as IPs—sanctions like electronic monitoring (EM) and house arrest—can be used at various points in the system, including pretrial, pre-imprisonment (front door sanctions like probation), and postimprisonment (backdoor sanctions like parole) and can be used at the county, state, and federal levels of corrections and with both juveniles and adults (Courtright, 2002). The extent of their use and variety of types and applications make for an eclectic list of potential and important ethical issues arising from their use. The sheer numbers of offenders on these sanctions make their fair and ethical use paramount.

Through the lens of a classic essay on this topic (von Hirsch, 1990), this article discusses why community corrections must be considered a profession and how some of the challenges facing p/p staff members compel them to confront ethical dilemmas unique to this subfield of corrections. (For a detailed list of ethical issues confronting community corrections, see Whitehead & Woodward, 2017.)

▶ Community Corrections as a Profession

In probation and parole training academies and college classrooms across the country, the story of John Augustus, the father of probation, is told and retold, often through the use of a historic video that was recently made available online (American Probation and Parole Association, 2018). A Boston boot maker and devout Christian who believed in abstinence from alcohol and kindness even toward those under its influence, Augustus was known in the Boston municipal courts in the 1840s for trying to assist and rehabilitate offenders. Although he stumbles on the idea of probation quite by accident in the Boston Municipal Court one day while returning a pair of boots he had mended for a judge, the "Man of Second Chances," credits Jesus Christ as the originator of the concept of probation.[2]

Guided by humanitarian ideals, John Augustus was one of probation's first volunteers. (Using volunteers who may not possess the required experience, training, and educational levels needed for full-time entry-level employment is itself an enduring ethical issue in community corrections.) His story is a powerful reminder of how one person can make a positive difference in many people's lives, but of course, p/p officers have this potential every day. Augustus' work influenced many of the practices of modern-day probation, such as screening offenders (and thus not accepting every client that he encountered), revocation of parole or probation, and release under certain conditions or rules to name a few. Augustus used what would today be called a "casework style of supervision" versus a "surveillance style of supervision," one emphasizing assistance, counseling, and a supportive one-to-one relationship (Seiter, 2020). In dealing with his clients, Augustus employed an ethical system heavily influenced by his religious beliefs, creating what Pollock (1998) would call a religious (ethical) perspective and some variation of the categorical imperative or the Golden Rule (Stohr, Walsh, & Hemmens, 2019). His work could also be considered in terms of an "ethics of care" framework, whereby "the care and concern for others is paramount" (p. 110). This seems to be the ethical foundation that dominated early probation practice. Augustus' humanitarian ideals are evident in his work, and he possessed a clear desire to assist his clients (see, e.g., Augustus, 1984).

Even though the nature of the job has changed greatly since Augustus' time, there are still aspects of p/p work that require sacrifice and a commitment to principles. Although the work provides a certain level of flexibility and autonomy (i.e., officers can often make their own work schedules as long as basic workweek parameters are followed), the pay scales for p/p work are lower when compared to those of other jobs related to criminal justice (CJ). However, scheduling flexibility may provide working parents with the ability to attend their children's school and sports-related events, which may compensate for the lower pay. Related to this positive aspect of flexible scheduling is the belief that p/p work provides a nice blend of indoor and outdoor work settings (e.g., seeing clients in the office and completing paperwork while also being out of the office to conduct home visits and make collateral contacts with associates of offenders). This sort of flexibility and autonomy often means that p/p officers are subject to less monitoring and supervision, making weekly reviews of caseloads (known as *case conferences*— conversations with supervisors about individual offenders) even more imperative. However, given the large amount of discretion inherent in p/p work (for instance, whether or not to return an offender to court for rules violations), officers who lack adequate supervision from supervisors could be under more pressure to act unethically or inappropriately (Stohr et al., 2019).

According to data from the Bureau of Labor Statistics (2017), the median annual pay for a probation officer (PO) is $56,630; $64,540 is the median for police officers. Annual pay for correctional officers and jailers generally lags behind that of POs by some $7,000 (Stohr et al., 2019). The median annual pay of p/p officers lags behind that of police officers because p/p occupations *require* a minimum of a four-year college degree and previous CJ-related work experience. This disparity in pay is even more surprising given that p/p occupations *require* a minimum of a four-year college degree and previous work experience, qualifications that many policing jobs don't have. This disparity in pay could be problematic because low pay can lead some individuals to engage in unethical behavior (Stohr et al., 2019) or be used to justify wrongdoing. Wages that are not family sustaining also result in the possibility of p/p officers working other part-time jobs to make ends meet or perhaps to pay off student loan debt accumulated simply to meet basic entry-level employment requirements. This need to hold one or more additional jobs results in further time away from home and family relationships and in some cases leads p/p officers to hold less desirable jobs such as doing security at entertainment venues, working as bouncers at local bars, and so on. Stohr et al. (2019) addressed this issue in part by compiling a list of ways "to prevent unethical behavior and promote ethical work practices." Stohr et al. state early in their list that governments should "pay people a professional wage as then they will be less likely to be tempted to engage in unethical behavior for personal gain" (p. 112). Other important items on their list include having a code of ethics in place and mandating ongoing ethics training. Although some agencies have their own code

The Code of Ethics of the American Probation and Parole Association (APPA)

I will render professional service to the justice system and the community at large in effecting the social adjustment of the offender.

I will uphold the law with dignity, displaying an awareness of my responsibility to offenders while recognizing the right of the public to be safeguarded from criminal activity.

I will strive to be objective in the performance of my duties, recognizing the inalienable right of all persons, appreciating the inherent worth of the individual, and respecting those confidences which can be reposed in me.

I will conduct my personal life with decorum, neither accepting nor granting favors in connection with my office.

I will cooperate with my co-workers and related agencies and will continually strive to improve my professional competence through the seeking and sharing of knowledge and understanding.

I will distinguish clearly, in public, between my statements and actions as an individual and as a representative of my profession.

I will encourage policy, procedures and personnel practices, which will enable others to conduct themselves in accordance with the values, goals and objectives of the American Probation and Parole Association. I recognize my office as a symbol of public faith and I accept it as a public trust to be held as long as I am true to the ethics of the American Probation and Parole Association.

I will constantly strive to achieve these objectives and ideals, dedicating myself to my chosen profession.

Reprinted with permission from the APPA.

of ethics, the American Probation and Parole Association (APPA) has developed one for its membership, which comprises community corrections professionals. Many p/p agencies use the code produced by the APPA.

The nature of the job continues to evolve. P/p officers work in increasingly dangerous environments and are being victimized more than ever before (Morgan, 2016). As a result, more and more POs are arming themselves (Ross, 2016), including those who work with juvenile offenders (Banks, 2017). The law clearly stipulates the specific training required of those who carry weapons, but there remains a larger ethical concern with regard to arming community supervision agents. Although parole officers carry firearms in two-thirds of the 50 states, some researchers argue that the presence of a firearm detracts from the rehabilitative role of the *probation* officer, particularly of *juvenile* probation officers (Banks, 2017). In the surveillance (i.e., crime control) era of the 1980s and 1990s, some CJ professionals believed that carrying firearms was a way to increase the credibility of the probation profession among other law enforcement agents and to help satiate the public's demand for punishment of offenders, a demand that seemed emblematic of the crime control era (Courtright, 2002). Today, the reality of the job and the changing nature of many cities (e.g., the prevalence of gun violence) seems to have driven the trend (see, e.g., Carroll, 2018). Many departments today mandate physical deadly force training for new hires whether or not they are later given the option to carry a firearm. As both a PO and a university professor, I have seen this trend steer new hires and college students who are considering this line of work *away* from the profession, and I worry that potentially good probation officers are being diverted from the profession because of their unwillingness to carry a firearm or because they have a physical disability of some kind that precludes their use of a firearm.

Lastly, any argument for increasing the pay of community supervision officers must consider to what extent p/p work constitutes a "profession." According to Stohr et al. (2019), any employment activity must have five basic characteristics to qualify as a profession: (1) prior educational attainment involving college, (2) formal training on the job or just before the start of the job, (3) pay and benefits that are commensurate with the work, (4) the right to exercise discretion, and (5) a code of ethics that guides those engaged in the work (p. 314). Although some correctional occupations would *not* meet these characteristics, p/p work would, with the *possible* exception of the third characteristic.

▶ Ethical Foundations of Community Corrections

Corrections, even community corrections to a certain extent, is a more hidden and less visible component of the CJ system, which makes ethical decision making even more paramount (Albanese, 2016). Police work, by comparison, is likely to be more visible to the public, especially given the use of body cameras worn by many police officers. Social media and smartphones have opened up new pathways that may facilitate potential misbehavior by p/p agents (see, e.g., "Warren County Probation Officer," 2014).

Except for departmental policies that mandate specific actions and disallow others (e.g., zero tolerance for drug use), p/p work entails a fair amount of discretion (the ability to make choices and to act or not act on them) (Stohr et al., 2019). Much has been written about the social work–law enforcement continuum in community corrections work. Community supervision officers have particular styles that are thought to exist along this continuum, and the specific role they play is situational and potentially varies by offender circumstance (e.g., they may function under some circumstances more like social workers than law enforcement officers). The inability of some p/p officers to reconcile these different roles has led some to suffer from stress and ultimately burnout that results in their leaving the field. All p/p officers also must be aware of the three human components involved in any criminal event: the offender, the victim, and the community. Given the multifaceted goals of p/p work, an officer's ethicality is paramount. Typically, a concern for all three human components of the criminal event seems overwhelmingly utilitarian (e.g., sometimes it is necessary to revoke an offender's probation and subsequently jail an offender to keep the victim and community safe), but there are also aspects of "ethics of care" philosophies when offenders get a second or third chance to stop using drugs or alcohol or to complete their conditions (i.e., rules) of probation. Multiple opportunities to attain sobriety are an increasing reality as we learn more about addiction and its effects on the brain and as the pendulum swings away from the crime control era. Of course, some p/p officers are more concerned for themselves and have already counted the days to their next vacation and retirement (egoism).

One lesson that the CJ community did learn courtesy of the decade of the IP (the 1990s), is that the ideal community supervision program appears to be a balance of accountability *and* treatment (Whitehead & Woodward, 2017) and that punishment alone has little or perhaps even a negative impact on offender reformation (Cullen, Jonson, & Mears, 2017).

In addition, community supervision officers sometimes work with offenders who are skilled at manipulation. Some p/p officers, especially if they are new to the job, are not always well versed and trained in the prevention of offender manipulation (although most professionals have stories to tell in this regard; see, e.g., Fuller, 2012).[3] New p/p officers who are manipulated by clients may take these attempts at manipulation personally, despite some of this being preventable with knowledge of the criminal personality and on-the-job experience. To some extent, this is a normal consequence of dealing with criminal offenders.

With any newly created sanction or diversion program comes the possibility of net widening—that is, unnecessarily increasing the scope of social control—and, indeed, community corrections have experienced such drawbacks (see, e.g., Bechard, Ireland, Berg, & Vogel, 2011). Although we typically consider net widening to be a problem at the front end of the system (e.g., a first-time offender gets sentenced to house arrest with EM instead of standard probation, thereby unnecessarily widening the net of social control), the IP "experiment" taught us that our net of social control can also be used at the back end. This "back-end net widening" (Whitehead & Woodward, 2017, p. 243) was a real consequence of the IP movement and made it difficult for many programs to claim success in reducing jail populations and thereby saving money; many offenders in these IP programs were returned to jail for rules violations, including failure to pay fines, fees, and restitution, and not necessarily for committing new crimes.

Ethical dilemmas are also inherent in interactions with offenders, and such dilemmas force p/p professionals to make difficult decisions. For instance, is it ever acceptable to lie to an offender? In the IP movement's infancy, there were real problems with the accuracy and dependability of the technology. When I was working as a probation officer, I remember an occasion when another probation officer and I were connecting a client to electronic monitoring (with a continuously signaling "active" EM bracelet). Although the technology continuously signaled and would alert a monitoring center if clients were not where they should be, it was capable of little else, including telling us where offenders were or if they had been drinking or using drugs. I remember on this occasion the client asking my work colleague if the technology had the capability to determine if an offender had been drinking. Particularly in the infancy of this monitoring technology, offenders sometimes thought that the devices had amazing power to detect violations, which of course they did not. But my colleague replied, "Yes." Afterward, I asked my colleague about his response to this offender. He replied, "If that little lie keeps him [the client] from drinking and violating his probation, then it was well worth it." I have kept this memory and lesson with me since. My colleague was using a more utilitarian (consequence-based) philosophy, whereas I was more of a "lying is always wrong" person regardless of the reason or the audience (ethical formalism and categorical imperative). Now, of course, the technology to detect drinking by an offender is now readily available and called *secure continuous remote alcohol monitoring* (SCRAM).[4] As this anecdote demonstrates, p/p officers vary in their exercise of ethical decision making.

▶ Acceptable Penal Content, Legalism, and Other "Common Fallacies of Intrusiveness"

In the heyday of the IP movement in the 1990s, Andrew von Hirsch (1990) wrote a groundbreaking, thought-provoking article that forced those of us working in or studying community corrections to reexamine from an ethical standpoint the sanctions imposed on offenders via the IP. The cautionary tales and questions von Hirsch raised are as relevant today as they were in the 1990s. He specifically examines the intrusiveness of CBCs, an area that is often overlooked even though it contains the majority of the correction population. A thorough discussion of von Hirsch's important article is beyond the scope of this article, but his work points to several ethical issues confronting community corrections today, and I address them here using some of the framework from his classic article.

Acceptable Penal Content

When considering sanctions against offenders, von Hirsch argues, we should always consider the person's individual dignity. However, CJ professionals have not thought about community-based sanctions to the same extent that we have considered legally and ethically custodial (i.e., incarcerative) punishments. So-called scarlet letter sanctions, or shame-based punishments, as conditions of probation, seem cyclically popular and were particularly in vogue in the retributive era of the 1980s and 1990s. These are important sanctions to consider from an ethical standpoint because their use is fundamentally an ethical rather than a legal issue; the courts have often ruled that these types of sanctions do not violate the Eighth Amendment's prohibition against cruel and unusual punishment (see, e.g., *U.S. v. Gementera*, 379 F. 3d 596 (9th Cir. 2004).[5] The courts have readily considered shame-based sanctions to be (1) rehabilitative, (2) necessary for the protection of the community, or (3) somehow related to the crime for which the offender was convicted, especially because probation is considered to be a "privilege" sanction and not a constitutional right (Filcik, 1990). However, according to Ziel (2005), the unique differences among criminal offenders mean that the rehabilitative "effect of shaming remains a true wild card" (p. 512); generating shame, which is a complex psychological emotion, can result in unintended consequences such as anger, violence, or suicide (Garvey, 2002). In addition, the deterrent effect of shaming remains questionable (Garvey, 2002). Von Hirsch (1990) offers an ethical threshold of sorts on the use of community-based sanctions; he argues that sanctions enforcing or monitoring legitimate conditions of community supervision are "acceptable," whereas sanctions or practices not specifically required for the enforcement of these conditions should not be allowed. For example, home visits to monitor compliance with court-ordered abstention from drug use or curfews would be acceptable for von Hirsch, but home visits simply to annoy or harass an offender would not be. Von Hirsch's stance on scarlet letter punishments is clear; these sanctions would constitute "unacceptable penal content" and would compromise the dignity of the offender. In von Hirsch's (1990) view, "there is no way a person can, with dignity, go about in public with a sign admitting himself or herself to be a moral pariah" (p. 168). Of course, he is not alone in considering these types of sanctions to be inappropriate (see, e.g., Ziel, 2005). Note that other and perhaps more restorative justice sanctions (such as letters of apology or victim–offender mediation sessions) that are conducted as conditions of probation or parole would be unlikely to constitute "unacceptable penal content" for von Hirsch.

Community supervision agents spend their careers pointing out to offenders the difference between p/p versus jail and prison and using the latter as a threat to induce compliance. Offender complaints about sanctions served in the community are often lobbed back with the threat of the more onerous sanction—jail or prison. Because of this typical reaction to their complaints about p/p, many offenders will consent to various sanctions or conditions of their release from incarceration as long as they can remain in the community, according to von Hirsch. Von Hirsch (1990, p. 165) refers to this as the "anything but prison theory," but this philosophy is yet another "common fallacy of intrusiveness" because we should justify individual sanctions in their own right, not in comparison to other sanctions. In my own brief career as a probation officer, I found this "theory" to be true and commonly used in practice. However, opponents of shaming-related punishments "argue that consent given when the only other option is confinement is bogus consent," reports Garvey (2002), "because imprisonment is usually not an acceptable sanction under [many] circumstances" (p. 1496).

The ethicality of home visits (not as an aspect of condition compliance) also reminds us that intrusiveness does not have to involve technology, which is a point made by von Hirsch. The increasing use of technology during the IP movement (particularly in the 1980s and 1990s) was a major concern for some (see, e.g., Corbett & Marx, 1991) and for good reason; the technology of offender monitoring advanced rapidly and represented a potential windfall for tech firms, whereas operating budgets for agencies remained stagnant. Von Hirsch has noted that "intrusion depends not on technology but on the extent to which the practice affects the dignity and privacy of those intruded upon" (p. 165). Frequent, unannounced home visits may be equally or more disturbing than an electronic monitor that verifies the offender's presence in the home.

Legalism

For von Hirsch, the common assumption that monitoring the activities of an offender, whatever the means, is intrusive and fails to address whether the practice infringes on specific constitutional requirements. The problem, he writes, is that the Constitution does not give much consideration to the treatment of convicted offenders. He does argue, however, that the state also has not just legal but *ethical* obligations to the offender. The Eighth Amendment outlaws only the "most grossly disproportionate punishments," (p. 166), but von Hirsch argues that states should go further in safeguarding proportionality requirements. When new p/p programs or practices are developed, administrators and sponsors should ask themselves not only whether they pass constitutional muster but also whether there are any *ethical* grounds for considering the sanction humiliating or overly intrusive. This is an important consideration for anyone dealing with court decisions that will impact criminal offenders over the years.

Sometimes, however, it appears as though even these lessons in constitutional mandates and their impact need to be relearned, particularly when for-profit agencies are involved. Most states have implemented an increasing number of supervision-related user fees that offenders in the community must pay at once or in installments (Cullen et al., 2017). This fee requirement has forced staff to take on the additional duty of collecting these fees, which have become integral to community corrections budgets. According to Cook (2017), private probation companies in Georgia collected approximately $16 million in the first nine months of 2016. Although these fees are collected by both public and private agencies, it is the private realm that seems to have generated the most legal concern of late. In 2017, Sentinel—a private, for-profit, probation-based company—settled several lawsuits brought by indigent offenders in Georgia for more than $2 million. The company was taken to task for mandating additional fees (not ordered by the courts) and subsequently violating probation terms for offender nonpayment (Cook, 2017; "Probation for Profit," 2014). Although some of us in corrections were hopeful that the Sentinel case would be heard by the Supreme Court of the United States, the parties involved recently reached a settlement. (As of 2018, other cases were pending.) As Cook (2017) notes,

> People who can't afford right away to pay fines for traffic offenses, misdemeanors and city ordinance violations are put on probation until they can pay off that debt. But in the recent lawsuit, probationers also had to pay $44-a-month supervision fees and cover the costs of drug testing or electronic monitoring even if a judge did not order it. (p. 1)

The actions of the private probation firms in these cases, potentially problematic on multiple levels, seemed remarkably inappropriate given the U.S. Supreme Court's 1983 ruling in *Bearden v. Georgia*. In that case, the Court ruled that probation agencies should always take into account an offender's ability to pay when deciding that an offender must pay supervision fees or fines for failure to pay or for other violations of the probation agencies' rules. In the *Bearden* case, the probationer's employment status had changed through no fault of his own, and his probation officer then filed a violation of probation report on the basis of failing to pay restitution in a timely manner. Sentinel's practices have been challenged in other locations as well. Cook (2017) has reported that the "Southern Center for Human Rights settled for $130,000 with Sentinel over a practice in its Cleveland office of requiring probationers to submit to drug testing that was not court ordered" (p. 2). These abuses seem likely to continue unless contract compliance monitoring of these private companies improves. These lawsuits are robust fuel for opponents of p/p privatization, who suggest that if government agencies have to spend time and money monitoring private companies for potential abuses, then the government should simply stop contracting out p/p functions. The lawsuits against Sentinel speak to the importance of contract compliance monitoring and the fact that the U.S. Constitution exists for everyone. According to Whitehead and Woodward (2017), "If state inspectors enforce the contract conditions, then problems can be prevented or quickly resolved" (p. 252). The issues surrounding the use of fees for offenders has undoubtedly created some of the "back-end net widening" (Whitehead & Woodward, 2017) described earlier. In addition, an ethical dilemma is created if and when agencies, public or private, emphasize fee collection at the expense of more traditional functions such as offender monitoring, supervision, and assistance.

The problems surrounding the use of fees stems from the privatization of certain functions of p/p work and, in some cases, the supervision process itself. The fact that the CJ and corrections communities have had seemingly little concern about these issues is once again remarkable given that the majority of the correctional population is part of the p/p system rather than the prison system. Ross (2016) summarized this irony best when he wrote, "Despite the rather large amount of scholarship and public debate about the privatization of corrections, little has been written on private entities running community corrections services and programs" (p. 265). Some jurisdictions—Georgia, Tennessee, and some counties in Florida (see Carlton, Sokol, & Martin, 2011)—have allowed misdemeanor probationers to be supervised by private companies. The trend toward privatization is increasing (Whitehead & Woodward, 2017) and not only for p/p-related agencies. The federal Bureau of Prisons contracts out community corrections centers operated by various privately run entities such as Volunteers of America and the Salvation Army, among others (Ross, 2016). The use of entities such as the Salvation Army and Sentinel is alive and well in community corrections. The Salvation Army has a long history of supervising misdemeanor probationers in several counties in Florida (see, e.g., Carlton et al., 2011).

Privatization is an enduring issue in corrections because it is ultimately an *ethical* rather than a legal issue, at least currently. Opponents believe that supervising and monitoring offenders should be a governmental function and that only the state should have the right to conduct those functions. Proponents of privatization, given their emphasis on profit, believe that private companies can provide these services at lower cost and perhaps more effectively and efficiently. Barring cases of gross or obvious wrongdoing and obvious violations of Eighth Amendment guarantees, the use of private companies in corrections, including community corrections, has survived legal challenges. Perhaps one day courts will consider privatization practices to exist within the realm of "evolving standards of decency" and subject them to a more critical light.

Another interesting point raised by von Hirsch (1990) in his timeless article is the extent to which third parties (i.e., those living with the offender) can be impacted by the community supervision experience, although the specific extent to which decision makers should consider the rights of third parties remains unclear. The rights of third parties are interesting to consider in CBCs, if perhaps only for that fact that this is a unique characteristic of the ethicality of these types of sanctions. When offender X goes to prison, other entities are generally not directly and personally *punished* by the sanction the offender is serving. Von Hirsch recommends limiting the method and scope of social control in the supervision process specifically to the offender (i.e. not singling out third parties for wrongdoing) and suggests that judges consider the ethical rights of third parties at the time of sentencing and act in such a way that the intrusiveness of such sanctions are minimized for them (Sloan, 2019).

▶ Conclusion

Although ideologies shift from time to time, perhaps from decade to decade, the reality is that the job of community supervision of offenders has always contained a mixture of both law enforcement and social work. The correctional pendulum seems to be on the move once again. Evidence of a changing correctional landscape seems to be upon us. Specialty courts for offenders with special needs continue to flourish; there is now greater emphasis on evidence-based practices in p/p practice (Morgan, 2016); we have witnessed a remarkable reduction of prison populations in several states (such as New York and Pennsylvania), resulting in the prison closures; some civil disabilities (e.g., legal restrictions against offenders disallowing certain kinds of occupational licensure and legal rights restrictions) placed on felons and offenders in general have been lessened or modified (see, for instance,

Pennsylvania's Clean Slate Law, which recently resulted in 30 million misdemeanor criminal cases being sealed—Carlson, 2019); supervision techniques such as cognitive-behavioral therapy and motivational interviewing are becoming more common in p/p practice; *reentry* no longer seems a bad or politically charged word; and continuing substance abuse by offenders is being met with more or increased *treatment*, instead of punishment, at least in some states such as Pennsylvania. As strange as this last point may seem (i.e., from treating substance abuse instead of punishing it), it was, after all, a lesson we learned from the IP movement (i.e., that punishment alone is unlikely to change behavior and have any positive impact on substance use or abuse). It is likely that the community supervision officers of the future will need to be cut from a different cloth, one that is more oriented toward rehabilitation and assistance. A successful reinvestment in community supervision will require new ways of doing things. Cullen, Jonson, and Mears (2017) lay out an eclectic plan for the decade ahead should the CJ community wish to develop new approaches to community supervision. A thorough discussion of this work goes beyond the space limitations of this article, but the Cullen et al. (2017) article should be required reading for p/p agencies throughout the country. The authors offer 10 recommendations for reinvesting in community corrections, and these suggestions are organized around incentivizing the use of community corrections (and disincentivizing prison use), reducing recidivism, and "doing less harm" to offenders. Suffice it to say, several of their recommendations (of both the short- and long-term varieties) focus on the importance of restoring offenders to their pre-conviction state. It is obvious that Cullen et al. (2017) see community corrections' largely untapped yet important potential.

The conditions that will enable us to provide p/p personnel with more resources and credibility are coming together. It is time for us to get serious about the system that controls, monitors, and assists the nearly 5 million people under correctional custody and to start realizing that this line of work represents a *profession* like any other whose pay should be family sustaining and sufficient to attract and retain young, college-educated professionals who desire to join its ranks. It is time to reinvest in community supervision (Cullen et al., 2017). As Cullen at al. (2017) have noted, "The future of effective community supervision does not lie in deterrence-oriented systems devoted to graduated sanctions, but in therapeutic-oriented systems devoted to human change" (p. 62). Part of their suggested plan for the future involves holding p/p personnel more accountable for successes and failures and giving them more responsibility as agents of behavioral change. For instance, they believe that more could and should be done with the time that we spend with p/p offenders, such as the office visit (when an offender checks in with his or her p/p agent at the office). Historically, these visits have been cursory, quick, and repetitive and have perhaps resulted in missed opportunities to impact or direct meaningful behavioral change. Another example offered by Cullen et al. (2017) is that we should make a much bigger deal of an offender who successfully completes his or her p/p term. I remember these encounters being rather anticlimatic and cursory. As a previous probation officer, these ideas (among others) resonated with me and seem doable, important, and certainly suggestive of a return to a previous casework style of community supervision. Of course, reducing large, and in some cases, enormous caseloads would be a necessary prerequisite to any of these changes. As educated and occupationally invested professionals, we owe it to p/p staff to make sure they are prepared for these tasks. This paradigm shift in community corrections will require not only practitioners who subscribe to this new philosophy but also continued attention to the ethicality of those on the frontlines who are assisting and monitoring millions of adjudicated persons who live among us. With these philosophical shifts in how we view crime, criminals, and the criminal justice system will come more questions, such as what we *owe* the offender (Whitehead & Woodward, 2017). I challenge readers to ask this important question: What do we owe the offender? If we can agree that we owe them a shot at redemption and a second chance, then we owe them the opportunity and assistance needed to achieve that redemption. I'm certain that John Augustus would approve.

▶ Endnotes

1. An earlier version of this paper was presented at the annual meeting of the Academy of Criminal Justice Sciences March 27, 2019, at the Baltimore Marriott Waterfront Hotel in Baltimore, MD.
2. A video on John Augustus (originally produced by the Christopher Movement and now reproduced and distributed by the American Probation and Parole Association) can be found at https://www.youtube.com/watch?v=vQRy3aSAGec
3. For a good discussion of the different types of manipulative clients that p/p officers can face, as well as how their gaming or manipulation can be prevented, see Cornelius (2009).
4. For a detailed description of SCRAM, see the company's website at https://www.scramsystems .com/
5. From time to time, we are reminded that what is legal is not always ethical.

▶ References

Albanese, J. S. (2016). *Professional ethics in criminal justice: Being ethical when no one is looking* (4th ed.). Boston, MA: Pearson.

American Probation and Parole Association. (2018). Sentence deferred: The story of John Augustus. Originally published by the Christophers in 1955. Retrieved from https://www.youtube.com /watch?v=vQRy3aSAGec

Augustus, J. (1984). *A report on the labors of John Augustus: Bicentennial edition.* Louisville, KY: American Probation and Parole Association.

Banks, C. (2017). *Criminal justice ethics: Theory and practice* (4th ed.). Thousand Oaks, CA: Sage.

Bearden v. Georgia, 461 U.S. 660 (1983)

Bechard, S., Ireland, C., Berg, B., & Vogel, B. (2011). Arbitrary arbitration: Diverting juveniles into the justice system—A reexamination after 22 years. *International Journal of Offender Therapy and Comparative Criminology, 55*, 605–625.

Bureau of Labor Statistics. (2017). *Occupational employment statistics survey program.* Washington, DC: U.S. Department of Labor. Retrieved from https://www.bls.gov/oes/current/oes_nat .htm#23-0000

Carlson, C. (2019, June 28). 30 million criminal cases to be sealed under Clean Slate Act. *Erie News Now.* Retrieved from https://www.erienewsnow.com/story/40723046/30-million-criminal -cases-to-be-sealed-under-clean-slate-act

Carlton, S., Sokol, M., & Martin, J. (2011, March 21). Salvation Army probation programs blur some lines. *St. Petersburg Times*, 4A.

Carroll, C. (2018, June 19). Erie county juvenile probation officers now carrying guns. *Erie News Now.* Retrieved from http://www.erienewsnow.com/story/38458018/erie-county-juvenile-probation -officers-now-carrying-guns

Cook, R. (2017, February 2). Private probation company settles lawsuits for more than $2 million. *Atlanta Journal-Constitution*. Retrieved from https://www.myajc.com/news/local/private-probation-company-settles-lawsuits-for-more-than- million/mkHQH9KFMSBNC4E8bK6QzM/

Corbett, R., & Marx, G. T. (1991). No soul in the new machine: Technofallacies in the electronic monitoring movement. *Justice Quarterly, 8*, 399–414.

Cornelius, G. (2009). *The art of the con: Avoiding offender manipulation* (2nd ed.). Lanham, MD: American Correctional Association.

Courtright, K. E. (2002). Intermediate sanctions. In D. Levinson (Ed.), *Encyclopedia of crime and punishment* (pp. 912–917). Thousand Oaks, CA: Sage.

Courtright, K. E., Berg, B. L., & Mutchnick, R. J. (1997). The cost effectiveness of using house arrest with electronic monitoring for drunk drivers. *Federal Probation, 61*, 19–22.

Cullen, F. T., Jonson, C. L., & Mears, D. P. (2017). Reinventing community corrections. *Crime & Justice, 46*(1), 27–93. doi:10.1086/688457

Filcik, J. C. (1990). Signs of the times: Scarlet letter probation conditions. *Washington University Journal of Urban and Contemporary Law, 37*, 291–323. Retrieved from http://openscholarship.wustl.edu/law_urbanlaw/vol37/iss1/11

Fuller, J. R. (2012). Looking back: Reflections of a probation and parole officer. In L. M. Johnson (Ed.), *Experiencing corrections: From practitioner to professor* (pp. 15–28). Los Angeles, CA: Sage.

Garvey, S. P. (2002). Shame penalties. In D. Levinson (Ed.), *Encyclopedia of crime and punishment* (pp. 1494–1497). Thousand Oaks, CA: Sage.

Kaeble, D., & Cowhig, M. (2018). *Correctional populations in the United States, 2016* (NCJ# 251211). Washington, DC: U.S. Department of Justice, Bureau of Justice Statistics.

Lutz, F. (2014). *Professional lives of community corrections officers: The invisible side of reentry*. Los Angeles, CA: Sage.

Morgan, K. (2016). *Probation, parole, and community corrections work in theory and practice: Preparing students for careers in probation and parole agencies*. Durham, NC: Carolina Academic Press.

Petersilia, J. (2011). Community corrections: Probation, parole, and prisoner reentry. In J. Q. Wilson & J. Petersilia (Eds.), *Crime and public policy* (2nd ed., pp. 499–531). New York, NY: Oxford University Press.

Pollock, J. M. (1998). *Ethics in crime and justice: Dilemmas and decisions* (3rd ed.). Belmont, CA: West/Wadsworth.

Probation for profit. (2014, August 28). *Religion & Ethics Newsweekly*. Retrieved from https://www.tpt.org/religion-ethics-newsweekly/video/religion-and-ethics-newsweekly-probation-profit-rebbes-legacy-comfort-dogs/

Ross, J. I. (2016). *Key issues in corrections*. Chicago, IL: Policy Press.

Seiter, R.P. (2020). *Corrections: An introduction* (6th ed.). Boston, MA: Pearson.

Sloan, J. J. (2019). *Criminal justice ethics: A framework for analysis*. New York, NY: Oxford University Press.

Stohr, M. K., Walsh, A., & Hemmens, C. (2019). *Corrections: A text/reader* (3rd ed.). Thousand Oaks, CA: Sage.

U.S. v. Gementera, 379 F. 3d 596 (9th Cir. 2004)

von Hirsch, A. (1990). The ethics of community-based sanctions. *Crime and Delinquency, 36*, 162–173.

Warren County probation officer allegedly groped, intimidated client. (2014, March 7). Associated Press—*TribLive*. Retrieved from https://triblive.com/state/pennsylvania/5725821-74/collins-probation-county

Whitehead, J. T., & Woodward, V. (2017). Ethical issues in probation, parole, and community corrections. In M. C. Braswell, B. R. McCarthy, & B. J. McCarthy (Eds.), *Justice, crime, and ethics* (9th ed., pp. 235–260). New York, NY: Routledge.

Ziel, P. (2005). Eighteenth century public humiliation penalties in twenty-first century America: The "shameful" return of "scarlet letter" punishments in *U.S. v. Gementera*. *Brigham Young University Journal of Public Law, 19*(2), 499–523. Retrieved from https://digitalcommons.law.byu.edu/jpl/vol19/iss2/9

SECTION 7

Ethics and Special Population

Special Populations in Criminal Justice

Beau Shine

▶ What Are "Special Populations"?

Special populations is a catchall term widely recognized and used in the social and behavioral sciences, as well as outside of academia. Despite the population's general familiarity with the term, its definition remains somewhat vague and nebulous. For instance, when it comes to education, *special populations* is defined by the Carl D. Perkins Career and Technical Education Improvement Act of 2006 (Perkins IV) as "individuals with disabilities; individuals from economically disadvantaged families, including foster children; individuals preparing for nontraditional training and employment; single parents, including single pregnant women; displaced homemakers; and individuals with other barriers to educational achievement, including individuals with limited English proficiency" (California Department of Education, 2018). However, the health-care field uses a different working definition, defining special populations as people who "require more health care services [or] specialized health care services than other people" (University of Iowa Public Policy Center, 2018).

How special populations is defined then is determined in part by the people served and overseen by a given department, agency, service provider, or professional field. In general, special populations possess some characteristic or set of characteristics that place them in a disadvantaged or vulnerable position. In their respective fields, professionals work to ameliorate this disadvantage or vulnerability by addressing the individual needs of the special populations they serve. Examples of special populations in criminal justice include people with physical or developmental disabilities, mental illnesses, and the elderly (Center for Substance Abuse Treatment, 1998).

▶ Special Populations and Legislation

Of the aforementioned groups of special populations in criminal justice, legislation has been passed that mandates additional care and resources for all but the elderly. This legislation includes the Rehabilitation Act of 1973 and the Americans with Disabilities Act of 1990.

The Rehabilitation Act of 1973

The Rehabilitation Act of 1973 banned discrimination of mentally and physically disabled people by any federal department or agency, as well as by any department or agency funded by the federal government (McEntee, 1995; Shine, 2019). The act provided a vast array of services for people with mental and physical disabilities. Drawing from the Civil Rights Act of 1964, which outlawed employment based on race and religion, the Rehabilitation Act of 1973 was developed to reduce barriers to employment while bolstering support for autonomous living, self-determination, and inclusion nationwide. Since its creation, the act has been amended twice: in 1993 and in 1998. Two sections of the act are relevant to the criminal justice system: Sections 504 and 508.

Section 504 of the Rehabilitation Act of 1973 is a federal law that protects disabled people from being discriminated against because of their disability (Wegner, 1984). The nondiscrimination mandate applies to organizations and employers that receive federal funding. Section 504 bans agencies, organizations, and employers from preventing people with disabilities equal access to benefits and services. People who have mental or physical impairments that "substantially limits one or more major life activities," are also protected. Major life activities include being able to learn, speak, hear, walk, work, and live independently. Since the Rehabilitation Act was passed, the federal government has spent billions on equipment for police departments and federal law enforcement agencies nationwide, including at the state and local levels (Williams, 2014). From fiscal years 2009 to 2014, the federal government provided almost $18 billion in support for state and local police departments. In addition, federal law enforcement agencies are completely funded by the federal government, making Section 504 of the Rehabilitation Act of 1973 applicable to every criminal justice department and agency nationwide.

The act's 1998 amendment required federal agencies to make their electronic and information technology accessible to people with disabilities. Section 508 was passed to minimize technological barriers and provide equal opportunities for individuals with disabilities and to prioritize the creation of technologies to reach these goals. As a result, the Department of Justice started using accessible software, video, and media programs designed to assist people with disabilities, including individuals with hearing and vision impairments.

The Americans with Disabilities Act of 1990

The Americans with Disabilities Act of 1990 (ADA) furthered the efforts of the Rehabilitation Act of 1973 by advancing equal opportunities and accessibility for people with disabilities. The act is an extensive addition to civil rights legislation that bans disability-based discrimination relating to state and local government, public accommodations, commercial facilities, transportation, and telecommunications (McEntee, 1995). The ADA applies to all individuals who qualify as disabled. According to the act, a person is considered disabled if he or she has a mental or physical impairment that significantly interferes with a "major life activity"—that is, a primary activity involved in day-to-day life, including learning, seeing, walking, talking, and hearing. The ADA does not explicitly identify all qualified disabilities, but common examples of disabilities include reliance on a wheelchair or other assistive device such as a cane or walker, learning and developmental disabilities, blindness, deafness, and some mental illnesses.

After the ADA was passed, several civil rights cases were heard by the United States Supreme Court. A series of Supreme Court decisions interpreted the ADA of 1990 in a way that made it difficult to prove that an impairment was a "disability," thus failing to aid the people whom the legislation was designed to protect (U.S. Department of Labor, 2015; U.S. Equal Employment Opportunity Commission, 2008). As a result, the ADA Amendments Act (ADAAA) was passed in 2008, codifying major changes to the ADA's definition of "disability" and expanding coverage under both the Rehabilitation Act of 1973 and the ADA of 1990. The changes clarified what had previously been implicit: An impairment that significantly hinders one major life activity is not required to obstruct additional major life activities in order to be deemed a disability (Long, 2008). In addition, the ADAAA of 2008 increased the types of "major life activities," including but not limited to caring for oneself, performing manual tasks, seeing, standing, walking, lifting, bending, hearing, speaking, eating, sleeping, breathing, learning, thinking, concentrating, communicating, and working.

In 2010, the ADA was revised with updated accessibility standards (Department of Justice, 2010). The standards, known as "ADA Standards for Accessible Design," were approved by Attorney General Eric Holder on July 23, 2010. On March 15, 2012, compliance with the 2010 accessibility standards became required for new construction and modifications under Titles II and III and became the compliance date for using the 2010 standards for program accessibility and barrier removal. All agencies, organizations, and businesses identified in Titles II and III are required to follow the updated accessibility standards, which were implemented to improve accessibility in newly constructed and reconstructed buildings for individuals with disabilities. These accessibility standards impacted the development and maintenance of criminal justice-related buildings nationwide and at every stage of the system.

▶ Civil Rights Violations: A Case Study

On July 24, 1997, Douglas McCray, a married, deaf African American man, took his two young children out for dinner to Quincy's in Dothan, Alabama (*McCray v. City of Dothan*, 169 F.Supp.2d 1260, 2001). On arriving, McCray parked his car next to a Corvette. As he and his children exited the car, his four-year-old daughter nicked the Corvette with their car door. Because he was deaf, McCray did not hear the impact; however, the owner of the Corvette, Wayne Hart, said he witnessed the incident from inside the restaurant.

After entering the restaurant, Mr. McCray and his children were approached by Hart, who attempted to address the issue with McCray. Unable to communicate with Hart, McCray instructed his daughter to tell Mr. Hart that he was deaf. She did so, and after the two men attempted to communicate unsuccessfully, Hart spoke with restaurant employees, who in turn contacted the police.

The Dothan Police Department dispatched Officer Woodruff to what she described as a "private property traffic incident." On her arrival, Mr. Hart spoke with Officer Woodruff, telling her what he had witnessed. Hart went on to tell Officer Woodruff that Mr. McCray was uncooperative when he approached him about the incident. During their conversation, Hart made Officer Woodruff aware that McCray was deaf and unable to communicate with him.

By the time Officer Woodruff approached Mr. McCray, he and his children were eating dinner. When Officer Woodruff approached, McCray pointed to his ears to signal that he was deaf. He also signaled that he was unable to read lips. Officer Woodruff then tried to communicate with McCray by writing questions down on paper. McCray, having been deaf before he was ever able to speak, could only communicate via American Sign Language (ASL), which does not translate verbatim to English. As such, he was unable to fully understand what Officer Woodruff was attempting to relay, and the attempted exchange was ineffective. At that point, Mr. McCray requested that his wife be called so she could interpret for him.

Although later acknowledging that she had no reason to think McCray had committed any crime and there was no indication he had personally caused any damage to Hart's Corvette, Officer Woodruff became irritated and left the restaurant, before returning to write a note asking McCray to show her his license. Mr. McCray, unaware of the situation in its entirety, wrote that his interpreter would be arriving soon to get the situation resolved. Once again, Officer Woodruff became upset and walked out of Quincy's, this time to call her supervisor and request an additional officer on the scene based on the unusual nature of the circumstance and so that "nobody got hurt," despite Woodruff admitting that Mr. McCray never did anything to indicate that he was violent or aggressive.

After Officer Woodruff's call, dispatch sent Officer Howell to the scene to deal with a "disorderly person." Officers Woodruff and Howell then went back into Quincy's to get Mr. McCray to fill out a property damage report. At this point, two additional officers, Officers Carpenter and Carmichael, arrived on the scene. Returning to the table where McCray and his children were sitting, Officers Woodruff and Howell attempted to communicate with McCray orally once again. McCray signaled with gestures that he wanted to communicate by writing notes, a request that was refused by one of the officers. Officer Woodruff signaled for him to stand up and come outside. Mr. McCray looked up and shook his head to indicate "No" and pointed to his children and continued eating. Officer Woodruff made contact with McCray's elbow twice, and he pulled away from her both times. Then, as Officers Woodruff and Howell both grabbed Mr. McCray to force him to stand up, McCray swung his arms because he thought he was going to be handcuffed. Both officers admitted at the time that McCray was not under arrest; however, Mr. McCray later stated that Officer Howell pulled him up and slammed him onto a table so hard it caused the table to break.

According to witnesses, Officers Carpenter and Carmichael were standing nearby and threw Mr. McCray onto the floor. Officers Woodruff and Carpenter held McCray's legs while Officer Carmichael held him down by pressing his forearms on Mr. McCray's throat. McCray testified that he was being choked, causing him pain and making it hard for him to breathe. McCray acknowledged that he attempted to free his head so that he could breathe but denied that he resisted arrest or fought back.

Mr. McCray was forcibly removed from Quincy's with his hands handcuffed behind his back, eliminating his ability to communicate. His wife, Kim Stanford, arrived shortly after McCray was brought outside and indicated she knew ASL and could communicate on his behalf if they freed his hands. The officers placed McCray in a squad car without allowing him to communicate with his wife and took him to the police station. McCray was neither asked if he was injured nor examined by paramedics. McCray's children, who witnessed the incident, were left alone in the restaurant while police responded to the incident. When their mother arrived, she found them distraught and in tears.

Mr. McCray was taken to the local jail. When Kim Stanford arrived at the jail, she was not allowed to interpret for him. However, McCray was able to communicate to his wife and a jailer that he was hurt and needed medical attention. His request to go to the hospital was denied, and he was placed in a cell. He had blood on his clothing and had pain in his throat and chest. When McCray's family was finally allowed to visit him, they asked that he be taken to the hospital. Jail employees responded by saying that he was not injured and denied their request.

Although Mr. McCray was eventually taken to the hospital, he could not communicate because he was handcuffed and denied access to an interpreter. McCray said he received minimal medical attention from a doctor after a lengthy wait. After being released from jail, McCray suffered from tenderness over his larynx, wrist and knee pain, and severe pain in both sides of his rib cage. X-rays indicated a possible rib fracture.

After leaving the hospital, Mr. McCray returned to jail until he was transported to court the next day. He was not granted his release until posting $10,000 for bail. His charges included two counts of second-degree assault, resisting arrest, and obstructing government operations. None of the officers involved testified that they heard or saw any of their fellow officers tell or signal to McCray that he was under arrest, nor did any of them know when the arrest took place. In addition, none of the officers involved could explain the basis for his obstruction charge. All of the charges were dismissed at a preliminary hearing because of a lack of probable cause, and Mr. McCray filed a civil suit against the city of Dothan on the basis that his mistreatment was a result of his deafness and violated the Americans with Disabilities Act, which prohibits discrimination and ensures equal opportunities for people with disabilities (U.S. Congress, 1990). He also sued for lack of reasonable accommodations on the basis of not being provided an interpreter. The lawsuit resulted in a settlement of $575,000 awarded to Mr. McCray, an expense picked up by taxpayers (Brodin, 2005).

▶ Additional Considerations

In addition to making sure criminal justice departments and agencies are adhering to legislative mandates, certain groups under the umbrella of special populations present their own sets of challenges and quandaries. For instance, given the disproportionately high medical costs associated with incarcerating aging offenders, should elderly inmates be eligible for geriatric release (also known as *geriatric parole*)? On one hand, geriatric release has the capacity to save taxpayers millions. In Virginia alone, inmates 60 and older accounted for $12,540,000 in off-site medical bills for the year 2015 (Dujardin, 2017). On the other hand, geriatric release undermines proportionality of punishment and introduces disparity in treatment via leniency toward elderly inmates. In addition, opponents of geriatric release argue that releasing offenders early, regardless of their age, may endanger public safety.

Another challenge criminal justice departments face is how to manage individuals with mental illness. According to the National Alliance on Mental Illness (2018), "in a mental health crisis, people are more likely to encounter police than get medical help. As a result, 2 million people with mental illness are booked into jails each year. Nearly 15% of men and 30% of women booked into jails have a serious mental health condition." Treating mental illness as a criminal justice issue rather than a social health issue places an enormous burden on police departments across the country, robbing them of time that could be spent fighting serious crime, and overpopulating their jails with people who need assistance, not punishment. Jails should not be repositories for mentally ill persons.

The concerns raised in this chapter are not exhaustive; many other issues and challenges face criminal justice departments and agencies when dealing with special populations. Given that equity is a fundamental tenet of the American criminal justice system, it is imperative that the system works with and for special populations to ensure equal treatment, access to resources, and justice for all.

▶ References

Brodin, R. (2005). Remedying a particularized form of discrimination: Why disabled plaintiffs can and should bring claims for police misconduct under the Americans with Disabilities Act. *University of Pennsylvania Law Review, 154*(1), 157–199.

California Department of Education. (2018). Special populations. Retrieved from https://www.cde .ca.gov/ci/ct/pk/pops.asp

Center for Substance Abuse Treatment. (1998). *Continuity of offender treatment for substance use disorders from institution to community.* Rockville, MD: Substance Abuse and Mental Health Services Administration.

Department of Justice. (2010). *2010* ADA standards for accessible design. Retrieved from http:// www.ada.gov/regs2010/2010ADAStandards/2010ADAstandards.htm

Dujardin, P. (2017). Should Virginia release more older prisoners to make room for younger ones? *Daily Press* [Newport News, VA]. Retrieved from http://www.dailypress.com/news/crime/dp -nws-parole-geriatric-inmates-20170423-story.html

Long, A. (2008). Introducing the new and improved Americans with Disabilities Act: Assessing the ADA Amendments Act of 2008. *Northwestern University Law Review Colloquy, 103,* 217–229.

McCray v. City of Dothan, 169 F. Supp. 2d 1260 (M.D. Ala. 2001). Retrieved from https://law.justia .com/cases/federal/district-courts/FSupp2/169/1260/2424055/

McEntee, M. (1995). Deaf and hard-of-hearing clients: Some legal implications. *Social Work, 40*(2), 183–187.

National Alliance on Mental Illness. (2018). Jailing people with mental illness. Retrieved from https://www.nami.org/Learn-More/Public-Policy/Jailing-People-with-Mental-Illness

Shine, B. (2019). Documenting current practices in the management of deaf suspects in the USA. *Policing: An International Journal of Police Strategies & Management, 42*(3), 347–361.

University of Iowa Public Policy Center. (2018). Populations with special healthcare needs. Retrieved from http://ppc.uiowa.edu/health/research/populations-special-health-care-needs-shcn

U.S. Congress. (1990). Americans with Disabilities Act. Retrieved from https://adata.org/factsheet /ADA-overview#targetText=The%20Americans%20with%20Disabilities%20Act,open%20 to%20the%20general%20public

U.S. Department of Labor. (2015). The ADA Amendments Act of 2008: Frequently asked questions. Washington, DC: Author. Retrieved from http://www.dol.gov/ofccp/regs/compliance/faqs /ADAfaqs.htm#Q4

U.S. Equal Employment Opportunity Commission (2008). *ADA Amendments Act of 2008.* Washington, DC: Author. Retrieved from http://www.eeoc.gov/laws/statutes/adaaa.cfm

Wegner, J. (1984). The antidiscrimination model reconsidered: Ensuring equal opportunity without respect to handicap under Section 504 of the Rehabilitation Act of 1973. *Cornell Law Review, 69*(3), 401–516.

Williams, T. (2014). Celebrating 24 years of the Americans with Disabilities Act. The White House. Retrieved from https://www.whitehouse.gov/blog/2014/07/25/celebrating-24-years-americans -disabilities-act

ARTICLE 29

Are We Not All Special? Doing Research with Correctional Populations Inside and Outside of Prison

Rosemary Ricciardelli and Stacy H. Haynes

D ebate about the ethics of prisoner research, particularly using prisoners as "subjects" in biomedical research, is a long-standing part of human history. The Nuremberg trials, conducted in Nuremberg, Germany, documented "murders, tortures, and other atrocities committed in the name of medical science" by respected physicians on concentration camp prisoners during World War II ("Ministries Case," 1949; see also Lerner, 2007; "Trials of War Criminals," 1949). These acts, however, were among too many instances of biomedical research on prisoners internationally (for interested readers, Hornblum, 1997, produces a great summary of prisoner biomedical experimentation; see also Butterfield, 1951; Lee, 1994; Pappworth, 1967; Stanley, 1922). The establishment of the Nuremberg Code in 1947, with its primary principle being that all research participants "should have legal capacity to give consent . . . exercise free power of choice, without the element of force . . . constraint or coercion," was a movement toward affirming and protecting the rights of carceral populations ("The Medical Case," 1949, p. 24). Nevertheless, debate continues about whether prisoners, or even releasees, are able to freely consent to participate in research (Moreno, 2001; Moser et al., 2004; Pont, 2008; Sharif, Singh, Trey & Lavee, 2014).

Despite much legislation and policy regulation about the use of prisoners in research—both biomedical research (see Gostin, 2007) and social scientific research—concerns about the ethics of conducting noninvasive biomedical or social science research remain. Some critics, for instance, are opposed to prison tours. Their opposition highlights the harm experienced when prisoners are denied "the opportunity to shape the content of these excursions and are reduced to objects deemed unsuitable for human interaction" (Pitche, Walby, Minogue, 2016, p. 176). In other words, there are concerns about how appropriate it is to put prisoners on display and how accurately these tours portray prison life. Alternatives to carceral tours and prisoner research have also been proposed, including collaborative research that includes the voices of prisoners as authors instead of as research "subjects" (see also Bosworth Campbell, Demby, Ferranti, & Santos, 2005; Dey, 2009; Minogue, 2009; Ross, 2015; Taylor, 2009). What these diverse authors recognize is that if any narrative created—albeit through research or through touring—is to be ethical and informed, then it must always include the voluntary voices of the protagonist and all of the accompanying players. Yet given that each person under correctional supervision—that is, those supervised in an institution and those supervised in the community—is without power and pressured to comply with their correctional plan, is it even possible to obtain consent that is truly informed, voluntary, and free?

Recognizing that the debate around whether prisoners can freely consent is likely to remain unresolved, in this article we will focus on the important ethical concerns associated with doing qualitative and quantitative research on correctional populations, both those under supervision in institutions and those under supervision in the community. Our aim is to highlight ethical areas that, to our knowledge, remain undocumented in the literature. We address select ethics of qualitative research before highlighting those of quantitative studies. We end the article with a few key points of consideration for our readers.

▶ Doing Research with Correctional Populations: Ethics of Qualitative Research

Everyone approaches research, both theoretically and empirically, from a personal standpoint, position, or perspective. Regardless of one's theoretical framework (e.g., from critical to interpretive paradigms) or methods (e.g., from ethnography to statistical analyses) of choice, it is always our ethics that define us as both researchers and people. Doing research with populations that are inherently vulnerable because of their legal and disempowered positions creates obvious challenges, as well as latent and unexpected ones. As previously highlighted, researchers have noted many of the initial and more recognizable challenges of doing such research, particularly in the fields of health and biomedical research (Hornblum, 1997; Lerner, 2007). In the social sciences, the challenges are slightly different as research outcomes and interactions are much more personal in nature; specifically, they are based on disclosures of private thoughts, experiences, and, at times, more intimate details. For examples, review the narratives in Ricciardelli (2014) or the first chapter in Ricciardelli and Peters (2017).

When doing research, particularly qualitative research, bonds may form as one listens intently to the interviewee, providing him or her with a nonjudgmental space to speak about experiences and thought processes. The resulting considerations—which may be ethical, personal, or professional—are numerous and often overlap (Adorjan & Ricciardelli, 2016; Carlen, 2012; Hammersley & Traianou, 2012; Israel & Hay, 2011). But what is often not discussed, yet of central importance, is how, as a researcher, one balances the effects of the focused attention and interest we display toward the research participant with the resulting sense of connection from said experiences for the participant. For example, many times after an interview, particularly when a strong rapport with the interviewee was felt to be developing (as evidenced by the flow of conversation, the continuation of the interview, and the vast information and experience the interviewee feels comfortable enough to share), Ricciardelli had to choose firmly how the interview and thus relationship would cease. On a personal level, she wanted to keep being there for the participant, to follow up, to be a person the interviewee could reach out to for support. Professionally, she wanted to limit follow-ups to the study components. Ethically, she was obligated to recognize that even if she felt inclined (which is common given the understanding felt or the desire to help one succeed in their desistance from crime processes), she had to recognize that it is not her place. In essence, creating any dependency or becoming anyone's support person, particularly given the challenges of prison life and reentry that would later require prisoners or clients to restructure and reestablish their support system is selfish and hurtful (although unintentional) to the interviewee.

A research-based relationship that creates a space for sharing information is not a relationship based on developed and long-term trust. The sharing is not genuinely reflective of a relationship in a traditional sense; it does not come about slowly as time is passed getting to know a person. Instead, sharing is tied to promises of confidentiality and anonymity and embedded in binding documents such as informed consent. Thus, a research relationship is not the foundation of any deep personal connection, and it does not teach or even emulate relationships in "real life." It skips the proper steps involved in relationship development and the participant, in essence, skips the growth processes required to establish such a relationship. Moreover, the participant may be doing this after having been removed from society for decades. But now, fresh in a prison or in the community, exposure to the nuances and vulnerabilities of community and social living are lost, intimidating, or downright terrifying (see Ricciardelli, 2014; Ricciardelli, 2018). Such processes are particularly important postincarceration because people learn to navigate the reentry process and must maneuver the stresses tied to learning to interact again in a free society. Releasees must figure out how and when to disclose their histories, a potentially consuming task that can induce anxiety, ruin relationships, and lead to a variety of diverse vulnerabilities: emotional, legal, physical, social, or financial.

Ricciardelli has personally witnessed releasees during reentry whose budding relationships with individuals, either as friends or possible romantic partners, have abruptly ended after they disclose their criminal history. Some have had employment terminated, and others have been evicted from their living spaces (see Chapter 1 in Ricciardelli and Peters, 2016; Ricciardelli & Mooney, 2017, 2018). An interview participant once explained that when he disclosed to his therapist that he had intentionally killed more than one person, his therapist was "a deer in headlights" and clearly uncomfortable. Yet, when telling Ricciardelli, he said "I didn't even blink" and just kept listening and talking. Had he never had that experience with his therapist, his perception could have been that reactions to admissions of murder would be rather benign, a perception that would have been misleading. Thus, although there is a potentially therapeutic element to sharing during interviews, for participants to actualize the benefits of participation, the interviewer needs to recognize and remember that the interviewer–interviewee relationship is unique and not reflective of most relationships in the community. This uniqueness also means that if the interviewer is operating as a "helper" or support person, it reduces or eliminates opportunities for the interviewee to turn to someone else to provide that help or support. Limiting or removing such opportunities, if a genuine ethical violation, is inappropriate because a researcher cannot (and should not) serve as an interviewee's "person" (i.e., the person an interviewee relies on for any and all support needs).

Prisoners and releasees need stable long-term relationships in society, and such relationships are not the point of research. Such a pursuit by any researcher, despite best intentions, is not only unfair but also unethical. In these instances, research becomes a form of *taking* rather than sharing or giving. This notion of taking is also tied to the second ethical challenge that is rarely noted in qualitative research: the idea of doing interviews post-theme saturation to increase sample sizes and "numbers." Although large samples "look good" and are more desirable for publication purposes, the practice of doing interviews for "numbers" is complicated and particularly concerning when working with prisoner–client populations. Each interview, focus group, day spent on ethnography, or other method takes something from the research participants. We learn their stories, we build rapport, and, often intentionally, we create the hope or the expectation that we can produce meaningful change. Thus, despite the pressures of the academy to build up samples and so on, it is fundamental as researchers that we do not "take" more than necessary for the purposes of research. Theme saturation—that is, when no new knowledge on a research question is produced because all emergent themes are covered—should be the point at which we stop the research on that specific topic or around that specific question. Failing to do so means we are doing research for numbers and using our privilege (i.e., our status and our access) rather than doing the research to learn from participants and expand knowledge. In other words, we start taking and increasing hopes and expectations for personal gain rather than for the pursuit of knowledge, and that is unethical. Of course, the focus on numbers is entirely different for quantitative studies, which tend to remove the relationship component altogether, and to which we now turn.

▶ Doing Research with Correctional Populations: Ethics of Quantitative Research

Quantitative research (largely in the form of surveys, at least among social scientists) with correctional populations also presents unique challenges. These challenges are related to issues of consent, as mentioned previously, as well as privacy, validity, and access to mental health resources. Issues regarding consent have been discussed in great detail elsewhere (see, for example, Moreno, 2001; Moser et al., 2004; Pont, 2008; Sharif et al., 2014), but the first and most general concern, as we noted, is that individuals are not truly "free" to choose whether or not to participate.

The second concern, related to privacy, is that correctional staff and other nonparticipating prisoners are almost always in the room for data collection (i.e., when other prisoners are filling out the surveys). For example, when administering surveys in prison, officers typically bring groups of prisoners to a central location (typically a lunchroom, classroom, or other meeting room). Once there, the researcher then describes the survey, provides an informed consent form, and administers the survey. When prisoners have completed (or opted out of) the survey, they are then escorted out; if necessary, additional groups of prisoners are brought to the same location and guided through the same survey process. The problem with conducting surveys in this manner is that prisoners who are being observed—by correctional officers and other prisoners—may feel pressured to complete the survey (or not) and respond to questions in a particular manner (for one example, see McCambridge, Witton, & Elbourne, 2014, and other discussions of the Hawthrone effect). If prisoners have questions or concerns about a particular item, they may hesitate to ask the researcher for clarification for fear of being overheard by others or simply fear of disclosing they do not understand a question or item.

The third concern is that of validity. Surveys require the ability to read, and unless researchers read the survey (which sometimes happens), some respondents simply "wing it," raising serious concerns about the validity of their responses. How frequently this occurs is not always apparent. For example, while assisting a graduate student who was surveying prisoners as part of her dissertation, Haynes observed several prisoners who were reluctant to complete the survey because they could not read the material, a problem some attributed to not being able to read and others to "forgetting their glasses." Of course, other prisoners experienced the same problem but did not speak up (e.g., issues of literacy are very central among prisoners and releasees). As researchers, we have a responsibility to identify these problems and assist individuals in completing the survey or not completing the survey but without revealing their illiteracy or making them feel vulnerable as a result.

A fourth concern, access to mental health resources, arises because participation in survey research may be uncomfortable for some individuals. Although every effort is made to ensure that these risks are minimal, responding to questions about the crime they committed, their lives before incarceration (or their involvement in the criminal justice system more generally), and the like may cause distress or anxiety. Informed consent forms typically include contact information for the researchers and, when necessary, counseling services. For surveys conducted outside prison, counseling resources may be more readily available. If the same survey is conducted *inside* prison, however, similar resources may not be available. If prisoners experience any discomforts as a result of completing the survey, how are researchers to ensure that they receive the same access to these services? Do researchers have an obligation to identify alternative resources, if none is available inside the facility?

Generalizability is one final concern that impacts qualitative and quantitative researchers doing work with correctional populations. Most prison samples eventually become convenience samples, in large part because researchers do not have equal access to all prisoners. Among incarcerated samples, for example, researchers likely have little or no access to individuals in solitary confinement or in the infirmary. It may also be that those involved in prison programs are unavailable while the researchers are present, further limiting who is likely to participate.

▶ Final Thoughts

Taken together, there are challenges when doing the qualitative and quantitative research with correctional populations. One of the biggest challenges—both inside and outside of prison—relates to issues of consent and process. Individuals under correctional supervision are not "free," at least in the same way others are, to make their own choices. Participation in any research project, whether qualitative or quantitative, is often unintentionally (or sometimes intentionally) coercive. Although institutional review boards make a concerted effort to ensure that this vulnerable population is afforded every possible protection, problems remain. Individuals' actions are constrained by the correctional environment or by the relationships they must maintain with their correctional supervisors. In other words, they must wrestle with concerns that their participation is somehow tied to their release or their access to correctional programs. Recognizing the centrality of the issue of consent, the lack of available mental health resources for prisoners and other such realities, it is of utmost importance that we remember not to "take" from our participants unnecessarily. Said another way, we must ensure we do not interview or survey prisoners simply to increase the numbers in our sample and that we always remember our place as researchers, particularly when doing qualitative research that requires building rapport and later ending relationships with our participants.

▶ References

Adorjan, M., & Ricciardelli, R. (2016). *Engaging with ethics in international criminological research.* Abingdon, UK: Routledge, Taylor, & Francis Group.

Bosworth, M., Campbell, D., Demby, B., Ferranti, S. M. & Santos, M. (2005). Doing prison research: Views from inside. *Qualitative Inquiry, 11*, 249–264.

Butterfield, W. J. H. (1951). Memorandum on "Observations on Volunteers from Penitentiary" 1951 and letters to Richard W. Copeland October 30, 1951 and Major W.F. Smyth, October 30, 1951. Archives of Medical College of Virginia, Richmond, VA.

Carlen, P. (2012). Criminological knowledge: Doing critique; doing politics. In S. Hall & S. Winlow (Eds.), *New directions in criminological theory* (pp. 35–47). Abingdon, UK: Routledge.

Dey, E. (2009). Prison tours as a research tool in the golden gulag. *Journal of Prisoners on Prisons, 18*(1–2), 119–25.

Gostin, L. O. (2007). Biomedical research involving prisoners: Ethical values and legal regulation. *Journal of the American Medical Association, 297*(7), 737–740.

Hammersley, M., & Traianou, A. (2012). *Ethics in qualitative research: Controversies and contexts.* Thousand Oaks, CA: Sage.

Hornblum, A. M. (1997). They were cheap and available: Prisoners as research subjects in twentieth century America. *BMJ, 315*(7120), 1437–1441.

Israel, M., & Hay, I. (2011). Research ethics in criminology. In *Sage handbook of criminological research methods* (pp. 500–509). London: Sage.

Lee, G. (1994, November 28). The lifelong harm to radiation's human guinea pigs. *Washington Post*, p. 33.

Lerner, B. H. (2007). Subjects or objects? Prisoners and human experimentation. *New England Journal of Medicine, 356*(18), 1806.

McCambridge, J., Witton, J., & Elbourne, D. R. (2014). Systematic review of the Hawthorne effect: New concepts are needed to study research participation effects. *Journal of Clinical Epidemiology, 67*(3), 267–277.

Medical Case, The. (1949). *Trials of war criminals before the Nuernberg military tribunals under Control Council Law No. 10.* (1949), Vol. 1. Washington, DC: Government Printing Office.

Ministries Case. (October 1946–April, 1949). *Trials of war criminals before the Nuernberg military tribunals under Control Council Law No. 10, 14.* Washington, DC: Government Printing Office.

Minogue, C. (2009). The engaged specific intellectual: Resisting unethical prison tourism and the hubris of the objectifying modality of the universal intellectual. *Journal of Prisoners on Prisons, 18*(1–2), 129–142.

Moreno, J. D. (2001). Goodbye to all that: The end of moderate protectionism in human subjects research. *Hastings Center Report, 31*(3), 9–17.

Moser, D. J., Arndt, S., Kanz, J. E., Benjamin, M. L., Bayless, J. D., Reese, R. L., . . . & Flaum, M. A. (2004). Coercion and informed consent in research involving prisoners. *Comprehensive Psychiatry, 45*(1), 1–9.

Pappworth, M. H. (1967). *Human guinea pigs.* Boston. MA: Beacon Press.

Pitche, J., Walby, K., & Minogue, C. (2016). Carceral tours and missed opportunities: Revisiting conceptual, ethical and pedagogical dilemmas. Pp. 175–191 in M. Adorjan & R. Ricciardelli, *Engaging with ethics in international criminological research.* Abingdon, UK: Routledge, Taylor, & Francis Group.

Pont, J. (2008). Ethics in research involving prisoners. *International Journal of Prisoner Health, 4*(4), 184–197.

Ricciardelli, R. (2014). *Surviving incarceration: Inside Canadian penitentiaries.* Waterloo, Ontario, Canada: Wilfrid Laurier University Press.

Ricciardelli, R. (2018). Parolees' perceptions of case management practices during reintegration. *Victims and Offenders: An International Journal of Evidence-based Research, Policy, and Practice, 13*(6), 777–797. https://www.tandfonline.com/doi/abs/10.1080/15564886.2018.1476997

Ricciardelli, R. (2019). Parolees' perceptions of case management practices during reintegration. *Victims and Offenders: An International Journal of Evidence-based Research, Policy, and Practice.* Advance online publication. doi: 10.1080/15564886.2018.1476997

Ricciardelli, R., & Mooney, T. (2017). Vulnerabilities and Barriers in Post-release Employment Reintegration as Indicated by Parolees. In R. Ricciardelli and A. Peters. (Eds.), *After prison: Navigating employment and reintegration.* Waterloo, Ontario, Canada: Wilfrid Laurier University Press.

Ricciardelli, R., & Mooney, T. (2018). The decision to disclose: Employment after prison. *Journal of Offender Rehabilitation, 57*(6), 343–366.

Ricciardelli, R., & Peters, A. (2017). *After prison: Navigating employment and reintegration.* Waterloo, Ontario, Canada: Wilfrid Laurier University Press.

Ross, J. I. (2015). Varieties of prison voyeurism: An analytic/interpretive framework. *The Prison Journal, 95*(3), 397–417.

Sharif, A., Singh, M. F., Trey, T., & Lavee, J. (2014). Organ procurement from executed prisoners in China. *American Journal of Transplantation, 14*(10), 2246–2252.

Stanley, L. L. (1922). An analysis of one thousand testicular substance implantations. *Endocrinology, 6*, 787–788.

Taylor, J. M. (2009). Diogenes still can't find his honest man. *Journal of Prisoners on Prisons, 18*(1–2), 91–110.

Trials of war criminals before the Nuremberg military tribunals. (1949). *Control Council Law, 10*, 181–182.

Ethical Issues with the Incarceration of the Mentally Ill

Sarah A. See
Eric S. See
Christopher M. Bellas

In 2016, approximately 45 million Americans were diagnosed with a mental illness. This means that 18.3% of the population—or one in five Americans—has a mental illness (National Institute of Mental Illness, 2017). The percentage of mentally ill is even higher in the nation's prisons and jails. According to Segal, Frasso, and Sisti (2018), approximately 20% to 25% of incarcerated individuals in the United States have been diagnosed with a serious mental illness.

Currently, more than 2 million people are incarcerated in the United States: approximately 1.3 million people in state prisons, 600,000 in local jails, and 225,000 in federal prisons. Estimates vary, but housing an inmate can cost anywhere from $30,000 to $60,000 per year (Wagner & Sawyer, 2018). This figure is for the average inmate and assumes no particular additional needs such as mental health care.

As total institutions, jails and prisons are responsible for meeting all of the basic needs of their inmates. This includes mental health needs. Individuals may enter the jail or prison with an existing mental illness or may develop one as they serve time. In any event, they are entitled to treatment. Too often, adequate treatment options are substandard or nonexistent. As will be discussed, the current legal standard of care for mentally ill inmates is unacceptable and well below the standard of care available in the community. Along with an inadequate legal standard, society is failing in its ethical duty to meet the needs of mentally ill inmates. This failure is taking place in both jails and prisons. Sadly, the specific failure to care for the mentally ill in the nation's institutions is a reflection of the general failure to care for the mentally ill in society. This article examines how this failure occurred and the consequences of neglecting the mentally ill in prisons and jails; in addition it offers policy recommendations designed to aid the criminal justice system in meeting its ethical obligations to a vulnerable and growing subset of the correctional population.

▶ Brief History of Mental Illness

Mental illness has been a taboo subject as far back as 5000 B.C.E. In ancient times, mental illness was viewed as a supernatural phenomenon and a demonic possession. One common treatment was to drill a hole in an individual's skull to allow demons to come out (Stanley, 2018). As the study of mental illness continued, during the fifth and third centuries B.C.E., it was seen as a condition that resulted from an imbalance in one's body. The way to reestablish balance was to restore the body, which is why treatment during this time included bloodletting and purging.

In the 15th and16th centuries, mentally ill individuals were removed from society because they were viewed as unmanageable and unable to be cared for by family members. They were often placed in workhouses or insane asylums against their will (Stanley, 2018). As the study of mental illness evolved in the 18th and 19th centuries, some reforms were made. Psychiatric hospitals were established as a place for the mentally ill to receive more humane treatment. Although mentally ill individuals were removed from society and isolated, the focus was on treatment and keeping individuals as well as society safe. This was a noted improvement from bloodletting and forced labor. Institutionalization of the mentally ill in hospitals or institutions became the new norm.

The institutionalization movement continued into the early 1900s and peaked in the 1950s. According to Bloom (2010), a total of 558,289 psychiatric beds were available within state and county facilities in the United States in 1955. After 1955, however, the movement to treat the mentally ill in hospitals and institutions began to rapidly decline. In 1980, there were 156,713 beds; in 2005, only 52,539 psychiatric beds were available within state and county facilities. As of 2016, a total of 37, 679 state hospital beds were reported in the United States (Treatment Advocacy Center, 2016a). Why the downfall? Why did the rise of mental health hospitals and institutions, a move hundreds of years in the making, collapse in a few short decades?

As noted by Geller (2006), several trends began forming in the 1950s to lead to the downfall of the institutionalization movement. These trends became stronger as the decades passed and simply overwhelmed the treatment system in place. The first factor was cost. Hospitals were unable to charge patients enough money to cover the cost of care and to make a profit. Second, a lack of psychiatrists for both the general population and for institutionalized patients made long-term treatment a challenge. Finally, the widespread use of new medications made treatment a possibility for many outside the hospital setting. As a result of these and other factors, the number of patients receiving care for mental issues in public and private hospitals peaked in 1955 and then decreased by 95% over the next 50 years (Fisher, Geller, & Pandiani, 2009). Were these patients magically cured? If not, where did these tens of thousands of patients go? Where would the next generation of mentally ill individuals receive treatment?

Although perhaps started with good intentions, the institutionalization of the mentally ill in public and private hospitals in this country was fraught with problems from the beginning. Patients were often warehoused as opposed to treated. Conditions were brutal, unsanitary, and not conducive to treating mental disorders. In fact, torture, abuse, assault, and medical experimentation were not uncommon (Stanley,

2018). Many of these problems were a result of a lack of proper funding. Institutions were often left to the states to manage, and the federal government only played a significant role between the end of World War II and the election of Ronald Reagan (Bloom, 2010). In general, despite the attempts by Presidents John F. Kennedy, Lyndon Johnson, and Jimmy Carter to improve the care and treatment of the mentally ill, little progress was made. By the time President Reagan was elected, the federal role in mental health treatment had effectively ended and the deinstitutionalization movement was in full force.

Even while effectively ending federal involvement in the treatment of the mentally ill, President Reagan attempted to shift the responsibility to the states through the use of block grants (Bloom, 2010). Budgets, however, have always been an issue. With the decrease of mental hospitals and budget cuts for federal, state, and local agencies, the mentally ill have faced difficulty with issues such as finding adequate access to health care and obtaining medication and appropriate housing. As a result, more mentally ill individuals have found themselves unemployed, homeless, and lacking even basic treatment plans. Between 2009 and 2012, there was approximately $4.35 billion cut in state budgets in public mental health spending alone (Ollove, 2016).

Budget cuts also caused a substantial reduction in the number of facilities that offered mental health services. Agencies that relied on government funding have been forced to close their doors. This has reduced the access for mentally ill individuals to mental health treatment in their communities (Markowitz, 2006). Such treatment includes but is not limited to counseling services, medication management, and case-management services. Because of these closures, mentally ill individuals have struggled to receive the services they need. The consequences of the lack of community resources have impacted the criminal justice system negatively (Markowitz, 2006).

As the more than 100-year movement of institutionalization came to a close and deinstitutionalization became the norm, the issue of homelessness became a factor related to both the mentally ill and jail and prison populations (Fischer, Shinn, Shrout, & Tsemberis, 2008; Markowitz 2006; Segal et al., 2018). Historically, homelessness or vagrancy has been a crime. It is an act that has been and continues to be treated as a crime that punishes an individual for simply not having a stable residence or a means of regular financial support. Unfortunately, there are a disproportionate number of homeless persons with a mental illness who are affected by these laws. According to a report given to Congress in December 2017 by the U.S. Department of Housing and Urban Development (Office of Community Planning and Development), on any given night in 2017, there were 553,742 homeless people in the United States. These numbers included homeless individuals who were in emergency shelters, transitional housing, and locations in which they were not sheltered.

Homelessness affects the mentally ill in everyday ways not often considered or discussed. Financial support often comes through governmental services from agencies and programs such as health departments, social service agencies, and the Medicaid and Medicare programs. Historically, these agencies may require an individual to have a permanent residence to receive services, along with an ID card or birth certificate. These requirements can prove especially challenging for an individual who is both mentally ill and homeless. Lack of a residence can also serve as a road block to receiving access to psychotropic medications. Without financial support and access to proper medications, many homeless individuals wind up in the nation's correctional systems as opposed to a competent community mental health system. As a result, jails and prisons have taken on the unintended consequence of providing mental health services to these individuals (Lamb & Weinberger, 2005).

▶ Mentally Ill in the Criminal Justice System

Since the number of psychiatric care facilities has declined, there has been an increase in the homeless population (Lamb & Weinberger, 2001) and a huge increase in the number of the mentally ill being incarcerated in jails and prisons (Amory Carr, Amrheim, & Dery, 2011). These populations are related. The country began to see an increase in the number of mentally ill in jails and prisons in the 1980s. However, these numbers began to dramatically increase in the early 2000s. It was then that the country started to see the impact of the deinstitutionalization of the mentally ill. There are 10 times as many mentally ill individuals incarcerated compared to those receiving treatment in psychiatric hospitals (Montross, 2016). What was once viewed as a public health crisis, prompting the last piece of major legislation from President Kennedy, has transformed into a criminal justice emergency resulting in the use of jails and prisons as a means to warehouse the mentally ill. Institutionalization has transformed into deinstitutionalization, which has morphed into mass incarceration.

Jail

As of 2016, approximately 20% of inmates in jail were estimated to have a serious mental illness (Treatment Advocacy Center, 2016b). According to the Bureau of Justice Statistics (BJS), in 2016 midyear, county and city jails had a population of 740,700 inmates in custody (BJS, 2018). This translates to approximately 148,140 inmates with a serious mental illness. Mentally ill inmates in jail face unique circumstances. They typically have longer stays in jail, often twice as long or more depending on the jurisdiction. Reasons for this include their lack of understanding or complying with jail rules and time spent waiting for evaluations or restoration for competency to stand trial. Inmates with a mental illness in the jail system have difficulty not only receiving initial mental health services but also receiving ongoing services (Segal et al., 2018). Jails are not designed to provide long term mental health care. They are often a revolving door for individuals with a mental illness.

The cost of providing mental health services is a serious problem. Jails are local facilities that rely on county funding. County facilities do not have the budgets of state-operated prison facilities. Because mentally ill inmates spend more days in jail than nonmentally ill inmates, the costs of incarceration often increase substantially. The costs depend on the level of care that is required, which can vary based on diagnosis, therapy, and medication needs (if any). Therapy needs can be identified by the forum (individual, group), the type (behavioral therapy, substance abuse therapy, etc.), and the frequency (once a week, once every two weeks, once a month, etc.)

Because a stay in jail is short term and typically less than one year, the mental health services that are provided are for the stabilization of particular mental health conditions or to make an individual mentally competent to stand trial. The limited mental health treatment that is provided is temporary and not necessarily the same treatment that would be provided if the goal were to return the mentally ill individual to society. There is often a difference between the mental health services needed to make inmates functional in the jail system and the treatment inmates need to reenter the community and reduce the likelihood of recidivism.

Jails are required to provide psychiatric care; however, the level of care varies greatly based on the jail requirements, regulations, policies, and the security needs of the institution. This is problematic because no single accepted standard of care exists for inmates with a mental illness. This makes meeting the ethical responsibility of the criminal justice system nearly impossible because no individual, agency, state, or government is ultimately held accountable.

Prison

Of the 1.3 million inmates incarcerated in state prisons approximately 17% have a serious mental illness (Wagner & Sawyer, 2018). That translates to approximately 221,000 inmates with a mental illness. These individuals tend to have committed more violent offenses or have a habitual history of incarceration. This population also tends to be found more frequently in segregation units for disciplinary reasons and in more secure long-term segregation units because of ongoing behavior problems (Galanek, 2015). However, segregation itself can be detrimental to inmates diagnosed with mental illnesses such as schizophrenia, bipolar disorder, major depression and posttraumatic stress disorder. Trestman (2014) notes the detrimental effects of solitary confinement and how it is often compared to torture. The impacts of such confinement are devastating. Inmates with a mental illness who have been placed in segregation for prolonged periods of time have reported increased levels of fear, agitation, and suicidal thoughts.

Housing a mentally ill person in prison has substantial costs: an average between $30,000 and $60,000 annually. The average cost of housing a mentally inmate is substantially more, depending on the treatment that is necessary. Psychotropic medications alone cost thousands of dollars per month per inmate, depending on the drug. Added expenses include psychologists, psychiatrists, therapists, and nurses.

Ethical issues that also must be considered, including but not limited to access to treatment, irregularity of continuous care, medication compliance, medication management, forced medication, and even confidentiality. Access to treatment can involve the ability to receive counseling, medication management, and appointments with a psychologist or psychiatrist. An inmate on psychotropic medication needs guaranteed routine doctor appointments to ensure that the medications are not creating additional medical problems. Some appointments may require that an inmate leave the prison and go to a hospital, depending on the level of need.

Prisons are on a strict schedule and inmates are usually not able to schedule appointments as needed. There are specific times for meals, recreation, lockdowns, and so on. These schedules are important for the safety and security of those in the institution and are not easily changed or modified. Therefore, mental health needs must work around those schedules. Inmates do not have immediate access to their medication as needed. They must wait for "pill call" to receive psychotropic medications. They must also wait to be seen for counseling when a therapist, psychologist, or psychiatrist is available at the institution. Mental health needs become secondary to an institution's safety and security needs, real or imagined. As a result, state prisons fail to meet the minimum ethical standard of mental health care.

The primary function of jails and prisons is to punish and rehabilitate offenders while keeping the community safe. The criminal justice system has become the primary system of providing mental health services in the United States. Jails and prisons have unfortunately taken the place of psychiatric hospitals to house the mentally ill. With the criminalization of the mentally ill the current trend, there has been a shift in the responsibility to care for this special population. Is the criminal justice system the best place to care for mentally ill offenders? Regardless of the correctional setting, inmates are entitled to medical care, including mental health care. How much care are they entitled to? In other words, how good does the medical or mental health care need to be? What is the standard of care?

The Eighth Amendment of the United States Constitution states: "Excessive bail shall not be required, nor excessive fines imposed, nor cruel and unusual punishment be inflicted." There has been considerable debate about the interpretation of cruel and unusual punishment with regard to the incarceration of mentally ill inmates. What justifies the placement of mentally ill individuals who engage in minor, nonviolent crimes in the criminal justice system? Can these individuals be punished while they are receiving treatment? Regarding the Eighth Amendment, at what point does punishment of the mentally ill become cruel and unusual?

The Eighth Amendment was at issue in the U.S. Supreme Court case of *Estelle v. Gamble*, 429 U.S. 97 (1976). This case established that inmates have a constitutional right to medical care. Inmates are dependent on the prison institutional staff to provide them with medical treatment because they have been deprived of liberty and the ability to care for themselves (*Estelle v. Gamble*, 1976; *Spicer v. Williamson*, 1926). Although this sounds like a victory for inmates, it is not. Although *Gamble* established that inmates are entitled to adequate medical care, what has been developed are best described as minimum levels of care (Hartman, Cook, & Persky, 2016). A minimum level of care describes mental health services in some of the nation's jails and prisons but greatly overstates the level of care typically offered to inmates.

How does one determine if ethical responsibilities are being met based on a criterion of minimum standards? The legal standard of concern is one of deliberate indifference. *Deliberate indifference* is defined as "the conscious or reckless disregard of the consequences of one's acts or omissions. It entails something more than negligence but is satisfied by something less than acts or omissions for the very purpose of causing harm or with knowledge that harm will result" (US Legal, n.d.). Deliberate indifference can apply to jail or prison staff members if they intentionally ignore safety concerns that can lead to imminent risk of harm either physically or mentally. However, there is often disagreement as to what deliberate indifference means in practice. What is knowledge of harm? A threat? An action? In theory, deliberate indifference is an act greater than malpractice. In practice, the standard of deliberate indifference officially sanctions the mistreatment and neglect of the mentally ill in custody.

The American Psychiatric Association (APA), recommends that "psychiatric care in jails and prisons be held to the standard of what 'should be available' in the community as opposed to the standard of what actually is available" (APA, 2000, p. 6). Mental health services in the community are inadequate. Although this is true, at least those in the community can control their treatment plans. They can shop for services and make basic choices about their own care. Inmates are unable to do the same. The holding in *Estelle v. Gamble* harms the mentally ill inmate because he or she is unable to seek other mental health services and must rely on what the jail or prison system provides. Community services are inadequate. The standard of care that exists in jails and prisons across the country is significantly lower than what can be accessed in the community, and it clearly fails to meet the spirit or intent of the APA.

▶ Recommendations

Several potential solutions can be used to reduce the number of mentally ill offenders in jails and prisons. This article began with a discussion of the large number of people suffering from a mental illness in society in general. First, to reduce the number of inmates with a mental illness, society must find a way to help those in need before they break the law. There must be increased access to mental health services in the community. Mental health services in general are lacking, particularly those designed for the homeless or those in extreme poverty. Roadblocks to treatment such as the lack of permanent residency, transportation, proper identification, and birth certificates must be eliminated as requirements for service. In addition, the high costs of psychotropic medications must be subsidized and recognized by the larger society as the last line of defense in keeping individuals in the community and out of correctional institutions.

Second, law enforcement needs to use more discretion and focus on diversion when dealing with minor offenses. Referring mentally ill individuals to established community resources would be more appropriate than charging and locking them up for offenses such as vagrancy or loitering. This includes mental health courts. Mental health courts have been around since the late 1990s and oversee mentally ill individuals with individualized treatment plans monitored by judicial officers along with community mental health services. Their purpose is to divert offenders from the traditional criminal justice system to minimize the number of people with a mental illness in jails and prisons (Mental Health America, 2018).

Third, mental health care must improve for inmates in jail and prison. Providing a minimum level of care is a disservice to those in need. Medical services that barely rise above malpractice standards would not be acceptable if provided to any other population in this country. Inmates are entitled to competent professionals, appropriate medications, proven treatment plans, and follow-up care. These individuals are coming back into the community, and we must treat them as though they will be living in our communities.

Finally, for those leaving an institution, specific, individualized reentry plans are essential to reduce recidivism among this specialized population. Including mental health services in the reentry process is an integral part of reducing the chances of reincarceration. Mental health services must include initial and follow-up appointments, monitoring, counseling, medication management, and case-management services. Reentry must assist with and monitor housing and employment.

▶ Conclusions

The treatment of the mentally ill is cyclical. If those in need had received the necessary mental health treatment in their communities, then it is possible they might not have become involved in the criminal justice system in the first place. In a similar vein, mentally ill inmates are often released from the institution back into a community that is no more equipped to meet their mental health needs than when the initial criminal act was committed. Society must ensure that only those mentally ill offenders who have committed serious crimes are incarcerated and use appropriate diversion programs for more minor offenders. Upon their release from the system, mentally ill individuals need to be referred to receive mental health services in the communities into which they are released.

Society as a whole has an ethical responsibility to help care for individuals who are unable or unwilling to care for themselves because of severe mental illness. We can no longer afford to rely on the criminal justice system to care for those individuals. Jails and prisons were never designed to take the place of psychiatric hospitals. Mentally ill offenders are perhaps the most vulnerable segment of a population already discarded and abandoned by society. How they are treated and cared for is a reflection of the entirety of the criminal justice system and the larger society. There is still time to right this historical wrong and develop an ethics-centered correctional system.

▶ References

American Psychiatric Association. (APA). (2000). *Psychiatric services in jails and prisons* (2nd ed.). Arlington, VA: American Psychiatric Association.

Amory Carr, W., Amrhein, C., & Dery, R. (2011). Research protections for diverted mentally ill individuals: Should they be considered prisoners? *Behavioral Sciences and the Law, 29*, 796–805.

Bloom, J. D. (2010, Winter). "The incarceration revolution": The abandonment of the seriously mentally ill to our jails and prisons. *Journal of Law, Medicine and Ethics*, 727–734.

Bureau of Justice Statistics (BJS). (2018). Jail inmates in 2016. Retrieved from https://www.bjs.gov/index.cfm?ty=pbdetail&iid=6186

Estelle v. Gamble, 429 U.S. 97 (1976).

Fischer, S. N., Shinn, M., Shrout, P., & Tsemberis, S. (2008). Homelessness, mental illness, and criminal activity: Examining patterns over time. *Journal of Community Psychology, 42*, 251–265.

Fisher, W. H., Geller, J. L., & Pandiani, J. A. (2009). The changing role of the state psychiatric hospital. *Health Affairs, 28*, 676–684.

Galanek, J. D. (2015). Correctional officers and the incarcerated mentally ill: Responses to psychiatric illness in prison. *Medical Anthropology Quarterly, 29*(1), 116–136.

Geller, J. L. (2006). A history of private psychiatric hospitals in the USA: From start to almost finished. *Psychiatric Quarterly, 77*(1), 1–41.

Hartman, L. E., Cook, G., & Persky, E. (2016) Standards and guidelines for correctional health care facilities. *Academy of Architecture for Justice*. Retrieved from https://network.aia.org/academyofarchitectureforjustice/blogs/kerry-feeney/2016/12/16/standards-and-guidelines-for-correctional-health-care-facilities

Lamb, H. R., & Weinberger, L. E. (Eds). (2001). *Deinstitutionalization: Promise and problems*. San Francisco, CA: Jossey-Bass.

Lamb, H. R., & Weinberger, L. E. (2005). The shift of psychiatric inpatient care from hospitals to jails and prisons. *Journal of the American Academy of Psychiatry and the Law, 33*, 529–534.

Markowitz, F. E. (2006). Psychiatric hospital capacity, homelessness, and crime and arrest rates. *Criminology, 44*(1), 45–72.

Mental Health America. (2018). Position statement 53: Mental health courts. Retrieved from http://www.mentalhealthamerica.net/positions/mental-health-courts

Montross, C. (2016). Hard time or hospital treatment? Mental illness and the criminal justice system. *New England Journal of Medicine, 375*(15), 1407–1409.

National Institute of Mental Health. (2017). Mental illness. Retrieved from https://www.nimh.nih.gov/health/statistics/mental-illness.shtml

Ollove, M. (2016, August 2). Amid shortage of psychiatric beds, mentally ill face long waits for treatment. PBS News Hour. Retrieved from https://www.pbs.org/newshour/nation/amid-shortage-psychiatric-beds-mentally-ill-face-long-waits-treatment

Segal, A., Frasso, R., & Sisti, D. (2018). County jail or psychiatric hospital? Ethical challenges in correctional mental health care. *Qualitative Health Research, 28*, 963–976.

Spicer v. Williamson, 191 NC 487 (1926).

Stanley, T. (2018). A beautiful mind: The history of the treatment of mental illness. History Cooperative. Retrieved from http://historycooperative.org/a-beautiful-mind-the-history-of-the-treatment-of-mental-illness/

Treatment Advocacy Center. (2016a) *Going, going, gone: Trends and consequences of eliminating state psychiatric beds*. Retrieved from http://www.treatmentadvocacycenter.org/storage/documents/going-going-gone.pdf

Treatment Advocacy Center. (2016b). Serious mental illness prevalence in jails and prisons. Office of Research and Public Affairs. Retrieved from https://www.treatmentadvocacycenter.org/evidence-and-research/learn-more-about/3695

Trestman, R. L. (2014). Ethics, the law, and prisoners: Protecting society, changing human behavior, and protecting human rights. *Bioethical Inquiry, 11*, 311–318.

U.S. Department of Housing and Urban Development. (2017). Point-in-time estimates of homelessness. *The 2017 Annual Homeless Assessment Report (AHAR) to Congress*. Washington, DC: Office of Community Planning and Development. Retrieved from https://www.hudexchange.info/resources/documents/2017-AHAR-Part-1.pdf

US Legal. (n.d.). Deliberate indifference law and legal definition. Retrieved from https://definitions.uslegal.com/d/deliberate-indifference/

Wagner, P. & Sawyer, W. (2018). Mass incarceration: The whole pie 2018. Prison Policy Initiative. Retrieved from https://www.prisonpolicy.org/reports/pie2018.html

The Ethics of Panhandling: Free Speech Intersects with Social Control

Arelys Madero-Hernandez

▶ Introduction

Panhandling is the act of soliciting charitable donations of cash or other gratuities in public places such as streets and sidewalks without offering goods or service in return (Lankenau, 1999). The most common form is *passive*, which refers to soliciting without coercion, primarily by holding a sign. *Aggressive* panhandling applies to repeated verbal requests or soliciting at times or places where it may be threatening to passersby (Scott, 2002). Panhandling is a relatively common feature of cities. After all, the same factors that make downtown areas thrive such as pedestrian traffic, renewed storefronts, and street activity, also attract panhandlers. Classic studies of life in urban areas—particularly downtown areas—portray beggars, scavengers, entertainers, and street vendors as natural inhabitants of sidewalks (Duneier, 1999; Whyte, 1988).

Systematic estimates of panhandling are not available, but a general picture on the extent of this problem can be inferred from recent surveys of homeless populations. The 2018 Annual Homeless Assessment Report estimated that there were approximately 552,830 sheltered and unsheltered homeless persons in the United States, according to point-in-time counts that include homeless persons in local shelters and unsheltered individuals living in the streets (U.S. Department of Housing and Human Development, 2018). Although research shows that not all homeless individuals panhandle and not all panhandlers are homeless, roughly 15% of homeless persons panhandle (Lee & Farrell, 2003). This translates to more than 80,000 panhandlers in cities across the nation, counting only those classified as homeless.

Considering these numbers, it is not surprising that local municipalities and cities have increasingly enacted ordinances to set limits on begging in public places. In 2014, 24% of the largest U.S. cities had bans on begging that applied citywide, and 76% had bans for specific public places (National Law Center on Homelessness and Poverty, 2014). The prohibitions imposed vary widely across cities, with some outlawing verbal requests for money donations or requests made at close distance, others banning begging in specific places. In Portland, Maine, for example, a past ordinance banned standing, sitting, driving, or parking on median strips (i.e., the paved or planted area dividing streets into lanes). The ordinance, which was enforced against panhandlers who solicited for donations on the median, was struck down by a court (*Cutting v. City of Portland*, 2015). In New York City, city regulations that prohibit begging in mass transit stations, including the subway and bus systems, were upheld in court (*Young v. New York City Transit Authority*, 1990). These opposing decisions on the constitutionality of antibegging ordinances not only highlight the legal complexity of this issue but also point to the need for alternatives other than criminalization to address this problem in the long term.

Panhandling criminalization policies are ordinary responses in a climate saturated by compassion fatigue syndrome—a rising disillusionment with the effectiveness of programs created to address begging and homelessness in general (Millich, 1994). There is evidence that such a climate existed in the United States in 1990s (Mitchell, 2011), but some research also shows that the American public views these problems as needing humane intervention and not simply as chronic nuisances to be eradicated from urban landscapes. Public opinion studies report that Americans support initiatives to address begging and homelessness regardless of whether they attribute their causes to individualistic factors (i.e., personal choice) or broader societal and structural factors (Guzewicz & Takooshian, 1992; Lee, Jones & Lewis, 1990; Link et al., 1995).

Both government and the general public see the need for social control of panhandling. What is less clear is what that social control should look like, what ethical issues emerge in doing so, and what alternatives exist to the way it is done now. The purpose of this chapter is to examine the issues in depth. The chapter begins by establishing the importance of panhandling as a social problem requiring humane and effective intervention. Next, the chapter presents an analysis of the free speech dilemmas that arise from the application of antipanhandling laws and ordinances as legal remedies to curb this problem. Last, the chapter closes with a discussion of promising alternatives for control that do not entail criminalization.

▶ The Social Control of Panhandling

Moral and Practical Justifications for Control

Despite consensus as to the need for interventions to curb panhandling, there are two different perspectives to justify why. First, a *deontologist* approach poses that helping panhandlers is the moral or right thing to do. Many social justice advocates and organizations argue that our society needs to ensure that every human being—regardless of socioeconomic status—has access to basic human rights such as access to food and shelter. This perspective also suggests that even if not all panhandlers are homeless, many suffer significant mental or physical disabilities that prevent them from working to sustain themselves, and they have a right to ask for help when in need. Second, a more *utilitarian* perspective emphasizes that controlling panhandling can yield substantial benefits and is worth doing for that reason alone. This is the position advocated by downtown property owners, most city officials, and local investors who perceive a negative impact of panhandlers on downtown economies. Panhandling can be an obstacle for public life expansion and a threat to businesses because it can prevent legitimate users such as city dwellers, workers, and visitors from interactions in sidewalks. With the recent trend toward revitalized downtown districts across the nation, it is not surprising that city planners are in search of alternatives that maximize the use of public spaces such as plazas, city gardens, pedestrian walkways, and shopping areas. There is no empirical evidence to support the notion that panhandlers drive businesses away; only a small proportion of all panhandled individuals report having changed their shopping, transportation, or entertainment routines to avoid exposure to panhandlers (Lee & Farrell, 2003). However, perceptions are a powerful driver of policy, and many people perceive panhandling as something that diminishes business for downtowns and is worth controlling.

Another powerful consideration for the need of control is the issue of safety—both the safety of the panhandler and the general public. Past research has depicted a high prevalence of criminal victimization among panhandlers. Simons, Whitbeck, and Bales (1989) reported that homeless individuals who panhandled or got food from dumpsters were significantly more likely than other homeless to be beaten up, robbed, sexually assaulted, threatened, or assaulted with a weapon. Ethnographic studies, on the other hand, describe panhandlers, homeless, and other types of street people as ordinary subjects of public humiliation and stigma (Lankenau, 1999; Snow & Anderson, 1987). Panhandlers tend to walk in the streets at late hours and alone, sleep in public areas, carry cash, and be intoxicated in public, and such risky routines put them at increased risk of theft and personal attacks (Lee & Schreck, 2005; Whitbeck & Simons, 1990).

Safety considerations also emerge in the context of public perceptions of street people as dangerous, and the presumed connection between signs of incivility or disorder (such as panhandling) and more serious crime as postulated by the broken windows theory (Wilson & Kelling, 1982). The empirical evidence to date offers mixed support to the disorder–serious crime link. Although some studies have shown that neighborhoods with higher levels of disorder also have higher robbery rates (Skogan, 1990), other studies have shown that such a relationship is not generalizable across contexts or becomes spurious after controlling for structural neighborhood characteristics (Harcourt, 1998; Sampson & Raudenbush, 1999). Studies have offered more consistent support to the disorder–fear of crime link, with some evidence pointing that citizens living in neighborhoods with high levels of disorder are more fearful and more likely to consider moving out (Skogan & Maxfield, 1981; Taylor, 2001). These findings imply that panhandling, as a form of social disorder, could possibly increase citizens' fear of crime. Duneier's (1999) ethnographic work in New York's Greenwich Village supports this argument. According to the author, village residents and especially women have a perception of street people as dangerous, panhandlers included. In sum, government's efforts to control panhandling appear highly justified on safety concerns.

Legal Controls on Panhandling: Free Speech Dilemmas

Advocates and civil right organizations criticize antipanhandling laws and ordinances on the fundamental issue of whether these laws are unconstitutional and "oppressive to free expression" (Lauricello, 2016, p. 1105). The argument is simple: The criminalization of panhandling is a violation of the right of free speech guaranteed by the First Amendment to the United States Constitution. Although courts have not always agreed with this argument but instead have been inconsistent in finding begging to be a form of protected speech, a recent Supreme Court ruling has challenged the constitutionality of antipanhandling laws (*Reed et al. v. Town of Gilbert, Arizona et al.*, 2015). As discussed in the following section, this precedent stands to drastically change the legal remedies cities have at their disposal to curb panhandling in the future.

Is Panhandling Protected Speech?

The First Amendment to the United States Constitution states that "Congress shall make no law . . . abridging the freedom of speech" (U.S. Constitution, Amendment I). The protection of speech is interpreted to stem from the vision that exchanging ideas is a necessary element of a free society, but it does not mean that any and all types of speech are protected; there is no protected right to forms of speech that involve defamation, indecency, or obscenity. Moreover, the Supreme Court has interpreted this protection as particularly relevant to speech relating to public issues (e.g., the expression of ideological and political viewpoints) and as applicable to public places (e.g., sidewalks, streets, parks, plazas), or what the Supreme Court describes as traditional public forums (Ellickson, 1996).

In this context, panhandling seems as a reasonable manifestation of constitutionally protected speech not only because panhandlers perform soliciting activities in public places but also because the act of asking for a donation communicates a message of public significance (Millich, 1994). When a person is holding a sign, for example, begging for food, it conveys something much larger than a personal need—it illustrates issues of inequality and a lack of basic human rights in our society. Overturning a California law that prohibited begging in *Blair v. Shanahan*, a federal court wrote: "A request for alms clearly conveys information regarding the speaker's plight. Begging gives the speaker an opportunity to spread his views and ideas on, among other things, the way our society treats its poor" (775 F. Supp. 1315, 1991 pp. 322–323).

Although panhandlers' speech would seem to be constitutionally protected, the matter is rather complex. The Supreme Court has interpreted the First Amendment as allowing for select instances of regulation of speech, particularly when it is narrowly applied to specific places, specific times, or when the prohibition is deemed "content neutral" rather than "content based." An antipanhandling law or ordinance is content neutral if it does not discriminate on viewpoint (Lauricello, 2016) if it is justified not as a mere restriction of the panhandler's message but on different grounds (e.g., deemed necessary to prevent blocking of sidewalks in specific areas). On the contrary, content-based prohibitions are those that restrict speech because of the content or subject matter of ideas being conveyed (Neidig, 2017).

Courts have different judicial review standards to examine content-based versus content-neutral restrictions of speech: Strict scrutiny applies in the former, and intermediate scrutiny applies in the latter. Strict scrutiny, being among the most stringent standards, is difficult to meet because it requires that the policy or law is "narrowly tailored to promote a compelling government interest" and no "less restrictive alternative would serve the government's purpose" (Neidig, 2017, p. 552). Antipanhandling regulations rarely meet this standard; it is more likely that they meet intermediate scrutiny. In that case, all that needs to be demonstrated is that the policy or law "furthers an important or substantial governmental interest; if the governmental interest is unrelated to the suppression of free expression" (Neidig, 2017, p. 552). Following this logic, a city could defend an ordinance prohibiting begging within certain distance from some facilities, for example, as justified by the interest of ensuring pedestrian flow, arguing that the spirit is not to ban beggars' messages and that the banning occurs only to the extent that it is attempted in specific locations in this case. In fact, this has been the main argument presented in past court cases where city ordinances or state laws have been challenged. This explains why cities around the United States have enacted antipanhandling ordinances to be applied narrowly to certain places or times far more often than they have enacted general no-panhandling ones.

The preceding discussion illustrates the complexities in the question of whether panhandling is protected speech. It is not surprising that courts had decidedly different opinions on this matter until recently, with some upholding and others overturning antipanhandling laws and ordinances. This situation changed since the decision of the Supreme Court in *Reed v. Town of Gilbert* (2015), which sets an important precedent that goes against past court rulings, potentially challenging the constitutionality of antipanhandling ordinances and reinforcing the notion that panhandling is protected speech.

The Legacy of Reed v. Town of Gilbert

In 2015, the Supreme Court decided *Reed v. Town of Gilbert*. The case was unique in that it was not about the restrictions of expression of panhandlers but about the regulation of signs (which are commonly used by panhandlers). The town of Gilbert, Arizona, had a sign code that prohibited the display of signs in outdoor spaces unless permitted by the town. The code exempted 23 categories or types of signs from the permit requirement and imposed various restrictions for each category in terms of time, place, and other aspects of the display. Local officials warned and cited the Good News Community Church for violating the code by posting signs advertising the time and location of Sunday services, which were held at different locations each week. As per the code, signs displayed by the church fell into the category of "temporary and directional signs," which were restricted in size, manner of display, and timing of posting. Because the church typically posted the signs between early Saturday and mid-Sunday each week, the town enforced a violation of the code in timing, stating that the type of sign in question would need to be posted no more than 12 hours in advance and removed no later than one hour after the event start time. The petitioner, Clyde Reed, acting on behalf of the church, sued the town claiming that the code violated their freedom of speech. Lower courts and an appellate court found the code restrictions to be content neutral and not against the First Amendment. However, the Supreme Court overturned the appellate court decision, concluding that: "The Sign Code's provisions are content-based regulations of speech that do not survive strict scrutiny" (576 US, pp. 1–2). The Court explained how the town's argued interests of "preserving aesthetic appeal and traffic safety" failed strict scrutiny, thereby violating the First Amendment (576 US, pp. 16–17). The ruling's significance, in a nutshell, is that it confirmed that laws restricting free speech targeted at specific subject matters are indeed content based and subject to the strictest judicial scrutiny—even if they do not openly discriminate against specific viewpoints.

Reed influenced subsequent decisions regarding city prohibitions in panhandling cases, most notably in two recent instances. In *Thayer v. City of Worcester* (2015), the American Civil Liberties Union (ACLU) filed a lawsuit against the city of Worcester, Massachusetts, over two ordinances that prohibited panhandling, one of which restricted soliciting within 20 feet of specific locations such as restaurants and bus stops and the other prohibiting standing on traffic islands. The district court originally denied ACLU's request for an injunction, ruling the ordinances as content neutral, a decision affirmed by the corresponding appellate court. The Supreme Court granted certiorari and remanded the case with the provision that it be decided considering *Reed*. Using this legal precedent, the district court found the panhandling ordinance to be content based and concluded it failed strict scrutiny. The Court found the traffic island ordinance content neutral yet not narrowly tailored, thereby violating the First Amendment. Similarly, in *Norton v. City of Springfield* (2015), a higher court reheard a petition for injunction against an ordinance that banned panhandling in the historic downtown of Springfield, Illinois. Under the guidelines of *Reed*, the Court changed its original opinion and mandated an injunction after concluding that the ordinance was content based because it restricted an entire subject matter of speech.

The Future of Legal Remedies to Panhandling

Along with the more general precedent set by *Reed*, the *Thayer* and *Norton* decisions signal the beginning of a new trend against criminalization of panhandling. Thus, as legal experts have noted, most antipanhandling laws that stood as constitutional before *Reed* would not currently sustain legal challenges (Lauricello, 2016; Neidig, 2017). This is not to say that all restrictions of panhandling activities will be considered unconstitutional from this point on; rather, the most general or "blanket" prohibitions would likely require substantial amendments to withstand strict scrutiny. City officials can still consider ordinances as legal remedies to panhandling if they are consistent with strict scrutiny. For example, new ordinances (or parts of old ones) that ban only aggressive panhandling will remain viable because of the exceedingly narrow application to a conduct that is "threatening" and with compelling safety interests in mind. However, it will be increasingly relevant to clearly define aggressive panhandling, including behaviorally specific definitions that not only can clarify legal matters but also can serve as a mechanism to prevent abuses of power against panhandlers (Szanto, 2010).

An interesting perspective on the future of legal remedies suggests that if cities and local governments find it increasingly challenging to enact antipanhandling laws and ordinances, then they may turn to the enforcement of other existing and more severe laws to accomplish their goal of keeping the streets clear of beggars and homeless individuals (Neidig, 2017). For example, officials can enforce against beggars misdemeanor violations that have nothing to do with the act of begging such as charges of disorderly conduct, harassment, or obstruction of public ways (Broderick, 1994). This displacement thesis is plausible and likely on a small scale. But judging from past research, it does not seem that a substantial increase in misdemeanor arrests of panhandlers will be a necessary consequence. During much of the 1990s, despite the proliferation of antibegging laws and ordinances, enforcement was still rather uncommon because police rarely resorted to arresting panhandlers (Goldstein, 1993). In fact, contemporary policing approaches that emphasize long-term solutions such as problem-oriented policing (POP) go against the idea of merely relying on arrests as a means to solve problems, and highlight the importance of engaging a broader set of services and agencies beyond the police. Clearly, effective policies will require considering more than just legal remedies. A few of the most promising and widely implemented solutions to panhandling are reviewed next.

Promising Controls on Panhandling: Is There A Better Way?

Formulating a long-term plan to address panhandling is not an easy task. Despite the widespread tendency to criminalize, only a handful of cities have implemented comprehensive strategies that humanely address the needs of panhandlers and tackle the broader circumstances that feed into it. Thus, there is limited empirical evidence on the effectiveness of alternative programs or strategies besides legal remedies (Neidig, 2017; Scott, 2002), and the available research comes from case studies rather than large-scale systematic program evaluations. The paragraphs that follow focus on three main programs or practices that had some success in addressing panhandling: educational campaigns for the public, environmental changes, and the provision of social services to panhandlers (Scott, 2002).

Educational Campaigns

These types of interventions focus on reducing the demand, or the pool of "donors" on which panhandlers rely. Mass media campaigns ask the public not to give donations to panhandlers and instead encourage them to donate to institutions and charities that provide services for those in need (Scott, 2002). Messages are typically spread via print sources (e.g., posters, pamphlets, billboards) and through social media platforms (e.g., Facebook and Twitter). In Fort Worth, Texas, for example, the downtown coalition launched an awareness campaign with the message "Don't enable panhandlers. There's a better way to offer change." It offered options for donors to send contributions via text message to support the local homeless coalition (Downtown Fort Worth Inc., 2019). These campaigns also remind the public that many panhandlers use the money to sustain substance-abuse lifestyles and that isolated donations do little to solve the problem at a societal level. The Evanston, Illinois, Police Department implemented a long-term plan using POP that included a public information campaign with this message: "Giving pocket change to panhandlers encourages and supports panhandling and, in most cases, puts the panhandler more at risk by supporting one's addiction to alcohol or drugs" (Evanston Police Department, 1995, p. 6). The department reported a 64% decrease in the number of panhandlers after the campaign was implemented (Mulholland, Sowa, & Steinhoff, 1997).

Apparently, the most effective educational campaigns are those targeted to specific places or audiences as opposed to entire cities. The stereotype that panhandlers' incomes come from many small donations is not supported by research; instead, most of it comes from a small group of consistent donors, or "regulars" who donate larger amounts (Madero-Hernandez, 2010). Regular donors typically work or live in the areas where panhandlers stand, so they have regular contact to the point of getting to know the panhandlers by name. Considering this finding, it makes intuitive sense to target these campaigns to this core group of donors. In the case of Evanston, Illinois, initial data collection suggested that students of Northwestern University were regular donors; thus, information sessions were carried out in conjunction with the university police tailored specifically to students (Evanston Police Department, 1995).

The case studies just mentioned offer preliminary evidence that educational campaigns have at least some impact in reducing panhandling. However, one notable reason why these campaigns may not be as effective as desired is that individuals donating may have preconceived philosophies or ideologies that guide their behavior, and they may be unlikely to change drastically with a campaign. Some studies suggest that persons who identify as political liberals and those with strong religious beliefs are more inclined to donate directly to panhandlers (Lee & Farrell, 2003). For liberals, the act of donating is conceivably a protest "against the system" (Smith, 2005, p. 560); for religious people, donating is part of the duties of their faith. To the extent that broader factors such as ideological viewpoints shape the "demand" for panhandling, educational campaigns will have somewhat limited effects.

Environmental Changes

Changes in the physical layout of places such as removal of unnecessary resting and enabling structures (e.g., places to rest and sit, water sources, public bathrooms) and clear demarcation of property may have the potential of reducing panhandling at specific spots. These types of interventions are informed by theories such as crime prevention through environmental design and situational crime prevention. Anecdotal evidence suggests that situational responses aimed at changing the physical layout of places to make panhandlers more uncomfortable have some success (Sampson & Scott, 1999). In California, the Santa Ana Police Department implemented a comprehensive plan that included several changes in the Harbor Plaza commercial district, including the relocation of water fountains and gate closures in areas where panhandlers used to sleep (Santa Ana Police Department, 1993). More recently, the city of Cincinnati, Ohio, removed a four-block segment of street benches located around a large stadium, a popular hotspot for panhandlers and the homeless (Knight, 2017).

As with educational campaigns, the limitations of environmental changes should also be considered. First, such changes will not affect other factors that allow for opportunities for panhandling such as a large pool of donors. Ideally, these types of responses may affect panhandlers' assessments of rewards and risks and persuade them to seriously consider an alternative lifestyle—insofar as opportunities for such lifestyle are available. Second, environmental modifications may have the unintended effect of displacement—that is, a panhandler simply moves to another location. Third, and perhaps more important, these types of changes can face substantial community backlash if not conducted simultaneously with the provision of services to address the panhandlers' basic needs. This would be the case, for example, if city officials decide to demolish a vacant plaza where homeless panhandlers sleep, knowing that there are no alternative places of shelter available for that population.

Provision of Social Services

One of the most popular and comprehensive interventions is the creation of entities that coordinate access to social services such as referrals to substance-abuse treatment, mental health services, temporary housing, welfare benefits, job readiness, and other employment-assistance programs. In the case of Cincinnati, Ohio, the downtown business district association implemented a model of centralized referrals with a full-time social worker hired to reach out to homeless individuals to offer a direct connection to social services (Madero-Hernandez, 2010). The logic of this model is to streamline assistance while also developing a close connection between the social worker and the panhandlers.

This model was implemented by the Fontana, California, Police Department, which connected transient populations to health, food, housing, and job-training services. The program was successful with a reported 90% of homeless individuals placed in housing or enrolled in rehabilitation programs with shelters (Fontana Police Department, 1998). A variation of this model is the voucher program implemented in Berkeley, California, that provides limited-use coupons that have no cash value but can be redeemed for goods and services at local grocery stores, restaurants, pharmacies, laundromats, and so on (Goldstein, 1993; Spector, 1996). As with the previously mentioned interventions, the provision of social services can have tempered results, particularly if panhandlers refuse to receive help for ideological reasons or see the help as undeserved or the process of referrals as cumbersome.

▶ Conclusion

Cities across the United States have experimented with a variety of solutions to the problem of panhandling. The American public views panhandling as a problem that requires intervention, and not simply as a minor nuisance. As Smith (2005) explains, city council members consider the passage of antibegging regulations beneficial when their constituencies demand that the city do something about a problem they perceive as out of control. Although it appears clear that governments must implement responses to deal with panhandling, it is not clear what responses are most ethical or effective. The predominant reliance on legal remedies and the criminalization of panhandling have historically been questioned on ethical grounds as mechanisms to silence the voice of the disenfranchised. Besides ethical issues, recent court rulings that held panhandling to be protected speech suggest the need to look for other means to regulate it. Although it seems unlikely that panhandling will be fully eliminated, cities can implement alternative mechanisms of social control that are more humane and widely endorsed by most segments of society such as the provision of social services.

▶ References

Broderick, K. S. (1994). Rejecting the parasite and motivating the laggard: A constitutional analysis of the District of Columbia's Aggressive Panhandling Statute. *D.C. Law Review, 2*(2) 179–235.

Downtown Fort Worth Inc. (2019). Panhandling awareness campaign. Retrieved January 15, 2019, from https://www.dfwi.org/about/ambassador-program/panhandling-awareness-campaign

Duneier, M. (1999). *Sidewalk.* New York, NY: Farrar, Straus & Giroux.

Ellickson, R. C. (1996). Controlling chronic misconduct in city spaces: Of panhandlers, skid rows and public-space zoning. *Yale Law Journal, 105*(5), 1160–1248.

Evanston Police Department. (1995). Anti-panhandling strategy. Submission for the Herman Goldstein Award for Excellence in Problem-Oriented Policing. Retrieved February 6, 2019, from https://popcenter.asu.edu/sites/default/files/library/awards/goldstein/1995/95-22.pdf

Fontana Police Department. (1998). Fontana Police Department submission for the 1998 Herman Goldstein Award for Excellence in Problem-Oriented Policing. Retrieved February 6, 2019, from https://popcenter.asu.edu/sites/default/files/library/awards/goldstein/1998/98-20(F).pdf

Goldstein, B. J. (1993). Panhandlers at Yale: A case study on the limits of law. *Indiana Law Review, 27*(2), 295–359.

Guzewicz, T. D., & Takooshian, H. (1992). Development of a short-form scale of public attitudes toward homelessness. *Journal of Social Distress and the Homeless, 1*(1), 67–79.

Harcourt, B. E. (1998). Reflecting on the subject: Critique of the social influence conception of deterrence, the broken windows theory, and order-maintenance policing New York style. *Michigan Law Review, 97*(2), 291–389.

Knight, C. (2017, September 21). Third St. benches, a spot for homeless, demolished over "lewd" behavior. *Cincinnati Enquirer.* Retrieved January 8, 2019, from https://www.cincinnati.com /story/news/politics/2017/09/21/third-st-benches-spot-homeless-demolished-over-lewd -behavior/689776001/

Lankenau, S. E. (1999). Stronger than dirt: Public humiliation and status enhancement among panhandlers. *Journal of Contemporary Ethnography, 28*(3), 288–318.

Lauricello, A. D. (2016). Panhandling regulation after *Reed v. Town of Gilbert. Columbia Law Review, 116*(4), 1105–1142.

Lee, B. A., & Farrell, C. R. (2003). Buddy, can you spare a dime? Homelessness, panhandling, and the public. *Urban Affairs Review, 38*(3), 299–324.

Lee, B. A., Jones, S. H., & Lewis, D. W. (1990). Public beliefs about the causes of homelessness. *Social Forces 69*(1), 253–265.

Lee B. A., & Schreck, C. J. (2005). Danger on the streets: Marginality and victimization among homeless people. *American Behavioral Scientist, 48*(8), 1055–1081.

Link, B. G., Schwartz, S., Moore, R., Phelan, J., Struening, E., & Stueve, A. (1995). Public knowledge, attitudes, and beliefs about homeless people: Evidence for compassion fatigue? *American Journal of Community Psychology, 23*(2), 533–555.

Madero-Hernandez, A. (2010). The physical environment of panhandling: Do panhandlers prefer specific areas of downtown? Unpublished manuscript.

Millich, N. A. (1994). Compassion fatigue and the First Amendment: Are the homeless constitutional castaways? *U.C. Davis Law Review, 27*(2), 255–355.

Mitchell, D. (2011). Homelessness, American style. *Urban Geography, 32*(7), 933–956.

Mulholland, J., Sowa, J. & Steinhoff, E. (1997). Evanston reduces aggressive panhandling by influencing the behavior of givers. *Problem-Solving Quarterly 10*(1), 9–12.

National Law Center on Homelessness & Poverty (2014). *No safe place: The criminalization of homelessness in U.S. cities.* Washington, DC: National Law Center on Homelessness & Poverty.

Neidig, N. P. (2017). The demise of anti-panhandling laws in America. *St. Mary's Law Journal, 48*(3), 543–572.

Sampson, R. & Scott, M. S. (1999). *Tackling crime and other public safety problems: Case studies in problem-solving.* Washington, DC: U.S Department of Justice, Office of Community Oriented Policing Services.

Sampson, R. J., & Raudenbush, S. W. (1999). Systematic social observation of public spaces: A new look at disorder in urban neighborhoods. *American Journal of Sociology, 105*(3), 603–651.

Santa Ana Police Department. (1993). Harbor Plaza: Saving a commercial district through targeted enforcement, environmental adjustments and public awareness. Submission for the Herman Goldstein Award for Excellence in Problem-Oriented Policing. Retrieved February 6, 2019, from https://popcenter.asu.edu/sites/default/files/library/awards/goldstein/1993/93-06(W).pdf

Scott, M. (2002). *Panhandling*. Washington, DC: U.S Department of Justice Office of Community Oriented Policing Services.

Simons, R. L., Whitbeck, L. B., & Bales, A. (1989). Life of the streets: Victimization and psychological distress among the adult homeless. *Journal of Interpersonal Violence, 4*(4), 482–501.

Skogan, W. (1990). *Disorder and decline: Crime and spiral of decay in American neighborhoods*. Berkeley, CA: University of California Press.

Skogan, W., & Maxfield, M. G. (1981). *Coping with crime: Individual and neighborhood reactions*. Beverly Hills, CA: Sage.

Smith, P. K. (2005). The economics of anti-begging regulations. *American Journal of Economics and Sociology, 64*(2), 549–576.

Snow, D. A., & Anderson, L. (1987). Identity work among the homeless: The verbal construction and avowal of personal identities. *American Journal of Sociology, 92*(6), 1336–1371.

Spector, R. (1996). Vouchers for panhandlers: Creative solutions to an old problem. *University of Pennsylvania Journal of Law and Social Change, 3*(6), 49–109.

Szanto, R. A. (2010). Excuse me! Can you spare some change . . . In this economy? A socio-economic history of anti-panhandling laws. *Phoenix Law Review 4*(2), 519–560.

Taylor, R. B. (2001). *Breaking away from broken windows: Baltimore neighborhoods and the nationwide fight against crime, fear and decline*. New York, NY: Westview.

U.S. Constitution, Amendment I.

U.S. Department of Housing and Urban Development (2018). *The 2018 annual homeless assessment report (AHAR) to Congress*. Washington, DC: Office of Community Planning and Development, U.S. Department of Housing and Urban Development.

Whitbeck, L. B., & Simons, R. L. (1990). Life on the streets: The victimization of runaway and homeless adolescents. *Youth and Society, 22*(1), 108–125.

Whyte, W. H. (1988). *City: Rediscovering the center*. New York, NY: Doubleday.

Wilson, J. Q., & Kelling, G. L. (1982). Broken windows: The police and neighborhood safety. *Atlantic Monthly, 249*(3) 29–38.

▶ Cases

Blair v. Shanahan, 775 F. Supp. 1315 (N.D. Cal. 1991).

Cutting v. City of Portland, 802 F.3d 79, 81–82 (1st Cir. 2015).

Norton v. City of Springfield, 768 F. 3d 713 (7th Cir. 2014), rev'd, 806 F.3d 411 (7th Cir. 2015).

Reed et al. v. Town of Gilbert, Arizona et al. (2015). Oyez. Retrieved February 1, 2019, from https://www.oyez.org/cases/2014/13-502

Thayer v. City of Worcester, 755 F. 3d 60, 64–71 (1st Cir. 2014), vacated, 135 S. Ct. 2887 (2015).

Young v. New York City Transit Authority, 903 F.2d 146 (2d Cir.), cert. denied, 111 S. Ct. 516 (1990).

Higher Learning: Race and the School-to-Prison Pipeline

Brandon J. Haas
Amy J. Samuels
Gregory L. Samuels

▶ Introduction

Race and race-related inequities and injustices are often perceived as uncomfortable and complex topics. Consequently, meaningful dialogue about racism is often perceived as off-limits and avoided, which allows unawareness and subjectivity to persist. Therefore, such social ills as economic inequality, the erosion of civil rights, mass incarceration, police brutality, racial profiling, and the school-to-prison pipeline frequently go unquestioned, and political, economic, and social issues that disfavor or marginalize many people of color go unchecked. Many White people are insulated from the reality of racism in America because it is not something they encounter or experience firsthand. For that reason, they might argue that the United States is a postracial society and fail to see or understand the critical need to actively work to counter the legacy of racism.

As Michelle Alexander (2012) states in *The New Jim Crow: Mass Incarceration in the Age of Colorblindness*, "racial caste systems do not require racial hostility or overt bigotry to thrive. They need only racial indifference, as Martin Luther King Jr. warned more than [45] years ago" (p. 14). Thus, the racial inequities and injustices that are evident in social cultural contexts, as well as educational experiences, are often tolerated because they are not perceived as individual or interpersonal racism. They often go unseen because they are built into the systems and institutions—that is, they are structurally intertwined. The vast disproportionality that is displayed in the school-to-prison pipeline, as well as the criminal justice system with its harsh overrepresentation of people of color behind bars, drives a narrative that actions and behaviors of people of color are problematic rather than prompting analysis of how discrimination and oppression reinforce social stratification and inequity.

"As a society, our decision to heap shame and contempt upon those who struggle and fail in a system designed to keep them locked up and locked out says far more about ourselves than it does about them" (Alexander, 2012, p. 176). This appears to indict American educational, legal, and social institutions with the crime of not taking onus or having continuity of thought regarding equal and just treatment of its citizens.

▶ School and Society

Education has always been part of life. Indigenous peoples educated their young as a part of community life, whereas schooling as we know it developed from the model of European colonialists. Since the 19th century, compulsory schooling laws have made schooling a thread that connects us. These early years remained crucial in the development of what has become foundational theory and practice in education (Cremin, 1955). Over time, schools have been shaped and reshaped based on the needs and context of society. Sadovnik, Cookson, Semel, and Coughlan (2017) point out two key ideas prevalent in the history of schools. First, the school was charged with assuming the roles once occupied by family, church, and community. Second, "the School continues to serve as a focal point in larger issues of societal needs" (p. 69).

Dewey (1899/2013) contends that schools should serve as embryonic communities through which children could learn how to exist and engage as members of a community, providing a third role of schooling. Reflecting on these ideas provides us with an avenue to consider the role and relationship of schools and society. One key role that schools maintain is that of agents of cultural and social transmission through socialization, the process through which the morals, values, and beliefs of society are instilled in an individual so he or she might assimilate into society.

Segregation of schools leading up to and following *Brown v. Board of Education* (1954) played a crucial role in perpetuating cultural beliefs and practices grounded in racism. Considering the three roles of schools previously mentioned, it is no surprise that we see the maintenance of the status quo through intentional or unintentional effects of schooling through curriculum, pedagogy, and school structure and practice. Sadovnik et al. (2017) emphasize that through a variety of practices, including tracking and academic stratification, "schools play a major role in determining who will get ahead in society and who will not" (p. 138). Through their interaction with society, schools remain segregated and continue to operate under the influence of a racialized society.

▶ Race and Society

Racism has historically been one of the most complex social issues since the founding of the United States. Socialization into collective groups shapes our group identities, which are then instrumental in our worldviews and actions based on choices that are driven by our perspectives. Robin DiAngelo (2018) points out:

> In addition to challenging our sense of ourselves as individuals, tackling group identity also challenges our belief in objectivity. If group membership is relevant, then we do not see the world from the universal human perspective, but from the perspective of a particular kind of human. (p. 11)

Socialization into collective groups begins at birth and is developed through schooling because schools are key sites of social learning (Dewey, 1899/2013). Examples of oppression can be seen throughout the history of the United States as manifested via class, ethnicity, and race in a continuous saga of establishing a hierarchy. In United States history, students often hear about the discrimination of Irish and Italian immigrants as they study early immigration. The racist idea presented in this narrative is that White immigrants were also victims of discrimination, just like people of color, making this less about race than class. But a closer look reveals something different.

During the 19th century, the Irish were oppressed as they sought a better life in the United States. They were forced into low-wage jobs, could live only in certain neighborhoods, and were often viewed as untrustworthy or lazy by employers who refused to hire them or paid them low wages. In theory, working together with people of color in the lower-class could have proven a powerful alliance for change. Instead, the Irish sought to escape their oppressors by engaging a well-established aspect of their identity that was simultaneously valued in society: Whiteness. By refocusing our perspective from the Irish *being* oppressed to *escaping* oppression, we see how race played a central role. The appeal to their White identity provided an escape from the bottom rung of the social ladder by situating them as superior to their Black lower-class brethren, thereby perpetuating racist ideas, behaviors, and structures that have been prevalent since European colonization.

Coates (2015) states, "But race is the child of racism, not the father" (p. 7) in explaining the idea of inferiority as a rationale for unequal treatment (DiAngelo, 2018). The notion of inferiority has been manifest in de facto and de jure segregation since Columbus "discovered America," a racist idea that school children are introduced to early in their education. Throughout history, we have seen expressions of racism in a multitude of forms, including slavery, Jim Crow, segregation, mass incarceration, and now the school-to-prison pipeline. Ibram Kendi (2017), author of *Stamped from the Beginning*, argues:

> the beneficiaries of slavery, segregation, and mass incarceration have produced racist ideas of Black people being best suited for or deserving the confines of slavery, segregation, or the jail cell. Consumers of these racist ideas have been led to believe there is something wrong with Black people, and not the policies that have enslaved, oppressed, and confined so many Black people. (p. 10)

Following the start of the Civil Rights Movement, a shift from overt to covert racism occurred. It is through the system of racism that the ideals of White supremacy are engaged and supported through legal means (Alexander, 2012; Anderson, 2016; DiAngelo, 2018). Social practices that preserve the status quo persist unbeknownst to White citizens. Practices and policies such as redlining (coding maps of neighborhoods by using red to show "undesirable" areas) and real-estate practices that prohibit brokers from selling to buyers who would upset the racial composition of a neighborhood (Tatum, 2017) continue to maintain segregation, thereby directly impacting students of color in local schools. Rodgers (2017) recognizes that the culture of the United States is built on a "tacit acceptance of [White] supremacy" (p. 223) and that we are unable to "productively discuss—much less resolve—racial tensions" (p. 222). This shift and the attention to coded language has led many Americans to believe we live in a postracial society. This has led many White people to say they "do not see color, only people" and that race is no longer a decisive factor in determining life chances and success. Shifts in policy, legislation, and institutions that remain subtle mechanisms for oppressing Black and other racial minorities from advancing in society are known as "color-blind racism" and "new racism" (Bonilla-Silva, 2013), with mass incarceration as the new Jim Crow (Alexander, 2012). If we were truly in a postracial society, then how might we explain legislation passed in 2018 that makes lynching a federal crime for the first time (BBC News, 2018), or 100 years after the first bill was introduced, or the recent law in New York City that bans discrimination based on hair (Stowe, 2019)?

Race is a complex social issue that requires thoughtful discussion, yet it is wholly unacceptable to refuse to acknowledge the role of race and the subtle and less subtle messages that society sends through popular culture, media, and literature. *Racism* is a term that often evokes images of the Ku Klux Klan, lynchings, burning crosses, slavery, and segregated facilities such as water fountains and lunch counters. For this reason, it can be difficult for White people to discuss and accept the prevalent existence and reality of racism in society, which is described as *White fragility* (DiAngelo, 2018), and the inherent advantage based on skin color or White privilege. Because of the images that likely come to mind when considering the word *racism*, prejudice and discrimination are tightly linked to the word and everyone has been taught that being prejudiced is bad. Except that all humans have prejudice. What you may be envisioning is discrimination, or actions based on prejudice. These actions show up ranging from fairly subtle discomfort to extreme acts of discrimination such as violence and hate speech.

Let us consider how these ideas pervade society and send often imperceptible messages with grave consequences. Children begin noticing differences between people at an early age, and they begin trying to make sense of these differences. Tatum (2017) recounts conversations with her children, who were younger than five years old, regarding race language such as Black, because they saw their skin as brown, and White, because it is more pinkish tan. Children's yearning to understand the world around them can lead to questions at inopportune public moments and result in being quickly hushed by an uncomfortable caretaker instead of being capitalized on as a teachable moment. This silencing sends the message that race is a taboo subject and not to be discussed.

Language and messages that necessitate a critical lens are pervasive in popular culture and transmit messages to children about race. Many books, films, and songs intended for children add to social stigma. Disney and Dr. Seuss are two examples. In Disney's films, issues related to race, class, gender, and colonization are often portrayed through plots and music. In *The Lion King*, the hyenas are racially identified through their language and voices and are the villains of the film who destroy the pride lands when they invade (Tatum, 2017). This pattern is further evidenced in the songs of multiple films that convey colonialist and gender-based messages through song lyrics and portrayals, such as *Snow White* and *Pocahontas* (Hawkman & Shear, 2017). Books such as Harper Lee's *To Kill a Mockingbird*, often held up as a standard for teaching tolerance, promote racist ideas of the White savior in which White characters play an instrumental role in helping or providing voice to people of color. Hollywood continuously exacerbates this issue in films such as *The Blind Side,* in which Sandra Bullock's character takes in Michael Oher, and Brad Pitt's role in *Twelve Years a Slave* (Roisin, 2017). The role of Hollywood is further complicit in the continuous casting of White actors and actresses as people of color. The realities of these issues are evident in backlashes such as the uproar over casting a Black actress to play Hermione Granger in *Harry Potter and the Cursed Child* or the depiction of *Black Panther*'s Shuri, a princess in the fictional kingdom of Wakanda, who was smarter than Bruce Banner and Tony Stark in *Avengers: Infinity War.* Children see and internalize these messages that subsequently shape their identity and worldview that is strengthened by contemporary events.

One such event was the murder of 18-year old Michael Brown by Darren Wilson, a White police officer in Ferguson, Missouri, on August 9, 2014. Following Brown's death, Ferguson erupted into protests that became violent and destructive. News media coverage focused on the rage of the Black community during the protests, and Michael Brown was often referred to by media as a "thug" (Anderson, 2016). This term was brought to the American consciousness through the writings of Mark Twain and Philip Meadows Taylor that linked the word to violence and the notion of being a "gangster," and it continues to be a racist epithet that has been described as a synonym for the N-word (Garber, 2015). This portrayal was worsened by the photos of Brown taken from social media that depicted him as unsmiling and "flashing gang signs" (Poniewozik, 2014). The combination of language and visuals of Michael Brown and the events in Ferguson propagated the image of anger, crime, and violence among the Black community instead of provoking people to look closer at the root causes of these issues.

▶ Race and Schooling

Now that we have explored the disparate impact of racism on social cultural contexts, let us consider how the legacy of racism influences our educational spaces, particularly in relation to K–12 schools. Race is a unique social construct that impacts economic, political, and social components of American society (Bonilla-Silva, 2013; Ladson-Billings, 2006, 2014; Oluo, 2018), and virtually no space goes untouched, including the four walls of the schoolhouse. Although it is comforting to believe that democratic ideals of equality, equity, and justice dominate the climate and culture of educational spaces, the unfortunate reality is that schools are not equal, equitable, or just, especially when it comes to treatment and access to resources. The deep-rooted biases, prejudices, discrimination, and oppression that characterize our economic, political, and social spaces are also insidiously problematic in our schools, resulting in academic and discipline disparities that frequently disfavor and marginalize students of color.

Although we have been aware of race-based educational inequities for decades (Coleman, Kelly, & Moore, 1975), these inequities and injustices continue to persist in schools and manifest themselves as academic disparities (Darling-Hammond, 2010; Gay, 2010; Ladson-Billings, 2006), unequal access and opportunity (Kozol, 2006; Sensoy & DiAngelo, 2017), lowered expectations for students from historically marginalized backgrounds (Anyon, 2014; Darling-Hammond, 2010; Kozol, 2006;

Ladson-Billings, 2006), implicit racial bias (Gilliam, Maupin, Reyes, Accavitti & Shic, 2016), and resegregation of schools (Hannah-Jones, 2017; Orfield, 2007). Consequently, as we consider the impact of race on schooling, we must consider the following questions:

> How much longer will we tolerate unequal and inequitable educational conditions for students of color?

> How much longer will we allow students to be subjected to substandard educational climates and vast disparities of resources and opportunities based on the zip code in which they live or the family from which they are from?

> How much longer will we allow implicit racial bias and a culture of lower expectations to drive the narrative and influence inequitable outcomes for Black and Brown students?

It is imperative that we respond strategically to challenge oppression, disempowerment, unjust policies, and inequities in education. We must consider how to proactively counter the institutional and structural racism that permeates the schooling experience, disrupt the narratives of silence and avoidance (DiAngelo, 2011; Pitts, 2016), and advocate sustainable change for justice and inclusion.

Racial disparities are pervasive within educational institutions (Darling-Hammond, 2010; Kozol, 2006; Sensoy & DiAngelo, 2017). They are often revealed in practices such as educational tracking, disproportionate access to rigorous coursework, and vast achievement gaps. According to data reported by Musu-Gillette et al. (2017) and related to National Assessment of Educational Progress test results from 2015, achievement gaps persist in both reading and math and are evident in all testing years (fourth, eighth, and 12th grades). Reading achievement of White students in fourth grade was 26 points higher than their Black peers and 24 points higher than their Latinx peers. In 12th grade, the achievement gap was even more disparaging for Black students, who scored 30 points less than their White peers. Regarding math proficiency, fourth-grade White students scored 24 points higher than their Black peers and 18 points higher than their Latinx peers. The gap was even wider in eighth grade, where White students scored 32 points higher than their Black peers and 22 points more than their Latinx peers. The gaps persisted through 12th grade, where the average mathematics scores for White students were higher than the scores for their Black and Latinx peers in every survey year since 2005.

Although the causes for such achievement gaps can seem obscure and multifaceted, the racist undertones cannot be overlooked. Even when comparing high-achieving students, racial disparities persist even when test scores are exactly the same. Grissom and Redding (2016) investigated the role of teacher discretion and bias on academic access. When comparing students with identical test scores, White students were twice as likely to be placed in gifted and talented programs than their Black peers. To investigate this further, let us consider an example from Broward County, Florida. Even though half of the student population is Black or Latinx, in 2005, only 25% of the third graders who were identified as gifted were Black or Latinx. Recognizing the danger of subjectivity, the district challenged this vast inequity by shifting from a referral process that used only feedback from teachers and parents to a more objective universal-screening program. The new screening program, which deliberately minimized the impact of bias and teacher discretion, resulted in a 130% increase for Latinx students in gifted programs and an 80% increase for Black students (Dynarski, 2016). Unfortunately, the intricacy of race-based implications does not end there. Grissom and Redding (2016) also found that when high-achieving Black students are taught by Black teachers, they are just as likely to be assigned to gifted programs as their high-achieving White peers. However, the elementary and secondary educator workforce in public schools is 82% White (U.S. Department of Education, 2016).

In addition to access to gifted programs, data also reveal inequitable access for students of color to rigorous coursework such as Advanced Placement (AP) and International Baccalaureate (IB) classes. Although Black and Latinx students make up 37% of high school students, they only represent 27% of students enrolled in at least one AP course and only 18% of the students who receive a passing score on an AP exam (U.S. Department of Education Office for Civil Rights, 2014). According to the National Center for Education Statistics (2017), although White students earn an average of 3.1 AP/IB credits in high school, Black students earn only an average of 2.7 credits (Musu-Gillette et al., 2017).

Along with well-documented achievement gaps and inequitable access to rigorous academic opportunities, teacher quality is a major issue because research highlights that students of color are more likely to be taught by less qualified teachers. Goldhaber, Lavery, and Theobald (2015) report that across grade levels teacher quality (measured by experience, licensure exam scores, and value-added components) serves to advantage White students and disadvantage racial minority students. Furthermore, when considering inequities in access, opportunity, and teacher quality, we must also examine the resegregation of schools, because it further underscores the legacy of racism. Jonathan Kozol, a respected activist in the field, asserts, "Among the many burning issues of concern to educators and educational ethicists during the past few years, none appears to provoke more heated controversy than the devastating backswing of our urban public schools to racial resegregation at a level of intensity the nation has not seen in decades" (Kozol, 2007, para. 1).

Notwithstanding the judicial success of *Brown v. Board of Education*, many schools did not desegregate "with all deliberate speed." Some schools simply closed their doors to avoid integration, including the school system of Prince Edward County in Virginia, which completely disbanded to avoid complying with desegregation orders (Glasrud, 1977). Reflecting on the 10 years after *Brown v. Board of Education*, Darling-Hammond (2010) states, "by 1964, fully a decade later, 98% of African American students in Southern schools were still enrolled in all-Black schools, and over 70% of Black students in the North were still enrolled in predominantly minority schools" (p. 35).

Rather than focusing on the goal of racially integrated and equitable schools, recent trends, policies, and court decisions indicate schools are further distancing themselves from addressing the evils of segregation, thereby failing to live up to the democratic ideas of liberty, equality, and justice (Orfield & Frankenberg, 2007). Schools are increasing the practice of racial segregation: White students attend schools where 80% of their peers are also White, whereas Latinx students attend schools where only 28% of the students are White, and Black students attend schools where only 31% of the students are White (Orfield & Lee, 2004).

▶ School Discipline and Race

In addition to academic disparities and inequitable access and opportunity, racism in schools is evident in the disproportionality of racial discipline rates and student data trends. It is imperative to consider the consequences of such disproportionality because it results in contentious educational experiences for many students and can lead to disconnection from the schooling experience or push out. Students of color are consistently disciplined more harshly, are more likely to be referred to the office, and face higher rates of suspension and expulsion. As highlighted in a jointly issued letter by the Department of Education and Department of Justice's Civil Rights Division (2014):

> significant and unexplained racial disparities in student discipline give rise to concerns that schools may be engaging in racial discrimination that violates the Federal civil rights laws . . . in our investigations we have found cases where African American students were disciplined more harshly and more frequently because of their race than similarly situated white students. In short, racial discrimination in school discipline is a real problem. (para. 5)

Black students are three times more likely to be suspended and expelled than White students. On average, approximately 5% of White students are suspended, compared to 16.4% of Black students (U.S. Department of Education Office for Civil Rights, 2014). The statistics are even more striking in the American South. A 2016 report from the University of Pennsylvania's Center for the Study of Race and Equity in Education found that 13 Southern states were responsible for 55% of the 1.2 million suspensions involving Black students nationwide (Smith & Harper, 2016). Moreover, Black and Latinx students are more likely than their White peers to be disciplined when receiving a referral for minor misbehavior (Nelson & Lind, 2015; Skiba et al., 2011); they also receive more severe punishments for the same types of infractions and are suspended for longer periods of time (Anderson & Ritter, 2018). Although White students are more likely to be disciplined for offenses such as using obscene language, smoking, and vandalism, Black students are more likely to be disciplined for subjective reasons such as being "disrespectful" or "disruptive" or for "disobedient" behavior (Nelson & Lind, 2015). Suspensions and expulsions not only result in decreased instructional time but also often lead to even more adverse outcomes. For instance, although Black students make up 16% of student enrollment in K–12 schools, they represent 27% of students referred to law enforcement and 31% of students subjected to a school-related arrest (U.S. Department of Education Office for Civil Rights, 2014). In addition, students who have been suspended or expelled are more likely to be retained at least one grade level and twice as likely to drop out of school (Nelson & Lind, 2015).

Many people may think that discipline-related disparities are more common in secondary settings, but such disparities begin even before students enter kindergarten (Gilliam et al., 2016). Black children make up 18% of preschool enrollment, but 42% of preschoolers who are suspended once and 48% of preschoolers who are suspended more than once (U.S. Department of Education Office for Civil Rights, 2014). To highlight the discriminatory nature of implicit bias,

Gilliam et al. (2016) revealed that preschool teachers were more likely to expect off-task behavior from Black students, particularly Black boys, and they monitored more closely situations involving Black students to see if such misbehavior was occurring. As such, it is essential to inquire if Black boys are engaging in more misbehavior or if their misbehavior is more likely to be identified because they are watched more closely. Nonetheless, it is impossible to deny that more severe disciplinary outcomes for students of color are partly the result of biases and discriminatory practices, intentional or not.

Although schools are supposed to be structured to engage, encourage, and empower students, the unfortunate reality is that current policies and practices of low expectations, racialized educational tracking, racialized behavior disparities, and resegregation result in disengaging, disfavoring, and disempowering many students. Next, we will examine how such disconnection and marginalization unjustly influences a school-to-prison pipeline trajectory that disproportionately affects youth of color and their entrance into the criminal justice system at alarming rates.

▶ School-to-Prison Pipeline

The term *school-to-prison pipeline* refers to a complex institutional problem that involves an array of disciplinary practices and policies that results in a pathway for punishments that begin in school and end in the criminal justice system. Given the increase in disciplinary actions that are connected to police involvement, particularly school resource officers (SROs), the likelihood of pushing students out of school and into the criminal justice system is escalating, making the school-to-prison pipeline one of the most pressing challenges facing public education. Just as students of color are disproportionately disciplined, suspended, and expelled, they are disproportionately represented in the school-to-prison pipeline and disproportionately subjected to the criminal justice system. As Senator Richard Durbin stated at a congressional hearing focused on calling for an end to the school-to-prison pipeline, "For many young people, our schools are increasingly a gateway to the criminal justice system. What is especially concerning about this phenomenon is that it deprives our kids of their fundamental right to an education." He continued, "A schoolyard fight that used to warrant a visit to the principal's office can now lead to a trip to the booking station and a judge" (St. George, 2012, para. 10).

Zero-tolerance policies are often perceived as the catalyst for creating and intensifying the school-to-prison pipeline. These policies were sparked by a desire for increased safety and were aligned with legislation such as the Gun-Free School Zones Act of 1990, which sought to reduce the threat of gun violence in schools by requiring a one-year suspension for any student possessing a firearm on a school campus, and the Safe and Drug-Free Schools and Community Act of 1989 (Scott & Saucedo, 2013). Zero-tolerance policies require administrators to issue specific punishments, typically suspensions or expulsions, when students violate certain rules, regardless of the student's individual circumstances or previous offenses. With zero-tolerance policies came increased police presence in schools and police involvement in non–zero-tolerance offenses on school campuses. For example, minor infractions of school rules are often criminalized and disciplinary issues that should be addressed by teachers and administrators are often handled by school police, many of whom have little training in working with youth or community policing. In addition, nonviolent offenses such as disruptive behavior are resulting in overuse of suspensions and expulsions, which is problematic because such consequences have implications that extend beyond the present. For example, after students develop a reputation for being "problem students," they are more likely to be involved in additional incidents with increased gravity. According to the NAACP Legal Defense and Educational Fund (2017), "a child who is expelled or suspended is more than twice as likely to be arrested within the same month as compared to a child who had not been previously suspended during the same month" (p.10). In addition, once a student enters the criminal justice system, issues compound. For example, incarceration decreases the likelihood of high school graduation and increases the prospect of future incarceration (NAACP Legal Defense and Educational Fund, 2017), which then directly influences one's ability to pursue future education and secure housing and employment.

Racial discipline disparities are widespread across all regions of the United States. Black male students are three times more likely to be arrested at school than their White male counterparts, and Black females are 1.5 times more likely to be arrested than their White male counterparts (Blad & Harwin, 2017). Although Black students made up 16% of the student population in 2011–2012, they represented 31% of in-school arrests (Nelson & Lind, 2015). Also, Black students are more likely to attend schools that have police officers present and are more likely to attend schools where arrests occur (Blad & Harwin, 2017).

Many people might argue that arrests are justifiable, but it is critical to emphasize that many arrests are the result of minor misbehaviors and misunderstandings that should be addressed through school-based counseling or mentoring, not police intervention. For example, in Prince William County, Virginia, "a 14-year-old boy was arrested on charges of disorderly conduct and petty larceny . . . after a school-based officer accused him of stealing a carton of milk. The boy, who qualified for free lunches, said he had gone back to the cafeteria cooler to get the milk after he forgot to pick one up when he first went through the serving line" (Blad & Harwin, 2017, para. 23). In addition, data reported from New York in 2012 revealed that nearly 20% of in-school arrests by SROs documented vague reasons such as resisting arrest or obstructing governmental administration (Nelson & Lind, 2015).

Considering the policies and practices that result in racial disparities in suspensions, expulsions, school-based arrests, and criminalization of our youth, it is no surprise similar disparities are observed in incarceration rates of adults in state prisons nationwide. According to the Sentencing Project (Nellis, 2016), the incarceration rates of Black adults are five times higher than those of Whites, and the incarceration rates for Latinx adults are four times higher than for Whites. In some states, the disparities are even more alarming. For example, in 12 states, Black people make up more than half the prison population, and in Maryland they represent 72% of the population. Alexander (2012) highlights that the United States has the highest incarceration rate in the world of 750 per 100,000 children and adults. In highlighting the causes for such disparities, comparable to what is observed in schools, the Sentencing Project (Nellis, 2016) highlights inequitable policies and practices, implicit biases, and structural disadvantages.

▶ Conclusion

Title VI of the Civil Rights Act of 1964 prohibits states, districts, and public schools from discriminating based on race, color, or national origin. In reality, schools discriminate based on race and color, whether deliberately or not. Racial inequities exist in schooling and society, and the disparities are irrefutable. Schools should promote a safe and welcoming climate and culture for all students; unfortunately, that is not the reality for many students of color. From the moment students begin school, as early as prekindergarten, they are predisposed to inequities and subjected to biases and prejudices that result in persistent discriminatory practices.

The school-to-prison pipeline presents overwhelming obstacles that further marginalize and exclude both Black and Brown students and deprive them of educational access and opportunity. Therefore, when examining the impact of race on schooling, it is essential to interrogate the disproportionality many students of color are forced to endure because it results in contentious educational experiences that cause many students to be unjustly funneled from school buildings to correctional facilities. Nevertheless, educators, policy makers, and community members have a responsibility to actively counter the unjust policies and practices that perpetuate the insidious dangers of implicit bias, reinforce the legacy of racism, and exacerbate the school-to-prison pipeline. Rather than promoting schooling that isolates, punishes, and pushes out students, we must find a way to promote caring, equitable, inclusive, and just educational environments that embrace all students.

▶ References

Alexander, M. (2012). *The new Jim Crow: Mass incarceration in the age of colorblindness.* New York, NY: The New Press.

Anderson, C. (2016). *White rage: The unspoken truth of our racial divide.* New York, NY: Bloomsbury Publishing USA.

Anderson, K. P., & Ritter, G. W. (2018). Do school discipline policies treat students fairly? Evidence from Arkansas. *Educational Policy.* doi:10.1177/0895904818802085

Anyon, J. (2014). *Radical possibilities: Public policy, urban education, and a new social movement.* New York, NY: Taylor & Francis.

BBC News. (2018, December 20). US passes first anti-lynching law after Senate vote. BBC. Retrieved from https://www.bbc.com/news/world-us-canada-46634184

Blad, E. & Harwin, A. (2017, February 27). Analysis reveals racial disparities in school arrests. PBS News Hour. Education. Retrieved from https://www.pbs.org/newshour/education/analysis-reveals-racial-disparities-school-arrests

Bonilla-Silva, E. (2013). *Racism without racists: Color-blind racism and the persistence of racial inequality in America* (4th ed.). Lanham, MD: Rowman & Littlefield.

Brown v. Board of Education, 347 U.S. 483 (1954).

Civil Rights Act of 1964 § 7, 42 U.S.C. § 2000e et seq (1964).

Coates, T. N. (2015). *Between the world and me.* New York, NY: Spiegel & Grau.

Coleman, J. S., Kelly, S. D., & Moore, J. A. (1975). *Trends in school segregation, 1968–1973.* Washington, DC: Urban Institute.

Cremin, L. A. (1955). The revolution in American secondary education, 1893–1918. *Teachers College Record, 56*(6), 295–308.

Dewey, J. (2013). *The school and society and the child and the curriculum.* University of Chicago Press. (Originally published 1899.)

Darling-Hammond, L. (2010). *The flat world and education: How America's commitment to equity will determine our future.* New York, NY: Teacher's College, Columbia University.

DiAngelo, R. (2011). White fragility. *International Journal of Critical Pedagogy, 3*(3), 54–70.

DiAngelo, R. (2018). *White fragility: Why it's so hard for white people to talk about racism.* Boston, MA: Beacon Press.

Dynarski, S. (2016, April 8). Why talented Black and Hispanic students can go undiscovered. *The New York Times.* Retrieved from https://www.nytimes.com/2016/04/10/upshot/why-talented-black-and-hispanic-students-can-go-undiscovered.html

Garber, M. (2015, April 28). The history of "thug": The surprisingly ancient and global etymology of a racially charged epithet. *Atlantic.* Retrieved from https://www.theatlantic.com/entertainment/archive/2015/04/thug/391682/

Gay, G. (2010). *Culturally responsive teaching: Theory, research, and practice* (2nd ed.), New York, NY: Teachers College.

Gilliam, W., Maupin, A., Reyes, C., Accavitti, M., & Shic, F. (2016). *Do early educators' implicit biases regarding sex and race relate to behavior expectations and recommendations of preschool expulsions and suspensions?* [Research study brief]. Yale University Child Study Center. Retrieved from http://ziglercenter.yale.edu/publications/Preschool%20Implicit%20Bias%20Policy%20Brief_final_9_26_276766_5379_v1.pdf

Glasrud, B. (1977). The crisis of conservative Virginia: The Byrd organization and the politics of massive resistance. (Book Review) *Journal of Southern History, 43*(2), 324–325.

Goldhaber, D., Lavery, L., & Theobald, R. (2015). Uneven playing field? Assessing the teacher quality gap between advantaged and disadvantaged students. *Educational Researcher, 44* (5), 293–307.

Grissom, J. A., & Redding, C. (2016). Discretion and disproportionality: Explaining the underrepresentation of high-achieving students of color in gifted programs. *AERA Open, 2*(1), 1–25.

Hannah-Jones, N. (2017, September 6). The resegregation of Jefferson County: What one Alabama town's attempt to secede from its school district tells us about the fragile progress of racial integration in America. *New York Times Magazine.* Education Issue. Retrieved from https://www.nytimes.com/2017/09/06/magazine/the-resegregation-of-jefferson-county.html

Hawkman, A. M., & Shear, S. B. (2017). Thinking and teaching with theory and Disney music for social studies. In W. Russell, W. & S. Waters (Eds.), *Cinematic social studies: A resource for teaching and learning social studies with film.* Charlotte, NC: Information Age Publishing.

Kendi, I. X. (2017). *Stamped from the beginning: The definitive history of racist ideas in America.* New York, NY: Random House.

Kozol, J. (2006). *The shame of the nation: The restoration of apartheid schooling in America.* New York, NY: Random House.

Kozol, J. (2007). Turning our ideals to concrete deeds. *Journal of Educational Controversy, 2*(1), Article 2.

Ladson-Billings, G. (2006). It's not the culture of poverty, it's the poverty of culture: The problem with teacher education. *Anthropology and Education Quarterly, 37*(2), 104–109.

Ladson-Billings, G. (2014). Culturally relevant pedagogy 2.0: a.k.a. the remix. *Harvard Educational Review, 84*(1), 74–84.

Musu-Gillette, L., de Brey, C., McFarland, J., Hussar, W., Sonnenberg, W., & Wilkinson-Flicker, S (2017). Status and trends in the education of racial and ethnic groups 2017. (NCES 2017-051) U.S. Department of Education. National Center for Education Statistics. Washington, DC. Retrieved from https://nces.ed.gov/pubs2017/2017051.pdf

NAACP Legal Defense and Educational Fund. (2017). *Locked out of the classroom: How implicit bias contributes to disparities in school discipline.* New York, NY. Retrieved from https://www.naacpldf.org/files/about-us/Bias_Reportv2017_30_11_FINAL.pdf

Nellis, A. (2016). *The color of justice: Racial and ethnic disparity in state prisons.* The Sentencing Project: Research and Advocacy for Reform. Washington, DC: The Sentencing Project. Retrieved from https://www.sentencingproject.org/publications/color-of-justice-racial-and-ethnic-disparity-in-state-prisons/

Nelson, L., & Lind, D. (2015). The school to prison pipeline, explained. *Justice Policy Institute News.* Retrieved from http://www.justicepolicy.org/news/8775

Oluo, I. (2018). *So you want to talk about race.* New York, NY: Seal Press.

Orfield, G. (2007). Excerpts from the 2006 report: Racial Transformation and the Changing Nature of Segregation. *Journal of Educational Controversy, 2*(1). Article 3. Retrieved from http://cedar.wwu.edu/jec/vol2/iss1/3

Orfield, G., & Frankenberg, E. (2007). The integration decision what's next for educators, and for society, after the U.S. Supreme Court's ruling? *Education Week, 26*(43), 1–18.

Orfield, G. & Lee, C. (2004). *Brown at 50: King's dream or Plessy's nightmare?* Cambridge, MA: Civil Rights Project, Harvard University.

Pitts, J. (2016). Don't say nothing. Teaching Tolerance. Southern Poverty Law Center. Retrieved from http://www.tolerance.org/magazine/tt54-fall-2016/feature/dont-say-nothing

Poniewozik, J. (2014, August 11). #Iftheygunnedmedown and what hashtag activism does right. *Time.* Retrieved from https://time.com/3101550/iftheygunnedmedown-hashtag-activism -michael-brown-twitter/

Rodgers, M. (2017). The pedagogical role of a white instructor's racial awareness narrative. In T. Kennedy, J. Middleton, & K. Ratcliffe (Eds.), *Rhetorics of whiteness: Postracial hauntings in popular culture, social media, and education.* Carbondale, IL: Southern Illinois University Press.

Roisin, F. (2017, September 14). Why Hollywood's white savior obsession is an extension of colonialism. *Teen Vogue.* Retrieved from https://www.teenvogue.com/story/hollywoods-white -savior-obsession-colonialism

Sadovnik, A. R., Cookson, P. W., Jr., Semel, S. F., & Coughlan, R. W. (2017). *Exploring education: An introduction to the foundations of education.* New York, NY: Routledge.

Scott, R., & Saucedo, M. (2013). Mass incarceration, the school-to-prison-pipeline, and the struggle over "Secure Communities" in Illinois. *Journal of Educational Controversy, 7*(1), Article 7. Retrieved from https://cedar.wwu.edu/jec/vol7/iss1/7

Sensoy, O., & DiAngelo, R. (2017). *Is everyone really equal? An introduction to key concepts in social justice education* (2nd ed.). New York, NY: Teachers College.

Skiba, R. J., Horner, R. H., Chung, C.-G., Rausch, M. K., May, S. L., & Tobin, T. (2011). Race is not neutral: A national investigation of African American and Latino disproportionality in school discipline. *School Psychology Review, 40*(1), 85–107.

Smith, E. J., & Harper, S. R. (2016). *Disproportionate impact of K-12 school suspensions and expulsion on Black students in southern states.* Philadelphia, PA: University of Pennsylvania, Center for the Study of Race and Equity in Education.

St. George, D. (2012, December 13). "School-to-prison pipeline" hearing puts spotlight on student discipline. *Washington Post.* Retrieved from https://www.washingtonpost.com/local /education/school-to-prison-pipeline-hearing-puts-spotlight-on-student-discipline/2012 /12/13/18503286-4524-11e2-9648-a2c323a991d6_story.html

Stowe, S. (2019, February 18). New York to ban discrimination based on hair. *The New York Times.* Retrieved from https://www.nytimes.com/2019/02/18/style/hair-discrimination-new-york-city .html

Tatum, B. D. (2017). *Why are all the Black kids sitting together in the cafeteria? And other conversations about race.* New York, NY: Basic Books.

U.S. Department of Education. (2016). The state of racial diversity in the educator workforce. Policy and Program Studies Service Office of Planning, Evaluation, and Policy Development. Washington, DC Retrieved from https://www2.ed.gov/rschstat/eval/highered/racial-diversity /state-racial-diversity-workforce.pdf

U.S. Department of Education Office for Civil Rights. (2014). Civil rights data collection: Data snapshot: School discipline. Washington, DC: Retrieved from https://ocrdata.ed.gov /downloads/crdc-school-discipline-snapshot.pdf

U.S. Department of Justice, Civil Rights Division. (2014, January 8). *Notice of language assistance: Dear colleague letter on the nondiscrimination of school discipline.* Washington, DC: Retrieved from: https://www2.ed.gov/about/offices/list/ocr/letters/colleague-201401-title-vi.html

SECTION 8

Surveillance, Security, and Crime Control

ARTICLE 33

Introduction to Surveillance, Technology, and Crime Control

Don Hummer

It is not hyperbole to state that our daily actions are currently being watched and monitored more so than at any other time in human history. Our lives are interwoven with technology and are under greater surveillance any time we venture from our homes and are in public spaces. Our movements are captured by cameras and recorded on video, sometimes without our knowledge (e.g., Alexandrie, 2017; Norris & Armstrong, 1998). Corporations and social media networks log our digital movements on the World Wide Web and note our preferences in terms of the material we peruse, the types of media we gravitate toward, and the goods and services we purchase. The Internet-connected devices we depend on daily can quickly provide a full summary of who we've contacted and where we've been. Those in the crime-prone age cohort (~15–29 years old) have the greatest likelihood of being "wired," and by extension have greater amounts of information about their movements and actions on view, even those engaged in criminal activity. All of this begs two key questions: (1) Does increased surveillance and monitoring make society safer by preventing crime? (2) Is it possible we've traded individual privacies for an illusion of crime reduction or, in a worst-case scenario, made ourselves more vulnerable to victimization as personal privacy has eroded?

Any examination of the interplay between technology and crime must consider both the pros and cons that emerging technologies bring to the table. There may be no greater aid to criminal investigators than perpetrators who document their actions and leave a digital footprint. Such evidence in a court of law carries weight equivalent to forensic evidence and is markedly better than eyewitness testimony. Therefore, a strong argument can be made that technology likely prevents criminal incidents as well as facilitates convictions of perpetrators who commit crimes. Technological innovations are also demonstrating new methods to assess the extent of criminal activity in specific areas. Analyses of social media posts on crime and disorder may provide a more valid assessment of the true prevalence of criminal acts than traditional crime measures (Williams, Burnap, & Sloan, 2017). When considered this way, it is no wonder the benefits of technology in the criminal justice system have been so eagerly discussed and new technologies employed. But there are downsides, and these are being realized as these new technologies come online and problems arise. Privacy issues are continuously litigated in the United States and around the globe, with the balance of power in terms of information control resting with the private sector. Currently, if individuals voluntarily provide personal, identifying information and agree to the terms of use of a digital platform, they have little recourse if their information is used in a manner that was unanticipated.

▶ The Criminal Justice System and Technology

One is hard-pressed to name a human services field that is more invested in and enamored with technology than the justice system. Throughout their rapid 20th-century growth, criminal justice agencies embraced technological advancements and employed them, even when little or no evidence was available on their effectiveness or unanticipated consequences (Marx, 1995, 2007). What has emerged is a "crime prevention" industry within which the justice system itself is but one major player. Law enforcement at all levels relies on outside entities (such as the U.S. Department of Defense and private companies such as Axon) to develop tools that can be adapted to everyday use by officers (Hummer, 2007; Hummer & Byrne, 2017). The key unanswered question is whether these advances actually help *prevent* crime, or do they simply facilitate detection and investigation of crimes that occur? Although it is impossible to state how much crime is actually prevented with any validity, it seems safe to conclude that crime prevention strategies deter some portion of potential criminal incidents in specific contexts (e.g., Chalfin & McCrary, 2017; Lim, Kim, Eck, & Kim, 2016; Lim & Wilcox, 2017; Welsh, Farrington, & Taheri, 2015; Wo, 2018). It is also difficult from a cost–benefit standpoint to determine if the fiscal expenditures on "hard" technology—such as closed-circuit television (CCTV) cameras, body-worn cameras, and less-than-lethal weaponry—or "soft" technology—such as "big data" and predictive analytics, record-management systems, and large-scale data storage—are the best use of public-sector funds.

If we believe that more traditional crime prevention strategies such as crime prevention through environmental design and saturation patrol are effective at preventing criminal acts, then it is certainly possible that new technologies enhance effectiveness. For example, urban planning to reduce crime in business districts may be enhanced with CCTV cameras (Han, Morcol, Hummer, & Peterson, 2017). Also, targeted patrol can be significantly aided by automatic vehicle-location systems that direct patrol units to known high crime locations (Weisburd et al., 2015). Further, a fundamental aspect of deterrence theory is the certainty of punishment or, conversely worded, the likelihood of getting caught. Technology can significantly increase both the real and perceived chances of observation and police intervention if someone commits a crime (Parveen, 2017), therefore changing the decision-making calculus of the potential offender. Lastly, large-scale data collection from police activities (responses to calls for service, arrests, traffic stops, miscellaneous contacts with citizens) can provide the basis for police to anticipate criminality in specific places at specific times (Mastrobuoni, 2014). Such predictive policing is not new—to be sure, there was ample opportunity for the 19th-century London bobbies to be "predictive" when they began an evening's watch. However, the growth of information technology and the ease of data collection, storage, and sharing has ushered in an era in policing specifically, and criminal justice generally, in which organizational strategies and initiatives are data driven and based less on theoretical or logical reasoning (see Brayne, 2017; Chan & Moses, 2015; Sanders, Weston, & Schott, 2015).

▶ Surveillance, Privacy, and Individual Liberties

The propensity toward embracing new technologies in criminal justice is perhaps rooted in how ubiquitous technology is in humans' everyday lives and the desire to "do something" systemically about problems that have proven trenchant. Even though it may be argued that many crime and justice issues are societal problems that the justice system is helpless to address (Stewart, Smith, Stewart, & Fullwood, 1994), given the context within which the system must operate, ideas and strategies incorporating new technologies are typically received enthusiastically. For example, in the early 1980s, the electronic monitoring of offenders under community supervision was a novel idea and used in few jurisdictions nationally in the United States. By 1989, electronic monitoring was in place in 33 states (Corbett & Marx, 1991), and today this is a primary means of offender control in noncarceral settings. By numerous measures, electronic monitoring would be labeled a wholesale success given the system's ability to provide greater supervision for more offenders at lower cost than if that supervision were performed by an increased number of probation or parole officers. However, any time the criminal justice system is able to accommodate more offenders, there is the risk of systemic net widening and that offenders now being brought into the system do not represent the entire offending population. Those new offenders brought into the system, in turn, will be subjected to increased levels of supervision and control.

Decades ago, critics of technological expansion and the "new surveillance" observed that American society was moving *toward* the curtailing of freedoms and privacy and away from constitutionally guaranteed liberties (Corbett & Marx, 1991; Marx, 1981). It's curious that American citizens, who for centuries have held dear to the premise of individual freedom, liberty, and democratic traditions, seem generally unconcerned about increased obtrusiveness from the justice system as facilitated by technology. More to the point, people globally are willing participants in their own surveillance via their digital footprints. Social media platforms (Facebook and Instagram, among others) have become rich sources of information for police investigators because people have increasingly made available images, textual comments, contact information, and links to friends and associates (Rice & Parkin, 2016).

From a positive slant, social media also have the potential to become the 21st century's vehicle for fostering positive relations in a manner similar to how police departments reinvigorated foot patrols for the same purpose (Hummer & Byrne, 2017). As individuals change their information-gathering practices more toward mobile, Web-based platforms, it has become imperative for law enforcement to connect with this demographic through its preferred method, either proactively or in a supervisory or investigatory fashion (Hummer & Byrne, 2017). As media consumption becomes predominantly digital and emanates from social media, criminologists and justice system actors will also need to ascertain the impact of this form of information gathering on how people view their own world. Some evidence demonstrates that social media consumption—in addition to the traditional predictors of age, sex, race, and residential area—are significantly associated with increasing fear of crime (Intravia, Wolff, Paez, & Gibbs, 2017). In addition, some evidence suggests that collective discontent shared via social media platforms can have an effect on criminal incidents, particularly in communities where that anger is felt most strongly, even when those communities are geographically distant from one another or the locus of an initiating incident (e.g., Pyrooz, Decker, Wolfe, & Shjarback, 2016).

Similarly, Internet-connected or "smart" devices have become useful tools for the justice system to ascertain an individual's movements and develop a timeline of their activities. These devices contain a user's activities, actions, words, and biostatistics (Kitchen, 2017). Privacy laws surrounding the ownership of such megadata have resulted in agencies essentially bypassing individuals and going straight to network and corporate entities that store information for access during an investigation (Kitchen, 2017). This places a large amount of power into the hands of companies such as Apple, Amazon, and Google because justice system investigations necessarily depend on the cooperation or expertise of those working for these entities. Currently, surveillance laws are nebulous when it comes to encrypted data stored privately (Finklea, 2016). The ramifications are fairly clear: These devices have grown exponentially more popular in a short amount of time because of the convenience users experience in requesting information, streaming music, ordering goods, or initiating home-security measures. This ease of use seems to override privacy concerns and is chalked up as part of living a "tech lifestyle." Few people give much consideration to what happens to the massive amount of data accumulated by corporate entities via Internet-connected devices, who has access to that information, how that information might be used, or the ramifications of that data being accessed by external actors.

▶ Technology and Victimization

The range of offenses that can be perpetrated virtually is almost as extensive as those that occur offline. Although identity theft, fraud, and cyberbullying and cyberstalking get a majority of the attention in cybercrime discussions, the Internet has broadened the definition of what must be protected via "guardianship." New applications simply extend the available platform for cybercriminality and expand the scope of victimizers to a global context (Saunders, 2017; Wright, 2017). Growing incident counts have demonstrated that no individual, organization, corporation, or government is immune from hacking and cyberaggression. It is becoming extremely difficult if not impossible for average citizens to maintain control over their personal information. Our banking and credit information, medical records, addresses and contact numbers, information about our property ownership, and social involvement all reside in cyberspace and are vulnerable to attack. Recently in the United States, hospitals, major hotel chains, and big-box retailers—just to give a few major examples—have been impacted by cyberactors. What is perhaps most troubling to individuals is the overall sense of helplessness when an attack occurs on an entity that has access to or has stored their personal information. Citizens can be diligent in changing passwords regularly, avoiding phishing scams, and protecting personal identification numbers, but hackers see a greater rate of return in large targets with extensive data stores.

Although fear is justifiable when doing everyday tasks such as opening emails, creating an online account through a health-care provider, or paying for gas at the pump with a credit card, that fear may be disproportionate to the threat. It is certainly true that financial losses from cybercrime are increasing substantially—to as much as $2 trillion in 2019 (Morgan, 2016). However, some observers contend that perceptions of the most feared threats, such as cyberterrorism or a crippling attack on digital infrastructure, may be significantly overblown (Bowman-Grieve, 2015; Kenney, 2015). Apart from crimes committed for financial motivation, governments, criminal organizations, and terrorist groups use the Internet—more often than not, illegitimately—to influence, recruit new followers, or initiate campaigns of disinformation. The highest-profile example of the latter perhaps being Russian interference in the 2016 U.S. presidential election (Ziegler, 2018), acts that may have violated international law (Ohlin, 2017). However, the types of threats and frequency are increasing on an annual basis and require innovative threat assessments to prevent attacks and mitigate damage from attacks that have occurred. The number of Internet-connected devices in existence necessarily makes systems more complex. As system complexity increases, so does threat vulnerability (Tounsi & Rais, 2018). The interdependence of the public sector on corporations is evidenced again when examining cybervictimization prevention. Although many of the tools for combating attacks on government servers and data are coordinated by the state, protections for individual consumers, at least in the United States, emanate predominantly from the private sector. These partnerships—and, most crucially, information sharing— must continue to evolve and receive financial support from a variety of sources as threat matrices expand.

▶ Conclusion

Advances in technology are not a panacea for the pervasive issues that must be addressed by the justice system, nor are innovations problem free. Each time a new technology is employed in the field, a set of unforeseen confounds inevitably arise that will need to be solved before that new technology is used to its full potential (Byrne & Marx, 2011). Like any tool in an arsenal, technology has appropriate uses, and the vast majority of those utilizations are extremely task specific. Perhaps the greatest danger new technologies face is the potential to oversell their benefits. Some of the applications discussed in this article walk a fine line toward realizing true benefits and promising outcomes that may not be delivered. Any crime prevention measure runs this risk given the inherent difficulties in demonstrating sustained effectiveness (Sherman, Gottfredson, MacKenzie, Reuter, & Bushway, 1998). Those who implement policy must identify and explicitly state the expectations for any new technology in the justice system and realistically present what the technology will accomplish along with possible consequences. This prevents setting an initiative up for failure even before it is fully launched because it is not being ascribed capabilities it cannot attain.

It cannot be argued that technology has changed—in some cases radically—the workings of the criminal justice system. Gunshot detection, CCTV, and electronic monitoring of offenders (to name a few examples) provide surveillance that could not be achieved by even doubling the number of personnel working in criminal justice agencies. However, the crime prevention capabilities of technology have a maximum capacity. These innovations do little to address the fundamental criminogenic macrostructural factors in society that cause criminal or deviant behavior. Whether one adheres to a criminological viewpoint that emphasizes structural inequality, degraded collective efficacy, or biological factors as the primary force driving criminal behavior is immaterial. Technology necessarily cannot impact these issues, so focusing resources on new technologies continues the legacy of a reactionary justice system and perhaps undermines efforts to address "root causes." The criminal justice system will always need to investigate, adjudicate, and sanction criminal offenses. Technology is a fundamental component of this effort and holds the most promise for potentially deterring crime, helping to ensure the safety of justice system personnel and suspects, and easing some of the burden on those working in the justice system. Progressing through the 21st century, the system needs to take advantage of these benefits while recognizing the limitations, drawbacks, and privacy threats inherent in new technologies and being proactive in response to problems that arise. This is achieved via independent evaluation of strategies and a willingness to revisit policy decisions when necessary, even if the political ramifications are unpopular. Concurrently, policy makers, criminologists, and the general public must continue efforts toward better understanding the etiology of offending and proffering solutions that lessen reliance on technology as a means of social control.

▶ References

Alexandrie, G. (2017). Surveillance cameras and crime: A review of randomized and natural experiments. *Journal of Scandinavian Studies in Criminology and Crime Prevention, 18*(2), 210–222. https://doi.org/10.1080/14043858.2017.1387410

Bowman-Grieve, L. (2015). Cyberterrorism and moral panics: a reflection on the discourse of cyberterrorism. In L. Jarvis, S. MacDonald, & T. Chen (Eds) *Terrorism online*. London, UK: Routledge.

Brayne, S. (2017). Big data surveillance: The case of policing. *American Sociological Review, 82*(5), 977–1008. https://doi.org/10.1177/0003122417725865

Byrne, J. M., & Marx, G. T. (2011). Technological innovations in crime prevention and policing: A review of the research on implementation and impact. *Journal of Police Studies, 3*, 17–40. Retrieved from https://www.ncjrs.gov/pdffiles1/nij/238011.pdf

Chalfin, A., & McCrary, J. (2017). Criminal deterrence: A review of the literature. *Journal of Economic Literature, 55*(1), 5–48. Retrieved from https://doi.org/10.1257/jel.20141147

Chan, J., & Moses, L. B. (2015). Is big data challenging criminology? *Theoretical Criminology, 20*(1), 21–39. https://doi.org/10.1177/1362480615586614

Corbett, R., & Marx, G. T. (1991). Critique: No soul in the new machine: Technofallacies in the electronic monitoring movement. *Justice Quarterly, 8*(3), 399–414. https://doi.org/10.1080/07418829100091111

Finklea, K. (2016). *Encryption and evolving technology: Implications for U.S. law enforcement investigations*. Washington, DC: Congressional Research Service. Retrieved from http://www.a51.nl/sites/default/files/pdf/R44187%20(1).pdf

Han, S., Morcol, G., Hummer, D., & Peterson, S.A. (2017). The effects of business improvement districts on property and nuisance crimes: Evidence from Philadelphia. *Journal of Urban Affairs 39*(5), 658–674. Retrieved from https://doi.org/10.1080/07352166.2016.1262691

Hummer, D. (2007). Policing and "hard" technology. In J. M. Byrne & D. J. Rebovich (Eds.), *The new technology of crime, law and social control.* Monsey, NY: Criminal Justice Press.

Hummer, D., & Byrne, J. M. (2017). Technology, innovation, and 21st century policing. In M. R. McGuire & T. J. Holt (Eds.), *The Routledge Handbook of Technology, Crime and Justice.* New York: Routledge, Taylor & Francis Group.

Intravia, J., Wolff, K. T., Paez, R., & Gibbs, B. R. (2017). Investigating the relationship between social media consumption and fear of crime: A partial analysis of mostly young adults. *Computers in Human Behavior, 77,* 158–168. Retrieved from https://doi.org/10.1016/j.chb.2017.08.047

Kenney, M. (2015). Cyber-terrorism in a post-Stuxnet world. *Orbis, 59*(1), 111–128. https://doi .org/10.1016/j.orbis.2014.11.009

Kitchen, A. N. (2017). Smart devices and criminal investigations: Protecting suspects' privacy and Fourth Amendment rights. *Criminal Law Bulletin, 54.* Retrieved from https://papers.ssrn .com/sol3/papers.cfm?abstract_id=3028119

Lim, H., Kim, C., Eck, J., & Kim, J. (2016). The crime-reduction effects of open-street CCTV in South Korea. *Security Journal, 29*(2), 241–255. Retrieved from https://doi.org/10.1057/sj.2013.10

Lim, H., & Wilcox, P. (2017). Crime-reduction effects of open-street CCTV: Conditionality considerations, *Justice Quarterly, 34*(4), 597–626. Retrieved from https://doi.org/10.1080/074 18825.2016.1194449

Marx, G. T. (1981). Ironies of social control: Authorities as contributors to deviance through escalation, nonenforcement and covert facilitation. *Social Problems 28*(3)221–246. Retrieved from https://doi.org/10.2307/800300

Marx, G. T. (1995). The engineering of social control: The search for the silver bullet. In J. Hagan & R. D. Peterson (Eds.) *Crime and inequality.* Palo Alto, CA: Stanford University Press.

Marx, G. T. (2007). The engineering of social control: Intended and unintended consequences. In J. M. Byrne & D. J. Rebovich (Eds.), *The new technology of crime, law and social control.* Monsey, NY: Criminal Justice Press.

Mastrobuoni, G. (2014). Crime is terribly revealing: Information technology and police productivity. Unpublished manuscript. Retrieved from http://www.hec.unil.ch/documents/seminars/deep /1587.pdf

Morgan, S. (2016). Cybercrime costs projected to reach $2 trillion by 2019. *Forbes.* Retrieved from http://www.forbes.com/sites/stevemorgan/2016/01/17/cyber-crime-costs-projected-to-reach -2-trillion-by-2019/

Norris, C., & Armstrong, G. (1998). Introduction: Power and vision. In C. Norris, J. Moran, & G. Armstrong (Eds.), *Surveillance, closed circuit television and social control.* Farnham, UK: Ashgate.

Ohlin, J. D. (2017). Did Russian cyber interference in the 2016 election violate international law? *Texas Law Review 95,* 1579–1598. Retrieved from https://scholarship.law.cornell.edu/cgi /viewcontent.cgi?article=2632&context=facpub

Parveen, R. (2017). Policing in India: Technology and crime prevention. *Social Science and Humanities Journal, 1*(2), 132–143. Retrieved from http://sshj.in/index.php/sshj/article /view/23/18

Pyrooz, D. C., Decker, S. H., Wolfe, S. E., & Shjarback, J. A. (2016). Was there a Ferguson Effect on crime rates in large U.S. cities? *Journal of Criminal Justice, 46,* 1–8. Retrieved from https://doi .org/10.1016/j.jcrimjus.2016.01.001

Rice, S. K., & Parkin, W. S. (2016). Social media and law enforcement investigations. Oxford Handbooks Online Scholarly Research Review. Retrieved from https://doi.org/10.1093 /oxfordhb/9780199935383.013.98

Sanders, C. B., Weston, C., & Schott, N. (2015). Police innovations, "secret squirrels" and accountability: Empirically studying intelligence-led policing in Canada. *British Journal of Criminology, 55*(4), 711–729. Retrieved from https://doi.org/10.1093/bjc/azv008

Saunders, J. (2017). Tackling cybercrime—The UK response. *Journal of Cyber Policy, 2*(1), 4–15. Retrieved from https://www.tandfonline.com/doi/abs/10.1080/23738871.2017.1293117

Sherman, L. W., Gottfredson D. C., MacKenzie D., Reuter P., & Bushway S. (1998). *Preventing crime: What works, what doesn't, what's promising.* Washington, DC: National Institute of Justice.

Stewart, J., Smith, D., Stewart, G., & Fullwood, C. (1994). *Understanding offending behaviour.* London, UK: Routledge.

Tounsi, W., & Rais, H. (2018). A survey on technical threat intelligence in the age of sophisticated cyber attacks. *Computers & Security, 72,* 212–233. Retrieved from https://doi.org/10.1016/j .cose.2017.09.001

Weisburd, D., Groff, E. R., Jones, G., Cave, B., Amendola, K. L., Yang, S. M., & Emison, R. F. (2015). The Dallas patrol management experiment: Can AVL technologies be used to harness unallocated patrol time for crime prevention? *Journal of Experimental Criminology, 11*(3), 367–391. Retrieved from https://doi.org/10.1007/s11292-015-9234-y

Welsh, B. C., Farrington, D. P., & Taheri, S.A. (2015). Effectiveness and social costs of public area surveillance for crime prevention. *Annual Review of Law and Social Science, 11*(1), 111–130. Retrieved from https://doi.org/10.1146/annurev-lawsocsci-120814-121649

Williams, M. L., Burnap, P., & Sloan, L. (2017). Crime sensing with big data: The affordances and limitations of using open-source communications to estimate crime patterns. *British Journal of Criminology, 57*(2), 320–340. Retrieved from https://doi.org/10.1093/bjc/azw031

Wo, J. C. (2018). Revisiting the crime control benefits of voluntary organizations: Organizational presence, organizational capacity, and crime rates in Los Angeles neighborhoods. *Crime & Delinquency.* Retrieved from https://doi.org/10.1177/0011128718787517

Wright, S. (2017). Mythology of cyber-crime—Insecurity & governance in cyberspace: Some critical perspectives. In J. Ramírez & L. García-Segura (Eds.), *Cyberspace: Risks and benefits for society, security and development.* Cham, Switzerland: Springer.

Ziegler, C. E. (2018). International dimensions of electoral processes: Russia, the USA, and the 2016 elections. *International Politics, 55*(5), 557–574. Retrieved from https://doi.org/10.1057 /s41311-017-0113-1

© Sergii Gnatiuk/Shutterstock

Studying Surveillance and Tech Through "Digital Punishment"

Dr. Sarah Lageson

Imagine getting arrested one time and for a minor misunderstanding. Perhaps you were hanging out with a group of students at a party and two people begin to fight. Maybe someone else calls the police and an entire group of you are arrested and taken down to the police station for booking. You are searched, fingerprinted, and your photo is taken by the jail staff.

A few hours later, though, you are released. Everything has calmed down, and the local prosecutor won't be pressing any charges. You go home, a bit shaken up, but otherwise OK. As time goes on, you forget the incident ever happened.

After graduation, you begin to apply for jobs but don't have much luck. At this point, you're also looking for a new apartment, but landlords aren't returning your phone calls. What's worse, you've moved to a new city and are trying your luck with online dating. Unfortunately, though, your new potential dates keep canceling right before you are supposed to meet up. As you sort through all this apparent bad luck, a friend recommends that you search for yourself on Google.

And there it is—the first search result. Your booking photo, your "mugshot," taken back in college the night you were arrested and briefly held in jail. Besides the photo, your full name and date of birth are posted on the Web site. What's worse, the caption underneath the mugshot says you were arrested for "assault and battery." To make things even more confusing, the photo and your personal information appear on dozens of other Web sites. You try to figure out how to have the posts removed, but most Web sites don't offer any information on who to talk to, and those that do demand that you pay hundreds or even thousands of dollars to have the mugshot taken down. You don't know where to turn—and now you suspect this is why the jobs, apartments, and dates aren't working out. You even call the police station, but they tell you there's nothing they can do to help. You send an email to Google, asking for your search results to be changed, but the company autoreply informs you that it can't change the content of Web sites. You'll have to go back to the owner of the Web site to plead your case. What do you do now?

This is a serious reality for the millions of people who are arrested in the United States every year, many of whom are neither charged nor convicted of a crime. Because things such as arrest records, booking photos, and court documents are considered public records in most states, it's completely legal for media entities, Web sites, and private citizens to make copies and release these records freely.

As a researcher, I had long been interested in studying the collateral consequences of contact with the criminal justice system, particularly what we might call "low-level" contact such as an arrest that never led to charges. For instance, I conducted studies with my colleagues Chris Uggen, Mike Vuolo, and Ebony Ruhland on the impact of nonconviction records on employment opportunities, finding that even these "minor brushes" with the system had consequences for individuals, often because of the stigma attached to a "criminal record."

However, digital technologies were rapidly changing how these interactions with the system were being documented. Increasingly, people who were arrested also automatically became part of a database, their fingerprints and photographs cataloged into massive sets of data that were of interest to a lot of parties within the criminal justice system (such as a judge who is setting bail and relies on a criminal history report) as well as outside the criminal justice system (such as commercial background-check companies). This proliferation of data was beginning to create massive webs of surveillance of people who were now officially deemed suspicious. In turn, having a digital mark created and justified more opportunities down the road for a person to be stopped, arrested, or added to another database.

Because criminal justice is a governmental operation, however, these digital records were also becoming increasingly public. And, of course, advances in digital technology have rapidly increased the spread of this information. Law enforcement and court records used to exist in paper-based filing cabinets, but this is no longer the case. Now that records are packaged digitally, they are duplicated and posted at the speed of light. Many laws allow for this; for instance, the Freedom of Information Act allows people to access government records, including criminal justice records. The Communications Decency Act allows Google to claim it doesn't have any power to control what sorts of things appear on Web sites because the company is simply a search platform. The First Amendment allows Web sites to post these public records as acts of free speech.

I first learned about the harms of online criminal records while conducting fieldwork at criminal-record expungement clinics. As I dug deeper into the various fields that constitute the world of online records, I began to call this phenomenon *digital punishment* to describe how the Internet has been a major game changer in how criminal records and stigma attach to people in the digital era. Clearly, these records that used to exist in "practical obscurity" now existed all over the Internet, becoming a Pandora's box.

Once I dug in, I realized that digital transformation has seriously affected an accused person in every stage of the criminal justice system. Take, for instance, this interview with Jaci, a woman who was seeking legal aid to explore her options for expunging her criminal record. Jaci was hoping to volunteer at her daughter's school, but her online record prevented her from doing so:

> They seen me on this thing called "Mugshots." And I actually seen myself, and it's pretty embarrassing. I got probably like five Facebook messages. They were like, "Dude, you're on Mugshots." I went and looked it up and seen myself. I was really pretty sure it has to do with like, online access, people exposing other people. . . . I would like to volunteer at my daughter's school but I am not allowed to because of the background check. They give you a list of what you're not supposed to have on your background. So I'm like, "Well I can't do that." And it's kinda hard telling that to your daughter, "I can't volunteer today." She knows I'm working a lot so I just let her think that's why. I haven't talked to other parents. I kinda keep my background to myself, because I don't want people to know or to get into a conversation like, "Oh, what happened?"

In this way, I realized that the ubiquity of online records produced a particular type of surveillance and social control. First, people like Jaci don't know where or when their record might "pop up" on the Internet. Further, because Web sites that repost records are not regulated, the information is often incorrect or outdated. This adds to the anxiety of people like Jaci, who aren't sure how to navigate their new digital stigma. Person after person I talked to who was dealing with online records described a similar set of social, professional, and psychological harms.

Take Shana, for example, who discovered her mugshot online after she was arrested once after being caught up in a hectic scene at a local bar. Her charges were dismissed, but her booking photo continued to haunt her. "It is rather devastating. It is public shaming. 'Embarrassment' is an understatement," she told me. "There is a sense of paranoia and fear of who might search your name and see the trail of tabloid sites. These thoughts are a daily thing now. It is beyond horrible."

I recognized patterns across interviewees in that people were often "opting out" of institutional contexts that might trigger a Google search. This meant they were often stuck in employment, housing, or social situations that were less than ideal— but trying to change their circumstances might reveal their online record. This is how digital punishment brought forth by technological changes translates into surveillance and social control, by which people feel they can never escape their digital stigma. So they change their real-life behavior instead.

I have found ways to transform my research into advocacy for better privacy rights for people who have interacted with the criminal justice system, though there is still much work to be done. Efforts are underway to reclassify local criminal justice records, especially booking photos and preconviction records, as private data (much like how the identities of juvenile arrestees and victims are obscured from public view). A movement is growing to hold search engines such as Google more accountable for allowing Web sites to profit from reposting public records through manipulating Internet search results. In Europe, citizens now have the "right to be forgotten," which means they can legally petition Google to remove search results that reveal old criminal records, giving individuals a bit more power over their online identities—and there's some hope similar legislation might someday make it to the United States.

In the meantime, however, researchers and advocates need to closely watch how digital technologies are transforming our fundamental knowledge about law and ethics. Key postconviction remedies such as exonerations, appeals, and expungements are increasingly ineffective in a digital society that "never forgets." Courts are rapidly turning toward algorithmic risk assessments to determine bail amounts and recidivism risks without careful assessment of the various data inputs of such tools, especially those that exacerbate race and class disparities but are justified by big data. Lawyers must now understand that their clients might face a lifetime of Internet stigma and shaming, even if they win in the courtroom. Finally, researchers must understand the mechanics of technological interventions to truly understand how our systems of justice operate today. The learning curve might seem steep, but this will be a valuable—perhaps essential—skill to develop within the legal system.

U.S. Ethical Issues and Considerations as They Relate to Immigration

John J. Rodríguez
Frank A. Rodriguez
Vivian Dorsett
Arthur Vasquez

▶ Ethical Issues and Immigration

Part of the problem of racism in the United States is that it has been predominately a Black and White dialog (Rodriguez, 2008). As a society, the United States has failed to recognize other marginalized groups such as Hispanics, Asians, members of the LGBTQ community, and immigrants to name a few (Rodriguez & Belshaw, 2010). More recently, immigrants as a marginalized group have come to the national platform in terms of questionable ethical practices.

The 2016 presidential election reintroduced the immigration debate as to whether crime and immigration are correlated—more specifically, do illegal immigrants commit more crime than native-born citizens? Although this issue has been researched and previously debated, it is an excellent example of an ideologically rooted ethical dilemma that should be investigated through objective data analysis rather than subjective data analysis. Consequently, many methodological challenges make the study of ethics and immigration difficult. One step to conduct research into ethics and immigration is to identify any bias or preconceptions. For example, people who favor a strict approach to reducing the number of immigrants here without authorization may be more likely to believe that so-called illegal immigrants are more likely than native-born Americans to be criminals. Advocates for such undocumented immigrants do not believe that they have higher crime rates than native-born Americans. Some interest groups publish reports that need to be evaluated with potential biases in mind. Academics are not immune from personal biases, so looking at their findings from an ethical standpoint is important. To help resolve this dilemma, data need to be triangulated to be objectively analyzed. To triangulate data, it must be collected from more than one source to see how consistent or inconsistent they may be.

The immigration debate has been a fixture in the news media for decades, and policy makers are attuned to increased public consciousness and awareness. This was heightened after the terrorist attacks of September 11, 2001 (9/11), which raised questions about potential flaws in how foreign-born citizens enter the United States. This debate led to various changes in the organizational configuration of the federal enforcement agencies. This led to routine concerns among policy makers regarding security at the border. The increased attention to border security and 9/11 threats was eventually merged with the consistent concerns related to illegal immigration. These two concerns were (1) about potential terrorists coming through the "weak" border and (2) the inflow of Mexican immigrants looking for work by coming through the southern border of the United States. Both concerns fueled the enactment of numerous state and federal policies and a renewed interest in having local and state law enforcement agencies help the federal government enforce federal statutes.

Could the increased concern over undocumented immigrants be related to a bias against just the Hispanic population? The question continues to be relevant as issues of race and justice are being tested again as the Hispanic population expands. The question is whether or not there is an ethical dilemma associated with immigration. However, one could argue that this dilemma of immigration is only important now because of both legal and illegal Hispanic immigration. In fact, Hispanics have now become the largest minority group in the United States, overtaking African Americans (Urbina, 2012). In addition, Hispanics are overrepresented in prisons and are often incarcerated for rather minor, nonviolent offenses. Hispanics in the criminal justice system are also reported to be less likely than other racial and ethnic groups to receive rehabilitative services such as treatment programs for addictions. It is likely that, as this population continues to grow, it will continue to flex its political muscle. These concerns and issues have a major impact on immigrants, both legal and undocumented.

▶ Immigration and Public Attitudes

In recent opinion polls, the public consistently indicated that it is concerned with illegal immigration. In 2015, a survey found that 50% of people thought that immigrants made the economy worse, 28% of people thought that immigrants made economy better, and 20% thought there was little difference either way. The same survey also found that 50% of Americans thought that immigrants had made the crime issue worse as compared to only 7% of people who thought that immigrants made crime conditions better. When science and technology were included in the survey, 29% thought that immigration helped to make the United States better, and only 12% thought that immigrants made science and technology worse. The survey also found that 50% thought that immigrants helped make America better as it relates to music, food, and the arts, whereas 11% thought that the immigrants made America worse (Pew Research Center, 2015).

▶ Immigration Laws and Ethics in the United States

The United States of America is known as a nation of laws. Some individuals believe laws are created to help control human behavior. Many Americans, however, may believe that our government itself has not always had ethical laws and policies, and there are some questionable ones to say the least. For example, consider the laws of slavery. For more than 200 years, entire families were sold and separated—according to the prevailing law of the land. Today's immigration laws and policies affect not only undocumented individuals but also entire families and their U.S.-born children (Rodriguez, Dorsett, & Rodriguez, 2018; Wolff, Intravia, Baglivio, & Piquero, 2015).

States such as Arizona, California, and Texas have long had influxes of Hispanic immigrants, and these states have responded with policies and laws that have affected these immigrant families for generations, many of them highly restrictive. Arizona, for example, has laws in place that explicitly bar students who are undocumented from attending college with in-state tuition, even if the student has been living in Arizona for several years (Androff, Ayón, Becerra, & Gurrola, 2011). On the other hand, the California Department of Social Services has established a Latino Practice Advisory Committee made of national and state specialists to simplify culturally responsive services among county child-welfare systems (Dettlaff, 2015).

In Texas, Governor Greg Abbott has requested additional U.S. Customs and Border Patrol agents and five supplementary aviation assets from the federal government, and the Texas Department of Public Safety is requesting more than $300 million above an already existing security budget of $750 million. A subsidy has also been requested to double the already 500 state troopers posted along the Rio Grande River on Texas' southern border (Ward, 2016).

Many Americans believe that immigrants commit more crime than U.S. born-citizens, and this myth is a big reason for increased border enforcement and stricter deportation policies (Hagan, Levi, & Dinovitzer, 2008; McCarthy, 2015; Sampson, 2008). This false perception about immigrants being criminal threats may come largely from the way immigrants are portrayed in television shows, movies, and the daily news (Rumbaut & Ewing, 2007). As such, this document will use the term *undocumented* and not *illegal* or *alien* when referring to immigrants residing in the United States without legal permanent residency or citizenship. Destructive terms such as *illegal* and *alien* underpin a frame of criminalization. These terms are popular with individuals who may not know the difference, including many U.S. politicians (Rodriguez & Dawkins, 2016).

Research conducted by Rodriguez (2013) declared that many undocumented, undetected, and unaccompanied immigrant youth are not perpetrators of crime but are instead victims of crime as soon as they set foot on U.S. soil. Nevertheless, numerous researchers over the last several years, including Bersani, Loughran, and Piquero (2014); Kubrin and Desmond (2015); Martinez, Stowell, and Lee (2010); Rodriguez and Dawkins (2016); and Rodriguez, Pirtle, and Henderson (2008); and Sampson (2018) and Wolff et al. (2015) have discovered that immigrants are not responsible for violence and crime and in many instances are inversely related to crime. This confirms that immigrant communities have less crime than places with fewer immigrant residents.

Wolff et al.'s innovative 2015 study found that immigrant communities may protect youths from reoffending by the presence of a healthy family, the likelihood of lower familial incarceration, and strong prosocial ties to members in the community that provide a more supportive environment for immigrant youth to desist. Therefore, it is vital to keep families together when possible.

▶ Hispanic Immigrant Children

Hispanic children make up the largest and fastest-growing ethnic immigrant youth population in the United States (Dettlaff, 2015; Dettlaff & Johnson, 2011). These children now make up 25% of our country's 75 million children, and they are projected to make up 33.3 million of the estimated 100 million children in the country by 2050 (Passel, 2011). The Annie E. Casey Foundation (2018) is a leading organization in foster care and a premier center of facts on families and children. In one project titled "Kids COUNT," the foundation determined that more than 16 million children live in immigrant households, and 90% of these children are U.S.-born citizens as Hispanic immigrants make up the largest populations. There are approximately 2.3 million mixed-status families, which simply means that a family member is a permanent legal resident, undocumented, or in legal limbo. The last category includes recipients designated of Temporary Protected Status or Deferred Action for Childhood Arrivals (Castañeda & Melo, 2014; Passel, 2011).

▶ Immigration Experiences

Emigrating from a Latin American country to the United States can be a life-threatening experience, especially for young women and children. Many of these immigrants have already experienced some type of violence, sexual assault, or robbery in their home countries and when they leave their own countries (Dawkins & Rodriguez, 2016; Gulbas & Zayas, 2017; Leyro, 2017; Rodriguez, 2013; Rodriguez, Dorsett, & Rodriguez, 2018). Migration can result in parents being separated from their children and other family members for long periods of time (Dawkins & Rodriguez, 2016; Gulbas & Zayas, 2017; Leyro, 2017; Rodriguez, 2013; Rodriguez & Dawkins, 2016). Many migrating women and children experience significant trauma during their trips to the United States and will develop anxiety disorders, including posttraumatic stress disorder (Smart & Smart, 1995; Weber 2015). To this end, why do we as a nation continue to exacerbate the victimization of immigrants through our laws?

▶ Social Services

Note that not all American states offer welfare assistance to undocumented immigrants. Immigration status is determined at the federal level, but state-level policies and practices vary from state to state. In fact, states determine whether immigrants will be allowed access to public services and benefits (Philbin, Flake, Hatzenbuehler, & Hirsch, 2018). Some of the services that are not available to noncitizens include public housing, Medicaid, and income assistance, and both state- and municipal-level governments have mixed policies for such benefits (Finno-Velasquez, 2013). Also, immigrant families and their children are likely to not have insurance, to have fair or even bad health, and are still unlikely to receive public benefits (Capps, Fix, Ost, Reardon-Anderson, & Passel, 2005; Dettlaff & Earner, 2012).

As mentioned, Hispanics constitute the fastest-growing ethnic population in the United States, yet Hispanic immigrant families use public and community services far less than U.S.-born citizens because of language barriers and help-seeking behavior (Ayón & Aisenberg, 2010; Dettlaff, 2015; Finno-Velasquez, 2013). In today's United States, more than 4 million children of undocumented immigrants are not allowed the benefits of U.S. citizens (Zayas, 2015), and Hispanic families are fearful of even trying to use social services because they believe they are an extension of the government and its authority (Kriz & Skivenes, 2012). A wealth of data links the underuse of public services with immigration status because of federal laws and fears of detection (Capps et al., 2005; Lopez, 2017). Also note that undocumented Hispanic immigrant families underuse public social services when compared to other ethnic immigrant individuals (Finno-Velasquez, 2013; Ortega et al., 2007).

Features of public service providers such as ethnic matches between clients and providers demonstrate ethnic proficiency, and Spanish-language proficiency is vital in meeting the needs of immigrant families (Ayón & Aisenberg, 2010; Finno-Velasquez, 2013; Gulbas & Zayas, 2017).

▶ Undocumented and Unaccompanied Children in the United States

The exact number of youth crossing the U.S.–Mexican border without documentation is not known. What is known and what is new is the increase in the number of children, especially unaccompanied children, whose numbers have increased drastically since 2012 (Roth & Grace, 2015). Haddal (2007) posited that nearly 80,000 Hispanic children are apprehended crossing the U.S.–Mexican border each year. More recent findings suggest that of the estimated 1 million people detected attempting to walk onto U.S. soil without proper documentation each year, close to 100,000 are unaccompanied children (Roth & Grace, 2015). These numbers do not include the numbers of children undetected by Immigration and Customs Enforcement or other U.S. law enforcement personnel. Rodriguez (2013) termed these youth *undocumented, unaccompanied,* and *undetected.*

Unaccompanied children detected by the Department of Homeland Security (DHS) are placed into a detention facility under the custody of the Office of Refugee Resettlement (ORR) (Aldarondo & Becker, 2011). The children are first screened by forensic exams to ensure they are younger than 18 years of age. The unaccompanied children are then handed to a division of ORR called the Division of Unaccompanied Children's Services (DUCS). In a DUCS detention facility, all medical needs are supposed to be met and tests are conducted within 90 days of the children's placement (Aldarondo & Becker, 2011). Social skills, classes in English as a second language, and other educational services are provided in these facilities. These children have a slim opportunity to become American citizens if they obtain the status of lawful permanent residency and meet the requirements to apply for special immigrant juvenile status (SIJS).

Immigration policy procedure has many inconsistencies when SIJS is available for these children. Several states are unaware of the law, fail to inform or encourage undocumented children, and are confused about how these children may apply for SIJS (Kriz & Skivenes, 2012). A study done by Garcia, Aisenberg, and Harachi (2012) found that many caseworkers were not aware of the SIJS. According to Byrne (2008), no child may be deprived of SIJS because of age as long as the child applied for SIJS before age 21. After living in the country for five years, these SIJS individuals may apply for U.S. citizenship. Nevertheless, children who were born in Mexico do not qualify for SIJS. Therefore, if these youths remain in the United States, they may not apply for college loans or other benefits or obtain legal employment, and they will remain susceptible to victimization and exploitation (Bronstein & Montgomery, 2011).

▶ Trauma and Deportations

A parent's potential deportation directly affects children's well-being (Brabeck & Xu, 2010). When a parent is deported, the children suffer a devastating loss because of the parents' roles in their families (Derby, 2012; Gulbas & Zayas, 2017). From January to the end of June 2011, 46,000 parents of U.S. citizen children were deported. Parents are not only aware of the possibility of being deported but also face the dreadful fear of separation from their children (Dettlaff & Rycraft, 2010; Gulbas & Zayas, 2017).

President Donald Trump has intensified this fear among immigrant families with two administrative orders that expand the power and scope of federal immigration enforcement (Cervantes & Walker, 2017). DHS has apprehended more than 40,000 people since President Trump signed the executive order, a 40% increase in apprehension over the same period the previous year (Duara, 2017). This executive order considered prioritizing the apprehension and deportation of approximately 8 million people living in the United States compared to President Barack Obama's executive order, with fewer than 1.5 million individuals considered priorities for removal and deportation.

The administrative change has been catastrophic for immigrant families. Many families are torn apart as children are left with one or sometimes no parents at all (Covarrubias & Hartman, 2015). The policies are damaging not only to immigrant families but also to their own communities. Many of these children are placed in the welfare system at an average cost of $26,000 annually (Derby, 2012). Children younger than five years old will likely be adopted, and these parents may never see their children again (Covarrubias & Hartman, 2015). The psychological trauma and economic hardship that goes along with deportations or detainment have irreversible effects on the children (Brabeck, Lykes, & Hunter, 2014; Gulbas & Zayas, 2017; Rodriguez & Dawkins, 2016).

During parental deportation, children fear and distrust law enforcement and other government entities. Many are beginning to have emotional and behavioral problems, including depression, anxiety, poor grades, and sleep deprivation (Baum, Jones, & Barry, 2010; Brabeck & Xu, 2010; Derby, 2012; Gulbas & Zayas, 2017). Some of these mental and emotional problems are irreversible (Allen, Cisneros, & Tellez, 2015; Gulbas & Zayas, 2017).

This increased enforcement of immigration laws has separated even more children from their parents, with research showing that Hispanic children are removed at higher rates and placed into child-welfare care across the country (Dorsett, 2012; Pecora et al., 2010; Scott, Faulkner, Cardoso, & Burstain, 2014). As such, these children are overrepresented in the child-welfare system and are more likely to be placed in out-of-home care more quickly and for longer periods of time than their White non-Hispanic counterparts (Salcedo, 2015).

Research has also found immigrant children in the welfare system are over-medicated, undereducated, malnourished, and separated from brothers and sisters, and a few have died in the custody of the state (Barth & Blackwell, 1998; Douglas & Poletti, 2016; Pecora et al., 2005, 2010; Roller-White et al., 2012). Failure to place these children in bilingual homes causes them to forget their native language and lose their cultural identity (Garcia et al., 2012). Thus, it is vital to keep families together when possible. This may not always be the law or policy in our country, but it may be the ethical thing to do. Immigrant children in the child-welfare system or foster-care system have also become an ethical concern.

▶ Immigration and Child Welfare in the United States

Historically, extended families, private groups, and organizations cared for orphaned or wayward youth in the United States. The so-called child savers movement began the ideology of social reform in the 19th century by assimilating and socializing these children to make them productive citizens (Krisberg, 2005). Today the United States child-welfare system assists close to 500,000 children yearly, with another estimated 25,000 aging out of the system per year. Each state has an individual responsibility to govern its child-welfare system with oversight by and funding from the federal government. A state typically becomes a legal guardian to a child when he or she is neglected, abused, or abandoned. "It thereby becomes the responsibility of the state to provide and care for, support and socialize youth (or ensure that other competent caregivers do this), until they emancipate out of care or are returned to their families" (Dorsett, 2012).

The relationship between immigration and child welfare in the United States has a distorted history of failure and ethical dilemmas. Beginning in the 1800s, welfare movements such as the child savers, which were operated by upper- and middle-class Protestants, institutionalized orphaned and immigrant children by placing them in children's homes and workhouses for reform, and shipped orphans from the East Coast to the West Coast on "orphan trains" (Krisberg, 2005). This sometimes led to separated siblings, and some children became indentured servants. Before and during this movement was the attempted assimilation of Native Indian children by White missionaries who separated one-third of Native families. The termination of Native Indian parental rights led to children being moved on trains, being institutionalized, and sometimes suffering abuse, exploitation, feelings of unworthiness, and separation from their cultures and families (Byrd, 2013; Kadushin, 1980; Kraimer-Rickabay, 2005; Krisberg, 2005).

The current public outcry over immigration and deportation has been covered by mainstream American news media outlets such as the *Washington Post* and National Public Radio. These outlets have covered the detention of families along the southern U.S. border and the incarceration of immigrant parents and children sent into the child-welfare system (Bump, 2018; Domonoske & Gonzales, 2018).

The U.S. child-welfare system was already burdened with shortages of foster parents (Friedman, 2017; Riley-Behringer & Cage, 2014), youths being medicated with psychotropic medications (Warner, Song, & Pottick, 2014), and children lingering in the foster-care system often until age 18 years of age and struggling in adulthood (Ahmann, 2017; Pecora, 2012; Shah et al., 2017). Immigrant children face the same issues and also receive the same services as U.S. children in child welfare such as assigned caseworkers and legal representation. However, immigrant children face additional challenges such as language and cultural barriers and parents being detained or incarcerated while the legal processes of immigration are sorted out. Immigrant children also face inadequate health care (Turney, 2017), a lack of culturally competent service providers (Rajendran & Chemtob, 2010), and issues of social attachment (Dorsett, 2012; Murray & Murray, 2010). Immigrant families crossing borders or seeking asylum have been detained and sometimes separated. Detention facilities for immigrant families were opened as early as 2001 in Pennsylvania and Texas. The Texas facility was shut down in 2009 because of abuses families were experiencing in the facility (Balcazar, 2016). Children of immigrant families whose parents are incarcerated risk being placed in the foster system if kinship care or family in the United States is not located to take in a child. So it begs the question, should immigrant children be placed in the U.S. foster-care system because of immigration issues when abuse, neglect, or abandonment is not the issue?

Another pressing issue for immigrant and American children in the foster-care system is exploitation. Children may seek to come to the United States to seek employment and are often exploited in sweatshops (Rodriguez et al., 2018). Sexual exploitation is another area of concern with children in foster care and immigrant children (Ayón, Messing, Gurrola, & Valencia-Garcia, 2018; Miller, Decker, Silverman, & Raj, 2007). This is where federal oversight is a must for foster care and the protection of immigrant children crossing borders into the United States.

Protections for the vulnerable population of children are necessary regardless of the child's status, whether as citizen, Native Indian, or immigrant. Support for such children is only approximately 40 years old; before that, the only humane welfare system in the United States was for pets. American children where first represented in 1912 at the first White House Conference for Children presented by President Theodore Roosevelts. This led to combating child exploitation through the establishment of the Children's Bureau (U.S. Department of Health & Human Services, n.d.). Other historical U.S. acts to protect children include:

- the 1974 Child Abuse Prevention and Treatment Act, which brought child welfare and child protection to center stage (www.nlihc.org);
- the 1978 Indian Child Welfare Act, which protects Native Indian children and their culture (Byrd, 2013);

- the 2000 Child Citizenship Act, which allows children born outside of the United States to become citizens under special conditions (U.S. Department of State, n.d.);
- the 2014 Preventing Sexual Exploitation and Strengthening Families Act, which brought the hard issue of the sexual exploitation of children to the forefront as both a national and global issue (Greenbaum, 2014); and
- the 2018 Family First Prevention Services Act (FFPSA), which sought to keep children out of foster care (see Annie E. Casey Foundation, www.aecf.org).

These acts put laws in place to protect children, a vulnerable population that otherwise does not always have representation. Whether or not a child is a natural-born citizen or an immigrant, the U.S. government is responsible for his or her welfare on American soil. Certain conditions govern the rights of immigrant children to be protected or gain citizenship when necessary, protecting their rights and protecting them from exploitation. These rights, however, do not replace the need for a child to live safely with biological parents and families. Passage of the FFPSA and recent child-welfare discussion focus on preventing children from entering foster care. Keeping families together and reunifying families in safe environments for children have been ongoing legal and ethical conversations and in the forefront with the recent border policy of separating children from parents. Research suggests reunification should be carefully considered so that children are not put into unsafe situations; this is what the federal government is tasked with in determining if children brought across the border are with biological parents or traffickers. Reunification of immigrant children with parents who were simply seeking asylum can prevent child-behavior problems, allow children to preserve their original cultures and native languages, and provide continued economic and social support (Gubernskaya & Dreby, 2017; Osterling & Han, 2011).

▶ Conclusion

The U.S. immigrant population in particular has recently been on the national stage for reasons that are not always positive, but at least there is now a conversation. The United States of America is a nation of immigrants; as such, we should be careful when creating laws and policies that affect not only immigrant families but also the communities in which these families reside. Ethical considerations as they relate to immigration include knowing the difference between what is legally allowable and the right thing to do.

▶ References

Ahmann, E., (2017). Supporting youth aging out of foster care. *Pediatric Nursing, 43*(1). 43.

Aldarondo, E., & Becker, R. (2011). Promoting the well-being of unaccompanied immigrant minors. In L. Buki & L. Piedra (Eds.), *Creating infrastructures for Latino mental health* (pp. 195–214). New York, NY: Springer.

Allen, B., Cisneros, E., & Tellez, A. (2015). The children left behind: The impact of parental deportation on mental health. *Journal of Child and Family Studies, 24*(2), 386–392.

Androff, D. K., Ayón, C., Becerra, D., & Gurrola, M. (2011). US immigration policy and immigrant children's well-being: The impact of policy shifts. *Journal of Sociology and Social Welfare, 38*, 77–98.

American Humane Association [AHA]. (n.d.). *How American Humane Association began.* Washington, DC: Author. Retrieved from www.americanhumane.org

Annie E. Casey Foundation. (2018). Family First Prevention Services Act will change the lives of children in foster care. Retrieved from https://www.aecf.org/blog/family-first-prevention -services-act-will-change-the-lives-of-children-in-f/

Ayón, C., & Aisenberg, E. (2010). Negotiating cultural values and expectations within the public child welfare system: A look at familismo and personalismo. *Child and Family Social Work, 15,* 335–344. Retrieved from doi:10.1111/j.1365-2206.2010.00682

Ayón, C., Messing, J. T., Gurrola, M., & Valencia-Garcia, D. (2018). The oppression of Latina mothers: Experiences of exploitation, violence, marginalization, cultural imperialism, And powerlessness in their everyday lives. *Violence Against Women, 242*(8), 879–900. Retrieved from doi:10,1177/1077801217724451

Balcazar, F. E. (2016). Policy statement on the incarceration of undocumented migrant families. *American Journal of Community Psychology, 57*(1–2), 255–263. Retrieved from doi:10.1002 /ajcp.12017

Barth, R. P., & Blackwell, D. L. (1998). Death rates among California's foster care and former foster care populations. *Children and Youth Services Review, 20*(7), 577–604. Retrieved from https:// doi.org/10.1016/S0190-7409(98)00027-9

Baum, J., Jones, R., & Barry, C. (2010). *In the child's best interest? The consequences of losing a lawful immigrant parent to deportation.* Retrieved from www.law.ucdavis.edu/news/images /childsbestinterest.pdf

Bersani, B. E., Loughran, T. A., & Piquero, A. R. (2014). Comparing patterns and predictors of immigrant offending among a sample of adjudicated youth. *Journal of Youth and Adolescence, 43*(11), 1914–1933.

Brabeck, K., Lykes, M., & Hunter, C. (2014). The psychosocial impact of detention and deportation on U.S. migrant children and families. *American Journal of Orthopsychiatry, 84*(5), 496–505. Retrieved from doi.org/10.1037/ort0000011

Brabeck, K., & Xu, Q. (2010). The impact of detention and deportation on Latino immigrant children and families: A quantitative exploration. *Hispanic Journal of Behavioral Sciences, 32*(3), 341–361. Retrieved from https://doi.org/10.1177/0739986310374053

Bronstein, I., & Montgomery, P. (2011). Psychological distress in refugee children: A systematic review. *Clinical Child and Family Psychology Review, 14,* 44–56. Retrieved from https://link .springer.com/article/10.1007/s10567-010-0081-0

Bump, P. (2018, July 9). *The children separated from their parents, by the numbers. Washington Post.* Retrieved from https://www.washingtonpost.com/news/politics/wp/2018/07/09/the -children-separated-from-their-parents-by-the-numbers/

Byrd, S. (2013). Learning from the past: Why termination of a non-citizen parent's rights should not be based on the child's best interest. *University of Miami Law Review, 68*(1), 323.

Byrne, O. (2008). *Unaccompanied children in the United States: A literature review.* New York, NY: Vera Institute of Justice. Retrieved from http://www.f2f.ca.gov/res/pdf/UnaccompaniedChildren-US.pdf

Capps, R., Fix, M., Ost, J., Reardon-Anderson, J., & Passel, J. S. (2005). *The health and well-being of young children of immigrants,* Washington, DC: Urban Institute. Retrieved from www.urban .org/UploadedPDF/311139_ChildrenImmigrants.pdf

Castañeda, H., & Melo, M. A. (2014). Health care access for Latino mixed-status families: Barriers, strategies, and implications for reform. *American Behavioral Scientist, 58*(14), 1891–1909. Retrieved from doi: 10.1177/0002764214550290

Cervantes, W., & Walker, C. (2017). *Five reasons Trump's immigration orders harm children.* Retrieved from www.clasp.org/resources-and-publications/publication-1/Five-Reasons -Immigration-Enforcement-Orders-Harm-Children.pdf

Covarrubias, N., & Hartman, A. (2015). *Information packet: Deportation and child welfare in mixed status families with unauthorized parents and citizen children.* New York, NY: National Center for Child Welfare Excellence. Retrieved from www.nccwe.org/downloads/info-packs /HartmanCovarrubias.pdf

Dawkins, M., & Rodriguez, F. (2016). Undocumented and unaccompanied Latino youth who are exposed to violence are more likely to turn to crime to overcome disadvantage. LSE US Centre. Retrieved from http://bit.ly/24UlxKW

Derby, J. (2012). The burden of deportation on children in Mexican immigrant families. *Journal of Marriage and Family, 74*, 829–845. Retrieved from https://onlinelibrary.wiley.com/doi/abs/10.1111/j.1741-3737.2012.00989.x

Dettlaff, A. J. (2015, January). Emerging strategies to address the needs of Latino children in the child welfare system: Innovations and advances in California. In *Society for Social Work and Research 19th Annual Conference: The Social and Behavioral Importance of Increased Longevity.* Fairfax, VA: SSWR.

Dettlaff, A., & Earner, I. (2012). Children of immigrants in the child welfare system: Characteristics, risk, and maltreatment. *Families in Society: The Journal of Contemporary Social Services, 93*(4), 295–303. Retrieved from https://doi.org/10.1606/1044-3894.4240

Dettlaff, A., & Johnson, M. (2011). Child maltreatment dynamics among immigrant and U.S. born Latino children: Findings from the National Survey of Child and Adolescent Well-Being (NSCAW). *Children and Youth Services Review, 33*, 936–944.

Dettlaff, A., & Rycraft, J. (2010). Adapting systems of care for child welfare practice with immigrant Latino children and families. *Evaluation and Program Planning, 33*, 303–310. Retrieved from doi:10.1016/j.evalprogplan.2009.07.003

Domonoske, C., & Gonzales, R. (2018, June 19). What we know: Family separation and "zero tolerance" at the border. National Public Radio. Retrieved from https://www.npr.org/2018/06/19/621065383/what-we-know-family-separation-and-zero-tolerance-at-the-border

Dorsett, V. J. (2012). A descriptive analysis of foster care transitional service and alumni outcomes. Doctoral dissertation. College Station, TX: Texas A&M University.

Douglas, K., & Poletti, A. (2016). *Life narratives and youth culture: Representation, agency and Participation.* New York, NY: Springer Publishing.

Duara, N. (2017, May 17). Arrest on civil immigration charges go up 38% in the first 100 days since Trump's executive order. *Los Angeles Times.* Retrieved from www.latimes.com/nation/la-na-ice-deport-trump-20170517-story.html

Finno-Velasquez, M. (2013). The relationship between parent immigration status and concrete support service use among Latinos in child welfare: Findings using the National Survey of Child and Adolescent Well-Being (NSCAW II). *Children and Youth Services Review, 35*(12), 2118–2127.

Friedman, L. (2017). Shortage of foster parents: An exploratory study of the attrition of prospective foster parents during the licensing process. Retrieved from https://repository.brynmawr.edu/dissertations/164/

Garcia, A., Aisenberg, E., & Harachi, T. (2012). Pathways to service equalities among Latinos in the child welfare system. *Children and Youth Services Review, 34*, 1060–1071.

Greenbaum, V. J. (2014) Commercial sexual exploitation and sex trafficking of children in the United States. *Current Problems in Pediatric and Adolescent Health Care, 44*(9), 245–269. Retrieved from https://www.ncbi.nlm.nih.gov/pubmed/25131563

Gubernskaya, Z., & Dreby, J. (2017) US immigrations policy and the case for family unity. *Journal of Migration and Human Security, 5*(2). Retrieved from https://cmsny.org/publications/jmhs-case-for-family-unity/

Gulbas, L. E., & Zayas, L. H. (2017). Exploring the effects of US immigration enforcement on the well-being of citizen children in Mexican immigrant families. *RSF: The Russell Sage Foundation Journal of the Social Sciences, 3*(4), 53–69.

Haddal, C. C. (2007, March). *Unaccompanied alien children: Policies and issues.* RL 33896. Washington, DC: Congressional Research Service.

Hagan, J., Levi, R., & Dinovitzer, R. (2008). The symbolic violence of the crime-immigration nexus: Migrant mythologies in the Americas. *Criminology & Public Policy, 7*, 95–112.

Kadushin, A. (1980). *Child welfare services* (3rd ed.). New York, NY: Macmillan.

Kraimer-Rickabay, L. (2005). A case study of the state of Connecticut Department of Children and Families' One-on-One Mentor Program for youth aging out of foster care. Storrs, CT: University of Connecticut.

Krisberg, B. (2005). *Juvenile justice: Redeeming our children.* Thousand Oaks, CA: Sage.

Kriz, K., & Skivenes, M. (2012). How child welfare workers perceive their work with undocumented families: An explorative study of challenges and coping strategies. *Children and Youth Services Review, 34*(4), 790–797.

Kubrin, C. E., & Desmond, S. (2015). The power of place revisited: Why immigrant communities have lower levels of adolescent violence. *Youth Violence and Juvenile Justice, 13*, 345–366.

Leyro, S. P. (2017). *The fear factor: Exploring the impact of the vulnerability to deportation on immigrants' lives.* New York, NY: CUNY Academic Works.

Lopez, C., Bergren, M. D., & Painter, S. G. (2008). Latino disparities in child mental health services. *Journal of Child and Adolescent Psychiatric Nursing, 21*(3), 137–145.

Martinez, R., Stowell, J., & Lee, M. (2010). Immigration and crime in an era of transformation: A longitudinal analysis of homicides in San Diego neighborhoods, 1980–2000. *Criminology, 48*, 797–829.

McCarthy, J. (2015, March 17). In U.S., worries about terrorism, race relations up sharply. Gallup. Retrieved from https://news.gallup.com/poll/182018/worries-terrorism-race-relations-sharply .aspx

Miller, E., Decker, M. R., Silverman, J. G., & Raj, A. (2007). Migration, sexual exploitation, and women's health: A case report from a community health center. *Violence Against Women, 13*(5), 486–497. Retrieved from https://journals.sagepub.com/doi/10.1177/1077801207301614

Murray, J., & Murray, L. (2010). Parental incarceration, attachment and child psychopathology. *Attachment & Human Development, 12*(4), 289–309. Retrieved from https://www.tandfonline .com/doi/abs/10.1080/14751790903416889

Ortega, A. N., Fang, H., Perez, V. H., Rizzo, J. A., Carter-Pokras, O., Wallace, S. P., & Gelberg, L. (2007). Health care access, use of services, and experiences among undocumented Mexicans and other Latinos. *Archives of Internal Medicine, 167*(21), 2354–2360.

Osterling, K. L., & Han, M. (2011). Reunification outcomes among Mexican immigrant families in the child welfare system. *Children and Youth Services Review, 33*(9), 1658–1666. Retrieved from http://cssr.berkeley.edu/cwscmsreports/LatinoPracticeAdvisory/RESEARCH_CWS _Outcomes/Reunification_outcomes_among_Mexican.pdf

Passel, J. S. (2011). Demography of immigrant youth: Past, present, and future. *The Future of Children, 21*(1), 19–41. Retrieved from www.jstor.org/stable/41229010

Pecora, P. J. (2012). Maximizing educational achievement of youth in foster care and alumni: Factors associated with success. *Children and Youth Services Review, 34*(6), 1121–1129. Retrieved from https://www.researchgate.net/publication/254408255_Maximizing_educational_achievement _of_youth_in_foster_care_and_alumni_Factors_associated_with_success

Pecora, P. J., Kessler, J. W., O'Brien, K., Downs, A. C., English, D., White, J., & Holmes, K. (2005). *Improving family foster care: Findings from the Northwest Foster Care Alumni Study.* Retrieved from https://caseyfamilypro-wpengine.netdna-ssl.com/media/AlumniStudies_NW _Report_ES.pdf

Pecora, P. J., Kessler, J. W., Williams, J., Downs, A. C., English, D. J., White, J., & O'Brien, K. (2010). *What works in family foster care? Key components of success from the Northwest Foster Care Alumni Study.* New York, NY: Oxford University Press.

Pew Research Center. (2015, September 28). Modern immigration wave brings 59 million to U.S., driving population growth and change through 2065. Retrieved from https://www.pewresearch .org/hispanic/2015/09/28/modern-immigration-wave-brings-59-million-to-u-s-driving -population-growth-and-change-through-2065/

Philbin, M. M., Flake, M., Hatzenbuehler, M. L., & Hirsch, J. S. (2018, February). State-level immigration and immigrant-focused policies as drivers of Latino health disparities in the United States. *Social Science & Medicine.* Retrieved from https://www.ncbi.nlm.nih.gov /pubmed/28410759

Rajendran, K., & Chemtob, C. M. (2010). Factors associated with service use among immigrants In the child welfare system. *Evaluation and Program Planning, 33*(3), 317–323. Retrieved from https://europepmc.org/abstract/med/19651442

Riley-Behringer, M., Cage, J., (2014) Barriers experienced by kinship and non-relative caregivers during the foster and adoptive parent licensure and home study process, *Journal of Public Child Welfare, 8*(2), 212–238. Retrieved from https://www.tandfonline.com/doi/abs/10.1080/155487 32.2014.893223

Rodriguez, F. A. (2013). Unaccompanied Latino youth on the United States–Mexico border: A qualitative study. (Unpublished doctoral dissertation). Prairie View, TX : Prairie View A&M University.

Rodriguez, F. A., Dorsett, V., Rodriguez, J. J. (2018, May). Undocumented immigrant Latina youth and the US child welfare system. In E. Trejos & N. Trevino (Eds.), *Handbook of Foster Youth.* London, UK: Routledge, Taylor & Francis Group.

Rodriguez, F. A., & Dawkins, M. (2016). Undocumented Latino youth: Migration experiences and the challenges of integrating into American society. *Journal of International Migration & Integration, 18*(2), 419–438. Retrieved from https://www.researchgate.net /publication/299346119_Undocumented_Latino_Youth_Migration_Experiences_and_the _Challenges_of_Integrating_into_American_Society

Rodriguez, J. J. (2008). The applicability of General Strain Theory to the Latino population. *Journal of Knowledge and Best Practices in Juvenile Justice and Psychology, 2,* 43–52.

Rodriguez, J. J., & Belshaw, S. (2010). General Strain Theory: A comparative analysis of Latino & White youths. *Southwest Journal of Criminal Justice, 7,* 138–158.

Rodriguez, J. J., Pirtle, D., & Henderson, H. (2008). Crime and Delinquency: Latinos in the United States. *International Journal of Crime, Criminal Justice, and Law, 3,* 19–29.

Roller-White, C., O'Brien, K., Pecora, P. J., Kessler, R. C., Sampson, N., & Hwang, I. (2012). *Texas Foster Care Alumni Study technical report: Outcomes at age 23 and 24.* Retrieved from www .casey.org/media/StateFosterCare_TX_fr.pdf

Roth, B. J., & Grace, B. L. (2015). Falling through the cracks: The paradox of post-release services for unaccompanied child migrants. *Children and Youth Services Review, 58,* 244–252. Retrieved from https://www.sciencedirect.com/science/article/pii/S0190740915300773?via%3Dihub

Rumbaut, R., & Ewing, W. (2007). *The myth of immigrant criminality and the paradox of assimilation: Incarceration rates among native and foreign-born men.* Washington, DC: Immigration Policy Center, American Immigration Law Foundation.

Salcedo, E. J. (2015, May). *Information packet: Latino youth and the foster care system.* New York, NY: National Center for Child Welfare Excellence. Retrieved from www.nccwe.org/downloads /info-packs/Salcedo.pdf

Sampson, R. (2008). Rethinking crime and immigration. *Contexts, 7,* 28–33.

Scott, J., Faulkner, M., Cardoso, J. B., & Burstain, J. (2014). Kinship care and undocumented Latino children in the Texas foster care system: Navigating the child welfare–immigration crossroads. *Child Welfare, 93*(4), 53–69.

Shah, M. F., Liu, Q., Mark Eddy, J., Barkan, S., Marshall, D., Mancuso, D., Lucenko, B., & Huber, A., (2017). Predicting homelessness among emerging adults aging out of foster care. American *Journal of Community Psychology, 60*(1–2), 33–44.

Smart, J. F., & Smart, D. W. (1995). Acculturative stress of Hispanics: Loss and challenge. *Journal of Counseling and Development, 73*(4), 390.

Turney, K. (2017). Unmet health care needs among children exposed to parental incarceration. *Maternal and Child Health Journal, 21*(5), 1194–1202. Retrieved from https://www.ncbi.nlm .nih.gov/pubmed/28108834

Urbina, Martin G. (2012). *Hispanics in the U.S. criminal justice system: The new American demography.* Springfield, IL: Charles C. Thomas.

U.S. Department of Health & Human Services. (n.d.). Historical highlights. Washington, DC: Author. Retrieved from https://www.hhs.gov/about/historical-highlights/index.html

U.S. Department of State. (n.d.). Child citizenship Act of 2000—Sections 320 and 322 of the INA. Washington DC: Bureau of Consular Affairs. Retrieved from https://travel.state.gov/content /travel/en/legal/travel-legal-considerations/us-citizenship/Child-Citizenship-2000-Sections -320-322-INA.html

Ward, M. (2016, August 29). Texas DPS seeks border-security budget hike increase to $1 billion. *Houston Chronicle.* Retrieved from www.chron.com/news/politics/texas/article/DPS-seeks -border-security-budget-hike-increase-to-9190661.php

Warner, L. A., Song, N. K., Pottick, K. J., (2014). Outpatient psychotropic medication use in the US: A comparison based on foster care status. *Journal of Child and Family Studies, 23*(4), 652–665. Retrieved from https://mijn.bsl.nl/outpatient-psychotropic-medication-use-in-the -us-a-comparison-ba/567196

Weber, C. (2015). Living in the shadows or government dependents: Immigrants and welfare in the United States. *Comparative Advantage, 3*(1), 4–20. Retrieved from https://stanfordcomparativeadvantage .files.wordpress.com/2016/12/comparative_advantage_spring_2015.pdf

Wolff, K. T., Baglivio, M. T., Intravia, J., & Piquero, A. R. (2015). The protective impact of immigrant concentration on juvenile recidivism: A statewide analysis of youth offenders. Journal of *Criminal Justice, 43*(6), 522–531.

Zayas, L. H. (2015). *Forgotten citizens: Deportation, children, and the making of American exiles and orphans.* Oxford, UK: Oxford University Press.

ARTICLE 36

Deleting Terror: Exploring the Ethical Aspects of Countering Online Extremism

W. Chris Hale

▶ Introduction

On April 15, 2013, two improvised explosive devices exploded a short distance from the finish line of the 117th running of the Boston Marathon. Carried out by two brothers, Dzhokhar and Tamerlan Tsarnaev, the attack killed three people and injured 264 others. Three days later, in preparation for a deadlier attack in Times Square, New York, the brothers hijacked a car and shot and killed Massachusetts Institute of Technology police officer Sean Collins. When the Tsarnaevs eventually had to refuel their car, the police caught up with them and killed Tamerlan, the older brother, in the subsequent firefight. Among other grievances, the Tsarnaev brothers were angered about the U.S. wars in Iraq and Afghanistan (Gunaratna & Haynal, 2013). Two years later, on June 17, 2015, Dylann Roof killed several Black parishioners at the Emanuel African Methodist Episcopal Church in Charleston, South Carolina. According to survivors, Roof attended that evening's bible study and sat quietly for approximately one hour. After which, he pulled out a .45-caliber Glock pistol and systematically murdered nine people. When he was not shooting, he was reloading his weapon, a reported five times. According to his manifesto, Roof was enraged by Black-on-White crime and concluded that it was time "to take drastic action" (Potok, 2015). Less than one year later, on June 12, 2016, in what has been described as the worst terrorist attack in the United States since September 11, 2001, Omar Mateen walked into the Pulse nightclub in Orlando, Florida and shot nearly one-third of the 320 club patrons. Armed with a Sig Sauer MCX semiautomatic rifle and a Glock handgun, Mateen slaughtered 49 people and wounded 53 others. Proclaiming allegiance to the Islamic State terrorist group during a 911 call, Mateen was eventually killed in the subsequent shootout with police (Alvarez & Perez-Pena, 2016). Despite differences in ideology, justifications, and rationalizations for their actions, the Tsarnaev brothers, Dylann Roof, and Omar Mateen were likely self-radicalized, in part though the consumption of online extremist material ("Radicalization in the U.S. and the Rise of Terrorism," 2016).

According to Gus Martin (2011), extremism "is characterized by intolerance toward opposing interests and divergent opinions and is the primary catalyst and motivation for terrorist behavior" (p. 4). Martin further argues that those who cross the line from extremism to terrorism "always develop noble arguments to rationalize and justify their acts of violence toward nations, people, religions, or other interests" (p. 4). Basically, extremism can be thought of as a precursor to terrorism and used to motivate and justify acts of terror. In addition, fueled in large part by popular social media platforms, extremists exploit controversial social and political issues, spread propaganda, recruit new members, and, in some cases, actually direct attacks (Hughes & Meleagrou-Hitchens, 2017; Rudner, 2017). Clearly, this has led governments around the world to be increasingly concerned about extremist and terrorist use of the Internet. Many, including that of the United States, repeatedly urge companies such as Facebook, Twitter, and Google (YouTube) to proactively monitor social media for terrorist content, modify or remove user posts and accounts, and promote countermessaging (Patel & Koushik, 2017). Nevertheless, despite a government's interest in countering online extremism (COE), some have argued that these policies risk violating fundamental ethical principles (Chima, 2016). The following examines ethical considerations in the context of COE. More specifically, this article will examine extremist and terrorist use of the Internet, how online radicalization works, how COE strategies are deployed, and the ethical concerns raised.

▶ Extremists' and Terrorists' Use of the Internet

Extremists use the Internet for a variety of reasons, including easy access, lack of government control, wider audiences, instant and anonymous communication with like-minded individuals, a multimedia environment, and the ability to shape traditional mass media coverage (Weimann, 2004). The following examines Internet facilitation of information sharing, social networking, recruitment, and publicity.

Information Sharing

Before the advent of the Internet, extremists spread their messages by placing fliers under windshield wipers or distributing books, newspapers, magazines, newsletters, and audiotapes (Stern, 1999). Although somewhat effective, these methods provided personal contact and direct ideological grooming, so they could reach only small audiences (Bipartisan Policy Center, 2018). Today, users can instantly download (in multiple languages) professional-quality pamphlets, books, magazines, and photo essays, as well as watch and listen to recorded or live-streaming audio and video in the privacy of their own homes.

Social Networking and Recruitment

Similar to other venues used to share information, the Internet has also proven to be an effective recruitment tool. Early recruitment methods included the roaming of public online chat rooms, where user demographics were tracked in an effort to find supporters (Weimann, 2004). Once located, potential recruits were flooded with religious decrees, training manuals, and anti-Western propaganda (Thomas, 2003; Zhou, Qin, Lai, Reid, & Chen, 2006). Today, social media platforms such as Twitter, Instagram, Facebook, and Google (YouTube) provide extremists with free, user-friendly services, and the ability to instantly reach a worldwide audience. Furthermore, social media platform algorithms are programmed to connect users to content the user already "likes." For example, Facebook personalizes user information based on past clicks and that of what is popular among users with similar interests. Likewise, Google returns search results largely based on previous search attempts. Essentially, these platforms place users in a "filter bubble" or feedback loop that anticipates, confirms, and strengthens users' preexisting beliefs (El-Bermawy, 2018).

Social media has also given rise to virtual entrepreneurs or virtual plotters. Virtual plotters are terrorist sympathizers who use social media platforms to reach out, recruit, foster connections, encourage, and mobilize radicalized Westerners (Hughes & Meleagrou-Hitchens, 2017). Infamous virtual plotters include Jalil Ibn Ameer Aziz, Mohamed Abdullahi Hassan, and Junaid Hussain. Jalil Ibn Ameer Aziz, a resident of Harrisburg, Pennsylvania, disseminated Islamic State propaganda and facilitated travel of foreign recruits over Twitter. He was also responsible for tweeting a "kill list" of more than 100 U.S. military members, including their names, addresses, and photographs. Muhammed Abdullahi Hassan, a Minnesota man of Somali descent, formed key relationships between Al-Shabaab (an East African jihadi group) and radicalized members of Minnesota's Somali–American community. Finally, Junaid Hussain, a British hacker and member of the Islamic State, used Twitter to inspire attacks in the United States and Britain on behalf of the Islamic State. He was also the most prominent member of "The Legion," a group of virtual plotters based in Raqqa, Syria, made up of British Islamic State operatives in direct contact with radicalized Americans. In fact, out of 38 U.S. plots and attacks inspired by the Islamic State between March 2014 and 2017, 21% involved communication with virtual plotters, mostly Legion members (Hughes & Meleagrou-Hitchens, 2017).

Publicity

Extremist propaganda relies on three rhetorical structures when justifying its reliance on violence to effect political, social, or religious change (Weimann, 2004). First, extremists portray their members as underdogs who have no choice but to defend themselves through violence. Organizations are portrayed as small, weak, and hunted, whereas governments are characterized as murderers seeking slaughter and genocide. Second, extremist organizations actively attempt to demonize and dehumanize the enemy. Using selected facts and misleading statements, extremist organizations effectively shift responsibility of violence from them toward their enemies (Potok, 2015). In addition, extremist web sites are increasingly using nonviolent communication in an attempt to contradict their violent image. This tactic is especially apparent with the rise of the so-called alt-right movement actively promoting social conflict rather than violence (Hankes & Amend, 2018). Nevertheless, to attract public attention, extremist groups must be able to publicize their causes and activities. In the past, the act of securing the public's attention required and often depended on attracting the attention of traditional television, radio, and print media (Bipartisan Policy Center, 2018). Today, social media have given extremist and terrorist groups unprecedented control over their messages, providing them the ability to directly shape public perception.

▶ Online Radicalization

Although Internet and social media use by extremists and terrorists is generally understood, the extent to which propaganda contributes to an individual's radicalization or actions continues to be debated (Borum, 2011; Weaver, 2015). According to John Horgan (as cited in Knefel, 2013), "Nobody watches YouTube or reads *Inspire* and becomes a terrorist. . . . YouTube videos and reading Al-Qaeda magazines tends to be far more relevant for sustaining commitment than inspiring it" (para. 2). In other words, an individual's radicalization process is not a simple linear path from limited initial exposure to radical ideas and subsequent violent actions. Likewise, Horgan adds that "there are the bigger social, political, and religious reasons people give for becoming involved" (para. 7). In addition, "hidden behind these bigger reasons, there are also hosts of littler reasons—personal fantasy, seeking adventure, camaraderie, purpose, identity" (para. 7). The following examines theories of online radicalization.

Content Immersion

According to Pyszczynski et al. (2006), the Internet and social media radicalize extremist beliefs only after extended periods of constant exposure. Resulting in mortality salience, this content immersion, especially that of promoting martyrdom and death, allows for a heightened sense of one's own mortality and therefore support for terrorist actions. Similarly, Sageman (2008) argues that content immersion results in moral outrage. He explains that extremist videos from conflict zones are intentionally powerful and emotionally arousing. These constant images of alleged Western atrocities contribute greatly to one's radicalization.

Social Environment

Other theories of radicalization stress the importance of the online social environment. According to Gerraerts (2012), an individual's extreme ideas are normalized and reinforced after constant interaction with like-minded others. These social media venues act as online echo chambers and have little or no editorial control, resulting in an environment in which hate and violent rhetoric flow unchallenged. Similarly, Suler (2004) concludes that the online social environment allows an individual to be anonymous, resulting in online disinhibition. In other words, the individual can effectively spread and absorb extreme beliefs in a hidden setting, thus avoiding responsibility for violent actions committed by them or others.

Role-Playing

Finally, and echoing the previously cited John Horgan, Brachman and Levine (2011) appear to argue that personal fantasy, adventure-seeking, purpose, and identity contribute to an individual's radicalization. Through role-playing, cyberspace allows people to project characteristics of their idealized selves. Unfortunately, radicalization results when individuals realize they actually do not possess these characteristics and must reconcile this gap through violence.

▶ Countering Violent Online Extremism

Regardless of how an individual becomes radicalized, the Internet and social media likely play an important role (Neumann, 2012). This has led governments around the world to be increasingly concerned about extremist and terrorist use of the Internet. Many governments, including that of the United States, have repeatedly urged companies such as Facebook, Twitter, and Google (YouTube) to proactively monitor social media for terrorist content, modify or remove user posts and accounts, and promote countermessaging (Patel & Koushik, 2017).

Removing the Threat

According to a recent Twitter government terms-of-service transparency report, between August 1, 2015, and December 31, 2017, the social media platform suspended 1,210,357 user accounts for content that violated Twitter's rules against promoting terrorism (Twitter, 2018). According to Twitter, this content was identified, in part, through its government referral system. Basically, governments are allowed to submit nonlegal requests concerning the removal of extremist content, and if Twitter determines a violation exists, content is promptly removed. Other content is flagged and removed through the company's internal algorithm, which purportedly suspends 75% of accounts before their first tweet (Darrah, 2017).

Also understanding the dangers of harmful content, Facebook is increasingly using artificial intelligence and algorithmic tools to identify and remove extremist content (Bickert & Fishman, 2018). These tools currently focus on Al-Qaeda, the Islamic State, and their affiliates, and include but are not limited to image matching and language understanding (Bickert & Fishman, 2017). Image matching works by comparing newly uploaded terrorist images and videos with already known and previously removed images or videos. This essentially allows Facebook to block other accounts from uploading the same content. Similarly, language matching employs algorithms to identify and remove text thought to advocate terrorism. According to Facebook, these technologies allowed the company to remove almost 2 million pieces of terrorist propaganda during the first four months of 2018, which was twice as much as previously removed through human-centered approaches alone (Bickert & Fishman, 2018).

Furthermore, in a recent blog, Google has described four steps it employs to combat terrorist content on YouTube, the company's popular video-sharing platform (YouTube, 2017a). The four steps include faster machine-learning technology to identify and remove violating videos, more content experts for its trusted flagger program, tougher standards for videos that are controversial yet do not violate existing policies, and countermessaging. According to Google (YouTube), the new algorithms allowed the company to remove more than 75% of all violating videos before a human flag was received.

Finally, in a combined attempt to fight online extremist content, Facebook, Microsoft, Twitter, and Google (YouTube) recently announced plans to share information through an industry database (Llanso, 2016). Participating companies can choose to submit *hashes*, or unique digital fingerprints of files depicting violent terrorist imagery, to this centralized database. Others will then be able to scan for matching files on their platforms. If the file is determined to be in violation, that platform can choose to remove it as well.

Countermessaging

Another strategy used to combat extremism is that of countermessaging. Online countermessaging is an attempt to shift the user's attention away from terrorist propaganda and toward material that contests it. One example includes Google (YouTube), which recently employed features from Jigsaw's Redirect Method (YouTube, 2017b). This algorithm allows Google (YouTube) to redirect users who have searched for extremist content (identified through sensitive keywords) to a playlist of carefully curated videos that confront and refute extremist propaganda.

▶ Ethical Considerations

Clearly, social media companies are now more proactively monitoring their platforms for terrorist content, removing user posts and accounts, and promoting countermessaging. Nevertheless, despite a government's interest in countering online extremism, some have argued that these policies risk violating fundamental ethical principles (Chima, 2016; Patel & Koushik, 2017). The following addresses the ethical concerns of countering online extremism.

Ethical Considerations of Removing the Threat

As previously indicated, Twitter, Facebook and Google (YouTube) are increasingly using artificial intelligence and algorithmic tools to identify and remove extremist content (Bickert & Fishman, 2018; Darrah, 2017; YouTube, 2017a). Patel and Koushik (2017) argue that this is problematic because it essentially requires social media companies, with no counterterrorism expertise, to determine what constitutes extremist speech or indications of potential violence. In addition, there is a lack of transparency in that little is known about what is actually being removed. Furthermore, Chima (2016) adds that because definitions of extremism vary greatly, these tools could disproportionately affect certain communities, religions, or ethnicities. For example, the American Civil Liberties Union (ACLU) of California found that police profiled Black activists by monitoring racially loaded hashtags such as #BlackLivesMatter and #DontShoot following the police killings of Michael Brown and Freddie Gray (Cagle, 2016). The ACLU of Massachusetts uncovered similar evidence of prejudice, finding that in 2014, 2015, and 2016, the Boston Police Department monitored religiously insensitive words and hashtags in their efforts to identify terrorist threats (Eledroos & Crockford, 2018). The more biased hashtags monitored included #MuslimLivesMatter and *Ummah*, the Arabic word for community.

In addition to the potential of falsely condemning an entire group of people, monitoring social media could indirectly discourage free speech. In other words, in the United States, even extremist speech is largely protected under the First Amendment. Nevertheless, knowledge of social media monitoring could dampen the free exchange of ideas (Waddell, 2016). This could ultimately create a slippery slope where posts and videos are removed, not for fostering extremist objectives or violence, but for just simply being unpopular (Patel & Koushik, 2017). These subjects include but are not limited to satire, journalism, activism, and political protest (Chima, 2016).

As with free speech, Americans are generally afforded some reasonable expectation of privacy. Nevertheless, according to Mund (2017), social media communications, even password-protected communications, currently receive no real expectation of privacy. Despite many other potential consequences, the likelihood of generating false positives or flagging the communications of innocent people is of great concern (Cope, York, & Gillula, 2017). Being labeled as an extremist unjustly could be a frightening experience and result in embarrassment, uncomfortable public exposure, and general distrust of the Internet (McCullough, 2016).

Ethical Considerations of Countermessaging

As previously described, another strategy in the ongoing battle against online extremism is countermessaging, or the promotion of messages that refute extremist views. According to Patel and Koushik (2017), Google's (YouTube) redirection algorithm, which essentially redirects users who have searched for extremist content to a playlist of selected videos that confront and refute extremism, raises several ethical questions. First, there is a general lack of transparency concerning how Google intends to identify "extremist" content or how it intends to "target" users who will be provided with the refuting content. Of concern is the fact that search terms likely targeted could be associated with unpopular political views, effectively blocking various forms of free expression and privileging only certain forms of speech (Llanso, 2016). In other words, who decides—or, in the case of machine-learning algorithms, what decides—what is appropriate is of considerable concern. Of further concern is the possibility of generating false positives or flagging the search results of innocent people (Patel & Koushik, 2017). Finally, as far as radicalization, Berger and Morgan (2015) warn that these strategies could frustrate, anger, and ultimately close avenues of counterdiscussion, effectively intensifying an individual's radicalization process.

Similar to efforts by social media companies, government countermessaging efforts have also generated ethical controversy. One example includes the U.S. Department of State's propaganda video for Islamic State recruits titled "Welcome to ISIS Land." Created and initial disseminated by the state department's now-defunct Center for Strategic Counterterrorism Communications, "Welcome to ISIS Land" used the Islamic State's own brutal footage in an attempt to challenge beliefs that potential recruits were fighting for a worthy cause (Miller & Higham, 2015). Becoming a viral phenomenon, the video showed prisoners being shot point-blank, headless corpses, and various forms of public execution juxtaposed with promises that recruits would learn valuable new skills. Ultimately becoming a source of embarrassment, the video did not deter recruits and most likely fueled extremism.

▶ Conclusion

In summary, extremists exploit controversial issues, spread propaganda, recruit new members, and sometimes actually direct attacks through social media platforms (Hughes & Meleagrou-Hitchens, 2017). This has led governments around the world to repeatedly urge companies such as Facebook, Twitter, and Google (YouTube) to proactively monitor social media for terrorist content, modify or remove user posts and accounts, and promote countermessaging (Patel & Koushik, 2017). Given the dangers posed by such content, including the likely self-radicalized attacks of Dzhokhar and Tamerlan Tsarnaev, Dylann Roof, Omar Mateen, and others ("Radicalization in the U.S.," 2016), it would appear that the motivations of governments and social media companies are sincere. Nonetheless, these platforms should make every attempt to avoid bias and prejudice, privilege only certain speech, discourage free expression, or violate one's privacy. This will most likely require social media companies to foster transparency and indicate the what, why, and how of what is being monitored, removed, or modified. Undoubtedly, it will be challenging to balance fundamental freedoms with the potential to prevent terrorist violence.

▶ References

Alvarez, L., & Perez-Pena, R. (2016, June 12). Praising ISIS, gunman attacks gay nightclub, leaving 50 dead in worst shooting on U.S. soil. *The New York Times*, p. A1.

Berger, J. M., & Morgan, J. (2015, March). *The ISIS Twitter census: Defining and describing the population of ISIS supporters on Twitter. The Brookings Project on U.S. Relations with the Islamic World - Analysis Paper, 20.* Retrieved from https://www.brookings.edu/wp-content /uploads/2016/06/isis_twitter_census_berger_morgan.pdf

Bickert, M., & Fishman, B. (2017, June 15). Hard questions: How we counter terrorism. Facebook Newsroom. Retrieved from https://newsroom.fb.com/news/2017/06/how-we-counter-terrorism/

Bickert, M., & Fishman, B. (2018, April 23). Hard questions: How effective is technology in keeping terrorists off Facebook? Facebook Newsroom. Retrieved from https://newsroom.fb.com/news /2018/04/keeping-terrorists-off-facebook/

Bipartisan Policy Center. (2018). Digital counterterrorism: Fighting jihadists online. Bipartisan Policy Center. Retrieved from https://bipartisanpolicy.org/event/digital-counterterrorism -fighting-jihadists-online/

Borum, R. (2011). Radicalization into violent extremism I: A review of social science theories. *Journal of Strategic Security, 4*(4), 7–36.

Brachman, J. M., & Levine, A. N. (2011). You too can be Awlaki. *Fletcher Forum of World Affairs* (1), 25–46.

Cagle, M. (2016, October 11). Facebook, Instagram, and Twitter provided data access for a surveillance product marketed to target activists of color. ACLU, Northern California. Retrieved from https://www.aclunc.org/blog/facebook-instagram-and-twitter-provided-data -access-surveillance-product-marketed-target

Chima, R. J. S. (2016). *Access Now position paper: A digital rights approach to proposals for preventing or countering violent extremism online.* Retrieved from https://www.accessnow.org /cms/assets/uploads/2016/10/CVE-online-10.27.pdf

Cope, S., York, J. C., & Gillula, J. (2017, July 12). Industry efforts to censor pro-terrorism online content pose risks to free speech. Electronic Frontier Foundation. Retrieved from https://www .eff.org/deeplinks/2017/07/industry-efforts-censor-pro-terrorism-online-content-pose-risks -free-speech

Darrah, K. (2017, September 20). Twitter algorithm detects terrorist accounts before they can tweet. The New Economy. Retrieved from https://www.theneweconomy.com/technology/twitter -algorithm-detects-terrorist-accounts-before-they-can-tweet

El-Bermawy, M. (2018, November 18). Your filter bubble is destroying democracy. *Wired*. Retrieved from https://www.wired.com/2016/11/filter-bubble-destroying-democracy/

Eledroos, N., & Crockford, K. (2018). Social media monitoring in Boston: Free speech in the crosshairs. Privacy SOS (ACLU of Massachusetts). Retrieved from https://privacysos.org/social-media-monitoring-boston-free-speech-crosshairs/

Gerraerts, S. (2012). Digital radicalization of youth. *Social Cosmos, 3*(1), 26–27.

Gunaratna, R., & Haynal, C. (2013). Current and emerging threats of homegrown terrorism: The case of the Boston bombings. *Perspectives on Terrorism, 7*(3), 44–63. Retrieved from http://www.jstor.org/stable/26296939

Hankes, K., & Amend, A. (2018, February 5). The alt-right is killing people. Southern Poverty Law Center. Retrieved from https://www.splcenter.org/20180205/alt-right-killing-people

Hughes, S., & Meleagrou-Hitchens, A. (2017). The threat to the United States from the Islamic State's virtual entrepreneurs. *CTC Sentinel*, (3), 1.

Knefel, J. (2013, May 6). Everything you've been told about radicalization is wrong. *Rolling Stone*. Retrieved from https://www.rollingstone.com/politics/politics-news/everything-youve-been-told-about-radicalization-is-wrong-80445/

Llanso, E. (2016, December 6). Takedown collaboration by private companies creates troubling precedent. Center for Democracy & Technology. Retrieved from https://cdt.org/blog/takedown-collaboration-by-private-companies-creates-troubling-precedent/

Martin, G. (2011). *Terrorism and Homeland Security*. Thousand Oaks, CA: Sage.

McCullough, K. (2016, May 6). Why government use of social media monitoring software is a direct threat to our liberty and privacy. ACLU of Oregon. Retrieved from https://www.aclu.org/blog/privacy-technology/surveillance-technologies/why-government-use-social-media-monitoring

Miller, G., & Higham, S. (2015, May 8). In a propaganda war against ISIS, the U.S. tried to play by the enemy's rules. *Washington Post*. Retrieved from https://www.washingtonpost.com/world/national-security/in-a-propaganda-war-us-tried-to-play-by-the-enemys-rules/2015/05/08/6eb6b732-e52f-11e4-81ea-0649268f729e_story.html?utm_term=.c3935125e26f

Mund, B. (2017). Social media searches and the reasonable expectation of privacy. *Yale Journal of Law and Technology, 19*(1), 238–273.

Neumann, P. (2012). Countering online radicalization in America. Bipartisan Policy Center. Retrieved from https://bipartisanpolicy.org/wp-content/uploads/2019/03/5086_BPC-_Online-Radicalization-Report-Executive-Summary-v4_web.pdf

Patel, F., & Koushik, M. (2017). *Countering violent extremism*. Brennan Center for Justice. Retrieved from https://www.brennancenter.org/sites/default/files/publications/Brennan%20Center%20CVE%20Report.pdf

Potok, M. (2015). Carnage in Charleston. *Intelligence Report, 159*, 20–25.

Pyszczynski, T., Abdollahi, A., Solomon, S., Greenberg, J., Cohen, F., & Weise, D. (2006). Mortality salience, martyrdom, and military might: The Great Satan versus the Axis of Evil. *Personality and Social Psychology Bulletin, 4*, 525.

Radicalization in the U.S. and the rise of terrorism. (2017). Joint hearing before the Subcommittee on National Security and the Subcommittee on Government Operations of the Committee on Oversight and Government Reform, House of Representatives, 104th Congress, second session, September 14, 2016. Retrieved from https://www.hsdl.org/?abstract&did=803987

Rudner, M. (2017). "Electronic Jihad": The Internet as Al Qaeda's catalyst for global terror. *Studies in Conflict and Terrorism, 40*(1), 10–23.

Sageman, M. (2008). *Leaderless jihad: Terror networks in the twenty-first century*. Philadelphia, PA: University of Pennsylvania Press.

Stern, K. S. (1999). *Hate and the Internet*. New York, NY: American Jewish Committee.

Suler, J. (2004). The online disinhibition effect. *Cyberpsychology and Behavior, 7*(3), 321–326.

Thomas, T. L. (2003, Spring). Al Qaeda and the Internet: The danger of "cyberplanning." [Electronic version] *Parameters, 33*(1), 112–123.

Twitter. (2018). Twitter rules enforcement. Retrieved from https://transparency.twitter.com/en/gov-tos-reports.html

Waddell, K. (2016, April 16). How surveillance stifles dissent on the Internet. *Atlantic*. Retrieved from https://www.theatlantic.com/technology/archive/2016/04/how-surveillance-mutes-dissent-on-the-internet/476955/

Weaver, M. (2015, July 20). Cameron's anti-terror strategy is "barking up wrong tree," says expert. *The Guardian* (London).

Weimann, G. (2004). www.terror.net: How modern terrorism uses the Internet. United States Institute of Peace, Special Report, p. 116.

YouTube. (2017a, August 1). An update on our commitment to fight terror content online. Official blog. Retrieved from https://youtube.googleblog.com/2017/08/an-update-on-our-commitment-to-fight.html

YouTube. (2017b, July 20). Bringing new redirect method features to YouTube. Official blog. Retrieved from https://youtube.googleblog.com/2017/07/bringing-new-redirect-method-features.html

Zhou, Y., Qin, J., Lai, G., Reid, E., & Chen, H. (2006). Exploring the dark side of the web: Collection and analysis of U.S. extremist online forums. In S. Mehrotra et al. (Eds.), *ISI 2006, LNCS 3975* (pp. 621–626). Verlag Berlin Heidelberg, Germany: Springer.

The Ethics of Catastrophic Incidents

David A. Mackey

When news segments chronicle the details of disasters across the globe, they bring the human toll of death, suffering, and injuries to a geographically disperse audience. Critical incidents can be naturally occurring or human-made, and both types result from a large variety of phenomena. Naturally occurring events, either related to weather or geological events, can include earthquakes, tsunamis, hurricanes, cyclones, droughts, and floods. Other types of critical incidents can include outbreaks of influenza, tuberculosis, anthrax, cholera, smallpox, Ebola, and efforts to introduce contamination into the food chain. In addition to accidents attributed to human error or faulty decision making, human-made critical incidents purposely intended to inflict physical and psychological damage on a population can involve nontraditional, violent, psychological, and economic approaches such as exploiting technological vulnerabilities, biological threats, and nuclear and chemical agents deployed against civilian targets. The National Infrastructure Protection Plan (NIPP) (NIPP, 2013) recognizes three aspects of critical infrastructure: physical, cyber, and human. The NIPP's focus on prevention, response, and mitigation of consequences of incidents targeting critical infrastructure has profound ethical issues.

Over time, because of the sophistication of our contemporary society in terms of our reliance on technology and the interconnectedness of society, our vulnerability to and potential consequences of several types of disasters have increased. For instance, the many facets of urbanization, numerous large public gatherings such as college and professional sporting events, and the relative ease of long-distance travel would certainly facilitate a swift transmission of a contagious disease among the U.S. population (Walsh, 2017). For societies across the globe, Walsh notes that geographic regions experiencing various forms of human conflict may be at greater risk for disease and illness because of interrupted international and national health monitoring and disease-surveillance efforts as well as the potential for a limited, organized international assistance once critical needs are identified. In addition, regional refugees may present challenges to the containment of various threats and response efforts, which may provide both a spread of infection to new people that refugees encounter and also a wider geographic dispersal that makes response and treatment more difficult. To illustrate recent disease outbreaks with the potential for widespread impact, Walsh cites Ebola, Zika, Middle East respiratory syndrome, and concerns with H7N9 influenza in China.

▶ Influenza

Although more exotic disease threats generate media attention because of their novelty, seasonal influenza inflicts a tremendous human toll each year. The domestic impact is illustrated by reports that 2018 was one of the worst years for the flu in the United States in nearly 40 years, killing 80,000 people and hospitalizing 900,000 (Scutti, 2018). To put this number into perspective, the FBI reports that an estimated 17,284 murders were reported in the United States in 2017 (U.S. Department of Justice, 2018). Although the 2018 influenza season was unusually virulent, according to the Centers for Disease Control and Prevention (2017), "between 291,000 and 646,000 people worldwide die from seasonal influenza-related respiratory illnesses each year, higher than a previous estimate of 250,000 to 500,000" (para 1). The average annual toll in the United States attributed to the seasonal flu is around 36,000 deaths (Agwunobi, 2007).

Along with medical, economic, and logistic concerns, pandemics of various origins have several ethical considerations concerning timely public information related to prevention and response. Walker (2016) contends the next pandemic event will be chronicled and communicated in minute detail through social media. There are benefits of a flattened communication hierarchy (i.e., many news platforms and media) during times of crisis. This flattened structure can be positive by disseminating timely news, public health instructions, and government alerts. Agencies and individuals can communicate directly to their audiences. Schwab and Beatley (2013) describe numerous efforts using social media to coordinate volunteer-response efforts as well as connecting individuals negatively impacted by a disaster to community resources such as temporary housing. Accurate and appropriate information about safeguards, precautions, and risks is critically important (Walker, 2016). On the negative side, Schwab and Beatley (2013) note that contemporary news programming's competition for ratings may lead to sensationalism; these issues are compounded by a constant news cycle and the need for continuous news. Inaccurate reports have consequences in times of crisis. "Hundreds of millions of people will receive unvetted and incorrect assertions, uncensored images, and unqualified guidance, all of which, if acted on, could endanger their own health, seriously damage their economies, and undermine the stability of their societies" (Walker, 2016, p. 43). Although sensationalism and shoddy reporting is problematic, to make matters even worse, communications during a public health crisis could be intentionally manipulated to create and intensify fear and incite panic among a population. For instance, Walker notes that social media may facilitate "intentional lies or highly disruptive bio-terror propaganda" (2016, p. 43). Walker notes that deliberate disinformation could be used to cause a run on grocery stores for food and water, as well as on pharmacies and hospitals for real or fictious antivirals or treatment. A psychological toll on a population might also be facilitated by uncensored visual details of suffering and death.

The 2018 flu season was historically significant in the United States and around the world, but it was not declared a pandemic. Bissell and Kirsch (2013b) note that a pandemic is classified on its geographic spread throughout the world rather than the magnitude of total reported cases or deaths; this scenario would be described as an epidemic. Just over a century ago, the pandemic of 1918 spanned the globe with successive waves of flu. Its transmission was aided by the movement and quartering of troops mobilized for World War I. Assembled masses of service members in barracks, trains, and transport ships provided fertile grounds for the transmission of influenza. Barry (2005) identifies the importance of the term *excess death toll*, which is the deaths attributed to influenza above and beyond those normally expected. Barry notes that "the 1918–19 epidemic caused an excess death toll of about 675,000 people. The nation then had a population between 105 and 110 million" (p. 238). Extrapolating the excess death toll to more current population numbers, Agwunobi (2007) contends that a contemporary pandemic on scale with the 1918 pandemic might produce as many as 2 million deaths. Crosby (2003) noted that the 4,597 deaths in Philadelphia in one week were attributed to influenza and pneumonia. Several issues would also emerge with these deaths: safe body removal, burial, orphaned children, and impacted services in the city.

Seasonal influenza exacts a physical toll, but according to Walker (2016), the dangers of genetically modified viruses created to serve as bioweapons would be even worse. Walker notes that bioweapons are not the exclusive domain of international superpowers requiring the vast expenditure of money and exclusive technical knowledge. Nonstate terror groups have the ability to genetically modify an existing disease or even resurrect a dormant virus from the past. As Walker notes, depending on the extent of genetic modifications, people's natural immunity to a virus as well as the lack of stockpiled of vaccines may not provide an effective defense against novel viruses.

No effective vaccine may be available at the onset of infection, and producing one might take six months because it would require the actual strain of virus in order to produce a vaccine (Agwunobi, 2007). Bissell and Kirsch (2013a) note that a future pandemic should be viewed as probable rather than a preposterous notion because contemporary humans would have little to no immunity to a novel virus.

Kotalik (2005) notes two additional global outbreaks in 1957 and 1968. Efforts at prevention and remediation occur at the federal, regional, state, and local levels. Planning and response involves ethical issues because allocating limited resources may have life-or-death implications. For instance, Thomas and Young (2011) examined influenza plans and the public health web sites of different states to determine the extent to which ethical considerations were specifically addressed and integrated into pandemic preparedness. They noted that recent state health plans emphasized ethical considerations to a greater extent than in the past once ethics was brought to national attention largely because of a national conference. Although they noted a recent increase in the attention to ethics, Thomas and Young note that only one in five states identified an ethical framework in their plans. Kotalik (2005, p. 424) notes that it is only recently that bioethics has developed a methodology to assess ethical considerations in pandemic plans.

▶ Vaccines

Peterson (2008) examined moral values and ethical considerations of vaccine distribution specifically in regard to the overall priority for vaccine distribution. An equal
right to vaccines would effectively require some type of lottery to give every person
an equal chance of being selected for vaccination. As Peterson noted, "None of the
contingency plans currently implemented by western democratic governments recognize that all citizens have equal rights to vaccine" (2008, p. 321). A vaccine cannot
be produced until the strain of the virus has been identified; therefore, the supply of
vaccines would be only gradually developed and probably could not be stockpiled
and prepositioned (Kotalik, 2005). The World Health Organization plans for vaccine distribution based on the premise that some individuals have a higher value
to society than others and should be prioritized for earlier vaccination to increase
their individual odds of survival. For example, several vaccination models prioritize
workers who are employed in the vaccine-production process as well as hospital
staff and first responders (e.g., doctors, nurses, and EMTs). Their survivability, in
turn, should lead to fewer infections and mortality because of the work they would
perform. In this model, groups having priority for vaccination would be those performing essential services related to medical response or the physical security of
those efforts.

Alternatively, Peterson (2011) notes that some models may include political
leaders in the priority category, along with health-care workers, to ensure political continuity. Peterson notes the unfairness of such an approach. In other models, a lottery system can be implemented in which every individual has a calculable
chance of being selected—but not necessarily an equal chance of being selected. For
instance, doctors and nurses would be weighted more heavily in the random draw.
As a related issue, Kotalik (2005) discusses the issue of forced, mandatory vaccinations, which may run counter to the wishes of individuals. Vaccination and disproportionately favorable access to medical care would also be advocated to reduce the
likelihood of medical personnel and first responders being disease-transmitting vectors (Bissell & Kirsch, 2013b; Kotalik, 2005). Prioritizing their vaccinations could be
based on two different reasons: the value of the work they perform or their increased
risk of infection because of the work they perform. Bissell and Kirsch (2013a) raise
an interesting point: Emergency responders and health-care providers may likely
have priority status for vaccinations, but whether they report to work or take care of
their own families highlights a real issue of conflicting duties. As an example, Crosby
(2003, p. 75) noted that 487 police officers in Philadelphia failed to report to work
during the 1918 pandemic.

Ethical questions remain as to whether the morally superior policy is one that
saves the greatest number of people by increasing chances that public health professionals survive or the one that creates a system that provides everyone an equal
chance of vaccination. The reality would be many people would need scarce medical
care such as antiviral treatment and access to ventilators, bed space, and access to
medical expertise (Kotalik, 2005). Schwab and Beatley (2013) raise the question as
to whether every human life has the same value. For instance, Peterson identifies
"a purely consequentialist account of morality: an action is right if and only if its
outcome is optimal" (2008, p. 324). Some theorists contend it is critical that everyone has some chance, however small, of receiving the vaccination as a basic issue of

fairness. In addition to vaccines, hospital care would most likely be rationed and individuals triaged for care. Depending on the surge of medical cases, most medical care might potentially be home-based palliative care rather than hospital care because of the number of beds and ventilators trying to control transmission vectors. The prevailing theme might well be the greatest good for the many. Although the discussion to this point has been about the distribution of a limited resource, a system of triage may be necessary because of the limited treatment resources available:

> [They] are designed to produce the greatest good for the greatest number by meeting human needs most effectively and efficiently under conditions of scarcity. They are structured to satisfy the formal criterion of justice (to treat similar cases similarly and equal cases equally), and their minimal material criteria for distribution of treatment is some combination of patients' needs and the probability of successful treatment. (Childress, 2004, para 7)

▶ Ethical Models

Disasters have immediate and long-term disruptions on businesses. Each type of disaster presents unique challenges for the continuity of operations. For instance, in a pandemic, employees not reporting for work either because they are sick or fear getting sick is a likely scenario. Many occupations may not lend themselves to working remotely from home so that a redesign of job tasks and responsibilities may be needed because of short staffing and the social-distancing measures that would need to be employed. The decision to stay home may be easier for some people but more complicated for others. For example, in the fictional work chronicling the impact of an influenza outbreak, the main characters in Konkoly's (2013) novel *The Jakarta Pandemic* had sufficient financial means to be able to take extended medical leave, and her spouse was able to quit his job when given the directive to report to work in a city experiencing many cases of influenza. The reality for some people is that not working may mean not getting paid. This reality would have a greater impact on the poor and disadvantaged. Baum, Jacobson, and Goold (2009) also identify the economic cost of staying home to watch children who may be sick or whose schools are closed to limit exposure. Likewise, if schools are closed to implement social-distancing measures, would youths stay confined at home and not socialize together if left unsupervised?

Baum, Jacobson, and Goold (2009) examined public perceptions of social-distancing measures as part of pandemic planning. Although mass transportation, school, and work may be places that challenge notions of social distancing, neighborhoods may seek to isolate themselves to limit exposure. Larger-scale social isolation presents operational challenges and ethical issues. Geographic quarantine may have limited effectiveness because of the time between exposure and the onset of symptoms (Agwunobi, 2007). Walker (2016) notes that these social-distancing measures are ideally dictated based on a scientific approach to the specific type of threat such as one spread by air, by bodily fluids, or by contaminated food or water sources. Organization and truly self-sufficient enclaves of communities may be rare. Agwunobi (2007) notes that schools may be closed for upward of 18 months in a pandemic. A quarantine would be only as effective as its physical barrier, which may be compromised by the arrival of close family members or strangers seeking refuge. For example, a child may arrive from an out-of-state university or in-laws may show up. Bissell and Kirsch (2013a) note that influenza would likely spread in waves over time. The initial lull after the first wave would not necessarily signal the end of the danger although some people might be tempted to declare the situation all clear.

One participant in Baum, Jacobson, and Goold's (2009) focus group on public perceptions of social-distancing measures enacted during a pandemic stated "the plan can't be created based on popularity and what . . . will make the most people happy because what will make the most people happy is certainly not the common good" (p. 9). Truly difficult choices would be made such as who would be let in, what functions would be critical to maintain, and what resources would be shared or consumed individually. Typical behavior patterns would be disrupted by social-distancing measures that restrict an individual's ability to freely move about and associate with others. One area of note is churches and houses of worship. Baum, Jacobson, and Goold (2009) continue: "Participants in our groups emphasized the importance of religious gatherings during times of crisis, suggesting that contingency plans to provide alternative avenues for spiritual guidance and support must be considered" (p. 11). Social-distancing measures slow transmission rates, which would allow time to develop and test a vaccine; these measures would need to be sustained over time to ensure their effectiveness. Social-distancing measures would close schools from preschool to college as well as nonessential workplaces, yet aspects of the economy would need to continue to function to avoid a financial collapse. Likewise, grocery stores present challenges to remain open and stocked on a near daily basis with a just-in-time distribution system. Stores would require trucking to restock, workers to shelve, and cashiers to remain open.

A key question when considering an individual's duty to help other people is whether this duty extends to those with whom the individual has no ongoing relationship, whether they are unfamiliar neighbors or complete strangers. To what extent do people have a duty to care for strangers in distant lands? How far out does our duty to care extend in terms of our geographic and social connections? Is there a moral duty to assist a neighbor in times of crisis if it may compromise one's safety and security? This distinction is also identified by Banks (2017) when discussing how far out this duty of care extends. Schwab and Beatley (2013) identify donor fatigue as a concern as each humanitarian crisis produces a plea for help typically in the form of cash donations. Does the motivation behind the assistance offered undermine or negate its moral worth? For example, based on a deontological perspective, people would have a duty to help their neighbors because they are neighbors. Alternatively, deontologists would see no moral value in helping one's neighbor if it was done with the motive of personal satisfaction in helping others. Likewise, helping others would have no moral value if the aid was offered as a way to strengthen one's own position by not having weak and desperate neighbors who may pose a threat to their safety and security.

Dudley (2003) notes that first responders, doctors, and nurses have a critical role in recognizing and responding to covert biological or chemical attacks. Dudley notes that smallpox is considered one of the more dangerous bioweapons because of its characteristics. As an illness, smallpox lasts around a month and is lethal in some 30% of cases. It is extremely contagious, can be spread from person to person, and can be passed to people from contaminated objects. Dudley notes that smallpox's potential as a bioweapon is enhanced by its latency period of seven to 21 days. Exposed individuals may be free of symptoms for as long as three weeks, which potentially increases its transmission. Economics plays a role in prevention efforts as well. Walsh (2017) notes there is little financial incentive to develop and market a vaccine for some infectious diseases such as Ebola, which has a 90% mortality rate. One of the more effective defenses against Ebola comes from its relatively short incubation period coupled with its high death rate. With limited exceptions, its cases have been limited geographically. Areas marked by poverty and conflict may be at risk. In poorer nations around the globe, health-care systems are already resource-strapped in terms of personnel and facilities.

Questions remain as to the prevalence and likelihood of a catastrophic event in the near future. Taleb (2010) describes so-called black swan events as low-probability but high-consequence events. These types of events can include disease outbreaks such as those previously mentioned as well as those incidents triggered by technological vulnerabilities such as power-grid vulnerabilities, water supplies, and financial networks. Koppel (2015) details the vulnerability of the nation's power grids to cyberintrusions and physical attacks. One type of physical attack could result from natural or human-made activities. For instance, an electromagnetic pulse (EMP) is caused by a high-altitude detonation of a nuclear device; EMP also can occur naturally by an extraterrestrial event as a solar flare. The potential consequences of the event were noted in the *Report of the Commission to Assess the Threat to the United States from Electromagnetic Pulse (EMP) Attack*:

> Depending on the specific characteristics of the attacks, unprecedented cascading failures of our major infrastructures could result. . . . The longer the outage, the more problematic and uncertain the recovery will be. It is possible for the functional outages to become mutually reinforcing until at some point the degradation of infrastructure could have irreversible effects on the country's ability to support its population. (Foster et al., 2004, pp. 1–2)

An EMP or cyberintrusion would disrupt electric-power production and distribution, resulting in serious degradation of infrastructure and essential services. This negative impact would include communications, public water systems, sewerage disposal, food delivery, and long-term medical care.

▶ Legal Concerns

Schwab and Beatley (2013) address issues related to equal protection under the law as it relates to disaster preparedness. Specific categories of people are protected by federal law—the aged, children, individuals with physical disabilities and prisoners—which should be considered during planning and response. Some groups may be at higher risk for secondary effects, which is the harm and injuries after catastrophes (Bissell and Kirsch, 2013b) that often involve safe food, water, and shelter. Tognotti (2013) notes this may require supplies to those individuals who are home confined, institutionalized, or less advantaged and therefore unprepared. Schwab and Beatley note that some individuals and families may not have the economic resources to prepare for an event, and this may accentuate their vulnerability if they cannot adhere to the fairly minimal recommendation set by the Federal Emergency Management Agency to stockpile three days' worth of food in case of emergency.

Ethical issues can be addressed by an individual's personal moral compass (which is shaped in part by upbringing, religion, and education), whereas some decisions are dictated by professional codes of conduct and professional ethics. For instance, Schwab and Beatley (2013) note emergency managers' code of ethics and its emphasis on respect, commitment, and professionalism. Legal aspects apply as well in terms of the treatment of people, especially vulnerable segments of the population (Schwab & Beatley, 2013). Likewise, doctors and nurses have their own professional ethics. Key aspects address professional duties to others while maintaining their own personal safety and limiting exposure to danger. Aspects of disaster preparedness such as a triage of care during a medical surge are based on objective decision making drawing from a utilitarian perspective of the greatest good for the many. Yet there remains an ethical duty based on moral obligations regardless of the consequences for human welfare (Tognotti, 2013).

▶ References

Agwunobi, J. O. (2007). Pandemic influenza: The threat, health system implications, and legal preparedness. *Journal of Law, Medicine & Ethics*, 3523–3527. Retrieved from https://journals.sagepub.com/doi/abs/10.1111/j.1748-720X.2007.00203.x?journalCode=lmec

Banks, C. (2017). *Criminal justice ethics: Theory and practice* (4th ed.). Los Angeles, CA: Sage.

Barry, J. M. (2005). *The great influenza: The epic story of the deadliest plague in history*. New York, NY: Penguin Books.

Baum, N. M., Jacobson, P. D., & Goold, S. D. (2009). "Listen to the people": Public deliberation about social distancing measures in a pandemic. *American Journal of Bioethics: AJOB*, 9(11), 4–14. Retrieved from https://www.tandfonline.com/doi/abs/10.1080/15265160903197531

Bissell, R., & Kirsch, T. (2013a). Pandemic scenario. In R. Bissell (Ed.), *Preparedness and response for catastrophic disasters* (pp. 301–317). Boca Raton, FL: CRC Press.

Bissell, R., & Kirsch, T. (2013b). Public health role in catastrophes. In R. Bissell (Ed.), *Preparedness and response for catastrophic disasters* (pp. 171–183). Boca Raton, FL: CRC Press.

Centers for Disease Control and Prevention. (2017). Seasonal flu death estimate increases worldwide. Retrieved from https://www.cdc.gov/media/releases/2017/p1213-flu-death-estimate.html

Childress, J. F. (2004). Disaster triage. *AMA Journal of Ethics*, 6(5). Retrieved from https://journalofethics.ama-assn.org/article/disaster-triage/2004-05

Crosby, A. W. (2003). *America's forgotten pandemic: The influenza of 1918* (2nd ed.). New York, NY: Cambridge University Press.

Dudley, J. P. (2003). New challenges for public health care: Biological and chemical weapons awareness, surveillance, and response. *Biological Research for Nursing*, 4(4), 244–250.

Foster, J. S., Jr., Gjelde, E., Graham, W. R., Hermann, R. J., Kluepfel, H. M., Lawson, R. L., . . . & Woodard, J. B. (2004). Report of the Commission to Assess the Threat to the United States from Electromagnetic Pulse (EMP) Attack. Volume 1: Executive report. Retrieved from http://www.empcommission.org/docs/empc_exec_rpt.pdf

Konkoly, S. (2013). *The Jakarta pandemic: A novel*. New York, NY: Stribling Media.

Koppel, T. (2015). *Lights out: A cyber attack A nation unprepared surviving the aftermath*. New York, NY: Crown Publishers.

Kotalik, J. (2005). Preparing for an influenza pandemic: Ethical issues. *Bioethics*, 19(4), 422–431.

National Infrastructure Protection Plan (NIPP). (2013). Partnering for critical infrastructure security and resilience. Washington, DC: Department of Homeland Security. Retrieved from https://www.dhs.gov/publication/nipp-2013-partnering-critical-infrastructure-security-and-resilience

Peterson, M. (2008). The moral importance of selecting people randomly. *Bioethics, 22*(6), 321–327. Retrieved from https://www.ncbi.nlm.nih.gov/pubmed/18445094

Peterson, M. (2011). Pandemic influenza and utilitarianism. *Bioethics, 25*(5), 290–291. Retrieved from https://onlinelibrary.wiley.com/doi/abs/10.1111/j.1467-8519.2010.01805.x

Schwab, A. K., & Beatley, T. (2013). Ethics in catastrophe readiness and response. In R. Bissell (Ed.), *Preparedness and response for catastrophic disasters* (pp. 45–75). Boca Raton, FL: CRC Press.

Scutti, S. (2018, September 27). Flu season deaths top 80,000 last year, CDC says. CNN. Retrieved from https://www.cnn.com/2018/09/26/health/flu-deaths-2017-2018-cdc-bn/index.html

Taleb, N. N. (2010). *The black swan: The impact of the highly improbable.* New York, NY: Random House.

Thomas, J. C., & Young, S. (2011). Wake me up when there's a crisis: Progress on state pandemic influenza ethics preparedness. *American Journal of Public Health, 101*(11), 2080–2082. Retrieved from https://www.ncbi.nlm.nih.gov/pubmed/21940921

Tognotti, E. (2013). Lessons from the history of quarantine, from plague to Influenza A. *Emerging Infectious Diseases, 19*(2) 254–259.

U.S. Department of Justice. (2018). *Crime in the United States, 2017.* Washington, DC: U.S. Dept. of Justice, Federal Bureau of Investigation. Retrieved from https://ucr.fbi.gov/crime-in-the -u.s/2017/crime-in-the-u.s.-2017/topic-pages/murder

Walker, J. (2016). Civil society's role in a public health crisis. *Issues in Science & Technology, 32*(4), 43–48.

Walsh, B. (2017). Warning: The next global security threat isn't what you think. *Time, 189*(18), 32–38.

SECTION 9

Ethics and Social Change

© Sergii Gnatiuk/Shutterstock.

Social Change and the U.S. Courts

Brendan Toner
Joshua L. Mitchell

▶ Introduction

More than 70 years ago, psychologist Kurt Lewin (1947) stated that social change and social stability should be analyzed together because both occur and often in tandem. For example, the monikers "Roaring 20s" and "Jazz Age" referred to the time period in the United States when the economy boomed, wages rose, and commercial radio and motion pictures appeared. The 1960s brought enhancements in civil rights and an increase in social protest, while other decades such as the 1950s were relatively stable. However, many of the events in the 1950s likely led to the changes that occurred in the 1960s, so both are of fundamental importance.

With social change, though, there are forces both driving and resisting change, which makes the issue complex. Although interest groups, citizens, and policy makers participate in this effort, the legal system in the United States itself has been a driver of social change. In periods of unresolved conflict, the U.S. Supreme Court has ruled on a wide variety of issues, including abortion, gay marriage, secularization, and racial segregation.

Since the founding of the United States there has been a connection between law and social change. Many current U.S. social norms would be unthinkable if not for the intervention of the courts. Some observers, though, have argued that the Supreme Court's role throughout most of history has been to block social change (Blake, 2015). We can see this opposition and support for change in how the Court dealt with legislation related to President Franklin Roosevelt's New Deal. In other periods in history, however, the Court led the way on social change, which is evident in the Court's support for desegregation and integration in the mid-to late 20th century. This article will look at these issues along with more recent controversies over rights for same-sex couples and how the courts have responded to those challenges.

This article is an overview of some of the controversies the courts have faced over the years. One of the challenges a student faces is being able to understand these historical debates and how they have framed many of the political and legal issues we see today in the United States. We hope the discussion will encourage students to learn more about these issues.

▶ Teaching of Evolution

Such social movements are not only confined to the Supreme Court. In 1925, national attention turned to Dayton, Tennessee, when two nationally known and high-profile attorneys clashed over the concepts of creationism and evolution and their places in society. In the John T. Scopes case, the issue was whether modern science, including the theory of evolution, could be taught in school. Scopes was a high school teacher who challenged Tennessee's Butler Act, which prohibited the teaching of evolution in state-funded schools.

On one side of the trial, former presidential candidate William Jennings Bryan, an opponent of teaching evolution, faced off against famed defense attorney Clarence Darrow, who defended Scopes teaching evolution. After an eight-day trial in July 1925, a jury ruled in favor of the state and fined Scopes $100; the decision was later overturned on a technicality (Greenberg, 2005). The Tennessee law stood for many more years before it was finally overturned.

Many years later in the case of *Epperson v. Arkansas* (1968), the U.S. Supreme Court struck down a law passed by the state in the 1920s (soon after the Scopes trial) banning the teaching of evolution in the classroom (Lancaster, 2017). This decision, however, did not end the controversy by any stretch of the imagination; debates still rage over what is being taught in public schools, including over the so-called theory of intelligent design, which some call a nonscientific belief similar to creationism (Addicott, 2002).

▶ New Deal

Going back to the turn of the 20th century, the Supreme Court ruled against states such as New York as evidenced by its decision in *Lochner v. New York* (Bernstein, 2015). This case involved New York's attempt to establish minimum wages and ban child labor to protect against Industrial Era abuses during a time of great social change. The Court at the time argued that businesses should have a right to conduct their business without having to deal with government intervention, which is known as *economic due process* (Stephens, Scheb, & Glennon, 2015). Therefore, in other words, the Court gave companies free rein to do as they saw fit, putting the burden on the government to provide a constitutional reason for the law to be enacted.

This line of thinking also inspired the Supreme Court to oppose much of Roosevelt's New Deal legislation during his first term, 1933 to 1937. Key rulings around this time invalidated the National Recovery Administration (which included minimum wages and workers' rights) and the Agricultural Adjustment Act (Shesol, 2010). This hostility toward social change even included decisions against minimum-wage laws passed by the states, not the federal government (Leuchtenburg, 2005).

Faced with such opposition to legislation to address social change, Roosevelt sought to have Congress pass a law that would add more justices to the Supreme Court for every justice age 70 or older in order to support his policy initiatives. Even though this was not traditional, the U.S. Constitution does not place a limit on the number of justices who can sit on the Supreme Court at one time. Despite this, the backlash to Roosevelt's plan was tremendous and ultimately doomed it because it did not garner enough support in Congress.

Despite this setback, however, Roosevelt ultimately came out on top as the Court changed its outlook on the New Deal, largely to protect its own institution from tinkering by the executive and legislative branches of government. Roosevelt's long tenure in the presidency also allowed him to outlast judicial opposition on the Court and to appoint new justices who would support his policy changes. This was evidenced by the Court's decision on a minimum-wage law from Washington state and two occasions when it voted to uphold the National Labor Relations Act, leading to what some called the "Constitutional Revolution of 1937" (Leuchtenburg, 2005).

▶ School Desegregation

The courts have not always been resistant to social change; in some cases, they have been at the forefront of such change. This maybe can be seen most clearly in the school-desegregation cases of the 1950s and 1960s. One of the most famous Supreme Court cases was decided in 1954 when the Court in *Brown v. Board of Education* struck down racial segregation in public schools. This highly controversial decision, especially in the South (although the case itself came from Kansas), came when segregated schools were the norm in many states. In fact, Chief Justice Earl Warren made it a point to establish unanimity on the Court even though it was not necessary to show how seriously the Court felt about this decision.

One of the first challenges to this decision came a few years later in 1957 in Little Rock, Arkansas, when African American students were attempting to integrate the city's public schools. After local resistance, including from the state's governor, the decision was enforced by the U.S. Army. As a result of this, the Little Rock school board challenged the desegregation order and went to court. Once again, the Supreme Court came out in favor of integration with a unanimous decision in the case of *Cooper v. Aaron* (1958).

Following decisions such as these, the Supreme Court then went beyond ending school segregation—because many schools had not integrated—by compelling integration in public schools. One major decision in this area was *Swann v. Charlotte-Mecklenburg Board of Education* (1971). The public schools in Charlotte, North Carolina, had not integrated much since the Supreme Court rulings from more than a decade earlier.

As with previous desegregation cases, the Court voted unanimously in favor of school integration. For Charlotte, specifically, the Court gave Federal District Judge James McMillan the authority to force the school district to submit an acceptable integration plan (Brabham, 2006). This model used in Charlotte was applied to other cities throughout the nation, including those outside the South such as Boston (McAndrews, 1997), where Federal District Judge Arthur Garrity issued a similar integration edict in that city's public schools (Lukas, 1985). This is an area in which the courts continued their involvement throughout the rest of the 20th century.

Since its founding, Boston had a highly segregated public school system as evidenced by the fact that schools in the Roxbury section of the city were mainly African American but schools in the South Boston area were almost exclusively White. To remedy this, Judge Garrity who became so closely associated with this situation was placed in charge of the decision only by lottery assignment (Goldberg, 1999), ensuring there was a plan for integration in place when he decided the case of *Morgan v. Hennigan* in 1974 (Formisano, 2004).

This was one of the most controversial issues in the Boston region because many residents protested the changes as approximately 18,000 children had to leave their traditional neighborhood schools and travel by bus to schools on the other side of town (Gellerman, 2014). These protests included marches at the homes and workplaces of Judge Garrity and Senator Edward Kennedy, who supported integration. This led to several violent incidents throughout the city and in the schools themselves; some observers even began calling Boston the "Little Rock of the North" (Formisano, 2004).

This situation continued for years as Garrity continued to oversee integration in the city. In 1989, busing was replaced by a system called "controlled choice," which still used race, but it was not much of a determinant as before. Only around the turn of the 21st century did the city finally put an end to the integration program which ironically happened soon before Judge Garrity died in 1999 (Goldberg, 1999). No matter how one views Garrity, most people might agree with the statement made by former Boston Mayor Thomas Menino at the time of Garrity's passing: "Whether you agreed or disagreed with his decision with his opinion a generation ago, everyone can agree Judge Garrity's influence on our city will be felt for a long time" (Gellerman, 2014).

▶ Abortion

During the 1970s, one of the most influential and controversial court rulings ever made by the Supreme Court was the case of *Roe v. Wade* in 1973. The decision legalized abortion in the United States. Before the *Roe* decision, states were left to create their own laws governing abortion rights. Whether or not one supported it, *Roe* had a far-reaching social effect in the United States.

In the years after the Roe decision, many challenges worked their way through state and federal courts. One major case that sought to weaken *Roe* was *Planned Parenthood of Southeastern Pennsylvania v. Casey* in 1992. Some legal scholars and observers felt that the case could undo *Roe v. Wade* because the Court had become far more conservative following appointments by President Ronald Reagan in the 1980s. The decision in this case, though, was mixed because it upheld *Roe* but also approved restrictions like those from Pennsylvania. Needless to say, it upset advocates on both sides (Daly, 1995).

This continues to be a major area of dispute into the 21st century with some prochoice advocates fearing that the *Roe* decision will be overturned following the 2018 retirement of Associate Justice Anthony Kennedy, one of the key votes upholding *Roe* in the 1990s. To replace Kennedy, President Donald Trump nominated U.S. Circuit Judge Brett Kavanaugh, a jurist who is decidedly more conservative on the issue (North, 2018). Some observers, however, feel that the *Casey* decision settled abortion law for the time being no matter who is added to the

Court (Devins, 2009). Regardless of outcome, the next few years will be extremely interesting.

▶ LGBT Rights

In the early hours on June 28, 1969, New York City police raided a gay club, the Stonewall Inn, in the city's Greenwich Village neighborhood. They police confiscated bootlegged alcohol and arrested 13 people employed at the bar or who had violated the city's gender-appropriate clothing code. The incident quickly led to rioting by club patrons and neighborhood residents, leading to six days of violence. This served as a nationwide and worldwide catalyst for the gay rights movement (Armstrong & Crage, 2006).

Another contemporary issue facing the Supreme Court is the argument over LGBTQ rights. In 2012, a cakeshop baker who held religious views against homosexuality refused to make a wedding cake for a same-sex couple. At that time, same-sex marriage was not recognized in Colorado. In 2018, the U.S. Supreme Court heard the case *Masterpiece Cakeshop v. Colorado Civil Rights Commission* and examined the issue of whether or not a business could exercise its First Amendment rights and refuse service to specific people (U.S. Supreme Court, 2018).

Colorado law prohibits businesses open to the public from refusing services based on an individual's race, religion, color, national origins, or sexual orientation. A complaint was filed with the Colorado Civil Rights Division, and the commission ruled that the bakery discriminated against the individuals. In 2015, the Colorado Court of Appeals affirmed the commission's ruling and also concluded that the state's Anti-Discrimination Act did not violate the bakery's freedom of speech or its free exercise of religion. The Colorado Supreme Court did not see case. In 2018, the U.S. Supreme reversed the decision in *Masterpiece Cakeshop v. Colorado Civil Rights Commission* based on concerns specific to the case (American Civil Liberties Union, 2018).

In the case *Obergefell v. Hodges* (2015), the Court ruled that the right to marry is guaranteed to same-sex couples under the equal protection and due process clauses of the 14th Amendment to the United States Constitution. This Court ruling afforded same-sex couples the same rights as heterosexual couples in all 50 states. This case also overturned *Baker v. Nelson* (1971), which had ruled that same-sex marriage bans were constitutional.

▶ Conclusion

As this article shows, the law and the courts at many different levels have played key roles in both advancing and sometimes slowing social change in the United States. This involvement has taken place in debates over religion, education policy, racial equality, abortion, and LGBTQ rights. Of course, this is not a complete list of the social issues the courts have been involved with, but they are among the most prominent. This judicial involvement has been happening since the nation's founding, continues to this day, and will likely continue into the future. The courts now will likely grapple with such issues far into the 21st century and beyond, especially with the advent of the Internet and related technologies that will have to be addressed.

▶ References

Addicott, J. F. (2002). Storm clouds on the horizon of Darwinism: Teaching the anthropic principle and intelligent design in the public schools. *Ohio State Law Journal, 63*, 1507–1599. Retrieved from https://kb.osu.edu/handle/1811/70516

American Civil Liberties Union. (2018). *Masterpiece Cakeshop v. Colorado Civil Rights Commission.* Retrieved from https://www.aclu.org/cases/masterpiece-cakeshop-v-colorado-civil-rights-commission

Armstrong, E. A., & Crage, S. M. (2006). Movements and memory: The making of the stonewall myth. *American Sociological Review, 71*(5), 724–751. Retrieved from https://journals.sagepub.com/doi/abs/10.1177/000312240607100502

Baker v. Nelson, 291 Minn. 310, 191 N.W.2d 185 (1971).

Bernstein, D. E. (2005). *Lochner v. New York*: A centennial retrospective. *Washington University Law Review, 83*(5), 1469–1527. Retrieved from https://wustllawreview.org/wp-content/uploads/2017/09/2-39.pdf

Blake, J. (2015, June 27). Supreme Court a force for change? Not so fast. CNN. Retrieved from https://www.cnn.com/2015/06/21/us/supreme-court-change/index.html

Brabham, R. (2006). *Swann v. Charlotte-Mecklenberg Board of Education. Encyclopedia of North Carolina*. Retrieved from https://www.ncpedia.org/swann-v-charlotte-mecklenburg-board

Cooper v. Aaron, 358 U.S. 1 (1958).

Daly, E. (1995). Reconsidering abortion law: Liberty, equality, and the new rhetoric of *Planned Parenthood v. Casey. American University Law Review, 45*(1), 77–150. Retrieved from https://digitalcommons.wcl.american.edu/cgi/viewcontent.cgi?article=1417&context=aulr

Devins, N. (2009). How "Planned Parenthood v. Casey" (pretty much) settled the abortion wars. *Yale Law Journal, 118*, 1318–1354. Retrieved from https://papers.ssrn.com/sol3/papers.cfm?abstract_id=1478487

Formisano, R. P. (2004). *Boston against busing: Race, class, and ethnicity in the 1960s and 1970s.* Chapel Hill, NC: University of North Carolina Press. Retrieved from https://www.researchgate.net/publication/319448697_Boston_against_busing_Race_class_and_ethnicity_in_the_1960s_and_1970s

Gellerman, B. (2014, September 5). "It was like a war zone": Busing in Boston. WBUR News. Retrieved from https://www.wbur.org/news/2014/09/05/boston-busing-anniversary

Goldberg, C. (1999, September 18). Judge W. Arthur Garrity is dead at 79. *The New York Times.* Retrieved from https://www.nytimes.com/1999/09/18/us/judge-w-arthur-garrity-jr-is-dead-at-79.html

Greenberg, D. (2005, September 8). The legend of the Scopes trial. *Slate*. Retrieved from https://slate.com/news-and-politics/2005/09/the-legend-of-the-scopes-trial.html

Lancaster, G. (2017, June 14). *Epperson v. Arkansas. The Encylopedia of Arkansas History and Culture*. Retrieved from https://encyclopediaofarkansas.net/entries/epperson-v-arkansas-2528/

Leuchtenburg, W. (2005, May). When Franklin Roosevelt clashed with the Supreme Court and lost. *Smithsonian Magazine*. Retrieved from https://www.smithsonianmag.com/history/when-franklin-roosevelt-clashed-with-the-supreme-court-and-lost-78497994/

Lewin, K. (1947). Frontiers in group dynamics: Concept, method and reality in social science; social equilibria and social change." *Human Relations, 1*(1), 5–41. Retrieved from https://www.scribd.com/document/349430927/Frontiers-in-Group-Dynamics-Concept-Method-and-Reality-in-Social-Science-Social-Equilibria-and-Social-Change

Lukas, J. A. (1985). *Common ground: A turbulent decade in the lives of three American families.* New York, NY: Vintage.

McAndrews, L. J. (1997). Missing the bus: Gerald Ford and school desegregation. *Presidential Studies Quarterly, 27*(4), 791–804.

Morgan v. Hennigan, 379 F. Supp. 410 (D. Mass. 1974) (June 21, 1974).

North, A. (2018, September 7). If Kavanaugh's confirmed, any of these 13 cases could end Roe. *Vox*. Retrieved from https://www.vox.com/2018/9/7/17818458/brett-kavanaugh-supreme-court-nominee-abortion-confirmation

Obergefell v. Hodges, 772 F. 3d 388, reversed (2015).

Planned Parenthood of Southeastern Pennsylvania v. Casey, 505 US 833 (1992).

Shesol, J. (2010). *Supreme power: Franklin Roosevelt vs. the Supreme Court*. New York, NY: W.W. Norton.

Stephens, O., Scheb, J., & Glennon, C. (2015). *American constitutional law*, 6th ed. Belmont, CA: Cengage.

U.S. Supreme Court. (2018). *Masterpiece Cakeshop v. Colorado Civil Rights Commission*, 584 U.S. 138 S. Ct. 1719; 201 L. Ed. 2d 35.

ARTICLE 39

Character in Context: "Do You Want to Do Something About It?"

Jim Obergefell

That simple question posed by civil rights attorney Al Gerhardstein set in a motion a process and experience that my late husband, John, and I had never imagined we'd embark upon, especially while John lay dying of amyotrophic lateral sclerosis (ALS), or Lou Gehrig's disease, in July 2013. Al referenced the fact that Ohio, the state where we lived, did not allow or recognize same-sex marriages and would therefore refuse to recognize our lawful Maryland marriage on John's death certificate when he died. Al wanted to know if we would consider filing a lawsuit in federal district court against the state of Ohio and the city of Cincinnati because of it.

John and I were faced with a decision that would have profound consequences not just for us but also our entire nation. We had to decide if our principles and desire to be treated as equal members of society were strong enough to initiate a legal fight against the government and see it to the end. We had to decide if we were willing to enter a world we knew only through popular culture, history, books, television, and the movies—the world of courtrooms, expert witnesses, precedents, decisions, confusing legal concepts, and writings.

Few decisions have been as easy to make.

On July 19, 2013, John and I filed suit against Ohio Governor John Kasich, Ohio Attorney General Mike DeWine, and Cincinnati Health Department Registrar Camille Jones, the city official responsible for death certificates, in United States District Court, Southern District of Ohio, Western Division. The case that would eventually morph into *Obergefell v. Hodges* was officially born.

In the years since making the decision to fight for our marriage, our rights, and our dignity, I'm constantly reminded that our choice to begin this battle wasn't just about us: It was about people and couples like us across the nation. It was about young people coming to terms with their sexual orientation or gender identity, facing a future where that most human of desires—to share life with someone you love—wasn't possible on the same terms as heterosexual couples. It was about giving parents hope that their children would grow up in a world where love and marriage were possibilities regardless of the person their child loved. It was about making marriage, as we interpret it in modern times, available to all.

For John and me, in the moment of our decision, it was about the two of us and our desire to have our relationship exist in the eyes of our government. We wanted John to die as a married man. We wanted the last official record of his life, his existence, to accurately reflect that he was married and that I was his surviving spouse. In our minds, few things were as clear-cut and simple as the need to be seen, to have our relationship respected, to be treated equally. We wanted validation. The irony is that although we had spent more than 20 years together in life being treated as unequal members of society, we were now willing to fight to be treated equally in death.

Marriage vows traditionally include promises to love, honor, and protect each other until death. John and I had made those promises informally over our decades together, but we didn't make them public and legal until July 11, 2013, two weeks after the Supreme Court struck down the Defense of Marriage Act with its decision in *United States v. Windsor*.

As the news broke of the Supreme Court decision on *Windsor*, the reality that the federal government would now have to recognize lawful same-sex marriages dawned, and I spontaneously proposed to John. After two decades together, we could finally marry and exist in the eyes of our government. We were faced with a terminal illness and we knew time was short, but we finally had the opportunity to say "I do" and have it carry legal weight. In a perfect world, we could have gone to our county courthouse six blocks away to get our marriage license. Because of Ohio's state-level defense of marriage act, our challenge now was to figure out the logistics of traveling to another state with a terminally ill, bedridden man to do something millions of others took for granted.

Discovering that Maryland does not require both parties to apply in person for a marriage license simplified one aspect of our wedding ceremony by allowing me to travel to Maryland alone to get the marriage license, thereby limiting travel, discomfort, and time away from home for John. We determined where we would marry, but the more complicated aspect was how we would get us both there together. John couldn't fly commercially, I wasn't willing to put him through a punishing ambulance ride of almost 1,000 miles, and sitting in his power wheelchair inside our wheelchair minivan was also not an option. We soon determined that chartering a medical jet was the only option for us to travel to Maryland while limiting John's pain and discomfort. Our generous family and friends covered the entire $13,000 cost of the chartered jet because they wanted us to be able to marry and wanted to help make it happen.

In a short ceremony performed by John's aunt Paulette, we finally got to say "I do" inside that cramped medical jet on the tarmac of the Baltimore–Washington International Airport. Because of Ohio's amendment banning same-sex marriage, we were forced to go to extreme lengths to be in another state for less than 45 minutes. Even though we resented that, we were thrilled because, for the first time as a couple, we were lawfully able to call each other "husband," something we did regularly in the days that followed. Being able to make our relationship public and legal changed things for us. We felt different, better, more complete. Our

20 years as a couple became something new, something more meaningful. To para-phrase Justice Anthony Kennedy (in *Obergefell v. Hodges*) we became something greater than we had been.

Five days after we married, Cincinnati civil rights attorney Al Gerhard-stein walked into our home and pulled out a blank Ohio death certificate. When Al explained Ohio would list John as single and would not include my name as John's surviving spouse, our hearts broke. We knew Ohio had its own version of the Defense of Marriage Act, but that knowledge was abstract. We knew Ohio wouldn't acknowledge our lawful Maryland marriage, but we had never considered it in rela-tion to John's last record as a person. This conversation made that abstract knowl-edge real and concrete, harmful and hateful.

Had we really jumped through all of these hoops to get married only to have it mean nothing in the state where we'd spent our entire 20 years together as a couple? Were we really undeserving of dignity and respect? Were we willing to allow John's death certificate to ignore our marriage, our relationship? Turns out we weren't. John and I decided to take a principled stand for ourselves and for couples like us.

Some people wondered how or why we could take on such a fight as John lay dying, nearing the end of his life. Do you really want to leave his side, Jim? Won't you have to spend time in court, or doing other things, that you could spend with John? It was simple, really. John and I had promised to love, honor, and protect each other. Yes, we would lose some of our time together during what would later turn out to be the last three months of John's life, but we'd taken our promises seriously, and here was our opportunity to actually do something eternal for each other and our marriage. We didn't want our marriage to be erased, wiped away, to no longer exist. We wanted John's last record as a person—as a citizen of the United States and resident of the state of Ohio—to be accurate. What would it say about our promises if we didn't fight to live up to them no matter what?

John fully supported filing a lawsuit, but he reminded me that I had to be com-fortable with taking on almost all of the effort because he could do nothing to help because of his health. ALS had stolen almost all physical abilities from him, but his mind and personality were still sharp, and he was willing to sacrifice time with me so that I could fight for our legal right to call each other "husband." John lived up to his promises to me by making it OK for me to take time away from him for court hearings, interviews, and more. John sacrificed his sense of comfort and safety for our marriage, for me.

The attorney we would work with was also a major consideration for our deci-sion to file. The legal profession suffers under a pop culture image of evil, self-serving ambulance chasers, attorneys who have no morals and will file any case for anyone because it means a "cut" of any settlement. Although we already knew that pop cul-ture image is inaccurate and unwarranted, Al Gerhardstein was also the antithesis of that negative caricature, and that gave us a measure of comfort and confidence.

Al is a kind and gentle man with a shrewd legal mind. More important for us, Al had dedicated his career to civil rights. Upon earning his JD at New York University School of Law in 1978, Ohio native Al returned home and opened a practice in Cincinnati focused on civil rights. At the time we met, after a career spanning almost four decades, Al had fought for prisoner rights, women's reproduc-tive freedom, victims of police misconduct, and more.

Our case also wouldn't be Al's first foray into the fight for LGBTQ rights, and that was important. One of his first cases as a practicing attorney was on behalf of his brother's partner, who was fighting an unfair job termination. A teacher in a Catholic school, the partner was terminated for being gay. It was no surprise that Al was unsuccessful in that case, but his early commitment to LGBTQ equality was on display again in the 1990s as he successfully fought an anti-LGBTQ Cincinnati city charter amendment in federal district court. Unfortunately, a loss in the Sixth Circuit remained standing after the United States Supreme Court remanded the case back to that court.

It was clear Al Gerhardstein was our advocate and experienced in the fight for LGBTQ rights. Perhaps more important, Al appreciated what John and I were going through with John's illness, and he always kept our well-being paramount in everything he did. For our first foray into the federal court system, we felt comfortable saying yes because we had a dedicated, intelligent, and kind attorney at our side.

Eight days after we married, we filed suit in federal court, charging that the state of Ohio and the city of Cincinnati were denying us equal protection under the law by refusing to recognize our lawful marriage on John's death certificate at the time he died. With the federal government now required to recognize lawful same-sex marriages because of the *Windsor* decision, shouldn't the state of Ohio be required to also recognize them?

Eleven days after we married inside that medical jet, I sat in U.S. District Judge Timothy Black's courtroom in Cincinnati for the hearing on our case. As I took the stand to read a statement to Judge Black, I found myself oddly calm. Yes, there were nerves—how could I not be nervous speaking in front of a federal judge in a packed courtroom, talking about the man I loved and what our marriage, our relationship, meant to us? I was calm because I knew we were right, I trusted Al's legal argument and acumen, and I refused to believe I lived in a nation that would allow a state government do something that the Supreme Court had just told the federal government it could no longer do.

And I had to live up to my promises to John.

By now, I'd also started to realize how our story and legal fight were resonating across the nation. I looked across that courtroom and saw friends, family, and strangers there to support John and me in our fight. From being recognized and thanked by passersby on the streets of Cincinnati to social media messages from strangers around the nation, our personal fight for our marriage was clearly becoming something much larger than just the two of us.

Al Gerhardstein brought that home to me during that first hearing with his response to the state's main defense that the state-level defense of marriage act was constitutional because a majority of voters had approved a 2004 ballot issuer banning same-sex marriage or its recognition. Without hesitation, Al responded that the surest way to curtail minority rights is to allow the majority to vote on them. Suddenly I saw this fight in a different way. We weren't just John and Jim, we were members of a minority in a courtroom fighting for our rights, and we could look to the many brave people who came before us as examples of turning a personal fight into a public fight for the rights of others. So many others had trod a similar path to ensure the majority didn't deny a minority its rights.

Al's response, along with the burgeoning media and public reaction to our case, helped me finally start to appreciate that what had started as a personal fight had become a highly public—and potentially far-reaching—fight. I was experiencing firsthand one of the core foundations of our nation's legal system: protecting the constitutional and civil rights of every citizen. Regardless of the cries of "activist judges," "wait for public opinion," and "handle this through the legislative process" that greeted our case, I found comfort knowing that we were availing ourselves of the very process our Constitution provides to ensure that all citizens experience equal justice under law.

Later that same day, Judge Black issued his decision. Starting with the words "this is not a complicated case," Judge Black found in our favor and issued a temporary restraining order requiring the city of Cincinnati and the state of Ohio to complete John's death certificate correctly at the time he died by showing him as married and listing my name as his surviving spouse. We finally felt that we existed as a couple in the eyes of our government. Our state would finally acknowledge and respect our relationship, our marriage. We matter. We count. We *are*.

This decision had a profound effect on us. John would die knowing his last record would be accurate. He could die knowing I could refer to him as my late husband, refer to myself as a widower, and have it actually mean something. John could die knowing he'd done what he could to live up to his promises to love, honor, and protect me.

John died three months to the day after the decision. Two months later, the state of Ohio appealed the ruling to the Sixth Circuit Court of Appeals. Even with Al's admonition not to be too confident because of this court's conservative leaning, I knew I had to continue fighting because that meant living up to my promises to John. In addition, I wouldn't be doing this on my own because our case was now part of a consolidated slate of cases from Ohio, Kentucky, Tennessee, and Michigan fighting state-level bans on same-sex marriage. John was gone, but I wasn't alone. I had more than 30 other plaintiffs by my side, not to mention the support I continued to experience firsthand across the country and in letters, cards, and messages from around the world. The fight was now about much more than John's and my marriage.

In late 2014, the Sixth Circuit ruled against us, siding with the states of Ohio, Kentucky, Tennessee, and Michigan. That loss prompted me to think back to our first meeting with Al when he asked if we wanted to file suit. I remembered that my high school government class had come to mind during that conversation. Cases can be appealed all the way to the Supreme Court of the United States. I remembered thinking that legal process couldn't possibly ever apply to someone I know, let alone myself.

Here I was, on the cusp of making just such a decision. Was this real? Was I willing to do this? Was I ready to take this fight as far as I could?

This was yet another easy decision, regardless of what becoming a Supreme Court plaintiff might entail or what it might do to my life. I couldn't let John down. I couldn't let down the millions of people across the nation who were watching this case, hoping that their relationships and their families would finally be on equal footing with opposite sex couples. I couldn't let down the rest of the plaintiffs in the consolidated case. I couldn't let down the countless couples across the nation who wanted to say "I do" to the person they loved, or the single people who hoped to one day be able to do that.

I knew I wouldn't be able to live with myself if I didn't file cert and keep fighting.

Even after filing cert, I wasn't expecting what happened next. Not only did the court accept the case, they announced that it would be known as *Obergefell v. Hodges*. I felt a sense of guilt because my name and face quickly became shorthand for the fight being waged by more than 30 plaintiffs, people with stories equally as compelling, people who were also taking a risk, making sacrifices, worrying about their children, and putting their lives on hold to be part of this fight. It wasn't just about me. And it still isn't.

This fight is about the closeted Asian American college student who told me before I spoke that she didn't think she'd ever be able to be open about who she is. After I finished, she came up to me again to say that she planned to come out on Facebook that evening.

It's about the straight couple who stopped me on the sidewalk in Philadelphia to ask for a photo of me with their toddler because they were happy that their child would one day be able to marry the person he or she loved, whoever that person happens to be.

This fight is about the countless couples who have shared photos of and stories about their proposals, their weddings, their lives together as a married couple. It's about the couples who have shared their relief that their marriage will exist no matter what state borders they cross.

It's for everyone who lived in fear that they would be unable to make decisions for or say goodbye to a spouse in the event of an accident or illness, for parents who feared for their children's welfare should something happen to the "legal" parent.

This fight is about allowing every American marriage to be legally formalized as a union of two people, to commit to love, to live openly and freely as an equal member of our society. It's about every child who feels different, every kid who is afraid to be open with his or her family. It's for every young person who has been disowned, kicked out of the house, or forced into damaging and discredited conversion therapy. It's for everyone who has been bullied, abused, harmed, or murdered because of who they are. It's for all LGBTQ persons who have taken their own lives.

I wasn't thinking that when John and I started this fight. We began from a deeply personal point of view—our marriage and protecting our more than two decades as a couple. As I sat in the courtroom of the Supreme Court of the United States of America on June 26, 2015, and realized we'd won, my immediate reaction was not surprising deeply personal. I burst into tears because I missed John and I wished he'd been able to experience this, to know that our marriage will forever exist in the eyes of the government. Then it hit me: For the first time in my life as an out gay man, I felt like an equal American.

Stepping out of the courthouse into the sea of people celebrating on the plaza of the Supreme Court building, I felt lighter than I had in years. A sense of comfort and safety, a sense of belonging came over me. Then the electric feeling of joy in the air washed over me as Al, other plaintiffs, attorneys, and I threaded our way through the jubilant crowd.

At one point I looked up at the courthouse and the words inscribed on the pediment: Equal Justice Under Law. Never had they meant as much to me, nor had they ever been so personal. In the years since the decision, I've frequently walked by the Supreme Court, and I've almost always taken a photo of those words. These words make me think about our decision to file suit. I think about the time together John and I sacrificed during the last months of his life. I think about how drastically my life has changed, how my previous world of anonymity has given way to a life of being recognized on sidewalks, in airplanes, and in so many other daily situations. I think about the countless people who have shaken my hand, hugged me, thanked me, told me stories, and cried. I think about the couples who came before us, who built a life together but were unable to legally call themselves married.

Knowing what I do now, I would make the same decisions. John and I wanted to live up to our promises to each other, and in the process we became part of something much greater, much more consequential than we ever imagined. Along the way I've realized that it really is up to "We the People" to make sure the words of and promises inherent in the Constitution mean something in real life. We were fortunate enough to find in Al Gerhardstein a stalwart defender of and believer in the words "Equal Justice Under Law." It's up to us to demand justice.

We must demand justice not only for ourselves but also for everyone. The LGBTQ community rightfully points to *Lawrence v. Texas, United States v. Windsor,* and *Obergefell v. Hodges* as major markers on our path to equality, but these cases hinge on principles underpinning previous decisions that impacted other minority groups. The arguments and rationales used to deny justice and equality to one minority are all too easily and frequently recycled in later years to deny justice and equality to a different minority. It's true that attitudes and understanding change, but those changes tend to happen slowly over time. Without our court system, attorneys dedicated to civil rights, and plaintiffs willing to demand justice and equality, those words inscribed in the Supreme Court pediment—Equal Justice Under Law—would just be words without meaning. There are times our society needs to be reminded that our Constitution begins with the words "We the People."

As a people, we're still working to create a nation that embodies those words. Every so often our nation takes a step forward with decisions like *Obergefell v. Hodges,* a day that President Obama described with these words:

"And then sometimes there are days like this, when that slow, steady effort is rewarded with justice that arrives like a thunderbolt."

Those days are worth fighting for, they're worth sacrificing for. I'm glad I did.

No "Piece of Cake": Applying Liberty and Equality in *Masterpiece Cakeshop*

Adam M. Carrington

▶ Introduction

On June 26, 2015, the U.S. Supreme Court handed down its decision in *Obergefell v. Hodges*. Justice Anthony Kennedy's majority opinion declared that states could not exclude same-sex couples from their legal definitions of marriage. In so doing, Kennedy argued that bans on marriage between gay couples violated two of our country's most fundamental principles: liberty and equality. The right to liberty included marriage as an expression of one's autonomy and dignity, and equality guaranteed this expression to all regardless of the spouses' gender (*Obergefell*, pp. 2599–2603). Moreover, the Constitution protected these principles through the Fourteenth Amendment's due process and equal protection clauses.

Obergefell effectively ended the legal debate over gay marriage. Same-sex couples would receive the same status and benefits as heterosexual relationships. But in ending one dispute, it opened up others. These new battles pertained to how we should integrate *Obergefell's* reasoning into our principles and within the laws following those principles. Some of the more pressing disputes involved those who continued to oppose same-sex marriage. Gay persons claimed that acting on such opposition often violated our new understanding of liberty and equality. Thus, laws, both constitutional and statutory, should protect gays from mistreatment rooted in their sexuality. Yet those opposed to gay marriage rested their own defense on principles of liberty and equal treatment. Instead of pointing to the Fourteenth Amendment, these persons claimed liberty and equality protections in the First Amendment, particularly its free exercise and free speech clauses. Thus, they claimed that the laws should accommodate their religious objections, not suppress them.

Court watchers believed the Supreme Court would first attempt to address these contentions in *Masterpiece Cakeshop v. Colorado Civil Rights Commission* (2018). The litigation originated in 2012. A gay couple—Charlie Craig and Dave Mullins—entered Masterpiece Cakeshop in a Denver, Colorado, suburb intending to order a cake for their wedding reception. Jack Phillips—the store's owner—refused to make one. He did so on religious grounds, believing that God ordained marriages involving only opposite-sex couples. Phillips thought that creating the cake constituted an approving participation in a same-sex wedding ceremony, thus violating his religious beliefs.

Craig and Mullins then brought a complaint to the Colorado Civil Rights Division, claiming that in refusing service Phillips violated the Colorado Anti-Discrimination Act (CADA). That state law prohibited places of public accommodation (including businesses like Masterpiece) from refusing service to persons for a series of reasons, including a person's sexual orientation. In his defense, Phillips did not challenge this law's constitutionality. Instead, he argued that the First Amendment granted him an exemption from the CADA on free exercise and free speech grounds. Phillips lost the case before the Colorado Civil Rights Division, the Colorado Civil Rights Commission, and on subsequent appeals through the state court system.

His appeal to the U.S. Supreme Court, however, went differently. By a 7–2 vote, that body reversed these prior decisions, siding with Phillips. Yet it did so on narrow grounds. Justice Kennedy's majority opinion argued that the state commission failed to give Phillips a fair hearing. First, members of the Colorado Civil Rights Commission made derogatory remarks about Phillips' religious motivations. Furthermore, it allowed bakers in another case to refuse to bake cakes with religiously based messages against gay marriage and homosexuality, doing so because they found the messages "offensive." Kennedy argued that this distinct outcome also showed animosity toward religion. In both cases, Colorado ultimately ruled against religious claims on the basis of what ideas it thought offensive.

Because of this hostility, the Court decided for Phillips, vacating the decisions of the lower tribunals. But in sidestepping the bigger issues, the Court led many observers to find the outcome underwhelming. The Court reached no conclusion about free exercise, free speech, or how those concepts related to discrimination. It did not even determine whether Phillips would win if he had received an unbiased review of his case. Kennedy acknowledged these points, concluding his opinion by stating that "[t]he outcome of cases like this in other circumstances must await further elaboration in the courts" (*Masterpiece*, p. 1732).

Yet we would be mistaken to leave the *Masterpiece* case at its majority opinion. A deeper discussion did occur within three concurring opinions filed by members of the seven-vote majority. These opinions jockeyed for positioning in those future cases, seeking to lay the groundwork on which a later Court could base its reasoning. Studying them presents us with two benefits. First, they preview two lines of argument likely to come before the Court down the road—the constitutional claims to liberty and equality. Second, the majority's reasoning showed an important but sometimes neglected factor in our current controversy. We see in these opinions an intricate debate not over fundamental principles but how to apply those principles to particular, sometimes messy, circumstances.

▶ Liberty and Free Speech

The First Amendment commands that "Congress shall make no law . . . abridging the freedom of speech."[1] Herein, the Constitution linked its Preamble's goal—"to secure the Blessings of Liberty to ourselves and to our Posterity"—with the particular purpose of protecting speech. Why is liberty in what we say so important? In *Palko v. Connecticut* (1937), the Supreme Court said regarding speech, "[o]f that freedom one may say that it is the matrix, the indispensable condition, of nearly every other form of freedom" (*Palko*, p. 327). Much of our lives involves some form of communication—from ordering a hamburger, to telling our significant other we love him or her, to declaring our opinions on religion, entertainment, fashion, or politics. To suppress speech is to suppress liberty in all of these areas—in much of our lives.

Everyone in this case agreed regarding the free speech clause's importance. But the problem resided in its application. Justice Clarence Thomas' concurring opinion took up this thorny question: Did Phillips' act of making a cake constitute an act of free speech? For forcing Phillips to speak what he did not believe would violate the freeness of his speech as much as would suppressing him from saying what he did think.

In a narrow sense, the answer seemed an obvious no. Phillips did not create the cake by his use of language; a cake's ingredients are not words measured, mixed, then baked in an oven. However, courts extend free speech protections beyond the mere act of speaking. They do so because human beings communicate in many ways beyond mere words. Justice Thomas listed several expressions that the Supreme Court has protected, "including nude dancing, burning the American flag, flying an upside-down American flag with a taped-on peace sign, wearing a military uniform, wearing a black armband, conducting a silent sit-in, refusing to salute the American flag, and flying a plain red flag" (*Masterpiece*, p. 1742). These symbolic actions fell under what courts have termed "free expression." To give full protection to free speech, judges accorded them First Amendment protection as well.

Therefore, whether Phillips' cake-making fell within free speech protections presented a more questionable issue. Did designing and baking a wedding cake communicate a message? Colorado, as well as Craig and Phillips, argued it did not. They noted, and Justice Thomas agreed, that the Supreme Court distinguished speech from what it called "conduct" (*Masterpiece*, p. 1741). Words and deeds made up distinct modes of operation, with constitutional protection extending only to the former. Following this distinction, the argument went that Phillips primarily acted, not spoke, in making the cake.

Drawing on precedent, Justice Thomas stated that the Court must consider two points to decide this issue. First, the justices had to examine Phillips' intention in baking cakes. To fall under expression, Phillips' actions must have "intended to be communicative" (*Masterpiece*, p. 1742). Little doubt existed on this count. Justice Thomas quoted testimony given by Phillips, saying that "[t]o him, a wedding cake inherently communicates that 'a wedding has occurred, a marriage has begun, and the couple should be celebrated'" (*Masterpiece*, p. 1743). Phillips clearly believed his cake-making entailed recognition and approval of any wedding he serviced.

Second, the court had to consider others' rational perception of Phillips' cake-making. Protected expression must be of the kind that, "in context, would reasonably be understood by the viewer to be communicative" (*Masterpiece*, p. 1742).

Here the main debate took place. Could someone at a same-sex wedding reasonably perceive Phillips' baking a cake as conveying approval of those nuptials?

Thomas argued that such a perception was reasonable. Looking back to English wedding history, Justice Thomas noted that wedding cakes, ubiquitous in such events, were not primarily intended for consumption. Instead, he pointed to an array of "symbolism" inhering in a wedding cake. Foremost among that symbolism, "[t]he cake's purpose is to mark the beginning of a new marriage and to celebrate the couple" (*Masterpiece*, p. 1743). Cakes, in other words, convey celebration of the event in which they are used (think also of birthdays and graduation parties). And celebration is a form of approval, an emphatic one, in fact.

Applied to this case, Justice Thomas declared that forcing Phillips to make cakes for gay weddings "requires him to, at the very least, acknowledge that same-sex weddings are 'weddings' and suggest that they should be celebrated—the precise message he believes his faith forbids" (*Masterpiece*, p. 1744). Thus, the law forced Phillips to express beliefs he did not hold. It forced him to speak and thus to speak un-freely. Under such reasoning, Thomas concluded, the First Amendment demanded an exemption for Phillips.

No other justice addressed Justice Thomas' free speech argument. But his opinion exemplified the bigger problem of application. For serious questions will arise if a future Supreme Court takes on his position. Foremost may be whether his understanding of expression threatens effectively to eliminate the distinction between speech and conduct. Is any activity merely conduct? Or could litigants find expression in the most mundane actions, from chewing gum to walking down the street? Courts have been extremely deferential to free speech claims, striking down most laws touching on them. To equate most action with speech, then, would invite the overthrow of most of our laws. Taken that far, Thomas' reasoning would turn freedom of speech into the tyranny of anarchy.

Justice Thomas, seemingly in anticipation of this objection, noted that "Phillips considers himself an artist" and takes special care in the design and creation of all of his baked goods (*Masterpiece*, p. 1742). Though itself debatable, this distinction would constitute some form of delineation. Some actions involve artistic action and thus are expressive. Some are not. But even on this score, Thomas' opinion leaves much unresolved. Whether future Courts take up this line of reasoning will depend in no small part on their ability to maintain clear and reasonable lines between speech and conduct.

▶ Equality and Free Exercise

I now turn to the other two concurring opinions, those written by Justices Elena Kagan and Neil Gorsuch. I consider them together because the justices wrote in response to each other's arguments. While Justice Thomas touched on liberty, Kagan and Gorsuch grappled over the principle of equality, particularly equality before the law.

To discuss this principle, we must understand that all laws *categorize*. They categorize actions as permissible or impermissible. They categorize persons according to certain characteristics, often affording protections or disadvantages to those with such traits. Equality requires that, in so categorizing, laws treat like things alike. Accomplishing this purpose first demands that legal categories make legitimate distinctions among actions and persons. The difference between dancing and physical battery legally matters; the distinction between the foxtrot and the electric slide should not. Second, equality then requires that governments rightly apply legal categories, treating that which the law equates the same and that which it distinguishes differently. If a state sets its drinking age at 21, for instance, then that law's enforcement can distinguish between someone who is 14 and someone who is 25. It could not add a distinction based on hair color, with one standard for blondes and another for redheads.

Kagan and Gorsuch agreed with these concepts. Moreover, neither questioned the legitimacy of the Colorado Anti-Discrimination Act regarding them. The CADA recognized categories of persons, including religious belief in addition to sexual orientation. It then established permissible and impermissible actions toward those holding such status. In so doing, the CADA sought equality. It did so by requiring most businesses and the state itself to act in a "neutral" fashion toward persons possessing these qualities. For businesses, neutrality meant that those establishments could not differentiate their service to customers based on their sexuality or religiosity. Regarding the government, the state must provide the same protections for discrimination of gay persons as for religious men and women.

While agreeing on these previous points, Kagan and Gorsuch divided sharply as to whether Colorado correctly applied the CADA. Fundamentally, the question hinged on how to compare Phillips' case and the other discussed by the majority opinion—William Jack's. As previously noted, these cases had different outcomes. The state decided against Phillips' refusal of service and for the baker's denial of Jack. Whether or not they rightly received different treatment depended on how one categorized their actions. If they acted in the same manner, then Colorado should grant them identical treatment. If their actions diverged according to the law, then that would warrant the distinct results. Heightening the issue was the question of the free exercise clause, which stated that "Congress shall make no law . . . prohibiting the free exercise" of religion. Court precedent defined this prohibition as requiring that laws be "generally applicable," meaning that they must act in neutral fashion toward religious and nonreligious entities (*Employment Division of Oregon v. Smith*). The CADA's text adhered to this requirement. But the question remained whether Colorado's enforcement of the law did the same.

Did the bakers in Jack's case treat religious customers in the same fashion that Phillips treated his gay patrons? Justice Kagan argued "a proper basis for distinguishing the cases was available—in fact, was obvious" (*Masterpiece*, p. 1733). Gorsuch countered that "[t]he facts show that the two cases share all legally salient features" (*Masterpiece*, p. 1735). Their divergence again showed the difficulty in applying principles in particular circumstances.

Fundamentally, Kagan and Gorsuch disagreed on why the different bakers refused service. In Jack's case, Kagan argued that the bakers distinguished between messages, not persons. She did so by emphasizing both the universality and the particularity of the bakers' rejection. Regarding universality, the ban on making cakes opposing gay marriage applied to anyone who asked. They "would not have made [the cake] for any customer" (*Masterpiece*, p. 1733). It did not matter whether the requested cake came from an Evangelical Protestant, a Roman Catholic, a Buddhist, or an atheist. "In refusing that request," Kagan thus reasoned, "the bakers did not single out Jack because of his religion, but instead treated him in the same way they would have treated anyone else" (*Masterpiece*, p. 1733). Therefore, the bakers in Jack's case did not treat Jack differently on the basis of his religion.

Furthermore, the bakers were particular in the message they rejected. Kagan noted that they did not refuse to bake *all* religiously themed cakes for Jack. She argued that "the bakers gave not the slightest indication that religious words . . . prompted the objection." Instead, it was only based on "the demeaning" messaging toward gay persons (*Masterpiece*, p. 1733). Other religiously themed orders would likely be accepted. Therefore, on both the universality of whose requests they rejected and on the particularity of the message rejected, the bakers in Jack's case did not violate the CADA.

Kagan then turned to Phillips. In contrast to Jack's bakers, Phillips refused service based on the particular persons ordering, not on a universal message. He did not decline to make wedding cakes. He declined to make a wedding cake for persons sharing a particular trait: homosexuality. Kagan emphasized this point, stating that "the same-sex couple in this case requested a wedding cake that Phillips would have made for an opposite-sex couple" (*Masterpiece*, p. 1733). Thus, unlike the bakers in Jack's case, Phillips refused service based on legally protected characteristics. Kagan argued that Phillips' distinction clearly lacked the required neutrality and thus obviously ran afoul of the CADA.

Justice Gorsuch countered by claiming that the bakers in both cases involved particular messages universally applied. In Jack's case, it was true that the refusing bakers said they would reject any cake like the one Jack requested, regardless of who asked for it. Gorsuch also agreed that those bakers therefore "were happy to provide religious persons with other cakes expressing other ideas" (*Masterpiece*, p. 1735). But Gorsuch argued that Phillips' refusal rested on the same ground. Phillips, Gorsuch claimed, also based his refusal in the message conveyed, not on the persons requesting service. Justice Gorsuch first called on reasoning found in Justice Thomas' opinion, arguing that making a cake for a wedding did communicate a message. Gorsuch said that a cake "celebrates a wedding, and if the wedding cake is made for a same-sex couple it celebrates a same-sex wedding" (*Masterpiece*, p. 1738). He even pointed out that lower tribunals had agreed, saying Craig and Mullins purchased a cake to "celebrate their same-sex wedding" (*Masterpiece*, p. 1738).

Phillips then rejected this message in universal fashion, regardless of who requested it. Gorsuch supported this claim along two lines. First, he pointed out that Phillips' refusal was not strictly tied to who ordered a wedding cake. He would refuse to bake one for a same-sex ceremony even if requested by a heterosexual person. Lest one assume such an example fanciful, Gorsuch pointed out that this very circumstance occurred in this case. After the initial rebuff, Craig's mother returned to the shop seeking to order the cake for the ceremony. Phillips denied her request as well, citing the same religious scruples to participating in the event (*Masterpiece*, p. 1735).

Second, the rejection was particular to the message, not to persons. Gorsuch pointed out that Phillips did not refuse *all* service to Craig and Mullins any more than the bakers in Jack's case did. According to the judicial record, "Mr. Phillips offered to make other baked goods for the couple, including cakes celebrating other occasions." *Masterpiece*, p. 1735). Moreover, Kagan's distinction, Gorsuch argued, inconsistently interpreted the relationship between the baker's message and its effect on the refused customers. In Phillips' case, Kagan as well as Colorado assumed that homosexuality as a legal status could not be separated from the act of entering into a same-sex marriage. Who usually requested cakes for same-sex weddings other than gay persons? Thus, to refuse to make the cake meant to refuse the men because of their homosexuality. But Gorsuch countered that the same reasoning should apply to Jack. He argued that "just as cakes celebrating same-sex weddings are (usually) requested by persons of a particular sexual orientation, so too are cakes expressing religious opposition to same-sex weddings (usually) requested by persons of particular religious faiths" (*Masterpiece*, p. 1736). Jack said his request came from his religious beliefs, a request not inconsistent with the history of his religion. Thus, under the reasoning applied to Phillips, to refuse to make the cake constituted discriminatory treatment based on his (protected) religious status.

Therefore, Gorsuch argued that Phillips' and Jack's cases were essentially the same. Both opposed a particular message: in Jack's case, messages demeaning gay persons; in Phillips' case, messages approving same-sex marriage. Both did so regardless of whether the request came from persons sharing characteristics protected by the free exercise clause or the CADA: in Jack's case religious belief, in Phillips' sexual orientation. Given these similarities, Gorsuch reasoned that for Colorado truly to uphold equality, truly to act in a neutral fashion, it must reach the same outcome in all of these cases.

▶ Conclusion

As concurrences, the opinions of Justices Thomas, Kagan, and Gorsuch did not legally settle the major issues raised. Yet they did describe two broad paths forward. One route will focus on free speech. Does legally enforced participation in a ceremony coerce persons into expressing approval? Or does so mandating merely stop actions discriminating against gay persons? Another will emphasize equality through government neutrality. However governments treat religiously based opposition to same-sex marriage, they must apply the same standards they use for other claims.

Which argument the Court will take up, much less how it will decide, remains for future cases. Nevertheless, the discussions found in *Masterpiece* lend themselves to current discussions. In *Obergefell*'s aftermath, our society faces significant questions regarding how to apply our deepest principles. Some of our disagreements are fundamental. Americans affirm the concepts of liberty and equality but hold significant disagreements on what those terms mean. Although this case eschewed that depth of debate, it showed another level of divergence. Agreement on principles of free speech and government neutrality still leave open thorny questions regarding application. This task of moving from principle to practice is far from fleeting, constituting a recurrent political problem. Yet the difficulty in applying these concepts should not dim our society's pursuit of them. Instead, it calls for citizens to reason together, to think and act both with rigor and humility. In such respect, we may begin to recognize equality. In such reasoning, we may responsibly exercise liberty.

▶ Endnote

[1]Through the doctrine of incorporation, this command now also applies to states through the Fourteenth Amendment.

▶ References

Colorado Anti-Discrimination Act. 2008. Colo. Rev. Stat. §24-34-601.

Masterpiece Cakeshop, Ltd. v. Colorado Civil Rights Commission, 2018. 138 S. Ct. 1719.

Obergefell v. Hodges, 2015. 135 S. Ct. 2584.

Palko v. Connecticut, 1937. 302 U.S. 319.

Employment Division, Department of Resources of Oregon v. Smith, 1990. 494 U.S. 872.

Ethics of School Desegregation in Little Rock, Arkansas

LaVerne Bell-Tolliver

Although the United States Supreme Court overturned segregation in public schools in 1954 via its historic ruling in *Brown v. Board of Education of Topeka* (1954), the Little Rock public schools did not officially begin desegregating until they were placed under legal and executive duress in 1957. A 1956 lawsuit filed by the parents of African American students who unsuccessfully attempted to desegregate the Little Rock public schools ultimately brought the matter to head. *Aaron v. Cooper* and its subsequent legal names and *Little Rock School District v. North Little Rock School District* became two of the longest-running lawsuits pertaining to public school desegregation (*Aaron v. Cooper*, 1956; *Arksansas Gazette*, 1956; *Little Rock School District v. Pulaski County Special School District No 1*, 1984).

The action of rendering a legal opinion in something so complex as school desegregation does not in and of itself make that action ethical. This article explores the avenues where the law and ethics collided or created areas of tension. Specifically, it will explore the voices of many African Americans who were silenced and devalued for many years. We will focus on this through the historical events that took place during the process of school desegregation in Little Rock, Arkansas.

The question of ethics in the activity of school desegregation may not have been overtly addressed at the time of its occurrence; however, as the subject is viewed over the course of history, we have the benefit of reflection on the phenomenon of school desegregation, specifically in Little Rock, Arkansas, through an ethical lens. Given the fact that the *Aaron v. Cooper* lawsuit and the Little Rock School Board's Pupil Assignment Law, also known as Act 461 of 1959, served as the genesis for school desegregation in the Little Rock public school system after the 1954 and 1955 *Brown v. Board of Education of Topeka* decisions were rendered by the

U.S. Supreme Court, those two legal actions will be explored along with court decisions that prompted the initial Brown decison (*Aaron v. Tucker*, 1960; *Brown v. Board of Education of Topeka*, 1954, 1955). Other legal actions, however, have continued to be a part of the desegregation and resegregation narratives of the Little Rock School District (LRSD). Therefore, legal actions subsequent to the desegregation of Little Rock Central High School will also be highlighted.

▶ Legal Standing of African Americans Before *Aaron v. Cooper*

A review of the legal history pertaining to the citizenship status of African Americans in the United States will set the context for the *Aaron v. Cooper* ruling concerning African American students in Little Rock, Arkansas. The following are highlights that led to the *Aaron v. Cooper* decision.

- Although slavery was the order of the day for most southern states, of which Arkansas was a part since receiving its statehood status in 1836, the Dred Scott decision of 1856 declared that African American slaves, even those set free by their masters, were not legally allowed to be called citizens of the United States (*Dred Scott v. Sandford*, 1856).

- The Emancipation Proclamation, issued by President Abraham Lincoln on January 1, 1863, was limited in that it provided freedom only to slaves who lived in many of the slaveholding states that seceded from the United States (Emancipation Proclamation, 1863).

- The 13th Amendment to the Constitution, ratified December 6, 1865, abolished slavery or involuntary servitude except for cases of crimes committed (Library of Congress, n.d.a).

- The 14th Amendment to the Constitution, ratified July 9, 1868, granted citizenship to all persons who were born or naturalized in the United States of America. No citizen could be denied life, liberty, property, or equal protection under the laws (Library of Congress, n.d.b).

- *Plessy v. Ferguson* (May 18, 1896) provided a major setback for African Americans when the U.S. Supreme Court officially established what came to be called "separate but equal." This ruling denied the right of African Americans to use the same public facilities, including schools and transportation, as Caucasian Americans (*Plessy v. Ferguson*, 1896; Smith, 1975).

- *Brown v. Board of Education of Topeka* (May 17, 1954) overturned *Plessy v. Ferguson* by declaring that allowing educational facilities to be separate made it "inherently unequal." Segregation of public schools *based solely on the issue of race* (italics added) was forbidden because it was a "denial of the equal protection of the laws," specifically those guaranteed by the 14th Amendment to the U.S. Constitution (*Brown v. Board of Education*, 1954).

- Brown II (*Brown v. Board of Education of Topeka*, 1955) rendered its decision on May 31, 1955, that desegregation was to be carried out in each public school system "with all deliberated speed." Unfortunately, the authority of deciding of how quickly full desegregation was to take place and in what manner was left up to each school system. The primary emphasis of this second Supreme Court ruling was that racial segregation of public schools was unconstitutional and that desegregation must take place. This failure on the part of the courts to more thoroughly define what "all deliberate speed" meant led to the lawsuit brought by Aaron and fellow students against superintendent Cooper and the entire school board of the Little Rock Public Schools in 1956.

In summary, legal actions such as the Dred Scott case and *Plessy v. Ferguson* silenced the voices of many African Americans for years. Although the 13th and 14th Amendments to the Constitution took the nation a step further in declaring African Americans as free citizens with limitations, Jim Crow laws existed in much of the South. *Brown v. Board of Education of Topeka* and Brown II took the country cautiously into the next chapter of racial change.

▶ *Aaron v. Cooper*

The plaintiffs of the original *Aaron v. Cooper* lawsuit argued that, as citizens of the United States and the State of Arkansas, they were being denied "rights, privileges, and immunities" that included the opportunity to attend desegregated public schools (*Aaron v. Cooper*, 1956). They petititioned the U.S. District Court for the Eastern District of Arkansas to prevent the school board and all other parties from allowing discrimination on the basis of race or color and to allow them to attend public Little Rock schools. The defendants—William Cooper, the president of the School Board . . . "and Secretary of the Board of Directors of Little Rock School District; the Superintendent of Little Rock School District; and the Little Rock School District itself" (*Aaron v. Cooper*, 1956)—denied that they were discriminating against the defendants who had attempted to desegregate five all-Caucasian schools. They argued first that they had to wait until the Supreme Court provided further clarification as to how to implement desegreation. This was done via Brown II (*Brown v. Board of Education of Topeka*, 1955). The board further argued that it had developed a "Plan of Integration" that would allow for an orderly way for it to implement desesegregation of the previously all-Caucasian schools in an organized fashion. The defendants further argued that the plan would not prompt them to act in a hasty fashion that would be "fraught with danger" as the plantiffs wanted them to do. This "Plan," sometimes identified as the "Blossom Plan" for superintendent Virgil Blossom, was developed and approved in May 1955. Given the fact that the plaintiffs initiated their lawsuit in 1956 means they were convinced that desegregation was not taking place.

In essence, the board rationalized that it needed to establish a plan that would include "the establishment of attendance areas, study of aptitudes of the children" among other systems. The plan called for additional schools to accommodate more students. It also recommended that desegregation should begin with phase one, which was the high school level (grades 10–12) in 1957 because there were fewer high school students and fewer schools would be needed at that level. The plan further endorsed beginning phase two of the desegregation process at the junior high level (grades 7–9) in 1959 or 1960, "following successful integration at the senior high school level" (*Aaron v. Cooper*, 1956). Finally, the plan for the launch of phase three—desegregation of the first six grades—was to be implemented "two or three years" after the implementation of the junior high schools. The plan stated that "complete integration would be effected not later than 1963" (*Aaron v. Cooper*, 1956).

In summary, Judge John Miller accepted the plan that allowed "gradual integration beginning with the high schools" (*Aaron v. Cooper*, 1956, 1959) by the school board on the basis of his belief that Superintendent Blossom had a knowledge of how to proceed with the desegregation process, that he and the other defendants were acting in good faith, and that the plan was sound and free from discrimination. "It would be an abuse of discretion for this court to fail to approve the plan or to interfere with its consummation so long as the defendants move in good faith, as they have done since immediately after the decision of May 17, 1954, to inaugurate and make effective a racially nondiscriminatory school system" (*Aaron v. Cooper*, 1956).

Recommended for his position by Governor Oval Faubus (Bell-Tolliver, 2017), Judge Miller made a ruling that was problematic in several ways. He allowed the school district that would create testing for African American students, rather than all students, to determine whether they would be able to meet an appropriate intelligence standard that would equip them to be able to attend school with Caucasian Americans. Second, he allowed the school board to establish "attendance areas" that ultimately reinforced segregation in the far west and far east corridors of Little Rock. The west sector of town was all Caucasian at the time, and the east part of the town where the 1956 high school was erected was in an all–African American area. Finally, the argument that additional schools had to be built to accommodate the number of students conflicted with the reality that the same number of students attending school in 1956 would be essentially the same number attending in 1957, with the exception of new first graders. If full desegregation were to take place at once and in all schools, no increase of schools would be needed beyond those demanded by natural population growth (*Aaron v. Cooper*, 1956).

Central High School was desegregated during the historically tumultous year of 1957 with a group of students who became known as the "Little Rock Nine." Although he was unsuccessful in stopping desegregation in 1957 when President Dwight Eisenhowever intervened (Lawrence, 1957), Governor Faubus was temporarily successful in interrupting the plan by closing Little Rock's public schools for the 1958–1959 school year. By doing so, he halted the plan of desegregation "under Act 4 of the General Assembly of the State of Arkansas" (*Aaron v. Tucker*, 1960; University of Arkansas, n.d.). *Cooper v. Aaron* (1958) ultimately overturned the district court's decision to allow the governor to close the high schools. The U.S. Supreme Court affirmed the judgment of the court of appeals that the schools were to proceed according to Brown II without interference from the govenor or state of Arkansas. "This Court cannot countenance a claim by the Governor and Legislature of a State that there is no duty on state officials to obey federal court orders resting on this Court's considered interpretation of the United States Constitution in *Brown v. Board of Education*, 347 U.S. 483. P. 358 U. S. 4" (*Cooper v. Aaron*, 1958).

Although Act 4 was finally ruled unconstitutional on June 18, 1989, closure allowed the school board to declare that desegregation did not fare well in its first year (*Dietz v. Arkansas*, 1989). Desegregation of the junior high schools, therefore, needed to be postponed until 1961. The fact that 39 African Americans applied for entry to the various junior high schools and were denied even after appealing (*Arkansas Gazette*, 1960; Little Rock Board of Education, 1960, p. 5) was disheartening to many families.

Ethical concerns abound. Judge Miller of *Aaron v. Cooper* (1956) used his legal power to dismiss the concerns of the complainants as he determined the Arkansas Plan of Desegration to be designed by a well-informed and well-meaning school board. He, therefore, intentially set the pace of implementing the plan for a "proper time and method of" desegregation to begin at a rate of speed that would not have been completed for hundreds of years. Second, Judge Miller left the matter of defining "successful integration in junior and senior high schools" up to the school board. The body of power, as mentioned earlier, rested in the hands of the courts and the school board.

A third ethical concern in this process continues to rest directly and indirectly on the actions of Governor Faubus and the Second Extraordinary Session of the General Assembly for 1958 (*Aaron v. Tucker*, 1960). Amendment 44 of the Constitution called on the state to "oppose in every Constitutional manner the Un-constitutional Desegregation decisions of May 17, 1954 and May 31, 1955, of the United States Supreme Court, including interposing the sovereignty of the state of Arkansas" (University of Arkansas, n.d., as cited in Bell-Tolliver, 2017, p. 267). As previously stated, the governor, the Arkansas General Assembly, and even the Arkansas Supreme Court successfully closed the high schools for one year and delayed the course of school desegregation for at least one year. In an indirect fashion, however, these actions fed the fears of many Caucasian citizens, who began the process of transferring their children to other types of schools or moving to other parts of the city or even away from Little Rock altogether. Little Rock real estate mogul William Rector, owner of Rector Means & Rowland Inc. and Rector Phillips Morse Inc., successfully encouraged and propelled the initial process of White flight. Rector purchased land and built housing in the far western section of Little Rock, an area that was redlined to African Americans, ultimately helping to create Pulaski Academy, a segregated private school (Johnson, 2007, p. 258; Walton College, n.d.).

▶ The Arkansas Pupil Assignment Law

The Arkansas Pupil Assignment Law, or Act 461 of 1959, arose from legislative actions that took place in a special legislative assembly called by the governor in another attempt to preempt the federal government from stopping the state's right to rule in its own way. Several acts were approved through Amendment 44 of the Arkansas Constitution, one of which was the Pupil Assignment Law (*Aaron v. Tucker*, 1960; *Garrett v. Faubus*, 1959; University of Arkansas, n.d.).

The Pupil Assignment Law, upheld in the courts at the *Aaron v. Tucker* hearing, was supposedly established to facilitate the integration process. Because race could no longer be used as a factor to determine placement, the following 16 placement criteria were established:

1. Available room and teaching capacity in the various schools.
2. Availability of transportation facilities.
3. The effect of the admission of new pupils upon established or proposed academic programs.
4. The suitability of established curricula for particular pupils.
5. The adequacy of the pupil's academic preparation for admission to a particular school and curriculum.

6. The scholastic aptitude and relative intelligence or mental energy or ability of the pupil.
7. The psychological qualifications of the pupil for the type of teaching and associations involved.
8. The effect of admission of the pupil upon the academic progress of other students in a particular school or facility thereof.
9. The effect of admission upon prevailing academic standards at a particular school.
10. The psychological effect upon the pupil of attendance at a particular school.
11. The possibility of breaches of the peace or ill will or economic retaliation within the community.
12. The home environment of the pupil.
13. The maintenance or severance of established and psychological relationships with other pupils and with teachers.
14. The choice and interests of the pupil.
15. The morals, conduct, health and personal standards of the pupil.
16. The request or consent of parents or guardians and the reasons assigned therefor (*Aaron v. Tucker*, 1960; Bell-Tolliver, 2017, pp. 21, 22).

Aside from the first criterion, all of the items related to this law posed at least four ethical concerns. First, each criterion was subject to the board's perspective in terms of determining whether individual students would qualify for attendance within a desegregated school. The Little Rock School Board was the final authority for developing the eligibility criteria and for selecting students to be admitted to the desegregated schools. If a student or his parents objected to the student's school assignment, the school board was also the authority to which the student or family could appeal. The responsibility for designing and reinforcing the plan lay with the same body.

A second ethical concern regarding the placement law is the fact that the 16 criteria largely applied only to African American students who were being considered for entry into previously all-Caucasian public schools. This made it suspect in terms of considering the motive for its use. An example of one such appeal among many is findings of a sixth-grade African American student who applied—and was denied—at a June 28, 1961, hearing by the school board to be reassigned from attending grade seven at Dunbar Junior High School to East Side Junior High for fall 1961. The findings rather than the usual transcript were provided in the July 27, 1961 minutes of the executive session of the Little Rock Board of Education (1961, p. 8). In summary, the student and her family provided an application for reassignment within the required 10-day time frame. Her rationale for requesting the reassignment was that the conditions at Dunbar were "unsatisfactory," and she would have "more transportation difficulties in attending Dunbar than" East Side. The board reviewed her records, which included her slightly above average IQ sore of 111, grade achievement at that time of 6.2 (sixth grade and second month), and her California Test of Personality results. She was viewed as having a lower-than-average grade ranking and considered to fall lower in social adjustment than the school board found acceptable. Finally, given the fact she lived three blocks closer to Dunbar than to East Side, she was denied admittance to East Side.

A third ethical concern is regarding criterion 10, the "psychological effect upon the pupil of attendance at a particular school." Although the criterion recognized that students would potentially be affected psychologically, neither the school board nor any educational agency related to the school system took measures to prepare students for the process of desegregating the schools. Bell-Tolliver (2017) reports that the majority of the 18 students she interviewed who were the first to desegregate the five public Little Rock junior high schools pointed to others as supportive in preparing them for this process. Those former students cited parents and nuclear or extended family members, supportive community members, African American churches, or organizations such as the NAACP or Urban League as being instrumental when they needed help.

In 1961, the Arkansas Pupil Assignment Law was in full effect when phase two of the Arkansas Plan for Desegregation commenced. This phase called for desegregating four of the five previously all-Caucasian junior high schools—East Side, Forest Heights, Southwest, and West Side (Bell-Tolliver, 2017). According to the September 4, 1961 *Arkansas Democrat*, no African American students applied to attend the fifth school, Pulaski Heights, in 1961. Reporter Bobbie Forster (as cited in Bell-Tolliver, 2017, pp. 22, 23) indicated in the *Arkansas Democrat* that 84 persons applied to enter the junior high schools, but only 25 persons were selected to attend the four junior high schools (Forester, 1961).

This statement from Forester points to the fourth ethical concern involving the placement law. In spite of having established selection criteria, no formal interviews were held with the 25 students selected by the board to attend the schools to determine whether they possessed the "psychological qualifications" or "mental energy" to be able to attend desegregated schools. No formal method of preparation was provided by the school board or the district staff to prepare these students to enter these schools. Instead, the names and addresses of each of the 25 selected students were published in the May 25, 1961, edition of the *Arkansas Democrat*. One person withdrew as a result of his home being attacked at least twice (Bell-Tolliver, 2017, p. 23). Two students desegregated Pulaski Heights, the fifth previously all-Caucasian junior high school in 1962.

Overall, in 1961 a total of 48 African American students were allowed to attend desegregated junior high and high schools (Bell-Tolliver, 2017). Although U.S. District Court Judge Gordon Young approved the limit of 48 students and explained that the district was making a good faith effort toward implementing desegregation, the fact that the African American students were the minority by far does not appear to be an ethically sound ruling. The distribution of African American students selected to attend junior high school was as follows: East Side, nine; Forest Heights, one; Southwest, two; and West Side, 11 (Forester, as cited in Bell-Tolliver, 2017, pp. 23, 24).

The June 30, 1963 minutes of the Little Rock Board of Directors special meeting indicated that the first and fourth grades were to be desegregated beginning in the fall of 1963. Somewhere between the origination of the 1956 Plan of Integration and 1963, the process of the implementation of school desegregation as a whole and phase three (grades one through six), particularly of the schools, slowed to a slight crawl. There was unanimous approval to begin the desegregation of the first grade, but the vote carried with four to two in favor of desegregating the fourth grade (p. 12). No explanation was given as to why these two grades were selected.

▶ Unfinished Business

The lack of sufficient progress concerning desegregation prompted action on the part of at least one community organization, the Council on Community Affairs represented by civil rights advocate Ozell Sutton. The council submitted a letter to the August 29, 1963 meeting of the LRSD Board of Education. Discussion was initially tabled until the October 31, 1963 meeting (Little Rock Board of Education Directors, June 30, 1963, p. 3) but was ultimately not heard until the November 21, 1963 meeting, just one day shy of the assassination of President John Fitzgerald Kennedy ("Integration—An Unfinished Business," as cited in Little Rock Board of Education Directors, November 21, 1963, pp. 2–6).

The council, described a letter as "a leadership group representing civic, religious, social and fraternal organizations," confronted the School District Board of Education about deliberately slowing the rate of desegregation.

> It is now more than nine years since the United States Supreme Court in the first Brown decision held racial segregation in public education to be unconstitutional. Eight years have elapsed since the second Brown decision requiring that desegregation proceed with "all deliberate speed." Six years have passed since the 1957 crisis and it was four years ago that our high schools were reopened. Yet less than two percent of the 6,500 Negro students enrolled in our public schools now enjoy the benefits of a desegregated education. Negro pupils will compose less than three-fourths of one percent of the total enrollment of formerly all-white schools when they open for the 1963–1964 school year. At the present rate of two percent in nine years it would take 450 years to completely desegregate our school system. We have yet to get to the business of desegregation. (Little Rock School District Board of Education Directors, November 21, 1963, pp. 2, 3)

Among the council's six recommendations, the first was that the school board "abandon the Pupil Assignment Plan," which also included the matter of students attending schools within their attendance zones (Little Rock School District Board, November 21, 1963, p. 3). The November 22, 1963 response from the board to the council denied all requests but specifically that pertaining to the Pupil Assignment Plan. "Our press in this area has been remarkably good and we are proud of the results achieved by our District, our community, and all our students. . . . If we follow your proposal we would require literally hundreds of children of each race to go to schools where forced attendance would obviously be detrimental to all" (Little Rock School District Board, November 21, 1963, p. 8).

Although a major change in terms of desegregation occurred at the March 24, 1964 meeting, the board continued to follow the pupil assignment plan with revisions. In that meeting, the board opted to desegregate all 12 grades for the 1964–1965 school year with the caveat that "the Superintendent shall cause enumeration forms (which shall include appropriate provision for indicating preference for initial assignment" for students in the first, third, fourth, sixth, seventh, and 10th grades. The same plan was set to continue for students of various grades in the 1965–1966 school year (Little Rock School District Board of Directors, March 24, 1964, p. 18), At the April 3, 1964 board meeting, a significant policy statement was approved that indicated the board would operate "without prejudice or bias." Five statements were adopted that focused on several items, including desegregating school organizations and extracurricular activities and pupil assignment (Little Rock Board of Directors, April 3, 1964, p. 3). In spite of the board's stated commitments to operate without prejudice, it continued to do so, as evidenced in the "Hearing on Request for Reassignment for the 1964–1965 School Year." Of the 77 appearances at the hearing with requests to be reassigned to predominantly Caucasian schools, almost half were disapproved (Little Rock Board of Directors, June 18, 1964, pp. 26–28).

▶ Tragedy Brings Change

The tragic death of President John Kennedy on November 22, 1963, brought about a significant change that affected the rights of citizens across the country and to the schools that were resistant to full desegregation. The 1964 Civil Rights Act proposed by President Kennedy before his assassination was signed into law on July 2, 1964 by his successor, President Lyndon Baines Johnson (National Archives, n.d.). This act made discrimination illegal in schools, places of employment, voting, housing, public accommodations, and so on. According to Section 401(b), which specifically refers to desegregation of public schools, "'Desegregation' means the assignment of students to public schools and within such schools without regard to their race, color, religion, or national origin, but 'desegregation' shall not mean the assignment of students to public schools in order to overcome racial imbalance" (Title IV, 1964).

▶ Public School Choice Act

Although the 1964 Civil Rights Act was signed into law to end all vestiges of desegregation, new barriers arose in Little Rock, Arkansas, as well as other areas of the country, which required legal action to remove them. *Clark v. Little Rock Board of Education* (1967) denied the complaint that freedom of choice was unfair to African American children, and *Swann v. Charlotte-Mecklenburg Board of Education* (1971) declared attendance zones found in pupil assignment laws were ineffective in eliminating segregation in the schools. Mandatory school busing of students to schools was ordered as an opportunity to remove remaining parts of segregation (Williams & Lovin, 1978).

The Public School Choice Act of 1989 granted students the right to "attend a school in a district in which the pupil does not reside" (Arkansas Public School Choice Act, 1989). This school choice act, however, did not provide transportation for the student. It stated specifically, "The responsibility for transportation for a nonresident pupil shall be borne generally by the pupil." That statement remains in current versions of the act.

The original school choice act was repealed (*Teague v. Arkansas Board of Education*) in 2012 because of racial restrictions and was replaced on April 16, 2013 with the School Choice Act of 2013, and included the statement, "A school district receiving transfers under the Public School Choice Act of 2013 and these rules shall not discriminate on the basis of gender, national origin, race, ethnicity, religion, or disability" (Anderson, Ash, Burks, & Ritter, 2013; Arkansas Public School Choice Act, 2013). The Teagues were Caucasian and were attempting to move away from schools that were becoming more racially diverse. The 2015 iteration of the school choice act (Arkansas Department of Education, 2015), was amended by Act 1066 of 2017 (Arkansas Department of Education, n.d.). It has continued until the present time to allow a legal process for students with financial privilege to leave the district by transferring to public or charter schools outside the district while legally moving funds from the school district as students transfer to other educational environments.

▶ From Desegregation to Resegregation

One final court case must be noted. *Little Rock School District et al. v. Pulaski County Special School District et al.* ended in 2014. This case was heard in the U.S. District Court for the Eastern District of Arkansas, Western Division, from 1982 until 2014 (Arkansas General Assembly, n.d.). According to the 1984 case, the judge ruled that three school districts—Little Rock, North Little Rock, and Pulaski County Special—had essentially become resegregated (Encyclopedia of Arkansas, 2014). Although the population was 65% White, 70% of the Little Rock schools' population in 1984 was African American. White students had either begun attending private schools or were transferring to Pulaski County Special School District or to the North Little Rock School District. All three districts were placed under supervision by the U.S. District Court until they could gain unitary status (Encyclopedia of Arkansas, 2014).

Economic and political power influences are linked with this demographic change. Although some persons simply transferred or placed their children in private religious or secular schools, followed later by charter schools, others physically moved to the suburbs to escape living in areas populated by African Americans (Swanson, McKenzie, & Ritter, 2016). In the 2018–2019 school year, 29 charter schools in total were allowed to operate throughout Arkansas. These schools are approved by the Arkansas Department of Education (Key, n.d.). Currently, 15 of those 29 charter schools exist in the city of Little Rock (Key, 2016). Student funds are shifted from public schools to the schools students choose to attend. In essence, the amendments from the Second Extraordinary Session of the General Assembly for the year 1958 have likely succeeded beyond the wildest dreams of Faubus, the General Assembly, and the Arkansas Supreme Court (*Aaron v. Tucker*, 1960) in that Act 84 of 1955 and Act 236 of 1959 stated that students would not be required to attend public schools together. Acts 5 and 151 of 1959 approved the transfer of funds from one school district to another when students opted to attend a school other than the one the student was assigned to attend (University of Arkansas, n.d., as cited in Bell-Tolliver, 2017, p. 268).

From 1984 until the present, the LRSD case has been overturned in some matters and upheld in others. The initial ruling was found to be too extreme, boundary lines were withdrawn or changed over time, and funding was provided to encourage the districts to improve their desegregation opportunities and otherwise retain Caucasian students (Encyclopedia of Arkansas, n.d.). The LRSD was finally declared unitary in 2007 (Arkansas General Assembly, n.d.; *Little Rock School District v. North Little Rock School District; Pulaski County Special School District*, 2009). The U.S. District Court for the Eastern District of Arkansas did not release Arkansas from the 1989 ruling, however, until all three school districts were declared unitary, which was finally granted in January 2014 (Encyclopedia of Arkansas, 2014; Education Week, 2018). Nevertheless, as of the date of this article, various components of this case continue to be under review by the United States District Court (*Little Rock School District v. Pulaski County Special School District et al.*, 2018).

One year following the January 2014 ruling, the Arkansas Department of Education intervened by removing the Little Rock School District's board. The department intervened, taking over the school district on January 28, 2015, after declaring the district to be in academic distress (Arkansas State Board of Education, 2015, p. 7). As of 2018, the Arkansas Department of Education remains in charge of the Little Rock School District. It operates the district in lieu of having a school board. The power of voice previously held by the board was removed, silenced. The state now has the authority to determine who will be heard within any limitation provided by the United States District Court (*Little Rock School District v. Pulaski County Special School District et al.*, 2018).

▶ Conclusion

"White flight," which began in the 1950s, had a tremendous impact on the Little Rock School District and its residents (Swanson et al., 2016). In 2015, the LRSD student population was less than 18% White. The city of Little Rock has made a 180-degree turn in that the majority of its students within the public school system are African American. Caucasian Americans with means of any sort have flown to charter or private schools or are being homeschooled. What began as an attempt by parents who hoped to provide their children with equal access to up-to-date equipment, textbooks, and schools has met with failure for the most part. Funds to provide these materials disappeared with the students who fled and with the closure of the federal desegregation cases.

"You can lead a horse to water, but you can't make him drink." Is that old adage the moral of the story? What advice can be given to the students, teachers, and administrators of the Little Rock School District who must perform just as well as other school districts but with fewer funds? It is evident that something must change. The 2015 action of the Arkansas Department of Education to remove the Little Rock School Board did not solve the problem of the district's school being in academic distress. In 2016–2017, only two schools in the district met the standard that qualified them to be in the "Achieving School" category. That title simply indicated that the school had met, not exceeded, "all of the annual measurable objectives (AMOs) set for it by the state for two consecutive years. AMOs are set in math, literacy, percent tested and graduation rate [high schools]" (Little Rock School District, 2017). The remaining public Little Rock Schools are in academic distress or meet the "needs improvement" criterion. The narrative of desegregation has not ended.

▶ References

Aaron v. Cooper, 143 F. Supp. 855 (E.D. Ark. 1956), U.S. District Court for the Eastern District of Arkansas, 143 F. Supp. 855 (E.D. Ark. 1956), August 27, 1956. Retrieved from https://law.justia .com/cases/federal/district-courts/FSupp/143/855/1417618/

Aaron v. Cooper, 261 F.2d 97, No. 16094, United States Court of Appeals Eighth Circuit. November 10, 1958. Retrieved from https://casetext.com/case/aaron-v-cooper-2

Aaron v. Cooper, 169 F. Supp. 325 (E.D. Ark. 1959) U.S. District Court for the Eastern District of Arkansas, January 9, 1959. Retrieved from https://law.justia.com/cases/federal/district-courts/ FSupp/169/325/1409468/

Aaron v. Tucker, 186 F. Supp. 913 (E.D. Ark. 1960) U.S. District Court E. D. Arkansas, W. D (September 2, 1960) Retrieved from http://law.justia.com/cases/federal/district-courts/FSupp /186/913/2374035/

Anderson, K. P, Ash, J. W., Burks, S. M., & Ritter, G. W. (2013). *Public school choice and desegregation in Arkansas*. Arkansas Education Report, *10*(2). Fayetteville, AR: Office for Education Policy, University of Arkansas. Retrieved from http://scholarworks.uark.edu/cgi/viewcontent.cgi ?article=1029&context=oepreport

Arkansas Democrat. (1961, September 4). Capacity enrollment expected in schools. Little Rock, AR: Butler Center for Arkansas Studies.

Arkansas Department of Education. (n.d.). School choice: Public School Choice Act of 2015. Retrieved from http://dese.ade.arkansas.gov/public/userfiles/rules/Current/FINAL_Public _School_Choice_August_2015.pdf#targetText=1.02%20The%20purpose%20of%20these ,School%20Choice%20Act%20of%202015.&targetText=2.01%20The%20Arkansas %20State%20Board,granted%20to%20it%20by%20Ark.

Arkansas Department of Education. (2015). Rules governing the Public School Choice Act of 2015. Retrieved from http://www.arkansased.gov/public/userfiles/rules/Current/FINAL_Public _School_Choice_August_2015.pdf

Arkansas Gazette. (1956, August 29). Here's the text of Judge Miller's opinion in the Little Rock integation case, p. 8a. Little Rock, AR: Butler Center for Arkansas Studies, Central Arkansas Library System.

Arkansas Gazette. (1960, June 14). "39 negroes seek integration in fall at Jr. high level." Little Rock, AR: Butler Center for Arkansas Studies.

Arkansas General Assembly. (n.d.). *Little Rock School District v. Pulaski County Special School District et al.*, Case No. 4:82:cv-00866-DPM. Little Rock, AR: State of Arkansas Bureau of Legislative Research. Retrieved from (http://www.arkleg.state.ar.us/education/K12/Pages/LitigationItem .aspx?LegItemId=4).

Arkansas Public School Choice Act of 1989. (1989). Act 609 of the 1989 Regular Session, General Assembly. Little Rock, AR: State of Arkansas. Retrieved from ftp://www.arkleg.state.ar.us /acts/1989/Public/609.pdf

Arkansas Public School Choice Act of 2013. (2013). Arkansas Department of Education Rules Governing the Public School Choice Act of 2013. Little Rock, AR: State of Arkansas. Retrieved from http://170.94.37.152/REGS/005.23.13-001F-13631.pdf

Arkansas State Board of Education. (2015, January 28). Minutes of the State Board of Education special meeting. Little Rock, AR: State Board of Education. Retrieved from http://www .arkansased.gov/public/userfiles/SBE_Minutes_2015/SBE_Minutes_January_28_2015.pdf

Bell-Tolliver, L. (Ed.). (2017). *The first twenty-five: An oral history of the desegregation of Little Rock's public junior high schools*. Fayetteville, AR: University of Arkansas Press

Brown v. Board of Education of Topeka, 347 U.S. 483, 1954. Retrieved from https://supreme.justia. com/cases/federal/us/347/483/

Brown v. Board of Education of Topeka, 349 U.S. 294, 1955. Retrieved from https://supreme.justia .com/cases/federal/us/349/294/

Clark v. Board of Education of Little Rock School District, 374 F. 2d 569 (March 31, 1967). Retrieved from https://openjurist.org/374/f2d/569

Cooper v. Aaron, 358 U.S. 1 (1958). Retrieved from https://supreme.justia.com/cases/federal/us /358/1/

Dietz v. Arkansas, 709 F. Supp. 902, 1989 U.S. Dist. LEXIS 3290 (E.D. Ark. 1989).

Dred Scott v. Sandford, 60 U.S. 393 (1856). https://supreme.justia.com/cases/federal/us/60/393/

Emancipation Proclamation. (1863). Washington, DC: National Archives. Retrieved from https://www.archives.gov/exhibits/featured-documents/emancipation-proclamation

Encyclopedia of Arkansas. (n.d.). Little Rock school desegregation cases (1982–2014). Little Rock, AR: Author. Retrieved from http://www.encyclopediaofarkansas.net/encyclopedia/entry-detail.aspx?entryID=7997

Encyclopedia of Arkansas. (2014). White flight. Retrieved from http://www.encyclopediaofarkansas.net/encyclopedia/entry-detail.aspx?search=1&entryID=4917

Forster, B. (1961, May 25). Negroes placed in white Jr. highs. *Arkansas Democrat*.

Garrett v. Faubus, 323 S.W.2d 877 (1959). Retrieved from https://law.justia.com/cases/arkansas/supreme-court/1959/5-1824-0.html

Johnson, B. F. (2007). After 1957: Resisting integration in Little Rock. *Arkansas Historical Quarterly*, 66(2), 258–283.

Key, J. (n.d.). Charter schools. Little Rock AR: Arkansas Department of Education. Retrieved from http://www.arkansased.gov/divisions/public-school-accountability/charter-schools

Key, J. (2016, February 24). Number of open-enrollment charters available. Little Rock, AR: Arkansas Department of Education. Retrieved from http://adecm.arkansas.gov/ViewApprovedMemo.aspx?Id=1822

Lawrence, W. H. (1957, September 6). President warns Governor Faubus he'll uphold law. *The New York Times*.

Library of Congress. (n.d.a). Primary documents in American history: 13th Amendment to the U.S. Constitution. Retrieved from https://www.loc.gov/rr/program/bib/ourdocs/13thamendment.html

Library of Congress. (n.d.b). Primary Documents in American History: 14th Amendment to the U.S. Constitution. Retrieved from http://www.loc.gov/rr/program/bib/ourdocs/14thamendment.html

Little Rock Board of Education. (1960, March 21). Minutes of the Little Rock Board of Education special meeting. Resolution of Board of Directors. Little Rock, AR: Board of Education.

Little Rock Board of Education. (1961, July 27). Minutes of the Little Rock Board of Education executive session Little Rock, AR: Board of Education.

Little Rock Board of Education Directors. (1963, June 30). Minutes of special meeting. Little Rock, AR: Board of Education.

Little Rock Board of Education Directors. (1963, November 21). Minutes of Board of Education directors meeting. Little Rock, AR: Board of Education.

Little Rock Board of Education Directors. (1964, March 24). Minutes of the Board of Directors regular meeting). Little Rock, AR: Board of Education.

Little Rock Board of Education Directors. (1964, April 3). Minutes of the Board of Directors executive meeting. Little Rock, AR: Board of Education.

Little Rock Board of Education Directors. (1964, June 18). Minutes of the Little Rock School District Board of Directors special meeting. Little Rock, AR: Board of Education.

Little Rock School District. (2017). School improvement designations for Little Rock School District 2015–16 and 2016–17. Little Rock, AR: Author. Retrieved from https://www.lrsd.org/cms/lib/AR02203631/Centricity/Domain/86/School%20Improvement%20and%20Distress%20Designations%20for%20LRSD%20and%20its%20Schools%202015-16%202016-17.pdf

Little Rock School District v. North Little Rock School District; Pulaski County Special School District; State of Arkansas. U.S. Court of Appeals for the Eighth Circuit Court of Appeals (No. 07-1866), 2009. Retrieved from http://media.ca8.uscourts.gov/opndir/09/04/071866P.pdf

Little Rock School District v. North Little Rock School District; Pulaski County Special School District; State of Arkansas, July 17, 2018. U.S. Court of Appeals for the Eighth Circuit Court of Appeals (No. 07-1866). Retrieved from http://media.arkansasonline.com/news/documents/2018/07/17/5412_1.pdf

Little Rock School District v. Pulaski County Special School District No 1, North Little Rock School District et al. U.S. District Court for the Eastern District of Arkansas—584 F. Supp. 328 (E.D. Ark. 1984). Retrieved from https://law.justia.com/cases/federal/district-courts/FSupp/584/328/2270128/

National Archives. (n.d.). Civil Rights Act of 1964. Retrieved from https://www.ourdocuments.gov /document_data/document_info_text/document_097_description.html

Plessy v. Ferguson, 163 U.S. 537 (May 18, 1896). Retrieved from https://supreme.justia.com/cases /federal/us/163/537/

Smith, C.U. (1975). Public school desegregation and the law. *Social Forces, 54*(2), 317–327.

Swann v. Charlotte-Mecklenburg Board of Education, 402 U.S. 1 (1971). Retrieved from https:// supreme.justia.com/cases/federal/us/402/1/ retrieved August 24, 2018.

Swanson, E., McKenzie, S. C., & Ritter, G. W. (2016). Integration in Little Rock, Part 1: Patterns in enrollment and characteristics of student movers. *Arkansas Education Report.* Fayetteville, AR: Office for Education Policy University of Arkansas. Retrieved from http://www .officeforeducationpolicy.org/downloads/2016/11/integration-in-little-rock-part-1.pdf

Title IV, Civil Rights Act of 1964. (1964). Retrieved from http://civilrights.findlaw.com /discrimination/title-iv-of-the-civil-rights-act-of-1964-desegregation-of-public.html

University of Arkansas. (n.d.). Sarah Alderman Murphy Papers, 1951–1994. Little Rock, AR: University of Arkansas. Retrieved from http://digitalcollections.uark.edu/cdm/compoundobject /collection/Civilrights/id/594/show/593

Walton College. (n.d.). William F. "Billy" Rector. Fayetteville, AR: University of Arkansas. Retrieved from http://walton.uark.edu/abhf/william-f-billy-rector.php

Williams, P. N., & Lovin, R. W. (1978). Rights and remedies: A study of desegregation in Boston. *Journal of Religious Ethics, 6*(2), 137–163.

© Sergii Gnatiuk/Shutterstock

Living and Dying

Michael Potts

▶ Introduction

Most ethical and legal issues in medicine cluster at the beginning and end points of life. This article focuses on end-of-life issues: the criteria for death and end-of-life decision making, including advance directives, medical futility policies, withdrawing and withholding care, euthanasia, and physician-assisted suicide. A person's worldview is key to which ethical theory influences his or her stance on end-of life issues; a traditional Roman Catholic, for instance, will hold radically different positions from the liberal secularist on whether physician-assisted suicide is morally right. Although law and morality are not synonymous, differences in moral stances are often reflected in differences in law. End-of-life issues illustrate the deep influence of morality on law.

▶ The Criteria for Death

The issue of organ transplantation was a driving force in contemporary attempts to develop alternative criteria for death (Beecher & Dorr, 1971). In the past, cessation of heartbeat and respiration were sufficient to declare a person dead. But some patients reveal little or no evidence of brain activity and are ventilator dependent, although their hearts continue to beat. The issue arose whether these patients are dead despite their beating hearts; if so, the "dead donor rule" that allows removal of organs only from dead individuals is followed, and it is morally acceptable to take their organs.

Determination of death has three facets: (1) the definition of death, (2) the criteria for death consistent with the definition, and (3) the medical tests determining whether the criteria have been met (Kass, 1974). The definition of death is a philosophical issue with an answer that depends on when human personhood ends. If personhood is identified with consciousness, then death occurs when an individual permanently loses the capacity for consciousness. If personhood is defined as a functioning organic body, then death occurs when that body is no longer functioning as an organic unity.

The issue of the proper criteria for death is partly philosophical and partly medical. Those who define death as a permanent lack of consciousness often support "higher brain death," the idea that death occurs with the permanent cessation of function in the parts of the brain essential for conscious experience. Those who believe we can accurately diagnose higher brain death usually argue that a patient in a persistent vegetative state, who can breathe on his or her own, and have wake–sleep cycles, is dead. So, too, are anencephalic infants, babies born without an upper brain (the cerebrum, including the cerebral cortex), which is thought to be the source of the content of consciousness. If these individuals are dead, then they would be suitable organ donors. Those who believe that we cannot accurately diagnose higher brain death may endorse a more stringent criterion, whole brain death, which holds that the entire brain, upper and lower, must permanently cease to function for a person to be dead. Some scholars who define death as the permanent loss of bodily integrity also support whole brain death. This is the majority position in the United States. In the United Kingdom, brain stem death is thought sufficient to eliminate bodily integrity and consciousness and is the legal standard of death there. Critics of all brain death criteria generally prefer a circulatory–respiratory criterion for death, which holds that death occurs with the destruction of the circulatory and respiratory systems (Potts, Byrne, & Nilges, 2000).

Donation after cardiac death (DCD) takes place in a person who decides in advance to be allowed to die by ventilator removal. When the heart stops for two minutes (or more, depending on the specific protocol), organs are removed and transplanted. One issue is that the patient may not be brain dead when organs are removed, and the removal of organs might be the direct cause of the patient's death. A defender of DCD could respond that organ removal is not the direct cause of death or argue that it does not matter if the donor is not dead. The donor freely decided to donate, withdrawal of care is moral and legal, and if the person is technically alive during organ removal, then the situation is one of justifiable homicide rather than murder.

▶ End-of-Life Decision Making

Until the social revolutions of the 1960s, the dominant view of end-of-life decision making was that the doctor made the decisions, and the patient unquestionably obeyed the doctor. Often the patient could not make an informed decision because, for instance, the patient was not told she had a terminal illness such as cancer. Such a policy, still followed in Japan and other Asian countries, is called *paternalism*. The doctor is like a parent who knows the patient's good and has the knowledge to make all medical decisions for the patient.

During the 1960s and 1970s, patients began to demand the right to make their own medical decisions ("the right of self-determination"). Applied to end-of-life issues, this view holds that a patient should be told of all essential information about a terminal illness and be given viable options for either treatment of the disease itself, or, if the patient decides, only palliative care to relieve pain and discomfort. The doctrine of *informed consent*—that the doctor must provide the patient with sufficient information to make an informed decision about his or her medical care—is now enshrined in law. It is based on the principle of autonomy, that all people have the right to make their own decisions about their bodies without interference from others.

This emphasis on autonomy led to the expansion of patients' rights over treatment at the end of life. The 1976 case of Karen Ann Quinlan, who was ventilator-dependent and unresponsive to others, led the New Jersey Supreme Court to rule that a patient (or the patient's surrogate or representative if the patient is incompetent to make an informed decision) is permitted to authorize the removal of a ventilator.

In another landmark case, the Nancy Cruzan case, the U.S. Supreme Court ruled in 1990 that a patient or surrogate can authorize withholding or withdrawing artificial nutrition and hydration. The justifications for such rights include the principle of autonomy along with the position that withdrawing or withholding care in the case of a terminal condition simply allows the disease process to take its course and is not equivalent to killing the patient. Roman Catholics appeal to their distinction between ordinary care (which must be offered by a doctor) and extraordinary care (burdensome care) that may be offered by the doctor, who is not morally obligated to do so. Although some utilitarians such as Tom Regan (1975), James Rachels (1979), and Peter Singer (2011) have argued that withholding or withdrawing care is killing the patient, this is neither the consensus of current law nor ethics.

An *advance directive* (AD) is a legal document designed to give health-care providers guidance on a patient's treatment in accordance with his or her wishes when that patient becomes mentally incompetent to make medical decisions. The simplest AD is a *Do Not Resuscitate* (DNR) order. A patient (or family member) signs a form in the presence of unrelated witnesses and has the document notarized. In case of a cardiac arrest, that patient will not receive CPR. The patient or surrogate can revoke the directive at any time.

A *living will* is an AD in which the patient specifies the kinds of care authorized and unauthorized if the patient becomes mentally incompetent. Thus, if a patient does not want a feeding tube or artificial hydration, then the living will can specify this. Living will forms vary from state to state, although states will generally honor out-of-state living wills. Critics argue that living wills can be interpreted in different ways by medical personnel, leading to either undertreatment or overtreatment. To lessen these possibilities, an individual can grant another person health-care power of attorney.

The *health-care power of attorney* (HPA) gives the person volunteering for that title the ability to make medical decisions in place of the patient should that patient become incompetent. Unless the person assigning HPA states otherwise, in case of that person's incompetence the surrogate will have the same health-care authority to make decisions as that person had while competent. It is important to make sure that one knows the potential HPA well so that the surrogate's decisions would reflect the patient's own values. If the person granting HPA does not wish to allow the HPA to make all decisions concerning health care, then forms allow for listing exceptions. Like living wills, health-care power of attorney forms are state specific, although other states usually honor them.

One of the fastest-growing and most common forms of AD in a hospital is the *Physician's Orders for Life-Sustaining Treatment* (POLST). These are forms signed by both the patient and the physician that inform the staff of the extent of allowable life-sustaining treatment such as CPR, kidney dialysis, or antibiotics. Some critics have argued that these forms do not have sufficient safeguards to avoid the physician imposing personal values on the patient, but given that a discussion with the patient is required (or with the patient's surrogate or family if the patient is incompetent and does not have a LW or HPA), this danger is mitigated. The name of the forms differs from state to state, although the actual content is similar.

Despite such a strong emphasis on autonomy and patient self-determination, many health-care providers and medical ethicists have backed away from the strong patient self-determination positions of the late 1970s through the early 1990s. In the 1990s, a debate over *futile* medical care flared. Futile care is "care" that does no good to the patient. The problem is defining what "good for the patient" means. CPR can sometimes start the heart of a terminal cancer patient in cardiac arrest, so it is not physiologically futile. Can "futility" be understood as broader than mere physiological futility? One possible understanding is that "futile care is care that cannot restore the patient to a good quality of life." Then the issue becomes defining "quality of life." This, along with futility in general, are value-laden concepts in which the physician's and patient's values may differ. In a case in which the physician's values win out because of futility policies, conflict can arise. Still, most hospitals have futility policies. They have been applied most often in the case of extremely low weight infants who have a near zero chance of survival once they suffer a brain hemorrhage. Parents who demand that the baby receive continued treatment can be denied their request by a hospital's futility policy. Proponents believe that such policies are for the patient's good; critics claim that such policies devalue human life and are mainly in place for financial reasons.

Whether to withhold or withdraw life-sustaining care is a classic issue in medical ethics. In the paternalistic era, doctors tended to treat patients aggressively. However, with the arrival of ventilators and feeding tubes, some patients were kept alive who may not have wished to live with the help of such devices. The two cases mentioned earlier, Quinlan and Cruzan, helped set precedent in these areas.

The Quinlan case concerns Karen Ann Quinlan, who mixed Quaaludes and alcohol and suffered a respiratory arrest in 1975 that led to her being in a persistent vegetative state. She was on a ventilator, and her parents asked the hospital to remove the ventilator, stating that their daughter had informed them she would not want to live dependent on machines. When the hospital refused, her parents sued, and the New Jersey Supreme Court, on March 31, 1976 (*In re Quinlan*, 1976), affirmed that the hospital had to follow Quinlan's prior wishes and remove the ventilator. The right to privacy to make one's own decisions (or the family serving as proxy) was inviolate. Although Karen Ann Quinlan began to breathe on her own after the removal of her ventilator until her death in 1985, precedent was set, and it is now legal for health-care providers to withdraw or withhold a ventilator, depending on the patient's or surrogate's wishes. The Quinlans, devout Catholics, received the support of the church because the Roman Catholic Church does not affirm that extraordinary (or burdensome) treatment must be given the patient (although it can be given if the patient consents).

The second case, *Cruzan v. Director, Missouri Department of Health* (1990), was decided by the Supreme Court of the United States (SCOTUS) and involved a young woman, Nancy Cruzan. She was thrown face down into a water-filled ditch from a traffic accident and left without a heartbeat or respiration. Although paramedics resuscitated her, she was in a persistent vegetative state (a state in which a patient can breathe spontaneously and has sleep–wake cycles but shows no signs of conscious awareness). Her parents asked the hospital to remove her feeding tube, and the case ended up in court. The SCOTUS majority opinion held that the parents had not shown "clear and convincing evidence" that Nancy Cruzan would have wanted her feeding tube removed. In her case, the parents later provided such evidence, and a lower court then allowed Cruzan's doctors to remove the feeding tube. This was done, and Cruzan died. The case revealed the urgent need for advance directives. As a result, Congress passed the Patient Self-Determination Act in 1991, which was signed into law by President George H. W. Bush. The law requires health-care institutions receiving federal funds to inform patients of advance directive options.

In the Cruzan ruling, Associate Justice Antonin Scalia illustrated one of the ethical problems with withdrawing a feeding tube: Is it the equivalent of suicide? In other words, is withdrawing life-sustaining care morally equivalent to the patient intentionally causing her own death by taking a drug prescribed specifically to kill her? Scalia believed that it is: To this extent, he was an ally of utilitarians such as Rachels, Regan, and Singer. Those three philosophers, however, believe that euthanasia is morally acceptable, something Scalia disagreed with. However, a consensus soon arose that instead of being mercy killing, withholding or withdrawing a feeding tube allows the disease process to take its course without interference by artificial means. This view is consistent with the Roman Catholic notion of double-effect reasoning. According to double effect, a good act may lead to bad consequences, but as long as the act itself is for a good goal and not for the purpose of an evil goal, the act is morally acceptable. For example, the issue sometimes arises of whether to increase the dose of barbiturates used for general and "proportionate palliative sedation" (Cavanaugh, 2019). According to double effect, it is acceptable to increase the dose because (1) the goal is to relieve pain, (2) barbiturate are drugs normally used to relieve pain, and (3) the purpose is not to kill the patient. Thus, even though the increased probability of the patient's death is foreknown, the act of increasing the dose of barbiturates remains morally good. Applied to the feeding tube issue, removing a feeding tube is for the purpose of removing extraordinary, burdensome care and allowing the disease process already present to take its natural course.

The same principle can apply to another famous case, that of Terri Schiavo. An eating disorder resulted in a low potassium level, and her heart stopped. After she was revived, she was in a persistent vegetative state. After 10 years in this condition, her husband, Michael Schiavo, said that Terri did not wish to live while dependent on a feeding tube. Her parents disagreed. Emotions grew overly tense on both sides—but the real issue was whether her prior wishes were accurately known during the time she was competent.

In the heat of the debate, some people made the claim that removing a feeding tube was a form of active euthanasia. Yet a feeding tube is making up for a bodily deficit caused by the disease process. In addition, one can argue that a feeding tube is extraordinary, burdensome care. Also, if those who believe (1) removing a feeding tube is wrong but also support (2) removal of a ventilator, there is no morally relevant difference between (1) and (2). Their claim that food and water are necessary for life is true, but so is oxygen.

Active euthanasia, or what I would call "euthanasia proper," is the intentional bringing about of the death of a patient, usually by means of a deadly drug. *Euthanasia* literally means "good death," but whether or not it is morally good is the issue here. Active euthanasia takes place today in the Netherlands, including cases in which doctors administered deadly drugs to patients without consulting family members. Sometimes this occurs in cases of comatose patients with no family or friends available who could state the patient's prior wishes. Utilitarian defenders of active euthanasia argue that the distinction between withdrawal of care and giving a deadly drug is verbal because they both result in the patient's death. They also argue that the relief of a terminally ill patient's pain is worth a relatively painless process of putting him or her to death, thereby ending suffering. Another argument stems from autonomy—the claim is that a person should have the right to determine the time and manner of his or her own death.

Opponents of active euthanasia argue that there is a morally significant difference between withdrawing care and giving a deadly drug. A key argument they use is that doctors should not be in the business of killing patients; that the line crossed violates the principle of nonmaleficence, "Do no harm," and sets a dangerous precedent for misuse of medical power. Other critics argue that people are not as autonomous as Western society believes, and that they do not, qua individuals, have the right to ask for euthanasia. In some Asian societies such as Japan, the family is more important than the individual, and it is the family who makes medical decisions instead of the individual patient.

Greater social cohesion results in more social support for the dying patient, and such support, as well as good palliative care such as pain control, may reduce the number of people who might otherwise desire euthanasia.

The issue of euthanasia shades into the debate over physician-assisted suicide (PAS). In the United States, PAS consists of a doctor writing a prescription for barbiturates for the patient along with directions for the amount that is a fatal dose. When the patient is ready, he or she decides the best time for her to commit suicide. In the United States, PAS is legal in Oregon, Washington, California, Montana, Vermont, and Hawaii. All are liberal states except for Montana, where a court ruling legalized PAS. The main argument for PAS is presented in the "Philosopher's Brief" to the U.S. Supreme Court, which was then considering whether PAS is a constitutional right (the Court later ruled unanimously that it is not). Philosophers Ronald Dworkin, Thomas Nagel, Robert Nozick, John Rawls, Thomas Scanlon, and Judith Jarvis Thomson argued from the standpoint of personal autonomy—that any competent individual has the right to determine the time and manner of his or her own death, and thus there is a "liberty interest" in making PAS a constitutional right (Dworkin et al., 1997).

Opponents of PAS argue either that suicide in general is wrong (either from theological bases or from a Kantian argument from human dignity) or that it is wrong for physicians to prescribe a deadly drug because of the violation of nonmaleficence. An argument can be given from the ends (goals) of medical practice—to help a vulnerable patient in need who comes to the physician, a person with knowledge and power, for help (Cavanaugh, 2018). The issue is whether prescribing a deadly drug is an abuse of physician power over vulnerable patients.

The fundamental issue uniting almost all the others is how to treat a dying person. Death was (and still often is) looked on as a failure by medical practitioners, and they tend to be uncomfortable dealing with dying patients. Discomfort, however, is no excuse for physicians failing in the fundamental end of medicine—to help a sick and vulnerable person in need, even if that person cannot be restored to health. The doctor can participate in palliative care, including pain control, and spend some time talking to the patient. If the doctor is too busy, other staff members—physician assistants, nurse practitioners, registered nurses, chaplains—can all spend time with the patient and help him or her during the frightening and often painful process of dying. Treatment for depression can also help ease the discomfort of a dying patient. Hospice and home care alternatives should be explored. If the patient has a sense that she is cared for during her dying days, then this can reduce the pressure for physician-assisted suicide or active euthanasia. Such care would also constitute evidence of the ethical practice of medicine in properly caring for the dying.

▶ References

Beecher, H. K., & Dorr, H. I. (1971). The new definition of death: Some opposing views. *Internationale Zeitshrift fur Pharmacologie, Therapie, und Toxokologie, 3*, 120–124.

Cavanaugh, T.A. (2018). *Hippocrates' Oath and Asclepius' snake: The birth of a medical profession.* New York, NY: Oxford University Press.

Cavanaugh, T. A. (2019). Personal communication, April 2.

Cruzan v. Director, Missouri Department of Health, 497 U.S. 261 (1990). Retrieved from https://www.law.cornell.edu/supremecourt/text/497/261

Dworkin, R., Nagel, T., Nozick, R., Rawls, J., Scanlon, T., & Thompson, J. J. (1997, March 27). Assisted suicide: The philosophers' brief. *The New York Review of Books.* Retrieved from https://www.nybooks.com/articles/1997/03/27/assisted-suicide-the-philosophers-brief/

In re Quinlan, 70 NJ. 10. 355 A.2d 647 (1976), cert. denied sub nom. Retrieved from https://law.justia.com/cases/new-jersey/supreme-court/1976/70-n-j-10-0.html

Kass, L. (1974). Death as an event: A commentary on Robert Morison. In P. L. Steinfels & R. M. Veatch (Eds.), *Death inside out: The Hastings Center report* (pp. 70–82). New York, NY: Harper & Row.

Potts, M., Byrne, P. A., & Nilges, R. G. (2000). *Beyond brain death: The case against brain-based criteria for human death.* Dordrecht, Holland: Kluwer Academic Publishers.

Rachels, J. (1979). Euthanasia, killing, and letting die. In J. Ladd (Ed.), *Ethical issues relating to life and death* (pp. 146–163). New York, NY: Oxford University Press.

Regan, T. (1975). *Active and passive euthanasia. New England Journal of Medicine, 292*, 78–80.

Singer, P. (2011). *Practical ethics* (3rd ed.). Cambridge, UK: Cambridge University Press.

SECTION 10

Juveniles and Ethics

Ethical Issues in Juvenile Justice

Shaun M. Gann

▶ Introduction

Before the 19th century, juveniles who came into contact with the criminal justice system were treated the same as adults. They had the same rights and expectations as adults, and they received the same punishments—including both corporal and capital punishments (Crowe, 2000). There was no separate juvenile justice system, and convicted juveniles and adults were housed in the same correctional facilities. For the purposes of the criminal justice system, juveniles were simply "little adults." This began to change, however, in the early 1800s. During this time, "children began to be viewed as persons at a unique stage of human development instead of smaller versions of adults with equal cognitive and moral capacities" (Crowe, 2000, p. 26). Adolescence became recognized as a distinctive stage of life characterized by physical, intellectual, social, emotional, and moral maturation (Crowe, 2000).

Contemporary research has shown that children and adolescents have cognitive, psychosocial, and neurobiological differences that distinguish them from adults and render them less blameworthy than adults when they commit crimes (Cauffman & Steinberg, 2012; Scott & Steinberg, 2008). For example, throughout adolescence, youth experience biological changes that affect brain functions associated with anti-social activities such as planning ahead, weighing costs and benefits, self-regulating emotions, controlling impulses, avoiding risks, and coordinating cognitive functions (Cauffman & Steinberg, 2012). Based on their review of adolescent development research, Scott and Steinberg (2008, p. 49) concluded that "ordinary teenagers differ from adults in their decision-making capacities, that their 'deficiencies' are developmental in nature, and that the psychological deficits that contribute to immature judgment are grounded in underlying neurobiological immaturity." Note, however, that these developmental deficiencies do not excuse juveniles from criminal responsibility. Rather, they simply mean that juveniles are less blameworthy for their actions and should not receive the same punishments an adult would receive for comparable criminal activity (Cauffman & Steinberg, 2012).

The beginning of the 20th century brought with it the new concept of specialized juvenile courts (Caldwell, 1961). The purpose of these early courts was to rehabilitate and educate delinquent and wayward youth. They were based on the *parens patriae* philosophy in which the court can assume responsibility over delinquent or unruly youths. It is then up to the court to take action that is in the best interest of the juvenile. Depending on the specific circumstances for each youth, this action may include—among others—probation, removing neglected or abused youths from their homes and placing them in safe settings, or placing delinquent youths in a secure confinement facility (i.e., the juvenile equivalent of an adult prison or jail).

The remainder of this article provides an overview of some of the ethical issues that are encountered in juvenile courts. The topics include the death penalty and life without parole for juvenile offenders, major Supreme Court cases involving juvenile court proceedings, disproportionate minority contact, and private correctional facilities for adjudicated youth. Each topic is discussed within the "children are different" perspective that permeates the juvenile justice system today. Note that the purpose of this article is not to argue in favor of one position or another. Instead, the aim is to present you—the reader—with certain aspects of juvenile justice that may involve ethical issues. After reading this article, it will be up to you to determine the ethical implications of these issues.

▶ The Death Penalty and Life Without Parole

One of the primary legal and ethical issues in juvenile justice in the 20th century has been whether capital punishment and life without parole (LWOP) sentences are permissible under the Eighth Amendment's ban on cruel and unusual punishment. Before the U.S. Supreme Court's decision in *Roper v. Simmons* (2005), juveniles who committed capital murder could receive the death penalty or LWOP, the same as adults. Indeed, since the founding of the United States, approximately 365 executions have occurred in which the offender was either a juvenile at the time of execution or at the time the crime was committed (Linn, 2016). However, only 22 of these executions occurred between 1976 (when the death penalty was reinstated after a short moratorium) and 2005 (when *Roper* was decided).

Though the use of capital punishment for those who committed murder as a juvenile decreased throughout the 20th century, it was officially abolished in the United States with the Court's ruling in *Roper v. Simmons* (2005). At 17 years old, Simmons committed a capital murder and was sentenced to death. On appeal, the Court relied on the "evolving standards of decency that mark the progress of a maturing society" to determine whether capital punishment should be considered cruel and unusual for certain groups of people. The Court argued that there was a national and international consensus that executing juveniles had become a rarity: "The objective indicia of consensus in this case—the rejection of the juvenile death penalty in the majority of states; the infrequency of its use even where it remains on the books; and the consistency in the trend toward abolition of the practice—provide sufficient evidence that today our society views juveniles as categorically less culpable than the average criminal" (*Roper v. Simmons*, p. 567). The Court also stated that there are three differences between juveniles and adults that demonstrate that juveniles cannot be classified among the worst offenders and thus deserve the death penalty: (1) Scientific research has shown that juveniles have a lack of maturity and an underdeveloped sense of responsibility, (2) juveniles are more susceptible to outside influences, and (3) a juvenile's character is not as well formed as that of an adult. Based on these arguments, the Court ruled that offenders who commit murder under age 18 cannot be executed for their crimes.

Though *Roper* prohibited the death penalty for crimes committed by juveniles, many states at the time still sentenced juveniles to life without parole—the second most severe penalty permitted by law—for both homicide and nonhomicide offenses. Court cases in 2010 and 2012 limited the use of LWOP for juvenile offenders, though they did not completely prohibit the sanction. In *Graham v. Florida* (2010), 17-year-old Terrance Graham was already on felony probation when he was arrested for robbery and possession of a firearm. He was sentenced to life in prison without the possibility of parole. On appeal, the Supreme Court again relied on the "evolving standards of decency" criteria and ruled that the Eighth Amendment prohibits LWOP for juvenile nonhomicide offenders. Two years later, in *Miller v. Alabama* (2012), the Court struck down the use of *mandatory* LWOP statutes that required all juveniles convicted of homicide—without exception—to receive a sentence of life without parole. Note, however, that the *Graham* and *Miller* rulings do not prevent juvenile offenders from spending the rest of their lives in prison. Instead, these offenders must simply be given the opportunity for parole at some point; if the paroling authority determines that the offender is still a threat to society, it may deny parole and the offender will remain in custody.

▶ Supreme Court Cases Involving Juvenile Court Proceedings

When the juvenile court was first introduced, court hearings involving allegedly delinquent youth were considered to be civil proceedings as opposed to criminal proceedings (Hemmens, Steiner, & Mueller, 2004). This was because of the court's reliance on the parens patriae philosophy and the assertion that youths in the juvenile court were not being punished (and thus did not require a criminal proceeding). Instead, the court process was likened to civil proceedings in which the goal was to make decisions that were in the best interest of all parties involved, particularly the accused youth (Hemmens et al., 2004). However, because these hearings were not considered criminal in nature, youths who came in front of the juvenile court were not guaranteed any of the constitutional protections that adult defendants received such as the right to counsel, the right against self-incrimination, and the right to notice of the charges against them.

During the first half of the 20th century, because of the potential ethical violations and judicial misconduct inherent in adjudication hearings where juveniles had no constitutional rights, many advocates argued that youth should share the same rights afforded to adults in court proceedings (Hemmens et al., 2004). Not until 1966, however, did the U.S. Supreme Court began to apply constitutional safeguards to juvenile court proceedings. This section discusses some of the major Court cases—most borne from ethical issues—that have had lasting effects on the juvenile justice system.

The first case in which the Court addressed constitutional rights in the juvenile court process was *Kent v. U.S.* (1966). At 16 years old, Morris Kent was arrested for housebreaking, robbery, and rape. He was waived to adult court without a hearing. On appeal, the issue before the Supreme Court was whether juveniles have any due process rights in situations where their case is transferred, or waived, from juvenile court to criminal court. Because the transfer decision is a "critically important stage" in the judicial process, the Court ruled that juveniles must be provided four safeguards before transfer: (1) a transfer hearing, (2) right to counsel at the hearing, (3) access to the records used by the juvenile court when making the transfer decision, and (4) a written statement of the reasons for the judge's decision. Though this case applied only to transfer hearings, it is significant for being the first case in which the Court provided oversight into the juvenile court process (Hemmens et al., 2004).

The next major case decided by the Court was *In re Gault* (1967). Gerald Gault was 15 years old when he was arrested for making an obscene phone call. His court hearing was held the next day, and the petition filed against him did not include an actual charge; it simply stated he was a "delinquent minor." Without representation by an attorney, Gault was ultimately committed to a training school (i.e., a juvenile prison) until his 21st birthday, or a total of six years. The maximum sentence for an adult convicted of the same crime would have been a $50 fine or a maximum of two months in jail. On appeal, the Supreme Court held that Gault had been denied due process because the court hearing did not meet the minimum requirements for fair treatment under the Constitution (Hemmens et al., 2004). The *Gault* ruling required that juveniles be provided with four due process rights during delinquency hearings when there is a possibility of placement in a secure facility: (1) the right to counsel, (2) the right to confront and cross-examine witnesses, (3) the right against self-incrimination, and (4) the right to notice of the hearing and the charges. These safeguards, the Court argued, would protect juveniles from "unbridled discretion and well-intended state intervention" (Hemmens et al., 2004, p. 80).

The issue in front of the Court in *In re Winship* (1970) was whether the Due Process Clause of the 14th Amendment requires "proof beyond a reasonable doubt" in adjudication hearings. Before *Winship*, prosecutors in most states had only to prove their case against juveniles by a "preponderance of the evidence," a step below "beyond a reasonable doubt." In *Winship*, the Court ruled that "the constitutional safeguard of proof beyond a reasonable doubt is as much required during the adjudicatory stage of a delinquency proceeding as are those constitutional safeguards applied in *Gault*" (*In re Winship*, p. 368).

In *Breed v. Jones* (1975), the Court had to determine whether the Fifth Amendment's protection against double jeopardy (i.e., being tried twice for the same offense) applied to juveniles. At age 17, Gary Jones was arrested for robbery. He was adjudicated delinquent in juvenile court but was determined to be unfit for treatment as a juvenile. As such, he was transferred to criminal court, where he was tried again for the same crime and found guilty. On appeal, the Supreme Court ruled that being tried in both juvenile and criminal court for the same crime constituted double jeopardy: "[Jones] was subjected to the burden of two trials for the same offense; he was twice put to the task of marshaling his resources against those of the State, twice subjected to the 'heavy personal strain' that such an experience represents" (*Breed v. Jones*, 1975, p. 533). The result of this case is that whichever court (juvenile or criminal) hears the facts of the case must also issue the sanction if the youth is found guilty.

Finally, one constitutional right has not been extended to juvenile courts. In *McKeiver v. Pennsylvania* (1971), the Supreme Court ruled that although prior cases had given juveniles many of the same rights enjoyed by adult defendants, the Constitution does not require jury trials in the juvenile court. The Court argued that "in our legal system, the jury is not a necessary component of accurate factfinding. . . . The imposition of the jury trial on the juvenile court system would not strengthen greatly, if at all, the factfinding function, and would, contrarily, provide an attrition of the juvenile court's assumed ability to function in a unique manner" (*McKeiver v. Pennsylvania*, p. 547).

▶ Disproportionate Minority Contact

One of the most often documented aspects of the juvenile justice system has been the pronounced disproportionality in the processing of White and non-White juveniles in juvenile courts (Bishop, 2005). Research consistently finds that minority youth are overrepresented at every stage in the juvenile court process. More specifically, minority youth are disproportionately petitioned to juvenile court, held in preadjudication detention, adjudicated delinquent, committed to secure-placement facilities after adjudication, and waived to criminal court (Brown & Sorensen, 2013; Davis & Sorensen, 2013; Leiber, 2015; Leiber, Bishop, & Chamlin, 2011; Moak, Thomas, Walker, & Gann, 2012). This knowledge is so ingrained that the U.S. Department of Justice's Office of Juvenile Justice and Delinquency Prevention (OJJDP) has termed the phenomenon *disproportionate minority contact* (DMC), which refers to the disproportionate number of minority youth who come into contact with the juvenile justice system relative to their representation in the general population (OJJDP, 2009). Indeed, Platt (1969) argued that the first juvenile court in Chicago, Illinois, was created to address the perceived "urban disenchantment" that contributed to juvenile delinquency in large cities. Because racial minorities and those with little financial resources were—and are—more likely to reside in these urban areas, the underlying philosophies of early juvenile courts essentially guaranteed that non-White youth would come into contact with the juvenile justice system more frequently than White youth.

The original juvenile court was based on a social welfare model and the parens patriae philosophy (Armstrong & Rodriguez, 2005; Bishop & Leiber, 2011). As such, judicial decision making was based less on the current offense and more on the individualized needs of each youth coming before the court. In other words, dispositions for adjudicated youth were chosen based on what was in the best rehabilitative interest of the youth. However, the level of informality of the juvenile court, coupled with the large amount of discretion given to juvenile court judges, created an atmosphere that seemed to invite the possibility of racial discrimination (Armstrong & Rodriguez, 2005). For example, if court actors—specifically, juvenile court judges and probation officers—assess minority juveniles as being higher risk based on both legal and extralegal factors, then some level of racial disparity at various decision-making points in the system is inevitable (Bridges & Steen, 1998). Platt (1969) made a similar argument that the original advocates of the juvenile court in the late 19th century lobbied for the creation of the court not as a means of helping despondent children but as a method to maintain the middle-class status quo in an era of prolific immigration to large Midwestern and Northeastern cities.

Although rehabilitation remains the primary purpose of most juvenile courts, multiple societal and legal changes in the 1960s and 1970s led to the modification of juvenile court philosophy and policy to include punishment and public safety as primary objectives. Although some theorists have argued that this shift from rehabilitative to punitive ideals could have the side effect of reducing racial disparity in juvenile processing (for example, via the use of sentencing guidelines), most recent studies show that DMC still exists—to varying degrees—in all states and at a variety of stages in the juvenile court process (Davis & Sorensen, 2013; Owen & Takahashi, 2014; Sullivan, Mueller, Gann, Spiegel, & McManus, 2016).

▶ Private Correctional Facilities for Juveniles

Since the inception of the juvenile court, serious delinquent youth were typically placed in training schools—the juvenile equivalent of adult prisons—managed by state governments. These institutions often faced the same problems found in adult prisons: poor living conditions, minimal rehabilitative programming, and overcrowding (Feeley, 2002). In 1974, Congress passed the Juvenile Justice and Delinquency Prevention Act (JJDPA) that, among other things, called for states to develop alternatives to traditional incarceration for juvenile offenders (Bayer & Pozen, 2005). Soon after the JJDPA was passed, many private correctional companies stepped in to offer their services to state and local jurisdictions (DiIulio, 1988). The participation of private companies in certain aspects of corrections was not new at the time; many states had previously contracted out certain services within facilities such as providing food services, education, religion, and rehabilitation programs. It is a relatively new phenomenon, however, when governments contract with private companies to operate *every* aspect of a facility (Feeley, 2002).

In 2015, private residential facilities for juveniles made up 48% of all facilities holding juvenile offenders (Hockenberry, 2018). However, only 31% of all juvenile offenders in secure placement were housed in these private facilities. This equated to more than 15,000 juvenile offenders being housed in private facilities in 2015. Though it is relatively common today, the issue of privatizing corrections remains controversial, especially when it involves youth involved with the juvenile justice system.

One primary area of debate on the use of private facilities is whether private companies should be able to administer punishment to citizens, a duty typically reserved for government agencies (Armstrong & MacKenzie, 2003; Feeley, 2002). DiIulio (1988, p. 68) further explains the ethical issue: "Should the authority to administer criminal justice programs and facilities, to deprive citizens of their liberty, and to coerce them, be delegated to contractually deputized private individuals and groups, or ought it remain wholly within the hands of duly constituted public officials?"

Supporters of private facilities claim that they can construct and manage correctional facilities significantly more cheaply and more effectively than government-controlled facilities, thus saving the state money if it contracts with the company (Armstrong & MacKenzie, 2003; DiIulio, 1998; Feeley, 2002). Proponents also argue that because private corrections companies are motivated by profit, they have a strong incentive to maintain a safe environment and to improve rehabilitative programming for their charges. Furthermore, this might also force state departments of corrections to increase the quality of prison conditions and programming in public correctional facilities.

Conversely, opponents of private correctional facilities argue that the only way these companies can save money is by cutting costs elsewhere—through subpar construction and maintenance, poor programming, ill-trained and undereducated staff, and poor living conditions (Armstrong & MacKenzie, 2003; DiIulio, 1998). Furthermore, Feeley (2002) argued that the increased use of private facilities has actually increased public spending on corrections because private companies have created new forms of sanctioning, thus expanding the number of people who come under some form of social control. In addition, private companies have no incentive to reduce prison crowding because they are typically paid according to the number of offenders housed in their facilities. Finally, opponents of private, for-profit correctional facilities point to the "Kids for Cash" scandal in Luzerne County, Pennsylvania, as a prime example of the bribery and corruption that can occur when incarceration is privatized. From 2000 until the scandal's discovery in 2008, two juvenile court judges received more than $2.6 million in bribes and kickbacks from PA Child Care—a private company that operated juvenile correctional facilities in Pennsylvania—as payments for helping the company obtain a contract with the state to house delinquent youth and for helping ensure that the facilities' beds were consistently occupied (Chen, 2009; Clarke, 2009; Neitz, 2011).

▶ Conclusion

This article presented four areas of juvenile justice where ethical or moral issues have been encountered. Each issue arose in the juvenile system because of the knowledge that children are developmentally distinct from adults and, as such, should be treated differently when they commit criminal or delinquent acts. All of these issues also revolve around questions of fairness. For example, the Supreme Court case *In re Gault* addressed the question of whether it was fair, or *ethical*, to deny juveniles the due process rights guaranteed by the Constitution in juvenile court proceedings. Finally, the ethical issues discussed in this article are by no means the only ones encountered in the juvenile justice system. The next four articles in this text delve further into these topics.

▶ References

Armstrong, G. S., & MacKenzie, D. L. (2003). Private versus public juvenile correctional facilities: Do differences in environmental quality exist? *Crime & Delinquency, 49*, 542–563.

Armstrong, G. S., & Rodriguez, N. (2005). Effects on individual and contextual characteristics on preadjudication detention of juvenile delinquents. *Justice Quarterly, 22*, 521–539.

Bayer, P., & Pozen, D. E. (2005). The effectiveness of juvenile correctional facilities: Public versus private management. *Journal of Law and Economics, 48*, 549–589.

Bishop, D. M. (2005). The role of race and ethnicity in juvenile justice processing. In D. F. Hawkins & K. Kempf-Leonard (Eds.), *Our children, their children: Confronting racial and ethnic differences in American juvenile justice* (pp. 23–82). Chicago, IL: The University of Chicago Press.

Bishop, D. M., & Leiber, M. J. (2011). Racial and ethnic differences in delinquency and justice system responses. In D. M. Bishop & B. C. Feld (Eds.), *The Oxford handbook of juvenile crime and juvenile justice* (pp. 446–484). New York, NY: Oxford University Press.

Breed v. Jones, 421 U.S. 519 (1975).

Bridges, G. S., & Steen, S. (1998). Racial disparities in official assessments of juvenile offenders: Attributional stereotypes as mediating mechanisms. *American Sociological Review, 63*, 554–570.

Brown, J. M., & Sorensen, J. R. (2013). Race, ethnicity, gender, and waiver to adult court. *Journal of Ethnicity in Criminal Justice, 11*, 181–195.

Caldwell, R. G. (1961). The juvenile court: Its development and some major problems. *Journal of Criminal Law & Criminology, 51*, 493–511.

Cauffman, E., & Steinberg, L. (2012). Emerging findings from research on adolescent development and juvenile justice. *Victims & Offenders, 7*, 428–449.

Chen, S. (2009). Pennsylvania rocked by "jailing kids for cash" scandal. Retrieved from http://www .cnn.com/2009/CRIME/02/23/pennsylvania.corrupt.judges/

Clarke, M. (2009). Caging kids for cash: Two Pennsylvania judges guilty of selling out juvenile justice system. *Prison Legal News, 20*, 20–23.

Crowe, A. H. (2000). *Jurisdictional technical assistance package for juvenile corrections.* Washington, DC: U.S. Department of Justice, Office of Juvenile Justice and Delinquency Prediction.

Davis, J., & Sorensen, J. R. (2013). Disproportionate minority confinement of juveniles: A national examination of black-white disparity in placements, 1997–2006. *Crime & Delinquency, 59*, 115–139.

DiIulio, J. J. (1988). What's wrong with private prisons. *Public Interest, 92*, 66–83.

Feeley, M. M. (2002). Entrepreneurs of punishment: The legacy of privatization. *Punishment & Society, 4*, 321–344.

Graham v. Florida, 560 U.S. 48 (2010).

Hemmens, C., Steiner, B., & Mueller, D. (2004). *Significant cases in juvenile justice.* New York, NY: Oxford University Press.

Hockenberry, S. (2018). *Juveniles in residential placement, 2015.* Washington, DC: U.S. Department of Justice, Office of Juvenile Justice and Delinquency Prevention.

In re Gault, 387 U.S. 1 (1967).

In re Winship, 397 U.S. 358 (1970).

Kent v. U.S., 383 U.S. 541 (1966).

Leiber, M. J. (2015). Race, prior offending, and juvenile court outcomes. *Journal of Crime and Justice, 39*, 88–106.

Leiber, M. J., Bishop, D., & Chamlin, M. B. (2011). Juvenile justice decision-making before and after the implementation of the disproportionate minority contact (DMC) mandate. *Justice Quarterly, 28*, 460–492.

Linn, A. (2016). History of death penalty for juvenile offenders. Juvenile Justice Information Exchange. Retrieved from https://jjie.org/2016/02/13/history-of-death-penalty-for-juvenile -offenders/

McKeiver v. Pennsylvania, 403 U.S. 528 (1971).

Miller v. Alabama, 567 U.S. 460 (2012).

Moak, S. C., Thomas, S. A., Walker, J. T., & Gann, S. M. (2012). The influence of race on preadjudication detention: Applying the symbolic threat hypothesis to disproportionate minority contact. *Journal of Juvenile Justice, 2*(1), 73–90.

Neitz, M. B. (2011). A unique bench, a common code: Evaluating judicial ethics in juvenile court. *Juvenile and Family Court Journal, 62*, 32–53.

Office of Juvenile Justice and Delinquency Prevention (OJJDP). (2009). *Disproportionate minority contact.* Washington, DC: U.S. Department of Justice, Office of Justice Programs, Office of Juvenile Justice and Delinquency Prevention.

Owen, J., & Takahashi, Y. (2014). Disproportionate minority contact in a Latino majority county: A descriptive study. *Journal of Ethnicity in Criminal Justice, 12*, 264–288.

Platt, A. M. (1969). *The child savers: The invention of delinquency.* Chicago, IL: University of Chicago Press.

Roper v. Simmons, 543 U.S. 551 (2005).

Scott, E. S., & Steinberg, L. (2008). *Rethinking juvenile justice.* Cambridge, MA: Harvard University Press.

Sullivan, C. J., Mueller, D. J., Gann, S. M., Spiegel, S. N., & McManus, H. D. (2016). Weapon and drug offenses and juvenile disproportionate minority contact: An impact assessment and practical discussion. *Journal of Crime & Justice, 39*, 107–130.

ARTICLE 44

Youth Cybercrime

Kweilin T. Lucas

▶ Introduction

It is easy to say that young people are more connected and exposed than ever before. Technology provides users with accessibility to a wealth of information and various means to communicate with others. A recent study from the Pew Research Center found that 95% of teens between ages 13 and 17 have access to a smartphone, whereas 45% are almost constantly connected through social media platforms, especially Snapchat (35%), YouTube (32%), and Instagram (15%). Findings from the study also suggested that teens demonstrate mixed views on the impact of social media in their lives. For example, although 31% of the sample viewed social media positively, 24% believed that it has a mostly negative effect, mainly because it allows opportunities for bullying and rumor spreading. Youth who maintained negative perceptions also indicated that social media harmed relationships, offered unrealistic portrayals of others' lives, caused distractions, and perpetuated peer pressure. In addition, youth noted that social media can cause mental health issues and additional drama (Anderson & Jiang, 2018). As these findings indicate, although the Internet and modern communication devices are widely used for positive purposes, they are also used to engage in various forms of Internet harm, more commonly known as *cybercrime*.

Cybercrime, a broad concept that includes crimes that are committed using computers and other online or electronic networks and platforms (Jewkes & Yar, 2013). Victims of cybercrime range from larger-scale targets (e.g., governments, institutions, or multinational operations (Hansen et al., 2007) to individual targets where the assailants know their victims or target them specifically (Näsi et al., 2015), which has resulted in an overwhelming amount of implications for prevention and future policy. Fortunately, our knowledge and understanding of cybercrime and interpersonal Internet behavior is increasingly growing, as researchers have taken notice of these important issues.

An estimated 65% of people worldwide have been victims of cybercrime. Moreover, only 9% of people feel safe online (Norton, 2012). To understand more about cybercrime among teenagers and young adults, who are among the most vulnerable populations on the Internet, empirical studies have been conducted to test theoretical perspectives and gather evidence about youth involvement in cybercrime. For example, research indicates that anywhere between 4% and 20% of young American Internet users have been victims of cybercrime, including being victims of online scams and phishing attacks (Wolak, Mitchell, & Finkelhor, 2006). In addition, studies have found that 16% of youth engaged in cyberbullying using the Internet or their cell phones, with 23% of teens experiencing peer-perpetrated victimization (Dehue, Bolman, & Vollink, 2008). Overall, researchers estimate that one-third of all teenagers who use the Internet have been targeted in a variety of ways, including but not limited to receiving threatening messages, having private emails or text messages forwarded without their consent, having an embarrassing picture posted without their permission, or having rumors about them spread online (Lenhart, 2007).

In one notable study, Näsi, Oksanenb, Keipia, and Räsänen (2015) used a multinational sample to examine the common characteristics and predictors of cybercrime victimization among a combined sample of teenagers and young adults ages 15 to 30 years old (n = 3,506) from Finland, the United States, Germany, and the United Kingdom. The respondents' perceptions of their cybercrime victimization were measured using a question that asked if someone had committed a crime against them online in the past three years. If it applied to them, respondents then classified their victimization as slander, coercion or a threat of violence, identity theft, fraud, or sexual harassment. Data were then aggregated to reflect cybercrime victimization rates. Overall, 6.5% of the respondents reported cybercrime victimization. Further, the victimization rates were almost identical across the four countries Most respondents had been victims of slander or defamation, coercion, fraud, and identity theft. Only a small portion of respondents had experienced sexual victimization online (Näsi et al., 2015). Although these findings cannot be generalized to other populations, they contribute to our current knowledge of cybercrime victimization across nations. Every issue related to cybercrime researchers and policy makers with unique challenges to consider and overcome. Fortunately, prior studies have led much groundwork for what is known about each of these offenses that affect youth and their interactions with others online.

▶ Examples of Youth Cybercrime

Cyberbullying

Cyberbullying is perhaps the most prevalent cybercrime that youth are involved with as perpetrators, victims, or third-party witnesses. *Cyberbullying* refers to a modern form of bullying carried out through various forms of electronic technology (David-Ferdon & Hertz, 2007; Patchin & Hinduja, 2006; Vandebosch & Van Cleemput, 2009). Many researchers conceptualize cyberbullying as a multitude of problems experienced with online aggression, but others focus only on specific types of harm (Patchin & Hinduja, 2012); therefore it maintains a wide range of interpretations, and researchers have not developed a standard definition of the term (Cesaroni, Downing, & Alvi, 2012; Vandebosch & Van Cleemput, 2008; Wolak, Mitchell, & Finkelhor, 2007). Cyberbullying is unique because it can take on many forms, including flaming (posting or sending offensive messages over the Internet), online harassment (repeatedly sending messages), cyberstalking (making threats of potential harm by intimidating an individual), denigration (defamation by written or printed words), masquerading (pretending to be someone else), outing (sharing personal information about a person without his or her permission), and exclusion (maliciously leaving a person out of a group) (Li, 2007). In addition, seven distinct subcategories of cyberbullying are based on the way victims are targeted, including through text messages, picture and video clips, phone calls, emails, chat rooms, instant messages, and web sites (Smith et al., 2008). Cyberbullying has become a primary concern for schools and communities because of the emotional, psychological, and physical harm it causes victims (Hinduja & Patchin, 2007). In the most tragic instances, youth have taken their own lives because of cyberbullying. This phenomenon, known as *cyberbullicide*, is a serious concern; studies suggest that victims of cyberbullying are almost twice as likely to have attempted suicide than youths who had not experienced cyberbullying (Hinduja & Patchin, 2010).

Certainly, cyberbullying is serious in any context and at any age, but findings suggest that teens and young adults are easy targets for perpetrators, especially because they use technology on a regular basis and have a lot of freedom to browse the Internet. Evidence suggests that most students in grades six through nine experience cyberbullying, especially if they are in positions that are vulnerable to attack by peers. For example, Cassidy, Jackson, and Brown (2009) found that individuals with special needs; students with high academic, athletic, or artistic abilities; and young boys and girls who are considered unpopular or unattractive by the larger populations are often targets of cyberbullies. In addition, between 10% and 20% of students ($n = 365$) were occasionally cyberbullied because of their race or identity (Cassidy et al., 2009).

Findings of prevalence rates for cyberbullying among adolescent populations are mixed. For example, Dehue, Bollman, and Vollink (2008) found that 16% of students ($n = 1,211$) had engaged in cyberbullying via the Internet and text messages, whereas 23% had been targeted online with name-calling and gossiping occurring most frequently. In addition, Hinduja and Patchin (2007) found that between 32% of males and 36% of females ($n = 1,388$) had been victims of cyberbullying, with victimization occurring most often in chat rooms and via computer text message. For perpetrators, evidence suggests that between 8% and 18% of youth cyberbullied others at one point during their lives. Moreover, girls (15.6%) report participation in cyberbullying almost as often as boys (18%), many times because they were seeking revenge (22.5%) or because they felt that the victim deserved it (18.7%) (Hinduja & Patchin, 2009).

Cyberbullying is just as damaging to adolescents as traditional forms of bullying for several reasons. For one, the Internet and technology allow bullies opportunities to constantly monitor and access other Internet users, especially those they are targeting. Bullies can also share different form of media on the Internet (e.g., text messages, pictures, video, emails, screenshots) where they can be repeatedly viewed by victims and other online users. In addition, once material is online, it is difficult to delete (Hinduja & Patchin, 2010. One aspect of cyberbullying makes it stand out among other types of cybercrimes: Bullies can pose anonymously on the Internet and target their victims anytime technology allows (Hinduja & Patchin, 2010; Ybarra & Mitchell, 2004). Studies suggest that only a fraction of youth know the identity of the persons targeting them. For example, Juvonen and Gross (2008) found that around two-thirds of students who reported being cyberbullied knew their perpetrators; half knew their bully from school (Juvonen & Gross, 2008). In comparison, Kowalski and Limber (2007) found that half of cyberbullying victims do not know their perpetrators (Kowalski & Limber, 2007). Unfortunately, because new forms of technology are constantly evolving, perpetrators are always presented with new opportunities to target their victims (Hinduja & Patchin, 2010).

Cyberstalking

The rapid advancement in technology has enhanced individuals' ability to communication with others, but it has also increased risks of personal intrusion (Pittaro, 2007). Research indicates that a significant portion of individuals experience cyberstalking (Alexy et al., 2005; Baum et al., 2009; D'Ovidio & Doyle, 2003; Fisher, Cullen, & Turner, 2002; Jerin & Dolinsky, 2001; Sheridan & Grant, 2007; Spitzberg & Hoobler, 2002). *Cyberstalking* is described as the repeated pursuit of an individual using online media or technology (Reyns, Henson, & Fisher, 2011). Cyberstalking is unique to other forms of cybervictimization because perpetrators target their victims using several online behaviors, including harassment or threats via email, messenger systems, chat rooms, or various Internet sites (Baum et al., 2009). Cyberstalkers also use electronic devices in the form of cameras, audio devices, computer programs, and global-positioning systems to track and monitor their victims (D'Ovidio & Doyle, 2003; Finkelhor, Mitchell, & Wolak, 2000; Finn, 2004; Holt & Bossler, 2009; Jerin & Dolinsky, 2001; Marcum, Higgins, & Ricketts, 2010; Sheridan & Grant, 2007; Spitzberg & Hoobler, 2002). There are few empirical assessments of cyberstalking, so not much is known about the phenomenon (Parsons-Pollard & Moriarty, 2009). In addition, few studies have examined cyberstalking using theoretical foundations (Reyns et al., 2011).

Fortunately, researchers have laid the groundwork for future works by exploring this issue in more depth. For example, Reyns, Henson, and Fisher (2011) were among the first to examine factors that increase or decrease risk of cyberstalking victimization using lifestyle-routine activities theory. Interestingly, this study revealed that the number of photos someone posts of themselves online significantly predicts online harassment. In addition, the number of updates someone posts on social media or through Internet messaging applications increases their likelihood to receive unwanted, sexual attention from other online media users (Reyns et al., 2011).

Researchers have also begun to examine *Internet addiction*, which is a potentially new disorder characterized by a person's problematic use of the Internet that consumes their time and causes damage to their everyday functioning (Chakraborty, Basu, & Kumar, 2010; Young, 1998). For example, studies indicate that individuals who are dependent on the Internet maintain poor time-management skills and suffer negative consequences that affect their personal and family lives and their occupation (Young, 1998). Young adults are especially vulnerable to developing problematic Internet habits (Anderson 2001; Castiglione 2008; Christakis et al., 2011; Young, Yue, & Ying 2011). In addition, individuals who are socially inclined and unprepared to deal with the challenges that life brings may seek virtual relationships as opposed to those that occur in the real world (Anderson, 2001).

Navarro, Marcum, Higgins, and Ricketts (2016) were among the first to find a significant relationship between Internet addiction and the cyberstalking behaviors of juveniles. Their findings suggest that prevention and intervention activities that address cyberstalking behaviors should also consider treating underlying symptoms of Internet addiction. The researchers also note that in addressing the problem of cyberstalking among young populations it is important to not dismiss or neutralize the behavior as typical juvenile behavior. Instead, young people should be educated about the seriousness of cyberstalking, especially because misusing the Internet is considered a felony in some cases (Navarro, et al., 2016).

Sexting

Sexting refers to the sending or receiving sexually suggestive or explicit material from one electronic device to another (Hinduja & Patchin, 2018; Judge, 2012; Lenhart, 2009; Mitchell et al., 2012). The behavior is of concern among adults because images can be saved, forwarded to others, or posted on social media web sites without the consent or knowledge of the person being targeted (Ling & Yttri, 2005; Wastler, 2010). Sexting is even more concerning for adolescents, considering the legal consequences they face that are specific to juvenile populations (Ricketts et al., 2014). The legal risk escalates further when sexually based media involves someone under age 18 as outlined by U.S. pornography statutes (18 U.S.C. § 2,251) (Klettke, Hallford, & Mellor, 2014; Ricketts et al., 2014).

In addition to legal risks, adolescents who engage in sexting risk varying degrees of social and emotional consequences. The consequences escalate further in situations where pictures are forwarded among peers or classmates or posted online via social media web sites (Barak, 2005; Barkacs & Barkacs, 2010; Hinduja & Patchin, 2010; Judge, 2012; Strassberg et al., 2013). The individuals featured in the photos risk being ridiculed and ostracized by peers, bullying, and cybervictimization (Reyns, Burek, Henson, & Fisher, 2011; Ricketts et al., 2014). In severe cases, young people have been bullied so severely over an image that they committed suicide (Dake, Price, & Maziarz, 2012; Dilberto & Mattey, 2009; Smith et al., 2008). Although these cases are rare, they demonstrate the seriousness of consequences associated with sexting (Ricketts et al., 2014; Strassberg et al., 2013).

Theoretically sound studies on adolescent sexting are limited (Ricketts et al., 2014). In addition, the available research on the extent of sexting among adolescents is both limited and quite varied in its findings, although studies point to several emerging patterns that are worthy of future exploration (Ricketts et al., 2014). For example, according to Ricketts, Maloney, Marcum, and Higgins (2014), nationally based studies (Lenhart, 2009; Mitchell et al., 2012) demonstrate lower overall rates of youth sexting compared to studies that have used samples of local youth, which may suggest geographic variation in the behavior. Future studies that explore sexting behaviors among youth should consider using theoretical foundations to identify possible correlates to this behavior. Research should also explore prevalence rates and gender, as well as the relationship between individuals who create sext messages and those who send them to others online (Ricketts et al., 2014).

Sexual Solicitation

Also of concern is that studies have documented cases of adolescents forwarding sexually based images to unintended recipients (Ostrager, 2010; Peskin et al., 2013; Strassberg et al., 2013). In these situations, youth who engage in sexually explicit behavior on the Internet or through media face additional risk of experiencing victimization in various forms, including sextortion (Lamphere & Pikciunas, 2015; Patchin & Hinduja, 2018; Wolak et al., 2018), image-based sexual abuse

(O'Connor et al., 2018; Quayle & Cooper, 2015), and being exploited through the production and dissemination of child pornography (Prichard et al., 2012). *Sextortion* refers to the threatened dissemination of explicit, intimate, or embarrassing images of a sexual nature without consent of the individual involved (Patchin & Hinduja, 2018). Once the perpetrators acquire the sexually explicit images, either voluntarily or through other means, they threaten to disseminate them to obtain additional images, sexual acts, money, or something else the perpetrators wants (Patchin & Hinduja, 2018).

According to the U.S. Department of Justice, sextortion is the most important and fastest-growing threat that young people face on the Internet with "more minor victims per offender than all other child sexual exploitation offenses" (Lynch, 2016, p. 75; Patchin & Hinduja, 2018). Researchers note that the behavior may manifest from incidents of teen dating violence if the offender is a current or former boyfriend or girlfriend (Korchmaros et al., 2013; Van Ouytsel, Ponnet, & Walrave, 2018; Zweig et al., 2014). In these situations, the perpetrator may threaten the victim using images that were shared in privacy during a consensual relationship to prevent a breakup from occurring (Zweig et al., 2013). Likewise, perpetrators can obtain their partners' private information (e.g., social media accounts, text messages, emails) by hacking into their devices, or they can create a hate web site to encourage others to post cruel comments and stories about the victim (Zweig et al., 2013). Offenders of sextortion can also take on different roles, including relatives (Kopecký, 2017; Quayle, 2017; Taylor & Quayle, 2003), strangers who later turn into online friends (Krone, 2004; O'Connell, 2003), and cyberbullies (Hinduja & Patchin, 2015; Patchin & Hinduja, 2016). Researchers of sextortion classify the behavior as different from revenge porn, a behavior that also includes the unauthorized sharing of sexually explicit images (Patchin & Hinduja, 2018).

Revenge porn, also referred to as *image-based sexual abuse* (Quayle & Cooper, 2015) or *nonconsensual pornography* (Citron & Franks, 2014; O'Connor et al., 2018), is defined as the posting of sexually explicit media without the consent of the subject to cause the victim distress or embarrassment (O'Connor et al., 2018; Quayle & Cooper, 2015; "Revenge Porn," 2017). When the images are used to extort sexual favors or money from the victim, the behavior is then considered to be sextortion (Hinduja, 2016; O'Connor et al., 2018; Wittes et al., 2016). An estimated 10 million people in the United States have been threatened with nonconsensual image sharing or are victims (Lenhart, Ybarra, & Price-Feeny, 2016). Most often, these encounters occur via social media, messaging applications, video voice calls, and emails, although they also occur on dating applications and gaming platforms (Pollack, 2017). Indeed, the Internet serves as an ideal place for risk-taking behaviors and opportunities to engage in the solicitation and grooming of youth (Quayle & Cooper, 2015).

Finally, youth who engage in risky behaviors online are at an increased risk of becoming victims of *child pornography* or child-exploitation material (Prichard et al., 2012). According to researchers, it is difficult to measure the scale of child-exploitation material on the Internet because the number of people who access it is unknown, and it is difficult to determine the number of children and youth who are affected by its production (Prichard et al., 2012). What can be observed is that the crime has reached unprecedented rates since the Internet came into existence (Bourke & Hernandez, 2009; Leary, 2007; Martellozzo, Nehring, & Taylor, 2010). Sexually exploitive material of this nature can have significant negative psychological

(Fergusson, Boden, & Horwood, 2008; Jonas et al., 2011; Kendler et al., 2000; Leary, 2007; Paolucci, Genius, & Violato, 2001) and physical consequences on victims (Prichard et al., 2012). In addition, victims experience trauma because of their knowledge of their abusive images circulating the Internet (Beech et al., 2008; Leary, 2007).

Researchers are becoming increasingly concerned with how young people interact with pornography in general, including how it impacts their attitudes to sexual relations (Bryant 2009; Flood, 2009a, 2009b; Greenfield, 2004). Moreover, studies have examined youths' risk of exposure to child exploitive material online through peer-to-peer networks (Prichard et al., 2012). For example, Prichard, Spiranovic, Walters, and Lueg (2012) argue that young people may encounter a degree of acceptance toward and normalization of child exploitive material through their interactions with online peers. Therefore, they continue, it is possible that this may influence young people's attitudes toward child pornography. More research is needed, however, to establish this finding further (Prichard et al., 2012).

Computer Crimes

In addition to interpersonal cybercrimes, the Internet exposes youth to computer crimes as either victims or perpetrators. Computer crimes include offenses that use an electronic device such as a computer or smartphone during the commission of a crime (Taylor, Fritsch, & Liederbach, 2015). Technological advancements allow youth ideal opportunities to engage in such offenses as hacking (Marcum et al., 2014; Richet, 2013; Yar, 2005) and piracy (Aaltonen & Salmi, 2013).

The term *hacking* refers to the access and unauthorized use of a computer system for criminal purposes (Taylor et al., 2010). The term has gone through a series of conceptual changes since it first emerged in the 1960s—that is, during the same time the counterculture movement was occurring (Muncie, 1999; Yar, 2005). Historically, the hacker subculture has emphasized the implementation of ethical practices, as well as the right to freely access and exchange knowledge and information (Taylor, 1999). Indeed, perpetrators are in a powerful position because they can inflict considerable harm on victims in the form of viruses, destroying or altering files, theft, theft of services, credit card fraud, and infiltrating software (Rogers, Smoak, & Liu, 2005).

According to researchers, hackers have generally expressed distrust of political, military, and corporate authorities, and they often resist conventional lifestyles and attitudes, as well as social hierarchies (Taylor, 1999). In addition, studies note that hackers are a skilled population (Holt, 2007) and have a keen and admirable knowledge of technology (Baker, Hylender, & Valentine, 2008). Studies also indicate that hackers neutralize their behaviors and claim innocence by insisting that they engage in hacking for exploratory purposes, although the practice is generally looked at as unethical behavior (Yar, 2005). One recent study found that young people attack computer networks for various reasons, ranging from a way to impress their friends to challenging the political system (Weaver, 2017).

Like other types of cybercrime, the hacker subculture generated interest and gained considerable attention among researchers as the Internet became more established (Fream & Skinner, 1997; Taylor, 1999, 2000; Thomas, 2000; Yar, 2005). Social scientists have examined hacking among youth in various ways. For example, Yar (2005) applied concepts of Becker's (1963) labeling theory to hacking, implying that that label in which hackers obtain from agents of social control, such as the criminal justice system, will either reject the label (by claiming to be misunderstood) or embrace it (thereby continuing to engage in the behavior).

More recently, Marcum, Higgins, Ricketts, and Wolfe (2014) investigated the hacking behaviors of adolescents and the predictors of the behaviors using the general theory of crime (Gottfredson & Hirschi, 1990) and social learning theory (Akers, 1998), both of which were found to be associated with youth hacking behaviors. The findings suggested that respondents who associated with deviant peers were more likely to log into another person's email without permission and send an email, which provided support for social learning theory. In addition, both low self-control and deviant peer association were found to be predictors of hacking into a web site or another person's social media account without permission. Finally, hacking behaviors were more likely to be performed by individuals who perform well in school (Marcum et al., 2014). Although these studies have shed light on the hacker subculture, more research is needed to understand the phenomenon as it occurs among young offenders (Marcum et al., 2010; Richet, 2013).

In addition to hacking, there is also evidence that youth are pirating music and movies (Aaltonen & Salmi, 2013; Malin & Fowers, 2009). *Piracy* is the illegal downloading of commercially available music or movies, copyrighted material, and intellectual property to avoid fees or making unauthorized copies of these materials for personal use or distribution (Malin & Fowers, 2009). According to researchers, this form of theft is often perceived as being acceptable by society because people engage in the behavior privately in their own homes and it appears to be a victimless crime. Estimates, however, suggest that millions of dollars in sales of music and movie sales are lost each year because of piracy, forcing both industries to intervene and demand that piracy be considered a criminal, ethically wrong behavior (Evans et al., 1997; Kini, Ramakrishna, & Vijayaraman, 2004; Kini, Rominger, & Vijayaraman, 2000; Malin & Fowers, 2009; Zentner, 2006).

Concerningly, piracy behaviors are emerging as common among youth (Bhattachariee, Gopal, & Sanders, 2003) and are becoming increasingly acceptable (Malin & Fowers, 2009). Fortunately, researchers have begun to explore piracy to understand more about the behavior, including youths' attitudes toward piracy and their associations with peers who engage in piracy (Eining & Christensen, 1991; Liang & Yan, 2005; Malin & Fowers, 2009; Rahim, Seyal, & Rahman, 2001). For example, young populations, including students in high school and college, indicate willingness to participate in piracy (Higgins, Fell, & Wilson, 2006; Higgins & Makin, 2004; Malin & Fowers, 2009). In addition, studies indicate that self-control is a strong predictor of attitudes toward piracy (Higgins & Makin, 2004; Higgins et al., 2006; Malin & Fowers, 2009).

▶ Conclusion

The rapid expansion of the Internet and technology dramatically changed the way that people socialize with one another (Kraft & Wang, 2010). As this article demonstrated, youths who use the Internet are at increased risk of involvement in a variety of cybercrimes, including cyberbullying, cyberstalking, sexting, online sexual solicitation, hacking, and piracy. Each offense is unique, complex, and leads to various types of harm, including negative physical and psychosocial consequences. Researchers have made several suggestions for handling cybercrime by individuals and communities. For example, evidence suggests that youth cybercrime is linked to peer influence and low self-control, which reinforces the need for parents to be more aware of their children's friends and Internet activities (Holt, Bosler, & May, 2010). In addition, there is evidence to suggest that the term *cyberbullying* is dated (Crosslin & Golman, 2014) or perceived by youth as becoming normalized in society (Paullet & Pinchot, 2014). It has also been suggested that the term *online harassment* be used to describe behaviors that represent cyberbullying (Crosslin & Golman, 2014).

Considering the questions and issues that emerge regarding youth involvement in cybercrime, it is easy to see that there remains a need for more critical, theoretical analysis of youths' online experiences. Indeed, researchers are met with the challenge of exploring cybercrime from many angles. Given the progression of the Internet and technology, however, it appears there are unlimited opportunities to do so.

▶ References

Aaltonen, M., & Salmi, V. (2013). Versatile delinquents or specialized pirates? A comparison of correlates of illegal downloading and traditional juvenile crime. *Journal of Scandinavian Studies in Criminology and Crime Prevention, 14,* 188–195.

Akers, R. (1998). *Social learning and social structure: A general theory of crime and deviance.* Boston, MA: Northeastern University Press.

Alexy, E. M., Burgess, A. W., Baker, T., & Smoyak, S. A. (2005). Perceptions of cyberstalking among college students. *Brief Treatment and Crisis Intervention, 5,* 279–289.

Anderson, K. (2001). Internet use among college students: An exploratory study. *Journal of American College Health, 50*(1), 21–26.

Anderson, M., & Jiang, J. (2018, May 31). Teens, social media & technology 2018. Pew Research Center. Retrieved from http://www.pewinternet.org/2018/05/31/teens-social-media-technology -2018/

Baker, W. H. , Hylender, D., & Valentine, A. (2008). Verizon Business 2008 data breach investigation report. Retrieved from https://www.wired.com/images_blogs/threatlevel/files /databreachreport.pdf?intcid=inline_amp

Barak, A. (2005). Sexual harassment on the Internet. *Social Science Computer Review, 23,* 77–92.

Barkacs, L., & Barkacs, C. (2010). Do you think I'm sexty? Minors and sexting: Teenage fad or child pornography? *Journal of Legal Ethical and Regulatory Issues, 13,* 23–31.

Baum, K., Catalano, S., Rand, M., & Rose, K. (2009). *Stalking victimization in the United States.* Washington, DC: U.S. Department of Justice.

Becker, H. (1963). *Outsiders: Studies in the sociology of deviance.* New York, NY: Free Press.

Beech, A., Elliot, I., Birgden, A., & Findlater, D. (2008). The Internet and child sexual offending: A criminological review. *Aggression and Violent Behaviour, 13,* 216–228.

Bhattachariee, S., Gopal, R. D., & Sanders, G. L. (2003). Digital music and online sharing: Software piracy 2.0? *Communication of the ACM, 46*(7), 107–111.

Bourke, M., & Hernandez, A. (2009). The "Butner Study" redux: A report of the incidence of hands-on child victimization by child pornography offenders. *Journal of Family Violence, 24*(3), 183–191.

Bryant, C. (2009, February). Adolescence, pornography and harm. *Trends & Issues in Crime and Criminal Justice* (No. 368). Canberra, ACT: Australian Institute of Criminology.

Cassidy, W., Jackson, M., & Brown, K. (2009). Sticks and stones can break my bones, but how can pixels hurt me? Students' experiences with cyber-bullying. *School Psychology International, 30,* 383–402.

Castiglione, J. (2008). Internet abuse and possible addiction among undergraduates: A developing concern for library and university administrators. *Library Review, 57*(5), 358–371.

Cesaroni, C., Downing, S., & Alvi, S. (2012). Bullying enters the 21st century? Turning a critical eye to cyber-bullying research. *Youth Justice, 12*(3), 199-211.

Chakraborty, K., Basu, D., & Kumar, K. (2010). Internet addiction: Consensus, controversies, and the way ahead. *East Asian Archives of Psychiatry 20*, 123-132.

Christakis, D., Moreno, M., Jelenchick, L., Myaing, M., & Zhou, C. (2011). Problematic Internet usage in US college students: A pilot study. *BMC Medicine, 9*(1), 77-83.

Citron, D. K., & Franks, M. A. (2014). Criminalizing revenge porn. *Wake Forest Law Review, 49*, 345-391.

Crosslin, K. L., & Golman, M. (2014). "Maybe you don't want to face it"—College students' perspectives on cyberbullying. *Computers in Human Behavior, 41*, 14-20.

Dake, J. A., Price, J. H., & Maziarz, L. (2012). Prevalence and correlates of sexting behavior in adolescents. *American Journal of Sexuality Education, 7*, 1-15.

David-Ferdon, C., & Hertz, M. F. (2007). Electronic media, violence, and adolescents: An emerging public health problem. *Journal of Adolescent Health, 41*(6), 51-55.

Dehue, F., Bollman, C., & Vollink, T. (2008). Cyberbullying: Youngsters' experiences and parental perception. *CyberPsychology & Behavior, 11*, 217-223.

Dilberto, G., & Mattey, E. (2009). Sexting: Just how much of a danger is it and what can school nurses do about it? *NASN School Nurse, 24*, 262-267.

D'Ovidio, R., & Doyle, J. (2003). A study on cyberstalking: Understanding investigative hurdles. *FBI Law Enforcement Bulletin, 73*, 10-17.

Eining, M. M., & Christensen, A. L. (1991). *A psycho-social model of software piracy: The development and test of a model. Ethical issues in information systems.* Boston, MA: Boyd & Fraser.

Evans, D. T., Cullen, F. T., Burton, V. S., Dunaway, R. G., & Benson, M. L. (1997). The social consequences of self-control: Testing the general theory of crime. *Criminology, 35*, 475-504.

Fergusson, D.M., Boden, J.M., & Horwood, J.L. (2008). Exposure to childhood sexual and physical abuse and adjustment in early adulthood. *Child Abuse & Neglect, 32*, 607-619.

Finkelhor, D., Mitchell, K. J., & Wolak, J. (2000). *Online victimization: A report on the nation's youth.* Washington, DC: U.S. Department of Justice.

Finn, J. (2004). A survey of online harassment at a university campus. *Journal of Interpersonal Violence, 19*, 468-483.

Fisher, B. S., Cullen, F. T., & Turner, M. G. (2002). Being pursued: Stalking victimization in a national study of college women. *Criminology & Public Policy, 1*, 257-308.

Flood, M. (2009a). The harms of pornography exposure among children and young people. *Child Abuse Review, 18*, 384-400.

Flood, M. (2009b). Youth, sex, and the Internet. *Counselling, Psychotherapy, and Health, 5*(1), 131-147. The Use of Technology in Mental Health Special Issue.

Fream, A., & Skinner, W. (1997). Social learning theory analysis of computer crime among college students. *Journal of Research in Crime and Delinquency, 34*, 495-518.

Gottfredson, M., & Hirschi, T. (1990). *A general theory of crime.* Stanford, CA: Stanford University Press.

Greenfield, P. M. (2004). Inadvertent exposure to pornography on the Internet: Implications of peer-to-peer file-sharing networks for child development and families. *Applied Developmental Psychology, 25*, 741-750.

Hansen, J. V., Lowry, P. B., Meservy, R. D., & McDonald, D. M. (2007). Genetic programming for prevention of cyberterrorism through dynamic and evolving intrusion detection. *Decision Support Systems, 43*, 1362-1374.

Higgins, G. E., Fell, B. D., & Wilson, A. L. (2006). Digital piracy: Assessing the contributions of an integrated self-control theory and social learning theory using structural equation modeling. *Criminal Justice Studies, 19*, 3-22.

Higgins, G. E., & Makin, D. A. (2004). Self-control, deviant peers, and software piracy. *Psychological Reports, 95*(3), 921-933.

Hinduja, S. (2016, June 28). Sextortion. Cyberbullying Research Center. Retrieved from https://cyberbullying.org/sextortion

Hinduja, S., & Patchin, J. W. (2007). Offline consequences of online victimization: School violence and delinquency. *Journal of School Violence, 6*(3), 89-112.

Hinduja, S., & Patchin, J. W. (2009). *Bullying beyond the schoolyard: Preventing and responding to cyberbullying.* Thousand Oaks, CA: Sage.

Hinduja, S., & Patchin, J. W. (2010). Bullying, cyberbullying, and suicide. *Archives of Suicide Research, 14,* 206–221.

Hinduja, S., & Patchin, J. W. (2015). *Bullying beyond the schoolyard: Preventing and responding to cyberbullying* (2nd ed.). Thousand Oaks, CA: Sage.

Hinduja, S., & Patchin, J. W. (2018). Teen sexting: a brief guide for educators and parents [online]. Cyberbullying Research Center. Retrieved from http://www.cyberbullying.us

Holt, T. J. (2007). Subcultural evolution? Examining the influence of on- and off-line experiences on deviant subcultures. *Deviant Behavior, 28,* 171–198.

Holt, T. J., & Bossler, A. M. (2009). Examining the applicability of lifestyle–routine activities theory for cybercrime victimization. *Deviant Behavior, 30,* 1–25.

Holt, T. J., Bossler, A. M., & May, D. C. (2010). Low self-control, deviant peer associations, and juvenile cyberdeviance. *American Journal of Criminal Justice, 37*(3), 1–18.

Jerin, R., & Dolinsky, B. (2001). You've got mail! You don't want it: Cyber-victimization and on-line dating. *Journal of Criminal Justice and Popular Culture, 9,* 15–21.

Jewkes, Y., & Yar, M. (2013). Introduction: The Internet, cybercrime and the challenges of the twenty-first century. In Y. Jewkes & M. Yar (Eds.), *Handbook of Internet crime* (pp. 1–8). Devon, UK: Willan Publishing.

Jonas, S., Bebbington, P., McManus, S., Meltzer, H., Jenkins, R., Kuipers, E., . . . Brugha, T. (2011). Sexual abuse and psychiatric disorder in England: Results from the 2007 Adult Psychiatric Morbidity Study. *Psychological Medicine, 41,* 709–719.

Judge, A. M. (2012). Sexting among U. S. adolescents: Psychological and legal perspectives. *Harvard Review of Psychiatry, 20,* 86–96.

Juvonen, J., & Gross, E. F. (2008). Extending the school grounds? Bullying experiences in cyberspace. *Journal of School Health, 78,* 496–505.

Kendler, K. S., Bulik, C. M., Silberg, J., Hettema, J. M., Myers, J., & Prescott, C. A. (2000). Childhood sexual abuse and adult psychiatric and substance use disorders in women: An epidemiological and cotwin control analysis. *Archives of General Psychiatry, 57,* 953–959.

Kini, R. B., Ramakrishna, H. V., & Vijayaraman, B. S. (2004). Shaping of moral intensity regarding software piracy: A comparison between Thailand and U.S. students. *Journal of Business Ethics, 49,* 91–104.

Kini, R. B., Rominger, A., & Vijayaraman, B. S. (2000). An empirical study of software piracy and moral intensity among university students. *Journal of Computer Information Systems, 40,* 62–72.

Klettke, B., Hallford, D. J., & Mellor, D. J. (2014). Sexting prevalence and correlates: A systematic literature review. *Clinical Psychology Review, 34,* 44–53.

Kopecký, K. (2017). Online blackmail of Czech children focused on so-called "sextortion" (analysis of culprit and victim behaviors). *Telematics and Informatics, 34,* 11–19.

Korchmaros, J. D., Ybarra, M. L., Langhinrichsen-Rohling, J., Boyd, D., & Lenhart, A. (2013). Perpetration of teen dating violence in a networked society. *Cyberpsychology, Behavior, and Social Networking, 16,* 561–567.

Kowalski, R. M., & Limber, S. P. (2007). Electronic bullying among middle school students. *Journal of Adolescent Health, 41,* 22–30.

Kraft, E., & Wang, J. (2010). An exploratory study of the cyberbullying and cyberstalking experiences and factors related to victimization of students at a public liberal arts college. *International Journal of Technologies, 1*(4), 74–91.

Krone, T. (2004). A typology of online child pornography offending. Australian Institute of Criminology. Canberra, Australia: Australian Institute of Criminology. Retrieved from https://aic.gov.au/publications/tandi/tandi279

Lamphere, R. D., & Pikciunas, K. T. (2015). Sexting, sextortion and other Internet sexual offenses. In J. N. Navarro, S. Clevenger, & C. D. Marcum (Eds.). *The virtual enemy: The intersection between intimate partner abuse, technology, and cybercrime.* Durham, NC: Carolina Academic Press.

Leary, M. G. (2007). Self-produced child pornography: The appropriate societal response to juvenile self-sexual exploitation. *Virginia Journal of Social Policy & the Law, 15*(1), 1–50.

Lenhart, A. (2007). Cyberbullying. Pew Research Center. Retrieved from http://www.pewinternet .org/Reports/2007/Cyberbullying.aspx

Lenhart, A. (2009). Teens and sexting. Pew Research Center. Retrieved from https://www .pewinternet.org/2009/12/15/teens-and-sexting/

Lenhart, A., Ybarra, M., & Price-Feeny, M. (2016). Nonconsensual image sharing: One in 25 Americans has been the victim of revenge porn. Retrieved from https://datasociety.net /pubs/oh/Nonconsensual_Image_Sharing_2016.pdf

Li, Q. (2007). Bullying in the new playground: Research into cyberbullying and cyber victimization. *Australasian Journal of Educational Technology, 23*(4), 435–454.

Liang, Z., & Yan, Z. (2005). Software piracy among college students: A comprehensive review of contributing factors, underlying processes, and tackling strategies. *Journal of Educational Computing Research, 33*, 115–140.

Ling, R., & Yttri, B. (2005). Control, emancipation, and status: The mobile telephone in teen's parental and peer group control relationships. In R. Kraut, M. Brynin, & S. Kiesler (Eds.), *New information technologies at home: The domestic impact of computing and telecommunications* (pp. 219–235). Oxford, UK: Oxford University Press.

Lynch, L. E. (2016). The national strategy for child exploitation prevention and interdiction: A report to congress. Retrieved from https://www.justice.gov/psc/file/842411/download

Malin, J., & Fowers, B. J. (2009). Adolescent self-control and music and movie piracy. *Computers in Human Behavior, 25*, 718–722.

Marcum, C. D., Higgins, G. E., & Ricketts, M. L. (2010). Potential factors of online victimization of youth: An examination of adolescent online behaviors utilizing routine activity theory. *Deviant Behavior, 31*, 381–410.

Marcum, C. D., Higgins, G. E., Ricketts, M. L., & Wolfe, S. E. (2014). Hacking in high school: Cybercrime perpetration by juveniles. *Deviant Behavior, 35*, 581–591.

Martellozzo, E., Nehring, D., & Taylor, H. (2010). Online child sexual abuse by female offenders: An Exploratory study. *International Journal of Cyber Criminology, 4*(1–2), 592–609.

Mitchell, K. J., Finkelhor, D., Jones, L. M., & Wolak, J. (2012). Prevalence and characteristics of youth sexting: A national study. *Pediatrics, 129*, 13–20.

Muncie, J. (1999). *Youth and crime: A critical introduction.* London: Sage.

Näsi, M., Oksanen. A., Keipia, T., & Räsänen, P. (2015). Cybercrime victimization among young people: A multi-nation study. *Journal of Scandinavian Studies in Criminology and Crime Prevention, 16*(2), 203–210.

Navarro, J. N., Marcum, C. D., Higgins, G. E., & Ricketts, M. L. (2016). Addicted to the thrill of the virtual hunt: Examining the effects of Internet addiction on the cyberstalking behavior of juveniles. *Deviant Behavior, 37*(8), 893–903.

Norton. (2012). Norton cybercrime report: The human impact. Retrieved from https://www .symantec.com/content/en/us/home_homeoffice/media/pdf/cybercrime_report/Norton _USA-Human%20Impact-A4_Aug4-2.pdf

O'Connell, R. (2003). *A typology of child cybersexploitation and online grooming practices.* Preston, UK: University of Central Lancashire.

O'Connor, K., Drouin, M., Davis, D., & Thompson, H. (2018). Cyberbullying, revenge porn, and the midsized university: Victim characteristics, prevalence and students' knowledge of university policy and reporting procedures. *Higher Education Quarterly, 72*, 344–359.

Ostrager, B. (2010). SMS. OMG! TTYL: Translating the law to accommodate today's teens and the evolution from texting to sexting. *Family Court Review, 48*(4), 712–726.

Paolucci, E. O., Genius, M. I., & Violato, C. (2001). A meta-analysis of the published research on the effects of child sexual abuse. *Journal of Psychology, 135*, 17–36.

Parsons-Pollard, N., & Moriarty, L. J. (2009). Cyberstalking: Utilizing what we do know. *Victims and Offenders, 4*, 435–441.

Patchin, J. W., & Hinduja, S. (2006). Bullies move beyond the schoolyard: A preliminary look at cyberbullying. *Youth Violence and Justice, 4*(2), 148–169.

Patchin, J. W., & Hinduja, S. (2012). *Preventing and responding to cyberbullying: Expert perspectives.* Thousand Oaks, CA: Routledge.

Patchin, J. W., & Hinduja, S. (2016). *Bullying today: Bullet points and best practices.* Thousand Oaks, CA: Sage.

Patchin, J. W., & Hinduja, S. (2018). Sextortion among adolescents: Results from a national survey of U.S. youth. *Sexual Abuse*, 1–25.

Paullet, K., & Pinchot, J. (2014). Behind the screen where today's bully plays: Perceptions of college students on cyberbullying. *Journal of Information Systems Education, 25*(1), 63–69.

Peskin, M. F., Markham, C. M., Addy, R. C., Shegog, R., Thiel, M., & Tortolero, S. R. (2013). Prevalence and patterns of sexting among ethnic minority urban high school students. *Cyberpsychology, Behavior and Social Networking, 16*, 454–459.

Pittaro, M. (2007). Cyber stalking: An analysis of online harassment and intimidation. *International Journal of Cyber Criminology, 1*(2), 180–197.

Pollack, J. (2017). Getting even: empowering victims of revenge porn with a civil cause of action. *Albany Law Review, 80*, 353–380.

Prichard, J., Spiranovic, C., Watters, P., & Lueg, C. (2012). Young people, child pornography, and subcultural norms on the Internet. *Journal of the American Society for Information Science and Technology, 64*(5), 992–1000.

Quayle, E. (2017). Over the Internet, under the radar: Online child sexual abuse and exploitation [Brief]. Retrieved from http://www.barnardos.org.uk/over_the_internet__under_the_radar_literature_review.pdf

Quayle, E., & Cooper, K. (2015). The role of child sexual abuse images in coercive and non-coercive relationships with adolescents: A thematic review of the literature. *Child & Youth Services, 36*(4), 312–328.

Rahim, M. M., Seyal, A. H., & Rahman, M. N. A. (2001). Factors affecting softlifting intention of computing students: An empirical study. *Journal of Educational Computing Research, 24*, 385–405.

Revenge porn. (2017). In Oxford English Dictionary. Retrieved from https://en.oxforddictionaries.com/definition/us/revenge_porn

Reyns, B. W., Burek, M. W., Henson, B., & Fisher, B. S. (2011). The unintended consequences of digital technology: Exploring the relationship between sexting and cybervictimization. *Journal of Crime and Justice, 36*(1), 1–17.

Reyns, B. W., Henson, B., & Fisher, B. S. (2011). Being pursued online: Applying cyberlifestyle-routine activities theory to cyberstalking victimization. *Criminal Justice and Behavior, 38*(11), 1149–1169.

Richet, J., (2013). From young hackers to crackers. *International Journal of Technology and Human Interaction, 9*(3), 53–62.

Ricketts, M. L., Maloney, C., Marcum, C. D., & Higgins, G. E. (2014). The effect of Internet related problems on the sexting behavior of juveniles. *American Journal of Criminal Justice, 40*, 270–284.

Rogers, M., Smoak, N., & Liu, J. (2005). Self-reported deviant computer behavior: A big-5 moral choice, and manipulative exploitive behavior analysis. *Deviant Behavior, 27*, 245–268.

Sheridan, L. P., & Grant, T. (2007). Is cyberstalking different? Psychology, *Crime & Law, 13*, 627–640.

Smith, P. K., Mahdavi, J., Carvalho, M., Fisher, S., Russell, S., & Tippett, N. (2008). Cyberbullying: Its nature and impact in secondary school pupils. *Journal of Child Psychology and Psychiatry, 49*(4), 376–385.

Spitzberg, B. H., & Hoobler, G. (2002). Cyberstalking and the technologies of interpersonal terrorism. *New Media & Society, 4*, 71–92.

Strassberg, D. S., McKinnon, R. K., Sustaita, M. A., & Rullo, J. (2013). Sexting by high school students: An exploratory and descriptive study. *Archives of Sexual Behavior, 42*, 15–21.

Taylor, M., & Quayle, E. (2003). *Child pornography: An Internet crime*. New York, NY: Routledge.

Taylor, P. (1999). *Hackers: Crime in the digital sublime*. London, UK: Routledge.

Taylor, P. (2000). Hackers—Cyberpunks or microserfs? In D. Thomas & B. Loader (Eds.), *Cybercrime: Law enforcement, security and surveillance in the Information Age*, London, UK: Routledge.

Taylor, R. W., Fritsch, E. J., & Liederbach, J. (2015). *Digital crime and digital terrorism* (3rd ed.). Boston, MA: Pearson.

Taylor, R. W., Fritsch, E. J., Liederbach, J., & Holt, T. J. (2010). *Digital crime and digital terrorism* (2nd ed.). Upper Saddle River, NJ: Pearson.

Thomas, D. (2000). Criminality on the electronic frontier: Corporality and the judicial construction of the hacker. In D. Thomas & B. Loader (Eds.), *Cybercrime: Law enforcement, security and surveillance in the Information Age*, London. UK: Routledge.

Vandebosch, H., & Van Cleemput, K. (2008). Defining cyberbullying: A qualitative research into perceptions of youngsters. *CyberPsychology & Behavior, 11*, 499–503.

Vandebosch, H., & Van Cleemput, K. (2009). Cyberbullying among youngsters: Profiles of bullies and victims. *New Media & Society, 11*(8), 1349–1371.

Van Ouytsel, J., Ponnet, K., & Walrave, M. (2018). Cyber dating abuse victimization among secondary school students from a lifestyle-routine activities theory perspective. *Journal of Interpersonal Violence, 33*, 2767–2776.

Wastler, S. (2010). The harm in "sexting"? Analyzing the constitutionality of child pornography statutes that prohibit the voluntary production, possession, and dissemination of sexually explicit images by teenagers. *Harvard Journal of Law and Gender, 33*, 687–702.

Weaver, M. (2017, April 21). Teenage hackers motivated by morality not money, study finds. *The Guardian* [London]. Retrieved from https://www.theguardian.com/society/2017/apr/21/teenage-hackers-motivated-moral-crusade-money-cybercrime

Wittes, B., Poplin, C., Jurecic, Q., & Spera, C. (2016, May 11). Sextortion: Cybersecurity, teenagers, and remote sexual assault. Brookings Report. Washington, DC: Brookings Institution. Retrieved from https://www.brookings.edu/research/sextortion-cybersecurity-teenagers-and-remote-sexual-assault/

Wolak, J., Mitchell, K. J., & Finkelhor, D. (2006). Online victimization of youth: Five years later. *National Center for Missing and Exploited Children Bulletin.* Retrieved from http://unh.edu/ccrc/pdf/CV138.pdf

Wolak, J., Mitchell, K. J., & Finkelhor, D. (2007). Does online harassment constitute bullying? An exploration of online harassment by known peers and online-only contacts. *Journal of Adolescent Health, 41*(6), 51–58.

Wolak, J. D., Finkelhor, D., Walsh, W., & Treitman, L. (2018). Sextortion of minors: Characteristics and dynamics. *Journal of Adolescent Health, 62*, 72–79.

Yar, M. (2005). Computer hacking: Just another case of juvenile delinquency? *The Howard Journal, 44*(4), 387–399.

Ybarra, M. L., & Mitchell, J. K. (2004). Online aggressor/targets, aggressors and targets: A comparison of associated youth characteristics. *Journal of Child Psychology and Psychiatry, 45*, 1308–1316.

Young, K. (1998). Internet addiction: The emergence of a new clinical disorder. *CyberPsychology & Behavior, 1*(3), 237–244.

Young, K., Yue, X. D., & Ying, L. (2011). Prevalence estimates and etiologic models of Internet addiction. In K. Young & C. N. de Abreu (Eds.), *Internet addiction: A handbook and guide to evaluation and treatment.* Hoboken, NJ: John Wiley & Sons.

Zentner, A. (2006). Measuring the effect of online music piracy on music purchases . The *Journal of Law & Economics, 49*(1), 63–90.

Zweig, J. M., Dank, M., Yahner, J., & Lachman, P. (2013). The rate of cyber dating abuse among teens and how it relates to other forms of teen dating violence. *Journal of Youth and Adolescence, 42*, 1063–1077.

Zweig, J. M., Lachman, P., Yahner, J., & Dank, M. (2014). Correlates of cyber dating abuse among teens. *Journal of Youth and Adolescence, 43*, 1306–1321.

Ethics of Juvenile Waivers

Danielle Marie Carkin
Rimonda R. Maroun

A s society progressed, it became quite evident that youth differ greatly from adults in development, maturity, and potential for change. In acknowledging this, it became evident that treatment of juvenile offenders needed to change. Thus, the juvenile justice system was developed with the intent to offer a more informal process with more focus on rehabilitation.

However, as youth crime seemed to increase and fear of so-called superpredators intensified, this rationale diminished (DiIulio, 1995). As a result, changes in policy and attitude were made that increased the transfer of youth offenders to the adult criminal justice system (Jordan, 2006; Myers, 2005). The mechanisms that make this possible are known as *juvenile waivers*. The following sections will discuss the various waivers used in the juvenile justice system, their historical basis, and the ethical concerns regarding their use.

▶ Juvenile Waivers

Juvenile waivers (sometimes referred to as *transfers, remands, bind over,* or *certifications*) allow for youthful offenders to be transferred to criminal court despite their age (Bernard & Kurlycheck, 2010). For example, if a 15-year-old commits a crime, the youth could still face adult charges if he or she is waived to adult court. This would occur as a result of one of the three waiver types: judicial waiver, direct file, and statutory exclusion. Judicial waivers occur when the judge sends the case from juvenile court to adult court, whereas direct files are done by the prosecutor; both types are based on the individual case at hand. The third method stems from the legislation that exists in which a juvenile is automatically sent to criminal court based on the offense committed, which falls under the statutory exclusions category.

The increase in violent youth crime from the mid-1980s into the 1990s increased fear and panic among communities, leading states to expand the eligibility criteria for transfer to the adult criminal justice system (Freiburger & Jordan, 2016). Traditionally, judicial waivers were the most common mechanisms for transferring youth to adult court. Judicial waivers exist in various forms but are primarily of three distinctions: discretionary, presumptive, and mandatory (Means, Heller, & Janofsky, 2012). With discretionary waiver, enacted in 46 states, judges consider various factors, including public safety, academic involvement, family involvement, and victim injury in determining whether or not to waive a youth to adult court. Traditional discretion was taken away from judges in the juvenile justice system as states expanded their eligibility criteria and more youth were transferred, strictly focusing on age, offense, and offense severity.

The second type of judicial waiver, available in 15 states, is presumptive waiver, which permits juvenile transfer unless the juvenile offender can show cause that he or she is more amenable to the rehabilitative nature of the juvenile justice system (Griffin, Torbet, & Szymanski, 1998). Presumptive waiver shifts the burden of proof, which is typically on the state, to the juvenile to present mitigating evidence that establishes that he or she should not be transferred to adult court. If the youth is unable to rebut the presumption that transfer is warranted, then the juvenile court must waive jurisdiction.

The third type of judicial waiver, established in 14 states, is mandatory waiver (Griffin et al., 1998). This method mandates that a judge determine whether the case at hand meets the predetermined criteria determined by the legislature. The criteria vary by state. With mandatory waiver, the judge does not retain any discretionary authority. Once the criteria are confirmed, the youth is subsequently waived.

As judicial discretion and waiver waned, direct file (also known as *prosecutorial waiver*) and statutory exclusion (also known as *legislative waiver*) became more popular. As previously stated, through direct file, which is available in 15 states, it is the prosecutor who determines whether a case should remain in the juvenile justice system or be waived to the adult system (Griffin et al., 1998). The criteria for direct file vary among states, each emphasizing different legal factors such as age, offense severity, and prior record.

Through statutory exclusion or legislative waiver, available in 28 states, youth do not interact with the juvenile justice system at all but rather are processed entirely in the adult criminal justice system (Freiburger & Jordan, 2016). Several states exclude specific offenses, sometimes in conjunction with age and other legal factors, from processing in the juvenile justice system. In such cases, youth will be automatically processed through the adult criminal justice system without the involvement of judges or prosecutors. In this way, statutory exclusion is distinct from mandatory waiver—which originates in the juvenile justice system and is reviewed by the judge to evaluate the criteria (Griffin et al., 1998).

Thirty-one state legislatures have also passed "once waived, always waived" statutes. Under this legislation, once a juvenile is waived to adult court, he or she must be processed in the adult criminal justice system, despite age or offense (Griffin et al., 1998). In most jurisdictions, this requires a conviction.

Reverse waiver is also available in approximately half of the United States (Jordan & Myers, 2007). Reverse waiver permits juveniles who have been waived or transferred to adult court to be reverse waived back to the juvenile justice system. If a youth who has been transferred petitions the court to be decertified, or reverse waived, the judge will consider the same factors as juvenile court judges do when considering transfer, including age, offense severity, and prior record (Jordan & Myers, 2007). If decertified, the youth is subsequently processed in the juvenile justice system.

▶ Historical Basis for Juvenile Waivers

At its inception in 1899, based on the principle of *parens patriae,* the ultimate goal was to advocate for the best interests of youth. Rehabilitation and treatment of delinquents through a more informal system focused on the individual were the original intent (Besharov, 1974). Though the concept of transfer has existed since the development of the juvenile justice system (Bernard & Kurlychek, 2010), its practice significantly increased with the spike in violent youth crime beginning in the mid-1980s (Freiburger & Jordan, 2016; Myers, 2005). This created moral panic and fear among communities, prompting a shift in the legislature and juvenile justice system (DiIulio, 1995; Houston & Barton, 2005). According to Feld (1987), the historical and traditional intent of juvenile transfer was individualized, considering in each case the youth's amenability to treatment in the juvenile justice system. In the case of *Kent v. United States* (1966), the U.S. Supreme Court formalized the process of juvenile waiver to criminal court.

Morris Kent first made contact with the juvenile justice system at age 14. At 16, he was arrested, interrogated, and charged with housebreaking, robbery, and rape when his fingerprints were found in the victim's apartment. Despite the need for a hearing, Kent was waived to adult court, where he was tried and convicted. The waiver, which was invalid because of the lack of a hearing, was challenged multiple times. Each time he was denied, until the case was brought to the Supreme Court through the use of a writ of certiorari. As a result, *Kent vs. United States* (1966) set the standard for due process for juvenile waivers, ensuring that juveniles are afforded the right to a formal hearing before their case is sent to criminal court. Associate Justice Abe Fortas did not believe the juvenile court was operating in the best interest of the child, stating "that there may be grounds for concern that the child receives the worst of both worlds [in juvenile courts]: that he gets neither the protections accorded to adults nor the solicitous care and regenerative treatment postulated for children" (383 U.S., p. 541). Writing for the majority, Fortas expressed that youth are entitled not only to a hearing but also to a statement of the reasons for the decision to transfer, access to counsel, and counsel's right to access pertinent documents.

Four years later, many states began changing or considering reducing the age of majority, making it possible to try prosecute more youth offenders as adults. In *Breed v. Jones* (1975), the Supreme Court ruled that a juvenile could be processed in either juvenile or adult court but that trying the youth for the same offense in both courts constitutes double jeopardy (Ferro, 2003). The treatment of juveniles as adults continued to increase. In 1994, the number of youth transferred to adult criminal court totaled 11,700 (Ferro, 2003). Even though the juvenile justice system itself is also becoming more punitive, transfer of youth to adult court remains a common occurrence.

▶ Use of Waivers

The United States leads the world in incarceration rates in general, and this also holds true for the rate of which we incarcerate youth. In the United States, the use of waivers led to approximately 250,000 youth a year being prosecuted as adults by the beginning of the 21st century (Ziedenberg, 2011). Approximately 4,200 youth are now incarcerated in adult facilities (Sickmund & Puzzanchera, 2014), even though these facilities are not equipped by any means to hold juveniles.

Over the years, the use of judicial waivers has increased and decreased, not only in general but also for specific types of offenses (property, drug, public order, and person):

- The largest number of youths were incarcerated in state prisons at a rate that doubled between 1985 and 1997 (Strom, 2000). These rates have gone down between 1997 and 2016 (Carson, 2016).
- Property offenses were judicially waived at their highest rate in 1994, declined to their lowest level in 2004, and then saw a slight increase in 2013 (Hockenberry & Puzzanchera, 2015).
- Drug offense cases saw their first increase between 1985 and 1991, when they hit their highest point, before decreasing to their lowest point in 2013. It is no surprise that drug offenses were the most judicially waived offense between 1989 and 1992 (Hockenberry & Puzzanchera, 2015).
- Public order offenses and person offenses saw decreases in judicial waivers between 1985 and 2013. In 2013, however, person offenses made up 50% of the waived caseload, and property offenses declined (Hockenberry & Puzzanchera, 2015).

▶ Ethical Concerns

Many ethical issues are pertinent to the process of waiving a juvenile to criminal court. First and foremost is the fact that juveniles are juveniles, not adults, and thus should be treated accordingly. Youth tried as adults are then relieved of the protections their age ought to provide them. Youth under age 18 are in the midst of developing, which could be negatively impacted by processing through adult court. The purpose of the juvenile justice system is to provide youth with a more informal approach to justice. Along with the typical social, physical, and intellectual development youth undergo, many suffer from mental health and substance-use issues.

When juvenile offenders were acknowledged to be different from adult offenders, it was understood that there should be a separate juvenile court. With the inception of the House of Refuge and later the formal creation of the juvenile court, a system was created to treat and shape youth offenders in a way that promoted positive development and encouraged law-abiding behavior (Bernard & Kurlychek, 2010). Over time, the court has evolved in numerous ways, including applying due process procedures and shifting focus from the intent of the system to its actual performance, mirroring various aspects of the adult court. The intention of working in the best interests of the child and the goal of treatment also shifted to punishment with the so called get-tough movement, further paralleling the juvenile courts with the adult courts. With harsher sentencing outcomes, the development of blended sentencing, and options to transfer youths to the adult court, the boundary between the juvenile and adult criminal court has been obscured, prompting the need to reevaluate the transfer of juveniles to adult court.

Various court decisions have impacted juvenile sanctioning in a way that suggests we should reconsider juvenile waiver to adult court. *Miller v. Alabama* (2012) concluded that mandatory sentencing of life without parole violated the Eighth

Amendment. It was also decided that judges must consider each offender's individual circumstances when determining sanctions. Juveniles are inherently different from adults, and although life in prison without parole is not cruel and unusual for adults, it is disproportionate for juveniles. *Montgomery v. Louisiana* (2016) made *Miller* retroactive, further solidifying that the courts consider juveniles to be different from adults and not just smaller criminals. The decision in *Graham v. Florida* (2010) prohibited the use of life without parole for any offender not convicted of a homicide; this is the only crime for which this punishment is appropriate. In *Roper v. Simmons* (2005), the Court ruled that capital punishment for offenders younger than 18 at the time of their offense is a violation of the Eighth and 14th Amendments. The Court reasoned that the death penalty should be reserved for only the most serious crimes and offenders whose culpability warrants this severe punishment; juvenile offenders do not fit under this category (Bernard & Kurlychek, 2010). Referencing various scientific research, Associate Justice Anthony Kennedy reasoned that youth have diminished maturity and sense of responsibility and therefore lack proper impulse control, are significantly influenced by negative influences and peers, and do not have a fully developed personality or character in comparison to adults (Bernard & Kurlychek, 2010). These three fundamental differences explain that youths have diminished culpability and therefore cannot be sanctioned in the same manner and with the same severity as adults.

Considering the rationale for the aforementioned cases, there needs to be a reevaluation of whether juveniles should be transferred to adult court. The rulings are based on the reasoning that juveniles are fundamentally and developmentally different from adults. Adults are more responsible and culpable for their offenses than juvenile offenders; therefore harsher and more severe punishments are warranted. If juveniles have less culpability and should not receive the same harsh sentences as adult offenders, then they should not be transferred to adult court. The punishments that are proportionate for their culpability and offending can be given in juvenile court. However, some people argue that transfer of offenders is necessary because adult courts can better handle these cases (Jordan, 2012). Transfer is typically reserved for the most serious youth offenders, who are essentially different from other juvenile offenders, and findings in this study indicate that youth processed in juvenile court have greater rates of recidivism than those processed in adult court, a finding that is contrary to previously conducted research (Jordan, 2012). However, this finding may be explained by stricter supervision of transferred youths or because youths processed in juvenile court are released sooner than those processed and convicted in adult court—therefore having more time to recidivate.

Despite the results in Jordan (2012), if we consider the precedent set in *Miller v. Alabama*, *Montgomery v. Louisiana*, and *Roper v. Simmons*, then transfer laws must be reconsidered. The rationale for the decisions in these cases concerns why juveniles are prohibited from receiving life sentences without parole and capital punishment. Such reasons can also apply to transfer, and the boundary between the adult and juvenile court is no longer distinct.

It is not surprising that juveniles waived to criminal court are less likely to receive a sentence with emphasis on rehabilitation but rather are given harsher punishment (Jordan, 2014; Zimring, 2005). The juvenile justice system places a heavy emphasis on rehabilitation and restoration. Juvenile facilities encourage positive relationships between staff and youths, skill building and education, and opportunities for treatment and counseling; these are opportunities that youths are not afforded when incarcerated in adult facilities.

Further, juveniles who are treated as adults tend to receive more severe sentences than those who are tried as juveniles for similar offenses (Jordan & Myers, 2011; Lemmon, Austin, Verrecchia, & Fetzer, 2005). In a way, it seems that transferring youths to the adult system pushes the get-tough approach on crime and even further emphasizes the need to punish these particular juveniles more harshly because of their adult status.

Furthermore, juveniles also face higher rates of victimization, both sexually and physically, when incarcerated in adult facilities (Mistrett & Thomas, 2017). Fagan, Forst, and Vivona (1989) conducted a study in which they found juveniles are five times more likely to be sexually assaulted and twice as likely to be harmed by staff.

Developmentally, juveniles are significantly different from adults, so what justifies punishing them as such? Despite being offenders, they are youths going through the same hormonal and physical changes as nonoffending youth. Steinberg (1999) notes that five psychosocial developments are especially important to healthy development including self-identity, autonomy, intimacy, sexuality, and achievement. For youths spending time in an adult facility, these five developmental periods are negatively impacted.

When incarcerating youth as adults, we are setting them up to be harmed developmentally, physically, and mentally. Transferring juveniles to criminal court is far more dangerous than anticipated, making it not only unethical in many respects but also damaging. It is also important to consider the deterrent effect, or lack thereof, of juvenile transfer (Redding, 2008).

Juveniles transferred to adult courts are more likely not only to recidivate (Fagan, 1995), but also to commit a violent offense (Lanza-Kaduce, Lane, Bishop, and Frazier, 2005). More specifically, Lanza-Kaduce et al. (2005) found that 49% of transferred youth reoffended compared to 35% who did not. When broken down by offense, 24% of waived violent offenders reoffended, a significant figure when compared to 16% of nontransferred violent offenders; 11% of waived drug offenders reoffended compared to 9% of those not transferred; and 14% of waived property offenders reoffended compared to 10% of those not transferred. Similar results are consistently found by various researchers in the field as noted by Mistrett and Thomas (2017). Although the numbers are not drastically different, rather than deterring the youth from committing more criminal activities, there appears to be more of a criminogenic effect. Thus, transfers do more harm than good, yet they continue to occur (Fagan, 1995).

Not to be ignored is the racially disparate use of waivers. In fact, the level of disproportionate minority contact at the juvenile level is concerning given that minority youth are so vulnerable to juvenile transfer (Zeidenberg, 2001). Studies have consistently noted that minority youth are waived to criminal court at higher rates than Whites (Fagan, Forst, & Vivona, 1987; Males & Maccallair, 2000; Schiraldi & Ziedenberg, 1999; Snyder, Sickmund, & Poe-Yamagata, 2000; Zeidenberg, 2001 et al.). More specifically, older males who are African American or Hispanic have higher rates of transfer than females, non-Hispanics, and younger juveniles (Washburn et al., 2015). If waivers were to be used in an ethical, consistent manner, perhaps this would not be such a problem, and juveniles would not be at higher risk for the consequences of being treated as adult offenders.

▶ Conclusion

From the racial disparities to the lack of opportunities and treatment for youth and every concern between them, there are many ethical concerns about the use of waivers. It is imperative that we refer to the initial development of the juvenile justice system with its focus on rehabilitation and transition away from the use of waivers. We owe it to the youth to give them the opportunity to develop without further harm against them. The least we could do is develop more research to determine at what age these harms dissipate and when adult facilities are the necessary consequence for criminal behavior.

▶ References

Bernard, T. J., & Kurlychek, M. C. (2010). *The cycle of juvenile justice* (2nd ed.). New York, NY: Oxford University Press.

Besharov, D. J. (1974). *Juvenile justice advocacy: Practice in a unique court.* New York, NY: Practicing Law Institute. *Breed v. Jones*, 421 US 519, 95 S. Ct. 1779, 44 L. Ed. 2d 346 (1975).

Carson, E.A. (2018, January). Prisoners in 2016. NCJ 251149. Washington, DC: U.S. Department of Justice, Bureau of Justice Statistics.

DiIulio, J. J. (1995). The coming of the super-predators. *Weekly Standard, I,* 23–28.

Fagan, J. (1995). Separating the men from the boys: The comparative advantage of juvenile versus criminal court sanctions on recidivism among adolescent felony offenders. In J. C. Howell, B. Krisberg, J. D. Hawkins, & J. J. Wilson (Eds.), *A sourcebook: Serious, violent, and chronic juvenile offenders* (pp. 238–260). Thousand Oaks, CA: Sage.

Fagan, J., Forst, M., & Vivona, T. (1987). Racial determinants of the judicial transfer decision: Prosecuting violent youth in criminal court. *Crime & Delinquency, 33*(2), 259–286.

Fagan, J., Forst, M., & Vivona, T. S. (1989). Youth in prisons and training schools: Perceptions and the consequences of the treatment custody dichotomy. *Juvenile and Family Court, 2,* 10.

Feld, B. C. (1987). The juvenile court meets the principle of the offense: Legislative changes in juvenile waiver statutes. *Journal of Criminal Law and Criminology, 78,* 471–533.

Ferro, J. (2003). *Library in a book: Juvenile crime.* New York, NY: Facts on File.

Freiburger, T. L., & Jordan, K. L. (2016). *Race and ethnicity in the juvenile justice system.* Durham, NC: Carolina Academic Press.

Griffin, P., Torbet, P., & Szymanski, L. 1998. *Trying juveniles as adults in criminal court: An analysis of state transfer provisions.* Washington, DC: U.S. Department of Justice, Office of Justice Programs, Office of Juvenile Justice and Delinquency Prevention.

Hockenberry, S., & Puzzanchera, C. (2015). *Juvenile court statistics 2013.* Pittsburgh, PA: National Center for Juvenile Justice.

Houston, J., & Barton, S. M. (2005). *Juvenile justice: Theory, systems, and organization.* Upper Saddle River, NJ: Pearson Education.

Jordan, K. L. (2006). *Violent youth in adult court; The decertification of transferred offender.* New York, NY: LFB Scholarly.

Jordan, K. L. (2012). Juvenile transfer and recidivism: A propensity score matching approach. *Journal of Crime and Justice, 35*(1), 53–67.

Jordan, K. L. (2014). Juvenile status and criminal sentencing: Does it matter in the adult system? *Youth Violence and Juvenile Justice, 12*(4), 315–331.

Jordan, K. L., & Myers, D. L. (2007). The decertification of transferred youth: Examining the determinants of reverse waiver. *Youth Violence and Juvenile Justice,* 188–206.

Jordan, K. L., & Myers, D. L. (2011). Juvenile transfer and deterrence: Re-examining the effectiveness of a "get tough" policy. *Crime and Delinquency, 57,* 240–270.

Kent v. United States, 383 U.S. 541 (1966).

Lanza-Kaduce, L., Lane, J., Bishop, D. M., & Frazier, C. E. 2005. Juvenile offenders and adult felony recidivism: The impact of transfer. *Journal of Crime and Justice, 28*, 59–77.

Lemmon, J., Austin, T., Verrecchia, P., & Fetzer, M. (2005). The effect of legal and extralegal factors on statutory exclusion of juvenile offenders. *Youth Violence and Juvenile Justice, 3*, 214–234.

Males, M., & .Macallair, D. (2000). *The color of justice: An analysis of juvenile justice adult court transfers in California.* Washington, DC: Justice Policy Institute, January.

Means, R. F., Heller, L. D., & Janofsky, J. S. (2012). Transferring juvenile defendants from adult to juvenile court: How Maryland forensic evaluators and judges reach their decisions. *Journal of the American Academy of Psychiatry and the Law, 40*(3), 333–340.

Mistrett, M., & Thomas, J. (2017). A campaign approach to challenging the prosecution of youth as adults. *South Dakota Law Review, 62*, 705–727.

Myers, D.L. (2005). *Boys among men; Trying and sentencing juveniles as adults.* Westport, CT: Praeger.

Redding, R. (2010). Juvenile transfer laws: An effective deterrent to delinquency? Washington, DC: U.S. Department of Justice, Office of Juvenile Justice and Delinquency Prevention.

Schiraldi, V., & Ziedenberg, J. (1999). *The Florida experiment: an analysis of the impact of granting prosecutors discretion to try juveniles as adults.* Washington, DC: Justice Policy Institute.

Sickmund, M., and Puzzanchera, C. (Eds.). (2014). *Juvenile offenders and victims: 2014 national report.* Pittsburgh, PA: National Center for Juvenile Justice.

Snyder, H., Sickmund, M., & Poe-Yamagata, E. (2000, August). *Juvenile transfers to criminal court in the 1990s: Lessons learned from four studies.* Washington, DC: Office of Juvenile Justice and Delinquency Prevention.

Steinberg, L. (1999). *Adolescence* (5th ed.). Boston, MA: McGraw-Hill College.

Strom, K. (2000). *Profile of state prisoners under age 18, 1985–97.* Washington, DC: U.S. Department of Justice, Office of Justice Programs, Bureau of Justice Statistics.

Washburn, J. J., Teplin, L. A., Voss, L. S., Simon, C. D., Abram, K. M., McClelland, G. M., & Olson, N. (2015). *Detained youth processed in juvenile and adult court: Psychiatric disorders and mental health needs.* Washington, DC: U.S. Department of Justice, Office of Juvenile Justice and Delinquency Prevention.

Ziedenberg, J. (2001). *Drugs and disparity: The racial impact of Illinois' practice of transferring young drug offenders to adult court.* Washington, DC: Justice Policy Institute.

Ziedenberg, J. (2011). *You're an adult now: Youth in adult criminal justice system.* Washington, DC: National Institute of Corrections.

Zimring, F. E. 2005. *American Juvenile Justice.* New York, NY: Oxford University Press.

Legal and Ethical Issues for Students[1]

David A. Mackey

S tudents have the right to a public education in a safe environment that is conducive to learning. In fact, with compulsory education laws, they must attend school until they reach a certain age, which varies by state. However, students who remain in school also need to conduct themselves in a manner that does not interfere with the right of other students to receive an education. The Supreme Court of the United States recognizes that school officials have inherent authority over students and that this authority is necessary to maintain an environment conducive to learning. The existence of this authority need not be expressly stated in school manuals, but the courts have recognized it in the concept of *in loco parentis*, meaning "to stand in the place of parents." Teachers and school administrators thus have authority over youths while they are at school and must ensure an appropriate level of discipline and civility to maintain an environment conducive to learning.

Although the concept of in loco parentis governing the exercise of authority in the schools is fairly straightforward, complexities arise when it comes to defining the balance between the administration's ability to make and enforce rules and students' ability to enjoy their constitutional rights, such as freedom from unreasonable searches and seizures, free speech, and due process. For example, in a landmark school rights case (*Tinker v. Des Moines Independent Community School District*, 1969), Associate Justice Abe Fortas stated, "It can hardly be argued that either students or teachers shed their constitutional rights to freedom of speech or expression at the schoolhouse gate." He went on to state that,

> in our system, state-operated schools may not be enclaves of totalitarianism. School officials do not possess absolute authority over their students. Students in school, as well as out of school, are "persons" under our Constitution. They are possessed of fundamental rights which the State must respect, just as they themselves must respect their obligations to the State.

▶ Student Privacy Interests

Searching students suspected of possessing contraband, drugs, or weapons is one tactic administrators may employ to minimize crime in school and to enforce school rules. To what extent does the Fourth Amendment, which protects individuals from unreasonable searches and seizures, apply to students? Under what circumstances can school officials conduct searches of students, their belongings, or even their vehicles in the school parking lot? An increasingly prominent issue has been the desire of school officials to discipline students for infractions of school rules during nonschool hours or away from school property when such incidents have an impact on the educational environment.

New Jersey v. T.L.O. (1984)

"T.L.O." was a 14-year-old female freshman who was smoking cigarettes in the restroom when a teacher caught her in the act. The teacher took her to the principal's office; on questioning by the vice principal, she claimed she did not smoke. A school official searched her purse to recover the remaining cigarettes. The school official found marijuana, rolling papers, a list of names of students who owed her money, a pipe, and a letter she had written to a friend describing her activities selling marijuana at school. School officials notified the police, and the student was later adjudicated delinquent. The decision was eventually overturned by the New Jersey Supreme Court, and the case reached the Supreme Court of the United States. The case featured several issues of key importance. In Associate Justice Byron White's majority opinion in *New Jersey v. T.L.O.* (1984), he noted that the Constitution protects students against unreasonable searches and seizures. The Court noted that the search of T.L.O.'s purse to discover whether school rules were being violated was reasonable at the inception of the search. The search must be justified when it begins; it cannot be justified retroactively based on what is found or recovered during the search. Of particular importance was the Court's statement that school officials are not held to the same standard as police—the probable cause standard—when conducting a search, and they are not required to obtain a warrant. Her later adjudication and the resulting declaration of delinquency rested on the evidence school officials seized. In its decision, the Court noted that a search of a student by a school official is

> justified at its inception when there are reasonable grounds for suspecting that the search will turn up evidence that the student has violated or is violating either the law or the rules of the school. Such a search will be permissible in its scope when the measures adopted are reasonably related to the objectives of the search and not excessively intrusive in light of the age and sex of the student and the nature of the infraction. (*New Jersey v. T.L.O.*, U.S. 343, 1984, p. 469)

Strip Searches

The issue of searching students for contraband that school officials believe will negatively affect school safety and detract from the learning environment reappeared with the controversy surrounding the strip search of a 13-year-old female student,

Savana Redding, with the intent to uncover prescription ibuprofen (*Safford Unified School District #1 et al. v. Redding*, 2009). A key principle came into play in the controversy over whether the strip search was reasonable given the nature of the infraction and the age and gender of the student. Before the search, the principal was aware that another student had become ill after taking another person's prescription drugs and that yet another student claimed to have gotten a pill from Savana. During a search of her person, the student who provided Savana's name to the principal was caught with a blue pill (later determined to be naproxen), several white pills, and a razor blade. The principal searched Savana's backpack and did not find any pills. In the presence of the school nurse, Savana was asked to pull her bra and underwear away from her body, and no pills were found to be concealed. In the majority opinion, Associate Justice David Souter noted that the intrusiveness of the search was not justified given the circumstances. Although it did not create a prohibition on the use of strip searches, the decision does provide some guidance in terms of when searches would be appropriate in maintaining a safe and secure environment.

School Lockers

Do students have a reasonable expectation of privacy in their school lockers? By their nature, school lockers are no doubt perceived as providing some level of privacy and security for students. After all, students may be assigned individual lockers, which do not permit contents to be examined from the outside, and students may be provided with a key or combination lock. These factors can create a reasonable expectation of privacy on the part of students. With a widely perceived expectation of privacy because of the very nature of school lockers, it stands to reason that schools should communicate to students an understanding of the actual level of privacy they can expect with regard to their school lockers. An interesting example of such communication is the Milwaukee Public Schools locker policy, which clarifies the "reasonable expectation of privacy" with an "expressed understanding to the contrary." The policy states,

> School lockers are the property of Milwaukee Public Schools. At no time does the Milwaukee Public School District relinquish its exclusive control of lockers provided for the convenience of students. School authorities for any reason may conduct periodic general inspections of lockers at any time, without notice, without student consent, and without a search warrant. (Schimel 2016, p. 6)

An effective policy communication such as the Milwaukee example would ideally be distributed to students and parents as part of the student handbook outlining rights and responsibilities of students.

Metal Detectors

In *People v. Dukes* (1992), the New York Criminal Court upheld the use of a walk-through metal detector at a high school. In justifying the need for metal detectors, the school provided documentation that it had confiscated more than 2,000 weapons during a specified time period. The U.S. Supreme Court ruled that although individuals have a reasonable expectation of privacy in their persons and effects and are also protected against unreasonable searches and seizures, the government has a legitimate interest in maintaining a safe, orderly, and disciplined environment in schools. As a practical matter, though, few schools use metal detectors. They are expensive to operate because of equipment costs and the personnel hired to run the machines, training and supervision for those personnel, gender and sensitivity issues, and the costs of making the physical setting conducive to the operation. Schools traditionally have many doors and windows because of the long-held view that the greatest danger facing a school is fire and that students need to be able to exit in a hurry. Many points of entry are not conducive to the installation and operation of metal detectors. Furthermore, individuals may bring weapons into the school through windows or side entries and then stash them in drop ceilings, restrooms, lockers, classrooms, and libraries.

Drug Dogs

In *United States v. Place* (1983), the U.S. Supreme Court ruled that a search with a drug dog does not necessarily amount to a search under the Fourth Amendment. In the *Place* case, Drug Enforcement Administration agents seized luggage from a passenger when he arrived at LaGuardia Airport and took it to Kennedy Airport, where there was a drug dog. Ninety minutes after agents seized the passenger's luggage, a canine sniff detected the presence of drugs, and agents obtained a warrant to open the luggage and discovered drugs. The Court ruled that the 90-minute seizure was unreasonable, especially because officials knew when the passenger's flight was arriving from Miami, where he had originally raised suspicion. However, the Court did note that the use of a drug dog can be highly intrusive and can affect the dignity of those individuals who are searched, especially children.

Drug Testing

Drugs in school pose many concerns for both students and school officials. The negative impact of drugs can include debasing the school environment and students' health as well as promoting intimidation and the involvement of gangs. Schools face multiple challenges and options when attempting to reduce the presence of drugs in schools and students' drug use in general. One response is to implement drug testing for segments of the student population. In the first of two significant cases involving drug testing for students, the Supreme Court was asked to address whether drug testing for student athletes was reasonable. In *Vernonia School District 47J v. Acton* (1995), the Court upheld the use of drug testing for student athletes as a condition of their participation in school-sponsored athletics. The Court reasoned that the testing procedure outlined in this particular case met a clear and narrowly defined purpose, was objectively administered, and provided student athletes with an appropriate level of due process protection. The school district's policy of testing stated that circumstances must demonstrate a compelling need for drug testing, the program must have clearly defined goals and be limited in scope, the school district must have already attempted less intrusive methods, personnel who administer the program must have limits to their discretion (i.e., determining who gets tested and why), and the drug test must be used to investigate violations of school rules rather than to seek evidence of criminal activity. The Court also recognized that student athletes have a lower expectation of privacy than do other students because they already undergo physical exams, have a somewhat public image, and interact in a locker room environment.

The Court would later expand the scope of permissible drug testing in public schools with its decision in *Board of Education of Independent School District No. 92 of Pottawatomie County et al. v. Earls et al.* (2002). In this case, the school district's policy required all middle and high school students to consent to drug testing in order to participate in any extracurricular activity such as athletics, Future Farmers of America, or the band, but school officials used the drug test results to determine the student's eligibility to participate in extracurricular activities and not as part of a criminal investigation against the student.

Free Speech

Students' right to free speech presents a contemporary challenge for some school districts. In the wake of rapid technology change, controversy has focused on the ability of schools to address web- and cell phone–based bullying and harassment, but two court cases addressing more basic free speech issues are worth noting in addition to one in which new technology takes center stage. The Supreme Court upheld students' free speech rights in *Tinker v. Des Moines Independent Community School District* (1969). The case involved students wearing black armbands in school to protest U.S. involvement in Vietnam. A teacher told the students to remove the armbands and cited a recently enacted school policy that prohibited wearing them. In the majority opinion, Justice Fortas stated that, "in our system, undifferentiated fear or apprehension of disturbance is not enough to overcome the right to freedom of expression" (*Tinker v. Des Moines Independent Community School District*, 1969, para. 13). The Court ruled that schools can limit any speech, whether active or passive, that substantially interferes with the learning environment and not just speech that some may find offensive or unpopular. The Supreme Court ruled in favor of the students in the *Tinker* case, citing students' free speech rights. The Court later sided with the school in limiting active speech by students in *Bethel School District No. 403 v. Fraser* (1986). The case arose as the result of a speech delivered in front of some 600 14-year-olds by a student whose name had been on a list of potential graduation speakers. One part of the speech (quoted here from Justice Brennan's concurring opinion, para. 1) in particular led the school to suspend the student and remove his name from the list of potential graduation speakers:

> I know a man who is firm—he's firm in his pants, he's firm in his shirt, his character is firm—but most . . . of all, his belief in you, the students of Bethel, is firm. Jeff Kuhlman is a man who takes his point and pounds it in. If necessary, he'll take an issue and nail it to the wall. He doesn't attack things in spurts—he drives hard, pushing and pushing until finally—he succeeds. Jeff is a man who will go to the very end—even the climax, for each and every one of you. So vote for Jeff for A.S.B. vice-president—he'll never come between you and the best our high school can be.

Siding with the school's interest in banning speech considered vulgar and offensive, the Court upheld the school's decision.

A more recent case, *Morse et al. v. Frederick* (2007), popularly known as "Bong hits for Jesus," addressed the issue of whether a school can limit student speech that occurs off campus. Before the beginning of the 2002 Winter Olympics, in conjunction with a school-sanctioned event, school officials allowed students to watch the Olympic torch relay as it passed in front of the school during the day on its way to Utah. Officials allowed students to watch the event from either side of the street. As the torch and the trailing camera crews neared, students unfurled a 14-foot banner that read "BONG HITS 4 JESUS." The school principal demanded that the banner be lowered. Later, the principal suspended a student for 10 days for violating the school's policy against advocating the use of illegal substances.

Students face new forms of harassment and bullying via social networking web sites and text messaging, and school officials are grappling with ways to address such abuse. In some student bullying cases, either the perpetrators' actions or school administrators' inadequate responses may violate federal antidiscrimination laws (Ali, 2010). Federal statutes would be triggered if harassment is based on race, color, national origin, sex, or disability and is considered serious enough to create a hostile environment. Ali (2010, pp. 2–3) notes that, "if an investigation reveals that discriminatory harassment has occurred, a school must take prompt and effective steps reasonably calculated to end the harassment, eliminate any hostile environment and its effects, and prevent the harassment from recurring." Additional due process considerations apply in situations involving bullying based on disabilities. Among the scenarios outlined in the U.S. Department of Education memo (Ali, 2010) depicting a school's failure to recognize civil rights violations, one included a situation in which students posted bullying comments on social networking web sites.

New Hampshire is one state that has amended its school safety laws to incorporate protections against cyberbullying. The relevant section of New Hampshire's revised statutes states in part,

(a)   "Bullying" means a single significant incident or a pattern of incidents involving a written, verbal, or electronic communication, or a physical act or gesture, or any combination thereof, directed at another pupil which:
   (1)   Physically harms a pupil or damages the pupil's property;
   (2)   Causes emotional distress to a pupil;
   (3)   Interferes with a pupil's educational opportunities;
   (4)   Creates a hostile educational environment; or
   (5)   Substantially disrupts the orderly operation of the school.

(b)   "Bullying" shall include actions motivated by an imbalance of power based on a pupil's actual or perceived personal characteristics, behaviors, or beliefs, or motivated by the pupil's association with another person and based on the other person's characteristics, behaviors, or beliefs. (Title XV Education, 2010)

Key provisions of the law protect youths from cyberbullying, which can originate off campus, and identify five conditions that would trigger action under the law, including the potential to disrupt the orderly operation of the school. Federal appeals courts have been split as to whether school officials have constitutional authority to limit and discipline students for conduct some people consider off-campus protected speech.

▶ Due Process Considerations

Schools face several limitations when it comes to disciplining students. As previously noted, school principals historically had power and authority very much like those of prison wardens; they could administer a range of punishments without review and appeal. Society gave both principals and wardens considerable power and discretion in running their institutions, and they performed their duties without much public oversight or court involvement. In the 1960s, this situation began to change as several court cases introduced due process, or the idea of fundamental fairness, into school-discipline proceedings. These cases focused on reducing the arbitrary nature of decision making, thus replacing individual authority with substantive rules and documented procedures to follow. According to the documentation for *Goss v. Lopez* (1975), a student named Lopez received a 10-day suspension for allegedly taking part in a disturbance in the school cafeteria. He was one of 75 students suspended for 10 days without a hearing, without any presentation of evidence or testimony alleging the nature of the evidence for a violation of school rules, and without recourse to an appeal. The case eventually reached the U.S. Supreme Court, which ruled that the suspension was unconstitutional because the school had not held any sort of hearing to consider evidence or testimony.

Corporal punishment in schools refers to the infliction of physical punishments as a penalty for violating a school rule. Can and should schools use corporal punishment, such as paddling, to deter students from violating school rules? The Supreme Court has ruled that school administrators' use of corporal punishment against students does not violate the Constitution (*Ingraham v. Wright*, 1977). Approximately 19 states have legislation authorizing the use of corporal punishment in schools, but some school districts and individual schools in states that do not have laws prohibiting corporal punishment do not allow it within their own jurisdictions. Of the states that allow corporal punishment in schools, the majority of instances of its use are reported in Texas, Mississippi, and Alabama (Gershoff & Font, 2016).

▶ Endnotes

1. Excerpted from Mackey, D. A. (2013). Primary interventions: Crime prevention in the family and schools. In D. A. Mackey & K. Levan (Eds.), *Crime prevention* (pp. 31–59). Burlington, MA: Jones and Bartlett Learning.

▶ References

Ali, R. (2010, October 26). Dear colleague letter: Harassment and bullying. Washington, DC: U.S. Department of Education, Office for Civil Rights. Retrieved from http://www2.ed.gov/about/offices/list/ocr/letters/colleague-201010.pdf

Bethel School District No. 403 v. Fraser, 478 U.S. 675 (1986). Retrieved from https://caselaw.findlaw.com/us-supreme-court/478/675.html

Board of Education of Independent School District No. 92 of Pottawatomie County et al. v. Earls et al. (2002). No. 01-332. Retrieved from https://www.oyez.org/cases/2001/01-332

Gershoff, E. T., & Font, S. A. (2016). Corporal punishment in U.S. public schools: Prevalence, disparities in use, and status in state and federal policy. *Social Policy Report, 30*(1), 3–25.

Goss v. Lopez, 419 U.S. 565 (1975). https://caselaw.findlaw.com/us-supreme-court/419/565.html

Ingraham v. Wright, 430 U.S. 651 (1977). Retrieved from https://caselaw.findlaw.com/us-supreme-court/430/651.html

Morse et al. v. Frederick, No. 06-278. (2007). Retrieved from https://caselaw.findlaw.com/us-supreme-court/551/393.html

New Jersey v. T.L.O., 469 U.S. 325 (1984). Retrieved from https://caselaw.findlaw.com/us-supreme-court/468/1214.html

People v. Dukes, 580 NY2d 850, NY Crim. Ct. (1992). Retrieved from http://ny.findacase.com/research/wfrmDocViewer.aspx/xq/fac.19920131_0041269.NY.htm/qx

Safford Unified School District #1 et al. v. Redding, No. 08-479. (2009). Retrieved from https://caselaw.findlaw.com/us-supreme-court/557/364.html

Schimel, B. D. (2016). *Safe schools legal resource manual*. Madison, WI: Wisconsin Department of Justice. Retrieved from ttps://www.doj.state.wi.us/sites/default/files/school-safety/safe-schools-manual-2016.pdf

Tinker v. Des Moines Independent Community School District, No. 21, 383 F.2d 988 (1969). Retrieved from https://caselaw.findlaw.com/us-supreme-court/393/503.html

Title XV Education, N.H. Stat., RSA chap. 193-F: Pupil safety and violence prevention, §193-F:3 (2010). Retrieved from http://www.gencourt.state.nh.us/rsa/html/XV/193-F/193-F-3.htm

United States v. Place, 462 U.S. 696 (1983). Retrieved from http://laws.findlaw.com/us/462/696.html

Vernonia School District 47J v. Acton, No. 94-590 (1995). Retrieved from https://caselaw.findlaw.com/us-supreme-court/515/646.html

Contextual Considerations When Serving Justice-Involved Youth with Exceptionalities

Michele P. Bratina
Kelly M. Carrero

▶ Introduction

Serving youth involved with the justice system requires a unique set of skills and understanding. Breakthroughs in neurological research indicate the continuous maturation and development of the brain throughout childhood and late adolescence. The complexity of navigating such exceptional emotional, physical, and intellectual changes may lead to heightened vulnerability for victimization, offending, and perhaps an overall increase in risk-taking behaviors (Colver & Dovey-Pearce, 2018). For some youths, the risk of involvement in juvenile justice and other systems of care (e.g., child welfare) is exceptional; when coupled with continued reoffending, it can be difficult for youths to transition out of these systems (Vidal et al., 2017). Furthermore, data collected in relation to the prevalence of distinct histories of mental health–related issues and underlying trauma among juveniles in detention consistently reveal significantly higher rates among this group in comparison with those of their community-dwelling counterparts (Vitopoulos, Peterson-Badali, Brown, & Skilling, 2018). Consequently, it can be challenging to discern the extent to which maladaptive behaviors and infractions are the result of the erratic nature of adolescent development, underlying mental and behavioral health disorders, or simple deviance.

Given these complexities, educators, human services professionals, and justice practitioners are often faced with ethical challenges in their efforts to engage and manage youth across the multiple systems of care (Farn & Adams, 2016). Professionals serving youth who are court-involved must consider a myriad of contextual factors to better design programming, interventions, and supports to facilitate rehabilitation. The purpose of this article is to highlight some common contextual factors pertaining to youth with exceptionalities who are at risk for court involvement.

Justice-Involved Youth

Approximately 856,000 youths under age 18 are arrested in the United States in any given year—most commonly for property offenses such as theft, larceny, and vandalism (National Center for Juvenile Justice, 2017a). Approximately 53,000 youths 21 or younger are detained or confined in private or public U.S. correctional institutions (e.g., detention centers, boot camps, group homes, and ranches—see Sawyer, 2018). Of those youths, the majority are male (i.e., 86%; National Center for Juvenile Justice, 2017b) and disproportionately from ethnic minority backgrounds (see **TABLE 47.1**). Low socioeconomic status, lack of parental involvement, and having parents with high stress levels are common risk factors for juvenile justice involvement (Rekker, Keijsers, Branje, Koot, & Meeus, 2017). Some of these risk factors may be related to the fact that a majority of court-involved youth live in single-parent homes.

Research indicates that a majority of youth detained in the juvenile justice system meet diagnostic criteria for mental health disorders, including distinct histories of trauma and co-occurring substance-use disorders (Underwood & Washington, 2016). For example, although the number of offending youth in adult prisons has declined over the last decade, juveniles housed in adult prisons are still twice as likely to commit suicide as adults in adult facilities and 36 times more likely to commit suicide than juveniles in detention (Lind, 2015).

Proper classification and placement of offending youths present challenges for correctional officials. Various screening tools and comprehensive risk- and needs-assessment instruments are used to determine placement and housing for offending youth who present with behavioral health and other issues that may

TABLE 47.1 Comparison of Proportion of Detained Youth by Race/Ethnicity

	General Population (%)*	Detained Youth (%)
American Indian	1	2
Asian	6	1
Black	13	42
Hispanic/Latino	18	22
White	61	31

*Data represent population estimates in 2017 and are derived from https://www.census.gov/quickfacts/fact/table/US/AGE295217

render them at risk for decompensation, victimization, or disciplinary infractions (Vincent et al., 2018). Decisions for this population are often based on a complex mix of (1) age, (2) offense (i.e., level of violence), or (3) other extralegal factors that may present extreme ethical challenges to policy and practice (Valentine, Restivo, & Wright, 2019).

Despite the prevalence of trauma and self-harm, a persistent dilemma is a general lack of training among staff that is consistent across settings (e.g., detention, school) and centers on appropriate responses to youth with diverse needs (e.g., behavioral health, cognitive, social emotional, trauma). For instance, research on exclusionary discipline practices in U.S schools consistently reveals the disproportionality related to infractions for minor transgressions among minority students leading to negative school outcomes (e.g., suspensions; Aud, Fox, & KewalRamani, 2010; Whitford, Katsiyannis, & Counts, 2016). Moreover, a lack of understanding and consideration may further perpetuate a cycle of delinquency that begins in early childhood and persists throughout the life course (Branson, Baetz, Horwitz, & Hoagwood, 2017).

Throughout the remainder of this article, we present ethical challenges encountered by a variety of practitioners when responding to justice-involved youth, with a determined focus on youth with exceptionalities. We also examine effective school-based responses to and interventions for youth with behavioral health concerns, as well as trauma-informed care approaches for youth who may be court involved.

▶ Exceptionality and the Risk of Offending

Exceptionality is a term used in the field of education to refer to students who have an identified disability and require specially designed instruction or accommodations and modifications to access learning (Hallahan, Kauffman, & Pullen, 2015). At the federal level, the Individuals with Disabilities Education Improvement Act (IDEA) of 2004 delineates 13 categories of exceptionalities that can be further categorized under the following four types: (1) intellectual disabilities, (2) developmental or physical disabilities, (3) learning disabilities, and (4) emotional and behavioral disabilities (EBDs). Many findings reveal that youth with exceptionalities commit more offenses, have a higher risk of reoffending, and enter the system at a younger age than other youth (U.S. Department of Justice, 2017). Note also that youth with exceptionalities are three times more likely to be victims of maltreatment (Child Welfare Information Gateway, 2018).

In terms of the type of exceptionalities conducive to offending risk, research further indicates that approximately 70% of justice-involved juveniles who are placed in residential facilities have been diagnosed with one or more psychiatric disorders, and at least 20% have severe and persistent mental illness (Shufelt & Cocozza, 2006; Voisin, Kiim, Takahashi, Morotta, & Bocanegra, 2017). Specifically, close to 50% of incarcerated youth have an EBD such as depression, conduct disorder, obsessive–compulsive disorder, posttraumatic stress disorder (PTSD), and, more rarely, schizophrenia. Moreover, as many as 65% of juveniles experiencing comorbid issues—such as drug addiction—are unlikely to receive adequate treatment plans (Kapp, Petr, Robbins, & Choi, 2013). These findings warrant vigilant prioritization of a cross-systems approach to analyzing and addressing maladaptive behaviors in a school setting.

Exclusionary School Discipline for Youth with Disabilities

Youth with exceptionalities—particularly those identified with EBD—are suspended and expelled at a disproportionately higher rate than their nondisabled same-aged peers (U.S. Department of Education [USDOE], 2018). Suspending or expelling a student leads to deleterious student outcomes (e.g., behavioral problems, dropping out of school, incarceration) (American Psychological Association, 2008; Aud et al., 2010). The Individuals with Disabilities Education Improvement Act (IDEA) (2004) has clear guidance for schools seeking to respond to behavioral infractions committed on school grounds by youths with identified disabilities. Specifically, students with disabilities may be removed (i.e., in-school or out-of-school suspension) from current placement for as many as 10 days per school year without having to make a formal change of placement. After the 10th day of exclusionary discipline—either consecutive or simply cumulative in that year—or if the behavioral incidents resulting in removal indicate a pattern in behavior, then the student's individualized educational programming (IEP) team will have to meet and discuss a formal change of placement to conduct a manifestation determination review (Individuals with Disabilities Education Act [IDEA] Regulations, 2013; U.S. Code Title 20, 1415(k); U.S. Code Title 34, 300.536, n.d.).

Manifestation determination review (MDR) is a process that the IEP team employs to ascertain whether the problematic behaviors resulting in disciplinary actions were because of (1) impairments inherent in or related to the student's disability or (2) failure to implement the IEP (IDEA Regulations, 2013). MDR is designed as a protection for students with disabilities so they do not receive discriminatory treatment because of their disability status. Using the unique expertise of each member of the IEP team and adhering to the ethical codes that the IEP team (1) identify the least intrusive interventions possible and (2) provide students with therapeutic and educational environments (Behavioral Analyst Certification Board, 2017; Council for Exceptional Children, 2015), the IEP team reviews available data about behavioral infractions and the implementation of the student's IEP. In addition, the IEP team seeks to identify additional assessments, intervention strategies, or supports that may mitigate the likelihood of the student committing future behavioral infractions. If the MDR reveals there is a pattern to the behavior but it does not appear to be related to the student's disability or the school's failure to implement the IEP, then the school is able to administer disciplinary sanctions in the same manner as it would for a student who does not have a disability (U.S. Code Title 20, n.d.). Moreover, if the IEP team determines that a change in placement is appropriate, the student could be placed in a disciplinary setting or simply a more restrictive setting. Youth with disabilities are disproportionately represented in juvenile correctional facilities and other court-involved programs (Gagnon, Barber, Van Loan, & Leone, 2009; USDOE, 2014).

However, if the IEP team concludes that problematic behaviors are likely the result of impairments associated with the student's disability, then the team will often conduct a functional behavioral assessment, design a behavior-intervention plan, and revise the student's IEP. A *functional behavioral assessment* (FBA) is often conducted to (1) identify predicable patterns of behavior (including environmental factors likely to incite the behavior), (2) analyze potential skill or performance deficits involved in preventing the student from using desirable behaviors, and (3) determine how the problematic behaviors are serving the student (i.e., what does the student gain or avoid by using the problematic behaviors). Once the FBA has been completed, the IEP team drafts a behavior-intervention plan (BIP) that identifies (1) desirable replacement behaviors (i.e., those that the serve the same function as the problematic behavior but are socially acceptable), (2) intervention strategies to teach and support the replacement behaviors, (3) accommodations or environmental supports to prevent problem behaviors, and (4) response protocols when the problematic behavior occurs despite the implementation of the other BIP elements. When school personnel do not adhere to the procedures and regulations delineated in IDEA and the ethical codes published by their professional associations (e.g., Behavior Analysts Certification Board, Council for Exceptional Children, National Association of School Psychology), youth with disabilities are at greater risk of academic failure and possibly incarceration.

Trauma and the Risk of Offending

As previously stated, research indicates that a significant number of court-involved youth have been exposed to traumatic events; this leaves many of these youth with complex mixes of emotional, social, and physical health problems that may persist throughout their lives (Baglivio, Wolff, Epps, & Nelson, 2015; Griffin, Germaine, & Wilkinson, 2012). High rates of trauma histories have been especially reported for detained youth. For example, Abram et al. (2013) found that 93% of youths in a carceral setting had experienced at least one trauma, 84% had experienced more than one, and 57% had experienced some form of trauma more than six times. Furthermore, one in 10 of the detained children had PTSD; of those, 93% had at least one comorbid psychiatric disorder (males with PTSD had a higher risk). Almost all of the males and females reported trauma (i.e., 93% and 84%, respectively). Older juveniles (i.e., ages 14–18) report more trauma when compared to younger juveniles (i.e., ages 10–13). The highest reported traumas were (1) witnessing violence (74%), (2) being threatened with a weapon (58%), and (3) being in a situation in which the individual thought someone would die (53%). Some one-third of reporting youth reported (1) being attacked physically or beaten badly (35%), (2) being involved in an accident (33%), and (3) seeing the dead body of someone they knew (24%).

A growing line of research is developing on the life-span impact of multiple exposures to adverse childhood experiences (ACEs). Based on the original work done by Felitti and colleagues (1998), in collaboration with the Centers for Disease Control and Prevention, researchers have developed and implemented an ACE scale to measure varying types of adverse experiences during the course of childhood, including exposure to physical, sexual, and emotional abuse and household dysfunction. A respondent's total score on the instrument is referred to as his or her "ACE score," and is a cumulative total number of exposures, with scores ranging from 1 to 10. High ACE scores (≥4) have been found to be directly correlated with poor health outcomes and adult risk behaviors (Felitti, et al., 1998). Furthermore, a significant correlation has been found between exposure to multiple ACEs and juvenile offending behaviors (Baglivio et al., 2014; Craig, Piquero, Farrington, & Ttofi, 2017), including serious and chronic violent offending (Fox, Perez, Cass, Baglivio, & Epps, 2015).

According to the literature, some populations are more vulnerable to experiencing childhood trauma (ACEs) because of the nature of lifestyles that place them at a high risk for adverse outcomes—mostly those immersed in poor socioeconomic and social conditions (Baglivio et al., 2014; Felitti, et al, 1998). For example, in their study of more than 59,000 juvenile offenders in more than 3,900 neighborhoods, Baglivio and colleagues (2017) found that the number of ACEs in their sample was related to concentrated household disadvantage and affluence, with youth living in lower socioeconomic conditions more likely to have experienced a higher number of ACEs. This finding was significant even after controlling for factors such as race, age, and other parental characteristics (e.g., employment issues, level of family support).

Trauma-Informed Approaches to Treatment

For juveniles, the systematic goal should be rehabilitation as opposed to punishment. To best facilitate that, juveniles must be taught healthy coping mechanisms to overcome traumatic experiences. One of the most timely and effective strategies is the implementation of a *trauma-informed care* (TIC) strategy in agencies serving at-risk youth and those already justice-involved (Hanson & Lang, 2016). Such agencies may include (1) screening or catchment centers, (2) detention and rehabilitation facilities, and (3) community-based family and child service and support networks. A trauma-informed strategy or approach is one in which all staff are involved in understanding the existence and prevalence of trauma and its relationship to offending behaviors. A trauma-informed agency is one in which staff and administration understand and support the use of evidence-based strategies and programs designed to more effectively respond to risks and needs of at-risk youth and their families so to mediate any further involvement in multiple systems of care, including the juvenile justice system. A program that is based on a TIC model will employ a more respectful and accepting view of clients; the atmosphere is nonjudgmental, and the use of negative labels is avoided (Oral et al., 2016). A TIC can be integrated within existing treatment models or practices, including relapse prevention, cognitive-behavioral therapy, and risk–needs–responsivity models (Substance Abuse and Mental Health Services Administration [SAMHSA], 2014).

A TIC simply delivers clinical services in a way that recognizes the prevalence and impact of early childhood trauma on behavior over the life span. In this way, therapists can establish a nonthreatening treatment environment that facilitates trust, emotional safety, empowerment, and intimacy, and responds to maladaptive behavior in the context of traumatic experiences (Hanson & Lang, 2016; Oral et al., 2016). Although cumulative traumatic experiences during early childhood can result in irreversible neurodevelopmental deficits, the neuroplasticity of the brain allows for reorganization and accommodation of new experiences (SAMHSA, 2014). When clinicians respond to traumatized clients with compassion, validation, and respect, corrective emotional experiences allow new skills to be learned, enhanced, practiced, and reinforced.

The use of trauma-informed treatment in the juvenile justice system has become more widespread in recent years, with many programs and models available. Training programs frequently address (1) the impact of trauma on childhood development, (2) the relationship between trauma and behavioral problems (including delinquency/crime), (3) the common signs of a trauma history and triggers, (4) the appropriate responses to a traumatized youth's reactions, and (5) the strategies for managing stress (e.g., compassion fatigues) caused by working with a traumatized population (sometimes referred to as *vicarious trauma*; National Center for Mental Health and Juvenile Justice, 2016).

The National Child Traumatic Stress Network (NCTSN) was also designed and implemented to support the emerging focus on trauma-informed care in juvenile justice settings. The Network has effectively established a juvenile justice workgroup as well as a learning collaborative. The collaborative has been piloting trauma intervention in justice settings or with justice-involved children and youth. Another primary task has been the development of resources, including the NCTSN Bench Card for the Trauma-Informed Judge—an effort designed to provide support to criminal justice professionals as they consider adopting trauma-informed principles (DeCandia, Guarino, & Chervil, 2014). TIC programs involve multiple steps, including knowledge acquisition, cultural and organizational paradigm shifts, and policy and procedural change at every level in the agency hierarchy.

▶ Conclusions

The behavioral health–education nexus is a profound topic in that it requires actors from multiple systems or agencies to collaborate in unique ways so that more efficient problem solving can occur to best serve the client—that is, the child. Best-practice strategies are often framed with an integrative, trauma-informed multidisciplinary approach, including perspectives from interrelated disciplines such as criminal justice, social work, psychology (mental health and addiction counseling), and education. Whenever possible, a team-based approach should be taken to enhance service engagement and improve outcomes.

Although diversion options are available throughout the course of the juvenile justice system, significant gaps remain that affect treatment outcomes and the rates of recidivism—unfortunately, these gaps exist across multiple systems. The juvenile or criminal justice systems should not become the lead agencies charged with the majority of these functions. Ultimately, the most comprehensive approach encompasses collaboration between stakeholders from multiple systems of care, and an array of treatment programs and services would be accessible, recovery oriented, evidence based, and driven by the needs of consumers (Council of State Governments, 2002; Griffin et al., 2012). In brief, this relates to a cross-systems approach to treatment and rehabilitation in which an array of services will be accessible to all partner agencies (e.g., Children & Youth Services, Juvenile Justice, Education, and Mental Health & Disability).

All youths have challenges problem solving and regulating emotions during adolescence: It is no different for youths with exceptionalities. As stated previously, an unfortunate result of a lack of training with regard to behavioral assessment and management has often been youth involvement in the school-to-prison pipeline (SPP), which refers to the unanticipated trajectory of youths who succumb to school zero-tolerance policies (in particular, youths who are non-White, of lower socioeconomic status, or have EBD) when classroom behaviors become unmanageable, and the only perceived recourse involves disciplinary measures that may lead to suspension or expulsion from school (Pigott, Stearns, & Khey, 2018). Therefore, at all points of contact throughout the SPP, specific goals for teaching and treatment should be the focus and not simply punitive approaches. Diversion practices at the juvenile court level also allow for juveniles to remain free of the SPP. Many jurisdictions have diversion programs in place for those youths deemed appropriate. Youth courts and youth treatment courts are also being implemented for students with minor disciplinary infractions as a means of teaching normative behavioral expectations and restorative responses to delinquent behaviors. Youths attend court that is made up of their peers for disposition, which entails sentences such as community service, written apologies, and mediation (Brasof & Peterson, 2018).

Although youths with exceptionalities may exhibit abhorrent behaviors, they still have the right to a supportive, therapeutic environment (Behavioral Analyst Certification Board, 2017) and a free and appropriate education (IDEA, 2004). Service providers working with justice-involved youth with exceptionalities must also be supported in their efforts to teach, train, and support the youths in their care. All of society benefits when a child is cared for and taught well. All of society suffers when even one of our children is denied the opportunity to reach his or her maximum potential and become a contributing member of our community.

▶ References

Abram, K. M., Teplin, L. A., King, D. C., Longworth, S. L., Emanuel, K.M., Romero, E. G., McClelland, G. M., Dulcan, M. K., Washburn, J. J., Welty, L. J., & Olson, N. D. (2013). PTSD, trauma, and comorbid psychiatric disorders in detained youth. Washington, DC: Department of Justice, Office of Juvenile Justice and Delinquency Prevention. Retrieved from https://www.ojjdp.gov/pubs/239603.pdf

American Psychological Association. (2008). Are zero tolerance policies effective in the schools? An evidentiary review and recommendations. *American Psychologist, 63*(9), 852–862. Retrieved from doi:10.1037/0003-066X.63.9.852

Aud, S., Fox, M. A., & KewalRamani, A. (2010). *Status and trends in the education of racial and ethnic groups* (NCES 2010-015). Washington, DC: U.S. Department of Education, National Center for Education Statistics. Retrieved from https://nces.ed.gov/pubs2010/2010015.pdf

Baglivio, M. T., Epps, N., Swartz, K., Huq, M. S., Sheer, A., & Hardt, N. S. (2014). The prevalence of adverse childhood experiences (ACE) in the lives of juvenile offenders. *Journal of Juvenile Justice, 3*(2), 1–17.

Baglivio, M. T., Wolff, K. T., Epps, N., & Nelson, R. (2017). Predicting adverse childhood experiences: The importance of neighborhood context in youth trauma among delinquent youth. *Crime & Delinquency, 63*(2), 166–188.

Behavioral Analyst Certification Board. (2017, July 6). *Professional and ethical compliance code for behavior analysts.* Retrieved from https://www.bacb.com/wp-content/uploads/2017/09/170706-compliance-code-english.pdf

Branson, C. E., Baetz, C. L., Horwitz, S. M., & Hoagwood, K. E. (2017, November). Trauma informed juvenile justice systems: A systematic review of definitions and core components. *Psychological Trauma: Theory, Research, Practice, and Policy, 9*(6), 635–646. Retrieved from http://dx.doi.org/10.1037/tra0000255

Brasof, M., & Peterson, K. (2018, May 9). Creating procedural justice and legitimate authority within school discipline systems through youth court. *Psychology in the Schools, 55*(7). Retrieved from https://doi.org/10.1002/pits.22137

Child Welfare Information Gateway. (2018). *The risk and prevention of maltreatment of children with disabilities.* Washington, DC: U.S. Department of Health and Human Services, Children's Bureau. Retrieved from https://www.childwelfare.gov/pubs/prevenres/focus/

Colver, A., & Dovey-Pearce, G. (2018). The relationships of adolescent behaviours to adolescent brain changes and their relevance to the transition of adolescents and young adults with chronic illness and disability. Pp. 21–29 in *Health Care Transition.* Springer, Cham.

Council for Exceptional Children. (2015). *Ethical principles and professional practice standards for special educators*. Retrieved from https://www.cec.sped.org/Standards/Ethical-Principles-and-Practice-Standards

Craig, J. M., Piquero, A. R., Farrington, D. P., & Ttofi, M. M. (2017). A little early risk goes a long bad way: Adverse childhood experiences and life-course offending in the Cambridge study. *Journal of Criminal Justice, 53,* 34–45.

DeCandia, C., Guarino, K., & Chervil, R. (2014). *Trauma-informed care and trauma-specific services: A comprehensive approach to trauma intervention.* Washington, DC: American Institutes for Research. Retrieved from https://www.air.org/sites/default/files/downloads/report/Trauma-Informed%20Care%20White%20Paper_October%202014.pdf

Farn, A., & Adams, J. (2016). *Education and interagency collaboration: A lifeline for justice involved youth.* Washington, DC: Center for Juvenile Justice Reform. Retrieved from https://cjjr.georgetown.edu/wp-content/uploads/2016/08/Lifeline-for-Justice-Involved-Youth-August_2016.pdf

Felitti, V. J., Anda, R. F., Nordenberg, D., & Williamson, D. F. (1998). Adverse childhood experiences and health outcomes in adults: The Ace study. *Journal of Family and Consumer Sciences, 90*(3), 31.

Fox, B. H., Perez, N., Cass, E., Baglivio, M. T., & Epps, N. (2015). Trauma changes everything: Examining the relationship between adverse childhood experiences and serious, violent and chronic juvenile offenders. *Child Abuse & Neglect, 46,* 163–173.

Gagnon, J. C., Barber, B. R., Van Loan, C., & Leone, P. E. (2009). Juvenile correctional schools: Characteristics and approaches to curriculum. *Education and Treatment of Children, 32*(4), 673–696.

Griffin, G., Germain, E. J., & Wilkerson, R. G. (2012). Using a trauma-informed approach in juvenile justice institutions. *Journal of Child & Adolescent Trauma 5*(3), 271–83.

Hallahan, D. P., Kauffman, J. M., & Pullen, P. C. (2015). *Exceptional learners: An introduction to special education* (13th ed.). Boston, MA: Pearson.

Hanson, R. F., & Lang, J. (2016). A critical look at trauma-informed care among agencies and systems serving maltreated youth and their families. *Child Maltreatment, 21*(2), 95–100.

Individuals with Disabilities Education Improvement Act, Public Law 108-446, 108th Congress, (2004).

Individuals with Disabilities Education Act Regulations. (2013). § 34. C.F.R. 300.1 et seq.

Kapp, S. A., Petr, C. G., Robbins, M. L., & Choi, J. J. (2013). Collaboration between community mental health and juvenile justice systems: Barriers and facilitators. *Child and Adolescent Social Work Journal, 30*(6), 505–517.

Lind, D. (2015, June 17). Teenagers in prison have a shockingly high suicide rate. *Vox.* Retrieved from https://www.vox.com/2014/10/10/6957497/suicide-prison-rate-juvenile-teenager-prisoners

National Center for Juvenile Justice. (2017a). Estimated number of juvenile arrests, 2016. Statistical Briefing Book. Retrieved from https://www.ojjdp.gov/ojstatbb/crime/qa05101.asp?qaDate=2016

National Center for Juvenile Justice. (2017b). Female proportion of minority juveniles in residential placement, 2015. Statistical Briefing Book. Retrieved from https://www.ojjdp.gov/ojstatbb/corrections/qa08206.asp?qaDate=2015

National Center for Mental Health and Juvenile Justice. (2016). *Trauma among youth in the juvenile justice system.* Retrieved from https://www.ncmhjj.com/wp-content/uploads/2016/09/Trauma-Among-Youth-in-the-Juvenile-Justice-System-for-WEBSITE.pdf

Oral, R., Ramirez, M., Coohey, C., Nakada, S., Walz, A., Kuntz, A., . . . & Peek-Asa, C. (2016). Adverse childhood experiences and trauma informed care: the future of health care. *Pediatric Research, 79*(1–2), 227.

Pigott, C., Stearns, A. E., & Khey, D. N. (2018). School resource officers and the school to prison pipeline: Discovering trends of expulsions in public schools. *American Journal of Criminal Justice, 43*(1), 120–138.

Rekker, R., Keijsers, L., Branje, S., Koot, H., & Meeus, W. (2017). The interplay of parental monitoring of socioeconomic status predicting minor delinquency between and within adolescents. *Journal of Adolescence, 59,* 155–165.

Substance Abuse and Mental Health Services Administration. (2014). *SAMHSA's concept of trauma and guidance for a trauma-informed approach.* HHS Publication No. (SMA) 14-4884. Rockville, MD: Author.

Sawyer, W. (2018). Youth confinement: The whole pie. Prison Policy Initiative. Retrieved from https://www.prisonpolicy.org/reports/youth2018.html

Shufelt, J. L., & Cocozza, J. J. (2006). *Youth with mental disorders in the juvenile justice system: Results from a multi-state prevalence study* (pp. 1–16). Delmar, NY: National Center for Mental Health and Juvenile Justice.

Underwood, L. A., & Washington, A. (2016). Mental illness and juvenile offenders. *International Journal of Environmental Research and Public Health, 13*(2), 228.

U.S. Code Title 20. (n.d.). Education. Chapter 33. Education of individuals with disabilities. Subchapter II. Assistance for education of all children with disabilities Section 1415. Procedural safeguards.

U.S. Code Title 34. (n.d.). Education Subtitle B. Regulations of the Offices of the Department of Education Chapter III. Part 300. Assistance to states for the education of children with disabilities. Subpart E. Procedural safeguards due process procedures for parents and children. Subjgrp 60. Discipline Procedures Section 300.536. Change of placement because of disciplinary removals. Washington, DC: Office of Special Education and Rehabilitative Services, Department Of Education.

U.S. Department of Education [USDOE]. (2018). Civil rights data collection (CRDC). Washington, DC: Office for Civil Rights. Retrieved from https://www2.ed.gov/about/offices/list/ocr/data .html?src=rt

U.S. Department of Education [USDOE]. (2014). Office of Special Education and Rehabilitative Services (2014). *36th Annual Report to Congress on the Implementation of the Individuals with Disabilities Act*. Washington, DC.

U.S. Department of Justice, Office of Juvenile Justice and Delinquency Prevention. (2017). Youths with intellectual and developmental disabilities in the juvenile justice system. Retrieved from https://www.ojjdp.gov/mpg/litreviews/Intellectual-Developmental-Disabilities.pdf

Valentine, C. L., Restivo, E., & Wright, K. (2019). Prolonged isolation as a predictor of mental health for waived juveniles. *Journal of Offender Rehabilitation, 58*(4), 352–369.

Vidal, S., Prince, D., Connell, C. M., Caron, C. M., Kaufman, J. S., & Tebes, J. K. (2017). Maltreatment, family environment, and social risk factors: Determinants of the child welfare to juvenile justice transition among maltreated children and adolescents. *Child Abuse & Neglect, 63*, 7–18.

Vincent, G., Sullivan, C. J., Sullivan, C., Guy, L., Latessa, E., Tyson, J., & Adams, B. (2018, December). Studying drivers of risk and needs assessment instrument implementation in juvenile justice. U.S. Department of Justice, Office of Justice Programs, Office of Juvenile Justice and Delinquency Prevention. Retrieved from https://www.ojjdp.gov/pubs/251809.pdf

Vitopoulos, N. A., Peterson-Badali, M., Brown, S., & Skilling, T. A. (2018). The relationship between trauma, recidivism risk, and reoffending in male and female juvenile offenders. *Journal of Child & Adolescent Trauma*, 1–14.

Voisin, D. R., Kim, D., Takahashi, L., Morotta, P., & Bocanegra, K. (2017). Involvement in the juvenile justice system for African American adolescents: Examining associations with behavioral health problems. *Journal of Social Service Research, 43*(1), 129–140.

Whitford, D. K., Katsiyannis, A., & Counts, J. (2016). Discriminatory discipline: Trends and issues. *NASSP Bulletin, 100*(2), 117–135. Retrieved from https://journals.sagepub.com/doi /abs/10.1177/0192636516677340?journalCode=buld

College Students' Rights and Ethics

© Sergii Gnatiuk/Shutterstock

Ethical Dilemmas: Finding the Right Behavior in College Life

Christopher Benedetti

Colleges are facing increased scrutiny for their position and handling of a variety of social issues, including freedom of choice, economic equality, and academic integrity. Although these issues are often associated with laws and policies, the regular appearance of these issues in mainstream news and social media indicates a potential disconnect between law, policy, and practice. These disconnects often exist because of ethical dilemmas that are difficult to navigate and effectively resolve. Colleges continuously grapple with incidents while trying to find the *right* thing to do, often reacting to avoid legal fallout or diminished public perception (Patel, 2019) without clearly understanding the ethical dilemmas the incidents are based on and those the incidents have created. Students are caught in the middle of the confusion and receive little training, education, or guidance on ethics (Dowd, 2012), increasing the likelihood they will fail to meet a college's standard of behavior and find themselves penalized. But is there a *right* behavior for college students? Maybe the answer lies within the laws and policies that guide colleges' and students' rights . . . or perhaps it is not that simple.

▶ Ethical Dilemmas in Colleges

An ethical dilemma arises when a situation is without a clear path of resolution (Figar & Dordevic, 2016). There is not a *right* or *wrong* choice. As a result, the available choices to resolve the situation include some level of unintended (or understood) consequence that may seem injurious to the beliefs and values of those not in agreement with the resolution. All of us have a set of beliefs and values that form the core of who we are as individuals. For most of us, these beliefs and values are non-negotiable, especially in situations that may require compromise of those beliefs and values. Challenges to beliefs and values are often the precursors to ethical dilemmas because challenges can be seen as personal attacks, thus eliciting emotional responses that make the resolution of issues difficult.

Colleges regularly face ethical dilemmas when their beliefs and values are a mismatch to those of the students. The nature of the parental role of colleges is one such common ethical dilemma because the shift from high school and parental supervision to college can be jarring, spurring the college to take control. The college can assume the philosophy of *in loco parentis*, translated as "in place of the parent," which is the belief that the college can assume some of the physical and moral responsibilities and functions of a parent (Patel, 2019) as a way to aid that shift from the home into college. With this belief, the college can monitor student safety and well-being and take corrective steps if these are jeopardized. Although this appears to be an altruistic and even logical effort on the surface, an ethical dilemma arises when the college's beliefs and values related to safety and well-being contradict those of the individual student. After all, college students are legally adults and thus seek the same freedoms that those who work within the college enjoy. So, whose beliefs and values are *right*? The college's or the student's? Unfortunately, the answer is not easy. Colleges are under immense pressure to protect their students from a seemingly endless list of threats, which gives colleges a level of authority in assuming in loco parentis to apply the protection that meets their beliefs and values of safety and well-being. Because the larger society is experiencing similar threats, it is no surprise that these threats are reflected in colleges (Janosik, Creamer, & Humphrey, 2004), which further compels colleges to restrict behavior they may deem harmful.

▶ Colleges as a Reflection of Society

Colleges have largely shifted away from their historically homogeneous, privileged past in pursuit of a broader, more diverse student population that more accurately reflects current societal needs and ideals. This diversity includes the common demographic attributes such as gender, race and ethnicity, sexual identity, and socioeconomic status, but also a variety of viewpoints, including those that may be divergent or nonconforming with the college's own viewpoints. The college's desired outcome of this diverse student body is to create a rich, robust, and dynamic discourse that promotes a deeper level of learning for students to foster growth in the larger, increasingly pluralistic society (Locks, Hurtado, Bowman, & Oseguera, 2008). This convergent opportunity is what makes the college experience so novel for students and valuable to communities beyond the campus. The relationship between college and society is not only mirrored in each other (Janosik et al., 2004) but also is symbiotic in some cases.

Socioeconomics is one ethical dilemma facing colleges that is reflected in society—specifically, rising costs and their impact on quality of life, also known as cost of living. It is not unusual for local and national economies to ebb and flow, but the cost of living has steadily increased over time, which puts a strain on the funds available to individuals and families, especially without a significant increase in revenue to offset some of those increased costs. Similarly, the costs of college have steadily increased to accommodate increases in expenses, as well as reductions in revenue from local, state, and federal taxes. With a decrease in tax-based revenue, colleges are forced to look at increasing other forms of revenue, primarily through student tuition. In the past, earning a college degree was considered a wise decision, regardless of the cost because a college education was shown to increase an individual's earning potential. However, this thought has led to college students succumbing to significant debt that cannot be easily paid back, which stands only to worsen with rising tuition costs (Gecowets, 2017). Colleges are considering efforts to cut costs, but these cuts are sometimes at the expense of student programs and services. If there is a desire to retain these programs and services, then the burden is shifted back to increasing tuition and related costs. One can begin to see this dilemma from an economic standpoint, but the dilemma is even more ethically problematic. Without affordable higher education, society is at risk of allowing colleges to regress to their homogenous, privileged past in which only the affluent can access education beyond high school. With cost of living expenses projected to continue to increase, what should be done? Is it the responsibility of the college or the student? There is no *right* or *wrong* here, just a complex dilemma.

▶ Following the Letter of the Law

A seemingly commonsense approach to mitigating ethical dilemmas might be to simply follow what is written in law or policy. All of those who attend and work for the college are governed by law and policy, some of which were developed by the college, so this would be a logical thought. Unfortunately, this path is fraught with ethical dilemmas because laws and policies are not written with every possible context or situation in mind. Instead, following the "letter of the law" often prompts an ethical dilemma, particularly when those laws or polices that are ambiguous are employed. Misinterpretations and challenges to laws occur locally and nationally on a regular basis, and because colleges reflect society, they experience similar misinterpretations and challenges. In other words, colleges are just as vulnerable, which is why they develop stringent, even absolute policies to encourage following the letter of the law to reduce their vulnerability. Seems reasonable, right?

College policies with a zero-tolerance requirement for major student behavior infractions are an example of efforts to reduce misinterpretations and challenges to policy. Zero tolerance essentially means that colleges must apply a predetermined consequence, often significant to severe, to an individual or group in violation of the associated policy (Reynolds et al., 2008). As a result of the absolute nature of this type of policy, colleges are expected to act; when they are unable to do so, such as when there is insufficient evidence of a violation, then an ethical dilemma may emerge. For example, many colleges treat violations of their academic integrity policy, such as plagiarism, with zero tolerance. This may include consequences such as suspension and expulsion from the college, which are significant and severe. When an academic integrity violation is reported, the college reviews the evidence to determine the presence, degree, and intent of the violation in order to determine guilt and assign a consequence. In many cases, the accuser, typically an instructor or other college employee, and the accused student are not in agreement on the degree and intent of the violation, which sets up an ethical dilemma that must be navigated by those reviewing the evidence. The zero-tolerance aspect of the policy requires a determination of guilt. Regardless of the decision, one side will be dissatisfied: Either the accuser will be disappointed that a consequence was not assigned, or the accused will be saddened that his or her college enrollment will be potentially suspended or ended. Either way, someone will not feel that the *right* decision was made.

So, why do colleges develop and employ policy with absolute components given the potential for ethical dilemmas? Sometimes, this is in response to societal pressure to manage a perceived or real threat to safety and well-being (i.e., in loco parentis) that is occurring on campus or in society. Other times, it is an overcorrection to a previously ambiguous policy or law so that it is easier to follow the letter of the law to reach the hopefully *right* decision. However, the *right* decision is not always the best decision when working through an ethical dilemma. Following the letter of the law does provide some advantages, however, particularly in the form of due process. In the event of an unfavorable decision related to a law or policy, due process allows for the opportunity to have arguments and evidence heard by another audience (Lee, 2011). Given increased scrutiny, colleges may make reactive, overcorrective decisions based on ethical dilemmas in hopes of preventing future issues from occurring. Due process is a way to mitigate the possible mishandling of those ethical dilemma.

▶ Moving Past *Right* and *Wrong*

Because colleges exist within a diverse society, ethical dilemmas are inevitable. Ethical burdens are shared across the college campus as everyone adjusts to an ever-changing, unpredictable reality. The 21st century has revealed a society in a state of constant change as cultural and social norms continuously shift (Patel, 2019). Individually, we have beliefs and values that shape our perspective and level of importance on a variety of topics, which may fluctuate based on new knowledge and experience over time, further contributing to those shifts. Unfortunately, college students are often caught in the middle of these shifts as they navigate their rights and responsibilities to identify what is the *right* behavior for college. The specific ethical dilemmas identified throughout this text arise because an individual, group, policy, or law seeks a definitively *right* answer to a situation when that is not possible.

Collectively, there must be an effort to move past the need for a universal *right* and *wrong* regarding ethical behavior and instead accept existence on an ethical spectrum, somewhere between the ambiguous and absolute . . . between *right* and *wrong*. Existing on this spectrum requires thoughtfulness, honesty, and precision, but, most important of all, fairness. Engaging fairness in an ethical dilemma encourages a consideration of all perspectives and viewpoints for the best opportunity to reach a balanced resolution. Fairness is what exists between the *right* and *wrong* ends of the ethical spectrum, which allows for the navigation of ethical dilemmas with thoughtfulness, honesty, and precision to obtain a better understanding of the laws and policies that are an integral part of college student life.

Consider the following set of ethical principles developed by Kitchener (1985), which have been shown to be useful in considering college student behavior (Dowd, 2012) as a guide for moving within the ethical spectrum.

- Autonomy—freely think and act as individuals but without negatively impacting others
- Fidelity—treat individuals with loyalty, trustworthiness, and respect to avoid limiting the autonomy of others

- Beneficence—engage in thoughts and behaviors that are beneficial to others
- Nonmaleficence—avoid any thought or behavior that may harm others
- Justice—thinking and behaving fairly by being balanced and impartial

The key is that none of these principles identifies what is *right*. Rather, each principle provides a general guideline for how to think and behave to lessen the negative impacts of an ethical dilemma. Then, instead of forming judgments in a given situation based on individual beliefs and values, decisions based on these ethical principles can be made to identify what is fair. Jones (1991) distilled the essence of several classic ethical decision-making theories, which are captured in the following steps:

1. Identify the ethical dilemma.
2. Assess the nature of the dilemma.
3. Understand the intent of all involved.
4. Decide what is fair to resolve the dilemma.

By following these steps, guided by the ethical principles, one can be better equipped to navigate any ethical dilemma that will inevitably arise as a part of college life.

So, is there a *right* behavior for college students? The answer to this question is both yes and no, ultimately decided by how one thinks and acts given a situation and its impact on others. Certainly, colleges and students must adhere to the established laws and policies that govern behavior, but one can and should be thoughtful, honest, and precise in doing so. Students have a unique and valuable perspective of the ethics that is intertwined in college life. With this perspective comes a degree of power to influence change. Over the years, students have been the drivers of moving colleges beyond ethical dilemmas through divergent discourse, civil activism, and general application of their rights. Students have the right to think and act in responsible ways, which is arguably the most important right to have in college and beyond.

▶ References

Dowd, M. (2012). *A national study of the ethical dilemmas faced by student conduct administrators.* (Doctoral dissertation). Minnesota State University, Mankato. Mankato, Minnesota.

Figar, N., & Dordevic, B. (2016). Managing an ethical dilemma. *Economic Themes, 54*(3), 345–362.

Gecowets, K. (2017). At what cost? The ethics of student debt. *Siegel Institute Journal of Applied Ethics, 1*(1), 1–24.

Janosik, S., Creamer, D., & Humphrey, E. (2004). An analysis of ethical problems facing student affairs administrators. *NASPA Journal, 41*(2), 356–374.

Jones, T. (1991). Ethical decision making by individuals in organizations: An issue-contingent model. *Academy of Management Review, 16*(2), 366–395.

Kitchener, K. (1985). Ethical principles and ethical decisions in student affairs. In H. J. Canon and R. D. Brown (Eds.), *Applied ethics in student services* (pp. 17–29). San Francisco, CA: Jossey-Bass.

Lee, P. (2011). The curious life of "In loco parentis" at American universities. *Higher Education in Review, 8*, 65–90.

Locks, A., Hurtado, S., Bowman, N., & Oseguera, L. (2008). Extending notions of campus climate and diversity to students' transition to college. *Review of Higher Education, 31*(3), 257–285.

Patel, V. (2019, February). The new "In loco parentis." *Chronicle of Higher Education.* Retrieved from https://www.chronicle.com/interactives/Trend19-InLoco-Main

Reynolds, C., Skiba, R., Graham, S., Sheras, P., Conoley, J., & Garcia-Vazquez, E. (2008). Are zero tolerance policies effective in the schools? An evidentiary review and recommendations. *American Psychologist, 63*(9), 852–862.

© Sergii Gnatiuk/Shutterstock

Character in Context: My Life as an Academic Student Advocate

David Zehr

When I began my university teaching career more than 35 years ago, a student gave me an end-of-semester gift he'd found in a used bookstore—a copy of Oliver Kolstoe's (1975), *College Professoring: Or Through Academia with Gun and Camera.*

It has been years since I read that book, so my recollections are vague, but I remember it as a humorous take on the complications, convolutions, and the "you can't make this stuff up" episodes characteristic of higher education. I have more than my fair share of such stories that could easily fill a book, and if I ever put thought to word processor, a working title, in homage to Kolstoe, could be *College Professoring: Or Through Academia with Camera, an Ethicist, and Legal Counsel.* The camera piece aside, I do think it's important to talk about why I included both ethical and legal dimensions in my facetious book title. And that will entail a brief description of my career path in higher education.

Like many university faculty members, when I started out as an assistant professor I didn't think I'd have to regularly think about and deal with significant ethical and legal issues. For more than 20 years I was a full-time faculty member, and I spent my time on what was expected of me and what I thought was most important to my career: teaching, service to the institution, and scholarly engagement. For the past 13 years, however, I have served in various administrative capacities, and my responsibilities have focused more on issues that not infrequently necessitate navigating the ethical and legal dimensions of academic life at a university. So how did I get to my current position?

In 2006, I was asked to step away from full-time teaching and serve as an interim associate vice president for academic affairs. One year turned into two, two into three, and then I was appointed to the position on a noninterim basis after a national search. With the arrival of a new president in 2016, an administrative reorganization was put in place and my position was eliminated. I expected to simply return to the faculty on a full-time basis but was approached by senior administration about creating a new position that capitalized on my understanding of university policies and my record of helping students solve both simple and complicated matters affecting their academic progress. And with that, my new position, the Academic Student Advocate and Policy Advisor came into being.

As Academic Student Advocate, I am the point person for students who present with a myriad of concerns that include but are certainly not limited to grade disputes, academic integrity violations, excused absences, leaves of absence, late course withdrawals, faculty–student conflict, academic accommodations, missing graduation requirements and advising issues, and curricular substitutions. My position requires extensive communication and collaboration with campus constituencies, including the faculty, registrar, residential life, student account and financial aid services, admissions, and the provost's and president's offices. Working directly with me is a program assistant who has financial expertise, allowing us to jointly assist students navigating the complexities of academic progress and billing and loan issues. And physically we are housed with our dean of students, student conduct officers, and our Title IX coordinator because behavioral and health issues more often than not have implications for academic performance.

With that context, what follows is a sampling of issues I commonly deal with to illustrate that any journey through academia requires constant vigilance for ethical, moral, and legal pitfalls. Cameras are optional.

▶ Academic Integrity

Probably every college or university has a formal policy that frames the importance of academic integrity and offers guidelines for reporting and adjudicating violations. In spite of such policies and in spite of explicit efforts to educate students about the consequences of plagiarism, cheating, data fabrication, and the like, some students at some point in their academic program will still be accused of a policy violation. Perhaps cynically, I offer that the problem is never going to go away. And I dare say the problem isn't always just with students. On the flip side of student violations, I have heard of far too many alleged violations going unreported by faculty. This is as much an ethical lapse of judgment as the violation itself because it creates a situation in which some students are subject to formal procedures and sanctions and others are not. The most frequently heard excuses for not reporting violations are that formal procedures for hearing cases are too adversarial, too time consuming, and too emotionally draining, and that sanctions are either too harsh or not harsh enough. My institution struggled with this for years before crafting a new policy that, from a student perspective, focuses more on education than on punishment. Students are still held accountable for intentional violations of the policy, but they have greater opportunities to learn about making better choices. Faculty were given greater control over handing alleged violations without necessarily having to go through a formal hearing, allowing for less confrontational resolutions and sanctioning. Faculty are required to submit an electronic report of any violation and recommended outcome, and that is reviewed for consistency and fairness by my office. The key point to remember is that accountability for ensuring standards of integrity belongs jointly to students and faculty. Those who would undermine those standards, either by commission of a violation or by a blatant disregard of reporting and sanctioning processes, harm the educational mission of the institution.

▶ Federally Mandated Academic Accommodations

One might think there is little need to discuss compliance with federally mandated academic accommodations in an overview of ethical and legal issues in higher education, but indeed there is. To start, every campus receiving federal monies has professional staff dedicated to the oversight of legitimate academic accommodations. Those staff meet with students, process required documentation, and provide relevant information to professors about specific accommodations for specific students. Professors are expected to comply and maintain confidentiality. Most professors do those very things, but some fail to grasp the import of accommodations and therefore may undermine the process whether intentionally or unintentionally. Two quick examples of this include professors telling students they must take an exam in a classroom with others when the accommodation allows for proctored testing in a quiet and different setting and faculty restricting the use of technology in the classroom (e.g., laptops, cell phones) but explicitly exempting those with accommodations that allow the use of technology. Such things occur and persist even with reminders to faculty of their obligations, the availability of training and informational workshops, and feedback from explicit student complaints that I receive in my office. Failure to comply with federally mandated accommodations is an open invitation for a student to file a complaint with the Office for Civil Rights (OCR). And because an OCR complaint may have both personal and institutional repercussions, a college or university is obligated to protect students and educate faculty about what accommodations are for and why they so greatly matter.

▶ Title IX

Students' lives are a continually shifting amalgam of coursework, social relationships, financial concerns, and personal and family dynamics. That is undoubtedly an over-simplification, but our local organizational structure reflects the need and desire to provide integrated support services without regard to traditional and rigid divisional boundaries. As for Title IX specifically, I work closely with the coordinator to ensure academic support for students who report instances of sexual assault, harassment, or discrimination. That might entail meeting directly with students to discuss how an incident could affect their academic performance and class attendance; I reach out to faculty on behalf of students to document excused absences; and I have the authority to authorize late course withdrawals. While an allegation is being investigated, the responding party may also need assistance with these matters.

No one would ever dispute the need to provide broad support to anyone who discloses a legitimate Title IX incident. But what is important to be mindful of here is that support should not be confused with compromising academic standards or deviations from treating all students equally. Faculty members need to be flexible with, among other things, exam schedules, due dates, and absences—but not to a point where a student's learning of crucial skills or content is compromised. Likewise, students involved in Title IX cases, be they reporting parties or responding parties, need to be mindful that they are not absolved of fulfilling academic obligations. Balancing student needs, staff support, and faculty involvement requires sensitivity and strong, consistent communication. Title IX cases are by their nature fraught with significant legal implications, so my job is to minimize, to the greatest extent possible, disruptions or setbacks in a student's academic progress.

▶ Behavioral and Mental Health Issues

The newfound freedoms that await college students provide opportunities for growth and maturity, but they also offer windows of opportunity for a student to make poor behavioral choices. I am rarely directly involved in common rule-based infractions (e.g., underage drinking, drug use, residence hall violations) as these are competently handled by our professional conduct officers. When I am involved, it is as a student's advocate to ensure that outcomes of hearings and sanctions are fair and appropriate. But I do work frequently with our dean of students when behavioral issues, often with a significant mental health component, spill into the classroom. In some cases, a student's behavior may disrupt the learning environment for others. In extreme cases, a faculty member, students, and support staff may feel there is a legitimate threat to safety. Minor disruptions of the learning environment are typically resolved through a joint meeting with the student, myself, and the dean of students. We make it clear that repeated episodes are likely to have significant consequences because no one has the right to interfere with the instruction and learning of others. When any member of the university community feels threatened by student behavior, timeliness in responding is absolutely essential. In addition to myself and the dean of students, other members of our behavioral response team—university police, counseling center staff, conduct and residential life staff—are actively engaged in assessing the threat and responding with appropriate measures. With regard to threat assessment, we collectively must respect anyone's fears or concerns but must do so without violating the rights of the person deemed a threat. If a direct and intentional threat is not imminent, then we may also consult with university counsel on a case-by-case and as-needed basis to ensure that our interventions are suited to the context of an incident.

It is worth noting that the behavioral response team is, of necessity, sometimes reactive in its actions because as some threats have no clear warning signs. But because we also have a well-established formal reporting culture for concerns about students (academic and behavioral), the team, which meets regularly, can monitor, review, and intervene in cases before they rise to a more serious level.

▶ Student–Faculty Conflict: Classroom Management

Most of the conflicts between students and faculty that come to my attention are related to pedagogy, classroom management, and grades. It is not a surprise that many classroom management disputes are about inappropriate uses of technology. Smartphones and social media can be a toxic mix in a classroom, and faculty may have good reasons to want to minimize their influence during class time. More than a few faculty have approached me demanding that there be an institutional policy banning electronic devices in the classroom. I do my best to gently explain that getting a comprehensive and effective policy written, let alone passed by the faculty, is unlikely for many reasons. First, many students do use technology in the classroom for legitimate reasons (e.g., note-taking). Second, monitoring and policing the use of technology is burdensome and confrontational. Third, many faculty have been exceptionally creative in incorporating technology in their pedagogy. Last, students may have legitimate nonacademic needs to have access to their devices (e.g., for receipt of campus emergency alerts, for family or work-related issues). So instead of contemplating bans on technology or fretting about grandiose policies that will never see the light of day, faculty would be better served by engaging students directly in conversations about the proper place and use of technology in educational settings. Top-down, authoritative directives are probably going to prove ineffective in comparison to open and respectful conversations that engage students as active participants in shaping a classroom environment.

▶ Student–Faculty Conflict: Grades

The ubiquity of grade disputes makes it absolutely essential for any institution to have formal policies that ensure fairness in grading and articulate clear processes for resolving conflicts. More often than not, students, especially those not doing well in a course, ask about "extra credit" or submitting late work. Such pleas may also be accompanied by appeals designed to evoke faculty sympathy (e.g., "I'll lose my scholarship or financial aid," "I won't be able to participate in athletics," "I will be academically ineligible to register for future coursework"). Students probably don't realize that asking for special consideration means they are asking to be treated differently than other students. Most faculty are unswayed by such appeals even in the absence of any formal policy prohibiting special treatment, but I have had others approach me asking if it was OK to help a desperate student. In such cases, reminding faculty about the need to maintain fair and equitable grading standards—backed by formal policy—is sufficient for tempering their desire to help inappropriately.

For the most part, the preceding example is straightforward from a faculty perspective; it is not ethical to give selected students academic advantages not available to others. There are, however, more subtle ways faculty sometimes stray from sound grading principles. Students, for example, are entitled to know of all courses' assessments from the first day of a course. They have a right to know the weight of those assessments for the final grade. Those assessments should be graded in a timely manner, and students should receive appropriate feedback on assessments. When these things don't happen, students usually seek me out for help, and I do see a few cases each year. For example, I have been shown a syllabus that has an explicit no-tolerance policy for using the restroom during class but lacks a clear explanation for how homework assignments would be graded (it turned out those assignments weren't even collected). I have seen faculty tell students they must attend an event outside of class but make no provisions for cases where a student has a conflict with another obligation (e.g., another class, a job). I have been told directly by a faculty member that she doesn't "have time" to comment on student papers. And a final example: I mediated a case in which students in two different sections of the same course and taught by the same instructor received different final grades for identical scores. The instructor defended the practice by invoking "the curve made me do it." On behalf of the student, I took the matter to a grade appeals committee; panel members disagreed with the instructor.

As I tell students when they ask for help in resolving a grade dispute, a faculty member must be able to explicitly explain and adequately defend any assigned grade. It remains a mystery to me why some faculty, in spite of clear expectations for syllabus content and in spite of faculty-crafted policies about grading, nonetheless choose pathways that inevitably will lead to conflict. And in rare but not unheard of occurrences, that conflict can escalate to a point where senior administration and legal counsel need to be involved.

▶ Academic Advising

Effective academic advising is crucial for a student's understanding of all degree requirements and progress toward a degree. Students are, of course, responsible for knowing what their degree requirements are and where they stand at any given point in time. Toward this end, most institutions have sophisticated electronic tools (e.g., Degree Works) that allow students and advisers to precisely track what courses have been completed and what courses are outstanding. Many schools also have professional advisers and advising centers in addition to faculty advisers. So with dedicated staff and readily available tools to make advising uncomplicated, one might think this is an area that brings little traffic my way. To the contrary. I regularly deal with confusion and complaints about advisers and the advising process.

Why are there problems with advising? One prominent issue that I have expressed my discontent with for many years is curricular complexity. Certain majors have minimal requirements with lots of free electives. Advising in these programs is straightforward. Other programs are complicated and rigid with regard to structure, often leaving only a token free elective or two. This is an invitation to confusion and advising complications. Compounding this is the fact that faculty members frequently tinker with a curriculum. Courses are changed from three credits to four, new accreditation "requirements" invite curricular modifications, an external program review suggests a need for restructuring. . . . I could go on. I am not questioning the need for or value of curricular change. What I wish to stress is that when changes are made, faculty advisers are obligated to know the impact of those changes on students, especially with regard to their own majors. That doesn't always happen. In addition, sometimes curricular modification will necessitate that an institution make a reasonable accommodation for a student; that is, sometimes curricular exceptions or substitutions will need to be made, and a strong adviser knows what sorts of exceptions maintain the integrity of a program's requirements and what sorts ought not to be considered at all. Unfortunately, I have seen more than my fair share of proposed exceptions that make no sense, violate academic policy, or are not applied consistently to students. Often times, unreasonable exceptions are proposed because a faculty member wants to help a student. But a student is not helped when the vetting process for a curricular exception denies it. That is a source of student frustration and anger, frequently leading to the refrain of "My adviser said it was OK." Again, students are expected to be responsible for knowing their program requirements and should not passively accept the word of an adviser; but it is also incumbent on advisers to know their curricula and to be able to clearly explain it to a student, a parent, a staff member, or a colleague. Given the litigious proclivities of those who declare they have been poorly advised, institutions need to prioritize the importance of advising at all levels and hold poor advisers accountable for their mistakes.

▶ Freedom of Expression

Strident partisanship is a lamentable feature of contemporary American culture. One consequence of partisanship is an unwillingness to meaningfully engage the ideas of those who differ from you. This is a serious problem in local and national governance but is also, sadly, overtly creeping into higher education where there have been blatant attempts to vilify freedom of expression. High-profile cases have been documented at Evergreen State, Yale, Harvard, Williams, and Middlebury. The details across institutions may vary, but the overarching theme is that some students (and some faculty) don't like the ideas, politics, or facts of an invited speaker or a member of the university community—faculty, administrator, other students. When confronted with those with whom they disagree, some students (and some administrative and faculty enablers) employ tactics utterly at odds with the purpose and values of an institution of higher learning. Common are calls for the revocation of invitations to outside speakers, active disruptions of presentations, verbal and physical assaults against invited guests and sponsors, and, in cases involving employees, demands for their firing. The troubling reality is that in some cases these tactics are reinforced through institutional cowardice; administrators fail to denounce or hold accountable the perpetrators, and faculty fail to speak up on behalf of beleaguered colleagues.

The reasons for the rise of attacks on freedom of expression and inquiry are complicated, and others—for example, Lukianoff and Haidt (2018)—have provided thoughtful reviews of possible causes. But just as causes are multifaceted, stemming the anti-intellectual fervor of those too offended and too fragile to confront ideas head-on is neither simple nor straightforward. But it is worth noting that those who care deeply about the unfettered exchange of ideas can, at minimum, do two things. First, faculty and administrators can model appropriate responses to controversy. That entails listening to others with respect and confronting what one might deem "wrong" or "offensive" with rigorous counterclaims and evidence. Directly engaging with ideas is a far better way to display one's maturity and thought processes than closing oneself off from "them" by way of tantrums and force. Modeling intellectual exchange is an ethical imperative if higher education, already viewed unfavorably by many, is to sustain its preeminent status as a way of changing peoples' lives for the better. Students who have made their way to my office to report being offended in a classroom or other campus venue may or may not have a legitimate complaint. Supporting those with a genuine issue is essential. For those who simply don't like things they hear, I offer a respectful reminder that an education is of little value if it merely parrots and reinforces one's long-standing belief system, and that suppressing debate around controversial or unpopular ideas topics is an abdication of one's ethical responsibilities as a member of an academic community.

The second thing that might help is for faculty to reflect on how, when, and why they introduce politicized ideas into the classroom. For certain curricula, this is absolutely necessary and desirable. But some faculty members express their own partiality in such a way that students may feel they are constrained in expressing contrary opinions. It is not surprising that students perceive that those faculty members may allow their biases to affect their grading—and in some instances it has. A slightly different but related problem surfaces when faculty members stray from what they should be focusing on and intentionally introduce their own biases about topics that are irrelevant to course content. I have fielded complaints from students about faculty who opine on political candidates, judicial rulings, and the like when such topics are extraneous to a course. Faculty, when confronted about their biased presentations usually deny they have done anything untoward. But because human beings are keenly prone to self-deception, denial in the absence of a substantive rationale for politicizing the classroom is all the more reason to consider the possibility that students are on to something.

▶ Conclusion

The illustrative examples described in this article are but a partial sampling of things I have seen along the way in my journey through college professoring (and administrating). It truly has been a career path that could never have been predicted when I was in graduate school or starting out as a new assistant professor. It has been, however, a fortuitous redirection as it has deepened my understanding of and appreciation for the mundane problems, emerging crises, and emergencies that occur regularly as a part of university life. In my role, I cannot solve every problem that comes my way, nor can I always provide the answer that those who seek my support would like to hear. But I am grateful for the opportunity to try; it is the right thing to do.

▶ References

Kolstoe, O. P. (1975). *College professoring: Or through academia with gun and camera.* Carbondale, IL. Southern Illinois University Press.
Lukianoff, G., & Haidt, J. (2018). *The coddling of the American mind.* New York, NY: Penguin Press.

Addressing Plagiarism Among Undergraduate Students: It's Time to Adopt a Restorative Justice Approach

Robert Fitzpatrick

▶ Introduction

Taking credit for another's words, works, or ideas and claiming them as one's own is plagiarism, an ethical transgression not limited to students. Properly understood, plagiarism is always a moral breach. It is theft, and when it deprives the original author of potential income, it is also illegal. Whether intentional or unintentional, plagiarism has sullied the reputations of politicians, journalists, and authors, including at least one Pulitzer Prize winner. Sometimes, plagiarism is merely embarrassing, such as when First Lady Melania Trump addressed the 2016 Republican National Convention using passages from First Lady Michelle Obama's speech to the Democratic National Convention just four years earlier. But plagiarism can be far more serious, resulting in the loss of a reputation or the end of a career. It sometimes happens that authors intentionally or unintentionally plagiarize a copyrighted work. In these cases, the original author can justifiably seek damages—that is, a financial settlement. According to federal law, "The copyright owner is entitled to recover the actual damages suffered by him or her as a result of the infringement, and any profits of the infringer that are attributable to the infringement" (17 U.S. Code § 504(b)). Yet, despite repeated threats and warnings, many students don't view plagiarism as a moral offense at all (East, 2010), and those outside academia are likely to view the level of moral offense quite differently from those within it (Green, 2002).

The usual institutional response to academic plagiarism is to seek retributive justice—that is, punish the offender (Gullifer & Tyson, 2010). Plagiarists usually receive a failing grade for a course, or even expulsion—what one academic, Rebecca Moore Howard, has termed the "academic death penalty" (Blum, 2009, p. 20). Although this author has no intention of downplaying the seriousness of plagiarism, these extreme penalties need to be recognized as an outdated legacy handed down through years of unquestioned policy and tradition. In almost all undergraduate academic settings, punishment is of no use to the original authors and does nothing to educate offenders about the essential role careful research plays in the advancement of knowledge. It's time to look at plagiarism from the points of view of the faculty and the student and to reconsider how to deal with this increasing problem (McCabe & Treviño, 2002). In this article we argue for the replacement of the current negative retributive justice approach with a positive restorative justice model. This model will help address a more important issue: that even though students may understand they shouldn't plagiarize, they don't understand why it matters (Power, 2009; Voelker, Love, & Pentina, 2012).

▶ The Moral Basis for Plagiarism Punishments

Plagiarism encompasses a spectrum of behavior from an innocent mistake to intentional cheating. For example, a student who misattributes or fails to attribute a direct quotation may be merely ignorant or careless. However, a student who buys or copies an entire paper and passes it off as his or her own is intentionally cheating by misrepresenting his or her knowledge and ability.

At the most obvious level, the academic degree awarded to a plagiarist is a lie. An employer justifiably interprets a college degree as assurance of knowledge and skill. When the employee is discovered not to have that knowledge or skill, both the employee and the institution suffer damage to their reputations. A doubt is planted in the employer's mind that perhaps graduates of that institution are not to be trusted. One student can put into doubt the worth of all of the institution's graduates.

Retributive Justice

Most colleges and universities appear to assume cases of plagiarism are the result of students' deliberate intention to plagiarize or their deliberate indifference to plagiarizing. In an informal look at policies from academic institutions in each of the 50 states, the author found only one example, the University of Notre Dame, at which the penalty for plagiarism did not focus on retributive justice. Nearly all policies dictate that the student be sent to an academic integrity panel that functions to find guilt and assign punishment. Generally, the academic world appears to view plagiarism as a moral issue of right or wrong.

Kohlberg's Levels of Moral Development

The current academic reaction to plagiarism may only have validity for students who believe they have committed a moral transgression—an attitude that we might assume is held by many but surely not by all students. Julianne East may have been among the first to discuss Kohlberg's levels of moral development in relation to student attitudes toward plagiarism (2010). Kohlberg's theory (1973) describes three levels of moral self-awareness that describe offenders.

TABLE 50.1 Kohlberg's Levels of Moral Development				
Level of Moral Self-Awareness	**Behavior**	**Seeks**	**Avoids**	**Perceived Victim**
Preconventional	Selfish; often contrary to the expectations of society; no moral principle	Personal gratification	Being caught or punished	Someone else
Conventional	Normative; conforms to the expectations of society	Fitting into the social contract of acceptable behavior	The negative perception of others	The social order
Postconventional	Autonomous; principled	To live up to a personal moral code	Personal dishonor	Self

This table is an adaptation of the ideas described in "Kohlberg, L. (1973). The claim to moral adequacy of a highest stage of moral judgement. *Journal of Philosophy, 70*(18). p. 65.

If we were willing to accept the premise that all students believe they have committed a moral transgression by plagiarizing, we could match Kohlberg's three levels to the three possible student attitudes shown in **TABLE 50.1**. The preconventional level can be used to describe students who might be deterred from plagiarizing because of their fear of being caught and punished. The conventional level describes students who might be deterred from plagiarism by their belief that students should operate within the accepted social understanding that plagiarism is wrong. Finally, the postconventional level describes students who believe plagiarizing would violate their personal moral codes.

Assuming students recognize that plagiarism is a moral wrong, current penalties and practices used to deter plagiarism can be neatly matched to Kohlberg's model: (1) failure or expulsion is designed to scare the *preconventional* character; (2) preaching that plagiarism is simply not acceptable in academic society helps deter plagiarism by the *conventional* character; and (3) honor codes curb plagiarism (Sledge & Pringle, 2010) by appealing to the *postconventional* character. But are any of these levels valid predictors of behavior if offenders truly don't understand or believe they are doing anything wrong?

▶ Reconsidering Plagiarism as a Moral Transgression

It's a surprising fact that when it comes to plagiarism: professors don't agree on a clear definition of where to draw the line between influence and theft. Students receive confusing and contradictory instruction about what constitutes plagiarism (Blum, 2009;

Gullifer & Tyson, 2010). Nevertheless, based on our informal review of academic integrity policies, faculty members do appear to agree on, or at least don't feel inclined to question, extreme penalties for transgressors. But, as with most important issues, plagiarism is rarely black or white. The shades of gray are countless, and punishment might be the worst way to address most of them (Gullifer & Tyson, 2010).

Key points in determining guilt in plagiarism are intention and indifference (Blum, 2009). Students who intentionally steal ideas or text from others to avoid doing the assigned work or those who just don't care if they cheat, are, under most academic policies, equally culpable of an offense deserving a retributive response. Intent and indifference are also discussed by Green in his article about the legal perspective of plagiarism:

> If theft requires intent, and plagiarism derives much of its meaning from theft law, it seems to follow that plagiarism should also require intent. At the same time, I would modify this requirement to say that the element of intent can be satisfied by "deliberate indifference" to the obligation to attribute. That is, if the reason a person was unaware that he was copying or failing to attribute is that he was deliberately indifferent to the requirements of attribution, he should be viewed as having committed plagiarism. (Green, 2002, p. 182)

It's this point—that students somehow know that plagiarism is a moral offense—that justifies academia's hard stance. It appears that many institutions simply believe all students fall into Kohlberg's first stage of moral development: They have no moral principle. As a result, they employ retributive justice as a deterrent and threaten those who might dare to transgress with extreme penalties.

A Cultural Rather than a Moral Offense

But what if plagiarism isn't a moral offense? Jeroen Van Broeck provides a useful definition for considering plagiarism as a cultural offense:

> A cultural offence is an act by a member of a minority culture, which is considered an offence by the legal system of the dominant culture. That same act is nevertheless, within the cultural group of the offender, condoned, accepted as normal behavior and approved or even endorsed and promoted in the given situation. (Van-Boreck, 2001, p. 5)

For example, among many people in Tanzania, there is such a strong fear of albinos that the minority culture (in this case, the group without political power) encourages the practice of killing albino babies because they are believed to have supernatural powers that will inevitably be used for evil purposes when they grow older. Most Tanzanians cannot understand why the dominant culture, the government and the legal system, wants to end this age-old tradition. The practice persists despite efforts to stop it (Byrnes, 2014).

Although this example is admittedly extreme, it might be useful to view students and faculty as members of the minority and dominant cultures, respectively. The following quote briefly explains the divide:

> Students and lecturers can have different understandings of plagiarism. . . .
> [One researcher] positions lecturers on the moral high ground and claims

that lecturers understand plagiarism as a breach of trust undermining academic traditions, while students prioritize success as more important than avoiding plagiarism. (East, 2010, p. 71)

But why do faculty members react so strongly to plagiarism? To answer this question, we have to look at the cultural differences between faculty and students.

The Faculty Culture Point of View

Faculty members cherish a culture of knowledge and intellectual property, but their work doesn't have the same legal protections of, for example, a property owner. Real estate developers have property deeds providing legal protection from any conceivable manner by which their investments might be stolen or destroyed—for example, trespassers, lease violators, and arsonists. Society views such property infringements as financial losses, and a real estate developer can collect damages for such violations. However, when it comes to words, artistic works, or ideas, the concept of ownership is radically different. In the academic world, authors may also *own* their published words—as noted earlier, however, there is no law against plagiarism. It requires effort for authors to protect their ideas. The legal system will help authors only if they can prove particular instances of plagiarism violate their copyrights and cause damage in the form of lost income or harm to their reputations. The reticence to legislate the ownership of ideas is easy to understand. Unlike physical property, ideas flow into each other as streams flow into rivers. How do you identify the origin of a single drop of water in a wide river?

Nevertheless, it's by the association of an author with his or her ideas that a faculty member builds a reputation and rises in the academic ranks from lowly lecturer to full professor. Reputations and careers depend in large part on their publications. Therefore, an academic's ideas and publications are a most essential marker of status in the academic world; by providing a glimpse into the mind of the academic, publications have a particularly revered status.

As a reaction against plagiarism, an academic's respect for a fellow author's work eventually became (along with not falsifying research data) one of the most important ethical constructs of the academic world. Before the Internet, it took centuries for the academic world to build its own protective ethos against plagiarism. For most of the time there have been scholars, information was scarce and access to it was difficult. In the 15th century, for example, if an unscrupulous scholar stole an unknown work he happened on in an obscure library in a foreign country, he might easily translate that work, publish it in his own country under his own name, and likely never be discovered. Today, by contrast, discovering a plagiarist often only requires a suspicious reader and a Google search.

The Student Culture Viewpoint

From 1963 to 2003, several surveys have found around half of college students admit to copying a few sentences from written sources without appropriate citations (McCabe, Butterfield, & Treviño, 2004). There can be little doubt that the Internet has changed perspectives about what might constitute plagiarism or copyright infringement. The ease with which one can copy music, images, and text makes it difficult for the original authors to maintain control over their property (Aatonen & Salmi, 2013; Green, 2002).

Neutralization Theory

It is useful to examine student attitudes regarding plagiarism using the rationalizations described by Sykes and Matza in their 1957 article "Techniques of Neutralization: A Theory of Delinquency." These authors argue that a transgressor who commits a crime against society "frequently exhibits guilt or shame when he violates its proscription" (1957, p. 666). Offenders know they're wrong but have to rationalize their behavior to continue feeling good about their place in the social structure. In accord with neutralization theory, students usually seek to deny, or rationalize, personal responsibility for plagiarism using a variety

TABLE 50.2 Neutralization Theory: Rationalizations and Common Student Examples

Rationalization	Common Student Example
(1) Denial of responsibility: "By learning to view himself as more acted upon than acting, the delinquent prepares the way for deviance from the dominant normative system without the necessity of a frontal assault on the norms themselves" (Sykes & Matza, 1957, p. 667).	"We weren't given enough time to do the assignment."
(2) Denial of injury: The offender "[f]eels that his behavior does not really cause any great harm despite the fact that it runs counter to law" (Sykes & Matza, 1957, p. 667).	"I'm paying for this course. I can do whatever I want."
(3) Denial of the victim: The offender sees the offense as "a form of rightful retaliation" (Sykes & Matza, 1957, p. 668).	"This course is a waste of time. I'm only taking this because they say I need this for my general education requirement."
(4) Condemnation of the condemners: "The delinquent shifts the focus of attention from his own deviant acts to the motives and behavior of those who disapprove of his violation" (Sykes & Matza, 1957, p. 668).	"That professor can't teach. He doesn't know what he's doing."
(5) The appeal to higher loyalties: "[I]nternal and external social controls may be neutralized by sacrificing the demands of the larger society for the demands of the smaller social groups to which the delinquent belongs" (Sykes & Matza, 1957, p. 668).	"I let my roommate copy my paper because he will lose his scholarship if he fails."

This table is derived from Sykes, G. M., & Matza, D. (1957), Techniques of neutralization: A theory of delinquency. *American Sociological Review, 22*(6), 664–670.

of arguments. Most of these rationalizations have some validity within the student culture.

Sykes and Matza argue that "much delinquency is based on what is essentially an unrecognized extension of defenses to crimes, in the form of justifications for deviance that are seen as *valid by the delinquent but not by the legal system or society at large*" [emphasis added] (1957, p. 666). In this case, plagiarism is the deviant behavior the student seeks to justify.

Neutralization theory offers five rationalizations for illegal or unethical behavior: (1) denial of responsibility, (2) denial of injury, (3) denial of the victim, (4) condemnation of the condemners, and (5) appeal to higher loyalties (Sykes & Matza, 1957).

A justification for plagiarism implies an understanding of right and wrong with regard to what level of use of the ideas of another is acceptable without proper attribution. To the student who is not skilled at evaluating information sources, the Internet seems to provide information as definitively and as efficiently as a light bulb dispels total darkness. The landscape is floodlit by information. There is, in fact, so much information that many students find it difficult to see any particular value in information beyond its utility in accomplishing their personal academic goal: a degree. The analogy of streams feeding into a river is again useful here. Because information is now so plentiful and readily available, it is hard for students to care if the information has a relevant origin—let alone value. For many in the student culture, the lack of value of information beyond its immediate utility seems so obvious that it's difficult, or meaningless, to make the effort of seeing information from the point of view of the faculty culture.

▶ Seeking Common Ground

Undergraduate writing assignments are in part intended to train students how to intelligently and responsibly take part in the academic conversation, a conversation based on facts and previous scholarship. Credit for a fact or an idea is as important for the scholar as a deed is for a property owner. The ability to trace an idea back to its origin is often vital to scholarly progress, and it's an essential tool for the reader who may wish to look deeper into issues raised by the author. As we have seen, academia grounds its retributive justice approach on the premise that students have committed a moral wrong that justifies the academic world to take revenge for a moral transgression. The current approach assumes most students exist on the pre-conventional level of Kohlberg's moral hierarchy. It also assumes that students are aware of their transgression when plagiarizing and seek to rationalize their act in keeping with neutralization theory. But what if plagiarism isn't a moral issue? What if the social and information landscapes have changed to the extent that students have real difficulty seeing the issue of plagiarism from the cultural standpoint of the faculty? This difficulty doesn't justify plagiarism, but it does mean that more of an effort needs to be made to have students understand what plagiarism is and why it's not acceptable. For the current retributive justice approach to make sense, both cultures would have to agree that plagiarism is a moral issue. How is it possible to effectively address plagiarism if the offender and the victim have such culturally opposing views?

On one hand, students receive confusing instruction about what constitutes plagiarism. In her book, *My Word! Plagiarism and College Culture*, Suzan Blum succinctly summarizes the students' viewpoint:

> I think we do an injustice to students by overlooking the genuinely contentious nature of citation. By pretending that the standards are firm and fixed—despite students' experience of often getting very different instructions from different professors, sometimes within the same department— we reject an educational opportunity and force students to conclude, on their own, that the rules don't make any sense. That makes it easier for them to disregard them entirely. (2009, p. 15)

As this quote implies, all faculty members assume everyone in their culture agrees on a single and well-understood definition of plagiarism. But even if faculty don't agree on a clear definition of plagiarism, the *belief* of a single definition is well established in the academic culture, and faculty members may assume students are equally aware and share their antipathy for it. In reality, they do not, and numerous studies have documented students' varied perceptions of plagiarism (Gullifer & Tyson, 2010).

Plagiarism and Education

The concept of plagiarism is so horrific within the faculty culture that many may feel uncomfortable talking about it. In some cases, faculty members don't mention it because they don't want to appear to be threatening their students. So, faculty treat the instruction of plagiarism in a variety of ways. Approaches to plagiarism run the gamut from not mentioning it at all to referring to the policy in the syllabus to making students sign honesty pledges. Most often, faculty members assume the matter was taught somewhere else such as in a required English composition course or in a first-year seminar.

▶ Rethinking Ways to Address Plagiarism

The inspiration for the content of the following section came from an article by Farzana Kara and David MacAlister, "Responding to Academic Dishonesty in Universities: A Restorative Justice Approach" (Kara & MacAlister, 2010). It's easy to say plagiarism is wrong, but it's not always as easy to say what plagiarism is. There are many shades of gray.

Years of experience chairing academic integrity panels have made it clear to the author that the retributive model is unsatisfying and unproductive for both victims and offenders. In many instances, however, institutional policy requires faculty to bring cases of plagiarism before an academic integrity panel. The victim, the professor, is then essentially removed from the process and becomes a spectator as the offender is found guilty and punished. In cases of deliberate plagiarism or deliberate indifference, a punitive policy might be appropriate. But in the many cases where intent is more difficult to determine, retribution is unsatisfactory for the professor and uninstructive for the student. The retributive reaction effectively ends the possibility of positive interaction between the student and the faculty member. That door closes when the panel decides that the student must fail the assignment or the course. The policy doesn't allow for the victim professor to intervene on behalf of the offender student, nor does it allow the student to learn much beyond being more careful not to get caught. Retribution is, in fact, contrary to education.

The Restorative Justice Approach

Howard Zehr and Mark Umbreit were the first to articulate four stages or elements of restorative justice (Zehr & Umbreit, 1982): (1) the victim experience, (2) restitution, (3) offender accountability, and (4) mediation.

Faranza Kara and David McAlister (2010) have shown how well this approach works when addressing academic plagiarism. Notice how well these stages work in relation to the issues covered in this article.

TABLE 50.3 Using the Restorative Justice Model to Address Plagiarism Infractions

Components of Restorative Justice	Desired Outcomes	Relationship to Ideas Discussed in This Article
The victim experience	Resolution process gives the professor victim a voice to explain how he or she has been wronged. Allows the professor victim to explain why this particular example of plagiarism is an offense.	Cultural offense vs. moral offense
Restitution	Student offender comes to a respectful understanding of the point of view of the professor victim. The offender comes to understand that a moral transgression has been committed that personally affects a professor victim.	Kohlberg's levels of moral development
Offender accountability	The student offender comes to understand that the rationalizations expressed in neutralization theory have no validity. The offender comes to realize restitution is warranted.	Neutralization theory
Mediation	Victim, offender, and mediator meet to discuss the seriousness of this particular offense and to plan for a fair and commensurate resolution.	Retributive vs. restorative justice

This table is built on the ideas of restorative justice as outlined by Zehr, H., & Umbreit, M. (1982). Victim offender reconciliation: An incarceration substitute? *Federal Probation: A Journal of Correctional Philosophy and Practice, 46*(4), 64–68.

The Victim Experience

As we have seen, the dominant faculty culture views plagiarism as a crime against the most sacred tenet of education—the sanctity of research and the principle of giving credit to the originators of knowledge. The accusing faculty member is forced into the role of passive victim. As the harshness of current penalties indicate, plagiarism is the ultimate crime against knowledge for which there is only one sentence, "the academic death penalty." Yet it's difficult to imagine that the offender has any awareness of the magnitude of his offense. Although Zehr and Umbreit were writing about crime, they well describe the goal of the dominant culture: Punish the offender: "As one judge put it, 'I don't care what the victim or offender needs or wants, this crime . . . was against the state, and I'll take care of it as I see fit'" (Zehr & Umbreit, 1982, p. 64). Zehr and Umbreit point out that this harsh attitude ignores the fact that the crime, as in the case of plagiarism, is not understood by the student as a crime against the "state." It is more personal; it's an offense involving a victim professor who, we will assume, is in good faith trying to fulfill the role of educator. The offender student, perhaps unknowingly, has subverted this effort, and by doing so has offended the goal of education. More personally, he or she has caused an affront to the professor. Again, Zehr and Umbreit state it well when they say, "victims need to be given a voice and listened to if they are to experience that restoration of power which is necessary for psychological wholeness" (1982, p. 64).

Restitution

Zehr and Umbreit (1982) list restitution as the second requirement for restorative justice. This presents a special problem if the plagiarist genuinely doesn't believe an injustice has been committed. For example, if a delinquent steals a watch, he probably realizes this is an act against the dominant culture. Society hopes guilt might compel him to make restitution by returning the watch to its owner. As we have seen, in the academic or dominant culture, the view of plagiarism is that it is a crime against the most sacred tenet of education—the sanctity of research and the principle of giving credit to the originators of knowledge. Consider Kohlberg's three stages of moral development. At the preconventional stage, the offender may have stolen the watch for selfish reasons and been willing to take the risk. At the conventional level, the offender will understand that he has transgressed against the expectations of society. And at the postconventional level, the thief would have realized that stealing the watch was a crime not only against the owner but also against his personal code of behavior. The faculty member is looking for restitution in the form of having the student realize that plagiarism is theft, and that the student owes it to the original author and, in fact, to the highest academic principles, to understand this.

Offender Accountability

If offenders are truly not aware of an offense, it will be difficult to hold them accountable. "To commit offenses and live with their behavior, offenders, like the rest of us, often construct elaborate rationalizations about their actions and employ stereotypes about the persons involved" (Zehr & Umbreit, 1982, p. 65). It is unlikely that students, whose first inclination will be to justify their behavior as described in the theory of neutralization, has the slightest conception of the magnitude of the offense as seen from a professor's point of view. The gap between the cultures is great indeed. Mediation will be required to guide students into an understanding of their accountability and that restitution is necessary.

Mediation

As a final stage of the restorative justice model, a disinterested third party, the faculty member, and the student meet to discuss the transgression. It is hoped that at this meeting, the offender will see the transgression from the viewpoint of the victim. What's more important, however, is that both the victim and the offender will have the opportunity to discuss what went wrong, why it matters, and how to avoid a repetition of the offense. The mediator helps ensure a fair discussion and an equitable solution. Zehr and Umbreit describe the most promising outcome: "Stereotypes about offenders may be laid to rest, resulting not only in greater understanding of the offender but also reduced anxiety and suspicion for the victim" (1982, p. 66).

Much has been said in this article about stereotypical students and their rationalization of plagiarism. Through restorative justice, however, Howard Zehr and Mark Umbreit may have a more positive approach to dealing with the problem. As they have pointed out, "Nothing in our criminal process ever challenges those rationalizations and stereotypes. Offenders are rarely made to see the real human costs of what they have done. . . . Real accountability includes an opportunity to understand the human consequence of one's acts" (1982, p. 65).

▶ Conclusion

In this article, we have seen how the current practice of retributive justice widens the divide between faculty and student cultures. In cases of plagiarism, the current practice of retributive justice serves only to separate students from the learning experience. By refusing to listen to the student, retributive justice encourages an attitude of contempt of the educational goals the professor hopes to accomplish in assigning a research project.

When the only outcome of many of the current cases of plagiarism is failure or expulsion, it slams the door on further educational progress. Retributive justice has as its one goal the branding of students as intellectual outlaws as described in Kohlberg's preconventional level. The plagiarizer is seen as an immoral, self-serving agent intent on personal gratification whose only motivation toward acceptable behavior is the fear of being caught. Retributive justice reinforces the idea that the professor merely wants to catch students doing something wrong and then punish them. This attitude can lead only to the rationalizations described by neutralization theory.

Restorative justice, however, provides an opportunity to impress on even the most recalcitrant student the idea that his or her intellectual contributions are valid, important, and, most important of all, worth correcting when necessary. Restorative justice encourages students to see the value of a research assignment and to develop respect for the efforts of fellow scholars. Through restorative justice, students might be led to the understanding that a moral wrong has been committed against the professor and against scholarship. It opens a dialogue between the professor and the student that has the potential for great psychological healing between the two.

Students who have plagiarized are given an opportunity to see that their research papers are valid training for participation in the world of honest, intellectual dialogue. Restorative justice aims to bring students into an understanding of how careful research and citation practices contribute to the progress of knowledge and that their efforts should merit respectful consideration from their professors and, even more important, from themselves. Restorative justice promotes the idea that scholarship is a conversation in which they may take an active and responsible part.

Ideally, the faculty culture should be more aware of teaching the *why* of careful citation, but when students miss this point, a restorative justice approach to remediation can create an opportunity for students to realize the value of careful research to their own development as educated citizens who can accurately trace support for their opinions and decisions to verifiable, published facts.

Of course, there is no way to guarantee restorative justice will achieve the goals outlined in this article. Surely, when it is successful, the effort is more worthy of both faculty and students and of the educational enterprise. The "academic death penalty" should be reserved for the indifferent, repeat offender.

▶ Author Note

The author is grateful to Plymouth State University criminal justice student Garrett Hall and his librarian colleagues, Professors Christin Wixson and Alice Pearman, for sharing their thoughts and reviewing this manuscript before submission for publication consideration.

▶ References

Aatonen, M., & Salmi, V. (2013). Versatile delinquents or specialized pirates? A comparison of corelates of illegal downloading and traditional juvenile crime. *Journal of Scandinavian Studies in Criminology and Crime Prevention, 14*(2), 188–195. doi:10.1080/14043858.2013.837267

Blum, S. D. (2009). *My word! Plagiarism and college culture.* Ithaca, NY: Cornell University.

Byrnes, E. (2014). Albinism myths persist. *New Internationalist, 476,* 10.

East, J. (2010). Judging plagiarism: A problem of morality and convention. *Higher Education, 59*(1), 69–83.

Green, S. P. (2002). Plagiarism, norms, and the limits of theft law: Some observations on the use of criminal sanctions in enforcing intellectual property rights. *Hastings Law Journal, 54,* 167–242.

Gullifer, J., & Tyson, G. A. (2010). Exploring university students' perceptions of plagiarism; A focus group study. *Studies in Higher Education, 35*(4), 463–481.

Kara, F., & MacAlister, D. (2010). Responding to academic dishonesty in universities: A restorative justice approach. *Contemporary Justice Review, 13*(4), 443–453.

Kohlberg, L. (1973). The claim to moral adequacy of a highest stage of moral judgement. *Journal of Philosophy, 70*(18), 630–646.

McCabe, D. L., Butterfield, K. D., & Treviño, L. K. (2004). Academic integrity: How widespread is cheating and plagiarism? In D. R. Karp, & T. Allena (Eds.), *Restorative justice on the college campus: Promoting student growth and responsibility, and reawakening the spirit of campus community* (pp. 124–135). Springfield, IL: Charles C. Thomas.

McCabe, D., & Treviño, L. K. (2002). Honesty and honor codes. *Academe, 88*(1), 37–41.

Power, L. (2009). University students' perceptions of plagiarism. *Journal of Higher Education, 80*(6), 643–662.

Sledge, S., & Pringle, P. (2010). Assessing honor code effectiveness: Results of a multipronged approach from a five year study. *Research & Practice in Assessment, 5,* 4–15.

Sykes, G. M., & Matza, D. (1957). Techniques of neutralization: A theory of delinquency. *American Sociological Review, 22*(6), 664–670.

Van-Boreck, J. (2001). Cultural defense and culturally motivated crimes. *European Journal of Crime, Criminal Law & Criminal Justice, 9*(1), 1–32.

Voelker, T. A., Love, L. G., & Pentina, I. (2012). Plagiarism: What don't they know? *Journal of Education for Business, 87*(1), 36–41.

Zehr, H., & Umbreit, M. (1982). Victim offender reconciliation: An incarceration substitute? *Federal Probation: A Journal of Correctional Philosophy and Practice, 46*(4), 64–68.

ARTICLE 51

The Problem of Title IX

Kathryn Elvey

▶ Introduction

Gender equality may seem like a no-brainer. Few educated people in America today would argue that men and women are not equal. Furthermore, few would argue that men and women do not deserve the same access to education. However, this has not always been the case. It was not until 1837 that Oberlin College became the first institution of higher learning to admit women (Lapidus, Martin, & Luthara, 2009), and even though many advances have been made since 1837, many issues of sexism still linger in higher education. To combat issues in sexism, many laws and statutes—at the federal, state, and even university levels—have been passed since 1837 to help advance women in higher education. One such law that is consistently discussed is Title IX.

Title IX of the Education Amendments of 1972 (2018) states:

> No person in the United States shall, on the basis of sex, be excluded in, be denied the benefits of, or be subject to discrimination under any education program or activity receiving Federal financial assistance.

In other words, universities—public or private—that receive federal funding are not allowed to discriminate based on gender. This provision applies to *all* programs and activities that are provided by a university for their students beyond just education, including sports and clubs. Although this rule may sound fairly straightforward, it has led to some of most controversial issues across colleges and universities nationwide.

The implications for Title IX are far reaching. Most recently, Title IX has been applied to issues concerning sexual victimization and how colleges have responded to these accusations. Although this article will focus on issues surrounding sexual victimization and how Title IX has been used to combat those issues, it will also discuss how Title IX highlights issues in theory versus practice, due process rights and the burden of proof in the U.S. legal system, and the constantly changing legal and university systems. All of these issues are intimately related to the college student population and affect their lives daily, whether they realize it or not.

▶ History of Title IX

Although Title IX is probably most well known for its implications concerning sports programs, it was not originally meant to be applied to sports. It was intended to be a means by which women and men could achieve equal access to education (Schwarz, 2104). At the time the legislation was being debated, Senator John Tower of Texas wanted to create an amendment to Title IX that excluded sports from the legislation; it was aptly named the Tower Amendment (Schwarz, 2014). However, the Tower Amendment did not pass; in its place, Senator Jacob Javits of New York recommended a set of regulations for "intercollegiate athletic activities" (Javits Amendment, 1974). The amendment provided that men and women have their needs met regarding sports at institutions provided that "reasonable provisions considering the nature of particular sports" are attended to (Javits Amendment, 1974; Schwarz, 2014).

Title IX proved pivotal to the acceleration and and growth of women's sports programs across universities throughout the country. As an example, between 1972, the year Title IX was passed, and the first Women's World Cup in 1991, soccer saw a 17,000% increase in female participants (Donegan, 2019). Many people have attributed the popularity and success of women's soccer in the United States to Title IX and the role it played in creating equality across sports at the college level (Butler, 2019; Donegan, 2019).

▶ Sexual Victimization and Title IX

However, as time has passed, Title IX has been used as a means to ensure equal access to not just sports but also to education in the face of sexual victimization. In April 2011, the Obama administration through the Department of Education's Office for Civil Rights (OCR), released its "Dear Colleague Letter" (Ali, 2011). The letter asserted that "[s]exual harassment of students, which includes acts of sexual violence, is a form of sex discrimination prohibited by Title IX" (p. 1). The letter went on to tell universities how they must handle reported cases of sexual victimization; if they failed to abide by these procedures, they would lose all federal funding. Some of the controversial conditions that the letter outlined included that cases be handled using the evidentiary standard of a preponderance of the evidence (pp. 10–11), and it strongly discouraged cross-examination (p. 12). Furthermore, universities began to dispense with "live" hearings and instead followed "a single-investigator model," by which the investigator of the case would rule on the outcome after collecting evidence without a hearing (Bartholet, Gertner, Halley, & Gersen, 2017; Creeley, 2016; Joyce, 2017).

It is important to explain why these items are considered so controversial to some people: They limit the rights of the accused and seemingly do not consider a presumption of innocence. First, the evidentiary standard of preponderance of the evidence was defined in the Dear Colleague Letter as being "more likely than not that sexual harassment or violence occurred" (Ali, 2011, p. 11). This standard is compared to "clear and convincing evidence," which was defined as being "highly probable or reasonably certain that the sexual harassment or violence occurred"

(Ali, 2011, p. 11). This means that the investigator only has to be slightly more than 50% sure that an act of sexual victimization took place for the accused to be found guilty.

Second, by discouraging cross-examination, the Dear Colleague Letter made it so that the accused could not confront or question their accusers. The Dear Colleague Letter explained that there could be irreparable physiological and emotional harm done to the accuser if she or he had to confront the person who allegedly assaulted them (Ali, 2011, p. 12). However, some people (Bartholet et al., 2017; Creeley, 2016; Joyce, 2017; Rudovsky et al., 2015) contend that this flies in the face of due process rights such as those established in the Sixth and 14th Amendments, which gives the accused the right to face an accuser.

Finally, after the Dear Colleague Letter, many universities adopted the single-investigator model to examine accusations of sexual misconduct. The single-investigator model allowed one person to collect evidence, conduct interviews, and then make a decision on the guilt or innocence of the accused after fact-finding was completed. This model would make "the investigator all powerful" (Bartholet et al., 2017, p. 3). The problem with this model is that the accused have no way of knowing what evidence was collected against them, what was said about them, or what facts may have come to light; therefore, there was no way to refute or explain claims made against them.

Then in 2014 the Department of Education Office for Civil Rights went a step further releasing "Questions and Answers on Title IX and Sexual Violence" (Lhamon, 2014). This 2014 letter was meant to address specific issues that arose from the perceived lack of clarity in the Dear Colleague Letter (Ali, 2011) as well as to address concrete steps universities can take to institute prevention and intervention measures to help protect students from sexual violence.

As a result of the release of the Dear Colleague Letter (Ali, 2011) and the 2014 letter (Lhamon), universities began to react with "panicked over compliance" (Gersen, 2019, p. 1) in the face of losing funding. This was described as schools being "instructed, under penalty of potentially losing federal funds, to take a very aggressive approach to investigating alleged assaults and harassment" (Singal, 2017, para. 2). Furthermore, it created confusion in the face of enforcement, "producing deeply weird and troubling unintended consequences" (Singal, 2017, para. 3). Thousands of students were tried and punished for sexual misconduct on their campuses. This then resulted in hundreds of lawsuits being brought against universities by accused students, who claimed the universities were biased against males and had failed to provide them their due process rights (Joyce, 2017).

In 2016, Donald Trump was elected as president of the United States and appointed Betsy DeVos to be secretary of education. Under DeVos, the Department of Education's Office for Civil Rights rescinded the Dear Colleague Letter as well as the 2014 Questions and Answer Letters in September 2017 (Jackson, 2017). In rescinding these letters, the Department of Education noted that although both letters were well intentioned, they led to issues in which "schools face a confusing and counterproductive set of regulatory mandates, and the objective of regulatory compliance has displaced Title IX's goal of educational equity" (Jackson, 2017, p. 2).

Then at the end of 2018, DeVos and the Department of Education released proposed rule changes to Title IX. The rule changes directly addressed the issues discussed here. First, the proposed rule changes stated that universities could use either preponderance of the evidence or the standard of clear and convincing evidence. However, a college can use only the preponderance standard if it uses that standard for other conduct code violations (Department of Education, 2018). For example, if a student was to be brought forth on allegations of assault, the university would have to use a preponderance of the evidence in its hearing. Second, schools would be required to have a live hearing as well as require cross-examination. Finally, schools would not be allowed to use a single-investigator model (Department of Education, 2018). Some of these changes have been hailed as a success in terms of due process rights for those accused of committing sexual crimes, but some people have called this a giant step backward in terms of protecting victims of sexual violence (Gersen, 2019; Smith, 2019).

In addition, the rule proposed by DeVos would not require schools to investigate or respond to allegations of sexual misconduct that took place off school grounds (Department of Education, 2018). The Obama-era regulations required that these off-campus allegations between two students be addressed on campus (Ali, 2011; Lhamon, 2014). Opponents to this rule change contend this can create issues for victims of sexual violence where they are now required to attend class or possibly even live in the same building as their offenders; clearly, this could lead to intimidation as well as emotional and psychological distress (Ali, 2011; Gersen, 2019; Smith, 2019).

▶ Theory Versus Practice

Although there is no question that sexual victimization on college campuses should be investigated and prevented, the question arises about the application of Title IX. Some people did not feel as though Title IX was the correct law under which schools should be required to adjudicate students, stating there was no legal basis for making these claims (Lankford, 2016; Rudovsky et al., 2015). Furthermore, what was originally "well intentioned" did not secure the rights of all parties involved and appeared to support a model of guilty until proven innocent (Bartholet et al., 2017; Department of Education, 2018). The issue at hand is that implementing laws is easier than completely understanding their ramifications. Many legal rulings and policy implementations at the federal, state, and even university levels are well intentioned, but how they actually play out can result in unforeseen consequences. In the case of Title IX, these consequences can be life altering for either victims or accused offenders. Under both the Obama-era regulations and the new DeVos rules, individuals on both sides of the debate are critical of one another.

It is easy to criticize both mandates for their shortcomings, whether protecting the rights of victims or of the accused (Gersen, 2019; Smith, 2019). However, the nuances of laws and policies can be difficult to understand. One resolution that has been recommended to address Title IX issues is that all sexual victimization cases be turned over to the police (Joyce, 2017). Since 2013, at least six states and Congress have considered bills that would require some type of law enforcement reporting (Brodsky, 2017). These laws would require "mandatory reporting" by the university to law enforcement, even against the victims wishes, which victim-support advocates claim would decrease reporting of sexual victimization (Brodsky, 2017, p. 830).

Furthermore, Harvard law professors have deemed that it would be irresponsible for schools to shirk their responsibilities to students in the face of sexual violence (Bartholet et al., 2017, p. 4). Therefore, the question becomes, is there a reasonable way that universities can institute policies that protect victims and make them more comfortable in their learning environments while also ensuring the rights of the accused without involving the police?

▶ Due Process and the Burden of Proof

Due process can be distilled down to ensuring the rights of the accused to ensure that any judgment against them is fair. The loudest critics of the Obama-era regulations stated that the due process rights of the accused were mostly, if not completely, ignored. For example, 28 Harvard law professors (Bartholet et al., 2014) and 16 University of Pennsylvania law professors (Rudovsky et al., 2015) released public statements condemning the Obama-era regulations for violating the due process rights of accused students. Rudovsky et al. (2015) stated that "[d]ue process of law is not window dressing; it is the distillation of centuries of experience, and we ignore the lessons of history at our peril" (p. 5). The professors went on to say that by failing to afford due process rights for the accused, universities are failing to properly conduct fair examinations of accusations:

> We believe that OCR's approach exerts improper pressure upon universities to adopt procedures that do not afford fundamental fairness. We do not believe that providing justice for victims of sexual assault requires subordinating so many protections long deemed necessary to protect from injustice those accused of serious offenses. (p. 1)

Going further, Harvard law school professors stated that the processes that were adopted by universities "for deciding cases of alleged sexual misconduct . . . lack the most basic elements of fairness and due process, are overwhelmingly stacked against the accused" (Bartholet et al., 2014, p. 10).

The proposed DeVos rule changes (Department of Education, 2018) were aimed at mitigating the issues of due process rights—specifically, issues concerning cross-examination, the burden-of-proof standard, and the use of a single-investigator model that did not allow for the accused to refute claims against them. However, the proposed DeVos rule changes are not without their critics. One of the most glaring issues concerning the DeVos rule changes is the standard for the burden of proof. As previously stated, universities could use either preponderance of the evidence or the clear-and-convincing-evidence standard. However, a college can only use the preponderance standard if it uses that standard for other conduct code violations. Conversely, a school can use clear and convincing evidence in sexual victimization cases but continue using the preponderance-of-the-evidence standard for other rule violations, which seems skewed and discriminatory, as some have pointed out (Department of Education, 2018; Gersen, 2019).

▶ Cases for Consideration

Considering the issues involving due process and rights for the accused, hundreds of cases have been brought against universities that have punished students for sexual misconduct (Brodsky, 2017; Flanagan, 2018; Gersen, 2019; Joyce, 2017). Some of these cases have addressed complex issues and point out the flaws of system that is trying to protect students in the face of life-altering incidents of victimization. *Campus Safety Magazine* reported (Malafronte, 2019) that every two weeks a school is sued by a student who has been accused of sexual assault. The article goes on to point out that:

> [s]ince the "Dear Colleague" letter, there have been 319 federal cases where some type of action took place. Universities have lost 137 decisions, most of which were to dismiss the lawsuit. Universities have won 119 times and the cases have ended with confidential settlements 63 times. (p. 1)

While it is clear that there are many cases that can be discussed, below is just an examination of a few cases that highlight many of the issues reviewed above.

Jane Roe v. University of Cincinnati et al. (2017)

In the case of *Jane Roe v. University of Cincinnati et al.* (2017), Jane stated that she believed that the university was biased against her in its investigation and that the university withheld information that would have helped her make her case, including the ability to cross-examine the alleged victim and question witnesses. In this case, Jane walked John Doe home after a party; both John and Jane were familiar with one another given their involvement in the university's Reserve Officers' Training Corps (ROTC) program. John was heavily intoxicated, and Jane claimed she "just wanted to make sure she got home safe" (*Jane Roe v. University of Cincinnati et al.*, 2017, p. 2). John Doe requested she leave, and so did John's roommates. Then Jane allegedly told John's roommates "I promise you, nothing is going to happen. I'm just gonna give him his water, look him over, that's it" (p. 2). At this point, Jane locked them in John's bedroom, took his clothes off, and started sexual assaulting him. The next morning John reported the assault to his ROTC unit and then to the school's Title IX office.

Jane Doe was found guilty of sexually victimizing John Doe, and "UC suspended Ms. Roe until Mr. Doe graduated or stopped attending UC to prevent fear, concern, or emotional trauma to Mr. Doe" (*Jane Roe v. University of Cincinnati et al.*, 2017, p. 6). In her appeal, Jane stated that she did not have the ability to cross-examine John and that her witnesses were turned down when they should not have been. In the case of her witnesses, Jane wanted them to speak about a prior incident from April 2017 (p. 6). In that alleged incident, Jane had accused "CB" of sexually assaulting her; she took this complaint to her ROTC unit and the school's Title IX office. CB was not found responsible by the university but was dismissed from the school's ROTC program because of the accusation. An important point to note is that John Doe had testified as a witness on CB's behalf. Jane Roe believed that John was making the accusations against her in order to get back at her because he "harbored a grudge" based on the results of her accusations against CB (p. 6). Jane believes she should have been allowed to call her witnesses from the CB case and that their testimony should have been heard by the investigators; however, the university disagreed and did not feel as though it was pertinent to this case. The appellate court agreed. This is clearly a complex and complicated case, with many feelings and lives at stake. The question becomes, what should universities do in the face of such a complex landscape?

John Doe v. Purdue University et al. (2019)

In the case of *John Doe v. Purdue University et al.* (2019) John's girlfriend alleged that she woke up to John fondling her without her permission. She then alleged that John had admitted to touching her genitals while she slept on an earlier occasion. Immediately, John was suspended from Purdue's ROTC program and banned from being in any of the buildings where his now ex-girlfriend had classes. John denied all of the allegations against him and presented text messages to the investigators that he believed refuted his ex-girlfriend's claims. Eventually a report was written by the lead investigator and sent to a panel of three individuals charged with deciding John's guilt or innocence. John claimed he was only allowed to review a redacted copy of the investigation, and the report that was sent to the panel for a few brief minutes before the hearing. At the hearing:

> Doe appeared before the three-person panel, but the female student did not. . . Two members of the group allegedly stated they had not read the report, and the third apparently asked questions of Doe that already presumed his guilt. Doe said he could not speak to any of the evidence against him in the report because he had not seen a full version. (Bauer-Wolf, 2019, para. 10)

John won his appeal on the grounds that "he adequately alleged violations of both the Fourteenth Amendment and Title IX" (*John Doe v. Purdue University*, 2019, p. 2) by Purdue University. The question becomes, how was this even Purdue University's policy to begin with? It seems like an institution with a reputation for excellence would have better standards for punishing students in the face of life-altering consequences.

Matt Boermeester v. USC

Matt Boermeester was a kicker at University of Southern California (USC). In 2017, he was suspended, barred from campus, and from meeting with the football team and coaches after he was found guilty of Title IX allegations (Helfand, 2017; Singal, 2017). However, in this case the complaint against him was not from the victim but from a neighbor who allegedly saw Boermeester assault his girlfriend, Zoe Katz (Helfand, 2017; Singal, 2017). Katz denied the allegations repeatedly and said that she was just joking around with Boermeester. Katz alleged that investigators told her she must not be aware of the abuse or was a battered woman. She felt she was demeaned during the investigation and did not support the accusations against Boermeester. Despite Katz not supporting the accusations, USC still ruled that Boermeester was guilty of violating Title IX and suspended him. This particular case raised questions about victims' rights in the opposite direction: If victims are to be believed, then why should Katz be ignored when she is defending Boermeester?

▶ Conclusion

Title IX has changed how universities have responded to sexual victimization whether for better or for worse. There is little question that those 35 words in the original Title IX (1972) document have changed the landscape of higher education, but the question remains, at what cost? It is clear victims need protection, and the accused have rights. But how can universities adequately navigate such a complex set of laws and rights in face of legal penalties, where lives—of both the victim and accused—can be significantly altered forever? Is there really a policy that could be put into practice that would satisfy all parties on this issue?

▶ References

Ali, R. (2011, April 4). Dear colleague letter. Washington, DC: U.S. Department of Education, Office for Civil Rights.

Bartholet, E., Gertner, N., Halley, J., & Gersen, J. S. (2017, August 21). Fairness for all students under Title IX. Harvard. Retrieved from https://dash.harvard.edu/bitstream/handle/1/33789434/Fairness%20for%20All%20Students.pdf?sequence=1

Bartholet, E., Brewer, S., Clark, R., Dershowitz, A., Desan, A., Donahue, C., . . . Wilkins, D. (2014, January 14). Rethink Harvard's sexual harassment policy. *Boston Globe*. Retrieved from https://www.bostonglobe.com/opinion/2014/10/14/rethink-harvard-sexual-harassment-policy/HFDDiZN7nU2UwuUuWMnqbM/story.html

Bauer-Wolf, J. (2019, July 1). Another win for an accused student. *Inside Higher Ed*. Retrieved from https://www.insidehighered.com/news/2019/07/01/appeals-court-finds-purdue-may-have-been-biased-against-man-accused-sexual-assault

Brodsky, A. (2017) A rising tide: Learning about fair disciplinary process from Title IX. *Journal of Legal Education (77)*4. 822–849.

Butler, B. (2019, July 11). Captivated by the U.S. women's soccer team victory? Thank Title IX. Retrieved from https://www.latimes.com/opinion/op-ed/la-oe-butler-us-womens-soccer-title-nine-20190710-story.html

Creeley, W. (2016, January 13). "Single Investigator" at UCLA means hearings available only on appeal. FIRE. Retrieved from https://www.thefire.org/single-investigator-at-ucla-means-hearings-available-only-on-appeal/

Department of Education. (2018). Background and summary of the Education Department's proposed Title IX regulation. Retrieved from https://www2.ed.gov/about/offices/list/ocr/docs/background-summary-proposed-ttle-ix-regulation.pdf

Donegan, M. (2019, July 6). USA's formidable women's soccer team is no accident. It's a product of public policy. *The Guardian* [UK]. Retrieved from https://www.theguardian.com/commentisfree/2019/jul/06/usa-womens-world-cup-netherlands-title-xi

Education Amendments Act of 1972, 20 U.S.C. §§1681–1688 (2018).

Flanagan, C. (2018, June 1). Mutually nonconsensual sex. *The Atlantic*. Retrieved from https://www.theatlantic.com/ideas/archive/2018/06/title-ix-is-too-easy-to-abuse/561650/

Helfand, Z. (2017, July 30). Kicker Matt Boermeester was removed from USC after an unfair investigation, girlfriend says. *Los Angeles Times*. Retrieved from https://www.latimes.com/sports/usc/la-sp-matt-boermeester-removed-unfairly-girlfriend-says-20170730-story.html

Lhamon, C. (2014, April 29). Questions and answers on Title IX and sexual violence. Washington, DC: U.S. Department of Education, Office for Civil Rights. Retrieved from https://www2.ed.gov/about/offices/list/ocr/docs/qa-201404-title-ix.pdf

Lankford, J. (2016, January 7). Letter to John B. King. Retrieved from https://www.lankford.senate.gov/imo/media/doc/Sen.%20Lankford%20letter%20to%20Dept.%20of%20Education%201.7.16.pdf

Lapidus, L. M., Martin, E. J, & Luthra, N. (2009). *The rights of women: The authoritative ACLU guide to women's rights* (4th ed.). New York, NY: New York University Press.

Malafronte, K. (2019, April 19). Every 2 weeks, a student accused of sexual assault sues their school. *Campus Safety Magazine*. Retrieved from https://www.campussafetymagazine.com/clery/student -accused-sexual-sues-school/

Jackson, C. (2017). Notice of language assistance. Washington, DC: U.S. Department of Education, Office for Civil Rights. Retrieved from https://www.cmu.edu/title-ix/colleague-title-ix-201709 .pdf

Jane Roe v. University of Cincinnati et al. (2017). Case number 1-18—cv—312 in the United States District Court for the Southern District of Ohio, Western Division. Retrieved from https:// kcjohnson.files.wordpress.com/2018/08/roe-v-cincinnati-pi-denial.pdf

John Doe v. Purdue University et al. (2019). Appeal from the United States District Court for the Northern District of Indiana, Hammond Division. No. 2:17—cv—00033-PRC. Retrieved from http://media.ca7.uscourts.gov/cgi-bin/rssExec.pl?Submit=Display&Path=Y2019/D06-28 /C:17-3565:J:Barrett:aut:T:fnOp:N:2362429:S:0

Gersen, J. S. (2019, February 1). Assessing Betsy DeVos's proposed rules on Title IX and sexual assault. *The New Yorker*. Retrieved from https://www.newyorker.com/news/our-columnists /assessing-betsy-devos-proposed-rules-on-title-ix-and-sexual-assault

Javits Amendment. (1974). Regulations; Nature of particular sports: Intercollegiate athletic activities. 1974 Education Amendments of 1974, Pub. L. No. 93-380, § 844, 88 Stat. 484 (1974) (codified in 20 U.S.C. §§ 1681–1688). Retrieved from https://www.justice.gov/crt/title-ix-education -amendments-1972

Joyce, K. (2017, December 5). The takedown of Title IX: Inside the fight over federal rules on campus sexual assault. *The New York Times Magazine*. Retrieved from https://www.nytimes .com/2017/12/05/magazine/the-takedown-of-title-ix.html

Rudovsky, D., Bibas, S., Balganesh, S., Berman, M., Burbank, S., Fisch, J., . . . Wax, A. (2015, February 18). Open letter from members of the Penn Law School faculty. Sexual assault complaints: Protecting complainants and the accused students at universities. *Wall Street Journal* [online]. Retrieved from https://online.wsj.com/public/resources/documents/2015_0218_upenn.pdf

Schwarz, R. (2014). Timeout! Getting back to what Title IX intended and encouraging courts and the Office of Civil Rights to re-evaluate the three-prong compliance test. *Washington and Lee Journal of Civil Rights and Social Justice, 20*(2) 633-677.

Singal, J. (2017, August 4). A bizarre case at USC shows how broken Title IX enforcement Is right now. *New York Magazine*. Retrieved from http://nymag.com/intelligencer/2017/08/a-bizarre -usc-case-shows-how-broken-title-ix-enforcement-is.html

Smith, T. (2019, January 30). Trump administration gets an earful on new campus sexual assault rules. NPR. Retrieved from https://www.npr.org/2019/01/30/689879689/education -department-gathers-feedback-on-new-campus-sexual-assault-rules

Yoffe, E. (2018, September 4). Reining in the excesses of Title IX: The Department of Education's proposed rule changes aren't without their flaws—but they move the policy in a more just direction. *The Atlantic*. https://www.theatlantic.com/ideas/archive/2018/09/title-ix-reforms -are-overdue/569215/

Research Ethics in Criminal Justice

Edward Gregory Weeks III

▶ Introduction

Ethical practices in criminal justice research are of significant consideration when planning, conducting, and presenting original research. Historically, research with human participants had fewer guidelines, policies, and laws. The research relied on the researchers' best judgment. Past research practices commonly resulted in harm to research participants and sometimes those conducting the research. Criminal justice and other social science research are challenging endeavors. Researchers who collect original data must take careful steps to protect research participants from significant harms that may occur during the normal execution of a study. Criminal justice researchers must weigh the risks and benefits of the proposed research and decide how useful it would be to the field of criminal justice and society. It is important that ethical research protects research participants' anonymity and confidentiality. In addition, research participants must be able to opt out of a study if they do not want to participate at any time. Ultimately, criminal justice research is conducted for good or benevolent purposes while protecting all involved.

▶ The Law and Policy of Conducting Ethical Research

The Origins of Institutional Review

Human participant research rights are socially constructed. It took the prosecution of the war crimes of Nazi physicians during the Nuremberg trials of 1947 to begin discussing the importance of protecting individuals from harmful research practices. As a result of the war crime trials, the Nuremberg Code of ethics was established. As described in the code, the principles of voluntary consent, the necessity of the experiment, preventing harm to individuals through careful preparation by qualified researchers, and the ability to end an experiment if there is observable harm identified are essential to performing ethical research that involves people (Nuremberg Code, 1949). After the creation of the code, not until 1953 did the U.S. federal government create its first policy for the protection of human subjects. However, the National Institutes of Health Clinical Center used the code first. Research proposals are evaluated by an institutional review board (IRB) that determines whether a study follows the ethical guidelines. The IRB is independent of the research proposed and provides an independent assessment. The 1953 model forms the basis of our current process.

In 1979, the National Commission for the Protection of Human Rights published the *Belmont Report* in response to a clear ethical violation of medical experiments that had taken place in the United States. It was partly a result of the Tuskegee Syphilis Study in which an exploited and marginalized population of African Americans was used by U.S. Public Health researchers who observed the physical effects of syphilis, a sexually transmitted disease, even though a medical cure had been discovered (Brandt, 1978). The research study began in 1932, and its purpose was to observe the effects of latent syphilis in 400 African American males from Macon County, Alabama (Brandt, 1978). According to Brandt (1978), researchers were purposefully letting the dangerous experiment continue, causing significant injury to those suffering from the disease. Making matters worse, penicillin became commonly available in the 1950s as a treatment for the disease. If it had been administered, it would have saved as many as 100 of the males who had died as a direct result of the disease by 1972 (Brandt, 1987). This human tragedy was a direct result of poor research ethics.

Ethically, the researchers had a duty to end the experiment when the cure was made known to them. According to proper ethical reasoning, human virtues of protecting lives supersede any nationalistic and professional merits of obtaining the research results for the U.S. government and the researchers carrying out their observations validly (Souryal, 2014). After the Tuskegee Syphilis Study, the United States government decided it needed a better system to protect human research participants from harm with an independent assessment of the risks and rewards of research.

The Institutional Review Board

The IRB provides oversight for all criminal justice research conducted across the country (CFR, 2018), overseeing projects within research institutions, colleges, and universities. The IRB consists of a committee of colleagues who evaluate the risks and rewards of conducting the proposed research and whether the proposed study is kind and essential to the field of criminal justice (CFR, 2018). Most important of all, the IRB determines if the proposed study has considered the confidentiality and anonymity of its human participants. When there are human participants, a full review takes place. The Health and Human Services department of the U.S. government provides the federal law, policy, and guidelines that are followed for reviewing each research proposal. For more information on submitting a research proposal to an institutional review board and on the process, visit the National Institutes of Health at https://humansubjects.nih.gov/

Exempt Research

The IRB does not require all research be submitted to it. Exemptions exist for particular categories of analysis. Educational outcomes and assessments of students are usually exempt as long as a study is anonymous and confidential. A study should not put participants at risk of criminal or civil damages (CFR, 2018). In addition, secondary data analysis or reuse of another researcher's data could be exempt as long as the identity of the participants cannot be found in any of the data set variables. Other exempt categories involve making observations in public areas of people and things (CFR, 2018). For example, if students wanted to record the speed of cars on an open road or watch a car stopping at a crosswalk, they would be free under the federal guidelines to analyze and share that information as long as they did not identify the citizens they witnessed. Finally, research that does not involve using humans is exempt (CFR, 2018). For example, a student is interested in researching where police call boxes on a college campus. For a more detailed flowchart of information regarding whether research is exempt, researchers can visit the website of the Department of Health and Human Services at https://www.hhs.gov/ohrp/regulations-and-policy/decision-charts/index.html

Special Populations

Criminal justice researchers can find themselves working with special populations as well. Conducting ethical research means that children and prisons are protected populations that need extra consideration when they are part of a study. For example, a child and his or her parental guardian must agree to the informed consent and be able to stop their participation at any time they choose (CFR, 2018). According to the *Code of Federal Regulations* (2018), children should participate in research with only minimal risk. For example, a child could participate in a private interview in a safe environment and take a survey with minimally invasive questions.

Particular attention should be paid to studies involving child maltreatment. Children who are interviewed regarding child maltreatment may relive their abuse and be psychologically harmed (Coles & Mudaly, 2010). In some cases, an ethical dilemma may arise if a child discloses to a researcher that severe abuse is ongoing with his or her current caretaker (Steinberg, Pynoos, Goenjian, Sossanabadi, & Sherr, 1999). Researchers must consider ending the study for the child and decide how to report the abuse to the police or department of child services. They must weigh protecting the confidentiality of the child participant and preventing future harm. Complications can follow if they are mandated to report child abuse under the law of the state they are in—and they may be held criminally liable. However, according to Steinberg, Pynoos, Goenjian, Sossanabadi, and Sherr (1999), it is unclear whether the certificate of confidentiality granted by the IRB would preempt mandated-reporting laws.

Like children, inmates are a protected population. Inmate participants in criminal justice research deserve protection from harm. Historically, inmates who were in the Holocaust were intentionally harmed in medical experiments (Quinn, 2018). After the Nuremberg trials, the United States created special protections for inmates. Currently, debate is ongoing over the use of secondary data collected by Nazi scientists during World War II (Quinn, 2018) when Nazis conducted medical experiments on concentration camp prisoners, most of whom were Jewish. The Germans performed cruel experiments to test wartime conditions on the human body (Quinn, 2018), and many people died as a result of the research.

After the war, the U.S. soldiers who liberated the concentration camp at Dachau in Germany discovered the documents of the medical experiments. Major Leo Alexander evaluated the data from one test and determined that the information was valid even though it was collected criminally (Quinn, 2018). The data were from a study of the effects of hypothermia on the human body. The victims were placed against their will in cold water until they went into shock or passed away (Quinn, 2018). Alexander went on to publish an article, "The Treatment of Shock from Prolonged Exposure to Cold, Especially from Water" (1945) (Quinn, 2018). According to Quinn (2018), Nazi scientist research in many scientific areas was used for continued study until the late 1980s, and there was not much protest from the scientific community. The methods in which the illegal research was collected raised the moral dilemma of whether it is acceptable to use research data that was obtained illegally in newer studies. According to Quinn (2018), using historically collected data unlawfully is protected under the First Amendment to the U.S. Constitution. Those who support the use of the data claim that it had lifesaving potential, although the families of the victims consider it an offensive indignity. In contemporary and more civil times, researchers protect inmates involved with research by carefully following the legal guidelines.

According to § 46.305 of the *Code of Federal Regulations*, the following requirements must be met in addition to the usual protections for human participants:

1. The research under review represents one of the categories of research permissible under 45 CFR 46.306(a)(2);
    a. Any possible advantages accruing to the prisoner through his or her participation in the research—when compared to the general living conditions, medical care, quality of food, amenities, and opportunity for earnings in the prison—are not of such a magnitude that the inmate is impaired in being able to weigh the risks of the research against the value of receiving such advantages in the limited-choice prison environment;
2. The risks involved in the research are commensurate with risks that would be accepted by nonprisoner volunteers;
3. Procedures for the selection of subjects within the prison are fair to all prisoners and immune from arbitrary intervention by prison authorities or prisoners. Unless the principal investigator provides the IRB with written justification for following other procedures, control subjects must be selected randomly from the group of available prisoners who meet the characteristics needed for that particular research proposal;
4. The information is presented in language that is understandable to the subject population;
5. Adequate assurance exists that parole boards will not take into account a prisoner's participation in the research in making decisions regarding parole, and each prisoner is informed in advance that participation in the research will have no effect on his or her parole; and
6. Where the IRB finds a need for follow-up examination or care of participants after the end of their participation, adequate provision has been made for such examination or care, taking into account the varying lengths of individual prisoners' sentences and for informing participants of this fact (45 CFR 46.305(a)).

For more information on the CFR regulations, students and researchers can visit the Electronic Code of Federal Regulations at www.ecfr.gov

Informed Consent

The informed consent document is provided to research participants to inform them of all potential risks and benefits from participating in the study. The informed consent is not a contract that requires a signature like purchasing a car. Instead, it is information that make participants aware that they are free to end their participation even when they do not want to. The informed consent document should be written in plain language that participants can easily understand. Before the current laws, informed consent was not required, and documents similar to a business contract were used.

In 1971, informed consent did not exist as a requirement from an institutional review board. Social Psychologist Phillip Zimbardo decided to simulate a prison in the basement of his Stanford University psychology building. In this classic experiment, he randomly assigned males to be prisoners or guards from a sample of college students who would sign a contract and agree to participate for 2 weeks. The purpose of the experiment was to test the hypothesis that a negative environment could cause good people to misbehave (Zimbardo, 1971). Zimbardo relied on his best estimation that the study would not be harmful to the students because they would debrief after the study in case they had any adverse psychological effects.

During the study, the guards became aggressive and psychologically abusive toward the inmates. The inmates then decided to go on a hunger strike and rebel against the guards. The revolt led to more psychological abuse from the guards, and the prisoners began to mentally break down (Zimbardo, 1971). The study had to be ended early because the inmates started suffering from acute anxiety and stress and could not handle the pressure of the escalated situation. Zimbardo (1971) had the inmates debriefed, and many of them felt temporarily psychologically harmed. Separate from any research findings, the classic experiment highlighted the need for participants to be able to quit their participation when they think it is necessary even without signing a research contract.

Confidentiality

Confidentiality of the proposed research ensures that the collected data, information, tools, and materials are not disclosed to unauthorized individuals outside of the study. Often, researchers will explain to their participants through the informed consent that their information is protected. The IRB will grant the research study a certificate of confidentiality after it approves of the research and how it will be conducted. Protecting research could mean that the encrypted data are kept under lock and key, protected with strong passwords, and even stored on devices not connected to the Internet. Often, researchers will have to consider how to back up their information while providing confidentiality to participants, which may even mean storing their data on multiple secure servers. The most secure places a researcher could work would be in a Sensitive Compartmented Information Facility. This type of research could be conducted to study terrorism or to protect matters of national security. Other types of criminal justice research involves working with offenders and victims. Offenders' identities must be protected to ensure that the information provided is the most truthful and freely offered without fear of being charged with a crime.

In addition, working with victims presents its own set of challenges. Victims need to know that their identity is protected from being released. These vulnerable participants can reexperience past trauma when they are asked to describe their lived experiences. Victims also can suffer from the stigma of being labeled as victims, which would cause them additional harm if their identities were released. For example, a person who experiences a violent or sexual crime may admit to being diagnosed with a medical condition if they wish to keep their actual experience private.

Anonymity

Anonymity is the second concept that ethical researchers provide to their participants. Ensuring that participants are anonymous adds a layer of protection and also allows researchers the ability to publish and share their research and data. One fundamental way in which researchers provide anonymity to their participants is by removing any identifying information from surveys and data files. Instead, a serial number is used to keep track of cases. During recorded interviews and transcription, an interviewer can assign a code name to an individual to make him or her feel more comfortable sharing sensitive information and to protect his or her identity.

Ultimately, it is up to ethical researchers to build into their research protections for participants. The IRB must assess whether they are adequate and will not be too risky. The data may even be submitted to a public database, so anonymous and de-identified data are required to be provided.

▶ The Irish Republican Army and the Boston College Incident

Conducting criminal justice research can include many risks. Often researchers are studying sensitive topics and interviewing victims and offenders who have direct knowledge of specific crimes, so confidentiality must be maintained. Boston College researcher Ed Moloney and Anthony McIntyre, a former Irish Republican Army (IRA) member, interviewed Northern Ireland republicans and loyal paramilitary members who knew about the bombings, kidnappings, and murders that took place in that country during the turbulent time that came to be known as "the Troubles" (Palys & Lowman, 2012). The severe and violent crimes committed by IRA members drew the attention of the government of the United Kingdom (U.K.). Under an agreement with the United States, the United Kingdom requested that the interviews be turned over to its investigators. The researchers claimed it was their moral and ethical responsibility not to release the information because of the informed consent of confidentiality provided to the participants.

In May 2011, warrants were issued in the United States against Moloney and McIntyre and Boston College's librarian, Robert O'Neill (Palys & Lowman, 2012). According to the original court documents ("Motion to Quash," 2018), the U.S. Department of Justice, in partnership with the British government and acting on behalf of the Police Service of Northern Ireland and the office of the Director of Public Prosecution in Belfast, requested the interviews of study participants Brendan Hughs and Dolours Price:

1. the original tape recordings of any and all interviews of Brendan Hughes and Dolours Price;
2. any and all written documents, including but not limited to any and all transcripts, relating to any and all tape recordings of any and all interviews of Brendan Hughes and Dolours Price;
3. any and all written notes created in connection with any and all interviews of Brendan Hughes and Dolours Price; and
4. any and all computer records created in connection with any and all interviews of Brendan Hughes and Dolours Price.

After receiving the subpoena, Boston College had a challenging decision to make but decided to hand over the interviews with little resistance (Palys & Lowman, 2012). According to Palys and Lowman (2012), the American Civil Liberties Union criticized Boston College's decision to turn over the interviews without hiring of legal experts who could have scrutinized the legal code surrounding the case.

Two months later, the United Kingdom requested two more interviews. Boston College quickly sent them to the United Kingdom. When conducting criminal justice research, it is rare to receive a warrant for research, and it is not unreasonable for researchers and institutions to feel challenged and overwhelmed when a government arrives with an order. In this case, Boston College turned over the second set of interviews even though the information contained nothing about any IRA murder. According to Palys and Lowman (2012), Boston College showed a disregard for the confidentiality of the participants by not honoring their informed consent. Palys and Lowman (2012) suggest that institutions such as Boston College work with researchers to form clear policies and support for research projects that uphold the ethical standards of research.

Outside of the case study, the implications of turning over interviews could mean that potential participants will refuse to participate out of fear. Participants could now be less likely to tell the truth in research studies that could potentially save human lives.

▶ Conclusion

Ethics in criminal justice research is an essential part of conducting research that is valid and reliable. It ensures that human research participants are treated with dignity and respect while being prompted to be truthful. Researchers must weigh the risks of research using human participants by bringing their proposal to an institutional review board. They must consider all reasonable risks to themselves as well as the participants and install safeguards that promote confidentiality and anonymity. When conducting research, participants must be informed and agree to participate knowing the risks and benefits of participation and be able to end their involvement at any time. Research data should be kept private and secure from those not involved with the study.

Prior research studies such as the Tuskegee Syphilis Study, the Stanford Prison Experiment, and the Boston College–IRA case all provide insight into the social construction and evolution of research ethics. Criminal justice research often involves sensitive topics and risks to participants and researchers. By applying the CFR guidelines for conducting research ethically, researchers can protect their participants. However, if ethical reasoning and guidelines are not followed, a wide range of harm can occur to institutions, researchers, participants, and the greater society. It is up to researchers to design their research so it can contribute to the body of knowledge of criminal justice. If it is not done so ethically, all possible knowledge could be lost.

▶ **References**

Brandt, A. M. (1978). Racism and research: The case of the Tuskegee Syphilis Study. *Hastings Center Report, 8*(6), 21–29.

Code of Federal Regulations (CFR). (2018). Electronic Code of Federal Regulations. Retrieved from https://www.ecfr.gov/

Coles, J., & Mudaly, N. (2010). Staying safe: Strategies for qualitative child abuse researchers. *Child Abuse Review, 19*(1), 56–69.

Nuremberg Code. (1949). Trials of war criminals before the Nuremberg military tribunals under control council law, *10*, 181–182.

Palys, T., & Lowman, J. (2012). Defending research confidentiality "to the extent the law allows": Lessons from the Boston College subpoenas. *Journal of Academic Ethics, 10*(4), 271–297.

Motion to quash. (2012, February 17). Retrieved from http://bostoncollegesubpoena.wordpress.com/ court-documents/motion-to-quash/

Souryal, S. S. (2014). *Ethics in criminal justice: In search of the truth.* Philadelphia, PA: Routledge.

Steinberg, A. M., Pynoos, R. S., Goenjian, A. K., Sossanabadi, H., & Sherr, L. (1999). Are researchers bound by child abuse reporting laws? *Child Abuse & Neglect, 23*(8), 771–777.

Quinn, C. V. (2018). *Dignity, justice, and the Nazi data debate: On violating the violated anew.* New York, NY: Lexington Books.

Zimbardo, P. (1971). *The Stanford Prison Experiment: A simulation study of the psychology of imprisonment.* [Pdf]. Stanford Digital Repository, Stanford University, Stanford, CA.

Ethics and Popular Culture

Tweets, Snaps, Streaming, Hashtags, and @s: Pop Culture and the Ethical Landscape

Shavonne Arthurs

▶ Introduction

There are various definitions of the term *pop culture*. The *Oxford Dictionary* defines it as modern popular culture transmitted via the mass media and aimed particularly at younger people. The *Cambridge English Dictionary* defines it as music, TV, cinema, books, and so on that are popular and enjoyed by ordinary people rather than by experts or highly educated people. It seems as though by definition we do not give pop culture much credit. Only young or adaptable minds are susceptible to falling into the trends of popular influences. Some people think the rest of the population is far too intelligent to be swayed by viewership. Could this actually be the case? Can any single person state with confidence that the news, social media, print ads, and so on have never swayed them? This might be an issue of social denial. Realistically, pop culture is thrown at us from many angles, whether or not we are willing consumers. We are told certain products are better than others, certain foods will help us become healthier, certain music is better to listen to, certain clothing is trendy, and certain television shows should be watched by everyone—and be judged for not watching!

Popular culture is more than the largest hit song or new television show everyone cannot stop talking about. Culture, in general, is what molds and shapes our worldviews. We create value systems and draw lines in the sand between what is right and what is wrong. Beyond this, popular culture is taken and cultivated by the majority. It defines our personal identities, along with others, and various group identities. Because of this, popular culture has the potential to be a powerful agent of change for both good and bad. It can create positive social change while simultaneously further stigmatizing groups. It can create cohesiveness while also creating divisiveness.

The fluidity of popular culture causes these waves. It trends in and out, targeting certain social elements for a brief period and then moving on to something brighter and shinier to focus on. Social media is a specific form of popular culture that has significantly aided in the "flash in the pan" mentality of popular culture. Before the development of social media, we were largely (maybe blissfully?) unaware of things going on outside our immediate surroundings. We checked in with long-distance family and friends every so often. We knew of our own community events and checked into local and national news sources for major issues across states and international boundaries. Currently, we find information in a matter of seconds from across the globe. Because of its immediate accessibility, there is simply too much information to process and focus on for a sustainable amount of time. So, we have grown accustomed to short attention spans for topical issues, as well as limited focus on what we, as individuals, are passionate about.

▶ Managing Media

Not all of current popular culture is gloom and doom, though. With knowledge comes power. We have grown more open to other cultures' viewpoints. We engage at more international levels. Our television, music, and other types of media scopes have broadened. There is more social awareness attached to what happens on a daily basis. It is not so much the ease of access and the amount of information at our fingertips that is the main worry. What is concerning is how rapidly forms of media have developed and how they are regulated. For example, Facebook began as an exclusive group, and those interested in joining had to have a college address to join. In its earliest days, applicants even had to attend a certain college to join. Various universities created their own style Facebook-like pages in attempts to compete. Eventually, though, Facebook won and significantly broadened itself to become an all-inclusive online entity. With the momentum came other forms of social media such as Twitter, Instagram, and Snapchat. Each argues that it offers its own individual spin on socialness, but the knowledge base remains the same. The rapid growth has brought minimal regulations. Although there have always been user policies in place, many users have been ignorant about the standards of posting in these forums. Also, on the social media company side, it has become increasingly difficult to counter every development that arises. Mark Zuckerberg himself probably could not have predicted the current state of Facebook when he created the program as a college student at Harvard.

Difficulties in managing media have come to a head in recent news. First, Mark Zuckerberg's quick-paced success of Facebook caught up with the platform in 2018 when he sat through multiple congressional hearings to address privacy practice issues. It was determined that a company named Cambridge Analytica had obtained profile information data for an estimated 80 million Facebook users. The hearings brought about conversations beyond that of data sharing. They called into question the type of individuals who have access to the platform and what types of information could be shared with the masses. Zuckerberg himself admitted to the serious nature of the issues at the beginning of the hearings:

> Facebook is an idealistic and optimistic company. For most of our existence, we focused on all the good that connecting people can bring. As Facebook has grown, people everywhere have gotten a powerful new tool to stay connected to the people they love, make their voices heard, and build communities and businesses. Just recently, we've seen the #metoo movement and the March for Our Lives, organized, at least in part, on Facebook. After Hurricane Harvey, people raised more than $20 million for relief. And more than 70 million small businesses now use Facebook to grow and create jobs.
>
> But it's clear now that we didn't do enough to prevent those tools from being used for harm as well. That goes for fake news, foreign interference in elections, and hate speech, as well as developers and data privacy. We didn't take a broad enough view of our responsibility, and that was a big mistake. It was my mistake, and I'm sorry. I started Facebook, I run it, and I'm responsible for what happens here. (Facebook, 2018, p. 1)

Although there are updates to privacy settings and structures in the works at Facebook, they remain confusing to general consumers. Along with this, issues in content regulation are still ongoing.

In other recent discussions, President Donald Trump has blasted media outlets for publicizing so-called fake news. President Trump feels media outlets publish lies as facts, and it is difficult for laypeople to distinguish between the two. Socially, many people have latched onto this term, which has trended on various platforms since the beginning of his presidency. People have used this term to identify various elements of media tampering: influencing viewpoints, pushing political agendas, causing confusion, and masking other topical issues.

The issue of fake news is especially relevant with social media. What prevents people from posting any type of content on these platforms? Sure, people have been sentenced to "Facebook jail" for lewd comments and spamming. User accounts have been disabled for being fake and used for hacking and to promote businesses. Rightful users are able to report issues and maliciousness themselves. All are great updates. This, however, still does not address the fake news issue. For example, what would prevent someone from sharing a fake article that a celebrity died? In 2018, a Yahoo! news site reported that Michael J. Fox had died from pneumonia related to his Parkinson's disease. Luckily, this was disproven, with Fox himself posting on an unrelated topic on his Instagram page days after his supposed death (Fox, 2018).

Content is difficult to regulate on social media because it is difficult to regulate on the Internet itself. Part of the issue is figuring out how to draw the line between how the government should (or could) regulate the Internet while maintaining individual rights and freedom of press. Punishments are now being imposed for malicious content (as stated previously), such as bans and restrictions from websites to criminal charges. The content is also removed from the specific sites. These types of regulations have not worked because media content functions much like Hydra, the multiheaded serpent in Greek mythology. Cut off one head and two grow back. Screenshots and reposting have made it next to impossible to completely wipe an item from the Web.

The continued development of artificial intelligence is another recent issue. Currently, videos and images can be manipulated through face and voice in such a way that the naked eye finds it difficult to recognize the difference. The social term is called *deepfaking*, which is essentially the ability for computers to produce extremely realistic videos that display events or individuals and messages that never actually happened (Andrews, 2019). The issue became more prominent in 2018 when comedian and actor Jordan Peele simulated former President Barack Obama in a mock public service announcement as a warning of sorts to the dangers of the technology (Romano, 2018). It seems to have fallen on deaf ears because deepfake videos continue to be created; in a recent one, Jim Carrey starred in a deepfake production of *The Shining*, impersonating actor Jack Nicholson in the original portrayal (ctrl shift face, 2019). It is already difficult for laypeople to figure out false content, and the problem is being compounded with our increasing inability to discern fakes from reality.

▶ The Issue of Influencers

Along with false information and deepfakes is the added concern of media influencers. Celebrities (think movie and TV stars, music stars, and sports players) used to be role models. Younger generations looked to these celebrities for their views on trends anywhere from fashion to serious political issues. Social media platforms allowed more people into the fold. Various companies hire spokespeople for their products who have many followers on various platforms and garner many "likes." In one sense, they are "pseudo-celebrities." For example, Cameron Dallas got his start creating videos on the social media app Vine. With the initial attention he garnered there, he now has an Instagram page with more than 21 million followers (Dallas, n.d.). Garnering followers is becoming such an important thing that parents are even creating accounts for their children before they're born, both to claim certain handles (names) and to begin the process of gathering followers.

Role models are becoming more expansive, which means more people are weighing in on various social issues. Media outlets are highly influential and able to shape our worldviews about all types of social issues. But what about social media influencers? Are they just as influential? To examine this topic, the Twitter account of former National Football League (NFL) quarterback Colin Kaepernick was analyzed for his influencing status in the aftermath of incidents in which he knelt during the national anthem.

▶ Kaepernick's Tweet Ball

To understand Kaepernick's current social influence, it is important to know the history behind his actions. During an NFL preseason game against the Green Bay Packers on August 26, 2016, Colin Kaepernick—then a starting quarterback for the San Francisco 49ers—was viewed on camera sitting on the bench during the playing of the national anthem. Soon after, imagery of him sitting on the bench went viral on social media. The attention (and social discussion) was swift. The next day, Kaepernick conducted an interview with NFL.com and explained his rationale for sitting by stating: "I am not going to stand up to show pride in a flag for a country that oppresses black people and people of color. To me, this is bigger than football and it would be selfish on my part to look the other way. There are bodies in the street and people getting paid leave and getting away with murder" (Wyche, 2016). From this quote, it was clear his initial stance was based on the topic of police misuse of force and mistreatment of minorities in general.

After the initial bench sitting, other NFL players got involved, and the topic was further highlighted as a social movement. One of Kaepernick's teammates, Eric Reid, kneeled with Kaepernick during the game against the San Diego Chargers on September 1, 2016. NFL players from other teams began to kneel as well. Soon, coaches were asked to weigh in on kneeling during the national anthem. There were varying opinions. Some viewed the NFL as a job and an inappropriate spot for social reform. Some viewed it as disrespecting the military. Some viewed it as an inherent right as a United States citizen. Some coaches and owners required players to stand or they would not play. Some coaches and owners did not enforce any requirements of their players. As ever, it is a topic that manifests vast social divisions. The movement gained support beyond the NFL. Various sports (basketball, soccer, volleyball, to name a few) at various levels (high school, college, and national leagues) reported players kneeling during the national anthem.

Kaepernick, the NFL, and Social Media

The NFL has been a steady social media force for years. It seems, though, that Kaepernick's movement affected the league's social media stance. NFL viewership decreased during the 2016 season, and along with that came a decline in social media followers and impact (Laing, 2018). It took two football seasons for the NFL to see a marked increase on its social media platforms again. Twitter is one social media venue that allows fans to gain more personal relationships with their favorite teams and the league in general. People are able to see noted updates about their teams, as well as have actual social interaction with the accounts. Twitter is said to provide more value (and more loyalty) to fan bases.

Because the NFL accounts are influential, it only makes sense that individual player accounts are also influential. Colin Kaepernick's Twitter account (@Kaepernick7) to date has 2.13 million followers (Kaepernick, n.d.). He is also highly active on his account, with approximately 115,000 tweets. It is clear he would be considered an influencer with those numbers. The larger question surrounding media, social media, and the concept of influencers is, how much social influence is actually occurring? Does Twitter have enduring social influence? Do certain tweets garner more attention and influence? Are there variations in time and trends? Do other outside social variables have an effect? It is not easy to measure influence, but some analysis can provide insight. Remember the multiheaded serpent example previously mentioned? Well, social media platforms allow users to access all published individual account information. That means individual accounts can be measured by trends, likes, and so on. Analyzing Kaepernick's tweets could provide insight into his potential influence on followers.

@Kaepernick7 Tweet Analysis

The analysis was dated back to the initial bench-sitting incident on August 26, 2016. Something interesting to note is that Kaepernick became much more involved in tweeting after the incident than before. He tended to post a few times a month compared with multiple times a week after the incident. Kaepernick was mentioned (by his Twitter handle) approximately 6 million times from August 26 to September 30, 2016. The largest trend in mentions happened just after the bench-sitting incident until the end of August, with smaller spikes occurring thereafter.

Kaepernick's account had a total of 220 original tweets from July 1, 2016, through December 31, 2018. Through coding the tweets, a few overreaching trends were noted. First was his work with the million-dollar pledge. He made a pact to donate $1 million to charities that serve oppressed communities across the United States. He donated to various charities in smaller increments from $10,000 to $100,000. An example of a donation was to a group called Helping Oppressed Mothers Endure (HOME) in Lithonia, Georgia (n.d.). The group focuses on rebuilding and restoring homes to single mothers who have recently gone through some sort of hardship such as divorce or domestic violence. The second trend was focused on camps that emphasized knowing your rights. The camps were founded by Kaepernick and focus on raising youth awareness regarding topics of higher education, self-empowerment, and proper interactions with law enforcement. The overreaching goal is "to help build a stronger generation of people that will create the change that is much needed in this world" (Know Your Rights Camp, 2018). The third trend was birthday wishes. Kaepernick provided birthday "shout outs" to noted influencers related to minority rights. Examples include Malcolm X, Muhammed Ali, and his former teammate Eric Reid.

After the initial trends from Kaepernick's sitting during the national anthem in 2016, his influence waned until the 2017 NFL football season began. Kaepernick had approximately 5 million mentions from September 1 to October 10, 2017. A few significant events related to Kaepernick's initial kneeling in 2016 may have influenced this trend. First, on September 22, 2017, during a rally in Alabama, President Trump stated the NFL should fire any player who didn't stand for the national anthem (Tsuji, 2017). Second, on October 8, 2017, Vice President Mike Pence walked out of a game between the Indianapolis Colts and the 49ers to protest a player kneeling during the national anthem (Johnson, 2017). Third, on the same date, Dallas Cowboys owner Jerry Jones stated any player on his team who did not stand for the anthem would not play (Florio, 2017). His trending and mentions once again trailed off after these points.

Kaepernick trended again through the month of September 2018 at the start of the NFL season. He peaked again with approximately 5 million mentions in the time span. The major consideration during this period was the release of his ad campaign with Nike. Kaepernick posted the initial ad on his Twitter account under a close-up of his face: "Believe in something. Even if it means sacrificing everything" (Kaepernick, n.d.). Before the campaign, Kaepernick was released from the San Francisco 49ers and has not been picked up by another NFL team. His NFL firing was most likely related to his social stance because he has not played in the league since the 2016 season.

Kaepernick's 220 tweets were analyzed and categorized from July 2016 until December 2018. The tweets were coded into four main categories: (1) personal, (2) activism without citation, (3) activism with citation, and (4) social. Personal tweets were ones regarding his family, general personal life activities, and product branding. Activism without citation tweets were those regarding social issues

TABLE 53.1 Tweet Influence		
Tweet Type	**Retweets (Mean)**	**Likes (Mean)**
Personal	9,344.66	34,788.31
Activism without citation	7,029.09	19,117.28
Activism with citation	10,921.45	30,379.16
Social	7,218.60	21,443.50

without citing another influencer. Activism with citation tweets were about social issues that included tagged influencers. Social tweets were those regarding general comments such as well wishes for NFL players during the season. The tweet categories were then examined by average retweets and likes. Comments were avoided for impact because there are often false accounts and trolling that do not provide an accurate picture of attention to the specific topic at hand. Kaepernick's personal tweets acquired the most likes. This could potentially be the result of attraction of branding and product placement. Also, his Nike campaign drew considerable attention. Activism with citation acquired the most retweets. It makes sense that additional celebrity influence would have added effect on the various topics discussed (see **TABLE 53.1**).

During this period, Kaepernick's most popular tweet (in both retweets and likes) was a shout-out to rapper Eminem. In October 2017, Eminem released a rap video that was a "diss" track about President Trump. Kaepernick's tweet was a post of the video with the caption "I appreciate you @Eminem." The tweet garnered 385,017 retweets and 956,438 likes.

What the Tweet Does This All Mean?

So, what can be said about Kaepernick's Twitter account? It is clear Kaepernick has sustained attention and influence on the social media platform. There are a few interesting things to note beyond that. First, Kaepernick tends to trend during the fall months of the NFL season. It seems that, for sustainability, it is important to have the topic remain a discussion point by the NFL for Kaepernick's name to be brought into the fold. Also, it gives him a reason for further discussion. If the NFL handled the situation differently (and, potentially, if Kaepernick still played in the NFL), his Twitter account may have trended a bit differently. Also, the peaks and valleys demonstrate the fluidity of social media influences. As previously mentioned, people tend to trend on to different topics with short attention spans to a certain issue. Kaepernick's tweet influences follow that general trend.

In further examining Kaepernick's tweet topics more specifically, the only activism references that had significantly more impact was when policing was referenced. Various other comparisons were examined: content type (personal, social, activism, activism with influence), activism type (racial, ethnic, gender, other), and sports reference (present or not present). None were found to be significantly different in retweets and likes. It is interesting to note the policing reference as the standout influential topic because that was Kaepernick's initial rationale and stance when first sitting on the bench during the 2016 preseason game. It seems that he is still most widely noted for that specific topic, even though he has branched out to discuss various minority-driven social topics thereafter. Also, another interesting point is that Kaepernick's personal activism tweets garnered the least attention. Those for the million-dollar pledge [$t(218) = 1.505$, $p = 0.039$] and know-your-rights campaign [$t(218) = 1.179$, $p = 0.05$] were liked and retweeted significantly less than other tweets.

Based on Kaepernick's trends, his influence seems to be spotty at best and tends to trend off related topics. Also, the trends are more focused around more sensationalized topics such as media hype, politics, and celebrities. It is also surprising that his physical and personal philanthropic events garner less attention than minority discussion topics. Kaepernick's influence does not appear to stand alone and relies on branding and additional celebrity promotion. The low interest in his actual philanthropic events also highlights the interest in social media activism. The influence of social media platforms has created hashtag campaigns and various discussions without the physical "do something" nature of older-style activism. There is not as much of a need to stand outside and physically protest when it can be done at home behind the anonymity of a computer.

▶ The Future of Pop Culture Ethics

Even with the question of the actual influence of a specific person like Colin Kaepernick, it is clear that there is an impact when forces align. For the July 4 holiday in 2019, Nike planned to release a themed shoe with the colonial flag on the heel. Kaepernick took a stance and said the shoe was offensive in representing slavery and white supremacy. Largely because of Kaepernick's comments, Nike pulled the Air Max 1 Quick Strike Fourth of July shoe (Hargrove, 2019). What might be more interesting is that Nike had a 2% stock increase and an additional $3 billion in market value after pulling the shoes (Hale, 2019). Thoughts should not go to the worst-case scenario but are marketing ploys the stronger influence? It could be that situations are predicted for interactions in this way.

Overall, there is no clear picture of how much influence pop culture has or what type of influence it has. Did Nike see a peak in sales because of support for Kaepernick's cause *or* was it toward patriotism for America in the adverse? Other companies also released their own products with colonial flag designs that garnered significant social media attention. What is clear is that there is an influence, although it may not necessarily be easily measured. It is seen on social media and in public, and it is discussed in conversations. What may be more important for us to learn is how to become critical consumers. It may seem negative to call into question every single thing we view and every single conversation we have. Luckily, as quickly as we can retrieve misinformation, we can also retrieve proper information. We just need to be able to discern the difference.

▶ References

Andrews, J. (2019, June 12). Fake news is real—A.I. is going to make it much worse. CNBC. Retrieved from https://www.cnbc.com/2019/07/12/fake-news-is-real-ai-is-going-to-make-it -much-worse.html

ctrl shift face. (2019, July 8). *The Shining starring Jim Carrey: Episode 1—Concentration [DeepFake]* [Video file]. Retrieved from https://www.youtube.com/watch?v=HG_NZpkttXE&amp=&has _verified=1

Dallas, C. A. (n.d.). @camerondallas. Instagram.

Facebook. (2018). Transparency and use of consumer data: Testimony of Mark Zuckerberg in hearing before the United States Senate Committee on the Judiciary and the United States Senate Committee on Commerce, Science, and Transportation.

Florio, M. (2017, October 10). NFL reiterates that standing for the anthem is not mandatory, sort of. NBC Sports. Retrieved from https://profootballtalk.nbcsports.com/2017/10/10/nfl-reiterates -that-standing-for-the-anthem-is-not-mandatory-sort-of/

Fox, M. J. (2018, June 20). @Tracy.pollan is finally on instagram! Check it out. Instagram. Retrieved June 20, 2019, from https://www.instagram.com/p/Bl_4EwQB0Pc/?utm_source=ig_embed

Hale, K. (2019, July 8). Colin Kaepernick spurs Nike's stock after it pulled "Betsey Ross Flag" sneaker. *Forbes*. Retrieved from https://www.forbes.com/sites/korihale/2019/07/08/colin-kaepernick -spurs-nikes-stock-after-it-pulled-betsy-ross-flag-sneaker/#7424ed127ff6

Hargrove, C. (2019, July 3). Colin Kaepernick told Nike to pull a Betsey Ross flag shoe—& they did. Refinery29. Retrieved from https://www.refinery29.com/en-us/2019/07/236941/nikecolin -kaepernick-betsey-ross-sneaker

Helping Oppressed Mothers Endure (HOME) (n.d.). Retrieved from http://www.home2heart.org/

Johnson, A. (2017, October 8). VP Pence walks out of NFL game over players' kneeling protest. NBC News. Retrieved from https://www.nbcnews.com/politics/white-house/vp-pence-walks -out-nfl-game-over-players-kneeling-protest-n808866

Kaepernick, C. (n.d.). @Kaepernick7. Twitter.

Know Your Rights Camp. (2018). Retrieved from https://www.knowyourrightscamp.com/

Laing, D. (2018, November 14). Study finds NFL social media relevance up 9.38%. Samford University. Retrieved from https://www.samford.edu/sports-analytics/fans/2018/Study-Finds -NFL-Social-Media-Relevance-Up-9-38

Romano, A. (2018, April 12). Jordan Peele's simulated Obama PSA is a double-edged warning against fake news. *Vox*. Retrieved from https://www.vox.com/2018/4/18/17252410/jordan -peele-obama-deepfake-buzzfeed

Tsuji, A. (2017, September 22). President Trump says NFL players who protest anthem should be fired. *USA Today Sports*. Retrieved from https://ftw.usatoday.com/2017/09/donald-trump-nfl -anthem-protest-alabama-rally-video-quotes-kneeling-fired-soft-concussion

Wyche, S. (2016, August 27). Colin Kaepernick explains why he sat during national anthem. NFL.com. Retrieved from http://www.nfl.com/news/story/0ap3000000691077/article/colin -kaepernick-explains-why-he-sat-during-national-anthem

Character in Context: Mass Incarceration Creates Monsters

Dennis J. Stevens

What I lecture most about in classrooms and at law academies relates to two titles from my 28 textbooks: *The Failure of the American Correctional Complex: Let's Abolish it* (Stevens, 2014) and *An Introduction to American Policing* (2nd ed.) (Stevens, 2018). In those works, among others, I reveal how Justice Writers of America (JWA) (see crimeprofessor.com for details) serves as a guide in most of my work. This organization guides criminal justice personnel (by invitation only) in their personal construction of journal articles, documents, books, and data. My website is a platform toward careers and education in the American criminal justice system and is linked to reliable and cutting-edge detection, apprehension, and careful gathering of evidence, including careful psychological profiles of high-risk offenders. One tentative conclusion emerging from my research (almost 100 peer-reviewed studies) and from my experience as a high-risk, prison-treatment provider (e.g., Alcoholics Anonymous, Narcotics Anonymous, and prisoner educator, among other programs) is that the American prison complex (which includes law enforcement agencies and the courts) requires a huge upgrade, including resources, to serve and protect American residents including those in custody (Stevens, 2014, 2018, 2019).

Why? Maybe this is a good place to explain my concerns so you can decide whether those concerns are understandable or just misguided or misunderstood on my part. In all my years as a university professor at UMass Boston, the University of North Carolina—Charlotte, and Loyola University of New Orleans (among other institutions of higher education), students want to know if the facts presented by their professors are reliable so they can decide for themselves how they feel about those issues. I'll keep the following stats brief and rounded.

▶ Correctional Supervision Statistics

The Bureau of Justice Statistics (BJS, 2018a) reports that in the year ending 2016, approximately 6.3 million individuals were under the supervision of corrections departments across the country, which includes 2.2 million prisoners in jails and prisons as well as those on probation and parole.

▶ Recidivism

What you need to know right now is the facts about recidivism—the arrests of prisoners who have been released and returned to prison. Over a 9-year period (2005–2014), BJS (2018b) reported that an estimated 68% of released prisoners were rearrested within 3 years of release, 79% were arrested within 6 years, and a total of 83% were arrested within 9 years. **TABLE 54.1** provides a closer look at those released in 2005.

TABLE 54.1 Characteristics of Prisoners Released in 30 States in 2005

Characteristic		Percentage (%)
Gender	Male	89
	Female	11
Racial origin	White	40
	Black/African American	40
	Hispanic/Latino	18
	Other	2
Most serious offense	Violent	26
	Property	30
	Drug	32
	Public Order	13
Number of released prisoners: 401,300		

BJS (2018b). All statistics rounded.

▶ Uniform Crime Report: Reported Crimes

The Uniform Crime Report (UCR) program of the Federal Bureau of Investigation (FBI) collects the number of offenses that come to the attention of law enforcement for violent crimes and property crimes (FBI, 2016b) (see **FIGURE 54.1** and **TABLE 54.2**).

UCR: Arrests

The FBI's UCR program counts one arrest for each separate instance in which a person is arrested, cited, or summoned for an offense (FBI, 2016a).

- Nationwide, law enforcement made an estimated 10,662,252 arrests in 2016.
- Of these arrests, 515,151 were for violent crimes, and 1,353,283 were for property crimes. The highest number of arrests—estimated at 1,572,579 arrests—were for drug abuse violations.

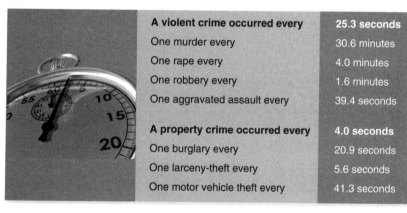

A violent crime occurred every	25.3 seconds
One murder every	30.6 minutes
One rape every	4.0 minutes
One robbery every	1.6 minutes
One aggravated assault every	39.4 seconds
A property crime occurred every	4.0 seconds
One burglary every	20.9 seconds
One larceny-theft every	5.6 seconds
One motor vehicle theft every	41.3 seconds

FIGURE 54.1 2016 Crime clock statistics.

Left: © Paul Fleet/Shutterstock; Right: FBI (2016c)

TABLE 54.2 Offense Analysis 2012–2016: Crimes Reported to Police

Crime	Total Number
Murder	17,250
Rape	130,603
Robbery	332,198
Burglary	1,151,096
Larceny	5,638,455
Motor vehicle theft	765,484

Data from (FBI, 2016d).

UCR: Clearance Rates

In the UCR program, law enforcement agencies can clear or "close" offenses in one of two ways: by arrest or by exceptional means (FBI, 2016e).

Cleared by Arrest

In 2016, 46% of violent crimes and 18% of property crimes were cleared by arrest or exceptional means. When considering clearances of violent crimes, 59% of murder offenses, 53% of aggravated assault offenses, 37% of rape offenses, and 30% of robbery offenses were cleared (see **FIGURE 54.2**).

In a closer look at the preceding in round numbers, six of 10 murderers (not convicted), four of 10 rapists, three of 10 robbers, almost six of 10 aggravated assault perpetrators, one of 10 burglars, two of 10 larceny–theft suspects, and a little more than one of 10 motor vehicle theft villains are apprehended. Therefore, we could argue that most criminals are never apprehended regardless of the nature of their crimes. Now what you don't know is how many of those arrested are tried and convicted.

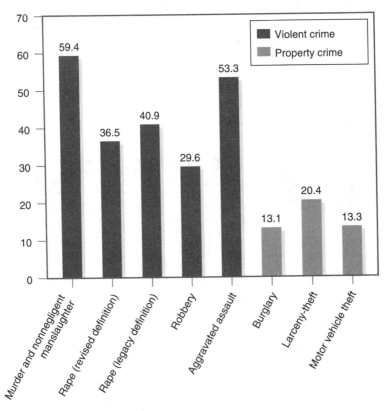

FIGURE 54.2 Percent of crimes cleared by arrest or exceptional means, 2016.

FBI (2016f).

▶ Conviction Rates

Among felony defendants whose cases were adjudicated (89% of cases), 68% were convicted (BJS, 2018a). Felony conviction rates were highest for defendants originally charged with motor vehicle theft (74%), a driving-related offense (73%), murder (70%), burglary (69%), or drug trafficking (67%). They were lowest for defendants originally charged with assault (45%). BJS reports that approximately seven of 10 felony defendants were convicted—including murderers. The nation's state courts had a record-high 102.4 million incoming cases in 2006 (BJS, 2018b).

▶ Violent Crimes Not Reported

Most violent crimes such as rape are never reported (Englander, 2017, p. 182). Similar to the myth about prison and crime deterrence, most Americans believe that the violence we are most likely to encounter would be away from home and on the streets. In fact, a female is far more likely to be assaulted in her own home by someone she knows, according to Englander (2017, pp. 5, 9).

Almost one in five unreported victimizations were never reported because the victim believed the crime was not important enough. Those crimes were rape or sexual assault, robbery, or aggravated assault (National Crime Victimization Survey, 2011). In 2016, more than 5 million victims aged 12 or older experienced violent victimization, and serious violent crimes were reported by more than 1.7 million of those victims (Morgan & Kena, 2018). To better understand unreported crime, see **FIGURE 54.3**.

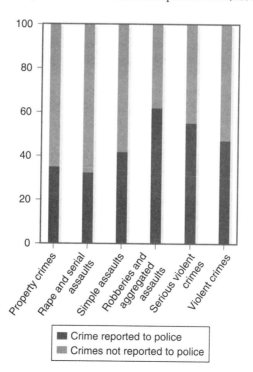

FIGURE 54.3 Percentages of crimes reported and not reported to police in 2015.

Truman, Jennifer, L. & Morgan, Rachel E. (2018, 2016). Criminal victimization, 2015. Bureau of Justice Statistics. Retrieved from https://www.bjs.gov/content/pub/pdf/cv15.pdf

Most reported crimes do not end in an arrest, which suggests that those who commit criminally violent crimes continue to prey on the rest of us without interference.

▶ Relationship Between Unemployment and Mass Incarceration

Young people who leave school in the middle of a recession are significantly more likely to lead a life of crime than those who enter a buoyant labor market. Crime scars resulting from higher entry-level unemployment rates prove to be both long lasting and substantial (Bell, Bindler, & Machin, 2018). The relationship between both the social environment and unemployment, arrest, and subsequent incarceration is strong.

Adam Looney (2018) reports that around one-third of all 30-year-old men who aren't working are either in prison or jail or are unemployed ex-prisoners. Most grew up in "poverty and many weren't working—or were earning very little—before incarceration. A disproportionate share grew up in racially segregated neighborhoods where child poverty rates were high, most parents were unmarried, and few men were employed" (Looney, 2018).

Living in poverty increases the chance of incarceration (Looney & Turner, 2018). But does that mean that affluent persons don't commit crime; they might not be identified, arrested, convicted, or incarcerated as often as the vulnerable person who may or may not in reality be guilty of a crime but look good for the crime. The bottom line is that most often cops arrest vulnerable populations, courts convict those vulnerable defendants more often than others, and prison sentences are typically handed out to those defendants more than others (Nagel, 2013; Nocella, 2013; Stevens, 2011a, 2014, 2018, 2019).

▶ Prison Industrial Complex and Prison Industries

Prisons have become home for growing prison enterprises (Foroohar, 2016). Two examples follow, yet most jurisdictions that include jails have a growing industrial component within their institutions. Although slavery was technically abolished in the United States in 1865, a loophole in the 13th Amendment has allowed a form of slavery to continue "as a punishment for crimes" well into the 21st century (Return to Now, 2016). It is not a surprise that corporations have lobbied for a broader and broader definition of "crime" in the last 150 years. As a result, more people are performing mandatory and essentially unpaid hard labor in America today than in 1830—and most have darker skin or are poor.

New Mexico Corrections Industries

The corrections industries (CIs) make purchasing tasks simple for states, cities, counties, and tribal, federal, educational, and not-for-profit agencies, which can purchase directly from them without the need for competitive bidding. CIs' one-stop shopping can fill all orders for furniture, moving, printing, and janitorial supplies as well as custom-designed shirts and uniforms. Their staffs are available for free consultation on any product or service offered. New Mexico Corrections Industries

(NMCI) contributes approximately $3 million per year to the New Mexico economy through purchases from local suppliers and payment of staff salaries (NMCI, 2018). With wages earned through CI jobs, prisoners contribute to crime victim funds, family and child support; pay legal financial obligations, court-ordered restitution, and court costs; and pay into mandatory savings for use on their release.

Indiana Department of Corrections

Joint ventures include partnerships with private-sector businesses to manufacture or assemble products and perform services within the walls and fences of Indiana's state prison system as operated by the Indiana Department of Correction (IDOC) (Indiana Correctional Industries, 2019). Private industry traditionally relies on its own plant and production facilities, so correctional industries are a viable alternative to meet production needs. Businesses benefit from a dependable labor pool, ample production space, and capacity inside Indiana's correctional facilities. IDOC provides a map that shows the locations of its facilities, and other documents provide information on products, prices, and delivery (Indiana Correctional Industries, 2019).

IDOC talks about its private-sector partnerships (PEN) and emphasizes how it can increase offender jobs through joint ventures with private-sector companies so that products can be manufactured or assembled within the walls and fences of IDOC properties and to perform services (SI, 2018). Private industry traditionally relies on its own plant and production facilities, so correctional industries are viable alternatives to meeting production needs. Businesses benefit from a dependable labor pool, ample production space, and capacity inside Indiana's correctional facilities.

▶ Prison Enterprises Are Big Business

Prison enterprises are booming businesses in the 21st century. One reason private corporations might have a vested interest in obtaining contracts to operate private prisons can be seen in the prisons' lucrative industrial potential. Thanks to prison labor, the United States is once again an attractive investment for Third World labor markets. A good example is the company that operated a maquiladora (an assembly plant in Mexico near the border) and closed that plant to relocate it to San Quentin State Prison in California (Pelaez, 2019). In Texas, a factory fired its 150 workers and contracted the services of prisoner workers from the private Lockhart, Texas, prison, where circuit boards are assembled for companies such as IBM and Compaq. Former Oregon State Representative Kevin Mannix recently urged Nike to cut its production in Indonesia and bring it back to his state, Nike's headquarter state, telling the shoe manufacturer that "there won't be any transportation costs; we're offering you competitive prison labor (here)" (Pelaez, 2019).

Pelaez (2019) notes that human rights organizations are condemning this new form of inhumane exploitation. For tycoons who have invested in the prison industry, it has been like finding a pot of gold, Pelaez (2019) remarked. The advantages are that prisoners aren't unionized, so there are no strikes, no unemployment insurance to pay, no vacations to schedule, and no comp time to reimburse. All prisoners are full-time, are never late or absent, and make things profitable. Also, if prisoners don't like the pay of 25 cents on every two dollars made or if they refuse to work, they're locked up in isolation.

The federal prison industry produces 100% of all military helmets, ammunition belts, bulletproof vests, ID tags, shirts, pants, tents, bags, and canteens (Pelaez, 2019). Along with war supplies, prison workers supply 98% of the entire market for equipment-assembly services; 93% of paints and paintbrushes; 92% of stove assemblies; 46% of body armor; 36% of home appliances; 30% of headphones, microphones, and speakers; and 21% of office furniture. Other products include airplane parts and medical supplies. Prisoners are even raising Seeing Eye dogs for blind people.

Cheap Labor

At least 37 states have legalized contracting prison labor by private corporations that mount their operations inside state prisons, according to Pelaez (2019). The list of companies includes the cream of U.S. corporate society: IBM, Boeing, Motorola, Microsoft, AT&T, Wireless, Texas Instruments, Dell, Compaq, Honeywell, Hewlett-Packard, Nortel, Lucent Technologies, 3Com, Intel, Northern Telecom, TWA, Nordstrom's, Revlon, Macy's, Pierre Cardin, and Target Stores. Between 1980 and 1994, profits went up from $392 million to $1.31 billion. Payrolls are low. The highest-paying private prison is CCA in Tennessee, where prisoners receive 50 cents per hour for what they call "highly skilled positions."

▶ Challenges Presented by Prison Industries

Some argue that the United States is the most civilized society to ever exist because of its affluence and technological and intellectual achievements (Yuen, 2019). It is the home of democracy, free will, and individuality. Yet the U.S. government, without putting its policies and strategies to a vote or allowing its population a say-so or even the knowledge that they restricted the use of 1,230,637 km² of land (almost 13% of the total U.S. land mass), restricted 3.5 million km² marine area (41% of total marina area), and 607 national designations, and it restricts the use of almost 28% of the land mass of the country and tends to emphasize governmental abuses, reports the World Database on Protected Areas (2017). If government can get away with that without a vote or even a say-so, then certainly deciding who is the criminal is not a far reach. At the core of this chapter is the perspective that Americas have little say-so or knowledge about governmental policies about detainment, arrest, conviction, and mass incarceration, particularly of marginalized or vulnerable populations. The American government, in league with social media constructs and media propaganda, suggests that mass incarceration is the most adventurous way out of America's crime problems (Stevens, 2011a). A thought of John Locke when establishing the U.S. government is that through "[publicly] agreed laws that correspond to a common set of public restrictions, the 'people as a sovereign body' serves to protect against violations of individual liberty and despotic power," quotes Queiroz (2018).

Think about what has been promoted about immigrants in 2019 by U.S. authorities at the highest level. For example, a government official has said of undocumented immigrants, "These aren't people. These are animals" (Korte & Gomez, 2018). So, how would law enforcement and corrections personnel respond to undocumented immigrants and other politically profiled individuals even when those individuals have never committed a crime or never been tried in a court of law? Violating the democratic rights of American residents (all residents) is a topic that Aguilar and Chiprin (2013) respond to this way: "The United States' criminal justice industrial complex has become a sprawling, massive enterprise. Policing and incarceration had evolved a sociopolitical mythology that applies regardless of law or method"; that is, the justice system has priority over individual democratic rights, and that includes how those individuals are treated once imprisoned.

This means that a criminal is whoever the state says is a criminal. A quote by Russian novelist Fyodor Dostoevsky (1821–1881) is appropriate here: "The degree of civilization in a society can be judged by entering its prisons." Based on the evidence presented thus far, in a country that increasingly resembles one huge prison, the only intelligent choice is to plan a prison break.

▶ Corporate and Managerial Crime

Perhaps the largest growth sector for illegal behavior in the United States is among corporations and corporate managers in pursuit of organizational and individual goals. For example, researchers argue that a significant relationship exists between the pursuit and maintenance of industry profits and dynamism in the industry, and illegal behavior is represented through price-fixing by business cartels (Kunsch, Schnarr, & Rowe, 2016). Those researchers also conclude that illegal behavior among corporate managers is rampant as they pursue individual corporate profits and the munificence associated with these cartels. Little doubt that corporate crime is out of control, advises another expert (Uhlmann, 2016). Corporate wrongdoing has pernicious effects on our communities, the economy, and the environment, which warrants the condemnation that criminal law provides, Uhlmann (2016) adds. Criminal prosecution of corporations upholds the rule of law, validates the choices of law-abiding companies, and promotes accountability. Together those values contribute to our sense that justice has been done when crime occurs, which enhances trust in the legal system, provides the opportunity for societal catharsis, and allows us to move forward in the aftermath of criminal activity. "When corporations face no consequences for their criminal behavior, we minimize their lawlessness and increase cynicism about the outsized influence of corporations" (Uhlmann, 2016).

▶ Goals of the American Justice Community

The ultimate goal of the justice community is to maintain a balance between public safety and the due process guarantees of the U.S. Constitution, a founding document that many people, including this author, have defended in foreign counties. In the final analysis, the job of everyone in criminal justice is public safety; this goal is accomplished by reducing dangers and stopping crime. Reducing risk means just that: In volatile encounters, justice personnel do not escalate danger but instead work to reduce it. Nonetheless, justice personnel know they cannot stop crime but can control it within a legal framework. In part, that means justice personnel, including correctional and police officers, volunteers, and contract venders, must:

- defuse danger where it exists particularly among law enforcement;
- provide services without compromising individual constitutional guarantees, especially due process guarantees, unless under correctional supervision or confinement, which limits constitutional guarantees; and
- control prison populations by using "custody with care."

For now, just know that in a free society, the justice system should conduct its business without violating the individual rights of any individual, including prisoners, even though their rights are diminished.

▶ My Challenges

Often the practices of the justice community and even public education and social services and their policies, including compliance issues, create a huge imbalance for personnel, many of whom contribute to JWA and others who were students in my classes more than 25 years. In some cases, practices that violate compliance issues are criminalized through federal litigation, so justice practitioners (and other public personnel) learn different techniques to avoid prosecution such as developing police reports that comply with regulations (Stevens, 2019, p. 14; 2018, p. 329). This brings to mind the evil twin concept.

Evil Twin Concept

Among other scholars, Deering (2016) has thoughts about the imbalance between democracy and governmental protection—for example, in prisons—and the personnel practices of those correctional officers who carry out policy. Rosemary Radford Ruether (2007, p. 1) addressed this idea of democracy and justice practitioner conduct as the double identity of America: "It is about the ideology of God and love, peace and law, democracy and freedom, and the evil twin that is concealed behind this rhetoric of positive national values and beliefs." On the one hand is the rule of law and the public servants who take oaths to defend the U.S. Constitution before their employment; on the other hand are those who might easily deviate from the rule of law when engaged with individuals. For instance:

> Correctional officers adhere to a code of ethics and professional conduct, which is a set of standards pertaining to morals and the effective discharge of duties. There is no uniform text for the code, with each jurisdiction or facility allowed to craft its own. However, the overarching goal is to administer justice with integrity, and within the bounds of the law. The code serves as the basis of policies and directives, rules and regulations, protocols and procedures, all of which are observed and undertaken in relation to facility management and operations. It embodies such core values as discipline, judiciousness, truthfulness, vigilance, respect for human rights, and sense of responsibility. (Correctional Officer.Org, 2019)

Violations

However, consider the unlawful conduct of officers. For example, the U.S. Department of Justice (DOJ) (2017) announced that "four former corrections officers at the Jackson County Detention Center . . . have been indicted by a federal grand jury for their roles in a conspiracy to physically assault an inmate in violation of his

Constitutional protection against unreasonable force." The DOJ (2017) added that "the Constitution provides every citizen the right of due process and protects every citizen from the use of unreasonable force." However, BJS (2012) reports that:

- around 5% of former state prisoners reported an incident involving another inmate, and 5% reported an incident involving facility staff;

- an estimated 1% of former prisoners reported that they unwillingly had sex or sexual contact with facility staffers, and 5% reported that they "willingly" had sex or sexual contact with staffers; and

- among former state prisoners, the rate of inmate-on-inmate sexual victimization was at least three times higher for females (14%) than for males (4%).

Remember that most crimes are never reported; that might well be the case for prisoners, too. Also, the differences between ethical and sworn policy among correctional and law enforcement officers is similar to the differences between physicians and patients, mental health providers and patients, and even perhaps the ethical policies among teachers and students. Adding parents and children to that list is a definite fit. Personnel who might deviate from policy, particularly when they violate the rights of those whom they supervise, can easily fit into an evil twin perspective as advanced by Ruether (2007). The place of the prison industrial complex in the popular imagination reveals as much about the power of American mythmaking and the distorted way we view much of the world and how to control it.

▶ Neutralizing the Plague of Mass Incarceration

Many people see mass incarceration as the *sine qua non* of the criminal justice system. Maybe you agree with that thought. Without prison, they argue, we could not punish past crimes, deter future crimes, or keep dangerous criminals safely separate from the rest of society. Prison advocates who argue that prisons are an indispensable tool to minimize crime tend to neglect other forms of punishment that have proven to move an offender toward law-abiding behavior as opposed to creating monsters from nonviolent offenders such as community corrections. Switching the focus from punishment to rehabilitation has merit for society, the offender, and his or her family and friends, according to the American Psychological Association (2003). One fact is that once an offender is incarcerated, he or she will always be treated as a convict. You know how that works; it can be explained through the labeling theory (Becker, 1997). Once labeled a criminal, how many options would this individual have once outside the prison?

Incarceration as a method of controlling crimes is also flawed because prison imposes enormous but well-hidden societal losses. It is an inefficient device for serving the utilitarian aims of the criminal law system—namely, optimally deterring bad social actors while minimizing total social costs, according to Salib (2017). An alternative system of criminal punishment could serve societal goals more efficiently.

One repetitive conclusion advanced throughout this article is that the prison industrial complex, similar to slavery, cannot be improved—so let's abolish as we did slavery. Confinement should be reserved for the worst of the worst, and confinement should be administered by state and local governments rather than federal entities and their intrusions into what are clearly state obligations and responsibilities.

Bottom line—which should come as no surprise—is that a huge disproportion of those imprisoned are individuals largely from marginalized populations; that is, there are more minorities than any other ethnic group in prison populations (Goodwin, 2013; Stevens, 2014, p. 396-401; Stevens, 2019, p. 47). No more rounding up all the usual suspects based on status: vulnerable population members who might fit someone's image of a criminal as opposed to someone who actually committed a criminal act (Stevens, 2018, p. 85; 2019, p. 26).

In a final analysis of mass incarceration, regardless of the previous nonviolent nature of prisoners, personnel tend to assimilate or accept the norms and values (or the prisonization effect) of the prison complex. Think of it this way: Just as when you first entered college, you looked around to see how other students behaved and whether you wanted to be accepted by other students and instructors, so you conformed. Konnikova (2015), a reporter for *The New Yorker*, provides another thought about prison culture: "[T]he Stanford County Prison (as an example) was a heavily manipulated environment, and the guards and prisoners (regardless of their conviction crime) acted in ways that were largely predetermined by how their roles were presented." The fact is that around one in four state prisoners released in 30 states in 2005 had been in prison for violent offenses (BJS, 2018b). Violence is out of control, but all sorts of victimization continually happens and often to the same prisoners; for example, young male and female prisoners are often raped and beaten by other prisoners and a few corrupt correctional officers, and many prisoners out of desperation and circumstance turn to cocaine and violence to survive, and people wonder why recidivism is so high (Nocella, 2013; Stevens, 2011b; Wolff, Shi, & Siegel, 2009). The notion that both male and female prisons can create monsters is consistent among other reliable researchers (Nagel, 2013; Nocella, 2013; Samenow, 2001, 2014).

▶ References

American Psychological Association. (2003). Rehabilitate or punish? Retrieved from https://www.apa.org/monitor/julaug03/rehab

Bell, B., Bindler, A., & Machin, S. (2018). Crime scars: Recessions and the making of career criminals. *Review of Economics and Statistics, 100*(3), 392–404.

Becker, H. (1997). Outsiders: Studies in the sociology of deviance. New York: Free Press.

Bureau of Justice Statistics. (BJS). (2018a). Correctional populations in the United States, 2016. NCJ251211. Retrieved from https://www.bjs.gov/content/pub/pdf/cpus16.pdf

Bureau of Justice Statistics. (BJS). (2018b). Update on prisoner recidivism: A 9-year follow-up period 2005–2014. Retrieved from https://www.bjs.gov/content/pub/pdf/18upr9yfup0514.pdf

Bureau of Justice Statistics. (BJS). (2018c). What is the probability of conviction for felony defendants? Retrieved from https://www.bjs.gov/index.cfm?ty=qa&iid=403.

Bureau of Justice Statistics. (BJS). (2018d). Summary findings: courts. Retrieved from https://www.bjs.gov/index.cfm?ty=tp&tid=30

Bureau of Justice Statistics. (BJS). (2012). PREA Data Collection Activities, 2012. Retrieved from https://www.bjs.gov/content/pub/pdf/pdca12.pdf

Correctional Officer.Org. (2019). Code of Ethics and Professional Conduct. Retrieved from https://www.correctionalofficer.org/professional-conduct

Deering, J. (2016). *Probation practice and the new penology: Practitioner reflections*. New York, NY: Routledge.

Englander, E. K. L. (2017). *Understanding violence*. New York, NY: Routledge.

Federal Bureau of Investigation. (FBI). (2016a). Persons arrested. Retrieved from https://ucr.fbi.gov/crime-in-the-u.s/2016/crime-in-the-u.s.-2016/topic-pages/persons-arrested

Federal Bureau of Investigation. (FBI). (2016b). Offenses known to law enforcement. Retrieved from https://ucr.fbi.gov/crime-in-the-u.s/2016/crime-in-the-u.s.-2016/topic-pages/offenses-known-to-law-enforcement

Federal Bureau of Investigation. (FBI). (2016c). Crime clock statistics. Retrieved from https://ucr.fbi.gov/crime-in-the-u.s/2016/crime-in-the-u.s.-2016/figures/crime-clock

Federal Bureau of Investigation. (FBI). (2016d). Offense analysis. United States, 2012–2016. Retrieved from https://ucr.fbi.gov/crime-in-the-u.s/2016/crime-in-the-u.s.-2016/tables/table-5

Federal Bureau of Investigation. (FBI). (2016e). Clearance rates, 2016. Retrieved from https://ucr.fbi.gov/crime-in-the-u.s/2016/crime-in-the-u.s.-2016/topic-pages/clearances

Foroohar, R. (2016. May 16). American capitalism's great crisis. *Time*. Retrieved from http://time.com/4327419/american-capitalisms-great-crisis/

Goodwin, M. (2013, March 29). Panel 1: AIDS/HIV. Presentations at the University of Maryland, Carey Law School. Switch Point Stories. Retrieved from http://digitalcommons.law.umaryland.edu/switch/2013/mar29/7/

Indiana Correctional Industries. (2019). Prison industries. Retrieved from https://www.in.gov/idoc/penindustries/2566.htm

Konnikova, M. (2015). The real lesson of the Stanford prison experiment. *The New Yorker*. Retrieved from https://www.newyorker.com/science/maria-konnikova/the-real-lesson-of-the-stanford-prison-experiment

Korte, G., & Gomez, A. (2018). Trump ramps up rhetoric on undocumented immigrants: "These aren't people. These are animals." *USA Today*. Retrieved from https://www.usatoday.com/story/news/politics/2018/05/16/trump-immigrants-animals-mexico-democrats-sanctuary-cities/617252002/

Kunsch, D. W., Schnarr, K., & Rowe, W. G. (2016). Effects of the environment on illegal cartel activity. *Journal of Strategy and Management, 9*(3), 344–360.

Looney, A. (2018). 5 facts about prisoners and work, before and after incarceration. Brookings Institution. Retrieved from https://www.brookings.edu/blog/up-front/2018/03/14/5-facts-about-prisoners-and-work-before-and-after-incarceration/

Looney, A., & Turner, N. (2018). Work and opportunity before and after incarceration. Brookings Institution. Retrieved from https://www.brookings.edu/research/work-and-opportunity-before-and-after-incarceration/

Morgan, R. E., & Ken, G. (2018). Criminal victimization, 2016: Revised. NCJ 252121. U.S. Department of Justice. Retrieved from https://www.bjs.gov/content/pub/pdf/cv16.pdf

Nagel, M. E. (2013). An Ubuntu ethic of punishment. Pp. 177–186 in M. E. Nagel & A. J. Nocella II, *The End of Prisons*. New York, NY: Rodopi Publishing.

National Crime Victimization Survey. (2011). Criminal victimization, 2010 (NCJ 235508). Washington, DC: U.S. Department of Justice. Retrieved from http://bjs.gov/content/pub/pdf/cv10.pdf

New Mexico Corrections Industries (NMCI). (2018). Retrieved from http://cd.nm.gov/admin/ci.html

Nocella, A., II. (2013). The rise of terrorization of dissent. Pp. 13–30 in M. E. Nagel & A. J. Nocella, II, *The End of Prisons*. New York, NY: Rodopi Publishing.

Pelaez, V. (2019, September 13). The prison industry in the United States: Big business or a new form of slavery? Global Research. Retrieved from http://www.globalresearch.ca/the-prison-industry-in-the-united-states-big-business-or-a-new-form-of-slavery/8289

Queiroz, R. (2018). Individual liberty and the importance of the concept of the people. Palgrave Communications. Retrieved from https://www.nature.com/articles/s41599-018-0151-3

Return to Now. (2016, June 13). How prison labor is the new American slavery and most of us unknowingly support it. Retrieved from http://returntonow.net/2016/06/13/prison-labor-is-the-new-american-slavery/

Ruether, R. R. (2007). *America, Amerikkka: Elect nation and imperial violence*. London, UK: Equinoxpub.

Salib, P. N. (2017, Fall). Why prison? An economic critique. *Berkeley Journal of Criminal Law, 22*(2), 111–170. Retrieved from https://papers.ssrn.com/sol3/papers.cfm?abstract_id=2928219

Samenow, S. E. (2001). *Before it's too late*. New York, NY: Harmony.

Samenow, S. E. (2014). *Inside the criminal mind: Revised and updated edition*. New York, NY: Broadway Books.

Stevens, D. J. (2011a). *Media and criminal justice*. Burlington, MA: Jones & Bartlett.

Stevens, D. J. (2011b). *Wicked women: A journey of super predators*. Bloomington, IN: IUniverse.

Stevens, D. J. (2014). *The failure of the American prison complex: Let's abolish it*. Dubuque, IA: Kendall Hunt.

Stevens, D. J. (2018). *An introduction to American policing* (2nd ed). Burlington, MA: Jones & Bartlett.

Stevens, D. J. (2019). *Cops at risk: Homicide, litigation, and disease*. San Diego, CA: Cognella Academic Publishing.

Truman, J. L., & Morgan, R. E. (2018). *Criminal victimization, 2015*. Washington, DC: Bureau of Justice Statistics. Retrieved from https://www.bjs.gov/content/pub/pdf/cv15.pdf

Uhlmann, D. M. (2016). *The pendulum swings: Reconsidering corporate criminal prosecution*. University of Michigan Law School. Retrieved from http://repository.law.umich.edu/cgi/viewcontent.cgi?article=2759&context=articles

U.S. Department of Justice. (2017). Four former corrections officers indicted for civil rights violations. Retrieved from https://www.justice.gov/opa/pr/four-former-corrections-officers-indicted-civil-rights-violations

Wolff, N., Shi, J., & Siegel, J. A. (2009). Patterns of victimization among male and female inmates: Evidence of an enduring legacy. *Violence and Victims, 24*(4), 469–484.

World Database on Protected Areas. (2017). World commission on protected areas. Retrieved from https://protectedplanet.net/country/US

Yuen, F. K. (2019). Power as prestige in world politics. *International Affairs, 95*(1), 119–142.

An Immovable Object[1] and a Corruptible City: Ethical Considerations in *The Dark Knight* Trilogy

Kristine Levan

In comic book contexts, both heroes and villains may be prompted to engage in difficult decision-making processes. Such processes often involve a moral dilemma or ethical conundrum that the audience must contend with at the same as the characters do. In addition, themes involving crime and justice are commonplace in many comic worlds. These factors allow an ideal setting to analyze various ethical issues and complexities that are often contiguous to those made within the criminal justice system.

Many comic world characters—including Spider-Man, Superman, and Wonder Woman—involve some conceptualization of ethics, morality, crime, and justice. One of the more blatant illustrations of how those concepts translate into a fictional comic world is illustrated within the Batman comic universe. In 1939, Batman debuted in *Detective Comics*. Since then, the Caped Crusader has appeared in Batman comic books, numerous graphic novels, the Batman television series (Dozier, D'Angelo, & Horwitz, 1966–1968), *Batman: The Animated Series* (Timm & Radomski, 1992–1995), a litany of films, several video games, and various forms of licensed toys and items featuring Batman characters. From the standpoint of cultural criminology, comic books and the accompanying films, television shows, and other iterations of their characters are portions of the collective by which society ascribes meaning and understanding to important issues of crime and justice (Ferrell, Hayward, & Young, 2015).

This article will focus on ethical dilemmas and justice issues in *The Dark Knight* trilogy films: *Batman Begins* (Nolan, 2005), *The Dark Knight* (Nolan, 2008), and *The Dark Knight Rises* (Nolan, 2012). Although there are many permutations of Batman in the vast Gotham universe, these specific films were selected for a few reasons: They make up a definitive trilogy and the story arc and characters can be analyzed within a contained context (i.e., the story line has a beginning and an end). Furthermore, because the films were widely released, more readers are likely to be familiar with the characters, events, and themes discussed herein, making comparisons to ethical issues more salient.

▶ The Origins of Batman: Violation of the Social Contract

Even those who are not Batman aficionados are generally familiar with his origin story. Born to wealthy Thomas and Martha Wayne, a young Bruce Wayne watched as his parents were robbed and murdered in an alley by a man who would later be identified as Joe Chill. This critical moment is a turning point for Bruce Wayne, one that has prompted extensive analysis over the decades. It has been argued, for instance, that the Batman hero and protagonist was created because of a lack of duty fulfillment from society, or "where the 'social contract' between citizen and state is the most essential" (Spanakos, 2008, p. 59). As a child, Bruce Wayne was dependent on his parents, who themselves depended on agents of the state for protection and safety. Because of this lack of duty from the state (and society more generally), Bruce Wayne lost his parents, and this later became the impetus for his transition into the Batman persona.

As he emerges into adulthood, he begins to understand the value of the social contract. "What man loses by the social contract is his natural freedom and an unlimited right to anything by which he is tempted and can obtain; what he gains is civil freedom and the right of property over everything he possesses" (Rousseau, 1762/1999, p. 91). But following that fateful night, Bruce Wayne never makes peace with losing his parents. Because the state's obligation under the social contract offers protection to its citizens (Rousseau, 1762/1999, p. 102), there may be no clearer violation in the eyes of a child than watching his or her parents murdered before them by a criminal and wondering if the agents of the state might have been able to prevent this tragedy. Moreover, a similar breakdown in structure and morals may be likely to continue, and incidents such as those that befell the Wayne family are likely to occur to other Gotham residents.

Over the course of three films, viewers see the social order of Gotham becoming progressively more chaotic, descending into what has been described in other Gotham scenarios as "Hobbesian disorder" (Spanakos, 2008, p. 60). Gangs, mobs, and villains scramble to claim pieces of Gotham territory as their own (Patterson, 2008). In *Batman Begins*, Bruce Wayne distinctly expresses his mission to Henri Ducard while training with the League of Shadows by stating, "I seek the means to fight injustice. To turn fear against those who prey on the fearful." The Batman persona will evolve in time to seek justice by apprehending villains and criminals. But what is Batman's relationship to law enforcement agencies? Is he considered an agent of the law or an independent vigilante?

▶ Batman: Lone Vigilante or State Actor?

Batman works alongside law enforcement on several occasions, but one particular scene in *The Dark Knight* illustrates the question of whether he may be considered a state actor.[2] For instance, during an interrogation of the Joker at Gotham City Police Department (GCPD), Batman becomes physically aggressive. Here, we could argue that he is a state actor. In this scene, the police have permitted him into an interrogation room to produce a response from the Joker regarding the location of Harvey Dent and Rachel Dawes; the Joker is believed to be involved in their disappearance (Lisk, 2014). During their exchange, the Joker disagrees that Batman and law enforcement representatives (as well as Gotham's civilians) bear any similarities. In the following excerpt he explains to Batman how their two personalities are more alike than Batman may realize:

> THE JOKER: Don't talk like one of them. . . . You're not! Even if you'd like to be. To them, you're just a freak, like me. They need you right now . . . when they don't, they'll cast you out, like a leper. See their morals, their code, it's a bad joke. Dropped at the first sign of trouble. They're only as good as the world allows them to be. I'll show you—when the chips are down these, uh, these civilized people, they'll eat each other. See, I'm not a monster. I'm just ahead of the curve. (*The Dark Knight*)

The Joker is partially correct. At the end of *The Dark Knight*, Batman ultimately chooses to leave Gotham of his own accord to protect the name and work of District Attorney Harvey Dent. By taking the blame for Dent's murders, committed after Dent assumed the Two Face persona, Batman is able to make a selfless and utilitarian choice. Revealing the true identity of the murderer would have prevented the justice that Batman, Commissioner Gordon, and Harvey Dent had worked toward.

The inadequacy and corruption portrayed by the GCPD is partly why Batman feels compelled to his extreme methods of vigilante justice (Phillips & Strobl, 2013; Reyns & Henson, 2010). His methodology for justice, however, causes dismay for Commissioner Loeb, who tells James Gordon, "No one takes the law into their own hands in my city" (*Batman Begins*).

▶ Gotham City Police Department: A Case of Corruption

Corruption and inadequacy of the Gotham City Police Department is a consistent and driving force in the storyline (Phillips & Strobl, 2013; Giddens, 2015). In *Batman Begins*, Henri Ducard explains that the corruption in Gotham is so extensive because the League of Shadows "infiltrated every level of its infrastructure." Several law enforcement officers at the GCPD are shown to be corrupt or untrustworthy, allowing both organized and individual criminals to flourish in the city (Phillips & Strobl, 2013; Giddens, 2015). This is a typical result when law enforcement becomes corrupt, as Banks (2017) explains: "one implication of corruption is that corrupters gain influence over the police, subverting police from their proper role and creating conditions that favor crime in the sense that there is an increase in public tolerance for some crimes" (p. 43). With the GCPD ignoring major and minor criminal offenses, the city becomes a breeding ground for underground economies and violence, allowing for Mafia influence, as well as major crime villains such as Ra's al Ghul, the Scarecrow, the Joker, and Bane to infiltrate the city.

The audience is privy to corruption from several key and influential individuals in Gotham and observes several instances develop over time. For instance, in *Batman Begins*, Detective Flass is one example of a corrupt law enforcement agent, taking bribes and engaging in unethical conduct throughout the film. Psychologist Dr. Jonathan Crane (the Scarecrow) provides false testimonies during trials and smuggles fear-inducing psychological drugs into Gotham for nefarious purposes. In *The Dark Knight*, Lau, who worked for Sal Maroni and the organized crime ring as an accountant, is arrested and brought in to the GCPD for questioning. The intent is to have him testify against those whom he has been working with (in exchange for immunity). Jim Gordon and Harvey Dent disagree over where to hold Lau because they distrust both county and GCPD holding cells. Several GCPD officers have also been investigated while Dent was working in Internal Affairs (IA). "If I didn't work with cops you'd investigated while you were making your name at IA I'd be working alone. I don't get political points for being an idealist. . . . I have to do the best I can with what I have" (Jim Gordon, *The Dark Knight*).

In *The Dark Knight Rises,* Bane delivers the following in a speech just outside Blackgate Prison:

> BANE: We take Gotham from the corrupt! The rich! The oppressors of generations who have kept you down with myths of opportunity and we give it back to you—the people. Gotham is yours! None shall interfere. Do as you please, but start by storming Blackgate and freeing the oppressed! (*The Dark Knight Rises*)

Bane gives this speech just after telling Gotham that Commissioner Jim Gordon had been dishonest for the past eight years. Aside from Commissioner Gordon and Batman, nobody knew that Harvey Dent, Gotham's former district attorney and "White Knight," had become the villainous Two Face before his death. Batman and Gordon allowed him to die a hero, forcing Batman (and in many respects, Bruce Wayne) into seclusion by taking the blame for the murders Dent had committed as Two Face. Moreover, many of the inmates serving time in Blackgate Prison were prosecuted by Harvey Dent. With the passage of the Dent Act, many of these prisoners were denied parole. With this shocking news, residents view the GCPD as more untrustworthy than previously believed and are willing to engage in revolution to gain control of Gotham.

▶ Justice, Retribution, or Revenge? "Crime Cannot Be Tolerated"

As with most superhero stories, "the seduction of retribution is always present and many plots involve the heroes wrestling with their own emotional desire for retribution" (Phillips & Strobl, 2013, p. 205). But, as Ducard explains to Bruce Wayne in *Batman Begins*, the goal for the League of Shadows is justice. Crime cannot be tolerated. Criminals thrive on the indulgences on society's understandings." Delineation between retribution and justice can be difficult to decipher, and it seems that Bruce Wayne and the League of Shadows (including Ducard/Ra's al Ghul) have different perspectives on justice.

Concepts such as revenge, retribution, and justice can quickly become muddled. Aristotle's view of justice is "conduct which conforms to whatever constitutes an authoritative instrument of moral and social control" (Chroust & Osborn, 1942, p. 129). Rawls's perspective on justice is less concerned with procedural justice and more focused on morality and fairness, which are also inclusive of social justice (Banks, 2017). Retribution based on the concept of *lex talionis* seeks punishments equal to the crimes committed. Finally, the concept of revenge seeks vengeance for actions. Unlike justice and retribution, revenge, according to Nozick (1981) encompasses "a particular emotional tone, pleasure in the suffering of another" (p. 367, as quoted in Banks, 2017, p. 164).

Bruce Wayne grapples with this issue in *Batman Begins* when Joe Chill is up for release from prison in exchange for information on his former cellmate, Mafia boss Carmine Falcone. Bruce was initially present in the court, and afterward intended to shoot Chill with a gun he had hidden in his jacket sleeve, a clear act of revenge for the murders of his parents. However, one of Falcone's employees completes the job first. Initially, perhaps Bruce feels cheated that he was unable to personally exact retribution on his parents' murderer. In his exchange with Rachel afterward, she discusses her viewpoints on the difference between justice and revenge:[3]

> RACHEL: No, they're never the same, Bruce. Justice is about harmony. Revenge is about you making yourself feel better, which is why we have an impartial system.
>
> BRUCE: Well, your system is broken.
>
> RACHEL: You care about justice? Look beyond your own pain, Bruce. This city is rotting. They talk about the depression as if its history, and it's not. Things are worse than ever down here. Falcone floods our streets with crime and drugs, preying on the desperate, creating new Joe Chills every day. You know Falcone may not have killed your parents, Bruce, but he's destroying everything that they stood for. (*Batman Begins*)

Once Bruce Wayne transitions into his Batman persona, his idea of justice appears to be separate from the existing criminal justice system because Gotham's inept and corrupt structure necessitates that it be separate. His focus shifts from a perspective once focused on revenge or retribution to one more interested in justice. Viewers are apprised of the social and economic ills of Gotham. As Banks (2017) explains, "Raising the issue of the social causes of crime and questioning the effectiveness of punishment are irrelevant considerations to a retributivist" (p. 160). Gotham's criminal underworld and economic disparity contribute greatly to the criminogenic chaos of Gotham. Bruce Wayne acknowledges these as root causes and seeks to right them through justice.

Wayne is addressing the corruption of the players within the system, doling out justice for super villains and everyday criminals, and exacting justice for his parents. As Giddens (2015) explains, "not only does Batman exist because of the *failures* of the system, but . . . he is directly engaged in *improving and fixing* that system through his extra-legal activities" (p. 768). His role as crime fighter appears to be more complicated than some other superheroes, who can deliver villains to an agency that we assume to be corruption-free to be processed in the way that police, courts, and corrections view as just. In Gotham, criminal offenders may be released, sentenced to Blackgate Prison, or sent to Arkham Asylum, where any number of events may drastically alter their fictional lives and story arcs.

▶ Batman's Code of Ethics

Batman creates his own ethical rules and moral code, which becomes common knowledge among Gotham residents and law enforcement, as well as among the villainous population. For instance, Batman does not rely on firearms to accomplish justice, a fact known to the Scarecrow in the beginning of the *The Dark Knight* film as he exclaims "That's not him!" when he spots a Batman clone brandishing a gun. Batman also informs Catwoman of his rule, although she later urges him to rethink his stance on guns during particularly catastrophic events in *The Dark Knight Rises*. When Batman seeks information on the Joker from Sal Maroni in *The Dark Knight*, he explains how Batman's moral code is preventing him from capturing his nemesis, the Joker:

> MARONI: Nobody's gonna tell you nothin'. They're wise to your act. You got rules. The Joker . . . he's got no rules. Nobody's gonna cross him for you. You want this guy you got one way, but you already know what that is. Just take off that mask. Let him come and find ya. (*The Dark Knight*)

Of course, Batman's ethical code and motivations are in sharp contrast to those of the Joker. As Alfred attempts to explain the Joker's motivations (or lack thereof) to Bruce Wayne, "Some men aren't looking for anything logical, like money. They can't be bought, bullied, reasoned or negotiated with. Some men just want to watch the world burn" (*The Dark Knight*). This example is also provided as one potentially illustrating the Joker's "healthy sense of self-preservation" (Robichaud, 2008, p. 73).

Batman is most infamously aligned with the ethical rule of his avoidance of lethal violence (see Phillips & Strobl, 2013, pp. 128-129). In *Batman Begins*, Ducard and the League of Shadows request that Bruce Wayne execute a captured murderer, which he refuses to do. Throughout the film, Ducard intentionally continues to place Bruce Wayne in situations where he seems cornered to commit murder, yet he does not. At one point, he reminds Ducard that he saved his life back at the temple of the League of Shadows, to which Ducard simply responds, "I warned you about compassion, Bruce." Toward the end of the film, he states, "I won't kill you . . . but I don't have to save you," as he allows the train to crash from the tracks without rescuing him. This, of course, is in contrast to his rescue of Ducard years earlier from the League of Shadows temple. From the beginning of their interactions, Ducard views Bruce Wayne's empathy and compassion as weaknesses, but he remains steadfast in specifying lethality as a clear demarcation for ethical violations.

The Joker is another villain who consistently and intentionally puts himself in situations in which Batman could fatally injure him. Batman continues to thwart these attempts, finally trapping the Joker by dangling him from a high-rise building.

> THE JOKER: This is what happens when an unstoppable force meets an immovable object. You truly are incorruptible aren't you? Huh? You won't kill

me out of some misplaced sense of self-righteousness. And, I won't kill you because you're just too much fun. I think you and I are destined to do this forever. (*The Dark Knight*)

Hanging upside down from a high-rise building saved only by one of Batman's gadgets, the Joker taunts Batman's ethics. What he claims is a "misplaced sense of self-righteousness" is a respect for his own moral code and value for human life. As discussed next from a Kantian perspective, Batman views the Joker's life as worthy, regardless of whether he is moral in his actions.

▶ The Kantian Caped Crusader?

Kant describes moral worth as deriving from the "maxim by which it is determined" as opposed to "the purpose which is to be attained by it" (1785/2001, p. 158). A Kantian perspective would indicate that an individual who has been given superpowers has the duty to act with those superpowers (Robichaud, 2005). But Bruce Wayne has no physical superpowers. He has extreme wealth and a personal desire for justice, but he doesn't have super strength or power, unlike many superheroes in the comic universe. So, is it his duty to don a cape and mask, putting his own mortal life at risk for the sake of the populous? According to Kant and the concept of duty, the obligation should be based on rationality, not emotions (Banks, 2017). To comprehend whether Batman's actions are based on rational or emotional motives, his purposes throughout the trilogy should be revisited.

In *Batman Begins*, Wayne talks specifically about his anger when he visits the League of Shadows and begins his training with Henri Ducard. Although the death of his parents is the initial motivator for justice, it is a continued need for a sense of justice that seems to continue propelling Wayne's actions. In other words, his initial obligation to duty was based on duty he felt toward his parents, but this seems to become more focused on Gotham as a whole as the film trilogy progresses.

Kant's categorical imperatives to duty are acts that are unconditional. Two points are of particular relevance from Kant's discussions of categorical imperatives: (1) Individuals act on the principle of universality (individuals should act as though their conduct may become universal), and (2) individuals should have respect for all persons (Banks, 2017). This first point may be poorly conceived, as is demonstrated in *The Dark Knight* with the Batman clones. Everyday civilians (presumably with less wealth than Bruce Wayne) are shown to be unsuccessful at delivering justice to Gotham residents, and some are harmed or murdered in the process. However, in the absence of becoming a masked vigilante, perhaps the idea is that citizens can choose more ethical options than depending on crime and corruption.

The second point, maintaining respect for all persons, is particularly relevant for Batman's case. As Hill (2000) states: "This respect should not be based on social rank, individual talents, or even moral goodness, but is grounded in the dignity of humanity, a value possessed by everyone who has the capacity to be a moral agent" (p. 64, as quoted in Banks, 2017, p. 343). Bruce Wayne, and correspondingly Batman, displays value for humanity. This is exemplified in the ethical code that he dictates for himself. Although his primary concern is for those he cares the most about (i.e., Rachel Dawes, Alfred Pennyworth, Lucius Fox, etc.), his ethical code demonstrates that he cares for all humans. Despite having ample opportunities to execute his nemeses, he is an individual who does not seize on these opportunities.[4]

▶ Conclusion

At first, *The Dark Knight* film franchise appears to simply be a successful comic book transition into a series of major motion pictures. On further investigation, Gotham, its heroes, its villains, and its citizens provide myriad opportunities to discuss ideas about crime, justice, and ethical issues. Further, the various government agencies provide points that merit additional consideration and discussion.

Comic characters infiltrate the lives of many individuals, making their fictional decisions all the more pertinent to discussions in a realistic world. Considering the continued popularity of comic books and the entertainment venues produced by their creators, they are worthy of continued reflection. In particular, we should be aware of the messages individuals are gleaning with respect to crime, justice, morality, and ethics and how these messages are transmitted into our daily lives and culture.

▶ Endnotes

1. "An Immovable Object" is referencing a quote from *The Dark Knight* (2008).
2. For a complete discussion on this topic, please see Lisk (2014) as referenced herein.
3. This scene and dialogue are discussed elsewhere in the literature. See DeScioli and Kurzban (2008) and Giddens (2015), both as referenced herein.
4. The character of Dick Grayson (Robin) is beyond the scope of this article because he is not depicted in the same manner as in the comics or other representations of Batman. However, for more discussion of Kant as applied to Robin's character and his relationship with Batman, see Nielson (2008).

▶ References

Banks, C. (2017). *Criminal justice ethics: Theory and practice* (4th ed.). Los Angeles, CA: Sage.

Chroust, A., & Osborn, D. L. (1942). Aristotle's conception of justice. *Notre Dame Law Review, 17*(2), 129–143.

DeScioli, P., & Kurzban, R. (2008). Cracking the superhero's moral code. Pp. 245–259 in R. S. Rosenberg (Ed.), *The psychology of superheroes: An unauthorized exploration*. Dallas, TX: Smart Pop Books.

Dozier, W., D'Angelo, W.P., & Horwitz, H. (Producers). (1966–1968). *Batman* [Television series]. Hollywood, CA: American Broadcasting Company.

Ferrell, J., Hayward, K., & Young, J. (2015). *Cultural criminology: An invitation* (2nd ed.). Los Angeles, CA: Sage.

Giddens, T. (2015). Natural law and vengeance: Jurisprudence on the streets of Gotham. *International Journal of Semiotic Law, 28*, 756–785.

Hill, T. E. (2000). *Respect, pluralism, and justice: Kantian perspectives*. Oxford, UK: Oxford University Press.

Kant, I. (2001). Fundamental principles of the metaphysics of morals. Pp. 143–221 in *Basic Writings of Kant*. New York, NY: Modern Library/Random House. (Originally published 1785.)

Lisk, J. (2014). Is Batman a state actor? The Dark Knight's relationship with the Gotham City Police Department and the Fourth Amendment implications. *Case Western Reserve Law Review, 64*(3), 1419–1440.

Nielsen, C. F. (2008). Leaving the shadow of the bat: Aristotle, Kant, and Dick Grayson on moral education. Pp. 254–266 in *Batman and Philosophy: The Dark Knight of the Soul*. Hoboken, NJ: John Wiley & Sons.

Nolan, C. (Director). (2012). *The Dark Knight Rises* [Motion picture]. Los Angles, CA: Warner Bros. Pictures.

Nolan, C. (Director). (2008). *The Dark Knight* [Motion picture]. Los Angles, CA: Warner Bros. Pictures.

Nolan, C. (Director). (2005). *Batman Begins* [Motion picture]. Los Angles, CA: Warner Bros. Pictures.

Nozick, R. (1981). *Philosophical explanations*. Cambridge, MA: Harvard University Press.

Patterson, B. C. (2008). No man's land: Social order in Gotham City and New Orleans. Pp. 41–54 in M. D. White & R. Arp (Eds.), *Batman and philosophy: The Dark Knight of the soul*. Hoboken, NJ: John Wiley & Sons.

Phillips, N. D., & Strobl, S. (2013). *Comic book crime: Truth, justice, and the American way*. New York, NY: New York University Press.

Reyns, B. W., & Henson, B. (2010). Superhero justice: The depiction of crime and justice in modern-age comic books and graphic novels. *Sociology of Crime, Law, and Deviance, 14*, 45–66.

Robichaud, C. (2005). With great power comes great responsibility: On the moral duties of the super-powerful and super-heroic. Pp. 177–193 in T. M. Morris & M. Morris (Eds.), *Superheroes and philosophy: Truth, justice, and the Socratic way*. Chicago, IL: Open Court Publishing.

Robichaud, C. (2008). The Joker's wild: Can we hold the Clown Prince morally responsible? Pp. 70–81 in *Batman and Philosophy: The Dark Knight of the Soul*. Hoboken, NJ: John Wiley & Sons.

Rousseau, J. (1999). The social contract. In C. Betts (Ed.), *Discourse on Political Economy and the Social Contract*. Oxford, UK: Oxford University Press. (Originally published 1762.)

Spanakos, T. (2008). Governing Gotham. Pp. 55–69 in M. D. White & R. Arp (Eds.), *Batman and philosophy: The Dark Knight of the soul*. Hoboken, NJ: John Wiley & Sons.

Timm, B., & Radomski, E. (1992–1995). *Batman: The animated series* [Television series]. Los Angeles, CA: Fox.

Art, Entertainment, or Admission of Guilt? Contextualizing Crime in Rap Lyrics

Adam Dunbar

In a highly technological society, images of crime can be found in various forms of popular culture, including television, film, and music—all of which can be examined to illuminate public attitudes about crime and justice. One form of popular culture that has received a notable amount of attention is rap music. Scholars, the media, and the public have analyzed themes of violence and crime present in much of rap to explore the relationship between the music and crime in inner-city communities. Some conclude that rap promotes violence and, in some cases, may contribute to crime (Geliebter, Ziegler, & Mandery, 2015; Jackson, 2004; Lyddanne, 2006; Stickle & Tewksbury, 2015), whereas others contend that the prevalence of crime and violence in rap is a by-product of a larger entertainment media culture that glamorizes violent behavior (Negus, 2012; Quinn, 2013; Richardson & Scott, 2002; Serrianne, 2015; Watts, 2012). Still others maintain that rap is a form of artistic expression that highlights the consequences of structural inequality (Kubrin, 2005a; Payne, 2016; Perry, 2004; Quinn, 2013; Rose, 1994).

Regardless of which perspective is adopted, however, it is generally accepted that rap music—a genre that uses rhyme, rhythmic speech, and street vernacular—emerged on the American cultural scene in the mid-1970s as part of a larger hip-hop movement (Keyes, 2002). Hip-hop, which includes DJing, graffiti art, and break dancing, largely reflects efforts to "give voice to the tensions and contradictions in the public urban landscape" and "make it work on behalf of the dispossessed" (Rose, 1994, p. 22). Thus, the early years of rap, its "golden age," are often characterized as politically conscious and Afrocentric (Keyes, 2002; Martinez, 1997). In fact, many rappers and rap groups, including De La Soul, Public Enemy, and KRS-One—who referred to himself as "The Teacha"—used their music to highlight racism and inequality in the United States (Kubrin & Nielson, 2014).

As rap gained popularity, a new subgenre of rap, gangsta rap, exploded onto the scene. Although scholars characterize rap music as a representation of a general "Black experience," gangsta rap is distinguished by its focus on violence and crime endemic to poor and working-class Black neighborhoods (Keyes, 2002; Kitwana, 1994; Rose, 1994). Gangsta rap highlights the sociopolitical and socioeconomic concerns of people of color, but it often does so through graphic language and violent imagery. One consequence of this was a contentious relationship between gangsta rap and the criminal justice system (Blecha, 2004). As just one example, the group N.W.A, who produced the song "F*ck tha Police," was banned from many mainstream radio stations because of concerns that their music glorified drug use and crime (Blecha, 2004; Charnas, 2011; Russell-Brown, 2004).

Even amid public backlash from religious groups and political organizations, gangsta rap enjoyed commercial success during the 1990s. During this time, rappers who offered graphic accounts of violent behavior and sexual conquest were often viewed as more marketable by corporate record labels and were often more commercially successful (Krims, 2000; Light, 2012). The commercialization of gangsta rap corresponded with a marked lyrical emphasis on what Rose (2008) terms the "gangsta-pimp-ho trinity" (p. 13). In other words, as rap gained more commercial success, themes of violence and misogyny became more prominent in the music (Quinn, 2013; Rose, 2008).

Rap music remains one of the most popular music genres; in 2018, it surpassed rock as the most popular genre in the United States (Nielsen Media Research, 2018). During the same year, for the first time ever, a rapper earned a Pulitzer Prize. Regardless of the mainstream popularity of rap, a handful of themes have remained consistently present in the genre. The music commonly discusses poverty (Perry, 2004), loss of loved ones (Kubrin 2005b; Rose, 1994), police surveillance (Rose, 1994), distrust of the criminal justice system (Martinez, 1997; Steinmetz & Henderson, 2012), and crime and violence (Kubrin, 2005a; Kubrin, 2005b). Notably, references to crime and violence have received the most scrutiny from scholars, media pundits, and politicians. This article reviews the varied ways that the relationship between rap music and crime has been described and thus sheds light on racialized assumptions about the causes of crime.

The remainder of this article first reviews concerns that rap music promotes violence and, therefore, contributes to crime in inner-city communities. Second, it describes claims that present crime and violence in rap music as a function of consumer demands for racialized violent imagery. Third, arguments are reviewed that frame rap as a form of artistic expression, one that highlights the structural inequality present in many Black communities. Finally, we conclude with a discussion of the implications of adopting these different perspectives, particularly for the predominately young Black men who create the music. Ultimately, this article aims to reveal how representations of rap music have contributed to perceptions of crime in Black communities.

▶ Rap as Threat

Critics of rap music often point to the pervasive themes of violence, prostitution, and other criminal behavior present in the music as evidence that the genre glorifies violence (Gore, 1987), brags about criminal exploits (Jackson, 2004; Lyddanne, 2006; Stickle & Tewksbury, 2015), and, in some cases, causes violent behavior (Geliebter et al., 2015; Johnson, Jackson, & Gatto, 1995). For example, during the 1990s, parents, officials, and the media used studies showing a link between listening to rap music and acceptance of violence (e.g., Johnson et al., 1995) to validate concerns about the genre. More recently, research has suggested that rap music may contribute to criminal behavior because the musical style of the genre (e.g., minimal use of instruments) increases the chance that listeners attend to explicit lyrics (e.g., Geliebter et al., 2015). In one study, researchers had half of the participants listen to one minute of rapper Lil Wayne's "Lollipop," a song replete with graphic imagery about his sexual exploits with women; the other half of participants listened to the same song performed by a heavy metal band. The researchers found that people were able to better recollect the lyrics when they were presented as rap rather than heavy metal, concluding that rap lyrics are more susceptible to being "heard, taken to heart, and acted upon" (p. 149).

Fears about the relationship between rap music and crime are often articulated in the media. Studying how the news portrays rap and rock music, Binder (1993) finds that rap music is viewed through a "danger to society" frame that is based on the idea that listeners of rap music will become threats to society. Through her analysis of news and opinion articles from 118 nationally published periodicals, she underscores how the media are more likely to describe listeners of rap as prone to violence and criminality than are listeners of other music genres. An example of the perceived link between rap and crime can be found in a promotional segment for a podcast produced by Mississippi Republican Senator Chris McDaniel. In the segment, McDaniel explains that rising gun violence is not because of the proliferation of guns, but rather "a morally bankrupt culture . . . that's called 'hip-hop'" (Murphy, 2014). Echoing that sentiment, in 2015, Fox News correspondent Geraldo Rivera suggested that "hip-hop has done more damage to young African-Americans than racism in recent years" (Ra, 2015). Rivera suggests that the themes present in rap music largely explain poor police–community relations because the music turns youth against law enforcement.

The assumption that rap music is threatening and dangerous is not, however, just found in the media. Police and prosecutors have also assumed a link between rap and crime. During the 1980s and 1990s, rap music incurred severe censorship and was heavily policed (Kubrin & Nielson, 2014). In 1992, the gangster rap song "Cop Killer" by Body Count was removed from music store shelves because of a fear that the song would encourage violence against police (Fried, 1996). This form of sanctioning also occurred for rap group N.W.A when the FBI urged police departments to cancel N.W.A concerts and strongly encouraged Priority Records—which produced N.W.A's debut album *Straight Outta Compton*—not to distribute their music (Blecha, 2004; Marsh & Pollack, 1989).

More recently, the assumption that rap glorifies violence and brags about criminal exploits has resulted in prosecutors using defendant-authored rap lyrics as evidence in criminal trials. Across the United States, prosecutors are treating rap lyrics like autobiographical confessions to incriminate defendants, many of whom are young men of color from impoverished neighborhoods (Dennis, 2007; Kubrin & Nielson, 2014; Powell, 2009; Stoia, Adams, & Drakulich, 2017). In many of these cases, prosecutors characterize rappers as criminal offenders who are writing about their violent and illicit exploits in the form of music lyrics (Dennis, 2007). The assertion that rap lyrics are evidence of criminal behavior is also articulated in one prosecutor's training manual, which describes how introducing rap lyrics at trial can help reveal that the defendant is, in reality, "a criminal wearing a do-rag and throwing a gang sign" (Jackson, 2004, p. 16). Regardless of whether rap lyrics are viewed as promoting crime or as evidence of criminal activity, the argument remains generally the same. Critics of rap focus on themes of crime and violence present in the music to portray rappers as prone to violence and depict the genre as contributing to crime in communities of color.

▶ Rap as Commodity

Others have characterized references to crime and violence in rap as a by-product of a larger entertainment media culture that glamorizes flashiness and criminal behavior (Negus, 2012; Quinn, 2013; Richardson & Scott, 2002; Serrianne, 2015; Watts, 2012). Illicit drug use, prostitution, domestic violence, and homicide are consistently present in video games, movies, and television shows (e.g., Grier, 2001). Crime is also a highly visible theme across many music genres. Country music has been criticized for its depictions of substance use, murder, and other forms of violence, especially domestic violence (e.g., Armstrong, 1993; Lowell et al., 2014). Rock music, and heavy metal in particular, has often been characterized as a musical genre that promotes criminal behavior, including violence and illicit drug use (Blecha, 2004; Leveritt, 2002). Even opera is replete with violent and sexual themes (Stoia et al., 2017). It is not a surprise, then, that crime is a ubiquitous theme in rap music, yet representations of crime in the genre have varied since the "golden age" of rap.

Starting in the 1990s, the content of rap music underwent a notable shift from the political messages prominent in the late 1980s to a marked emphasis on the objectification of women's bodies and gang culture (Serrianne, 2015; Watts, 2012). In particular, the genre experienced a notable increase in the number of songs mentioning violence (Herd, 2009; Hunnicutt & Andrews, 2009) and substance use (Herd, 2008). Also during this time, rappers who offered graphic accounts of criminal activity and sexual exploits became more successful, while rappers whose lyrics were characterized as socially conscious struggled to find mainstream success (Charnas, 2011; Rose; 2008; Serrianne, 2015; Stoia et al., 2017). Thus, the popularization of rap coincided with a proliferation of graphic, violent songs.

In light of this, some argue that the shift in rap's content was largely based on demands from corporate record labels for rappers to depict certain types of images (Perry, 2004; Quinn, 2013; Rose, 2008; Weitzer & Kubrin 2009). One study examining the effect of corporatization on the genre finds a distinct shift in the content, sound, and style of the music as larger record labels bought out smaller, independent labels (Myer & Kleck, 2007). Analyzing "Hot 100 Airplay" charts from Billboard magazine from January 1990 to December 2005, Myer and Kleck (2007) found a growing number of popular records were produced by corporate record labels. In fact, the four largest record labels produced approximately 75% of the records during that time. The researchers conclude that commercialization of rap music, especially the monopolization of the genre by a handful of record labels, homogenized rap's content. Building on this point, scholars and rappers describe how major record labels often limit the genre to hyperaggressive and hypersexualized depictions of Black men and women (e.g., Fitts, 2008; Neal, 2012; Quinn, 2013), depictions that are arguably produced for the consumption of predominately White, middle-class audiences (Watts, 2012).

Adopting this perspective, the presence of crime and violence in rap music is not largely based on crime in Black communities or rappers with a criminal disposition but on a deliberate effort by record labels to produce images that tap into deep-seated racial stereotypes and anxieties (Rose, 2008; Watkins, 2005). As Quinn (2013) argues, the pervasiveness of crime in rap music is partly based on "the vast appetite for 'Black ghetto realness' in the popular culture marketplace" (Quinn, 2013, p. 32). The profitability of playing the "gangsta" or "thug" may explain why, in the 1990s and early 2000s, rappers such as 50 Cent, Ice Cube, Jay-Z, and Dr. Dre benefited from establishing their street reputations, personas that have far outlasted their performing careers. The model for success has been replicated with contemporary rappers such as Tay-K 47 and Kodak Black, both of whom rose to prominence after their criminal exploits were made public. In other words, presenting lyrical accounts of a rapper's toughness and willingness to engage in violence has become a critical ingredient for success in the industry (Kitwana, 1994; Kubrin & Nielson, 2014).

Even rappers who were never previously involved in criminal activity understand the importance of establishing an "authentic" street-identified persona (Krims, 2000). One such example is Rick Ross, a Florida-based rapper who chose the name "Rick Ross" to pay homage to "Freeway" Rick Ross, a former Los Angeles drug kingpin. Rick Ross presents himself to the public as a gangsta rapper from Miami who is immersed in gang culture. However, the Smoking Gun website released documents showing that Rick Ross was actually a college graduate who used to work as a prison guard, contradicting this constructed "Rick Ross" persona ("Screw Rick Ross," 2008). After this became public, the rapper, whose legal name is William Leonard Roberts II, admitted that he only plays the role of the gangsta rapper "Rick Ross" to maintain his image in the industry. In sum, references to violence and other illicit activity in rap may be more illustrative of a consumer demand for depictions of Black criminality than of actual crime.

▶ Rap as Street Knowledge

The previous explanations for the presence of violence and crime in rap music overlook that rap music is, in fact, a form of cultural expression meant to highlight the consequences of structural inequality that shape the identity and experiences of Black men and women (Payne, 2016; Perry, 2004; Quinn, 2013). As Kelley (1996) explains, rappers are "street ethnographers" who can articulate the varied perspectives and experiences found in many low-income Black communities. Artists such as Chuck D from Public Enemy have echoed this sentiment by describing rap as Black America's CNN (Light, 2012; Payne, 2016). Generally speaking, rappers are storytellers who report on hardships in low-income Black communities such as poverty, police surveillance, and the consequences of mass incarceration. In this way, discussions of violence, drug use, and other criminal exploits do more to illuminate the relationship between poverty and crime than simply glamorize a rapper's involvement in crime (Kubrin, 2005a; Lusane, 1993; Russell-Brown, 2004).

In many ways, rappers aim to educate listeners about the poverty and institutionalized discrimination that have consistently plagued communities of color. Through characterizations of neighborhoods, relationships, and daily life, rappers can provide a framework for understanding how structural inequality and violence affect their communities (Payne, 2016; Rose, 1994). For example, in 2002, gangsta rapper DMX wrote *E.A.R.L.: The Autobiography of DMX* to juxtapose his loud and often explicit music with his painful experiences with poverty, substance abuse, and incarceration; in doing so, he explains to audiences why he has constructed his particular rap persona (Payne, 2016). And Atlanta-based rapper Young Jeezy, who has referred to himself as "Mr. CNN," released the album *The Recession* (2008), which depicts his economically disadvantaged upbringing, past involvement in drug dealing, and experiences with the criminal justice system. However, as Payne (2016) notes, the music, while occasionally describing past criminal activity, is meant to convey the anger growing in many Black communities from consistently blocked social, economic, and political opportunities.

Although violence and crime are prevalent themes in rap music, the stories rappers tell do not always match their lived experience (Kubrin & Nielson, 2014). Lyrics may be based on the life of the artist, but they may also be based on the lives of loved ones or other members of the community. Regardless, the lyrics serve a social function. Kubrin (2005a) reveals that rap lyrics often embody the code of the streets, or "a code of conduct regulated by the threat of violence" (Anderson, 1999, p. 15). After analyzing 403 rap songs from 1992 to 2000, she concludes that consistent references to respect, material wealth, and threats of violence are meant to illustrate the need to prove one's toughness, often through violence, to command respect and deter potential assaults. In addition to articulating the importance of respect, rap lyrics demonstrate ways to achieve respect in communities where conventional means for doing so are limited (Anderson, 1999; Perry, 2004). Thus, using narratives told from the first-person perspective, rappers attempt to educate audiences about the relationship between violence and poverty in their communities.

Although rap is, in many ways, pedagogical, it can also be understood as "a form of resistance" and expression of an oppositional culture," wherein rappers can push back against marginalization and oppression (Martinez, 1997, p. 268). Stated alternatively, rap lyrics referencing crime and violence may not be accurate representations of an actual event but rather, an attempt to shatter taboos and satirize racial stereotypes through the use of metaphor (Gates, 2011; Perry, 2004; Rose, 1994). In rap music, for example, depictions of drug dealing can represent a disavowal of traditional means to achieve wealth (Kubrin, 2005b), and drug use can represent hedonism in the face of Draconian drug laws (Perry, 2004). References to violence and crime can be used metaphorically to represent self-reliance and, in particular, independence from traditional civic institutions such as police and schools, both of which can alienate people of color (Emdin, 2010). In this way, the music can serve as a vehicle of expression about marginalization while simultaneously empowering the marginalized group by highlighting structural inequality in impoverished communities, one aspect of which is violence and crime (Perry, 2004; Rose, 1994).

▶ Conclusion

This article reviewed various ways to understand the relationship between rap music and crime. As discussed, critics often characterize rap music as a genre that brags about criminal exploits and promotes criminal behavior (e.g., Stickle & Tewksbury, 2015). Others, however, contend that violence and crime in rap music reflect consumer demands for racialized violent fantasies (e.g., Quinn, 2013). And still others suggest that rap is a form of artistic expression in which themes present in the music, including references to crime and violence, articulate the pain and frustration of structural inequality (e.g., Payne, 2016, Rose, 1994).

Of course, listeners' attitudes about the genre can inform how they understand the music. In fact, studies have demonstrated that stereotypes about the genre can affect how threatening (Fischoff, 1999; Fried, 1996; Fried, 1999), obscene (Dixon & Linz, 1997), and literal lyrics are perceived to be (Dunbar, 2018; Dunbar, Kubrin, & Scurich, 2016). One study, for example, discovered that violent lyrics are judged to be more offensive and threatening when they are identified as rap rather than as a different music genre (Fried, 1996). More recently, Dunbar, Kubrin, and Scurich (2016) replicated Fried's (1996) original findings, while also revealing that lyrics are perceived to be more literal when they are identified as rap compared to another genre, suggesting that stereotypes about the genre shape judgments of the music.

Concerns exist regarding judgments about rap music that treat the genre as dangerous and threatening. For one thing, the lay public may not understand the sociohistorical context of rap music and instead rely on stereotypes about the genre to inform its judgments about the lyrics. If the lay public is evaluating rap music in this way, then it runs the risk of conflating the artist with his or her art, which can perpetuate racialized views about who is criminally predisposed (Dunbar & Kubrin, 2018). Ultimately, the fear and outrage evoked by rap's lyrical content, and the exploitation of this sentiment by media and politicians alike, parallel other racial dog whistle issues that play on anti-Black biases related to crime while avoiding explicitly mentioning race (e.g., Kubrin & Nielson, 2014; Stoia et al., 2017). For this reason, it is necessary to examine violence and crime in rap music. In doing so, we can consider the consequences of public reactions to the genre and their implications for specific communities, in addition to understanding the purpose of the themes in the music.

▶ References

Anderson, E. (1999). *Code of the street: Decency, violence, and the moral life of the inner city*. New York: W.W. Norton & Co.

Armstrong, E. G. (1993). The rhetoric of violence in rap and country music. *Sociological Inquiry, 63*(1), 64–78. doi: 10.1111/j.1475-682X.1993.tb00202.x

Binder, A. (1993). Constructing racial rhetoric: Media depiction of harm in heavy metal and rap music. *American Sociological Review, 58*(6), 753–767. Retrieved from http://www.jstor.org/stable/2095949

Blecha, P. (2004). *Taboo tunes: A history of banned bands and censored songs*. San Francisco, CA: Backbeat Books.

Charnas, D. (2011). *The big payback: The history of the business of hip-hop*. London, UK: Penguin.

Dennis, A. L. (2007). Poetic (in)justice? Rap music lyrics as art, life, and criminal evidence. *Columbia Journal of Law & the Arts, 31*, 1–41. Retrieved from http://ssrn.com/abstract=1104756

Dixon, T. L., & Linz, D. G. (1997). Obscenity law and sexually explicit rap music: Understanding the effects of sex, attitudes, and beliefs. *Journal of Applied Communication Research, 25*, 217–241. doi: 10.1080/00909889709365477

DMX & Fontaine, S. (2002). *E.A.R.L.: The autobiography of DMX.* New York, NY: Harper Collins.

Dunbar, A. (2018). Art or confession?: Evaluating rap lyrics as evidence in criminal cases. *Race and Justice.* doi.org/10.1177/2153368717749879

Dunbar, A., & Kubrin, C. E. (2018). Imagining violent criminals: An experimental investigation of music stereotypes and character judgments. *Journal of Experimental Criminology, 14*(4), 507–528. doi: 10.1007/s11292-018-9342-6

Dunbar, A., Kubrin, C. E., & Scurich, N. (2016). The threatening nature of "rap" music. *Psychology, Public Policy, and Law, 22*(3), 280–292. doi: 10.1037/law0000093

Emdin, C. (2010). Affiliation and alienation: Hip-hop, rap, and urban science education. *Journal of Curriculum Studies, 42*(1), 1–25. doi: 10.1080/00220270903161118

Fischoff, S. P. (1999). Gangsta' rap and a murder in Bakersfield. *Journal of Applied Social Psychology, 29*(4), 795–805. doi: 10.1111/j.1559-1816.1999.tb02025.x

Fitts, M. (2008). "Drop it like it's hot": Culture industry laborers and their perspectives on rap music video production. *Meridians,* 211–235. https://www.jstor.org/stable/40338918

Fried, C. B. (1996). Bad rap for rap: Bias in reactions to music lyrics. *Journal of Applied Social Psychology, 26*(23), 2135–2146. Retrieved from doi: 10.1111/j.1559-1816.1996.tb01791.x

Fried, C. B. (1999). Who's afraid of rap? Differential reactions to music lyrics. *Journal of Applied Social Psychology, 29*(4), 705–721. Retrieved from doi: 10.1111/j.1559-1816.1999.tb02020.x

Gates, H. L., Jr. (2011). Foreword. In A. Bradley & A. DuBois (Eds.), *The anthology of rap* (pp. 22–28). New Haven, CT: Yale University Press.

Geliebter, D., Ziegler, A. J., & Mandery, E. (2015). Lyrical stresses of heavy metal and rap. *Metal Music Studies, 1*(1), 143–153. Retrieved from doi: 10.1386/mms.1.1.143_1

Gore, T. (1987). *Raising PG kids and an X-rated society.* Nashville TN: Abingdon Press.

Grier, S. A. (2001). The Federal Trade Commission's report on the marketing of violent entertainment to youths: Developing policy-tuned research. *Journal of Public Policy & Marketing, 20*(1), 123–132. Retrieved from doi: 10.1509/jppm.20.1.123.17288

Herd, D. (2008). Changes in drug use prevalence in rap music songs, 1979–1997. *Addiction Research and Theory, 16*(2): 167–180. Retrieved from doi: 10.1080/16066350801993987

Herd, D. (2009). Changing images of violence in rap music lyrics: 1979–1997. *Journal of Public Health Policy, 30*(4), 395–406. Retrieved from doi: 10.1057/jphp.2009.36

Hunnicutt, G., & Andrews, K. H. (2009). Tragic narratives in popular culture: Depictions of homicide in rap music. *Sociological Forum, 24*(3), 611–636. Retrieved from doi:10.1111/j .1573 7861.2009.01122.x

Jackson, A. (2004). *Prosecuting local gang cases: What prosecutors need to know.* Alexandria, VA: American Prosecutors Research Institute. Retrieved from https://www.popmatters.com /050401-edutainment-2496103113.html

Jeezy, Y. (2008). *The recession.* Atlanta, GA/New York, NY: Corporate Thugz Entertainment/Def Jam Recordings.

Johnson, J. D., Jackson, L. A., & Gatto, L. (1995). Violent attitudes and deferred academic aspiration: Deleterious effects of exposure to rap music. *Basic and Applied Social Psychology, 16*(1), 27–41. doi: 10.1080/01973533.1995.9646099

Kelley, R. D. G. (1996). Kickin' reality, kickin' ballistics: Gangsta rap and postindustrial Los Angeles. In W. E. Perkins (Ed.), *Droppin' science: Critical essays on rap music and hip hop culture* (pp. 117–158). Philadelphia, PA: Temple University Press.

Keyes, C. (2002). *Rap music and street consciousness.* Urbana, IL: University of Illinois Press.

Kitwana, B. (1994). *The rap on gangsta rap.* Chicago, IL: Third World Press.

Krims, A. (2000). *Rap music and the poetics of identity.* Cambridge, MA: Cambridge University Press.

Kubrin, C. (2005a). Gangstas, thugs, and hustlas: Identity and the code of the street in rap music. *Social Problems, 52*, 360–378. doi: 10.1525/sp.2005.52.3.360

Kubrin, C. E. (2005b). "I see death around the corner": Nihilism in rap music. *Sociological Perspectives, 48*, 433–459. doi: 10.1525/sop.2005.48.4.433

Kubrin, C. E., & Nielson, E. (2014). Rap on trial. *Race and Justice, 4*(3), 185–211. doi: 10.1177/2153368714525411

Leveritt, M. (2002). *Devil's knot: The true story of the West Memphis Three.* New York, NY: Atria Books.

Light, A. (2012). About a salary or reality?—Rap's recurrent conflict. In M. Forman & M. A. Neal (Eds.), *That's the joint! The hip-hop studies reader* (pp. 137–146). London, UK: Routledge.

Lowell, J. L., Grymes, K. C., Hankel, R., Speer, A. D., Custis, C. L., & To, R. L. (2014). Sex, drugs, and country music? A content analysis of substance use, sex, violence, and weapons in country music. *Global Journal of Human-Social Science Research, 14*(2), 80–88. Retrieved from https://socialscienceresearch.org/index.php/GJHSS/article/view/1192

Lusane, C. (1993). Rap, race, and politics. *Race & Class, 35,* 41–56. doi: 10.1177/030639689303500105

Lyddane, D. (2006). Understanding gangs and gang mentality: Acquiring evidence of the gang conspiracy. The United States Attorneys' Bulletin, 54, 1–14. Retrieved from https://www.justice.gov/archive/olp/pdf/gangs.pdf

Marsh, D., & Pollack, P. (1989, October 10). Wanted for attitude. *Village Voice,* pp. 33–37.

Martinez, T. A. (1997). Popular culture as oppositional culture: Rap as resistance. *Sociological Perspectives, 40*(2), 265–286. doi: 10.2307/1389525

Myer, L., & Kleck, C. (2007). From independent to corporate: A political economic analysis of rap billboard toppers. *Popular Music and Society, 30*(2), 137–148. doi: 10.1080/03007760701267649

Murphy, T. (2014, January 7). Mississippi GOP senate candidate blames hip-hop for gun violence. Retrieved from https://www.motherjones.com/politics/2014/01/chris-mcdaniel-mississippi-hip-hop-gun-violence-audio/

Neal, M. A. (2012). No time for fake niggas: Hip-hop culture and the authenticity debates. In M. Forman & M. A. Neal (Eds.), *That's the joint! The hip-hop studies reader* (pp. 493–496). London, UK: Routledge.

Negus, K. (2012). The business of rap: Between the street and the executive suite. In M. Forman & M. A. Neal (Eds.), *That's the joint! The hip-hop studies reader* (pp. 525–540). London, UK: Routledge.

Nielsen Media Research. (2018). *U.S. music year-end report.* Retrieved from http://www.nielsen.com/us/en/insights/reports/2018/2017-music-us-year-end-report.html

Payne, Y. A. (2016). Young Jeezy and "The recession": What gangster rap can teach us about economic poverty in the black community. *Journal of Black Studies, 47*(2), 113–133. doi: 10.1177/0021934715618396

Perry, I. (2004). *Prophets of the hood: Politics and poetics in hip hop.* Durham, Ireland: Duke University Press.

Powell, J. (2009). R.A.P.: Rule against perps (who write rhymes). *Rutgers Law Journal, 41,* 479–526. Retrieved from https://heinonline.org/HOL/LandingPage?handle=hein.journals/rutlj41&div=15&id=&page=

Quinn, E. (2013). *Nuthin' but a" G" thang: the culture and commerce of gangsta rap.* New York, NY: Columbia University Press.

Ra, F. (2015, July 10). Kendrick Lamar explains "Hip-hop is not the problem our reality is" & shuts down Geraldo Rivera. Retrieved from https://urbanintellectuals.com/2015/07/10/kendrick-lamar-explains-hip-hop-is-not-the-problem-our-reality-is-shuts-down-geraldo-rivera/

Richardson, J. W., & Scott, K. A. (2002). Rap music and its violent progeny: America's culture of violence in context. *Journal of Negro Education,* 175–192. doi: 10.2307/3211235

Rose, T. (1994). *Black noise.* Hanover, Germany: Wesleyan University Press.

Rose, T. (2008). *The hip hop wars: What we talk about when we talk about hip hop--and why it matters.* New York, NY: Civitas Books.

Russell-Brown, K. (2004). *Underground codes: Race, crime, and related fires.* New York, NY: NYU Press.

Serrianne, N. E. (2015). *America in the Nineties.* Syracuse, NY: Syracuse University Press.

Screw Rick Ross. (2008, July 21). The Smoking Gun. Retrieved from http://www.thesmokinggun.com/documents/crime/screw-rick-ross

Steinmetz, K. F., & Henderson, H. (2012). Hip-hop and procedural justice hip-hop artists' perceptions of criminal justice. *Race and Justice, 2*(3), 155–178. doi: 10.1177/2153368712443969

Stickle, B., & Tewksbury, R. (2015). A lyrical analysis of rap, country, pop and Christian music. *Contemporary Journal of Anthropology and Sociology, 5*(1–2), 6–21.

Stoia, N., Adams, K., & Drakulich, K. (2017). Rap lyrics as evidence: What can music theory tell us?. *Race and Justice*, 1–36. doi: 10.1177/2153368716688739

Watkins, S. C. (2005). *Hip hop matters: Politics, pop culture, and the struggle for the soul of a movement*. Boston, MA: Beacon Press.

Watts, E. (2012). An exploration of spectacular consumption: Gangsta rap as cultural commodity. In M. Forman & M. A. Neal (Eds.), *That's the joint! The hip-hop studies reader* (pp. 593–610). London, UK: Routledge.

Weitzer, R., & Kubrin, C. E. (2009). Misogyny in rap music: A content analysis of prevalence and meanings. *Men and Masculinities, 12*(1), 3–29. doi: 10.1177/1097184X08327696

© Sergii Gnatiuk/Shutterstock

ARTICLE 57

Media, Ethics, and Crime

Daniel Trigoboff

L aw enforcement and journalism both bear important responsibilities for protecting the rights of the people in a free society. Each keeps a close eye on day-to-day activities. Each monitors breaches of the law and of the peace.

But members of each profession often show up in tough times, asking difficult and even upsetting questions. Their presence can cause concern and anxiety for the targets of their scrutiny, but these are times when they may do their most important work. It is sometimes an interdependent relationship. Journalists inform the public on issues of public safety—information that often comes from law enforcement itself. When reporters arrive at a crime scene or other emergency, it is the men or women in blue they typically seek first to answer their questions.

But there is a natural tension: Each entity has its own approach to making information public, and both want to be in control. The public may be drawn to lurid and tragic stories, frequently noting that the news is often bad. Those who battle crime often believe that reporting highlights—even extends—the trauma of loss and victimhood. Police sometimes claim too much public information released can endanger an investigation, invade victim privacy, or compromise some other government interest. Journalists believe they are the ones who should make that determination; when frustrated by police, they may seek legal redress for access to police reports and video evidence.

▶ Statutes, the Constitution, and Confidentiality

The Constitution itself treats law enforcement and the press differently. Where the Fourth Amendment prescribes the rights of the people to be protected from government overreach, the First Amendment gives broad leeway to the press to publish (Reporters Committee for Freedom of the Press [RCFP], 2011a).

Access to information, however, is largely statutory. Reporters seek information that law enforcement often seeks to protect, and the matter frequently ends up in court, testing federal and state freedom of information and "sunshine" laws (RCFP, 2011a).

Sometimes media rely on unnamed sources, and law enforcement may perceive the news media's protection of those confidential sources as impediments to investigation and bring journalists to court. Some states protect journalists from subpoenas, search warrants, discovery orders, and jail for contempt, but others do not. Regardless of how the legal issues resolve, each side believes in the ethics of its position.

Experts in the ethics of journalism advise caution and discretion when using confidential sources. They advise newsrooms to develop and disseminate policies regarding confidentiality to avoid confusion and inconsistency (Radio Television Digital News Association [RTDNA], n.d., "Guidelines for Using Confidential Sources"). A story relying on confidential sourcing should be of great public concern, the information itself should be important, and there should be no other way to get the information on the record. Journalists should have confidence in the source's knowledge and in the reason why confidentiality is necessary. Terms such as "on background," "not for attribution," and "off the record" need to be clear to both reporter and source. As they maintain confidentiality, journalists should be able to describe the source sufficiently for the audience to have confidence in the information. How would the information be perceived if the source's name were known?

Beyond the ethical duties, newsrooms need to consider legal responsibilities. Is the news organization capable of keeping its promise of confidentiality? Can it protect tapes, notes, and comments? Is the reporter willing to go to jail for contempt of court to protect the source (Tompkins, 2002)?

▶ Policing Under Scrutiny

As police and police conduct have increasingly become the subjects of reporters' stories in an ongoing controversy over charges of police brutality, the struggle for access or control of information intensifies, and the relationship becomes more contentious and more adversarial.

For the media, public and professional pressure have steered journalists to perceived underserved communities and issues, including issues of crime and law enforcement—often involving race and ethnicity—in a time when much of the media faces diminishing resources. Allegations of unwarranted police violence have turned the focus to issues of justice and accountability.

The high-profile coverage of controversial police violence has led some police officers to believe the media holds an antipolice bias. A poll conducted by the National Police Research Platform for the Pew Research Center found that more than eight in 10 officers in large departments (100 or more sworn officers) agreed with the proposition that the media treats them unfairly. Half of those *strongly* agree that the media is unfair to police. Only 18% of officers surveyed disagreed. Pew notes that the bias against police is perceived across gender, racial, and ethnic lines, although it is perceived to be stronger by officers who are White rather than Black or Hispanic and among officers older than 45 (Stepler, 2017).

For police, the scrutiny goes well beyond those who do it professionally, and law enforcement needs to take note and take more control. Digital technologies like cell-phone cameras and platforms such as social media have both democratized reporting and focused unprecedented attention on law enforcement, according to PoliceOne, a law enforcement publication.

The media machine is always hungry, and citizen journalism is becoming an increasingly popular method of feeding it. Do you want the first report on a critical incident or controversy involving your department to come from sources other than your own? Post-Ferguson, how an agency handles media relations is more important now than ever before.

▶ An Impartial Referee?

Clearly, the well-publicized shootings draw attention not only to issues involving police, community and use of force but also to the lack of media coverage given to concerns of marginalized communities.

In *The Elements of Journalism*, journalists and media critics Bill Kovach and Tom Rosenstiel offer guidance for journalists and journalism. Its practitioners must be allowed to exercise their personal conscience, they say. Serving as an independent monitor of power means "watching over the powerful few in society on behalf of the many to guard against tyranny," Kovach and Rosenstiel write. Journalistic independence does not mean neutrality (Kovach & Rosenstiel, 2001, pp. 114–115).

Iconic columnist H. L. Mencken is widely quoted as saying that "The job of the newspaper is to comfort the afflicted and afflict the comfortable." But according to journalism think-tank the Poynter Institute, the quote originated in 1902 as a less-than-complimentary observation from Mr. Dooley, a character created by satirist Finley Peter Dunne: "Th' newspaper does ivrything f'r us. It runs th' polis foorce an' th' banks, commands th' milishy, controls th' ligislachure, baptizes th' young, marries th' foolish, comforts th' afflicted, afflicts th' comfortable, buries th' dead an' roasts thim afterward" (Dunne, 1902; quoted by Snedden, 2014).

Media critics offer what they perceive as evidence of bias with sometimes strained examples. But in a case involving one of the most widely covered allegations of unlawful police violence, a symbolic act of TV anchors stood out as a breach not only of neutrality, critics say, but also fairness. In December 2014, CNN anchors and panelists closed an on-air segment by holding up their hands, a direct reference to stories reported about the shooting death in Ferguson, Missouri of young Michael Brown during a confrontation with Ferguson police officer Darren Wilson (CNN, 2014; Concha, 2014). One panelist held a sign related to the New York City choking death of African American street vendor Eric Garner, an incident that drew considerable attention after it was recorded by cell-phone camera and spread by social media (Sanburn, 2014).

Although sympathetic to protests over the perceived failure of a Staten Island grand jury to issue indictments in the death of Garner, Mediaite critic Joe Concha called the "hands exhibition" regarding the death of Brown "misleading" (Concha, 2014). The deaths by Brown and Garner, Concha said,

are two very different cases that just happened to have grand jury decisions within nine days of each other. . . . [CNN anchors] holding their hands up yesterday following a discussion around the protests . . . blurred the lines between the two cases, almost implying Ferguson and Staten Island are somehow connected. (Concha, 2014)

Scott Jones of FTV Live, which monitors TV news, wrote, "No longer can CNN claim [itself] as a down the middle newscast with no bias," and he called the episode "nothing short of an embarrassment for CNN" (Jones, 2014). Some commentators note that although the show was unclearly labeled and ran in CNN's news bloc, the anchors were clearly voicing opinions.

The anchors' hands-up demonstration proved more than misleading after a detailed investigation and report by the Department of Justice in 2015 that cleared and exonerated Wilson. Jonathan Capehart, an opinion writer for the *Washington Post*, noted that the "hands up, don't shoot" mantra was rooted in an interview with a friend of Brown's who told MSNBC that Brown was shot in the back by Wilson. A friend of Brown's said Brown then turned around and faced Wilson and told the officer he didn't have a gun and to "stop shooting!" (Capehart, 2015).

And, like that, wrote Capehart, "'hands up, don't shoot' became the mantra of a movement. But it was wrong, built on a lie." The justice department report, Capehart wrote, "forced me to deal with two uncomfortable truths: Brown never surrendered with his hands up, and Wilson was justified in shooting Brown" (Capehart, 2015).

In *The Atlantic*, progressive writer Ta-Nehisi Coates similarly, if less adamantly, cited the report to conclude Wilson was innocent (Coates, 2015). Both Coates and Capehart—and numerous other writers—turned quickly to a companion probe by the justice department that found oppressive and harmful law enforcement practices in Ferguson with disparate racial impact. Wilson was cleared, but a cloud nonetheless remained over his department.

Capehart said he hoped the protests over disparate treatment of minorities would continue, but, he said,

> we must never allow ourselves to march under the banner of a false narrative on behalf of someone who would otherwise offend our sense of right and wrong. And when we discover that we have, we must acknowledge it, admit our error and keep on marching. That's what I've done here. (Capehart, 2015)

Capehart and Coates are clearly commentators: Their job is to offer perspective or opinion. But, notes Mediaite critic Joe Concha, it was never clear whether the CNN show that featured the anchors with their "hands up" was part of the network's news or commentary (Concha, 2014).

▶ Skepticism May Be Necessary

The CNN anchors apparently exercised their personal conscience; they believed they were monitoring power. The narrative on which they acted—a narrative, critics argue, they promoted—was not verified, and more extensive investigation showed it to be false. Some eyewitnesses, the association says, require skepticism, and reporters need to weed out sources who may be trying to get on television or advance a political agenda (SPJ, n.d.).

Misinformation can move so quickly—especially in the digital age—that, to paraphrase a saying often and variously attributed to Winston Churchill, Cordell Hull, and Mark Twain—that a lie can spread halfway around the world while the truth is putting its pants on.

The Radio Television News Digital News Association (RTDNA) advises "respectful and thoughtful skepticism" in the case of some "eyewitness" accounts, who may be just hoping to get on the air or advance a political view. Reporters should press sources for specifics and consistency in their accounts and do as much preinterviewing as possible before going live (RTDNA, n.d., "Guidelines for Live Coverage").

▶ Ethical Guidelines for Live Coverage

Even with the ubiquity of cell-phone cameras and live-streaming apps, the RTDNA notes, electronic journalists maintain superior ability and opportunity to cover live events. Journalists, it says, have a special responsibility to be accurate and to report with a measured tone. According to the RTDNA, "A good guideline in such situations is to overreact in the newsroom and under-react on the air or online" (RTDNA, n.d., "Guidelines for Live Coverage").

RTDNA advises caution while covering "deadly and disturbing high profile cases" and to keep staff safe in dangerous situations and suggests news managers be directly involved. In the event that law enforcement tries to impede journalists' access, RTDNA advises that news managers need to ensure that reporters and photographers know their rights and responsibilities and to establish clear expectations and practical protocols before such incidents occur (RTDNA, n.d., "Guidelines for Live Coverage").

Live coverage of disasters, shooting scenes, protests, rallies, and other breaking news can bring additional risks and challenges. Newsrooms need to inform audiences of relevant background information and select both background and live information carefully, often a daunting task when events are moving quickly. Moreover, RTDNA cautions, newsrooms need to consider the worst possible outcomes from developing stories—such as a live suicide. The association suggests newsrooms consider the long- and short-term consequences of their reporting and ask whether they should go live with the information. "What are the consequences of waiting for additional confirmation or for a regular newscast?" Is the report contributing to fear while raising awareness of an event? How is accuracy being assessed? Who is monitoring the report for tone or graphic content? Has the newsroom considered tape and signal delays in case the story gets violent or dangerous? Is the live coverage coming at a time when children are likely to be watching? Is going live essential, or is there a better way to tell the story (RTDNA, n.d., "Guidelines for Live Coverage")?

Many in the media took stock following the shootings at Columbine High School in suburban Denver in 1999. The incident is often considered a benchmark in live coverage. Although Denver stations were praised for their tireless reporting, ethicists note that discretion is necessary with live shots. News helicopters usually take care not to reveal tactical police positions, as shots of escaping students could reveal dangerous locations to a still-active shooter. Information-hungry newsrooms also need also to be careful about taking calls by people claiming to be on the scene with cell phones because they could reveal information exposing the callers and others to danger or because the calls might be fake (Trigoboff, 2000a).

In a high-threat, high profile situation, writes media relations trainer Rick Rosenthal, "for law enforcement TV news crews can pose the biggest challenge." Rosenthal discussed a post-Columbine hostage crisis in Baltimore in March 2000 in which an unemployed electrician with a violent history shot and killed four people and held three others at gunpoint for nearly 100 hours. Four TV crews from nearby Washington, D.C., joined four local crews at the scene (Rosenthal, 2000).

But, Rosenthal notes, effective communication between police and news media had begun before this crisis. Media trusted local police to come through with information and avoided such excesses as calling the suspect on the phone. The suspect, in fact, called a local TV station twice. But the station followed the advice of police and did not air the call until after the incident ended. "Had [Baltimore station] WJZ aired news of either call," says Rosenthal, "it would have made a compelling report; it would also have been dangerous and irresponsible."

Rosenthal praised area media for behaving responsibly despite competitive pressures; others worried that the stations compromised their independence (Trigoboff, 2000b). Independence is among the key values promoted in journalism ethics codes (Society of Professional Journalists [SPJ], n.d.). Baltimore's TV news directors said they did not surrender independence but made their own decisions grounded in concern for the community and the lives at risk (Trigoboff, 2000b, p. 14).

▶ Problems of Publicity

Pretrial publicity typically favors law enforcement and can present problems for defendants, defense attorneys, judges, and ultimately the media. Competent journalists know to employ the presumption of innocence and include words such as *alleged, charged, accused*, and so on. But they also need to remember that after a high-profile crime, police and prosecutors typically present their versions of often dramatic and compelling facts and monopolize the conversation often until a defendant and his or her lawyers present their case at trial. And given the decreasing resources of local news, an accusation could be the final word the public hears about a defendant, even if a trial leads to acquittal.

Legally, courts recognize that a fair trial may be challenged by the extensive publicity given to particularly sensational crimes both before and during trial. Trials are presumed open to the public except under the narrowest of circumstances, where closure is seen as necessary to preserve such important government interests as safety of witnesses or to protect a defendant's right to a fair trial. But even where judges are compelled to keep a courtroom open, the means to neutralize publicity can include changes of venue or gag orders on trial principals, which can create obstacles to covering a trial.

▶ Impeding Investigations

The media's defiance of government prohibitions on publishing information previously kept secret is often contentious; a good example is the legendary Pentagon Papers case (*New York Times v. U.S.*, 1971). Police and press have also clashed over reporting that reveals information that could damage ongoing investigations (Reighstad, 2017). In its Code of Ethics, the Society of Professional Journalists (SPJ) asserts the importance of independence and calls on journalists to recognize that legal access to information does not necessarily justify publishing or broadcasting it from an ethical standpoint (SPJ, 2014).

Years ago, I worked at a magazine that covered television, radio, and the Internet. Although I had the title of senior editor and responsibility for sections of the magazine, I loved reporting and writing about the media, and did as much of it as I could. During that time, a source I trusted tipped me that the comptroller at a major market TV station, which was owned by an international conglomerate, was suspected of embezzlement; FBI agents were leading an investigation. A probe by the FBI into a top TV market is a pretty big story. The details made it an even bigger story—lots of money and lots of spending. The comptroller was believed to have stolen millions of dollars from the company, and there were stories of a lavish lifestyle and expensive trips—including a pricey Disney World vacation.

Decades earlier I had been a police reporter on a daily newspaper, and I spent many years covering courts and law after I returned to journalism as a lawyer. So, I had written a fair amount about investigations and law enforcement. An FBI investigation was an unusual story for the local TV beat. But the decision whether to publish the story raised ethical considerations for me. Before calling the company for comment, I consulted other editors. I had solid confirmation from reliable sources. But I had a concern: Should we run the story? I had been told the investigation was secret, and the FBI as a rule does not comment on ongoing investigations. So, if we ran the story, we would be informing or confirming to the suspect that an FBI investigation was underway. Public disclosure could damage and maybe even kill the investigation, and an embezzler might be getting away with a crime.

And what if the suspect was innocent? It is true that journalists write every day about people accused and acquitted of crimes, but this was not yet a formal charge. The suspect was not well known—but surely would be if we ran the story. The suspect had a young family (as suggested by the alleged Disney World trip). A story—even an accurate, well-reported story—about an FBI investigation could taint a reputation forever, even if the investigation led to no charges.

The SPJ's Code of Ethics advises balancing the public's need to know with the potential of harm, intrusion, and even discomfort; when weighing consequences, extra consideration should be given to subjects who are not public figures. Information gained legally and properly may still fail to meet ethical standards for publication or broadcast (SPJ, 2014).

Of course, even if we held off, other media organizations might not. Another reporter could have received a similar tip—possibly from the same source—and decided to go full speed ahead. There were good reporters covering television, and not all of them worked for us. What good would our internal deliberations be if the story got out there anyway—and from a competitor? We knew that the story might well be reported by a rival reporter and publication that practiced different ethical considerations. But we decided that we would be guided by our own standards.

Because the investigation went back a few generations of station leadership— TV station management is notoriously prone to change—I needed to go to corporate executives for comment. In a large company like this, the corporate spokespeople were at the vice president level. That meant they did not merely pass along requests for comment, but they had the authority to speak for the company on a broad range of issues.

Resourceful corporate spokespeople might try a trade-off: hold off on one story and we will give you a bigger story or two later. Covering media or entertainment, breaking stories are currency. That future scoop might be clearly identified; it might be a favor to be called in later.

A corporation's comments frequently included "No comment." If a reporter did not have the facts, higher-level public relations people—sometimes former journalists themselves—were smart enough not to be bluffed into confirming an unflattering story. They might participate in background or off-the-record conversations, and journalists had better abide by the rules or lose access. For beat reporters, poor relationships can mean poor journalism. If the public relations people lied or broke promises, then it might not help their reputations among the press, although it did not necessarily hurt with their employers (this is hardly unique to media).

My colleagues and I decided our ethics would not be subject to negotiation. I contacted the corporation, told managers what we had, and told them that we did not plan to run the story until the investigation became public. I did ask them to give us an early heads-up when an arrest was made or an indictment was issued. I told them we would appreciate background information for the time we did run the story. But unlike an embargoed story, where background is distributed in advance in exchange for an agreed-on publication time, our request for background was not conditional. Our magazine was not looking to bargain or for a quid pro quo. We had made our decision; future consideration was not a factor. And if we lost the story to a competitor, well, we lost the story. We would live with it.

I tell the story not to lionize our publication but to offer insight to the deliberation that can accompany an ethical challenge in media—and one that, had we gone another way, might have compromised law enforcement. As a lawyer—though years away from teaching media law and ethics—I knew that we were on safe ground legally. A libel charge requires that a story be published, that the plaintiff be identified, that the plaintiff be harmed, and that the harm be the fault of the defendant. Even if we didn't name the suspect, using her title or other accurate description of her work would have met the identification requirement, and clearly her reputation would have been harmed before a conviction or even indictment. A vague reference to a nameless employee without a title or description of duties in a story would cost the story compelling details and render it valueless.

But reporting and publishing the story would not have met the fault requirement. Our reporting of the investigation was accurate and well-sourced. We would have contacted the comptroller or her representative. I doubt I would have enjoyed interviewing the comptroller, but it would hardly have been the first or the last uncomfortable conversation between a reporter and a beleaguered subject. Reporters frequently talk with losing candidates, fired employees, the recently widowed, and victims of crime. Conflict and tension often make news.

But however grounded the story might have been legally, I am glad we considered the ethical implications. Our decision not to run the story as soon as we had it nailed down was certainly not the only decision we might have reached. Ethics does not work that way. If two lawyers can give you two opinions (at least) on the application of a statute, what chance do we have for a clear ethical path in a complicated situation?

As a younger reporter, I might not have thought twice about going with the story. I sometimes tell students that reporters might spend the first part of their career stepping on the gas, and the second half stepping on the brake, perhaps as editors. Some reporters may possess the maturity early on to consider the balance between compelling stories and their inevitable risks and consequences—questionable sourcing, missing information, and damage to a subject's reputation. Others might take years to learn. But it is an important lesson.

▶ References

Capehart, J. (2015, March 16). "Hands up, don't shoot" was built on a lie. *Washington Post.* Retrieved from https://www.washingtonpost.com/blogs/post-partisan/wp/2015/03/16/lesson-learned -from-the-shooting-of-michael-brown/

CNN. (2014). CNN hosts' hands-up display goes viral. https://www.cnn.com/videos/bestoftv/2014 /12/14/cnn-sat-nr-hands-up-hosts.cnn

Coates, T-N. (2015, March 25). The gangsters of Ferguson. *The Atlantic.* Retrieved from https:// www.theatlantic.com/politics/archive/2015/03/The-Gangsters-Of-Ferguson/386893/

Concha, J. (2014, December 14). CNN's untitled opinion show sparks controversy with hands-up display. Mediaite. Retrieved from https://www.mediaite.com/tv/concha-cnns-ambiguous -untitled-opinion-show-sparks-controversy-with-hands-up-display/

Dunne, F. P. (1902, October 7). Today in media history. Poynter Institute. Retrieved from https:// www.poynter.org/reporting-editing/2014/today-in-media-history-mr-dooley-the-job-of-the -newspaper-is-to-comfort-the-afflicted-and-afflict-the-comfortable/

Jones, S. (2014, December 15). So much for non-biased news. FTVLive. Retrieved from https:// www.ftvlive.com/todays-news/2014/12/14/so-much-for-non-biased-news

Kovach, B., & Rosenstiel, T. (2001). Journalists must serve as an independent monitor of power. NiemanReports. Retrieved from https://niemanreports.org/articles/category/chapter-five-journalists -must-serve-as-an-independent-monitor-of-power/

New York Times Co. v. U.S. 403 U.S., 713.

Radio Television Digital News Association (RTDNA). (n.d.). Guidelines for live coverage. Retrieved from https://www.rtdna.org/content/live_coverage

Radio Television Digital News Association (RTDNA). (n.d.). Guidelines for using confidential sources. Retrieved from https://www.rtdna.org/content/confidential_sources

Reighstad, L. (2017, December 21). Lagordiloca's arrest raises constitutional concerns. *Texas Monthly.* Retrieved from https://www.texasmonthly.com/articles/lagordilocas-arrest-laredo/

Reporters Committee for Freedom of the Press (RCFP). (2011a). *First Amendment handbook* (7th ed.) Retrieved from https://www.rcfp.org/resources/first-amendment-handbook/

Reporters Committee for Freedom of the Press (RCFP). (2011b). Open government guide. Retrieved from https://www.rcfp.org/open-government-guide/

Rosenthal, R. (2000, May). Gunman, hostages and the media. *Law & Order,* 16–17.

Sanburn, J. (2014, July 23). Behind the video of Eric Garner's deadly confrontation with New York Police. *Time.* Retrieved from https://time.com/3016326/eric-garner-video-police-chokehold -death/

Shedden, D. (2014, October 7). Mr. Dooley: "The job of the newspaper is to comfort the afflicted and afflict the comfortable". Today in Media History. Oct. 7. https://www.poynter.org/reporting -editing/2014/today-in-media-history-mr-dooley-the-job-of-the-newspaper-is-to-comfort -the-afflicted-and-afflict-the-comfortable/

Society of Professional Journalists (SPJ). (n.d.). Code of ethics. https://www.spj.org/pdf/spj-code -of-ethics.pdf

Stepler, R. (2017, January 11). Key findings on how police view their jobs amid protests and calls for reform. Pew Research Center. Retrieved from https://www.pewresearch.org/fact-tank/2017/01/11/police-key-findings/

Tompkins, A. (2002, August 13). Guidelines for interviewing confidential sources: Who, when, and why? Poynter [online]. Retrieved from https://www.poynter.org/archive/2002/guidelines-for-interviewing-confidential-sources-who-when-and-why/

Trigoboff, D. (2000a, April 3). Lessons of Columbine. *Broadcasting & Cable*, 26–31.

Trigoboff, D. (2000b, March 27). Stations restrained or manipulated? *Broadcasting & Cable*, 14

Index

© Sergii Gnatiuk/Shutterstock

F